THE
APSAC
HANDBOOK
ON
CHILD
MALTREATMENT

These chapters present the viewpoints of their authors, as opposed to any official position of APSAC or its members. Furthermore, because this book addresses controversies in the field, the reader may discover contradicting views between chapters. The editors view this mix of interpretations and positions as a good sign—evidence of the continuing growth of the field and of its willingness to continuously challenge and reevaluate its assumptions and conclusions.

THE
APSAC
HANDBOOK
ON
CHILD
MALTREATMENT

Editors:

John Briere
Lucy Berliner
Josephine A. Bulkley
Carole Jenny
Theresa Reid

APSAC

Published in cooperation with the
American Professional Society on the Abuse of Children

SAGE Publications
International Educational and Professional Publisher
Thousand Oaks London New Delhi

For information address:

SAGE Publications, Inc.
2455 Teller Road
Thousand Oaks, California 91320
E-mail: order@sagepub.com

SAGE Publications Ltd.
6 Bonhill Street
London EC2A 4PU
United Kingdom

SAGE Publications India Pvt. Ltd.
M-32 Market
Greater Kailash I
New Delhi 110 048 India

Printed in the United States of America

Library of Congress Cataloging-in-Publication Data

The APSAC handbook on child maltreatment / editors, John Briere . . .
    [et al.].
        p.   cm.
    Includes bibliographical references and index.
    ISBN 0-8039-5596-0 (cl.). — ISBN 0-8039-5597-9 (pbk.)
    1. Child abuse—Handbooks, manuals, etc.   2. Child abuse—
Prevention—Handbooks, manuals, etc.   I. Briere, John.
    II. American Professional Society on the Abuse of Children.
    HV6626.5.A83   1996
    362.7′6—dc20   95-41738

This book is printed on acid-free paper.

    99   10   9   8   7   6

Production Editor: *Tricia K. Bennett*
Typesetter: *Christina M. Hill*
Copy Editor: *Gillian Dickens*
Developmental Editor: *Raymond M. Berger*

Contents

Preface

THERESA REID

Several years ago, a number of colleagues—social workers, psychologists, attorneys, physicians, nurses, researchers, law enforcement officers, and protective services administrators—started talking when they met at conferences of their desire for a national interdisciplinary organization designed to meet their needs as professionals in the field of child maltreatment. This new society would give professionals from all of the different disciplines who respond to child maltreatment a common forum for addressing the difficult problems they face in their work. To build a knowledge base on which professionals could confidently practice, it would encourage research and disseminate research findings in a usable form to all professionals working in the field. This association would serve as a vehicle for approaching difficult policy and practice questions that require an interdisciplinary response and as a "home base" for all professionals whose main concern was how best to help those affected by child maltreatment.

In 1987, these leaders founded the American Professional Society on the Abuse of Children (APSAC). In the intervening years, thousands of professionals from all 50 states and around the world have joined, and APSAC has made steady progress toward realizing its founders' goals. It has published the *APSAC Advisor,* a highly regarded quarterly news journal that delivers current information from leading experts in an immediately useful form. It has submitted *amicus curiae* briefs to the U.S. Supreme Court in cases with important implications for child abuse practice; published guidelines for practice on critically important aspects of practice; offered advanced professional education in institutes, colloquia, and audiotapes; fostered the development of a nationwide network of chapters through which interdisciplinary professionals address issues with local import; and issued press releases and letters to editors to promote accurate public awareness of the complexities of child maltreatment. In 1996, APSAC is launching its official journal, *Child Maltreatment,* an interdisciplinary, policy- and practice-oriented journal that will address all aspects of child maltreatment.

The APSAC Handbook on Child Maltreatment is a natural extension of APSAC's mission. Its chapters address all facets of the professional response to child abuse and neglect: prevention, assessment, intervention, and treatment. Its contributors represent all of the major disciplines responding to child abuse and neglect, including mental health, law, medicine, nursing, child protective services, and law enforcement. *The APSAC Handbook on Child Maltreatment* covers all aspects of child maltreatment, including emotional neglect and other forms of neglect, psychological maltreatment, and physical and sexual abuse.

The chapters in this book are based solidly on the latest empirical research, with extensive references for further reading. Yet all chapters are written in plain language and with an eye to immediate application: Chapter authors admirably succeeded in writing to experts in the field who are *not* experts in the chapter's particular subject area.

The APSAC Handbook on Child Maltreatment is, like APSAC, a single place where all professionals can come for the latest information about their critically important work.

Finally, *The APSAC Handbook on Child Maltreatment* reflects the central wealth of APSAC, which is the unstinting labor of volunteers. The editors and chapter authors have donated their work so that all proceeds from the sale of the book directly benefit APSAC. These authors and hundreds of other busy professionals who have given so freely of their scarce and valuable time have made APSAC a living, breathing force for all professionals in the field of child abuse and neglect. With their help, through the publication of *The APSAC Handbook on Child Maltreatment,* APSAC has made another step forward in its central aim: to ensure that everyone affected by child maltreatment receives the best possible professional response.

Introduction

DAVID FINKELHOR

Professional concern about child abuse—now entering its fourth decade—is not the product of some epidemic increase in the scope or nature of the problem. It is rather the result of a broad social movement and a historic moral transformation.

Child Abuse as a Social Movement

The social movement around child protection has been gathering momentum for almost a century and is rooted in two profound social changes. One has been the rise of a new, large class of professional workers who specialize in dealing with children and families. These include specialized workers in health care, such as pediatricians and school nurses; specialized workers in education, such as school counselors and special education teachers; specialized workers in family law and child advocacy; and specialized workers in mental health and social service, such as child psychologists and family therapists.

The other social change behind the child abuse movement has been the emancipation of women from the domestic sphere and their widespread entry into the workforce and the professions. In a variety of ways, these two changes have catalyzed a moral transformation in our view of children and a social and political initiative to intervene on their behalf.

These changes have lifted the veil of privacy around many aspects of family life, revealing the existence of violence and abuse, which had previously been obscured. This happened in part because newly independent women with increased access to divorce could afford to acknowledge and disclose some of the seamier realities of family life. The new professionals for their part were in positions to confirm these realities and welcomed such opportunities to justify their expertise. Professional receptivity to such child welfare concerns was even further increased as women moved in larger numbers into the higher-status and influential professions such as medicine, law, and government and brought with them their interest in children.

Child Abuse as a Moral Transformation

The moral transformation brought about by these changes can be summarized in two propositions. The first was a growing consensus that children should be socialized primarily through love, not discipline, and harsh methods of child rearing, including the hitting and humiliating of children, were detrimental to their development. The second proposition was that parental authority was not absolute; parents were not in all cases the best judges of their children's own welfare nor entitled to unrestricted authority over them. The growing acceptance of these propositions created the basis for the concept of child maltreatment—the misuse of parental power—and the notion that professionals and public authorities had the right to intervene in families on behalf of children.

The modern "discovery" of child abuse is sometimes attributed to C. Henry Kempe, the University of Colorado pediatrician, and his colleagues, with the publication of their 1962 paper on the "battered child syndrome" (Kempe, Silverman, Steele, Droegemueller, & Silver, 1962). But in fact concern about child abuse in the United States has a much longer history, dating back to before the turn of the century (Gordon, 1988). What the Kempe work signaled, though, was that influential medical professionals had joined the ranks of those advocating for child protection and were prepared to lead a new social movement to greatly expand governmental activity in this area (Pfohl, 1977). The physicians had little problem mobilizing other child-oriented professionals, who readily saw this coalition as a chance to improve conditions for children, promote the new values, and in the process create new opportunities for their own authority and expertise (Nelson, 1983). The coalition was very successful in the early 1970s in establishing the current child protection system with its mandatory reporting laws, its codified definitions of child maltreatment, and its corps of state-funded child protection workers.

The cause of child abuse benefited from a second mobilization in the late 1970s, as the growing women's movement gave political momentum to the problem of sexual abuse. In consciousness-raising groups, women around the country had discovered the common experience of having suffered rapes and sexual abuse as children that they had never discussed (Brownmiller, 1975). They began to speak publicly and write about these experiences and eventually prevailed on young professionals to begin to seek such cases. The result was a flood of new knowledge, publicity, and governmental action around the problem of sexual abuse.

Unfortunately, to describe the concern about child abuse as the product of a moral transformation and a social movement, rather than a scientific discovery, sometimes sounds as though one is discounting of the problem itself. But nothing could be further from the truth. Many of our great social and humanitarian advances such as democracy and Social Security were just such products. And many serious social conditions have languished without attention for want of a social movement to highlight them. It is important to recognize the social movement behind the problem to understand how the problem is formulated and what its future may be (Spector & Kitsuse, 1977).

An Epidemic of Child Abuse?

One of the early tasks of many social movements is to provide evidence to substantiate the seriousness of their concern, and in the case of child abuse, this has not been hard. A variety of studies (cited in later chapters) have suggested that the various forms of child abuse touch the lives of an important fraction of all children in the United States (Garbarino, 1989; Russell, 1986; Straus, Gelles, & Steinmetz, 1980), a scope that has surprised both the public and professionals. Other studies have clearly implicated child abuse in the etiology in a broad spectrum of social and psychological problems, ranging from crime and spouse abuse to alcoholism and depression.

Up until recently, cases being reported to child welfare authorities continued to grow at the rate of more than 10% per year. This escalation in reporting has generated much discussion about whether child abuse has been increasing in the current era. Most observers believe that the large annual increases in reported cases of abuse were principally a result of new public and professional sensitivity to the problem (Sedlak, 1991). Reinforcing this view, retrospective studies of adults show large quantities of abuse suffered by earlier generations at a time when little was being disclosed (Finkelhor, Hotaling, Lewis, & Smith, 1990). But the rise of some contemporary social problems may have contributed to the exacerbation of certain forms of abuse and neglect that were previously unknown or less common. For example, the drug abuse epidemic is certainly responsible for a new problem with cocaine-addicted babies (Bays, 1990). The increase in isolated and poor households headed by a single parent has probably worsened the problem of neglected and latchkey children. And the creation of video technology has created a new market for child pornography (Lanning & Burgess, 1989). Because our ability to monitor undisclosed maltreatment is very limited, we may never be able to say whether the true incidence has been increasing.

Child Abuse: The Second Stage

Whether or not the underlying problem is changing, the nature of our professional response is. All social movements and social problems go through stages of development, and child abuse is no exception. In recent years, child abuse has been moving out of the stage in which advocates had to struggle for public attention and acceptance and has entered a second stage, that of a more mature social problem (Spector & Kitsuse, 1977). This second stage is characterized not only by increasing institutionalization and professional acceptance but also by the recognition of the need for greater accountability. Issues left over from the first stage are joined by new challenges.

One issue leftover from the first stage is the ongoing need to exact more political and financial commitment from governmental authorities, a commitment that is commensurate with the size and seriousness of the problem and the public's articulated concern. Child welfare has not received the kind of support that has gone into other social problem areas such as health care, crime control, and education. This penury of public funding is the result of two factors: the relatively recent arrival of the child abuse problem on the social agenda and the fact that its arrival coincided with a period when political philosophies opposed to state intervention have been ascendant. New funding does not seem imminent, but it is clear from opinion surveys that, in spite of cynicism about government, the public is strongly in favor of increased governmental action on behalf of abused children (Schulman, Ronca, & Bucuvalas, Inc., 1988).

Another ongoing challenge for the field of child abuse has been coping with its very interdisciplinary character. This has been an asset in establishing a robust political coalition supportive of the problem. But it has been a challenge to balance the often conflicting disciplinary priorities and styles (e.g., prosecution vs. therapy) and to provide a forum in which professional development and dialogue could occur. As the field moves into a more mature phase, it is replacing the old ad hoc structures for this dialogue with more permanent ones.

The American Professional Society on Abuse of Children (APSAC) is one of these new structures. Founded in 1987, APSAC has brought together the diverse disciplines concerned with child abuse to create an organization in which conflicts could be negotiated and standards established while providing a unified voice that could speak for professionals working in the field.

New Research Agenda

The second stage also has brought a transformation in the nature of child abuse research. Much of the early research in the field was dedicated to drawing attention to the problem. Thus, prevalence studies tried to establish its scope, impact studies tried to establish its seriousness and connection to other social and psychological problems, and studies of professionals tried to highlight the misconceptions that needed to be corrected.

As the field enters a more mature phase, the research agenda has shifted. Of much greater interest now are studies that evaluate programs and professional practice to find out what works (if anything) and what doesn't. As it has become more successful, the field has been able to be more self-critical and ask hard questions. Thus, recent studies have begun to scrutinize intervention programs (e.g., Daro, Jones, & McCurdy, 1993), treatment methods for abusers and victims (e.g., Finkelhor & Berliner, 1995; Marques, Day, Nelson, & West, 1994), and the practices of child protective agencies and investigators (e.g., Kendall-Tackett, 1992). Although these studies may result in some discouraging and possibly embarrassing findings, they also hold the promise of truly improving the work.

The Rise of an Organized Opposition

In this second stage of its development, one of the new challenges faced by the child abuse movement is responding to an increasingly well-organized political opposition. During its first stage, child abuse was unusual in being a social problem that had little organized opposition and drew very broad support from across the political spectrum.

In recent years, however, an opposition has coalesced and gained visibility on a number of fronts. An increasing number of parents who believe they have suffered wrongful investigations and accusations have begun to bring suits and lobby for restrictions on state child welfare authorities (Hechler, 1988). Efforts to teach children skills for avoiding abuse and sexual victimization have aroused opposition from some academic critics (Berrick & Gilbert, 1991) as well as from conservative and religious groups concerned about undermining parental authority and the teaching of sex education in the schools. The prosecution of child molesters has resulted in more and better organized and specialized defense attorneys, who have developed a systematic critique of investigative practices, therapeutic techniques, and research evidence as well as their own cadre of expert witnesses (Hechler, 1988). Meanwhile, the growing state child welfare bureaucracies, with their large budgets and diffuse man-dates, have become easy targets for the axes of state legislators and budget managers.

The rise of this opposition has been termed the *child abuse backlash*. It has complicated the work of some practitioners not used to operating in an adversarial environment, has been the source of anguish for others who have been personally targeted, and in some cases has badly compromised their ability to advocate on behalf of abused children. But it has also had potentially salutary effects in some cases, curbing excesses of zeal, introducing discussions of issues of efficiency and equity, and forcing consideration of the interests of some groups (e.g., parents under investigation) that may have been previously overlooked.

A perhaps even more serious long-term threat to the field of child abuse than the backlash is the problem of public saturation. Social problems tend to follow an "issue attention" cycle, such that after an issue has been in the spotlight for a certain period, the media, the public, and politicians tend to lose interest (Downs, 1972). Child abuse has resisted the problem of saturation, in part by the discovery of "new" aspects of the problem that have reinvigorated public interest. The focus on sexual abuse in the late 1970s had this reinvigorating effect after a decade of interest in physical abuse.

Although the fascination with the topic of sexual abuse shows no current signs of flagging, there will be at some time in the future an inevitable waning of the attention cycle. In the meantime, some other issues may arise to sustain public interest. One concerns children who are the victims of parents who abuse drugs and alcohol. Another concerns the problem of emotional maltreatment. Although these "fad cycles" in social problems are in many ways regrettable and do little to produce rational social policy, they are to some extent an unavoidable feature of maintaining interest in child abuse as a social problem.

The APSAC Handbook

The APSAC Handbook on Child Maltreatment is a welcome summary of where the field is today in this stage of growing maturity. The interdisciplinary richness of the field is very much on display, as demonstrated by the relevant juxtaposition of sections on medicine, law, and psychotherapy. A newfound capacity for self-evaluation and self-criticism is apparent. The field's growing foundation in research and evaluation is also evident. It is on the basis of a synthesis of the sort available in the following articles that a field creates a picture of where it has come from and where it has yet to go. It is clear that this field has taken on one of the larger moral and humanitarian challenges that exists in our society today. This volume testifies to the enormous fund of professional expertise, scientific objectivity, social activism, and human compassion that has been unleashed in that challenge.

References

Bays, J. (1990). Substance abuse and child abuse: Impact of addiction on the child. *Pediatric Clinics of North America, 37*(4), 881-903.

Berrick, J. D., & Gilbert, N. (1991). *With the best intentions: The child sexual abuse prevention movement.* New York: Guilford.

Brownmiller, S. (1975). *Against our will: Men, women and rape.* New York: Simon & Schuster.

Daro, D., Jones, E., & McCurdy, K. (1993). *Preventing child abuse: An evaluation of services to high-risk families.* Philadelphia: William Penn Foundation.

Downs, A. (1972, Summer). Up and down with ecology—The "issue-attention cycle." *Public Interest,* pp. 38-50.

Finkelhor, D., & Berliner, L. (1995). Research on the treatment of sexually abused children: A review and recommendations. *Journal of the American Academy of Child and Adolescent Psychiatry, 34,* 1408-1423.

Finkelhor, D., Hotaling, G. T., Lewis, I. A., & Smith, C. (1990). Sexual abuse in a national survey of adult men and women: Prevalence, characteristics, and risk factors. *Child Abuse & Neglect, 14,* 19-28.

Garbarino, J. (1989). The incidence and prevalence of child maltreatment. In L. Ohlin & M. Tonry (Eds.), *Family violence* (pp. 219-261). Chicago: University of Chicago Press.

Gordon, L. (1988). *Family violence and social control.* New York: Viking.

Hechler, D. (1988). *The battle and the backlash: The child sexual abuse war.* Lexington, MA: Lexington Books.

Kempe, C. H., Silverman, F. N., Steele, B. F., Droegemueller, W., & Silver, H. K. (1962). The battered child syndrome. *Journal of the American Medical Association, 181,* 17-24.

Kendall-Tackett, K. A. (1992). Professionals' standards of "normal" behavior with anatomical dolls and factors that influence these standards. *Child Abuse & Neglect, 16,* 727-733.

Lanning, K. V., & Burgess, A. W. (1989). Child pornography and sex rings. In D. Zillman & J. Bryant (Eds.), *Pornography: Research advances and policy considerations.* Hillsdale, NJ: Lawrence Erlbaum.

Marques, J. K., Day, D. M., Nelson, C., & West, M. A. (1994). Effects of cognitive and behavioral treatment on sex offender recidivism: Preliminary results of a longitudinal study. *Criminal Justice and Behavior, 21,* 28-54.

Nelson, B. J. (1983). *Making an issue of child abuse: Political agenda setting for social problems.* Chicago: University of Chicago Press.

Pfohl, S. J. (1977). The discovery of child abuse. *Social Problems, 24,* 310-323.

Russell, D. E. H. (1986). *The secret trauma: Incest in the lives of girls and women.* New York: Basic Books.

Schulman, Ronca, & Bucuvalas, Inc. (1988). *Public attitudes and actions regarding child abuse and its prevention: 1988.* Chicago: National Committee for Prevention of Child Abuse.

Sedlak, A. J. (1991). *National incidence and prevalence of child abuse and neglect: 1991* (Revised report). Rockville, MD: Westat.

Spector, M., & Kitsuse, J. I. (1977). *Constructing social problems.* Menlo Park, CA: Cummings.

Straus, M. A., Gelles, R. J., & Steinmetz, S. K. (1980). *Behind closed doors: Violence in the American family.* Beverly Hills, CA: Sage.

PART ONE

Overview

Aspects of Child Maltreatment

In Part One, chapter authors provide an overview of different types of child maltreatment: neglect, physical abuse, psychological maltreatment, and sexual abuse. This comprehensive overview closes with a review of the available literature on the ritualistic abuse of children.

The order of the chapters reflects the prevalence of the types of maltreatment they address: According to the latest incidence study conducted for the federal government, neglect is the primary concern in 45% of all reports to child protective services (CPS), physical abuse in 25% of reports, sexual abuse in 16%, and psychological maltreatment in 6% of reports (8% of reports involve "other" categories). Ritual abuse of children, which has garnered a great deal of media attention in recent years, accounts for a very small proportion of the maltreatment experienced by U.S. children.

Neglect is most often reported and least often addressed in the professional and popular literature. In Chapter 1, Martha Farrell Erickson and Byron Egeland point out that although neglect may be nearly invisible, its effects can be as serious as those of physical and sexual abuse. Whether or not neglect has physical repercussions (such as failure to thrive and developmental delay or organ damage due to malnourishment), it can have a devastating impact on the child's development through lasting damage to the child's sense of self. Erickson and Egeland discuss definitions and subtypes of neglect, parental motivation, cultural issues, and impact and identify three specific factors that help mothers break the cycle of neglect, pointing a way to effective prevention.

In Chapter 2, psychologist David J. Kolko focuses on physical abuse. Kolko stresses that although most abusive parents were themselves abused as children, most abused children do not grow up to be abusers. He reviews the factors that mediate abuse effects, including gender, depression, intelligence, socioeconomic status, social support, and stress. Among the difficult issues Kolko addresses is the role of child characteristics in etiology. Acknowledging as risk factors child characteristics such as distress due to health problems or temperamental resistance to soothing is important in developing effective, comprehensive interventions. Although we do not yet know how well most therapeutic interventions work, Kolko reviews many promising possibilities and suggests future directions for research to better inform our interventions.

In Chapter 3, Lucy Berliner and Diana M. Elliott address the definitions, incidence, characteristics, risk factors, and short-term and long-term effects of child sexual abuse. Berliner and Elliott discuss at some length the scientific literature on the process of disclosure, which has such serious implications for investigators, therapists, and prosecutors, as well as for researchers attempting to gauge the incidence of child sexual abuse. The authors note that fewer than half of victims tell at the time of abuse, and a large percentage never reveal sexual abuse until asked for research purposes. Even when abuse is disclosed, only 6% to 12% is reported to authorities. Delays, inconsistencies, tentativeness, and recantation are common even in disclosures of abuse that are later corroborated. Several of the factors that mediate the effects of abuse also provide clear direction for professional practice: for instance, the finding that multiple interviews with *different* interviewers—but not with the same interviewer—is stressful for the child. The authors follow their review of the research with a discussion of implications for assessment, treatment, and further research.

If these chapters were ordered to reflect actual prevalence rather than the primary concern of reports, the chapter on psychological maltreatment would likely be offered first. In Chapter 4, Stuart N. Hart, Marla R. Brassard, and Henry C. Karlson argue convincingly that psychological maltreatment not only is embedded in all other types of maltreatment but accounts for most of the trauma resulting from other forms of abuse and neglect. Hart, Brassard, and Karlson begin their chapter with a discussion of operational definitions, the lack of which for psychological maltreatment has severely impeded efforts to address this pervasive problem. They go on to discuss the effects of psychological maltreatment, which include attachment disorders, behavior problems, and limitations in social competence, social adjustment, cognitive ability, problem solving, and educational achievement. Of the theoretical models available for explaining these effects, the authors find

Abraham Maslow's basic human needs theory most useful: Psychological maltreatment prohibits the fulfillment of basic needs for safety, love and belonging, and esteem. The authors argue that schools should be central to prevention, intervention, and treatment efforts, and they close their chapter with a discussion of an agenda for research.

In Chapter 5, Susan J. Kelley reviews the perplexing and disturbing problem of ritual abuse of children, opening with a thoughtful discussion of definitional issues and proceeding with a thorough and balanced review of prevalence, characteristics, and impact.

Taken together, these chapters provide a detailed account of the developmental insults adults can inflict on children. They also provide an excellent bird's-eye view of the terrain lying behind us and before us as a field. The chapters reflect an impressive accumulation of knowledge, the result of two decades of painstaking research and clinical practice with abused and neglected children and their families. As such, they articulate the existing basis for developing interventions to prevent the maltreatment of our children and ameliorate its effects. They also provide a far-reaching look forward to what needs to be done to increase our knowledge and competence.

—T.R.

1

Child Neglect

MARTHA FARRELL ERICKSON

BYRON EGELAND

Although the bruises and scars of physical abuse are more readily apparent, the quiet assault of child neglect often does at least as much damage to its young victims. Typically defined as an act of omission rather than commission, neglect may or may not be intentional. It is sometimes apparent (as in the unkempt appearance of the child who comes to school without a bath or adequate clothing) and sometimes nearly invisible until it is too late. Neglect is often fatal, due to inadequate physical protection, nutrition, or health care. Sometimes, as in the case of "failure to thrive," it is fatal because of a lack of human contact and love. In some cases, neglect slowly and persistently eats away at children's spirits until they have little will to connect with others or explore the world.

In this chapter, we present a brief overview of what is known about child neglect. First, within the context of a historical look at society's increasing awareness of neglect, we discuss definitions of neglect and its various subtypes. Second, we review research findings on the impact of neglect on children's health and develop-ment, including data from our own longitudinal study of the consequences of emotional neglect. Then we discuss what is known about the underlying causes and correlates of neglect, with an emphasis on those factors that may be amenable to change through preventive intervention. Finally, we briefly discuss what this information suggests for future research and practice.

Developing Awareness of Neglect

Although children have been abused and neglected for centuries, the recognition of maltreatment as a social problem is relatively recent. Thirty years ago, Kempe's landmark paper on the "battered child" (Kempe, Silverman, Steele, Droegemueller, & Silver, 1962) spurred a dramatic increase in public awareness of the impact of overt, intentional physical abuse. Widespread recognition of neglect, however, lagged far behind, even though neglect is more prevalent than abuse (American Association for Protecting Children, 1988; National Center on Child Abuse and Neglect [NCCAN], 1992) and has been shown to have consequences that are just as serious (e.g., Erickson, Egeland, & Pianta, 1989). Some experts have contended that neglect (emotional neglect, in particular) is the central feature of all maltreatment. For example, Newberger wrote as early as 1973 that "the essential element in child abuse is not the intention to destroy a child but rather the inability of a parent to nurture [his or her] offspring" (p. 15). Nevertheless, neglect continued to receive far less attention than abuse, both publicly and professionally, even as recently as the mid-1980s (Wolock & Horowitz, 1984). A perusal of current popular publications suggests that public attention still is aimed primarily at sensational cases of severe physical assault and injury.

Furthermore, the attention given to neglect (and also to abuse) often has focused only on observable physical effects. Neglect often leaves obvious physical signs, as in the case of gross malnourishment or accidents stemming from a caregiver's failure to protect a child from injury. But many types of neglect, including emotional neglect, typically leave no physical marks. These less obvious forms of neglect nevertheless can have a devastating impact on the child's development (Egeland & Erickson, 1987).

Only recently has public awareness expanded to include a recognition of the often profound psychological consequences that stem from even the most subtle neglect. Many experts now contend that the psychological consequences are the unifying factor in all types of maltreatment (e.g., see Brassard, Germain, &

> *Only recently has public awareness expanded to include a recognition of the often profound psychological consequences that stem from even the most subtle neglect.*

Hart, 1987). Recent research by Crittenden and her associates presents a strong case for the impact of psychological maltreatment, regardless of the severity of physical injury (Claussen & Crittenden, 1991). Whether or not the child sustains physical injury, at the core of maltreatment is lasting damage to the child's sense of self and the resultant impairment of social, emotional, and cognitive functioning.

Definitions and Subtypes of Neglect

Neglect means many things to many people. Definitions may vary depending on whether one takes a legal, medical, psychological, social service, or lay perspective (see Chapter 13, this volume, for a discussion of neglect from the medical perspective). Out of necessity, legal definitions tend to be the most elaborate and at least aspire to some level of precision (Flannery, 1979; Giovannoni, 1989; Wald, 1976). But even within the legal arena, there is great variability among definitions of neglect. Some of that variability is due to the fact that maltreatment statutes fall into three different categories, each with a different purpose and therefore a somewhat different interpretation of what constitutes neglect. The three categories include reporting laws that define who should make reports of maltreatment and under what conditions, dependency statutes that define which children may be made wards of the court, and criminal statutes that define a criminal act for purposes of prosecution. Even within any given category of legislation, definitions often include a mixture of precision (i.e., spelling out various kinds and degrees of neglect) and vagueness (i.e., broad, ambiguous phrases, such as "interfering with the child's welfare") (Giovannoni, 1989).

Other perspectives beyond the legal system may take an even broader, more inclusive view of neglect. For example, some groups of professionals advocate intervention in neglect cases that would not necessarily meet the criteria of the law. In an early study of perceptions of neglect, Boehm (1962) surveyed a large sample of community leaders from various professions, asking them to respond to vignettes describing various kinds of neglect. Teachers, nurses, social workers, and clergy were more likely to judge the cases as requiring intervention than were lawyers.

An even broader view of neglect is put forth in *Today's Children: Creating a Future for a Generation in Crisis* (1992) by David Hamburg, president of the Carnegie Corporation Foundation. Calling attention to the plight of today's children, Hamburg indicts U.S. society for "collective neglect" in failing to provide adequate health care, child care, preschool education, and policies that support families in caring for their children.

A general definition of neglect was embedded in the Child Abuse Prevention and Treatment Act of 1974 (P.L. 93-247), which defined abuse and neglect as

> the physical or *mental injury,* sexual abuse or exploitation, *negligent treatment,* or maltreatment of a child under the age of 18, or the age specified by the child protection law of the state in question, by a person who is responsible for the child's welfare under circumstances which indicate that the child's health or welfare is harmed or threatened thereby as determined in accordance with regulations prescribed by the Secretary. (emphasis added)

It is common for states to define abuse and neglect together rather than provide separate legal definitions for each. According to Corson and Davidson (1987), it is a moot issue in most courts whether the child was injured through an act of commission (abuse) or omission (neglect).

Beyond such overarching definitions of maltreatment, specific interpretations of what "neglect" encompasses vary along several dimensions. One controversy centers on whether actions can be defined as neglectful regardless of their apparent impact on the child. Must there be clear, immediate evidence of harm or "mental injury," or is an apparent "threat" to the child's well-being sufficient? For example, Brassard et al. (1987) cite one definition of mental injury as referring to *substantial, observable impairment* in the child's ability to perform and behave within a normal range with due regard to his or her cultural background.

Others would argue that actions can be neglectful regardless of their immediate observable impact on the child's functioning (see Schakel, 1987, for a discussion of this and other definitional issues). Certainly our own research on the long-term consequences of various patterns of maltreatment, discussed later in this chapter, suggests that the impact of neglect may become apparent later in the child's development, even if it is not immediately obvious. Thus, a definition that demands immediate, observable effects would overlook many cases of neglect. At the 1983 International Conference on Psychological Abuse, the interdisciplinary group of participants proposed a definition of psychological maltreatment that included both immediate and ultimate (i.e., manifest at a later point) damage to the child's behavioral, cognitive, affective, or physical functioning (Brassard et al., 1987). This raises the question of whether we know enough about the impact of neglect to say with some confidence that a given act would be expected ultimately to do damage to the child. Many working in this field would argue strongly that we do know enough.

Another definitional issue regarding neglect that is of particular salience within the legal arena has to do with the intentionality of the act. Dubowitz and his colleagues argue for a definition based on the unmet needs of the child, regardless of parental intentions (Dubowitz, Black, Starr, & Zuravin, 1993). Although intentionality can be a critical variable in determining legal culpability, the end result for the child may be the same whether the parent is willfully neglectful (e.g., out of hostility) or neglectful due to such factors as ignorance, depression, or overwhelming stress and inadequate support. From either an intervention or prevention perspective, identifying the factors that underlie the neglect is important in order to eliminate or ameliorate those factors and ensure that children receive the care and protection they need and deserve.

In considering neglect, parental motives cannot be dichotomized simply as intentional or unintentional.

In considering neglect, parental motives cannot be dichotomized simply as intentional or unintentional. Motives also need to be considered within the context of the parent's culture and beliefs. Garbarino (1991) cites the example of Hispanic parents who sometimes avoid using car seats for their infants because they believe the infants will feel abandoned if they cannot be held in their parents' arms. Nevertheless, the law requires that infants be restrained in protective car seats, and parents who refuse to comply are neglecting their duty to protect their children from potential harm.

As health care providers, mental health professionals, and lawmakers have grown in their understanding of neglect, definitions have been refined and elaborated. Several subtypes of neglect have been identified, including the following:

Physical neglect. This is the most widely recognized and commonly identified form of neglect. It includes failure to protect from harm or danger and provide for the child's basic physical needs, including adequate shelter, food, or clothing. In 1990, approximately 1,200 children died from abuse and neglect (NCCAN, 1992) in the United States (based on data from 46 states), but it is not clear how many fatalities were attributable to neglect as opposed to overt abuse.

Emotional neglect. In many cases, this type of neglect is more difficult to document or substantiate because of the absence of clear physical evidence and the fact that it goes on quietly in the privacy of the home, often beginning when children are too young to speak out or even know that they are not receiving appropriate care (Egeland & Erickson, 1987). In its extreme form, however, emotional neglect can lead to nonorganic failure to thrive. This produces stunted growth and physical illness or anomalies (e.g., Gardner, 1972) and is often fatal.

In discussing definitions of emotional neglect, Brassard et al. (1987) cite the American Humane Association, which describes emotional neglect as "passive or passive/aggressive inattention to the child's emotional needs, nurturing, or emotional well-being" (p. 267). In our own research, we have used the term *psychologically unavailable* to describe parents who overlook their infants' cues and signals, particularly the children's cries and pleas for warmth and comfort. As discussed later in this chapter, we have found this subtle form of neglect to have serious long-term consequences for young victims. The antithesis of emotional neglect is emotional availability, thoughtfully discussed by Biringen and Robinson (1991). These authors reconceptualize availability as a relational construct, taking into account both parent and child behavior, and propose a multidimensional approach to describing emotional availability that includes parental sensitivity, child responsiveness, parental nonintrusiveness, and child involvement of the parent. In their representation of availability as a continuous variable, emotional neglect would be at the extreme end of that continuum.

Definitions of neglect, however, are in part a function of time and place. What we today call emotional neglect would not have been recognized as such not so many years ago. In fact, in the 1920s, experts advised parents against sentimental handling of babies and urged them to let their babies cry so that they would learn that their parents were in charge (Newson & Newson, 1974). (As we discuss later, that notion has not disappeared completely.)

Definitions of emotional neglect also may vary somewhat depending on cultural context. For example, Korbin (1980) has pointed out that in some cultures, our Western practice of making young children sleep alone in their rooms at night would be viewed as emotional neglect. This illustrates that although there is agreement that emotional neglect involves inattention to the child's needs, there is not universal agreement on exactly what those needs are.

Medical neglect. This refers to caregivers' failure to provide prescribed medical treatment for their children, including required immunizations, prescribed medication, recommended surgery, or other intervention in cases of serious disease or injury. This type of neglect has raised some of the most controversial legal issues in the field of child protection, particularly in regard to cases in which the parents' religious beliefs conflict with the recommendations of the medical community (see Chapter 13, this volume). No doubt the courts will continue to grapple with the painful issues raised when children's apparent need for medical intervention clashes with parents' freedom of religion and choice.

Mental health neglect. Similar to medical neglect, this refers to caregivers' refusal to comply with recommended corrective or therapeutic procedures in cases in which a child is found to have a serious emotional or behavioral disorder. Although not yet widely addressed as a form of maltreatment, Hart (1987) has proposed standards and procedures for legal and social service intervention in regard to this subtype of neglect.

Educational neglect. In the legal arena, educational neglect refers to caregivers' failure to comply with state requirements for school attendance. Among educators and mental health professionals, it also may be used more broadly to encompass the parents' lack of cooperation or involvement in their children's schooling or the parents' resistance to follow through with special programs or interventions recommended by the schools. However, given the scope of parental rights and choices in regard to their children's education, such broad definitions are not likely to be incorporated into legal definitions of neglect.

The Impact of Child Neglect

Although abuse garners more public attention, neglect is the most common type of reported maltreatment. Based on a 50-state survey of CPS agencies in the United States, an estimated 2.7 million children were reported as victims of child abuse and neglect in 1990. Of those, approximately 45% were reported for neglect, as compared to 25% for physical abuse, 16% for sexual abuse, 6% for emotional maltreatment (some of whom experience emotional neglect), and 8% for

"other" forms of maltreatment (NCCAN, 1992). Approximately 40% of reported neglect cases are substantiated. It is likely

---

Although abuse garners more public attention, neglect is the most common type of reported maltreatment.

---

that the actual incidence of neglect is much higher than reporting statistics indicate. Because neglect (particularly emotional neglect) often leaves no visible scars, it is likely to go undetected. Furthermore, many victims of neglect are infants who are too young to speak out about the treatment they experience. Because neglect is often chronic rather than episodic, these children also may grow up thinking this is the way life is, not realizing that their experience constitutes maltreatment.

Long-Term Developmental Consequences of Neglect

The 1970s saw a burgeoning interest in studies of the consequences of maltreatment. Early studies, which focused primarily on children who were physically abused, usually presented clinical evidence or descriptive statistics without using control groups. These studies pointed to a disproportionate number of children who performed below average on standardized intelligence tests (e.g., Martin, Beezley, Conway, & Kempe, 1974; Morse, Sahler, & Friedman, 1970; Sandgrund, Gaines, & Green, 1974) and who exhibited varied social and emotional problems, including hostility, aggression, and passive, withdrawn behavior (e.g., Galdston, 1971; Kempe & Kempe, 1978; Martin & Beezley, 1977). In one of the first studies specifically to include neglected children among maltreated subjects, Steele (1977) found learning problems, low self-esteem, and, in subsequent years, a high incidence of juvenile delinquency.

The 1980s saw reports from several studies comparing maltreated children with control groups of nonmaltreated children. Some studies also made comparisons between children who were abused and those who were neglected. For example, Reidy (1977) found that both abused and neglected children behaved more aggressively in school than nonmaltreated children, but abused children exhibited more aggression during fantasy and free play than the neglected children.

Hoffman-Plotkin and Twentyman (1984) reported that abused children were more aggressive than either neglected or nonmaltreated children, but the neglected children interacted less with peers than either abused or nonmaltreated children. Similarly, Crittenden (1985b; Crittenden & Ainsworth, 1989) found that abused children were described as having difficult temperaments, became angry under stress, and exhibited mild developmental delays. Neglected children, on the other hand, were passive, tended toward helplessness under stress, and showed significant developmental delays. In a review of studies from 1975 to 1992, Katz (1992) found that both abused and neglected children had language delays or disorders, but the problems of neglected children were more severe.

These findings on the apparent differences in developmental consequences of abuse and neglect point to the importance of separating types of maltreatment when studying their consequences. Otherwise, combining abused and neglected children for group data may obscure the ways in which they differ from nonmaltreated children. On the other hand, many children experience more than one type of maltreatment; groups will overlap, and the line between subtypes usually is blurred. Thus, it is important to keep this in perspective when considering differences between neglect and abuse and recognize that such research is not always the hard science we would hope it to be. Also, it may be important to consider the consequences of multiple types of maltreatment. (Our own Minnesota Mother-Child Project, discussed later, and the Harvard Child Maltreatment Project [e.g., Cicchetti, Carlson, Braunwald, & Aber, 1987] both have attempted to address these questions.)

Emotional neglect. As difficult as it is to draw a clear line between abused and neglected children, it is even more difficult to distinguish between children who are physically neglected and those who are emotionally neglected. Most, if not all, children who are physically neglected are also emotionally neglected at least to some extent. However, the converse is not always true. We have seen a number of cases of children who were emotionally but not physically neglected (e.g., Egeland & Erickson, 1987). They were fed adequately, well-clothed, and received proper health care, but their caregivers did not respond to their emotional needs.

As mentioned earlier, the most extreme consequences of emotional neglect are labeled as the *nonorganic failure to thrive syndrome,* which involves failure to grow—or sometimes even to survive—despite adequate nourishment (Gardner, 1972; MacCarthy, 1979; Patton & Gardner, 1962). Even after diagnosis and intervention, the psychological consequences of emotional neglect persist. In a clinical follow-up of infants who had been diagnosed as failure to thrive, MacCarthy (1979) reported notable attention-seeking behavior and superficial displays of affection after these children were placed out of the home. Later in their childhood, these children were described as spiteful and selfish, and they reportedly engaged in stealing. Likewise, Polansky, Chalmers, Buttenwieser, and Williams (1981) chronicled the defiant, hostile behavior of young adolescents who, in infancy, had been diagnosed as failure to thrive. Hufton and Oates (1977) also found that failure-to-thrive children presented varied academic and behavior problems in the early elementary grades.

Even in cases much less profound than failure to thrive, the long-term consequences of emotional neglect are remarkable. As reported in detail in earlier papers (Egeland & Erickson, 1987; Egeland, Sroufe, & Erickson, 1983; Erickson, Egeland, & Pianta, 1989), our own research on children with psychologically unavailable parents provides powerful testimony to the impact of this form of neglect. Recently, we examined the behavior of these same children further into the school years and again compared them to nonmaltreated children within our same high-risk sample. (These findings are preliminary and have not yet been published elsewhere.) Both our earlier findings and the more recent preliminary analyses of our follow-up data are summarized in a subsequent section of this chapter.

Some Methodological Considerations in Studying the Effects of Neglect

It is not easy to examine the impact of neglect and sort it from the many variables that influence a child's development. It often has been noted that many maltreated children live in poverty or in families characterized by other kinds of problems. Therefore, it can be difficult to ascertain to what extent a child's subsequent problems are due to the maltreatment itself or to other aspects of the environment. For example, in a frequently cited study, Elmer (1977) found few differences between abused and nonabused children within a poverty sample, leading her to conclude that the impact of poverty and other environmental factors associated with it may override the effects of abuse. It has been noted elsewhere, however (e.g., Aber & Cicchetti, 1984; Erickson et al., 1989), that the nonabused children in Elmer's sample were matched to the abused children not only for poverty but also for hospitalization experience. Specifically, the nonabused comparison groups included (a) children who were hospitalized for accidental injury and (b) children who were not victims of trauma but were matched for history of hospitalization (i.e., for such things as acute illness). This may have blurred the lines between abused and "nonabused" children in this study. Given the relation of neglect to accidental injury and illness, it is plausible that a number of these children in the so-called nonabused group actually had experienced neglect. (As described below, our own longitudinal research does provide strong evidence that maltreatment has consequences above and beyond the effects of poverty.)

Although it is relatively easy to control for poverty and other sociodemographic variables, it is more challenging to separate the effects of maltreatment from other aspects of the home environment and family functioning. For example, other researchers have pointed to the general dysfunction among families in which intrafamilial sexual abuse has occurred, and some contend that it is the general dysfunction, rather than the sexual abuse per se, that accounts for children's poor psychological outcomes (e.g., Giaretto, 1976; Herman & Hirschman, 1981; Rosenfeld, 1977). Likewise, child

neglect is often embedded in a larger pattern of dysfunction and, in many cases, environmental chaos, making it difficult or impossible to separate the impact of neglect from other environmental influences. Although this is problematic from a research perspective, such distinctions may be less meaningful from a prevention or treatment perspective; intervention efforts most likely will need to address the entire matrix of home and family variables that support or impede children's development.

Another critical methodological issue involves taking into account the age and developmental stage of the children being studied. Early studies of maltreatment described consequences with little regard for age, often combining children of widely varying ages. Yet given how rapidly and dramatically children's behavior changes over time, consequences of maltreatment will probably be manifest in different ways at different periods of development. Neglect may be operationalized differently, depending on the age and developmental needs of the child (Biringen & Robinson, 1991; Erickson & Egeland, 1987). More recently, cross-sectional studies have looked at children within a narrower age range, and longitudinal studies have followed children through different stages of development, assessing child behavior within the framework of salient issues at each stage.

Many of the developmentally sensitive studies have focused on infancy and early childhood. For example, Gaensbauer, Mrazek, and Harmon (1980) examined the development of affective communication between infants and their caregivers, comparing maltreated and nonmaltreated infants. They observed developmental and affective delays among one group of children who were hypothesized to have experienced extreme neglect. Other children who performed normally on developmental tasks but presented depressed affect were believed to have received adequate care in early infancy, followed by separation from their caregivers or emotional neglect due to maternal depression.

Much of the recent research on maltreated infants has been guided by attachment theory (Bowlby, 1969, 1973, 1980) and facilitated by the Strange Situation Procedure for assessing the quality of parent-infant attachment (Ainsworth, Blehar, Waters, & Wall, 1978). This assessment procedure, used most often when the child is 1 or 2 years of age, has been demonstrated to be a valid and reliable measure of the infant's adaptation within the context of the infant-caregiver relationship, and it is predictive of the child's subsequent behavior in a variety of situations (e.g., see Bretherton & Waters, 1985). Infants who have secure relationships with their primary caregivers are more competent at later ages than children whose attachment was classified as anxious-resistant or anxious-avoidant in the Strange Situation. Anxiously attached children are more likely to exhibit problems in cognitive and emotional functioning (e.g., Erickson, Sroufe, & Egeland, 1985; Sroufe, Fox, & Pancake, 1983).

Studies have found maltreated children to have a high incidence of anxious attachment.

Several studies have found maltreated children, including those who are neglected, to have a high incidence of anxious attachment. This is not surprising, because primary determinants of the quality of attachment are the parent's responsiveness and sensitivity to the baby's cues and signals—the antithesis of maltreatment (Egeland & Farber, 1984). In the Harvard Maltreatment Project, maltreated infants were more likely than nonmaltreated infants to be insecurely attached (Schneider-Rosen, Braunwald, Carlson, & Cicchetti, 1985). Lamb, Gaensbauer, Malkin, and Schultz (1985) also reported that children who were maltreated by their primary caregivers were more likely to have insecure relationships with their biological mothers and, to a lesser extent, with their foster mothers. Crittenden (1985b) also reported a high incidence of anxious attachment among abused and neglected children.

Illustrative of the importance of taking development into account when looking at the consequences of maltreatment, Crittenden found interesting differences between abused and neglected children at 2 years of age. Abused children appeared angry during their first year of life but inhibited that anger with their mothers at 2 years of age. Neglected children did not show such a change in strategy, and Crittenden contends that the abused children's inhibition reflects the 2-year-

olds' new ability to form expectancies about their parents' behavior (1985a, 1992).

The Minnesota Mother-Child Project. One of the first major studies to address systematically the methodological considerations discussed earlier was the Minnesota Mother-Child Project. This is a prospective, longitudinal study designed to follow the development of a sample of 267 children born to first-time mothers identified as being at risk for parenting problems due to poverty, youth, low education, lack of support, and unstable life circumstances. Recruited through obstetric clinics during the second trimester of pregnancy, these women, their children, and their social networks have been assessed regularly, using varied methods and measures, through the children's early adolescence (see Erickson et al., 1989; Pianta, Egeland, & Erickson, 1989, for detailed discussion of this study).

Although the Minnesota Mother-Child Project has examined the entire qualitative range of caregiving, a major focus has been on the antecedents of abuse and neglect, as well as the long-term consequences of maltreatment on children's development. When the children in the study were 2 years old, we identified four groups of children who were maltreated, based on observations and other data collected since birth: physically abused ($N = 24$), verbally abused ($N = 19$), neglected ($N = 24$), and children whose mothers were psychologically unavailable, that is, emotionally neglectful ($N = 19$). (Note that there was overlap in the groups, with some children experiencing physical abuse in addition to other types of maltreatment.)

Of particular interest for this chapter are the neglected children and those with psychologically unavailable caregivers. Mothers in the "neglectful" group did not provide appropriate health care, physical care, or protection for their children— either through incompetence or irresponsibility. Although these mothers sometimes expressed concern and interest in their children's welfare, their care for their children was inconsistent and inadequate. Mothers in the psychologically unavailable group appeared detached and unresponsive to their children's bids for care and attention. When they did interact with their children, it was in a mechanical and perfunctory manner, with no apparent joy or satisfaction in the relationship.

As reported in detail in previous publications, we compared each of these maltreatment groups to a group of nonmaltreated children from within the same high-risk sample (Egeland & Sroufe, 1981; Egeland et al., 1983; Erickson et al., 1989), using as outcomes a wide range of measures administered over time and across multiple situations. Children in all maltreatment groups functioned poorly in a variety of situations from infancy through the preschool period. There was a relatively high incidence of anxious attachment among all groups of maltreated children.

Among neglected children, two thirds were anxiously attached at 1 year of age. At almost 2 years of age, when videotaped in a problem-solving task with their mothers, neglected children lacked enthusiasm, were easily frustrated, displayed considerable anger, and were noncompliant. When videotaped with their mothers in a series of teaching tasks, neglected children showed little enthusiasm or persistence, were angry, noncompliant, and often avoidant and unaffectionate toward their mothers, even though they were highly dependent on them for help. Also at 42 months, in an independent problem-solving task, these children showed poor impulse control, rigidity, a lack of creativity, and more unhappiness than all other groups. Later, at 54 months of age, when observed in a preschool or child care setting, neglected children demonstrated poor impulse control, extreme dependence on their teachers, and general adjustment problems in the classroom.

In many ways, our study shows the consequences of *emotional neglect* (or what we call psychologically unavailable parenting) to be even more profound than physical neglect and the other types of maltreatment. Nearly all of the children in this group were anxiously attached, with the majority of those classified as anxious-avoidant. In each of the assessments at 24 and 42 months, they displayed anger, noncompliance, lack of persistence, and little positive affect. Probably the most dramatic finding for these children was their steep decline in performance on the Bayley Scales of Infant Development between 9 and 24 months. In the preschool classroom, at approximately 54 months of age, these children presented varied and serious behavior problems. They continued to be noncompliant and negativistic, impulsive, highly dependent on teachers, and they sometimes displayed nervous signs,

self-abusive behavior, and other behaviors considered to be indicators of psychopathology (Egeland et al., 1983). Although the maltreatment they experienced was the most subtle of all groups, the consequences for the children were the most striking.

Again, when the children were between 4 and 6 years of age, we identified groups of children who were being maltreated. Of all the maltreatment groups, the children who were physically neglected at this stage of life presented the most problems. In particular, they were inattentive and uninvolved in learning, anxious, aggressive, and unpopular with peers. Their performance on standardized tests of intellectual functioning and academic achievement were the lowest of all the maltreatment groups. Children who experienced emotional neglect (psychologically unavailable parents) at this stage of life also presented significant problems in the classroom. However, the impact was not as dramatic as for the children who experienced that kind of maltreatment during the first 2 years of life.

Follow-up assessments of emotionally neglected children. Recently, we began to analyze data based on follow-up assessments done when the children in this sample were in elementary school. We especially were interested in seeing whether the impact of having a psychologically unavailable parent during infancy continued to be evident through the elementary years. We gathered information from classroom teachers in Grades 1, 2, 3, and 6. Teachers completed the Child Behavior Checklist on each child (Achenbach & Edelbrock, 1980) and, before they knew who the target child was, they also rank-ordered all the students in their classroom on dimensions of peer acceptance and emotional health. Children also were administered the Peabody Individual Achievement Test (Dunn & Markwardt, 1970) in each of the four grades.

Preliminary analyses indicate that children who experienced psychologically unavailable parenting in the first 2 years of life continued to have problems throughout the elementary school years. When compared to nonmaltreated children from the same high-risk sample, these emotionally neglected children were ranked low by their teachers on both peer acceptance and overall emotional health. On the Child Behavior Checklist, they were rated at all grade levels as being more socially withdrawn, unpopular with peers, and, in general, exhibiting more problems of the internalizing type. In the early grades, they also were rated as more aggressive and less attentive. On the Peabody Individual Achievement Test, these children performed significantly lower at every grade level than the nonmaltreated children in the sample. When these emotionally neglected children were compared with children who had been physically abused in the early years of life, there were no variables on which the physically abused children did significantly worse than the emotionally neglected children, although the emotionally neglected children were more withdrawn and inattentive than the physically abused children.

In summary, the impact of neglect on children's development was at least as damaging as other more overt types of abuse. Physical neglect, particularly during the preschool and primary grades, seriously impaired the children's school behavior. And emotional neglect, especially during the first 2 years of life, had a particularly striking and long-lasting impact on children's adaptation within the family, with peers and teachers, and in regard to learning and problem solving. The effects of neglect are above and beyond the negative impact of poverty and its correlates on children's development.

Antecedents of Neglect

A critical research question that has important implications for prevention involves the identification of variables that predict which children are likely to be neglected. The more we know about the antecedents of neglect, the more precise our attempts will be to identify and support families most at risk. Unfortunately, little in the research points to specific antecedents of neglect as opposed to physical abuse or other types of maltreatment. However, several studies provide useful information about antecedents and concomitants of maltreatment in general. Historically, many studies followed a psychiatric model, whereby abuse was seen as a result of the parent's emotional illness, with little attention paid to child characteristics or to environmental conditions in which the family functioned. More recent literature, however, reflects a shift toward more interactive processes that take into account the multiple variables that influence quality of care. For example, in

1980 Belsky proposed an ecological model of maltreatment that included four levels of analysis: (a) ontogeny (the individual characteristics associated with being a perpetrator of maltreatment), (b) the microsystem (family factors), (c) the exosystem (community factors), and (d) the macrosystem (cultural values and beliefs that serve to perpetuate maltreatment). (See Belsky, 1993, for a more recent elaboration of these ideas.) Similarly, Cicchetti and Rizley (1981) elaborated a transactional model suggesting that maltreatment occurs when *potentiating factors* (i.e., factors that increase the likelihood of maltreatment) outweigh *compensatory factors* (i.e., those that decrease the risk for maltreatment). Factors were categorized further into (a) enduring vulnerability factors, (b) transient challengers, (c) enduring protective factors, and (d) transient buffers.

Acknowledging that no single factor is sufficient to explain maltreatment, recent studies have begun to shed light on how these multiple variables interact to render parents more or less able to sustain adequate, appropriate care for their children. Variables of interest can be grouped broadly into parental characteristics and attitudes, child characteristics, and environmental factors. The findings that have accumulated over the past decade can be summarized briefly as follows.

One set of variables that distinguishes well between maltreating and nonmaltreating parents has to do with social-cognitive and affective processes that are tied to the parents' perceptions of their children and the parent-child relationship. Specifically, maltreating parents often are characterized by a *lack of understanding* of the emotional complexity of human relationships, especially the parent-child relationship. They have difficulty seeing things from the child's perspective or understanding behavior in terms of the child's developmental level and the context or situation.

Maltreating parents tend to think in global, all-or-nothing terms rather than see the shades of gray that more realistically capture human behavior (Brunnquell, Crichton, & Egeland, 1981; Newberger & Cook, 1983; Sameroff & Feil, 1984). Aber and Zigler (1981) point to the importance of the parents' own developmental level as a determinant of how they think and behave in regard to their children. Parental development reflects the parents' own history of care, their struggles with issues of dependency and autonomy, and their level of cognitive functioning. Parents with unresolved issues of trust, dependency, and autonomy are more likely to have difficulty understanding and meeting the demands of their children and may seek to meet their own needs through the parent-child relationship (Pianta et al., 1989). Maltreating parents also have been found to have a high incidence of depression (Lahey, Conger, Atkenson, & Treiber, 1984) and lack impulse control, particularly when stressed (Altemeier, O'Connor, Vietze, Sandler, & Sherrod, 1982; Wolfe, 1985).

Some researchers have focused on child behavior as a contributing factor to child maltreatment. Bell (1968) was one of the first to call attention to the child's influence on the parent in his important paper on the bidirectionality of influence in the parent-child relationship. Research in the 1970s focused on infant irritability and fussiness as contributing factors (Gil, 1970; Parke & Collmer, 1975; Thomas & Chess, 1977). However, retrospective designs and reliance on temperament measures that may have reflected parental perception more than actual child behavior made it difficult to interpret findings from such studies (Vaughn, Deinard, & Egeland, 1980). Others have cited the relationship between maltreatment and such child features as disabilities, prematurity, and facial features (Belsky, 1980; McCabe, 1984). Biringen and Robinson (1991) summarize studies that provide some limited evidence of the child's contribution to parental availability or unavailability.

Although few would dispute that some children are more difficult to care for than others, there is strong evidence from observational studies that child characteristics alone do not account for maltreatment. Research taking a transactional view of parent-child relationships demonstrates the power of parental sensitivity and responsiveness in overcoming the child's difficulty (Brachfield, Goldberg, & Sloman, 1980; Sameroff & Chandler, 1975). To muster the emotional resources to counter the challenges posed by a difficult child, parents may need extra support, education, and encouragement.

Finally, research on the etiology of maltreatment points to several environmental characteristics that are contributing factors. Again, these findings are not specific to neglect but appear to be robust in regard to maltreatment in general.

Major environmental factors include violence in the marital relationship (Straus, 1983; Straus, Gelles, & Steinmetz, 1980), parental unemployment (e.g., Galdston, 1965; Gelles, 1973; Gil, 1970; Horowitz & Wolock, 1981; Steinmetz & Straus, 1974), general disorganization (Tonge, James, & Hillam, 1975), and the availability of a helpful, supportive social network (Garbarino, 1982; Garbarino & Sherman, 1980), perhaps especially among single parents who lack intimate emotional support (Crnic, Greenberg, Ragozin, Robinson, & Basham, 1983). Data from the Second National Incidence Study indicate that, of all subtypes of maltreatment, physical neglect is most clearly associated with poverty and AFDC status (Jones & McCurdy, 1992).

In our own data from the Minnesota Mother-Child Project, we examined the antecedents of specific subtypes of maltreatment, including physical abuse, verbal abuse, neglect, and emotional neglect (what we called psychologically unavailable parenting). This work is described in detail in Pianta et al. (1989). In general, our findings confirmed and expanded on what others have reported. Specifically, we found lack of social support and insularity to characterize families in all maltreatment groups. Maltreating families also experienced more stressful life events than nonmaltreating families within the same high-risk sample. The home environments of maltreating families differed from nonmaltreating homes in terms of provision of play materials and parental involvement and responsivity to the child. The homes of neglectful and sexually abusive families also were observed to be more disorganized than the homes of nonmaltreating families. Maltreating mothers also presented more mood disturbances. Psychologically unavailable mothers were more tense, depressed, angry, and confused than nonmaltreating mothers. Neglectful mothers also were more tense, and they functioned at a lower level intellectually than mothers who provided adequate care. Overall, the maltreating parents differed markedly from nonmaltreating parents on many variables, but the differences by specific type of maltreatment were small.

Another variable of particular interest in our study was the care the mother received in her own childhood. Among mothers who were abused or neglected when they were children, 40% maltreated their children in the early years of their children's lives, and an additional 30%

provided borderline care. This number decreased as the children reached school-age but still remained high. Among neglected mothers in particular, seven out of nine maltreated their own children in the first 2 years of life, and most of these were cases of neglect (Pianta et al., 1989).

Perhaps the most important question of all is, What characterizes parents who rise above their own history of abuse and provide good care for their children? As described elsewhere (Egeland, 1988), three major factors distinguished between mothers who broke the cycle of maltreatment and those who did not: (a) the presence of a loving, supportive adult during her childhood, someone who gave her a different view of herself and others; (b) a supportive partner at the time she became a parent; and (c) therapeutic intervention that enabled the mother to come to some resolution of her early issues and achieve greater emotional stability and maturity. This is consistent with what other researchers have found as well (e.g., Main & Goldwyn, 1984; Ricks, 1985). The reader is referred to Zeanah and Zeanah (1989) for an insightful exploration of the mechanisms by which patterns of maltreatment are transmitted from one generation to the next.

Summary and Discussion: Implications for Practice and Future Research

Based on the research summarized here, it is clear that neglect is a major societal problem. According to CPS, 1.2 million children were reported for this form of maltreatment in 1990 (NCCAN, 1992). And those were only the children who showed up in child protection reports. Considering how easily neglect can be overlooked, it seems impossible to estimate the actual scope of the problem.

We also can say with reasonable certainty that neglect has a serious impact on children's behavior across time and varied situations. Neglected children, if they survive physically, often fail to develop the confidence, concentration, and social skills that would enable them to succeed in school and in relationships. The behavior they bring to the classroom sets them up for a continuing cycle of failure and disappointment unless something happens to make a difference.

Even the most subtle kinds of emotional neglect have a dramatic effect on children's development, especially during the early years of life. As we have discussed in detail elsewhere (e.g., see Erickson et al., 1989), attachment theory provides a useful framework for understanding the impact of neglect. This theory proposes that the infant's relationships with primary caregivers are the prototypes for subsequent relationships. Within those early relationships, children develop expectancies about how others will respond and about how effective they will be in soliciting the responses they need and want. Children then behave in accordance with those expectancies, and that, in a way, helps to perpetuate the kind of relationship experiences they have had.

For example, the child whose mother fails to respond to his or her signals will eventually shut down, no longer seeking or accepting contact with her (as did the anxious-avoidant children in our sample of emotionally neglected children). Then, when the child enters the new social world of school, those old expectancies and behaviors continue to play out in regard to learning, peer relations, and response to teachers.

Emotionally neglected children expect not to get what they need from others, and so they do not even try to solicit care and warmth. They expect not to be effective and successful in tasks, and so they do not try to succeed. Or perhaps, as Aber contends (Aber, Allen, Carlson, & Cicchetti, 1989), these children's dependence needs are so overwhelming that they are barely able to concern themselves with being motivated and task oriented. As we have discussed elsewhere (e.g., Erickson & Pianta, 1989), teachers and peers are often put off by these children's behavior, thus perpetuating their previous relationship experience and reinforcing their negative expectations of others and self.

It is ironic that the impact of emotional neglect is most profound when it is least likely to be detected—when the child is too young to speak out to others. (It is not surprising that early neglect has such a strong influence, because an infant's whole world revolves around his or her primary caregivers.) It is also ironic that, unless the child shows clear physical signs of neglect (e.g., failure to thrive), intervention is not likely to be mandated in cases of emotional neglect. (At least that has been our experience; we have not seen data to that effect.)

An interesting and useful direction for research would be to see how professionals are able to secure intervention or supportive services for emotionally neglectful families and to what extent they can get the system to respond to these families who may not meet the criteria for intervention by CPS. Again, it has been our experience that it is easy to fall into a catch-22 situation: Neglectful families who may not qualify for mandated intervention also may be the most difficult to engage in voluntary service. Either their lives are extremely disorganized (as is often the case with the physically neglectful) or the parents are distancing and perhaps depressed (as is often the case with the emotionally neglectful). The same factors that make it difficult for parents to connect emotionally with their children probably also make it difficult for them to connect with service providers or other potential sources of support. If they feel that they are being judged as failures in parenting, it will not be any easier for parents to connect with service providers.

Although the effectiveness of intervention with neglecting families has not been studied adequately, limited evidence suggests that interventions are successful with no more than 50% of families. The most effective interventions are comprehensive and relatively long term (Gaudin, 1993).

Research does point to some of the early indicators of parents who are likely to be physically or emotionally neglectful, and models of family support and early intervention offer promise as prevention strategies (Wolfe, 1993). In particular, maltreatment is likely to occur among parents who lack an understanding of their children's behavior and the parent-child relationship, experience a great deal of stress, are socially isolated or unsupported, and have a history of inadequate care themselves.

It is important to use knowledge of the antecedents of maltreatment to find ways to identify families at risk and address those underlying factors in an effort to prevent neglect. Health care providers, especially in obstetric, perinatal, and pediatric settings, may be in the best position to identify potentially neglectful families. Because neglect is particularly damaging in infancy, it is important to work with families as early in the infant's life as possible—or, preferably, even before the baby is born. In our own preventive intervention program, Project STEEP (Egeland & Erickson, 1990; Erickson, 1989; Erickson, Korfmacher, & Egeland, 1992), we have found expectant parents to be open to supportive, therapeutic services prior to the birth of their first child. Because they are not parents yet, they do not feel that their child rearing is being judged. And, as they anticipate the new experiences of childbirth and parenting, they are relatively open to the idea of sharing that adventure with their STEEP home visitor and other parents who will be giving birth at about the same time.

In our opinion, one of the major directions for both practice and research in the area of child neglect is the implementation and careful evaluation of programs designed to prevent neglect. Neglect takes many forms and reflects a variety of underlying problems. It is likely that different strategies will be needed for different families facing different issues. (A recent analysis of 34 prevention studies pointed to individualization as a key to success [Wekerle & Wolfe, 1993].) Approaches will vary, depending on such factors as the age and gender of the child, the stage of family development, race, ethnicity, and age and education of the parents. Although it is impossible to design a program to suit each unique family situation, programs should be flexible enough to meet families where they are, identifying and building on individual and family strengths. We concur with Aber and his colleagues (Aber et al., 1989) that programs must be designed, targeted, and evaluated within a clearly articulated theory on the development of maltreated children and the factors that lead to and perpetuate maltreatment. We believe that attachment theory provides a good place to begin.

The challenge for research then will be to assess to what extent, for whom, and under what conditions a program is effective in preventing neglect and other types of maltreatment. As we discover what really helps to build strong families, we prevent harm not only to the children in those families but also to the children of subsequent generations.

References

Aber, J. L., Allen, J. P., Carlson, V., & Cicchetti, D. (1989). The effects of maltreatment on development during early childhood: Recent studies and their theoretical, clinical, and policy implications. In D. Cicchetti & V. Carlson (Eds.), *Child maltreatment: Theory and research on the causes and consequences of child abuse and neglect* (pp. 579-619). New York: Cambridge University Press.

Aber, J. L., & Cicchetti, D. (1984). The social-emotional development of maltreated children: An empirical and theoretical analysis. In H. Fitzgerald, B. Lester, & M. Yogman (Eds.), *Theory and research in behavioral pediatrics* (Vol. 2, pp. 147-205). New York: Plenum.

Aber, J. L., & Zigler, D. (1981). Developmental considerations in the definition of child maltreatment. In. R. Rizley & D. Cicchetti (Eds.), *New directions in child development: Developmental perspectives in child maltreatment* (pp. 1-29). San Francisco: Jossey-Bass.

Achenbach, T., & Edelbrock, C. (1980). *Child behavior checklist—Teacher's report form.* Burlington: University of Vermont.

Ainsworth, M. D. S., Blehar, M., Waters, E., & Wall, S. (1978). *Patterns of attachment.* Hillsdale, NJ: Lawrence Erlbaum.

Altemeier, W., O'Connor, S., Vietze, P., Sandler, H., & Sherrod, K. (1982). Antecedents of child abuse. *Journal of Pediatrics, 100,* 823-829.

American Association for Protecting Children. (1988). *Highlights of official child neglect and abuse reporting, 1986.* Denver, CO: American Humane Association.

Bell, R. (1968). A reinterpretation of the direction of effects in studies of socialization. *Psychological Review, 75,* 81-95.

Belsky, J. (1980). Child maltreatment: An ecological integration. *American Psychologist, 35,* 320-335.

Belsky, J. (1993). Etiology of child maltreatment: A developmental-ecological analysis. *Psychological Bulletin, 114*(3), 413-434.

Biringen, Z., & Robinson, J. (1991). Emotional availability in mother-child interactions: A reconceptualization for research. *American Journal of Orthopsychiatry, 61*(2), 258-271.

Boehm, B. (1962). An assessment of family adequacy in protective cases. *Child Welfare, 41,* 10-16.

Bowlby, J. (1969). *Attachment and loss: Vol. 1. Attachment.* New York: Basic Books.

Bowlby, J. (1973). *Attachment and loss: Vol. 2. Separation.* New York: Basic Books.

Bowlby, J. (1980). *Attachment and loss: Vol 3. Loss, sadness, and depression.* New York: Basic Books.

Brachfield, S., Goldberg, S., & Sloman, J. (1980). Parent-infant interaction in free play at 8 and 12 months: Effects of prematurity and immaturity. *Infant Behavior in Development, 3,* 289-305.

Brassard, M., Germain, R., & Hart, S. (1987). *Psychological maltreatment of children and youth.* Elmsford, NY: Pergamon.

Bretherton, I., & Waters, E. (Eds.). (1985). Growing points of attachment theory and research. *Monographs of the Society for Research in Child Development, 50*(1-2, Serial No. 209).

Brunnquell, D., Crichton, L., & Egeland, B. (1981). Maternal personality and attitude in disturbances of child rearing. *American Journal of Orthopsychiatry, 51,* 680-691.

Cicchetti, D., Carlson, V., Braunwald, K. G., & Aber, J. L. (1987). The sequelae of child maltreatment. In R. Gelles & J. Lancaster (Eds.), *Child abuse and neglect: Biosocial dimensions* (pp. 277-298). New York: Aldine.

Cicchetti, D., & Rizley, R. (1981). Developmental perspectives on the etiology, intergenerational transmission, and sequelae of child maltreatment. *New Directions for Child Development, 11,* 31-55.

Claussen, A. H., & Crittenden, P. M. (1991). Physical and psychological maltreatment: Relations among the types of maltreatment. *Child Abuse & Neglect, 15*(1/2), 5-18.

Corson, J., & Davidson, H. (1987). Emotional abuse and the law. In M. Brassard, B. Germain, & S. Hart (Eds.), *Psychological maltreatment of children and youth* (pp. 185-202). Elmsford, NY: Pergamon.

Crittenden, P. M. (1985a). Maltreated infants: Vulnerability and resilience. *Journal of Child Psychology and Psychiatry, 26*(1), 85-96.

Crittenden, P. M. (1985b). Social networks, quality of child-rearing, and child development. *Child Development, 56,* 1299-1313.

Crittenden, P. M. (1992). Children's strategies for coping with adverse home environments: An interpretation using attachment theory. *Child Abuse & Neglect, 16*(3), 329-343.

Crittenden, P. M., & Ainsworth, M. D. S. (1989). Child maltreatment and attachment theory. In D. Cicchetti & V. Carlson (Eds.), *Child maltreatment: Theory and research on the causes and consequences of child abuse and neglect* (pp. 432-463). New York: Cambridge University Press.

Crnic, K., Greenberg, M., Ragozin, A., Robinson, N., & Basham, R. (1983). Effects of stress and social support on mothers and premature and full term infants. *Child Development, 54,* 209-217.

Dubowitz, H., Black, M., Starr, R. H., & Zuravin, S. (1993). A conceptual definition of child neglect. *Criminal Justice and Behavior, 20*(1), 8-26.

Dunn, L. M., & Markwardt, F. C. (1970). *Peabody Individual Achievement Test.* Circle Pines, MN: American Guidance Service.

Egeland, B. (1988). Breaking the cycle of abuse: Implications for prediction and intervention. In K. D. Browne, C. Davies, & P. Stratton (Eds.), *Early prediction and prevention of child abuse* (pp. 87-99). New York: John Wiley.

Egeland, B., & Erickson, M. F. (1987). Psychologically unavailable caregiving. In M. Brassard, B. Germain, & S. Hart (Eds.), *Psychological maltreatment of children and youth* (pp. 110-120). Elmsford, NY: Pergamon.

Egeland, B., & Erickson, M. F. (1990). Rising above the past: Strategies for helping new mothers break the cycle of abuse and neglect. *Zero to Three, 11*(2), 29-35.

Egeland, B., & Farber, E. A. (1984). Infant-mother attachment: Factors related to its development and changes over time. *Child Development, 55,* 753-771.

Egeland, B., & Sroufe, L. A. (1981). Developmental sequelae of maltreatment in infancy. In B. Rizley & D. Cicchetti (Eds.), *New directions for child development: Developmental perspectives in child maltreatment* (pp. 77-92). San Francisco: Jossey-Bass.

Egeland, B., Sroufe, L. A., & Erickson, M. F. (1983). Developmental consequences of different patterns of maltreatment. *Child Abuse & Neglect, 7*(4), 456-469.

Elmer, E. (1977). A follow-up study of traumatized children. *Pediatrics, 59*(2), 273-314.

Erickson, M. F. (1989). The STEEP Program: Helping young families rise above "at-risk." *Family Resource Coalition Report, 3,* 14-15.

Erickson, M. F., & Egeland, B. (1987). A developmental view of the psychological consequences of maltreatment. *School Psychology Review, 16*(2), 156-168.

Erickson, M. F., Egeland, B., & Pianta, R. C. (1989). The effects of maltreatment on the development of young children. In D. Cicchetti & V. Carlson (Eds.), *Child maltreatment: Theory and research on the causes and consequences of child abuse and neglect* (pp. 647-684). New York: Cambridge University Press.

Erickson, M. F., Korfmacher, J., & Egeland, B. (1992). Attachments past and present: Implications for therapeutic intervention with mother-infant dyad. *Development and Psychopathology, 4,* 495-507.

Erickson, M. F., & Pianta, R. C. (1989). New lunchbox, old feelings: What kids bring to school. *Early Education and Development, 1*(1), 29-35.

Erickson, M. F., Sroufe, L. A., & Egeland, B. (1985). The relationship between quality of attachment and behavior problems in preschool in a high-risk sample. In I. Bretherton & E. Waters (Eds.), *Child development monographs* (pp. 147-166). Chicago: University of Chicago Press.

Flannery, E. J. (1979). Synopsis: Standards relating to abuse and neglect. In R. Bourne & E. H. Newberger (Eds.), *Critical perspectives on child abuse.* Lexington, MA: D. C. Health.

Gaensbauer, T. J., Mrazek, D., & Harmon, R. J. (1980). Affective behavior patterns in abused and/or neglected infants. In N. Frude (Ed.), *The understanding and prevention of child abuse: Psychological approaches.* London: Concord.

Galdston, R. (1965). Observations on children who have been physically abused and their parents. *American Journal of Psychiatry, 122,* 440-443.

Galdston, R. (1971). Violence begins at home. *Journal of the American Academy of Child Psychiatry, 10,* 336-350.

Garbarino, J. (1982). *Children and families in the social environment.* New York: Aldine.

Garbarino, J. (1991). Not all bad developmental outcomes are the result of child abuse. *Development and Psychopathology, 3,* 45-50.

Garbarino, J., & Sherman, D. (1980). High-risk neighborhoods and high-risk families: The human ecology of maltreatment. *Child Development, 51,* 188-196.

Gardner, L. I. (1972). Deprivation dwarfism. *Scientific American, 227,* 76-82.

Gaudin, J. M. (1993). Effective intervention with neglectful families. *Criminal Justice and Behavior, 20*(1), 66-89.

Gelles, R. (1973). Child abuse as psychopathology: A sociological critique and reformation. *American Journal of Orthopsychiatry, 43,* 611-621.

Giaretto, H. (1976). Humanistic treatment of father-daughter incest. In R. Helfer & H. Kempe (Eds.), *Child abuse and neglect* (pp. 143-162). Cambridge, MA: Ballinger.

Gil, D. G. (1970). *Violence against children: Physical abuse in the United States.* Cambridge, MA: Harvard University Press.

Giovannoni, J. (1989). Definitional issues in child maltreatment. In D. Cicchetti & V. Carlson (Eds.), *Child maltreatment: Theory and research on the causes and consequences of child abuse and neglect* (pp. 3-37). New York: Cambridge University Press.

Hamburg, D. (1992). *Today's children: Creating a future for a generation in crisis.* New York: Times Books.

Hart, S. (1987). Mental health neglect—Proposed definition, standards, and procedures for legal and social services intervention. In M. Brassard, B. Germain, & S. Hart (Eds.), *Psychological maltreatment of children and youth* (pp. 268-270). Elmsford, NY: Pergamon.

Herman, J., & Hirschman, L. (1981). Families at risk for father-daughter incest. *American Journal of Psychiatry, 138,* 967-970.

Hoffman-Plotkin, D., & Twentyman, C. T. (1984). A multimodal assessment of behavioral and cognitive deficits in abused and neglected preschoolers. *Child Development, 55,* 794-802.

Horowitz, B., & Wolock, I. (1981). Material deprivation, child maltreatment and agency interventions among poor families. In L. Pelton (Ed.), *The social context of child abuse and neglect.* New York: Human Sciences.

Hufton, I. W., & Oates, R. K. (1977). Non-organic failure to thrive: A long-term follow-up. *Pediatrics, 59,* 73-77.

Jones, E. D., & McCurdy, K. (1992). The links between types of maltreatment and demographic characteristics of children. *Child Abuse & Neglect, 16*(2), 201-215.

Katz, K. (1992). Communication problems in maltreated children: A tutorial. *Journal of Childhood Communication Disorders, 14*(2), 147-163.

Kempe, C. H., Silverman, F. N., Steele, B. F., Droegemueller, W., & Silver, H. K. (1962). The battered-child syndrome. *Journal of the American Medical Association, 181*(17), 17-24.

Kempe, R., & Kempe, C. H. (1978). *Child abuse.* London: Lontana/Open Books.

Korbin, J. E. (1980). The cultural context of child abuse and neglect. *Child Abuse & Neglect, 4,* 3-13.

Lahey, B., Conger, R., Atkenson, B., & Treiber, F. (1984). Parenting behavior and emotional status of physically abusive mothers. *Journal of Consulting and Clinical Psychology, 52,* 1062-1071.

Lamb, M. F., Gaensbauer, T. J., Malkin, C. M., & Schultz, L. A. (1985). The effects of child maltreatment on security of infant-adult attachment. *Infant Behavior and Development, 8,* 34-45.

MacCarthy, D. (1979). Recognition of signs of emotional deprivation: A form of child abuse. *Child Abuse & Neglect, 3,* 423-428.

Main, M., & Goldwyn, R. (1984). Predicting rejection of her infant from mother's representation of her own experience: Implications for the abused-abusing intergenerational cycle. *Child Abuse & Neglect, 8,* 203-217.

Martin, H. P., & Beezley, P. (1977). Behavioral observations of abused children. *Developmental Medicine in Child Neurology, 19,* 373-387.

Martin, H. P., Beezley, P., Conway, E. F., & Kempe, C. H. (1974). The development of abused children. In I. Schulman (Ed.), *Advances in pediatrics* (Vol. 21, pp. 25-73). Chicago: Year Book.

McCabe, V. (1984). Abstract perceptual information for age level: A risk factor for maltreatment? *Child Development, 55,* 267-276.

Morse, W., Sahler, O. J., & Friedman, S. B. (1970). A three-year follow-up study of abused and neglected children. *American Journal of Diseases of Children, 120,* 439-446.

National Center on Child Abuse and Neglect (NCCAN). (1992, April). *National child abuse and neglect data system: Working paper 1, 1990 summary data component* (DHHS Publication No. (ACF)92-30361). Washington, DC: Government Printing Office.

Newberger, C. M., & Cook, S. J. (1983). Parental awareness and child abuse: A cognitive developmental analysis of urban and rural samples. *American Journal of Orthopsychiatry, 53,* 512-524.

Newberger, E. H. (1973). The myth of the battered child syndrome. In R. Bourne & E. H. Newberger (Eds.), *Critical perspectives on child abuse.* Lexington, MA: Lexington Books.

Newson, J., & Newson, E. (1974). Cultural aspects of childrearing in the English-speaking world. In M. P. M. Richard (Ed.), *The integration of a child into a social world* (pp. 53-82). London: Cambridge University Press.

Parke, R. D., & Collmer, C. W. (1975). Child abuse: An interdisciplinary analysis. In F. D. Horowitz (Ed.), *Review of child development research* (pp. 509-590). Chicago: University of Chicago Press.

Patton, R. G., & Gardner, L. I. (1962). Influence of family environment of growth: The syndrome of "maternal deprivation." *Pediatrics, 30,* 957-962.

Pianta, R., Egeland, B., & Erickson, M. F. (1989). The antecedents of maltreatment: Results of the Mother-Child Interaction Research Project. In D. Cicchetti & V. Carlson (Eds.), *Child maltreatment: Theory and research on the causes and consequences of child abuse and neglect* (pp. 203-253). New York: Cambridge University Press.

Polansky, N. A., Chalmers, M. A., Buttenwieser, E., & Williams, D. P. (1981). *Damaged parents: An anatomy of child neglect.* Chicago: University of Chicago Press.

Reidy, T. J. (1977). Aggressive characteristics of abused and neglected children. *Journal of Clinical Psychology, 33,* 1140-1145.

Ricks, M. (1985). The social transmission of parental behavior: Attachment across generations. In I. Bretherton & E. Waters (Eds.), *Growing points of attachment theory and research: Monographs of the Society for Research in Child Development, 50*(1-2, Serial No. 209), 211-227.

Rosenfeld, A. (1977). Sexual misuse and the family. *Victimology: An International Journal, 2,* 226-235.

Sameroff, A. J., & Chandler, M. J. (1975). Reproductive risk and the continuum of caretaking casualty. In F. D. Horowitz (Ed.), *Review of child development research* (pp. 187-244). Chicago: University of Chicago Press.

Sameroff, A. J., & Feil, L. A. (1984). Parental concepts of development. In I. Sigel (Ed.), *Parental belief systems: The psychological consequences for children* (pp. 83-105). Hillsdale, NJ: Lawrence Erlbaum.

Sandgrund, A., Gaines, R., & Green, A. H. (1974). Child abuse and mental retardation: A problem of cause and effect. *American Journal of Mental Deficiency, 79,* 327-330.

Schakel, J. (1987). Emotional neglect and stimulus deprivation. In M. Brassard, B. Germain, & S. Hart (Eds.), *Psychological maltreatment of children and youth* (pp. 100-109). Elmsford, NY: Pergamon.

Schneider-Rosen, K., Braunwald, K. G., Carlson, V., & Cicchetti, D. (1985). Current perspectives in attachment theory: Illustration from the study of maltreated infants. In I. Bretherton & E. Waters (Eds.), *Monographs of the Society for Research in Child Development, 50*(1-2, Serial No. 209), 194-210.

Sroufe, L. A., Fox, N., & Pancake, V. (1983). Attachment and dependency in developmental perspective. *Child Development, 54*(6), 1615-1627.

Steele, B. F. (1977, February). *Psychological dimensions of child abuse.* Paper presented to the American Association for the Advancement of Science, Denver, CO.

Steinmetz, S., & Straus, M. A. (Eds.). (1974). *Violence in the family.* New York: Dodd Mead.

Straus, M. A. (1983). Ordinary violence, child abuse, and wife beating: What do they have in common? In D. Finkelhor, R. J. Gelles, G. T. Hotaling, & M. A. Straus (Eds.), *The dark side of families: Current family violence research* (pp. 213-234). Beverly Hills, CA: Sage.

Straus, M., Gelles, R., & Steinmetz, S. (1980). *Behind closed doors.* New York: Doubleday.

Thomas, A., & Chess, S. (1977). *Temperament and development.* New York: Bruner-Mazel.

Tonge, W., James, D., & Hillam, S. (Eds.). (1975). Families without hope [Special edition]. *British Journal of Psychiatry, 11.*

Vaughn, B., Deinard, A., & Egeland, B. (1980). Measuring temperament in pediatric practice. *Journal of Pediatrics, 96,* 510-514.

Wald, M. S. (1976). State intervention on behalf of "neglected" children: Standards for removal of children from their homes, monitoring the status of children in foster care, and termination of parental rights. *Standard Law Review, 28,* 628-706.

Wekerle, C., & Wolfe, D. A. (1993). Prevention of child physical abuse and neglect: Promising new directions. *Clinical Psychology Review, 13*(6), 501-540.

Wolfe, D. A. (1985). Child-abusive parents: An empirical review and analysis. *Psychological Bulletin, 97,* 462-482.

Wolfe, D. A. (1993). Prevention of child neglect: Emerging issues. *Criminal Justice and Behavior, 20*(1), 90-111.

Wolock, I., & Horowitz, B. (1984). Child maltreatment as a social problem: The neglect of neglect. *American Journal of Orthopsychiatry, 54,* 530-543.

Zeanah, C. H., & Zeanah, P. A. (1989). Intergenerational transmission of maltreatment: Insights from attachment theory and research. *Psychiatry, 52*(2), 177-196.

2

Child Physical Abuse

DAVID J. KOLKO

Significance of the Problem

Child physical abuse represents a significant physical and mental health concern of child practitioners in the United States. Statistics reflecting the daily frequency of various problem situations involving children reveal that each day 10 children die from guns, 6 teenagers commit suicide, 211 children are arrested for drug abuse, 623 teens get syphilis or gonorrhea, and 1,849 children are abused or neglected ("Safe & Sound," 1992). As the latter figure suggests, the physical abuse of children, in particular, is all too common. Researchers have begun to docu-

ment the consequences of abuse (e.g., developmental, psychological, medical), risk factors (e.g., child, parent), and interventions (e.g., individual, family systems). Because only some of this evidence can be described in this chapter, the reader is referred to several other sources for a more comprehensive review of the literature (see Ammerman, 1990a, 1991; Azar, 1991; Cicchetti & Carlson, 1989; Daro, 1988; Erickson, Egeland, & Pianta, 1989; Fantuzzo, 1990; Kaufman & Rudy, 1991; Kolko, 1992; Mash & Johnston, 1990; Widom, 1989b).

There is considerable variation in the topography, severity, and stability of abu-

AUTHOR'S NOTE: Preparation of this review was supported, in part, by the National Center on Child Abuse and Neglect (Grants No. 90CA1459 and 90CA1547). The author acknowledges the contribution of the clinical and research staff of Project IMPACT: Karen Ankrom, Brian Day, Karen Drudy, Audrey Fincher, Sandy Minor, Valerie Newell, Evelyn Savido, Patricia Stewart, and Dana Scheidhauer. Address reprint requests to David J. Kolko, Ph.D., Director, Child & Parent Behavior Clinic, Western Psychiatric Institute and Clinic, 3811 O'Hara St., Pittsburgh, PA 15213.

sive behavior that makes these acts difficult to evaluate and remediate. In recognition of the breadth of this topic and the various forms and definitions of abuse, this review emphasizes primarily recent studies that reflect substantiated cases of child physical abuse (CPA) as well as cases that do not satisfy legal definitions but still reflect more general forms of child physical maltreatment (CPM). Where pertinent, child sexual abuse (CSA) cases also will be reviewed. Presented herein are empirical findings regarding risk factors, developmental effects, treatment outcome evidence, and follow-up outcomes, as well as a description of their general implications for practice and research.

Body of Knowledge, Definitions, and Incidence/Prevalence

Prevalence and incidence rates have been reported during the past two decades in an effort to understand how widespread a problem CPA is (Starr, Dubowitz, & Bush, 1990). Among other factors, the type and specificity of the definition used to identify cases of physical abuse (CPA) may influence such estimates. Definitions vary because of their reliance on a social judgment process that seeks to integrate social-demographic details (e.g., risk factors, safety issues) with the child's physical or medical status (e.g., severity of injury) (Emery, 1989). Moreover, a fine distinction exists between CPA and some of the more extreme forms of parent-to-child discipline (e.g., beating vs. spanking or slapping). Other individual worker and systemic factors may influence reporting rates (e.g., caseload size, experience of worker, population size). Accordingly, the task of determining when parental behaviors are excessive, unwarranted, dangerous, and ultimately abusive remains a complex one. Rates of child abuse vary considerably across states primarily due to the level of restrictiveness in their definitions (e.g., 30% in Maryland, 34% in Pennsylvania, 43% in Missouri, 44% in Nevada) (American Association for Protecting Children [AAPC], 1988). To advance the investigation process, child abuse specialists have suggested that protective services be concerned only with cases in which caretaker acts or the failure to act

has resulted in "the death; serious physical, sexual, or emotional harm; or imminent risk for serious harm" to a juvenile (Rycraft, 1990, p. 15). This definition would restrict the number of clients served by protective services and thus has implications for prevalence and incidence rates and service delivery. Definitional ambiguities suggest the potential benefit of articulating further official CPA definitions and reporting procedures.

As these comments suggest, incidence and prevalence rates reveal variations in the scope of child maltreatment. Nationally, the incidence of CPA in 1986 has been estimated at 3.5/1,000 children (AAPC, 1988), or 4.9/1,000 or 311,200 children (National Center on Child Abuse and Neglect [NCCAN], 1988). When cases involving abuse, endangerment, and being at risk for harm are combined, the incidence is 5.7/1,000 or 358,300 children (Sedlak, 1990). This number is substantially higher than that reported in the original national incidence study of 1979 (NCCAN, 1981).

Prevalence estimates suggest that approximately 27% of all reports that made up the caseloads of U.S. child protective services (CPS) in 1992 involved charges of physical abuse (McCurdy & Daro, 1994). This report indicated that an estimated 2.9 million children were reported to CPS agencies as alleged victims of child maltreatment, of whom an estimated 1.16 million children were substantiated as victims. The report also found that an estimated 1,261 children (1.94/100,000) died from abuse or neglect in 1992, a 49% increase nationwide since 1985. At the state level, reports from Pennsylvania, which has one of the most restrictive definitions, indicated higher percentages of cases involving suspected CPM, child fatalities, reabuse, and foster care placement in 1991 than in prior years (Pennsylvania Department of Public Welfare, 1992).

Population survey findings estimate that approximately 700,000 children were subjected to very severe violent behavior in 1985 (Gelles & Straus, 1987), but this figure jumps to 6.9 million children when considering cases involving less severe parental assault (110 incidents/1,000 children) during a 12-month period (Gelles & Straus, 1990). That study concluded that the incidence rate of CPA fell from 36/1,000 to 19/1,000 from 1975 to 1985. Such estimates may be somewhat inaccurate due to methodological and reporting biases, such as the use of only two-parent families, examination of a small number of violent behaviors, use of families with children above the age of 3, and variations in the interview method (see Starr et al., 1990). Ironically, during this same period, the number of cases reported increased dramatically, perhaps because of greater societal recognition and vigilance. Currently underway is the third National Incidence Study that should provide more rigorous evidence for changes in the incidence and prevalence of CPM.

Etiology and Risk: Predisposing Characteristics

Conceptualization

Models of CPA are important because of their potential to help organize individual findings across studies, identify key processes or factors associated with the emergence of abusive behavior for empirical evaluation, and suggest the utility of intervention programs (see National Academy of Sciences, 1993). Theories and supporting data have been offered to explain the physical abuse of children (e.g., Ammerman, 1990a; Azar & Siegel, 1990; MacKinnon, Lamb, Belsky, & Baum, 1990), with one recent book providing an integration of 46 different theories of abuse, 25 of which were associated with CPA (Tzeng, Jackson, & Karlson, 1991). This work and another theoretical analysis of the dimensions and underlying principles of contemporary theories (Azar, 1991) show that theories differ widely on key issues that require greater clarification (e.g., definitions, assumptions of origins of abuse, complexity and level of analysis, individual vs. contextual emphasis, child vs. family focus). These theories bear implications for both prevention and treatment.

Although evaluation of individual theories is complicated, certain early formulations have been examined and found to be somewhat limited in scope. For example, traditional models that emphasize the salience of serious psychiatric disturbances in the parent (e.g., psychological and emotional deficiencies) or problems inherent in the family's sociocultural context have received partial support (see Ammerman, 1990b; Wolfe, 1987). Features of these approaches have been incorporated into multidimensional, interactional models that recognize the interplay between children's and parents' characteristics, especially their psychological functioning and social system context. Among individual developments in this area, for example, there is empirical support for elaborations of a cognitive-behavioral model that posits the influence of parents' cognitive and behavioral repertoire in helping their children to negotiate developmental tasks (Azar & Siegel, 1990). This model identifies key parental skills or behaviors that need to be understood, such as developmentally sensitive expectations, adaptive attributions, adequate child-rearing and problem-solving skills, and constructive self-management (coping and social) skills. The model also maintains that the child's competencies and challenges and other contextual obstacles to positive parenting influence parental behavior. Other innovative work has attempted to classify abusers based on observations of parent-child interaction (Oldershaw, Walters, & Hall, 1989).

Related ecologically based or transactional models have integrated dysfunctional child-caregiver-family-environment interactions in understanding the precipitants and correlates of CPM (e.g., Ammerman, 1990b; MacKinnon et al., 1990; Wolfe, 1987). Ecological theorists advocate evaluation of the association between parental behaviors that elicit harsh parent-child interactions (Azar, Barnes, & Twentyman, 1988; Wolfe, 1987) and children's coping strategies (Cicchetti, 1990), among other family system characteristics. Within the interactional perspective, CPM represents the interplay among child, parent, and family factors (see Mash & Johnston, 1990). As an extension of this perspective, Belsky's (1993) recent "developmental-ecological" model is heuristically important in its emphasis on developmental child and parental characteristics, immediate interactional processes, and broader social context associated with child maltreatment.

Numerous influences on the expression of punitive parental behavior toward children are consistent with these perspectives and require integration in model development. These influences on parental behavior include observational learning (via modeling) of aggressive response patterns, failure to acquire prosocial parenting competencies or skills (especially in the face of heightened anger arousal), and development of coercive behaviors due to exposure to aggressive family interaction patterns and reinforcement for aggression (see Ammerman, 1990b). A multifactor model is needed because no single individual characteristic, especially among child factors, consistently has been related to abusive behavior (Azar, 1991) and because few variables are directly related to abuse (Salzinger, Feldman, Hammer, & Rosario, 1991). What is needed is some integration of key variables and processes that can indicate how these characteristics contribute to the emergence of abuse, the accuracy of explanatory models, and the design of intervention strategies. To promote progress toward this end, I discuss some of the more salient abuse-related variables and processes in the next section.

Child Characteristics

Health/medical status. Early health and medical problems may place certain children at risk for abuse.

Medical, intellectual, or developmental aberrations (e.g., birth complications, physical disability, low IQ) are some of the characteristics that may contribute to the emergence of abusive interactions.

Medical, intellectual, or developmental aberrations (e.g., birth complications, physical disability, low IQ) are some of the characteristics that may contribute to the emergence of abusive interactions (Belsky & Vondra, 1989). However, there is mixed evidence that these characteristics significantly increase a child's risk above and beyond parental characteristics (see Ammerman, 1990a, 1990b, 1991). Instead, such problems are more likely to be consequences than causes of abuse (Youngblade & Belsky, 1990). Of course, health problems may increase parental responsibility and worry, financial burdens on the family, disruptions in routines, and, in cases of serious health complications, may result in long separations from parents.

Temperament/behavior. Other aspects of the child's general behavior have been emphasized in CPA formulations, including such attributes as difficult temperament (e.g., impulsivity, crying) and both behavioral and emotional deviance (e.g., aggression, depression; see Belsky & Vondra, 1989). Such characteristics (e.g., high activity level, limited sociability) may reduce parental tolerance and increase parental reliance on physical discipline. Although deviant child behaviors have contributed to abusive incidents (Herrenkohl, Herrenkohl, & Egolf, 1983; Youngblade & Belsky, 1990) and have differentiated abused from nonabused conduct-problem children (e.g., Whipple & Webster-Stratton, 1991), a child's behavioral deviance is an insufficient explanation of such events (Ammerman, 1991; Pianta, Egeland, & Erickson, 1989).

Nevertheless, a child's difficult temperament and conduct problems are potent stressors that can disrupt parenting practices and effective parent-child interactions (see Webster-Stratton, 1990). A feature common to both categories is an adverse effect on attachment history (Cicchetti, 1990). Difficulties occurring especially early in a child's life may create undue burden on parents while also limiting the development of positive parent-child bonds. Excessive child-rearing responsibilities or challenges created by these vulnerabilities may result in increased parental irritability and reduced patience, thus heightening the likelihood of inconsistent care or punitive treatment. That specific child characteristics have been so implicated in interactional models of child abuse highlights the importance of documenting a child's behavioral characteristics and prosocial repertoire.

Parental Characteristics

The extensive literature on parental or perpetrator characteristics has been reviewed thoroughly elsewhere (see Milner, 1991; Milner & Chilamkurti, 1991). Certain characteristics are discussed here because of their importance to the maintenance of abusive interactional patterns. The majority of these parental characteristics reflect heightened levels of distress or dysfunction (e.g., depression, physical symptoms) and inappropriate parenting strategies rather than specific psychiatric disorders (see Factor & Wolfe, 1990; Milner & Chilamkurti, 1991).

Childhood history of abuse. The connection between harsh punishment experienced as a child and subsequent family violence has been described as one primary interactional mechanism by which abusive behavior is "transmitted" (Straus, Gelles, & Steinmetz, 1980). Early physical punishment is related to heightened abuse potential (Milner, Robertson, & Rogers, 1990) or actual physical violence toward children (e.g., Gelles & Straus, 1987; Pianta et al., 1989; Whipple & Webster-Stratton, 1991). An excellent prospective study extended these findings in showing a relationship between a grandparent's practices and an adult's subsequent use of harsh parenting practices, especially among mothers (Simons, Whitbeck, Conger, & Chyi-In, 1991). Interestingly, support was not found for the position that aggressive parenting practices are transmitted indirectly by influencing parental personality or beliefs about the legitimacy of harsh parenting practices. Rather, adults who experience or witness abuse during childhood are exposed to aversive models and may learn to use aggressive methods of disciplining children (Milner & Chilamkurti, 1991).

Although the percentage of abused children who become abusive parents is not small (estimated at about 30%), most of them do not grow up to be abusers.

Although the percentage of abused children who become abusive parents is not small (estimated at about 30%) (Kaufman & Zigler, 1987), most of them do not grow up to be abusers (see Widom, 1989b), nor does early abuse always distinguish abusers from nonabusive parents (e.g., Salzinger et al., 1991). Early physical punishment is only one of the primary risk factors for CPM (Straus & Smith, 1990) and may be related more to whether a child becomes the target (vs. source) of aggression (Cappell & Heiner, 1990). Beyond childhood exposure, the likelihood of CPM is influenced by other psychological or contextual factors associated with general aggressivity, such as gender, maternal depression, high IQ, poverty, poor parenting practices, social support/competence, and stress, among other factors (Cappell & Heiner, 1990; Mash & Johnston, 1990; Simons et al.,

1991; Webster-Stratton, 1985, 1990; Whipple & Webster-Stratton, 1991; Widom, 1989b). Taken together, these studies suggest that early abuse and later CPM are related indirectly and that many variables are related to CPM.

Personality and psychiatric disturbances. Specific characteristics of parental personality may increase the likelihood of parental aggression. Hostile personality has been found to be significantly related to the use of harsh parenting (Simons et al., 1991), and parental explosiveness, as well as irritability and the use of threats, has been associated with aggression against children and disrupted discipline (Caspi & Elder, 1988; Patterson, DeBaryshe, & Ramsey, 1989). Although these characteristics may increase the probability of harsh parenting and aggression against children, further studies are needed to determine whether hostile or explosive personality is a precursor to or consequence of harsh parenting.

Psychiatric disturbances such as depression (Whipple & Webster-Stratton, 1991) and substance abuse (Famularo, Stone, Barnum, & Wharton, 1986; Murphy et al., 1991; Whipple & Webster-Stratton, 1991) have been implicated in cases of CPM. Both forms of dysfunction may render parents less able or willing to maintain a high level of involvement with a child and more likely to exhibit irritability or anger in response to child misbehavior. Substance abuse may increase the risk of court noncompliance and, along with alcohol abuse, may increase the chance of a child's removal from the home (Famularo, Kinscherff, & Fenton, 1992a; Murphy et al., 1991). Likewise, maternal drug use has been associated with child maltreatment and child removal (Kelley, 1992). Recent evidence based on structured interviews has shown that current and past affective disorder, substance abuse, and posttraumatic stress disorder (PTSD) are more common in abusive than control parents (Famularo, Kinscherff, & Fenton, 1992c). Psychiatric disorders are evaluated infrequently in this literature, however, so it is difficult to determine the representativeness of these selected findings and the significance of certain disorders (e.g., PTSD) relative to other forms of distress.

Cognitive style. Recent perspectives have suggested that abusers evince negative cognitive-attributional styles or perceive their children in a more negative light than nonabusive parents (Azar & Siegel, 1990). For example, abusive parents have displayed high expectations of their children's behavior (Azar, Robinson, Hekimian, & Twentyman, 1984), which may be paralleled by a perception that the child's behavior is deviant. In one study, abusive parents reported higher levels of behavioral dysfunction among their children than those of comparison parents, even though home observations failed to reveal group differences (Whipple & Webster-Stratton, 1991). Parents who believe in the appropriateness of strict physical discipline and who also have high expectations of their children's behavior are more likely to engage in harsh parenting (Simons et al., 1991). Indeed, abusive parents are more accepting of physical punishment than nonabusive parents (Kelly, Grace, & Elliot, 1990).

In suggesting the presence of negative child perceptions, these constructs imply that parents may view their children with limited acceptance or positivity (see Mash & Johnston, 1990), which, in turn, may influence their actual management practices at home. Plausible reasons for excessive parental negativity toward children's misbehavior include parental distortions regarding the child's responsibility for certain actions, parental unhappiness and psychiatric disturbances, and reduced tolerance for child problems, but the impact of these conditions among abusive parents awaits further inquiry (Azar, 1991).

The attributional bias that disposes abusive parents to viewing children in a more negative light than their behavior actually warrants may be compared to the distortion that has been documented among aggressive adolescents and supports the need to understand parents' attributional styles or perceptual functioning better (Bugental, Mantyla, & Lewis, 1989).

Behavioral functioning. Abusive parents have been noted to exhibit inconsistent child-rearing practices (Susman, Trickett, Iannotti, Hollenbeck, & Zahn-Waxler, 1985) that often reflect the presence of critical, hostile, or aggressive management styles (Trickett & Kuczynski, 1986; Whipple & Webster-Stratton, 1991). In addition, they may exhibit limited attention to their children, as reflected by low levels of positive affect and social behav-

ior (Kavanaugh, Youngblade, Reid, & Fagot, 1988; Salzinger, Samit, Krieger, Kaplan, & Kaplan, 1986; Schindler & Arkowitz, 1986), poor problem solving (Azar et al., 1984; Hansen, Pallotta, Tishelman, Conaway, & MacMillan, 1988), and less attention-directing verbal and physical strategies (Alessandri, 1992), with the latter study showing less mutual interaction in both free play and problem-solving situations. In some cases, abusive parents actually have responded aversively to child prosocial behavior (Reid, Kavanaugh, & Baldwin, 1987). A strength of many of these studies is their inclusion of structured behavioral observations.

Because deficits in parental coping skills may be identified in diverse areas (e.g., child management, anger control, finance), it is important to incorporate multidimensional measures that tap these broad domains of functioning. For example, self-reports of both positive and negative parenting behaviors would elaborate on the quality of parent-child relationships. The experience of serious parental stressors in some families (e.g., low parental social support, depression, marital discord) further may restrict parents' abilities to support their children's efforts to cope with adversity (see Erickson et al., 1989; Pianta et al., 1989; Webster-Stratton, 1985; Whipple & Webster-Stratton, 1991).

Biological factors. Few biological variables have been examined in relation to CPM, but one characteristic, hyperarousal to stressful child-related stimuli, has been documented among physical child abusers, especially in skin conductance, a measure of autonomic arousal (e.g., Friedrich, Tyler, & Clark, 1985; Wolfe, Fairbanks, Kelly, & Bradlyn, 1983). Greater autonomic activity also has been found in response to nonchild-related stimuli perceived as stressful (Casanova, Domanic, McCanne, & Milner, 1991), which may contribute to parents' impulsive behavior and problem-solving difficulties (see McCanne & Milner, 1991). Future studies are needed to document more fully the impact of biological responding on child-directed aggression and the possible relationship of parental reactivity to cognitive and behavioral response patterns related to abusive behavior.

Family-System Characteristics

Coercive parent-child interactions. Family influences on abusive behavior reflect a broad range of functional and structural characteristics. For example, observational studies have shown that abusive parents and their victimized children exhibit aggressive or coercive behavior toward one another (see Azar et al., 1988; Fantuzzo, 1990).

Parents' aversive behavior often is reinforced negatively during coercive interchanges because it terminates children's deviant behavior.

Parents' aversive behavior often is reinforced negatively during coercive interchanges because it terminates children's deviant behavior. Other factors contributing to coercive interactions include the use of ineffective child management techniques, such as the limited use of positive affect and general discussion (Bousha & Twentyman, 1984; Kavanaugh et al., 1988; Oldershaw, Walters, & Hall, 1986). Indeed, limited positive interactions actually may be more characteristic of abusive families than excessive negativity (Caliso & Milner, 1992).

Overall, social-interactional studies identify patterns characterized by excessive family coercion and limited positive exchanges, with some evidence for aversive child behaviors (Azar & Wolfe, 1989; Conaway & Hansen, 1989). These findings stress the potential significance of aversive confrontations with family members as antecedents to or consequences of CPM. It should be pointed out that gender effects sometimes qualify these overall patterns. For example, Whipple and Webster-Stratton (1991) found that increased harsh physical punishment was observed among fathers but not mothers in abusive families, but only mothers were more critical verbally.

Poor family relationships. Physically punitive family environments may support psychologically abusive or coercive communications that contribute to the level of psychopathology evinced by child victims (Claussen & Crittenden, 1991; Kaufman & Cicchetti, 1989). This family context of

hostility may interact with other child and parent variables that maintain abusive behavior (Wolfe, 1987), such as heightened conflict and decreased cohesion (Azar & Wolfe, 1989) or partner abuse (Fantuzzo et al., 1991; Salzinger et al., 1991). Although it follows that hostile relationships within the family contribute to abusive behavior, more empirical evidence examining this relationship is needed.

Other contextual and social system variables. Diverse stress-eliciting factors or family socioeconomic disadvantages (e.g., limited income, unemployment, family size, youthful parenthood, single parenthood) contribute to the expression of violent behavior (Belsky & Vondra, 1989). Abusive families have experienced numerous child and parent stressors (Holden, Willis, & Foltz, 1989) and social disadvantage (Pianta et al., 1989). Poverty alone has emerged as a significant predictor of abuse status (Whipple & Webster-Stratton, 1991), and parental insularity or isolation has been regarded as a significant correlate (Starr, 1988). The experience of few positive extrafamilial relationships and much frustration with family members may compromise parents' overall effectiveness.

In one recent study, the developmental ecologies of the families of abused children were found to be characterized by parental worries, dissatisfaction with their children and the parenting role, limited emotional expressiveness, social isolation, and lack of encouragement for the development and autonomy of their children (Trickett, Aber, Carlson, & Cicchetti, 1991). Interestingly, the findings differentiating abusive from nonabusive families were more pronounced among cases from higher rather than lower socioeconomic status. The social disadvantage of abusive families, then, involves impoverishment in both social and community resources.

Summary. Although many of the aforementioned characteristics have been noted in abusive parents, whether they are necessary antecedents or correlates of abuse for particular parents cannot be determined clearly. This is perhaps one reason why it is difficult to identify abusers by using individual self-report measures (see Milner, 1991). At present, the psychological characteristics of abusive parents do not conform consistently to any specific traits or diagnostic profile beyond concerns related to their parenting role and stressful family circumstances (National Academy of Sciences, 1993; Wolfe, 1987). Abusers tend to experience symptoms of affective, somatic, and behavioral distress believed to impair their parenting functions and may contribute to unrealistic expectations of their child's conduct and capabilities. The broad characteristics attributed to abusive families underscore the multidimensional nature of aggressive interactions and strongly argue against single-variable conceptualizations of etiology (Belsky, 1993). Greater consideration of the bases of parenting and parent-child relationships and the environmental conditions that precipitate extreme responses along a continuum of parenting experiences will further our understanding of abusive behavior.

Sequelae/Consequences

Medical/Physical Functioning

Commonly accepted definitions of CPM permit considerable diversity in the nature and severity of children's injuries whose medical risk would be expected to influence their daily functioning and health. Adverse health effects following physical punishment have been noted in several studies, although the overall evidence is equivocal with respect to particular injuries (see Augoustinos, 1987). Recent controlled studies have documented more neonatal problems and family disruption due to the child's mental illness and/or head injury in maltreated than in control children (Famularo, Fenton, & Kinscherff, 1992) and more early developmental delays, neurological soft signs, serious physical injuries, skin markings and scars, and stimulant drug use among hospitalized children with a history of CPA (Kolko, Moser, & Weldy, 1990). The latter study also found that CSA, but not CPA, was related to heightened sexuality and physical signs of genital manipulation. Neurological impairment has been documented in child victims of CPA (Lewis, Mallouh, & Webb, 1989). Indeed, CPA may have an impact on various aspects of physiological functioning, such as decreased serotonin and increased dopamine and testosterone (see Lewis, 1992).

Poor health and increased health costs are correlates of spousal abuse (Gelles & Straus, 1990) and prompt questions as to whether CPM produces similar effects on the health or medical status of children. Because so few studies have been conducted, questions still remain regarding the impact of CPM, such as the following: (a) Do abused children suffer from repeated physical injuries? (b) Do physical injuries affect psychosocial adjustment and long-term academic and social functioning? (c) Does injury status relate to treatment outcome? Routine medical and health screening of suspected child victims seems warranted to supplement the investigation process and identify targets for medical intervention. Given the potential severity of neurological problems, evaluation of physical symptoms would enhance the diagnosis and remediation of CPA.

Developmental/Intellectual Deficits

Exposure to severe CPM may produce cognitive or intellectual deficits or other related limitations in cognitive (e.g., limited intellectual functioning), language (e.g., limited verbal ability), or perceptual motor deficits (Elmer & Gregg, 1967; Tarter, Hegedus, Winsten, & Alterman, 1984). Recent controlled studies extend these findings in showing reduced task initiation and motivation (Aber & Allen, 1987; Allen & Tarnowski, 1989) as well as limited intellectual functioning among maltreated youngsters (Alessandri, 1991; Erickson et al., 1989) and schoolchildren (Salzinger, Kaplan, Pelcovitz, Samit, & Krieger, 1984). Some of these limitations in intellectual functioning have been documented at different points in time (Erickson et al., 1989). Other studies, however, have failed to find differences in these areas between abused and nonabused children (see Augoustinos, 1987; Azar et al., 1988; Fantuzzo, 1990; Slade, Steward, Morrison, & Abramowitz, 1984).

The varied outcomes in this area may be attributable to several background factors, such as the failure to distinguish between types and severity of maltreatment or use objective measures (Augoustinos, 1987). Cognitive functioning may be related closely to the quality of the caretaking environment, as shown in one study that found that young victims of CPM had more receptive language problems than nonabused children but did not differ from children residing in low socioeconomic status families (Vondra, Barnett, & Cicchetti, 1990). Given that the level of stimulation in the daily living environment may influence a child's cognitive abilities (see Aber, Allen, Carlson, & Cicchetti, 1989), family environmental variables merit further evaluation. More extensive evaluation of the impact of physical injuries on children's cognitive abilities also is warranted.

Children with a history of CPA may develop perceptions of physical discipline that are related to their experiences.

Cognitive-Attributional Deficits

Children with a history of CPA may develop perceptions of physical discipline that are related to their experiences. Although studies indicate that both nonabused and abused children infrequently suggest the use of physical punishment (Carlson, 1986, 1991), abused children show a greater willingness to use physical punishment. The increased attention to aggressive stimuli in maltreated versus control children is consistent with this finding (Rieder & Cicchetti, 1989). Moreover, abused children seem to have greater problems with perspective taking (e.g., Howes & Espinosa, 1985). For example, some evidence has shown that abused compared to control youngsters generate fewer alternative solutions to hypothetical social problems and are more likely to perseverate on negative solutions (Haskett, 1990).

These few findings provide only limited investigation of the cognitive deficits or distortions evinced by abused children. This area could be extended by examining other aspects of children's cognitive-constructive repertoire as they pertain to their acceptance of violent behavior. It would be instructive to learn, for example, whether victims of CPM show negative attributional biases comparable to those of aggressive children (Dodge, 1990) or the types of cognitive distortions of depressed children (Kendall, Stark, & Adam, 1990). If so, then specific methods designed to enhance children's use of prosocial, verbal mediation skills are

likely to have an effect on these cognitive processes.

Socioemotional Functioning/ Affective Symptoms

Attachment and self-esteem. Disturbances in the formation of stable attachments are of developmental importance due to their association with significant forms of child adjustment, such as the child's individuation, personal sense of competence, and ability to regulate affect (Cicchetti, 1989, 1990). Studies examining the quality of the parent-child relationship among maltreated youngsters consistently have shown insecure attachments as reflected by increased avoidance and resistance (Cicchetti & Barnett, 1991; Crittenden, 1988) and separation problems (Lynch & Cicchetti, 1991). Consistent with claims that attachment problems may set the foundation for subsequent problems (Youngblade & Belsky, 1990), evidence suggests that attachment disturbances may be related to children's roles as victims, victimizers, or nonvictims (Troy & Sroufe, 1987).

Maltreated children also have shown evidence of limited self-esteem on self-report (Allen & Tarnowski, 1989; Kinard, 1982; Oates, Forrest, & Peacock, 1985) and parental report measures (Kaufman & Cicchetti, 1989) relative to controls, with some exceptions (Stovall & Craig, 1990). Although these findings suggest that victims of CPM view themselves more negatively than their nonabused peers, it is not clear whether these differences reflect problems with self-esteem following CPA or the presence of broad aspects of personal and family dysfunction. Also, the long-term impact of lowered self-esteem among victims of CPA merits investigation.

Affective disturbances. Expanding on initial clinical descriptions of the development of affective symptoms (e.g., depressive states, anxiety) among traumatized children (Green, 1981, 1983), empirical evidence supports the presence of negative affect in younger (Schneider-Rosen & Cicchetti, 1984) and older abused children (Kinard, 1980, 1982). More recent studies using standardized measures and multiple informants have found higher levels of depression and hopelessness among abused versus nonabused psychiatric patients (Allen & Tarnowski, 1989; Kazdin, Moser, Colbus, & Bell, 1985).

At the same time, victims of CPM do not always differ from their nonabused peers on items reflecting affective symptoms (Kazdin et al., 1985), especially in terms of parental reports (Kolko, Moser, & Weldy, 1988). This may reflect the fact that parents may be less sensitive to or disturbed by their children's internalizing symptoms. Other work suggests that cognitive-perceptual (information-processing) skills deficits may contribute to abused children's limited affective expressiveness (Barahal, Waterman, & Martin, 1981; Camras, Grow, & Ribordy, 1983). Because few studies have used standardized diagnostic interviews with abused children, it is also plausible that the severity of depression may be underestimated.

Psychiatric disturbances/PTSD. Green's (1981, 1983) original work suggested that long-term (vs. acute) exposure to abuse may be associated with more diverse problems (e.g., poor impulse control, helplessness, poor attachment, self-destructive behavior), including PTSD.

In coping with repeated abuse, traumatized children exhibit similar reactions that include recurrent memories, post-traumatic (abuse-repetitive) behaviors, attitude or personality changes associated with the realization that one is different, and trauma-specific fears.

In coping with repeated abuse, traumatized children exhibit similar reactions that include recurrent memories, posttraumatic (abuse-repetitive) behaviors, attitude or personality changes associated with the realization that one is different, and trauma-specific fears (Terr, 1988, 1990, 1991). These symptoms appear to be highly stable over time and may reflect the presence of idiosyncratic defenses (e.g., repression, dissociation) or affective states that range from psychic numbing to rage or sadness.

Empirical studies of PTSD have found differences between children with a chronic versus acute history of maltreatment. Chronic child victims tend to show

detachment, estrangement, restricted affect, thoughts that life is difficult or hard, and unhappiness. Acute victims are more likely to be anxious or agitated (Famularo, Kinscherff, & Fenton, 1990b). A history of maltreatment also has been associated with borderline personality disorder (Famularo, Kinscherff, & Fenton, 1990a), attention deficit hyperactivity disorder, or oppositional disorder (Famularo, Kinscherff, & Fenton, 1992b). These studies are noteworthy for their finding that maltreated cases differed from controls in certain disorders, depending on whether children (e.g., greater psychotic symptoms, personality/adjustment disorders) or parents (conduct/mood disorders) were interviewed. Hypervigilance is one PTSD symptom found to be associated with CPM, especially in boys (Hill, Bleichfeld, Brunstetter, Hebert, & Steckler, 1989).

With emerging support for the presence of certain psychiatric disturbances among victims of CPM, diagnostic studies are needed to learn about the breadth of these disorders and their therapeutic implications. Other studies using standardized interviews are needed to determine the relationship between CPM and certain disorders (e.g., conduct disorder, major depressive disorder), using nonabused clinical controls for comparison purposes. As suggested in the case of CSA, it is not clear whether PTSD is a mental disorder, especially an anxiety disorder; instead, its consideration as a normal response to an abnormal situation deserves empirical study (O'Donohue & Elliott, 1992). Clearly, the clinical presentation of abused children is variable and may be a function of the type, duration, and severity of the trauma, among other factors (e.g., child age, family dysfunction). Researchers should develop models of the psychology of child trauma and its relationship to psychopathology. These models would promote research to expand knowledge about CPA (see Cicchetti, 1990).

Social Behavior/Academic Performance

Behavioral dysfunction. One of the most extensive clinical consequences documented among victims of CPM is heightened aggressivity (see Ammerman, 1989; Azar et al., 1988; Kolko, 1992; National

Academy of Sciences, 1993) based on adult ratings (Hoffman-Plotkin & Twentyman, 1984; Kravic, 1987; Salzinger et al., 1984), home observations (Bousha & Twentyman, 1984), and play and social settings (Alessandri, 1991; Howes & Espinosa, 1985; Kaufman & Cicchetti, 1989; Rieder & Cicchetti, 1989). Many of these studies are notable due to the use of objective measures and, in some cases, comparison groups. For example, child victims of CPM consistently are found to be more aggressive than neglected children (Hoffman-Plotkin & Twentyman, 1984; Kaufman & Cicchetti, 1989).

Other externalizing behavior problems have been documented, such as increased rule violations, oppositionalism, and delinquency (Trickett & Kuczynski, 1986; Walker, Downey, & Bergman, 1989). In some instances, high levels of aggression have been directed toward siblings, parents, and even nonfamily members (Hotaling, Straus, & Lincoln, 1990).

Beyond fighting in and out of the home, children experiencing severe violence are at risk for property offenses, drinking and drug use, criminal arrests, and other serious antisocial acts.

Beyond fighting in and out of the home, children experiencing severe violence are at risk for property offenses, drinking and drug use, criminal arrests (Gelles & Straus, 1990; Hotaling et al., 1990), and other serious antisocial acts (see Lewis, Mallouh, et al., 1989).

The level of externalizing dysfunction may be related to the experience of witnessing family violence and other adverse family environment factors, such as negative life events (Kolko, 1992; Wolfe, 1987). Both heightened family conflict that includes verbal and physical aggression (vs. verbal only) and shelter residence (vs. home) have been found to be related significantly to the clinical severity of children's conduct and emotional problems and diminished social functioning (Fantuzzo et al., 1991).

Prosocial/adaptive behaviors. Apart from their involvement in aggressive behavior, victims of CPM exhibit less prosocial be-

havior and may experience poor peer relations (see Conaway & Hansen, 1989; Youngblade & Belsky, 1990). Young maltreated children are less friendly or positive in their interactions with peers (Howes & Espinosa, 1985; Kaufman & Cicchetti, 1989). One study of maltreated preschoolers showed that they engaged in more repetitive motor play and less parallel or group play than their nonmaltreated peers, which may implicate the presence of developmental delays in play behavior (Alessandri, 1991). Other evidence suggests that abused youngsters are less likely to initiate positive peer interactions, are less well-liked by peers, and receive fewer peer responses to their initiations (Haskett & Kistner, 1991). Likewise, older child victims show limited social competence (Feldman et al., 1989), problems making friends (Gelles & Straus, 1990) and reciprocity, and greater peer isolation (Dean, Malik, Richards, & Stringer, 1986).

Children who do not sustain social relationships may be less likely to exhibit empathy or perspective taking (Burgess & Youngblade, 1989), though this outcome may relate to limited parental social competence and generalized exposure to an impoverished or aversive social environment (Azar et al., 1988; Cicchetti, 1990; Fantuzzo et al., 1991). Due to their limited social skills or friendship experiences, interventions designed to help maltreated children initiate, maintain, and enhance their peer interactions may be warranted (see Kolko, 1986). Of course, limited social competence may be a feature of other problem groups, such as nonabused problem children (Wolfe & Mosk, 1983) or victims of CSA (Stovall & Craig, 1990).

Academic performance. Limited adjustment to school has been documented in young victims of CPM (Erickson et al., 1989) and, among older victims, has included poor school achievement (Salzinger et al., 1984), failing grades, and school disciplinary problems (Gelles & Straus, 1990). A large controlled study of victims of CPM (CPA, CSA, or neglect) and matched controls similarly showed that maltreated children had lower reading and math scores and were 25 times more likely to repeat a grade (Eckenrode, Laird, & Doris, 1993). Physically abused and neglected children had more referrals to principals than controls, whereas physically abused children had the highest number of suspensions. These effects were not attributable to socioeconomic status, gender, and age. The authors concluded that the academic careers of maltreated children may be marked by considerable discontinuity due to frequent moves, school transfers, and tardiness, suggesting the potential utility of specialized school programs. According to Wolfe and Mosk (1983), the school conduct of abused children in treatment did not always differ from that of nonabused but otherwise dysfunctional children in treatment, although the use of primarily parental self-reports in this study may not reflect the child's overall school adjustment accurately.

Long-Term Follow-Up Adjustment

The experience of CPM may result in long-term physical and psychosocial adjustment problems (see Cicchetti, Carlson, Braunwald, & Aber, 1987; Herrenkohl, 1990; Oates, 1986). A rare 20-year follow-up of 19 abused children documented considerable variability in the adults' overall adjustment, especially in terms of their social, emotional, marital, and behavioral functioning (Martin & Elmer, 1992). Unfortunately, the absence of comparison parents in this and other studies precludes any definitive conclusions regarding the impact of abuse in childhood.

Turning to some representative rigorous studies, one series of studies has documented both developmental and externalizing problems, excessive anger, and observed compliance and negative emotions, but not social skill deficits, in both younger and older abused children (Egeland & Sroufe, 1981; Erickson et al., 1989). Likewise, hostile parental behavior has been associated with reduced social and school competence and increased angry-rejecting behaviors in children (Herrenkohl, Herrenkohl, Egolf, & Wu, 1991). This study found that a supportive parent figure, high intellectual functioning, and higher socioeconomic status helped to compensate for an early adverse parenting experience. A controlled study by Widom (1989a) found that a history of CPA or neglect was related independently to the commission of any subsequent violent crime but not as much as were sex, race, and age. Interestingly,

most of the maltreated children did not engage in any juvenile offenses (74%) or violent criminal acts (74%). The interaction of a history of abuse or family violence and intrinsic (biopsychosocial) vulnerabilities may help to predict childhood aggression (Scerbo & Kolko, 1995) and adult violent crime (Lewis, Lovely, Yeager, & Femina, 1989).

Although CPM and other variables may increase a child's subsequent risk for aggressive behavior, this relationship is not straightforward. Indeed, young children with a history of physical harm have shown problems in social information-processing skills (e.g., inattention to social cues, attributions of hostile intent, poor problem-solving abilities), which not only predicted their later aggressivity but also mediated the relationship between early physical harm and aggression (Dodge, Bates, & Pettit, 1990). Other moderators of the long-term impact of abuse include maltreatment characteristics and individual, family, and environmental factors (see Malinosky-Rummell & Hansen, 1993).

Summary. Early CPM may have long-term adverse effects, but more controlled studies should be conducted to determine the extent to which follow-up difficulties are related to the functional impairments of abusive parents (e.g., heightened stress, psychological distress/depression, dependency, dissociated views of abuse history from self-concept as caretakers) (Egeland, Jacobvitz, & Sroufe, 1988). Indeed, there is considerable continuity in classifications of maternal maltreatment across several years (Pianta et al., 1989). Ongoing longitudinal studies examining broad clinical outcomes with several abused and at-risk groups soon may be able to expand on these findings (Landsverk, 1994; Runyan, 1994).

Intervention/Treatment

Approaches/Programs

Clinical formulation. Because diverse forms of maladjustment have been documented among abused children and their parents and families, an understanding of the child's and family's strengths is an important prerequisite. Issues for consideration in a comprehensive clinical evaluation include the nature and extent of dysfunction, the child's adjustment problems and family functioning, and potential resources or compensatory skills (Azar & Wolfe, 1989). The evaluation may bear implications for the types of therapeutic problems that need to be pursued at different levels (e.g., child, parent, family). Problems such as excessive child misbehavior, parental anger hyperarousal, and family stress may place the child at heightened risk for reabuse, interfere with successful social adjustment, and increase personal distress.

Certainly, interventions to both promote a prosocial repertoire and minimize the psychological sequelae of abusive behavior can be selected only if each family's own characteristics and interactional style are considered (Graziano & Mills, 1992). Treatment programs directed at these and other mediating variables have been described, among them, self-help groups, parent training, and family counseling (see Daro, 1988). Only some of these approaches and clinical issues will be highlighted in this section (see Azar & Wolfe, 1989; Fantuzzo, 1990).

General models. Different dimensions and professional roles must be coordinated to help families make contact with and profit from therapeutic services. Because the boundaries among these roles rarely are articulated, Baglow (1992) describes a useful cooperative framework for managing complex cases, emphasizing several important treatment phases. The key questions posed in this model may facilitate cross-agency collaboration, the identification of case management priorities, and the prevention of casework breakdown (e.g., issues of therapy vs. containment, monitoring of intervention). Given the complexities inherent in most cases of abuse, Graziano and Mills (1992) suggest that parent-directed methods to eliminate abusive behavior be supplemented with the evaluation, education, treatment, and follow-up of abused children to promote their social-psychological development. Models of treatment with sexually abused children serve as a helpful framework for understanding some of the key ingredients of psychotherapy for child victims of physical abuse (see Mannarino & Cohen, 1990).

Child skills training/day treatment. Few direct services designed to address the

psychosocial adjustment problems documented earlier have been directed toward children (see Fantuzzo, 1990; Mannarino & Cohen, 1990). Child involvement generally has occurred in the context of parent-child and family treatment (e.g., Brunk, Henggeler, & Whelan, 1987; Lutzker, 1990; Wolfe, Edwards, Manion, & Koverola, 1988), where children have received some direct programming as case needs have dictated. These family-based interventions are reviewed in a subsequent section.

Given children's diverse needs and characteristics, existing direct services vary along a continuum of care ranging from minimal outpatient visits to intensive treatment in different contexts. Day and residential treatment programs, primarily serving maltreated preschoolers, offer access to various therapeutic activities (e.g., recreation, learning, play) and modalities (e.g., child play groups, family counseling) with trained staff who work closely with each group (Culp, Heide, & Richardson, 1987; Elmer, 1977; Howes & Espinosa, 1985; Parish, Myers, Brandner, & Templin, 1985; Sankey, Elmer, Halechko, & Schulberg, 1985). For example, one representative program provided children with intensive, group-based treatment programming aimed at encouraging supportive peer relationships and identification of personal feelings, along with play, speech, and physical therapy (mean duration = 8.9 months) (Culp, Little, Letts, & Lawrence, 1991). The program incorporated other family services (e.g., family and individual therapy, support group counseling, parent education, crisis line). Relative to a control group, treated children saw themselves as having higher cognitive competence, peer acceptance, and maternal acceptance and received higher developmental quotients on standardized measures. Teacher ratings supported these improvements. Still, most children scored below the "normal" range in most areas.

Participants in other programs also have evinced improvements on developmental evaluations (e.g., Culp et al., 1987; Elmer, 1977; Parish et al., 1985) and demonstrated more adaptive and skillful peer interactions (Howes & Espinosa, 1985). However, the incorporation of multiple therapeutic components makes it difficult to determine the specific contribution of the child's day treatment to these outcomes.

Structured and intensive day or residential treatment programs that combine skills training and experiential methods offer several advantages in addressing the various social-psychological problems of child victims.

Structured and intensive day or residential treatment programs that combine skills training and experiential methods offer several advantages in addressing the various social-psychological problems of child victims (e.g., Gabel, Swanson, & Shindledecker, 1990; Kaufman & Cicchetti, 1989; Mannarino & Cohen, 1990).

Specific cognitive-behavioral and social learning procedures have been directed toward improving the abused child's peer relations and social adjustment (Kolko, 1986). A series of studies with maltreated preschoolers by Fantuzzo and his colleagues examined peer- and adult-mediated socialization techniques. Peer social initiation techniques designed to encourage social overtures to peers were found to increase prosocial interactions in two children (Fantuzzo, Stovall, Schachtel, Goins, & Hall, 1987). This intervention has been found superior to adult initiations in improving children's social adjustment and peer initiations (Fantuzzo, Jurecic, Stovall, Hightower, & Goins, 1988). Subsequent evidence showed that abused preschoolers may respond differentially to peer- versus adult-mediated interventions, although both interventions were somewhat limited in overall efficacy (Davis & Fantuzzo, 1989). These excellent studies are among the few to target children, and their results suggest the need to expand intervention programs and conduct long-term follow-up studies of program maintenance.

Behavioral parent training/social learning. Emphasizing the social-interactional model, one of the most common intervention strategies entails parent training in positive and nonviolent child management practices (e.g., appropriate commands, time-out) (Golub, Espinosa, Damon, & Card, 1987; Szykula & Fleischman, 1985), anger-control skills, or stress management techniques (e.g., coping self-statements, relaxation) (Egan, 1983)

in an effort to modify the overall level of family coercion (see National Academy of Sciences, 1993). These brief interventions have been demonstrated to improve skills acquisition (e.g., more prosocial interaction, conflict resolution) and, to some extent, maintenance across time (see Azar & Siegel, 1990; Graziano & Mills, 1992). One recent extension of this approach examined the addition of individualized parent training in diverse child management procedures and parent-child stimulation training to standard, informational groups with at-risk families (Wolfe et al., 1988). The combined program was associated with improvements in both parent (e.g., child abuse potential, parental depression) and child (e.g., behavior problems) targets, but there was little improvement in family interaction. Other beneficial outcomes included reduced out-of-home placement for children from homes rated as low (but not high) in family difficulty (Szykula & Fleischman, 1985) and continued in-home improvements in parent-child interactions (Lutzker, 1990).

A significant development in working with parents is the increased emphasis on cognitive-behavioral models and procedures (e.g., Azar & Siegel, 1990), which are designed primarily to alter some of the aforementioned parents' cognitive-attributional, problem-solving, and affective processes that may mediate hostile or aggressive behavior (see Azar, 1989). For example, programs have helped parents become aware of their negative self-statements and generate prosocial alternatives to these statements. These programs also have delivered realistic developmental information (e.g., Barth, Blythe, Schinke, Stevens, & Schilling, 1983) or have provided training in anger management, communication, and problem-solving skills (Acton & During, 1992; Nurius, Lovell, & Edgar, 1988). The addition of cognitive restructuring and problem solving to other stress management methods has been associated with reduced child assault, lessened anger arousal and increased empathy in parents, and fewer complaints concerning child behavior problems (Acton & During, 1992; Whiteman, Fanshel, & Grundy, 1987).

In-home, family-based services. Related interventions have been directed at the more global or contextual risk factors associated with abuse. In-home, family-based services have sought to address such problems as excessive child care demands, financial and economic disadvantages, social isolation, marital discord, and substance abuse (Amundson, 1989; Frankel, 1988). Home visitors and parent aids can provide information, support, counseling, and mental health referral to parents and other family members in need (Barth, 1989). Some of the problems that have been addressed include depression, limited homemaker skills, aversive kinship relationships, and social insularity.

In-home services that promote family preservation use crisis-oriented, intensive, and brief services to serve families with children who are at risk for placement. By offering intensive counseling, casework, and concrete services to address multiple risk factors, programs such as Homebuilders are noteworthy for their individualized interventions, program intensity, flexible scheduling, small caseloads, goal orientation with time-limited services, and program evaluation efforts (Whittaker, Kinney, Tracy, & Booth, 1990). Homebuilders has reported gains in family functioning (e.g., problem behaviors, communication skills), but these improvements are difficult to interpret in the absence of comparison data (Amundson, 1989). One report of comparison data from projects in three different states showed that family preservation services did not significantly reduce child placements 6 to 12 months after termination of services relative to families receiving other types of interventions (Nelson, 1990). Although the Homebuilders program provides an innovative approach to working with highly dysfunctional families, including those that involve substance abuse, additional information is needed to document its clinical effectiveness (e.g., Blythe, Jiordano, & Kelly, 1991).

Ecological/contextual/multisystemic interventions. Multifaceted interventions targeting the functional relationships among diverse individual, family, and systemic problems may maximize client motivation and the durability of improvements across time (Belsky & Vondra, 1989). This approach is concerned with altering contextual factors that increase stress, weaken a family's ability to function properly, and elicit aggressive behavior. These factors include poverty, single

parenthood, marital discord, and family aggression (see Azar & Siegel, 1990; Hansen & MacMillan, 1990; McDonald & Jouriles, 1991). Clinicians incorporate diverse systemic interventions to address several problem areas concurrently (Asen, George, Piper, & Stevens, 1989; Ayoub & Willett, 1992; Brunk et al., 1987; Culp et al., 1987; Dale & Davies, 1985; Heide et al., 1987; Malinosky-Rummell et al., 1991; Nicol et al., 1988; Pardeck, 1989; Sankey et al., 1985; Willett, Ayoub, & Robinson, 1991).

Programs representative of this approach generally include both parents and children during intervention. For example, Brunk et al. (1987) compared behavioral group parent training in specific management principles with multisystemic family treatment in which various problems in child, parent, family, and social systems were targeted (e.g., peer training, child management, family communication). In another treatment outcome study, family casework using behavioral techniques (modeling, reinforcement) and play therapy were conducted to alter individual and family interactions (Nicol et al., 1988). One program, Project 12-Ways (Lutzker & Rice, 1987), has offered some of the most diverse, individualized services using skills training methods (e.g., child management training, social support, assertion training, job training, home safety and finances training).

Evaluations of such interventions have indicated improvements in several domains and reductions in abusive activity at follow-up (see Azar & Wolfe, 1989; Kaufman & Rudy, 1991; National Academy of Sciences, 1993). Significant improvements have been found in parent-child relationships and child behavior problems (Brunk et al., 1987), parent-identified goals, and reduced reabuse rates relative to comparison cases (Lutzker & Rice, 1987). Similar improvements have been reported in family coercion but not in positive behaviors (Nicol et al., 1988). These findings, however, are qualified by the absence of clear targets for certain conditions (Nicol et al., 1988), follow-up information (Brunk et al., 1987; Nicol et al., 1988), and minimal treatment conditions (Brunk et al., 1987). Moreover, some evidence does not support the maintenance of treatment effects (Lutzker, 1990), especially relative to comparison cases (Wesch & Lutzker,

1991). The clinical complexities inherent in working with abusive families often necessitate multiple services to stabilize the home environment and promote improvements in parent-child relations.

Across all types of intervention studies, it is not surprising that problems with engagement, compliance, and dropout commonly have been reported among abusive families (Cohn & Daro, 1987). Lower rates of clinic attendance have been found in maltreating than non-maltreating families, which may be influenced by certain procedures (e.g., court ordering, child removal) (Warner, Malinosky-Rummell, Ellis, & Hansen, 1990). Malinosky-Rummell et al. (1991), for example, also reported a 38% no-show rate at home, a 66% clinic no-show rate, and a 36% dropout rate among 45 abusing families. CPA was noted during treatment in 23% of the cases, and case reopening by CPS workers occurred in 21% of the cases. Researchers have reported high rates of recidivism during treatment (about one third) (Cohn & Daro, 1987) and after treatment (30%-47%) (Daro, 1988). These and other obstacles to successful resolution of family conflict provide a significant challenge to practitioners. Families characterized as multirisk and violent and who present with distressed parenting have shown the least improvement in family functioning during preventive intervention, based on monthly therapist ratings (Ayoub & Willett, 1992). Many of these families show no change at all, even after lengthy treatment (Willett et al., 1991).

Practice Implications

In the following sections, I review the collective findings discussed above. The purpose of this review is to enhance the potential of psychosocial interventions with this population.

Comprehensive psychosocial evaluation. Given the diversity in the clinical pictures of abused children and their parents, an effort should be made to conduct a careful but comprehensive intake evaluation that incorporates multiple domains of functioning (e.g., behavioral, social), informants (e.g., child, parent, siblings), and methods (e.g., interviews, checklists,

observations). Various aspects of child and parent functioning and competence (e.g., child symptoms, parental mood state) and the family environment (e.g., caretaking routines, stimulation, activities) deserve evaluation due to their relationship to CPM. Several innovative and specialized assessment measures are available (Hansen & MacMillan, 1990).

Documentation of the functional context and parameters of abusive interactions (e.g., frequency, severity, chronicity, situational context) also deserves greater clinical attention (see Barnett, Manly, & Cicchetti, 1991). Examples of such definitional details are reported in recent studies (e.g., Allen & Tarnowski, 1989; Kazdin et al., 1985; Widom, 1989a). These parameters may influence the nature and extent of the impact of CPM. Sufficient clinical information along these lines is needed to ensure the accuracy of judgments of "low-risk status" after initial case reviews that result in case closures. Premature closure may preclude discussion of the benefits of follow-up services or recommendations for treatment and reduce parents' motivation to seek assistance for existing family problems. From a research perspective, the use of operational criteria to select and describe samples would facilitate cross-study comparisons.

Goals and targets. Even with the accumulation of clinical data, the development of a constructive formulation of the case and the identification of realistic, individualized goals remain complicated tasks (Baglow, 1992). One primary consideration in articulating these goals is how to balance the child's needs with those of the parents and family and how much to emphasize a focus on individuals versus the family. Although children's needs and vulnerabilities often are addressed in initial evaluations of risk status, they receive less follow-up attention once service options are reviewed, which suggests that greater attention usually is paid to goals related to containment (i.e., prevention of reabuse) rather than to treatment of the sequelae of abuse (i.e., improving the quality of life) (Baglow, 1992). The initial emphasis on containment and protection is understandable, but adequate intervention services that target environmental risk factors and psychological reactions to abusive caretaking are equally important (Graziano & Mills, 1992).

Potential targets for child-focused intervention include health promotion, social and developmental stimulation, behavior management, and education.

Potential targets for child-focused intervention include health promotion, social and developmental stimulation, behavior management, and education (see Mannarino & Cohen, 1990). Potential targets for parents include parent management skills; individual counseling for problems with anger, drug abuse, and depression; self-control; developmental knowledge; and social support. Regardless of the specific nature of the goals selected in the treatment of children and parents, there should be a balance between the focus on negative or deviant behavior and personal competencies and strengths. This dual focus is justified, given findings that implicate both behavioral deficiencies and excesses among abused children and their parents.

Treatment process and practicalities. Families recommended for services following investigation may struggle as much in handling the investigation experience as they do with the sequelae of the abuse incident. Their reactions to both experiences also may be exacerbated by the lack of a supportive process of referral for intervention. Keeping in mind the presence of various problems at the individual and family levels, it may be important to consider ways to minimize any further "mistreatment" of the family and promote a sense of concerned collaboration with them. Efforts to promote this "joining" with the family include the development of a client agreement that identifies all services and responsibilities, orientations to the agency and assigned therapists or counselors, and quick response to establishing the first contact. In addition, therapists should conduct some sessions, such as the orientation meeting, in the family's home or a local community setting.

Because of the insularity and limited resources of many abusing families, it is often necessary to problem solve ways to minimize potential obstacles to consistent participation during intervention and provide assistance with specific needs (e.g., transportation, baby-sitting or other child care, and food). Apart from the receipt of low-cost affordable services, impoverished and chaotic families may respond to incentives or contracts that maximize their motivation to attend sessions, complete homework or practice, or practice new skills at home (Azar & Siegel, 1990; Fantuzzo, 1990; Malinosky-Rummell et al., 1991). Client participation also may be promoted through the use of culturally sensitive and specific intervention programs, although few studies actually have reported the application, much less evaluation, of such programs. Evidence from other areas suggests the clinical utility of programs developed for at-risk Hispanic boys and carried out by trained Hispanic therapists (e.g., Malgady, Rogler, & Costantino, 1990).

Advocacy services also are encouraged to promote parental autonomy or authority, hasten the receipt of requested materials or services, or establish an intermediary in special meetings or the legal arena. The maintenance of close communication among the family's service providers is especially important to ensure that all treatment goals and decisions are clear and up-to-date. At the same time, such close collaboration among providers requires an explicit discussion with clients of information that is confidential or that must be communicated to other agencies. Although this guarantee of partial confidentiality may be confusing and detrimental to a trusting therapeutic relationship, it is a better alternative to withholding mandated clinical information.

Multimodal/multisystemic interventions. In addressing the broad clinical features of abused families, multimodal interventions that integrate complementary services by targeting significant family contextual problems are most likely to exert an impact (Kaufman & Rudy, 1991). Although the most common individual element involves some form of parent training, an expanded focus of intervention has evolved that incorporates active participation with the family, attention to an array of positive child-rearing and caretaking functions, methods based on skills or competency-based training, and the use of a supportive staff. In so doing, training efforts may be more successful in increasing parents' sensitivity to their children's emotional and behavioral needs (Cicchetti et al., 1987; Crittenden & Ainsworth, 1989; Erickson et al., 1989).

Parallel to this development, the incorporation of such complementary program components as intensive crisis services, counseling, the provision of concrete services (as in the family preservation services; e.g., Homebuilders), and individualized multisystemic treatments (e.g., Brunk et al., 1987) may help to maintain the integrity, safety, and functioning of abusive families. By providing whatever services are needed in a site selected for the client's benefit (e.g., home) and on an intensive basis, clinical interventions may be best able to target multiple risk factors, bolster natural support systems, and identify other needed resources. Abusing families are affected by many contextual factors, such as limited intelligence, poverty, single parenthood, stress, marital discord, family instability, child-rearing attitudes and practices, and philosophy of violence. Practitioners may need to address these multiple factors with all the complexity that this involves. Empirical findings as to the continuity of child and family problems following CPM further indicate that follow-up services should be considered as an important extension of intervention (Daro, 1988). Because intervention studies have shown limited evidence for the maintenance of gains (e.g., Lutzker, 1990; Wolfe et al., 1988), an examination of therapeutic methods that promote greater stability of improvements is warranted (e.g., "check-ups," service calls). Much work still needs to be done to promote the development and application of psychosocial interventions directed at multiple risk factors for abuse (National Academy of Sciences, 1993).

Unresolved Issues

Models/Mechanisms

Evidence supports the interactional, transactional, or ecological model of CPM, which emphasizes the complex interplay of child, parent, family, and social system characteristics in the origins of CPM (Azar et al., 1988; Belsky & Vondra, 1989; Cicchetti, 1990; Wolfe, 1987). How-

ever, it is necessary to understand further the different ways in which specific characteristics in each system contribute to abusive interactions (Azar, 1991; Mash & Wolfe, 1991). Studies must begin to examine these relationships to determine the relative importance of key variables, the underlying mechanisms of abusive behavior, the severity of dysfunction associated with CPM, and whether certain consequences are accounted for by others. This might help us better understand what precedes and what follows abusive activities (e.g., Erickson et al., 1989; Herrenkohl et al., 1991; Widom, 1989a). Key variables to be examined include parental mood state, substance abuse, child-rearing practices, and family level of physical aggression, coercion, and stress. Because features of the child's environment are strong correlates of CPM or its effects (e.g., Vondra et al., 1990), more information is needed regarding primary family relationships (e.g., stimulation, structure, support, conflict, verbal aggression, child rejection) that may mediate children's adjustment (Claussen & Crittenden, 1991; Crittenden, 1988). Recent interview data highlight the importance of understanding abusers' attributions of their own behavior (Bugental et al., 1989) as well as child misbehavior, parental distress, and environmental stress (Dietrich, Berkowitz, Kadushin, & McGloin, 1990). Thus, it is important to determine which factors lead to specific outcomes or interact with other variables.

Sequelae/Consequences

A few unresolved issues regarding our understanding of the consequences of abuse are prompted by the findings reviewed earlier. One primary issue is the extent to which physically abusive behavior represents a traumatic experience and how the development of posttraumatic symptoms relates to the psychosocial context of CPM, such as disruptions in family life processes, deviations in child development, severe family dysfunction, and cultural context. The specificity of the attachment disturbance (Cicchetti, 1989, 1990) and types of PTSD symptoms (e.g., Famularo et al., 1990b) seen among victims of CPM could be examined in comparison with child victims of other forms of trauma, including violent crime and sexual abuse (Pynoos et al., 1987). These comparisons would help researchers to evaluate the unique clinical pictures associated with different traumatic experiences (Kolko et al., 1988, 1990), because recent findings highlight the trauma-specific experiences among child victims (Figley, 1992).

The strongest evidence regarding sequelae points to problems with aggression, peer social behavior, and parent-child interactions, all of which may reflect disturbances in attachment or the maintenance of relationships. However, it is important to determine how unique these symptoms are in comparison to those of other children seen in clinics or assumed to be at risk. We also need more evidence bearing on less frequently studied consequences (e.g., heightened anger, self-blame, depression) to determine the prevalence of certain types of symptoms and whether those symptoms are related functionally to symptoms in other areas.

A related issue for exploration is the nature and extent to which these sequelae persist into later childhood and adolescence (e.g., peer relations, school adjustment and academic progress, cognitive-attributional repertoire). Serious child problems worthy of evaluation at follow-up include neurological impairment, academic problems, social competence, depression, suicidality, drug use, and involvement in violent and criminal activities (Hotaling et al., 1990; Kolko et al., 1990; Terr, 1991; Widom, 1989b). The presence of psychiatric disturbances also requires greater standardized evaluation (Gelles & Straus, 1990).

Finally, it also may be important to evaluate other family problems such as coercion, verbal hostility, and poverty, because these may contribute to increased child dysfunction. Insofar as firm conclusions about the direct effects of CPM are not available (Widom, 1989b), results from ongoing longitudinal studies will soon contribute information to address this question. Such information will fill gaps in knowledge regarding rates of reabuse and the recurrence of child and family problems that contribute to a child's at-risk status.

Treatment

Despite progress in establishing and evaluating intervention programs, there is insufficient evidence to suggest the efficacy of specific therapeutic components for CPM per se. Clinical and methodological limitations must be addressed to enhance the potential of psychosocial interventions (Kaufman & Rudy, 1991; Mash & Wolfe, 1991). For example, treatment specialists should conduct comprehensive interventions to enhance participation, progress, and maintenance; include children during treatment to enhance the modification of family aggression and coercion; and provide ongoing assessment of treatment course and outcome. Comparative outcome studies that report follow-up information clearly are needed because the relationship between CPM and the outcomes of various treatment approaches is sometimes unclear (Gabel et al., 1990; Sankey et al., 1985).

The absence of evaluations of interventions with child participants is a primary gap in the literature, because controlled studies that directly target school-aged children and their parents have not been reported (Mannarino & Cohen, 1990; National Academy of Sciences, 1993). Interventions directed toward children not only are needed but also must extend their evaluations of the effectiveness of treatment on targeted symptoms to both general child adjustment and risk for reabuse (e.g., Fantuzzo et al., 1988). If certain victims of CPM suffer from PTSD, for example, treatments based on this model should be developed to ameliorate the internalizing symptoms that these children may experience (Famularo et al., 1992c; Terr, 1991).

There is little information about the effectiveness of treatments that differ in format, such as the manner in which children are integrated into intervention (e.g., individual child, separate child and parent training, family therapy), site (community systems vs. home vs. clinic), single versus multicomponent interventions, and the timing or sequence of intervention components (e.g., how interventions are tailored to children's developmental stages). The specificity of different interventions should be studied to elaborate on findings showing that certain outcomes are associated with parent training methods (e.g., improved social problems) and other outcomes with family-directed therapy (e.g., improved parent-child relationships) (Brunk et al., 1987). Other methodological and clinical advances are needed to evaluate the impact of intervention on family functioning (Willett et al., 1991). The field of child abuse needs evaluation studies that address issues of internal and external validity, employ experimental control, and are prospective in format. Child abuse researchers should use experimental and statistical methods to increase confidence in study conclusions and rule out alternative explanations of outcome. Evidence of this nature would encourage an understanding of the "key" ingredients of intervention with this population. Several researchers have identified issues for consideration in psychotherapy trials and outcome studies (see Beutler, 1993; Kazdin, 1993; Pilkonis, 1993).

Topics for Further Exploration

Because many questions remain open with respect to both practice and research in this field, professional efforts to address key issues would contribute important knowledge to the understanding of CPM and its aftermath. Salient issues for exploration include the following:

1. It is important to understand both background and professional characteristics that influence the filing and substantiation of and reactions to reports of suspected CPM, as well as the impact of specific aspects of the abusive experience in procuring appropriate clinical and social resources (Eckenrode, Powers, Doris, Munsch, & Bolger, 1988; Wissow & Wilson, 1992). Substantiation of abuse allegations in the absence of adequate service delivery could do more harm than good. Child abuse specialists know very little about CPA victims' processing and interpretations of their experiences. Researchers need to examine whether these children identify violent and traumatic acts as easily as adults. Children may fail to identify abuse because of their use of different definitions, limited recall abilities or retrieval strategies, or apprehension about revealing potentially damaging information (see Ceci & Bruck, 1993; Pynoos & Nader, 1993). Documentation of the level of traumatic emotional or behavioral reactions is necessary, because such reactions may interfere with children's accurate representation of the severity of family violence (Terr, 1991).

2. Because CPM is not distinguished exclusively by one or more focal events but rather by a caretaking and interactional style that represents an ongoing family-interactional process, more attention is needed to quantify and examine parameters of abusive caretaking (e.g., level of verbal hostility; use of nonabusive, physical punishment) and abusive incidents (e.g., severity, topography, frequency). Other related aspects of family and community violence ought to be evaluated in an attempt to understand the context of CPA, especially given the prevalence of family and community violence and its relationship to heightened levels of psychological distress (Martinez & Richters, 1993; Richters & Martinez, 1993).

3. Child abuse specialists also need to know how best to minimize perpetrators' and other family members' denial of abuse allegations and their disdain for the "system" for even raising questions about their child-rearing competency. Both reactions may be antagonistic to the initiation of services and can remain as primary targets for intervention. Also, should any member of the family be removed from the home either during or just subsequent to investigation or case review? If so, should this be the offender or the child? Likewise, when is prosecution of benefit? To what extent is prosecution delayed, resulting in minimal consequences that are poorly integrated into the overall disposition of the case?

4. What are the long-term effects of CPM and to what extent do the effects differ from those associated with exposure to nonabusive but inadequate caretaking? How does CPM manifest itself differently across developmental stages (e.g., the extent to which the correlates of abuse vary by age group; see Malinosky-Rummell & Hansen, 1993)? To what degree is there developmentally consistent progression in the symptoms that emerge following CPM, and how do these symptoms relate to the development of PTSD symptoms such as those that have been found among victims of sexual abuse (Miller-Perrin & Wurtele, 1990)?

5. With respect to intervention, more progress needs to be made in addressing salient therapeutic obstacles (cognitive limitations, chronic stress, family discord, limited resources, parental and child resistance, poor motivation, coer-

cion, frequent attrition, negative orientation to treatment). Practitioners need to know which strategies are practical and useful. To document the process and course of intervention, practitioners also need to know how both children and parents respond to treatment. Studies that describe treatment progress may provide useful information to determine whether the course of treatment is in accord with expectations of child protection or safety (e.g., Ayoub & Willett, 1992; Willett et al., 1991). Finally, much work needs to be done to evaluate mediators of treatment outcome.

6. Because few studies have been directed toward children, especially school-aged children, practitioners and researchers need to understand better the conceptualization, role, and impact of child treatment and family approaches, as has been reported in recent studies in the area of child sexual abuse (e.g., Lebowitz, Harvey, & Herman, 1993; Sullivan, Scanlan, Brookhouser, Schulte, & Knutson, 1992). In examining these domains, practitioners need to know how services are best identified and administered. Whether services should be delivered concurrently or in sequential fashion is an important clinical question (i.e., is it more effective to administer multiple interventions at once or to apply them selectively to prioritized targets?).

7. How do practitioners maximize the likelihood that improvements achieved during intervention are maintained over time? Are specialized interventions that are directed toward different subgroups or risk factors (age, gender, socioeconomic status) needed to achieve lasting improvement? It is important to provide greater attention to the unique backgrounds and clinical characteristics of various at-risk populations during treatment (e.g., fathers, blended families, older child victims, low income inner-city children).

8. What can be learned about the origins of parental aggression and children's responses to diverse forms of physical trauma, including CPM, from studies that incorporate psychosocial and biological perspectives or measures (see Burrowes, Hales, & Arrington, 1988)? For example, what are the effects of CPM on children's immune, autonomic, and neurological systems, and how are these similar to and different from those identified among other child victims? A psychobiological conceptualization of CPA may be of heuristic and clinical importance.

9. Studies need greater methodological and empirical rigor through the use of multiple measures, informants, and methods (multitrait-multimethod), multivariate analyses, repeated measures, control or comparison groups, and formal follow-up evaluations (e.g., Brunk et al., 1987; Wolfe et al., 1988). A primary direction for evaluation efforts is to enhance the assessment process by selecting measures having conceptual implications (clear ties to constructs of interest), population sensitivity (clear ties to unique features of study subjects and their developmental levels), and therapeutic specificity (clear ties to treatment procedures).

10. What is the role of psychopharmacology in treating adult offenders and child victims? Given the potential for certain medications in reducing parents' anger arousal and other symptoms (e.g., anxiety, depression, impulsivity), as well as related behavioral and emotional problems in children (e.g., hyperactivity), medication may serve as a useful adjunct in a multimodal intervention program.

Summary

This chapter has reviewed recent studies and clinical reports regarding the conceptualization, characteristics, assessment, and intervention and treatment of child physical abuse. Certain trends have been identified in each of these domains that may provide the basis for subsequent empirical study and clinical application. At the same time, many questions are raised by these studies, and much more information is needed to enhance our efforts to both evaluate and treat children who have been physically mistreated. As new knowledge regarding the impact of physical abuse emerges (e.g., Straus, 1994), further advances are needed to understand the clinical phenomenology associated with the exposure to and experience of physical violence. Ultimately, such advances may help to identify effective interventions designed to remediate the developmental sequelae of child physical abuse.

References

Aber, J. L., & Allen, J. P. (1987). Effects of maltreatment on young children's socioemotional development: An attachment theory perspective. *Developmental Psychology, 23,* 406-414.

Aber, J. L., Allen, J. P., Carlson, V., & Cicchetti, D. (1989). The effects of maltreatment on development during early childhood: Recent studies and their theoretical, clinical, and policy implications. In D. Cicchetti & V. Carlson (Eds.), *Child maltreatment* (pp. 579-616). New York: Cambridge University Press.

Acton, R. G., & During, S. M. (1992). Preliminary results of aggression management training for aggressive parents. *Journal of Interpersonal Violence, 7,* 410-417.

Allen, D. M., & Tarnowski, K. J. (1989). Depressive characteristics of physically abused children. *Journal of Abnormal Child Psychology, 17,* 1-11.

Alessandri, S. M. (1991). Play and social behavior in maltreated preschoolers. *Development and Psychopathology, 3,* 191-205.

Alessandri, S. M. (1992). Mother-child interactional correlates of maltreated and nonmaltreated children's play behavior. *Development and Psychopathology, 4,* 257-270.

American Association for Protecting Children. (1988). *Highlights of official child neglect and abuse reporting 1986.* Denver, CO: American Humane Association.

Ammerman, R. T. (1989). Child abuse and neglect. In M. Hersen (Ed.), *Innovations in child behavior therapy* (pp. 353-394). New York: Springer.

Ammerman, R. T. (1990a). Etiological models of child maltreatment. A behavioral perspective. *Behavior Modification, 14,* 230-254.

Ammerman, R. T. (1990b). Predisposing child factors. In R. T. Ammerman & M. Hersen (Eds.), *Children at risk: An evaluation of factors contributing to child abuse and neglect* (pp. 199-221). New York: Plenum.

Ammerman, R. T. (1991). The role of the child in physical abuse: A reappraisal. *Violence and Victims, 6,* 87-101.

Amundson, M. J. (1989). Family crisis care: A home-based intervention program for child abuse. *Issues in Mental Health Nursing, 10,* 285-296.

Asen, K., George, E., Piper, R., & Stevens, A. (1989). A systems approach to child abuse: Management and treatment issues. *Child Abuse & Neglect, 13,* 45-57.

Augoustinos, M. (1987). Developmental effects of child abuse: Recent findings. *Child Abuse & Neglect, 11,* 15-27.

Ayoub, C. C., & Willett, J. B. (1992). Families at risk of child maltreatment: Entry-level characteristics and growth in family functioning during treatment. *Child Abuse & Neglect, 16,* 495-511.

Azar, S. T. (1989). Training of abused children. In C. E. Schaefer & J. M. Briesmeister (Eds.), *Handbook of parent training* (pp. 414-441). New York: John Wiley.

Azar, S. T. (1991). Models of child abuse: A metatheoretical analysis. *Criminal Justice and Behavior, 18,* 30-46.

Azar, S. T., Barnes, K. T., & Twentyman, C. T. (1988). Developmental outcomes in abused children: Consequences of parental abuse or a more general breakdown in caregiver behavior? *Behavior Therapist, 11,* 27-32.

Azar, S. T., Robinson, D. R., Hekimian, E., & Twentyman, C. T. (1984). Unrealistic expectations and problem solving ability in maltreating and comparison mothers. *Journal of Consulting and Clinical Psychology, 52,* 687-691.

Azar, S. T., & Siegel, B. R. (1990). Behavioral treatment of child abuse. A developmental perspective. *Behavior Modification, 14,* 279-300.

Azar, S. T., & Wolfe, D. A. (1989). Child abuse and neglect. In E. J. Mash & R. A. Barkley (Eds.), *Treatment of childhood disorders* (pp. 451-489). New York: Guilford.

Baglow, L. J. (1992). A multidimensional model for treatment of child abuse: A framework for cooperation. *Child Abuse & Neglect, 14,* 387-395.

Barahal, R. M., Waterman, J., & Martin, H. P. (1981). The social cognitive development of abused children. *Journal of Consulting and Clinical Psychology, 49,* 508-516.

Barnett, D., Manly, J. T., & Cicchetti, D. (1991). Continuing toward an operational definition of psychological maltreatment. *Development and Psychopathology, 3,* 19-29.

Barth, R. P. (1989). Evaluation of a task-centered child abuse prevention program. *Children and Youth Services Review, 11,* 117-131.

Barth, R. P., Blythe, B. J., Schinke, S. P., Stevens, P., & Schilling, R. F. (1983). Self-control training with maltreating parents. *Child Welfare, 62,* 313-324.

Belsky, J. (1993). Etiology of child maltreatment: A developmental-ecological analysis. *Psychological Bulletin, 114,* 413-434.

Belsky, J., & Vondra, J. (1989). Lessons from child abuse: The determinants of parenting. In D. Cicchetti & V. Carlson (Eds.), *Child maltreatment: Theory and research on the causes and consequences of child abuse and neglect* (pp. 153-202). New York: Cambridge University Press.

Beutler, L. E. (1993). Designing outcome studies: Treatment of adult victims of childhood sexual abuse. *Journal of Interpersonal Violence, 8,* 402-414.

Blythe, B. J., Jiordano, M. J., & Kelly, S. A. (1991). Family preservation with substance abusing families: Help that works. *Child, Youth, and Family Services Quarterly, 14,* 12-13.

Bousha, D. M., & Twentyman, C. T. (1984). Mother-child interactional style in abuse, neglect, and control groups: Naturalistic observations in the home. *Child Development, 93,* 106-114.

Brunk, M., Henggeler, S. W., & Whelan, J. P. (1987). Comparison of multisystemic therapy and parent training in the brief treatment of child abuse and neglect. *Journal of Consulting and Clinical Psychology, 55,* 171-178.

Bugental, D. B., Mantyla, S. M., & Lewis, J. (1989). Parental attributions as moderates of affective communication to children at risk for physical abuse. In D. Cicchetti & V. Carlson (Eds.), *Child maltreatment: Theory and research on the causes and consequences of child abuse and neglect* (pp. 254-259). New York: Cambridge University Press.

Burgess, R. L., & Youngblade, L. M. (1989). Social incompetence and the intergenerational transmission of abusive parental-behavior. In R. J. Gelles, G. Hotaling, D. Finkelhor, & M. Straus (Eds.), *New directions in family violence research* (pp. 38-60). Newbury Park, CA: Sage.

Burrowes, K. L., Hales, R. E., & Arrington, E. (1988). Research on the biological aspects of violence. *Psychiatric Clinics of North America, 11,* 499-509.

Caliso, J. A., & Milner, J. S. (1992). Childhood history of abuse and child abuse screening. *Child Abuse & Neglect, 16,* 647-659.

Camras, L. A., Grow, J. G., & Ribordy, S. C. (1983). Recognition of emotional expression by abused children. *Journal of Clinical Child Psychology, 12,* 325-328.

Cappell, C., & Heiner, R. B. (1990). The intergenerational transmission of family aggression. *Journal of Family Violence, 5,* 135-151.

Carlson, B. E. (1986). Children's beliefs about punishment. *American Journal of Orthopsychiatry, 56,* 308-312.

Carlson, B. E. (1991). Emotionally disturbed children's beliefs and punishment. *Child Abuse & Neglect, 15,* 19-28.

Casanova, G. M., Domanic, J., McCanne, T. R., & Milner, J. S. (1991). Physiological responses to non-child-related stressors in mothers at risk for child abuse. *Child Abuse & Neglect, 16,* 31-44.

Caspi, A., & Elder, G. H. (1988). Emergent family patterns: The intergenerational construction of problem behaviour and relationships. In R. A. Hinde & J. Stevenson-Hinde (Eds.), *Relationships with families: Mutual influences* (pp. 218-240). Oxford, UK: Clarendon.

Ceci, S. J., & Bruck, M. (1993). The suggestibility of the child witness: A historical review and synthesis. *Psychological Bulletin, 113,* 403-439.

Cicchetti, D. (1989). How research on child maltreatment has informed the study of child development: Perspectives from developmental psychopathology. In D. Cicchetti & V. Carlson (Eds.), *Child maltreatment: Theory and research on the causes and consequences of child abuse and neglect* (pp. 377-431). New York: Cambridge University Press.

Cicchetti, D. (1990). The organization and coherence of socioemotional, cognitive, and representational development: Illustrations through a developmental psychopathology perspective on Down syndrome and child maltreatment. In R. Thompson (Ed.), *Nebraska symposium on motivation* (Vol. 36, pp. 259-366). Lincoln: University of Nebraska Press.

Cicchetti, D., & Barnett, D. (1991). Toward the development of a scientific nosology of child maltreatment. In D. Cicchetti & W. Grove (Eds.), *Thinking clearly about psychology: Essays in honor of Paul E. Meehl* (pp. 346-377). Minneapolis: University of Minnesota Press.

Cicchetti, D., & Carlson, V. (Eds.). (1989). *Child maltreatment: Theory and research on the causes and consequences of child abuse and neglect.* New York: Cambridge University Press.

Cicchetti, D., Carlson, V., Braunwald, K., & Aber, J. L. (1987). The sequelae of child maltreatment. In R. Gelles & J. Lancaster (Eds.), *Child abuse and neglect: Biosocial dimensions* (pp. 277-298). New York: Aldine.

Claussen, A. H., & Crittenden, P. M. (1991). Physical and psychological maltreatment: Relations among types of maltreatment. *Child Abuse & Neglect, 15,* 5-18.

Cohn, A. H., & Daro, D. (1987). Is treatment too late? What ten years of evaluative research tell us. *Child Abuse & Neglect, 11,* 433-442.

Conaway, L. P., & Hansen, D. J. (1989). Social behavior of physically abused and neglected children: A critical review. *Clinical Psychology Review, 9,* 627-652.

Crittenden, P. (1988). Family and dyadic patterns of functioning in maltreating families. In K. Browne, C. Davies, & P. Stratton (Eds.), *Early prediction and prevention of child abuse* (pp. 161-187). New York: John Wiley.

Crittenden, P. M., & Ainsworth, M. D. S. (1989). Child maltreatment and attachment theory. In D. Cicchetti & V. Carlson (Eds.), *Child maltreatment: Theory and research on the causes and consequences of child abuse and neglect* (pp. 432-463). New York: Cambridge University Press.

Culp, R. E., Heide, J. S., & Richardson, M. T. (1987). Maltreated children's developmental scores: Treatment versus nontreatment. *Child Abuse & Neglect, 11,* 29-34.

Culp, R. E., Little, V., Letts, D., Lawrence, H. (1991). Maltreated children's self-concept: Effects of a comprehensive treatment program. *American Journal of Orthopsychiatry, 61,* 114-121.

Dale, P., & Davies, M. (1985). A model of intervention in child-abusing families: A wider systems view. *Child Abuse & Neglect, 9,* 449-455.

Daro, D. (1988). *Confronting child abuse: Research for effective program design.* New York: Free Press.

Davis, S., & Fantuzzo, J. W. (1989). The effects of adult and peer social initiations on social behavior of withdrawn and aggressive maltreated preschool children. *Journal of Family Violence, 4,* 227-248.

Dean, A. L., Malik, M. M., Richards, W., & Stringer, S. A. (1986). Effects of parental maltreatment on children's conceptions of interpersonal relationships. *Developmental Psychology, 22,* 617-626.

Dietrich, D., Berkowitz, L., Kadushin, A., & McGloin, J. (1990). Some factors influencing abusers' justification of their child abuse. *Child Abuse & Neglect, 14,* 337-345.

Dodge, K. A. (1990). Nature versus nurture in childhood conduct disorder: It is time to ask a different question. *Developmental Psychology, 26,* 698-701.

Dodge, K. A., Bates, J. E., & Pettit, G. S. (1990). Mechanisms in the cycle of violence. *Science, 250,* 1678-1682.

Eckenrode, J., Laird, M., & Doris, J. (1993). School performance and disciplinary problems among abused and neglected children. *Developmental Psychology, 29,* 53-63.

Eckenrode, J., Powers, J., Doris, J., Munsch, J., & Bolger, N. (1988). Substantiation of child abuse and neglect reports. *Journal of Consulting and Clinical Psychology, 56,* 9-16.

Egan, K. (1983). Stress management and child management with abusive parents. *Journal of Clinical Child Psychology, 12,* 292-299.

Egeland, B., Jacobvitz, D., & Sroufe, L. A. (1988). Breaking the cycle of abuse. *Child Development, 59,* 1080-1088.

Egeland, B., & Sroufe, L. A. (1981). Developmental sequelae of maltreatment in infancy. *New Directions for Child Development, 11,* 77-92.

Elmer, E. (1977). A follow-up study of traumatized children. *Pediatrics, 59,* 273-279.

Elmer, E., & Gregg, G. S. (1967). Developmental characteristics of abused children. *Pediatrics, 40,* 596-602.

Emery, R. E. (1989). Family violence. *American Psychologist, 44,* 321-328.

Erickson, M. F., Egeland, B., & Pianta, R. (1989). The effects of maltreatment on the development of young children. In D. Cicchetti & V. Carlson (Eds.), *Child maltreatment: Theory and research on the causes and consequences of child abuse and neglect* (pp. 647-684). New York: Cambridge University Press.

Factor, D. C., & Wolfe, D. A. (1990). Parental psychopathology and high-risk children. In R. T. Ammerman & M. Hersen (Eds.), *Children at risk: An evaluation of factors contributing to child abuse and neglect* (pp. 171-198). New York: Plenum.

Famularo, R. A., Fenton, T., & Kinscherff, R. T. (1992). Medical and developmental histories of maltreated children. *Clinical Pediatrics, 31,* 536-541.

Famularo, R. A., Kinscherff, R., & Fenton, T. (1990a). Posttraumatic stress disorder among children clinically diagnosed as borderline disorder. *Journal of Nervous and Mental Diseases, 179,* 428-431.

Famularo, R., Kinscherff, R., & Fenton, T. (1990b). Symptom differences in acute and chronic presentation of childhood post-traumatic stress disorder. *Child Abuse & Neglect, 14,* 439-444.

Famularo, R. A., Kinscherff, R., & Fenton, T. (1992a). Parental substance abuse and the nature of child maltreatment. *Child Abuse & Neglect, 16,* 475-483.

Famularo, R. A., Kinscherff, R., & Fenton, T. (1992b). Psychiatric diagnoses of abusive mothers: A preliminary report. *Journal of Nervous and Mental Diseases, 180,* 658-661.

Famularo, R. A., Kinscherff, R., & Fenton, T. (1992c). Psychiatric diagnoses of maltreated children. *Journal of the American Academy of Child and Adolescent Psychiatry, 31,* 863-867.

Famularo, R. A., Stone, K., Barnum, R., & Wharton, R. (1986). Alcoholism and severe child maltreatment. *American Journal of Orthopsychiatry, 56,* 481-485.

Fantuzzo, J. W. (1990). Behavioral treatment of the victims of child abuse and neglect. *Behavior Modification, 14,* 316-339.

Fantuzzo, J. W., DePaola, L. M., Lambert, L., Martino, T., Anderson, G., & Sutton, S. (1991). Effects of interparental violence on the psychological adjustment and competencies of young children. *Journal of Consulting and Clinical Psychology, 59,* 258-265.

Fantuzzo, J. W., Jurecic, L., Stovall, A., Hightower, A. D., & Goins, C. (1988). Effects of adult and peer social initiations on the social behavior of withdrawn, maltreated preschool children. *Journal of Consulting and Clinical Psychology, 56,* 34-39.

Fantuzzo, J. W., Stovall, A., Schachtel, D., Goins, C., & Hall, R. (1987). The effects of peer social initiations on the social behavior of withdrawn maltreated preschool children. *Journal of Behavior Therapy and Experimental Psychiatry, 18,* 357-363.

Feldman, R., Salzinger, S., Rosario, M., Hammer, M., Alvarado, L., & Caraballo, L. (1989, October). *Parent and teacher ratings of abused and non-abused children's behavior.* Paper presented at the annual meeting of the American Academy of Child Psychiatry, New York.

Figley, C. R. (1992). Posttraumatic stress disorder: Part II. Relationship with various traumatic events. *Violence Update, 2,* 8-11.

Frankel, H. (1988). Family-centered, home-based services in child protection: A review of the research. *Social Service Review, 62,* 137-157.

Friedrich, W. N., Tyler, J. D., & Clark, J. A. (1985). Personality and psychophysiological variables in abusive, neglectful, and low-income control mothers. *Journal of Nervous and Mental Disease, 170,* 577-587.

Gabel, S., Swanson, A. J., & Shindledecker, R. (1990). Aggressive children in a day treatment program: Changed outcome and possible explanations. *Child Abuse & Neglect, 14,* 515-523.

Gelles, R. J., & Straus, M. A. (1987). Is violence toward children increasing? *Journal of Interpersonal Violence, 2,* 212-222.

Gelles, R. J., & Straus, M. A. (1990). The medical and psychological costs of family violence. In M. A. Straus & R. J. Gelles (Eds.), *Physical violence in American families: Risk factors and adaptations to violence in 8,145 families* (pp. 425-430). New Brunswick, NJ: Transaction Books.

Golub, J. S., Espinosa, M., Damon, L., & Card, J. (1987). A video-tape parent education program for abusive parents. *Child Abuse & Neglect, 11,* 255-265.

Graziano, A. M., & Mills, J. R. (1992). Treatment for abused children: When is a partial solution acceptable? *Child Abuse & Neglect, 16,* 217-228.

Green, A. H. (1981). Core affective disturbance in abused children. *Journal of the American Academy of Psychoanalysis, 9,* 435-446.

Green, A. H. (1983). Dimension of psychological trauma in abused children. *Journal of the American Academy of Child Psychiatry, 22,* 231-237.

Hansen, D. J., & MacMillan, V. M. (1990). Behavioral assessment of child-abusive and neglectful families. Recent developments and current issues. *Behavior Modification, 14,* 255-278.

Hansen, D. J., Pallotta, G. M., Tishelman, A. C., Conaway, L. P., & MacMillan, V. M. (1988). Parental problem-solving skills and child behavior problems: A comparison of physically abusive, neglectful, clinic, and community families. *Journal of Family Violence, 4,* 353-368.

Haskett, M. (1990). Social problem-solving skills of young physically abused children. *Child Psychiatry and Human Development, 21,* 109-118.

Haskett, M., & Kistner, J. A. (1991). Social interactions and peer perceptions of young physically abused children. *Child Development, 62,* 979-990.

Herrenkohl, R. C. (1990). Research directions related to child abuse and neglect. In R. T. Ammerman & M. Hersen (Eds.), *Children at risk: An evaluation of factors contributing to child abuse and neglect* (pp. 85-105). New York: Plenum.

Herrenkohl, R. C., Herrenkohl E. C., & Egolf, B. P. (1983). Circumstances surrounding the occurrence of child maltreatment. *Journal of Consulting and Clinical Psychology, 51,* 424-431.

Herrenkohl, R. C., Herrenkohl, E. C., Egolf, B. P., & Wu, P. (1991). *The developmental consequences of child abuse: The Lehigh longitudinal study* (Grant No. MH41109). Washington, DC: National Center on Child Abuse and Neglect.

Hill, S. D., Bleichfeld, B., Brunstetter, R. D., Hebert, J. E., & Steckler, S. (1989). Cognitive and physiological responsiveness of abused children. *Journal of the American Academy of Child and Adolescent Psychiatry, 28,* 219-284.

Hoffman-Plotkin, D., & Twentyman, C. T. (1984). A multimodal assessment of behavioral and cognitive deficits in abused and neglected preschoolers. *Child Development, 55,* 794-802.

Holden, E. W., Willis, D. J., & Foltz, L. (1989). Child abuse potential and parenting stress: Relationships in maltreating parents. *Psychological Assessment: A Journal of Consulting and Clinical Psychology, 1,* 64-67.

Hotaling, G. T., Straus, M. A., & Lincoln, A. J. (1990). Intrafamily violence and crime and violence outside the family. In M. A. Straus & R. J. Gelles (Eds.), *Physical violence in American families: Risk factors and adaptations to violence in 8,145 families* (pp. 431-470). New Brunswick, NJ: Transaction Books.

Howes, C., & Espinosa, M. P. (1985). The consequences of child abuse for the formation of relationships with peers. *Child Abuse & Neglect, 9,* 397-404.

Kaufman, J., & Cicchetti, D. (1989). The effects of maltreatment on school-aged children's socioemotional development: Assessments in a day-camp setting. *Developmental Psychology, 25,* 516-524.

Kaufman, J., & Zigler, E. (1987). Do abused children become abusive parents? *American Journal of Orthopsychiatry, 57,* 186-192.

Kaufman, K. L., & Rudy, L. (1991). Future directions in the treatment of physical child abuse. *Criminal Justice and Behavior, 18,* 82-97.

Kavanaugh, K. A., Youngblade, L., Reid, J. B., & Fagot, B. I. (1988). Interactions between children and abusive versus control parents. *Journal of Clinical Child Psychology, 17,* 137-142.

Kazdin, A. E. (1993). Evaluation in clinical practice: Clinically sensitive and systematic methods of treatment delivery. *Behavior Therapy, 24,* 11-45.

Kazdin, A. E., Moser, J., Colbus, D., & Bell, R. (1985). Depressive symptoms among physically abused and psychiatrically disturbed children. *Journal of Abnormal Psychology, 94,* 298-307.

Kelley, S. J. (1992). Parenting stress and child maltreatment in drug-exposed children. *Child Abuse & Neglect, 16,* 317-328.

Kelly, M. L., Grace, N., & Elliot, S. N. (1990). Acceptability of positive and punitive discipline methods: Comparisons among abusive, potentially abusive, and nonabusive parents. *Child Abuse & Neglect, 14,* 219-226.

Kendall, P. C., Stark, K. D., & Adam, T. (1990). Cognitive deficit or cognitive distortion in childhood depression. *Journal of Abnormal Child Psychology, 18,* 255-270.

Kinard, E. M. (1980). Emotional development in physically abused children. *American Journal of Orthopsychiatry, 50,* 686-696.

Kinard, E. M. (1982). Experiencing child abuse: Effects on emotional adjustment. *American Journal of Orthopsychiatry, 52,* 82-91.

Kolko, D. J. (1986). Social-cognitive skills training with an abused and abusive child psychiatric inpatient: Training, generalization, and follow-up. *Journal of Family Violence, 1,* 149-166.

Kolko, D. J. (1992). Characteristics of child victims of physical violence. Research findings and clinical implications. *Journal of Interpersonal Violence, 7,* 244-276.

Kolko, D. J., Moser, J. T., & Weldy, S. R. (1988). Behavioral/emotional indicators of child sexual abuse among child psychiatric inpatients: A comparison with physical abuse. *Child Abuse & Neglect, 12,* 529-541.

Kolko, D. J., Moser, J. T., & Weldy, S. R. (1990). Medical/health histories and physical evaluation of physically and sexually abused child psychiatric patients: A controlled study. *Journal of Family Violence, 5,* 249-267.

Kravic, J. N. (1987). Behavior problems and social competence of clinic-referred abused children. *Journal of Family Violence, 2,* 111-120.

Landsverk, J. (1994). Psychological impact of child maltreatment (Research grantees status report [NCCAN Grant No. 90-CA1458]). In NCCAN (Ed.), *Profiles of research grants funded by NCCAN.* Washington, DC: U.S. Department of Health and Human Services.

Lebowitz, L., Harvey, M. R., & Herman, J. L. (1993). A stage-by-dimension model of recovery from sexual trauma. *Journal of Interpersonal Violence, 8,* 378-391.

Lewis, D. O. (1992). From abuse to violence: Psychophysiological consequences of maltreatment. *Journal of the American Academy of Child and Adolescent Psychiatry, 31,* 383-391.

Lewis, D. O., Lovely, R., Yeager, C., & Femina, D. (1989). Toward a theory of the genesis of violence: A follow-up study of delinquents. *Journal of the American Academy of Child and Adolescent Psychiatry, 28,* 431-436.

Lewis, D. O., Mallouh, C., & Webb, V. (1989). Child abuse, delinquency, and violent criminality. In D. Cicchetti & V. Carlson (Eds.), *Child maltreatment: Theory and research on the causes and consequences of child abuse and neglect* (pp. 707-721). New York: Cambridge University Press.

Lutzker, J. R. (1990). Project 12-Ways: Treating child abuse and neglect from an ecobehavioral perspective. In R. F. Dangel & R. F. Polster (Eds.), *Parent training: Foundations of research and practice* (pp. 260-291). New York: Guilford.

Lutzker, J. R., & Rice, J. M. (1987). Using recidivism data to evaluate Project 12-Ways: An ecobehavioral approach to the treatment and prevention of child abuse and neglect. *Journal of Family Violence, 2,* 283-290.

Lynch, M., & Cicchetti, D. (1991). Patterns of relatedness in maltreated and nonmaltreated children: Connections among multiple representational models. *Development and Psychopathology, 3,* 207-226.

MacKinnon, C. E., Lamb, M. E., Belsky, J., & Baum, C. (1990). An affective-cognitive model of mother-child aggression. *Development and Psychopathology, 2,* 1-13.

Malgady, R. G., Rogler, L. H., & Costantino, G. (1990). Hero/heroine modeling for Puerto Rican adolescents: A preventive mental health intervention. *Journal of Consulting and Clinical Psychology, 58,* 469-474.

Malinosky-Rummell, R., Ellis, J. T., Warner, J. E., Ujcich, K., Carr, R. E., & Hansen, D. J. (1991, November). *Individualized behavioral intervention for physically abusive and neglectful families: An evaluation of the family interaction skills project.* Paper presented at the 25th annual conference of the Association for the Advancement of Behavior Therapy, New York.

Malinosky-Rummell, R., & Hansen, D. J. (1993). Long-term consequences of childhood physical abuse. *Psychological Bulletin, 114,* 68-79.

Mannarino, A. P., & Cohen, J. A. (1990). Treating the abused child. In R. T. Ammerman & M. Hersen (Eds.), *Children at risk: An evaluation of factors contributing to child abuse and neglect* (pp. 249-266). New York: Plenum.

Martin, J. A., & Elmer, E. (1992). Battered children grown up: A follow-up study of individuals severely maltreated as children. *Child Abuse & Neglect, 16,* 75-87.

Martinez, P., & Richters, J. E. (1993). The NIMH Community Violence Project: II. Children's distress symptoms associated with violence exposure. *Psychiatry, 56,* 22-35.

Mash, E. J., & Johnston, C. (1990). Determinants of parenting stress: Illustrations from families of hyperactive children and families of physically abused children. *Journal of Clinical Psychology, 19,* 313-328.

Mash, E. J., & Wolfe, D. A. (1991). Methodological issues in research on physical child abuse. *Criminal Justice and Behavior, 18,* 8-29.

McCanne, T. R., & Milner, J. S. (1991). Physiological reactivity of physically abusive and at-risk subjects to child-related stimuli. In J. S. Milner (Ed.), *Neuropsychology of aggression* (pp. 147-166). Norwell, MA: Kluwer.

McCurdy, K., & Daro, D. (1994). Current trends in child abuse reporting and fatalities. *Journal of Interpersonal Violence, 9*(4), 75-94.

McDonald, R., & Jouriles, E. N. (1991). Marital aggression and child behavior problems: Research findings, mechanisms, and intervention strategies. *The Behavior Therapist, 14,* 189-191.

Miller-Perrin, C. L., & Wurtele, S. K. (1990). Reactions to childhood sexual abuse: Implications for post-traumatic stress disorder. In C. I. Meed (Ed.), *Post-traumatic stress disorder: Assessment, differential diagnosis, and forensic evaluation* (pp. 91-135). Sarasota, FL: Professional Resources Exchange.

Milner, J. S. (1991). Physical child abuse perpetrator screening and evaluation. *Criminal Justice and Behavior, 18,* 47-63.

Milner, J. S., & Chilamkurti, C. (1991). Physical child abuse perpetrator characteristics: A review of the literature. *Journal of Interpersonal Violence, 6,* 345-366.

Milner, J. S., Robertson, K. R., & Rogers, D. L. (1990). Childhood history of abuse and adult child abuse potential. *Journal of Family Violence, 5,* 15-34.

Murphy, J. M., Jellinek, M., Quinn, D., Smith, G., Poitrast, F. G., & Goshko, M. (1991). Substance abuse and serious child mistreatment: Prevalence, risk, and outcome in a court sample. *Child Abuse & Neglect, 15,* 197-211.

National Academy of Sciences. (1993). *Understanding child abuse and neglect.* Washington, DC: National Academy Press.

National Center on Child Abuse and Neglect (NCCAN). (1981). *Study findings: National study of the incidence and severity of child abuse and neglect* (DHHS Publication No. OHDS 81-30325). Washington, DC: Department of Health and Human Services.

National Center on Child Abuse and Neglect (NCCAN). (1988). *Study findings: National study of the incidence and prevalence of child abuse and neglect: 1988.* Washington, DC: Department of Health and Human Services.

Nelson, K. (1990, Fall). How do we know that family-based services are effective? *The Prevention Report* (University of Iowa, National Resource Center on Family Based Services), pp. 1-3.

Nicol, A. R., Smith, J., Kay, B., Hall, D., Barlow, J., & Williams, B. (1988). A focused casework approach to the treatment of child abuse: A controlled comparison. *Journal of Child Psychology and Psychiatry, 29,* 703-711.

Nurius, P. S., Lovell, M., & Edgar, M. (1988). Self-appraisals of abusive parents: A contextual approach to study and treatment. *Journal of Interpersonal Violence, 3,* 458-467.

Oates, K. (1986). *Child abuse and neglect: What happens eventually?* New York: Brunner/Mazel.

Oates, R. K., Forrest, D., & Peacock, A. (1985). Self-esteem of abused children. *Child Abuse & Neglect, 9,* 159-163.

O'Donohue, W., & Elliott, A. N. (1992). The current status of post-traumatic stress disorder as a diagnostic category: Problems and proposals. *Journal of Traumatic Stress, 5,* 421-439.

Oldershaw, L., Walters, G. C., & Hall, D. K. (1986). Control strategies and noncompliance in abusive mother-child dyads: An observational study. *Child Development, 57,* 722-732.

Oldershaw, L., Walters, G. C., & Hall, D. K. (1989). A behavioral approach to the classification of different types of abusive mothers. *Merrill-Palmer Quarterly, 35,* 255-279.

Pardeck, J. T. (1989). Family therapy as a treatment approach to child abuse. *Family Therapy, 16,* 113-119.

Parish, R. A., Myers, P. A., Brandner, A., & Templin, K. H. (1985). Developmental milestones in abused children and their improvement with a family-oriented approach to the treatment of child abuse. *Child Abuse & Neglect, 9,* 245-250.

Patterson, G. R., DeBaryshe, B. D., & Ramsey, E. (1989). A developmental perspective on antisocial behavior. *American Psychologist, 44,* 329-335.

Pennsylvania Department of Public Welfare. (1992). *1991 child abuse report: 15 years of child protection.* Harrisburg: Commonwealth of Pennsylvania.

Pianta, R., Egeland, B., & Erickson, M. F. (1989). The antecedents of maltreatment: Results of the Mother-Child Interactions Research Project. In D. Cicchetti & V. Carlson (Eds.), *Child maltreatment: Theory and research on the causes and consequences of child abuse and neglect* (pp. 203-253). New York: Cambridge University Press.

Pilkonis, P. (1993). Studying the effects of treatment in victims of childhood sexual abuse. *Journal of Interpersonal Violence, 8,* 392-401.

Pynoos, R. S., Frederick, C., Nader, K., Arroyo, W., Steinberg, A., Eth, S., Nunez, F., & Fairbanks, L. (1987). Life threat and posttraumatic stress in school-age children. *Archives of General Psychiatry, 44,* 1057-1063.

Pynoos, R. S., & Nader, K. (1993). Issues in the treatment of posttraumatic stress in children and adolescents. In J. P. Wilson & B. Raphael (Eds.), *International handbook of traumatic stress syndromes* (pp. 535-549). New York: Plenum.

Reid, J. B., Kavanaugh, K., & Baldwin, D. V. (1987). Abusive parents' perceptions of child problem behavior: An example of parental bias. *Journal of Abnormal Psychology, 15,* 457-466.

Richters, J. E., & Martinez, P. (1993). The NIMH Community Violence Project: I. Children as victims of and witnesses to violence. *Psychiatry, 56,* 7-21.

Rieder, C., & Cicchetti, D. (1989). Organizational perspective on cognitive control functioning and cognitive-affective balance in maltreated children. *Developmental Psychology, 25,* 382-393.

Runyan, D. (1994). *Longitudinal Study Coordinating Center for Child Abuse and Neglect* (Research Grantees Progress report [NCCAN Grant No. 90-CA1467]). Washington, DC: U.S. Department of Health and Human Services.

Rycraft, J. R. (1990). Redefining abuse and neglect: A narrower focus could affect children at risk. *Public Welfare, 48,* 14-22.

Safe & sound: The Western Pennsylvania Committee for prevention of child abuse. (1992, Spring). *Safe & Sound News,* p. 4.

Salzinger, S., Feldman, R. S., Hammer, M., & Rosario, M. (1991). Risk for physical child abuse and the personal consequences for its victims. *Criminal Justice and Behavior, 18,* 64-81.

Salzinger, S., Kaplan, S., Pelcovitz, D., Samit, C., & Krieger, R. (1984). Parent and teacher assessment of children's behavior in child maltreating families. *Journal of the American Academy of Child Psychiatry, 23,* 458-464.

Salzinger, S., Samit, C., Krieger, R., Kaplan, S., & Kaplan, T. (1986). A controlled study of the life events of the mothers of maltreated children in suburban families. *Journal of the American Academy of Child Psychiatry, 25,* 419-426.

Sankey, C. C., Elmer, E., Halechko, A. D., & Schulberg, P. (1985). The development of abused and high-risk infants in different treatment modalities: Residential versus in-home care. *Child Abuse & Neglect, 9,* 237-243.

Scerbo, A. S., & Kolko, D. J. (1995). Child physical abuse and aggression: Preliminary findings on the role of internalizing problems. *Journal of the American Academy of Child and Adolescent Psychiatry, 34,* 1060-1066.

Schindler, F., & Arkowitz, H. (1986). The assessment of mother-child interactions in physically abusive and non-abusive families. *Journal of Family Violence, 1,* 247-257.

Schneider-Rosen, K., & Cicchetti, D. (1984). The relationship between affect and cognition in maltreated infants: Quality of attachment and the development of visual self-recognition. *Child Development, 55,* 648-658.

Sedlak, A. J. (1990). *Technical amendment to the study findings—National incidence and prevalence of child abuse and neglect: 1988.* Rockville, MD: Westat.

Simons, R. L., Whitbeck, L. B., Conger, R. D., & Chyi-In, W. (1991). Intergenerational transmission of harsh parenting. *Developmental Psychology, 27,* 159-171.

Slade, B. B., Steward, M. S., Morrison, T. L., & Abramowitz, S. I. (1984). Locus of control, persistence, and use of contingency information in physically abused children. *Child Abuse & Neglect, 8,* 447-457.

Starr, R. H., Jr. (1988). Physical abuse of children. In V. B. Van Hasselt, R. L. Morrison, A. S. Belleck, & M. Hersen (Eds.), *Handbook of family violence* (pp. 119-155). New York: Plenum.

Starr, R. H., Jr., Dubowitz, H., & Bush, B. A. (1990). The epidemiology of child maltreatment. In R. T. Ammerman & M. Hersen (Eds.), *Children at risk: An evaluation of factors contributing to child abuse and neglect* (pp. 23-53). New York: Plenum.

Stovall, G., & Craig, R. J. (1990). Mental representations of physically and sexually abused latency-aged females. *Child Abuse & Neglect, 14,* 233-242.

Straus, M. A. (1994). *Beating the devil out of them: Corporal punishment in American families.* Lexington, MA: Lexington Books.

Straus, M. A., Gelles, R. J., & Steinmetz, S. K. (1980). *Behind closed doors.* New York: Doubleday.

Straus, M. A., & Smith, C. (1990). Family patterns and child abuse. In M. A. Straus & R. J. Gelles (Eds.), *Physical violence in American families: Risk factors and adaptations to violence in 8,145 families* (pp. 258-259). New Brunswick, NJ: Transaction Books.

Sullivan, P. M., Scanlan, J. M., & Brookhouser, P. E., Schulte, L., & Knutson, J. (1992). The effects of psychotherapy on behavior problems of sexually abused deaf children. *Child Abuse & Neglect, 16,* 297-307.

Susman, E. J., Trickett, P. K., Iannotti, R. J., Hollenbeck, B. E., & Zahn-Waxler, C. (1985). Child-rearing patterns in depressed, abusive, and normal mothers. *American Journal of Orthopsychiatry, 55,* 237-251.

Szykula, S. A., & Fleischman, M. J. (1985). Reducing out of home placements of abused children: Two controlled field studies. *Child Abuse & Neglect, 9,* 277-283.

Tarter, R. E., Hegedus, A. M., Winsten, N. E., & Alterman, A. I. (1984). Neuropsychological, personality, and familial characteristics of physically abused delinquents. *Journal of the American Academy of Child and Adolescent Psychiatry, 23,* 668-674.

Terr, L. C. (1988). What happens to the memories of early childhood trauma? *Journal of the American Academy of Child and Adolescent Psychiatry, 27,* 96-104.

Terr, L. C. (1990). *Too scared to cry.* New York: Harper & Row.

Terr, L. C. (1991). Childhood traumas: An outline and overview. *American Journal of Psychiatry, 148,* 10-20.

Trickett, P. K., Aber, J. L., Carlson, V., & Cicchetti, D. (1991). Relationship of socioeconomic status to the etiology and developmental sequelae of physical child abuse. *Developmental Psychology, 27,* 148-158.

Trickett, P. K., & Kuczynski, L. (1986). Children's misbehaviors and parental discipline strategies in abusive and nonabusive families. *Developmental Psychology, 22,* 115-123.

Troy, M., & Sroufe, L. A. (1987). Victimization among preschoolers: Role of attachment relationship history. *Journal of the American Academy of Child and Adolescent Psychiatry, 26,* 166-172.

Tzeng, O. C. S., Jackson, J. W., & Karlson, H. C. (1991). *Theories of child abuse and neglect.* New York: Praeger.

Vondra, J. A., Barnett, D., & Cicchetti, D. (1990). Self-concept, motivation, and competence among preschoolers from maltreating and comparison families. *Child Abuse & Neglect, 14,* 525-540.

Walker, E., Downey, G., & Bergman, A. (1989). The effects of parental psychopathology and maltreatment on child behavior: A test of the diathesis-stress model. *Child Development, 60,* 15-24.

Warner, J. D., Malinosky-Rummell, R., Ellis, J. T., & Hansen, D. J. (1990, November). *An examination of demographic and treatment variables associated with session attendance of maltreating families*. Paper presented at the 24th annual conference of the Association for the Advancement of Behavior Therapy, San Francisco.

Webster-Stratton, C. (1985). Comparison of abusive and nonabusive families with conduct-disordered children. *American Journal of Orthopsychiatry, 55,* 59-68.

Webster-Stratton, C. (1990). Stress: A potential disruptor of parent perceptions and family interactions. *Journal of Clinical Child Psychology, 19,* 302-312.

Wesch, D., & Lutzker, J. R. (1991). A comprehensive 5-year evaluation of Project 12-Ways: An ecobehavioral program for treating and preventing child abuse and neglect. *Journal of Family Violence, 6,* 17-35.

Whipple, E. E., & Webster-Stratton, C. (1991). The role of parental stress in physically abusive families. *Child Abuse & Neglect, 15,* 279-291.

Whiteman, M., Fanshel, D., & Grundy, J. F. (1987, November-December). Cognitive-behavioral interventions aimed at anger of parents at risk of child abuse. *Social Work,* pp. 469-474.

Whittaker, J., Kinney, J., Tracy, E. M., & Booth, C. (Eds.). (1990). *Reaching high risk families: Intensive family preservation in human services.* New York: Aldine.

Widom, C. S. (1989a). Does violence beget violence? A critical examination of the literature. *Psychological Bulletin, 106,* 3-28.

Widom, C. S. (1989b). The cycle of violence. *Science, 244,* 160-165.

Willett, J. B., Ayoub, C. C., & Robinson, D. (1991). Using growth modeling to examine systematic differences in growth: An example of change in the functioning of families at risk of maladaptive parenting, child abuse, or neglect. *Journal of Consulting and Clinical Psychology, 59,* 38-47.

Wissow, L. S., & Wilson, M. E. H. (1992). Use of epidemiological data in the diagnosis of physical child abuse: Variations in response to hypothetical cases. *Child Abuse & Neglect, 16,* 45-55.

Wolfe, D. A. (1987). *Child abuse: Implications for child development and psychopathology.* Newbury Park, CA: Sage.

Wolfe, D., Edwards, B., Manion, I., & Koverola, C. (1988). Early intervention for parents at risk of child abuse and neglect: A preliminary report. *Journal of Consulting and Clinical Psychology, 56,* 40-47.

Wolfe, D. A., Fairbanks, J. A., Kelly, J. A., & Bradlyn, A. S. (1983). Child abusive parents' physiological responses to stressful and non-stressful behavior in children. *Behavioral Assessment, 5,* 363-371.

Wolfe, D. A., & Mosk, M. D. (1983). Behavioral comparisons of children from abusive and distressed families. *Journal of Consulting and Clinical Psychology, 51,* 702-708.

Youngblade, L. M., & Belsky, J. (1990). Social and emotional consequences of child maltreatment. In R. T. Ammerman & M. Hersen (Eds.), *Children at risk: An evaluation of factors contributing to child abuse and neglect* (pp. 109-140). New York: Plenum.

3

Sexual Abuse of Children

LUCY BERLINER

DIANA M. ELLIOTT

Incidence and Characteristics of Abuse

Sexual abuse involves any sexual activity with a child where consent is not or cannot be given (Finkelhor, 1979). This includes sexual contact that is accomplished by force or threat of force, regardless of the age of the participants, and all sexual contact between an adult and a child, regardless of whether there is deception or the child understands the sexual nature of the activity. Sexual contact between a teenager and a younger child also can be abusive if there is a significant disparity in age, development, or size rendering the younger child incapable of giving informed consent (Ryan, 1991). The sexual activity may include sexual penetration, sexual touching, or noncontact sexual acts such as exposure or voyeurism.

All states have laws prohibiting child molestation (Meyers, 1992). Each state individually defines child abuse, and thus criminal statutes vary from state to state. Child abuse statutes define sexually abusive behavior usually quite broadly but sometimes extend jurisdiction only to acts committed by caretakers. States identify an age that an individual can consent to sexual contact with an adult, usually between 14 and 18 years. Sexual contact between an adult and a minor under the age of consent is illegal. In addition, incest is generally illegal regardless of age or consent. Criminal statutes also can apply to teenagers and sometimes children, but for prosecution to proceed, it must be established that the offending child was capable of forming the intent to commit a crime.

Rates of Sexual Abuse

The exact incidence and prevalence of sexual abuse in the general population are not known precisely. It is difficult to establish incidence rates because most sexual abuse is not reported at the time it occurs (e.g., Finkelhor, Hotaling, Lewis, & Smith, 1990). In addition, it is impossible to know exactly how many cases of sexual abuse are reported on an annual basis nationwide. Because there is no national reporting system for crimes against children, official crime and child abuse statistics tend to be unreliable. Child abuse figures vary by state definitions and sometimes do not include sexual abuse committed by nonfamily members. Currently, the best mechanism for determining the scope of child sexual abuse is through retrospective surveys of adult nonclinical populations. Such surveys show considerable variability that can be best explained by differences in research methodology. The population surveyed, survey method, type and number of screening questions, and definitions of sexual abuse all influence the reported figures of abuse (Finkelhor, 1994).

Russell (1984) and Wyatt (1985) surveyed probability samples of adult women in two U.S. cities on the West Coast. Both studies had numerous screening questions, used broad definitions, and conducted in-person interviews. These studies found, respectively, 38% and 45% victimization by age 18 and, when noncontact offenses were included, 54% and 62% victimization rates. A telephone survey of a national probability sample of adults revealed 27% of women and 16% of men reported a contact sexual offense by age 18 (Finkelhor et al., 1990). Similarly, in a mail-out questionnaire to a national, stratified random sample, 32% of females and 13% of males reported a history of contact sexual abuse (Elliott & Briere, 1995).

Although reporting of sexual abuse has increased significantly in recent years, results of nonclinical studies do not support a conclusion that the rate of sexual abuse has changed dramatically (Feldman et al., 1991). Recent research on the impact of trauma on memory suggests that estimates of abuse rates based on self-report actually may underestimate its prevalence. For example, in a follow-up study of sexually abused girls who had been examined at a county hospital for sexual assault, more than one third did not recall that abusive experience an average of 17 years later (Williams, 1994). The women were not informed of the purpose of the study at follow-up but were asked questions about a sexual abuse history. Analysis of the responses of women who did not report the index case of abuse strongly suggests that they did not recall what had happened; they were not simply reluctant to report it, given that more than half of these subjects reported *other* abusive experiences in childhood. Williams's data suggest that at any given time, a significant number of individuals who had been sexually abused as children might respond negatively to questions inquiring into such a history because they did not recall the abuse.

Characteristics of Sexual Abuse Experiences

The reported characteristics of sexual abuse vary depending on the data source. For example, child abuse reporting systems and clinical programs tend to over-represent intrafamilial cases. Based on general population surveys (e.g., Finkelhor et al., 1990; Saunders, Kilpatrick, Resnick, Hanson, & Lipovsky, 1992), abuse by parent figures (parents and stepparents) constitutes between 6% and 16% of all cases, and abuse by any relative comprises approximately one fourth of cases. In these nonclinical samples, teenagers represent up to 40% of offenders, and strangers account for a relatively small proportion (5%-15%), with the remainder of cases involving individuals known to the child or family. In clinical samples, however, parent figures comprise about one third of the offenders and all relatives about one half (e.g., Elliott & Briere, 1994; Gomes-Schwartz, Horowitz, & Cardarelli, 1990). In both clinical and nonclinical samples, the vast majority of

Although reporting of sexual abuse has increased significantly in recent years, results of nonclinical studies do not support a conclusion that the rate of sexual abuse has changed dramatically.

offenders are male, although boys are more likely than girls to be abused by women (20% vs. 5%) (Finkelhor & Russell, 1984), and 40% of the reported cases of day care sexual abuse involve female offenders (Finkelhor, Williams, & Burns, 1988).

Multiple abuse episodes of sexual abuse are very common, occurring in more than half of the cases in nonclinical samples and in 75% of clinical samples of children (Conte & Schuerman, 1987; Elliott & Briere, 1994). Completed or attempted oral, anal, or vaginal penetration occurs in between 20% and 49% of nonclinical subjects (Finkelhor et al., 1990; Russell, 1984) and in more than 60% of forensic samples (Elliott & Briere, 1994; Gomes-Schwartz et al., 1990). The mean age for sexual abuse in nonclinical samples is approximately 9 years old, with a range from infancy to 17 years.

In clinical samples, both sex and race are associated with some differences in abuse experiences and circumstances. Compared to girls, boys are older at onset of victimization, more likely to be abused by nonfamily members, and more likely to be abused by women and by offenders who are known to have abused other children (e.g., Faller, 1989). Differences in abuse experience, offender relationship, family characteristics, and family response also are associated with ethnic background (Rao, DiClemente, & Ponton, 1992). Asians tend to be older at victimization, whereas African American children tend to be the youngest. Hispanic and African American children are more likely than Asian and Caucasian victims to experience penetration offenses. Asian victims are most likely to be abused by a male relative and Caucasian children by an acquaintance. A significant proportion of Asian and Hispanic children have immigrant parents, and Asian victims are most likely to be living with both parents. Reported retrospectively, nonclinical African American and Caucasian women have similar rates of child sexual abuse (Wyatt, 1985), the rates for Asian women are somewhat lower, and Hispanic women are at increased risk for incestuous abuse (Russell, 1984).

Families with a child who has been sexually abused are thought to have certain characteristics. Empirical studies have found that families of both incest and nonincest sexual abuse victims are reported as less cohesive, more disorganized, and generally more dysfunctional than families of nonabused individuals (Elliott, 1994; Harter, Alexander, & Neimeyer, 1988; Hoagwood & Stewart, 1989; Madonna, Van Scoyk, & Jones, 1991). The areas most often identified as problematic in incest cases are problems with communication, a lack of emotional closeness and flexibility, and social isolation (e.g., Dadds, Smith, Weber, & Robinson, 1991). Although it appears that families in which incest has occurred do exhibit greater dysfunction, it is possible that the pathology is at least as much a result of the incest as the cause (Briere & Elliott, 1993).

Some risk factors for sexual abuse have been identified. Girls are at higher risk for sexual abuse than boys. Both males and females are at increased risk if they have lived without one of their natural parents, have a mother who is unavailable, or perceive their family life as unhappy (Finkelhor & Baron, 1986; Finkelhor et al., 1990). There is speculation that children who have a psychological or cognitive vulnerability also may be at increased risk for sexual abuse (e.g., Tharinger, Horton, & Millea, 1990). The incidence of sexual abuse among children with a disability is 1.75 times the rate for children with no disability (National Center on Child Abuse and Neglect [NCCAN], 1993). To some extent, this confirms the report that offenders select children whom they perceive to be vulnerable to manipulation (Conte, Wolfe, & Smith, 1989). Unlike other forms of child abuse, socioeconomic status does not appear to be related to sexual abuse.

Sexual abuse is accomplished in a variety of ways. In some cases, even though the offender has a relationship with the child, the victimization occurs without warning. More typically, offenders engage in a gradual process of sexualizing the relationship over time (Berliner & Conte, 1990). They may conceal the sexual nature of the activity by characterizing it as nonsexual (e.g., sex education, hygiene) or may encourage the child to consider the relationship as mutual. Repeat offenders generally calculate and plan their approach to victimizing children, often employing elaborate strategies to involve the children, maintain their cooperation, and prevent reporting (Conte et al., 1989; Lang & Frenzel, 1988). In a substantial percentage of cases, offenders use force, threaten the child, or induce fear of injury or death (e.g., Elliott & Briere, 1994; Gomes-Schwartz et al., 1990; Saunders, Kilpatrick, et al., 1992). In other cases, the offender employs emotional coercion, offers tangible rewards, or misuses adult authority.

Disclosing and Reporting Sexual Abuse

Most sexual abuse is neither disclosed immediately nor reported to authorities subsequent to disclosure.

Studies of clinical and nonclinical populations of adults reveal that fewer than half of victims tell anyone at the time of the abuse, and a large percentage never reveal the victimization until asked for research purposes.

Studies of clinical and nonclinical populations of adults reveal that fewer than half of victims tell anyone at the time of the abuse, and a large percentage never reveal the victimization until asked for research purposes. For example, Finkelhor et al. (1990) found that only about 40% of both men and women had disclosed the abuse at the time it occurred, 24% of women and 14% of men told at a later time, and 33% of women and 42% of men had never told until the time of data collection. Similarly, Elliott (1993b) found that among professional women who were abused as children, immediate disclosures occurred in only 20% of the cases, whereas 40% of the sample had not disclosed the abuse until completing the survey. Even when abuse is disclosed, only 6% to 12% of cases are reported to authorities (Elliott, 1993b; Russell, 1984; Saunders, Kilpatrick, et al., 1992).

Research conducted in clinical and forensic samples of children similarly suggests that there is typically a delay in disclosure. Gomes-Schwartz et al. (1990) found that only 24% reported within a week of the last episode, and Elliott and Briere (1994) found that 75% of children did not disclose within the year of the first incident, and 18% waited more than 5 years. Many times the victimization comes to light because of an unintentional report from the child victim. Sometimes, for example, children confide in a friend without intending an official report. When children do disclose, they are most likely to tell a parent, usually their mother. Sgroi (1982) has discussed acci-

dental versus purposeful disclosure, and research suggests that preschool children are more likely than older children to make accidental disclosures (Sorensen & Snow, 1991). In 45% to 75% of all cases that come to the attention of authorities, the precipitating event is something other than the child's disclosure of abuse (Sauzier, 1989; Sorensen & Snow, 1991). Abuse may be uncovered because of suspicious behaviors or statements, medical findings of injury or infection, or because a witness interrupted the abuse, pornographic pictures were found, or an offender confessed.

It has been commonly noted that even when children who have been abused are questioned directly, they may deny the abuse initially or later recant. Sorensen and Snow (1991) found that in 116 confirmed cases of sexual abuse, almost three fourths of the children did not reveal abuse when first questioned, and only 11% provided initial disclosures without denying or demonstrating tentative features. Between 8% and 22% of children recant true allegations of sexual abuse (Elliott & Briere, 1994; Jones & McGraw, 1987; Sorensen & Snow, 1991). Children are thought to recant either because they have been subjected to pressure from the offender or family members or because their report has produced negative consequences to themselves or others. Many children report fears about telling or regret the disclosure because of the outcome (Sauzier, 1989). Even when children do report abuse that is later confirmed, their accounts frequently are marked by inconsistencies and tentativeness (Sorensen & Snow, 1991). Summit (1983) described a child sexual abuse accommodation syndrome that consists of several dynamics that can affect children's ability to disclose their abuse. These dynamics (secrecy, helplessness, entrapment, and accommodation) can lead to delayed, unconvincing disclosure or retraction.

Although children sometimes do not disclose when asked, it has been demonstrated in clinical samples that children and adult women are more likely to report abuse if they are asked. A study of child outpatients showed a marked increase in the reported rate of sexual abuse (from 6% to 31%) when the children were asked specifically about a possible abuse history (Lanktree, Briere, & Zaidi, 1991). Similarly, Briere and Zaidi (1989) found that the rate of sexual abuse history in adult female psychiatric emergency room patients increased from 6% to 70% after clinicians were instructed to screen for sexual abuse. The prevalence of sexual abuse in clinical samples and the hypothesized relationship between abuse and later psychological functioning support routine inquiry regarding sexual abuse for individuals who present in clinical settings.

Effects of Sexual Abuse

Research conducted over the past decade indicates that a wide range of psychological and interpersonal problems are more prevalent among those who have been sexually abused than among individuals with no such experiences. Although a definitive causal relationship between such difficulties and sexual abuse cannot be established using current retrospective research methodologies (Briere, 1992b), the aggregate of consistent findings in this literature has led many researchers and clinicians to conclude that childhood sexual abuse is a major risk factor for a variety of problems, both in the short term (e.g., Beitchman, Zucker, Hood, daCosta, & Ackman, 1991; Berliner, 1991; Kendall-Tackett, Williams, & Finkelhor, 1993) and in terms of later adult functioning (e.g., Browne & Finkelhor, 1986; Finkelhor, 1990). Fundamentally, the harm can be attributed to the fact that sexual abuse is always nonconsensual, frequently developmentally inappropriate, and invariably alters the nature of the relationship within which it occurs. It can be painful, frightening, and confusing and can lead to responses in childhood that interfere with normal developmental processes and increase the risk for subsequent maladjustment in adult life.

Effects on Children

The scientific study of the impact of sexual abuse on children is a relatively recent endeavor. However, a body of empirical literature specifically describing the effects of sexual abuse on child victims has accumulated. Unlike studies of adults that have been conducted with nonclinical as well as with clinical samples, most information on children is derived from clinical samples, virtually all of which have some involvement with child protection or criminal justice authorities. Thus, what is discussed below regarding the effects of sexual abuse on children is based primarily on clinical data. Consistent with the clinical data, however, two recent studies of nonclinical teenagers suggest that sexually abused adolescents report higher rates of emotional and behavioral problems than their nonabused peers (Boney-McCoy & Finkelhor, 1995; Hibbard, Ingersoll, & Orr, 1990).

Emotional distress and dysfunction. As a group, sexually abused children do not self-report clinically significant levels of distress on symptom checklist measures of depression, anxiety, and self-esteem and often do not differ from comparison groups of nonabused children on these measures (Einbender & Friedrich, 1989; Mannarino, Cohen, & Gregor, 1989; Wolfe, Gentile, & Wolfe, 1989). However, emotional disturbance has been found on personality tests (e.g., Basta & Peterson, 1990; German, Habernicht, & Futcher, 1990; Scott & Stone, 1986) and projective measures (Stovall & Craig, 1990). Projective measures may pick up aspects of functioning that children cannot or do not reveal symptomatically. For example, children who were reported by parents to have internalizing distress but did not themselves report depression revealed depressive symptomatology on their Rorschach responses (Shapiro, Leifer, Martone, & Kassem, 1990).

A number of factors may account for the lack of group differences in symptom checklist measures. It has been hypothesized that generic measures do not tap the abuse-specific effects of sexual molestation (Briere & Runtz, 1993). In addition, there is significant variation in the effects of abuse on children, mediated by a number of factors discussed in the next section. Finally, problems in certain areas of clinical interest appear to develop over time and may not be apparent when victims are screened initially (Briere, 1992b; Gomes-Schwartz et al., 1990).

Unlike with *child* victims, nonclinical *adolescent* samples of sexual abuse victims do report higher levels of depression and anxiety on generic measures (Gidycz & Koss, 1989). The group differences noted in adolescents may result from an increased ability of teenagers (compared to younger children) to report problems or, alternatively, may represent a delayed response to earlier sexual abuse experiences.

When sexually abused children in treatment are compared to their non-abused clinical cohorts, they tend to have different kinds of problems. They are more likely than their nonabused peers to be diagnosed with depression, exhibit suicidal behavior (Lanktree et al., 1991), and have lower self-esteem (Cavaiola & Schiff, 1989; Wozencraft, Wagner, & Pellegrin, 1991), greater symptoms of anxiety (Kolko, Moser, & Weldy, 1988), and more substance abuse problems (Singer, Petchers, & Hussey, 1989). When sexually abused girls from dysfunctional families are compared with nonabused girls from similarly disturbed families, the abused girls have lower self-esteem, more internalized aggression, and poorer relationships with their mothers (Hotte & Rafman, 1992).

Posttrauma effects. Posttraumatic stress disorder (PTSD) (American Psychiatric Association, 1994), a psychiatric diagnosis that describes anxiety responses to a significant stressor, has been found in abused children. Researchers assessing children specifically for PTSD using standard diagnostic criteria or interview schedules have found rates up to 48% (McLeer, Deblinger, Atkins, Ralphe, & Foa, 1988). Sexually abused children appear more likely than other maltreated children to receive the diagnosis (Deblinger, McLeer, Atkins, Ralphe, & Foa, 1988). Although the majority of sexually abused children do not meet full diagnostic criteria, many exhibit PTSD symptoms (McLeer, Deblinger, Henry, & Orvaschel, 1992; Wolfe et al., 1989). Conte and Schuerman (1987) found that sexually abused children differed significantly from a nonabused comparison group, especially in posttraumatic symptoms such as fear, anxiety, and concentration problems.

Behavioral problems. On standard measures of child behavioral problems, sexually abused children are reported by their parents to have more behavioral problems than nonabused children. The problems reach clinically significant elevations but are not as severe as in clinical populations (e.g., Cohen & Mannarino, 1988; Einbender & Friedrich, 1989; Gomes-Schwartz et al., 1990; Tong, Oates, & McDowell, 1986). In addition, maternal distress and lack of support for the child appear to be associated with reporting higher levels of child behavior problems (Everson, Hunter, Runyan, Edelsohn, &

Coulter, 1989). When sexually abused boys were compared to a clinical sample of boys with oppositional or conduct disorders, abused boys were less externalizing and more sexualized (Friedrich, Beilke, & Urquiza, 1988).

Adolescents who have been sexually abused are more likely than nonvictims to run away from home, use drugs, and be bulimic (Hibbard et al., 1990) than nonvictims. In addition, teenage mothers with a history of sexual abuse are more likely to abuse their children or have them taken away by child protective services (CPS) (Boyer & Fine, 1991).

A specific effect of sexual abuse is increased sexual behavior. Samples of sexually abused children are reported consistently as having more sexual behavior problems than samples of nonabused children. In addition, the increased sexualized behavior appears uniquely related to sexual abuse, with sexually abused children reported to have more sexual behavior than a clinical comparison of neglected, physically abused, and psychiatrically disturbed children in outpatient samples (Gale, Thompson, Moran, & Sack, 1988; Kolko et al., 1988; White, Halpin, Strom, & Santelli, 1988). Sexually aggressive boys generally have more serious abuse histories and more disturbed family functioning (Friedrich & Luecke, 1989).

Friedrich developed a parent report instrument to assess the presence and level of sexual behavior in children (Child Sexual Behavior Inventory [CSBI]) (Friedrich, Grambsch, Broughton, Kuiper, & Beilke, 1991). Their data suggest that some types of sexual behaviors are quite common in nonabused children. For example, more than 40% of parents report that their children touch their sex parts at home and undress in front of others. Other more explicit sexual behaviors appear quite rare. Oral-genital contact and the insertion of objects into the vagina or anus, for example, were observed by less than 1% of the parents. Parental nudity, exposure to explicit sexual behavior, and a history of life problems are associated with increased sexual behavior in children. When sexually abused children are compared with nonabused children, they tend to have more sexual behavior and engage in sexual behavior imitative of adult sexual activity (Friedrich et al., 1992). However, most sexually abused children do not engage in sexualized behavior (Friedrich, 1993).

Interpersonal consequences. Sexually abused children tend to be less socially competent, more aggressive, and more socially withdrawn than nonabused children (Friedrich, Beilke, & Urquiza, 1987). As a group, these children perceive themselves as different from others and tend to be less trusting of those in their immediate environment (Mannarino, Cohen, & Berman, 1994). On projective measures, abused children exhibit more disturbed object relations than do their nonabused peers (Stovall & Craig, 1990).

As previously stated, a specific effect of sexual abuse among children is that of increased sexual behavior. Such behavior not only may result in interpersonal rejection or stigmatization by the victim's peer milieu but may lead to social sanctions and punishments when such behavior escalates into the victimization of other children (Gil & Johnson, 1993).

Cognitive difficulties and distortions. Cognitive functioning appears to be affected by sexual abuse experiences. Einbender and Friedrich (1989) report greater cognitive impairment in a sample of sexually abused girls. Some effects of abuse on children who have been observed clinically have not been fully examined empirically. For example, guilt, shame, self-blame, loss of trust, and the effects of stigmatization are thought to be common in sexually abused children. Few measures are designed to assess these impacts, thus little data are available. Contrary to a common clinical impression, empirical studies find that most children do not blame themselves for what happened (e.g., Hunter, Goodwin, & Wilson, 1992). However, preliminary evidence supports the view that sexually abused children as a group tend to perceive themselves as different from peers and have heightened self-blame for other negative events and reduced interpersonal trust (Mannarino et al., 1994). Until further data are available, generalizations about these areas of potential impact should be made cautiously, because these relationships are apt to be complex and multidetermined.

Course of symptoms. The few available studies that document children's symptoms over time reveal a general pattern of improvement for most children. However, between 10% and 24% of child victims either do not improve or deteriorate (see Kendall-Tackett et al., 1993). In addition, Gomes-Schwartz et al. (1990) found that abused children who were initially least symptomatic had more problems at 18 months than did their initially more highly symptomatic peers. Friedrich and Reams (1987) note that in a series of case studies, symptoms tend to fluctuate over time rather than improve in linear fashion. In a longitudinal study of children in abuse-focused therapy, Lanktree and Briere (1995) demonstrated a positive impact of such treatment on symptomatology. Their data also suggest that certain symptoms, particularly dissociation, sexual concerns, and posttraumatic stress, require longer-term treatment before significant attenuation in distress is reported by children. Because the longest follow-up period has been 18 months, little is known about the long-term process of symptom development and subsequent recovery.

Effects on Adults

Sexual abuse constitutes a major risk factor for a variety of problems in adult life (Browne & Finkelhor, 1986; Finkelhor, 1990). However, the effects of abuse on adult living are not uniform; some survivors report very few symptoms, but others experience life as overwhelming in many domains. Of the latter group, those who seek treatment often present with a complex array of difficulties and concerns. Whether mild or severe, the symptoms evidenced by adult survivors are an extension of those found in child victims (Briere, 1989).

Like child victims, many adult survivors of sexual abuse internalize abuse-related pain (producing affective symptoms such as anxiety and depression) as well as externalize it (creating behavioral problems and interpersonal difficulties). This range of abuse-related difficulties has been documented across race and social class (Stein, Golding, Siegel, Burnam, & Sorensen, 1988).

Research on the long-term effects of sexual abuse has tended to focus on the sequelae in women. Studies that include males suggest that sexual abuse has lasting impacts on adult adjustment for both genders. However, there may be sex differences in symptomatology, reflected in a tendency for males to cope with their abuse by externalizing their distress (e.g., increased anger and aggression toward others) and for females to employ greater internalization in coping (e.g., depression; Lew, 1988; Urquiza & Crowley, 1986).

Emotional distress. As with sexually abused children, adult survivors report more dysphoria than do their nonabused peers. Depression is the most frequently reported symptom and has been documented in a variety of clinical and nonclinical samples (Browne & Finkelhor, 1986).

Sexual abuse victims may have as much as a fourfold greater lifetime risk for major depression than do individuals with no such abuse history.

Sexual abuse victims may have as much as a fourfold greater lifetime risk for major depression than do individuals with no such abuse history (Stein et al., 1988). The pervasiveness of depression among some survivors is thought to be the cumulative effects of chronic betrayal, disempowerment, feelings of guilt and helplessness, and low self-esteem (Finkelhor & Browne, 1985; Peters, 1988). Thus, it should not be surprising that increased suicidal ideation and behaviors have been linked to sexual abuse. In two studies of outpatient women, for example, patients with an abuse history were twice as likely to have attempted suicide than were their nonabused peers (Briere & Runtz, 1987; Briere & Zaidi, 1989). In a community sample, approximately 16% of survivors had attempted suicide, whereas less than 6% of their nonabused cohorts had made a similar attempt (Saunders, Villeponteaux, Lipovsky, & Kilpatrick, 1992).

Anxiety is also a well-documented sequel of sexual abuse (Donaldson & Gardner, 1985; Peters, 1988). In the general population, survivors are more likely than nonabused individuals to meet the criteria for generalized anxiety disorder, phobias, panic disorder, and/or obsessive compulsive disorder, with sexual abuse survivors having up to five times a greater likelihood of being diagnosed with at least one anxiety disorder than their nonabused peers (Saunders, Villeponteaux, et al., 1992; Stein et al., 1988). Adults with child abuse histories may manifest their anxiety in multiple dimensions: (a) cognitively (e.g., through excessive preoccu-

pation with and hypervigilance to danger) (Jehu, 1988), (b) with classically conditioned responses (e.g., sexual dysfunction), and (c) somatically, as a natural extension of sympathetic nervous system hyperarousal (e.g., headaches, gastrointestinal problems, back and pelvic pain, and muscle tension) (Springs & Friedrich, 1992).

In addition to chronic anxiety and depression, problems with anger often are reported by adult survivors of child sexual abuse. Survivors frequently report chronic irritability, unexpected feelings of rage, and fear of their own anger (Briere & Runtz, 1987; Donaldson & Gardner, 1985). Such feelings can be internalized as self-hatred and depression (Courtois, 1988) or externalized and result in the perpetration of abuse against others (Herman, 1988). The rage experienced by some survivors can intensify when it is restimulated by interpersonal events reminiscent of the original abuse scenario.

Posttrauma effects. Psychological distress that occurs in reaction to a traumatic event often manifests itself in the ongoing reexperiencing of that event through nightmares, flashbacks, intrusive thoughts, and other symptoms of PTSD. Child sexual abuse has been shown to result in PTSD in as many as 36% of adult survivors (Donaldson & Gardner, 1985; Saunders, Villeponteaux, et al., 1992). When the abuse included penetration, the risk for developing PTSD appears especially high, with as many as 66% of such victims developing the disorder at some point in their lives (Saunders, Villeponteaux, et al., 1992). Although many adult survivors do not meet the *DSM-III* criteria for PTSD, the experience of both intrusive and avoidant symptoms associated with PTSD is common (Elliott & Briere, 1994). The reliving of the original abuse experience (whether through flashbacks, intrusive thoughts, or nightmares) often is not perceived as under the control of the adult survivor and, therefore, is apt to reinforce the feelings of helplessness and victimization of the original experience.

Clinical writers suggest that, along with PTSD, dissociation is a common response to highly traumatic events and often is seen in adult survivors of sexual abuse (Kluft, 1985; Putnum, 1990). In addition, research studies demonstrate a relationship between dissociation and childhood sexual abuse (Briere & Runtz, 1987; Chu

& Dill, 1990). Dissociation is thought to be the psyche's defense against the complete awareness of abuse-related thoughts, feelings, and behaviors (van der Kolk & Kadish, 1987). For victims of especially severe abuse, the trauma may be overwhelming, making it difficult for the survivor to fully integrate the events cognitively and thus reinforcing any mechanism that reduces complete awareness of the trauma. The ability of the survivor to dissociate abuse-specific thoughts, affects, and memories allows for the reduction of the acute and continuing impacts of victimization by changing the nature or extent of abuse-related pain (Shengold, 1989).

Along with psychic numbing, depersonalization, and disengagement, dissociation may take the form of amnesia for the abuse. According to *DSM-IV* (APA, 1994), amnesia refers to a memory disturbance "characterized by an inability to recall important personal information, usually of a traumatic or stressful nature, that is too extensive to be explained by ordinary forgetfulness" (p. 478). Recent research suggests that a substantial proportion of sexual abuse survivors report partial or complete loss of memory for their abuse experiences (Briere & Conte, 1993; Elliott & Briere, 1995; Williams, 1994). It appears that dissociation of abuse-related memories may be correlated with maltreatment that began at a particularly early age, was long in duration, or was chronic or violent in nature (Briere & Conte, 1993; Herman & Schatzow, 1987). Dissociation also may be correlated with earlier abuse by a family member (Williams, 1994).

Dissociation of memories superficially may increase the survivor's level of behavioral and psychological functioning by numbing or partitioning off abuse-related affect and recollections (van der Kolk & Kadish, 1987) and thus can be a valuable defense in the presence of acute trauma. However, it can have negative long-term consequences for adaptive functioning later in life and ultimately may decrease the survivor's capacity for self-care and interfere with adaptive cognitive processes. Among sexual abuse survivors, for example, the use of avoidant and suppressing strategies as a means of coping with the abuse has been associated with poorer adult psychological adjustment (Leitenberg, Greenwald, & Cado, 1992).

Cognitive distortions. During childhood, internal templates for adult assumptions about self, others, and safety of the environment are created (Cole & Putnum, 1992). Sexual abuse survivors often are raised in intrusive and violent environments. As a result, abuse-related cognitions are common and reflect self-blame, low self-esteem, negative self-attributes, a disbelief in self-efficacy, and a perception of self as helpless and life as dangerous or hopeless (Gold, 1986; Jehu, 1988). Such cognitive disturbance is thought to arise from stigmatization associated with responses to the abuse and the victim's internalization of the assumptions regarding self, the abuser, and society at large (Finkelhor & Browne, 1985).

Clinical writers have stressed the role of the victim's need to make sense of his or her abuse as supporting the development of cognitive distortions (Briere, 1989).

The child who is victimized by a caretaker is forced into an "abuse dichotomy" when attempting to understand the perpetrator's behavior: "Either he or she is bad or I am the bad one."

The child who is victimized by a caretaker is forced into an "abuse dichotomy" when attempting to understand the perpetrator's behavior: "Either he or she is bad or I am the bad one." Because of children's developmental status and their acceptance of social messages regarding parent-child interactions (i.e., the caretaker is necessarily right in disagreements), children often assume that the abusive act is justifiable punishment for some misdeed. This conclusion logically leads to another: "It must be my fault that I am being hurt, and thus it follows that I am as bad as whatever was or is done to me" (Briere, 1989, p. 88). As a result, the survivor may internalize a sense of self-blame and inherent badness that lasts well into adulthood.

Externalized emotional distress. Child abuse can result in a constant challenge to the development and implementation of coping mechanisms because of the level of hyperarousal, emotional pain, and restimulation of abuse memories experienced by many survivors. Thus, any external activity that successfully reduces such internal tension (e.g., through distraction, self-soothing, or anesthesia) is reinforced. These activities include self-mutilatory activities such as cutting, burning, hitting oneself, or pulling out hair (van der Kolk, Perry, & Herman, 1991; Walsh & Rosen, 1988); using sexual activity during times of intense painful affect (Briere, 1992a); binging and purging to deal with feelings of emptiness (Piran, Lerner, Garfinkel, Kennedy, & Brouillette, 1988; Steiger & Zanko, 1990); and alcohol or substance abuse (Singer et al., 1989; Sullivan, 1988).

These patterns, although potential problems for family members and therapists, are often the survivor's attempt to reduce overwhelming pain and reestablish a sense of internal balance. They are activated most frequently when feelings of anger, anxiety, guilt, intrusion, isolation, or sadness overwhelm the survivor's internal resources. Subsequent to engaging in tension reduction behaviors, survivors often report an initial sense of escape, pleasure, relaxation, or relief. This, however, may be followed by increased feelings of guilt or self-loathing and may precipitate a repeat of the tension reduction behavior (Briere, 1992a).

Interpersonal difficulties. Given the emotional distress, the tendency toward distorted beliefs regarding self and others, the intrusion and destabilization associated with posttraumatic stress, and the often maladaptive efforts to deal with such difficulties experienced by many survivors, interpersonal problems in adulthood are a predictable sequel of childhood sexual abuse. Because the victimization typically occurs in the context of human relationships, sexual abuse can cause a disruption in the normal process of learning to trust, act autonomously, and form stable, secure relationships (Courtois, 1988; Elliott, 1994). Furthermore, the violation and betrayal of boundaries in the context of developing intimacy can create interpersonal ambivalence in many adult survivors.

As adults, female survivors report a greater fear of both men and women (e.g., Briere & Runtz, 1987). They are more likely to remain single, and once married they are more likely to divorce or separate from their husbands than are nonabused women (e.g., Russell, 1986). They report having fewer friends (Gold, 1986), less satisfaction in their relationships, greater discomfort and sensitivity, and more maladaptive interpersonal patterns (Elliott, 1994).

Of the interpersonal sequelae, perhaps the most common complaint of sexual abuse survivors is in the sexual domain. This may take the form of sexual dysfunction (Maltz & Holman, 1987), sexual preoccupation (Lew, 1988), fantasies of forced sexual contact (Briere, Smiljanich, & Henschel, 1994), or multiple brief and superficial sexual relationships (Courtois, 1988). In addition, sexual abuse survivors are more likely to become involved in abusive sexual or romantic relationships (Browne & Finkelhor, 1986) and experience revictimization in their adult lives (Russell, 1986; Sorensen, Siegel, Golding, & Stein, 1991).

Mediating Factors

Although the literature summarized earlier is relatively unanimous with regard to the potential negative psychological impacts of childhood sexual abuse, such victimization does not necessarily have inevitable or massive impact on victims. A careful examination of the data suggests that although child and adult survivors tend, as groups, to have more problems than their nonabused peers, there is no single universal or uniform impact of sexual abuse and no guarantee that any given person will develop any posttraumatic responses to sexual abuse. In fact, up to 40% of sexually abused children did not appear to have any of the expected abuse-related problems in a number of studies (Kendall-Tackett et al., 1993). This may reflect the fact that the term *sexual abuse* covers a range of abusive behaviors of varying intensity and duration. For example, survivors who experience a single incident of less intrusive sexual abuse and then disclose to a supportive parent who takes protective action may be more likely to report minimal or none of the typical sequelae documented in research studies and outlined in this chapter.

Certain characteristics of the abuse experience and the environment in which it took place appear to influence the ultimate development of distress. Abuse involving penetration, violence, a closer relationship to the offender, multiple offenders, longer duration, and more frequent contact usually are found to be related to more negative impact in both child (e.g., Conte & Schuerman, 1987) and adult survivors (Peters, 1988; Russell, 1986). Age and sex appear to be related more to the type of distress seen in children. Boys appear to have more externalizing problems than girls (Friedrich et al., 1988). As previously mentioned, children manifest different kinds of problems at different developmental stages, and adult symptomatology appears to be influenced by the developmental stage in which the abuse occurred (Cole & Putnam, 1992; Kendall-Tackett et al., 1993). Parents report more behavior problems in school-age children, and adolescents self-report higher levels of distress.

Cognitive appraisal and coping may be among the most important factors for the development of problems in sexually abused children.

Cognitive appraisal and coping may be among the most important factors for the development of problems in sexually abused children (Spaccarelli, 1994). Interestingly, higher levels of cognitive functioning are correlated with greater distress (Shapiro, Leifer, Martone, & Kassem, 1992), perhaps because older children or those with more sophisticated cognitive functioning are more able to appreciate the implications of having been abused. Greater distress also is found in children who (a) have a global, stable, and internal attributional style (Wolfe et al., 1989); (b) blame themselves for the abuse (Morrow, 1991); (c) view their experiences as threatening and use wishful thinking as a coping strategy (Johnson & Kenkel, 1991); and (d) form various other negative cognitive appraisals regarding the abuse (Spaccarelli, in press).

A number of studies document the contributory role of the victim's childhood family environment in symptomatology (Alexander, 1992; Briere & Elliott, 1993).

Family dysfunction not only may increase the likelihood of intrafamilial sexual abuse but also may exacerbate the effects of the abuse once it has occurred (Alexander, 1992; Courtois, 1988). Abused children are more distressed if their families have characteristics of negative family functioning (Conte & Schuerman, 1987), more conflict, and less cohesion (Friedrich et al., 1987). Families of abused children often have multiple additional problems, including parental divorce, violence, psychiatric problems, and substance abuse (Elliott & Briere, 1994; Finkelhor & Baron, 1986). More extreme psychological problems are predicted in adulthood by subsequent revictimization (Russell, 1986; Sorensen et al., 1991) and a lack of social support available to the adult survivor (Herman, 1992; Springs & Friedrich, 1992).

Maternal belief in the child's disclosure and support following disclosure have a significant impact on later functioning. In contrast to conventional wisdom, most parents believe their children and take some protective action (Conte & Schuerman, 1987; Elliott & Briere, 1994; Gomes-Schwartz et al., 1990). Maternal support (Everson et al., 1989; Gomes-Schwartz et al., 1990; Runyan, Hunter, & Everson, 1992) or a supportive relationship with an adult (Conte & Schuerman, 1987) is associated with decreased psychological distress.

In general, the closer the relationship of the offender to the mother, the more likely that support will be compromised. The highest risk of failure to support is found when the offender is a stepfather or the mother's live-in boyfriend (Elliott & Briere, 1994; Gomes-Schwartz et al., 1990). In incest cases, mothers are more likely to believe if the child is younger, has not also been physically abused, and when the offender does not have a history of alcohol abuse (Sirles & Franke, 1989). Similarly, in combined incest and nonincest cases, lack of maternal support was predicted by physical abuse or neglect of the victim, spousal abuse, and substance abuse of the caretaker (Elliott & Briere, 1994). Lack of maternal support also is associated with the impact of intervention. The most important variable predicting out-of-home placement is whether the mother believes and supports the child (Hunter, Coulter, Runyan, & Everson, 1990). Children who lack maternal support are more likely to recant the original allegation of abuse or refuse to report it, even in the face of clear evidence that the abuse occurred (Elliott & Briere, 1994; Lawson & Chaffin, 1992). Finally, maternal support also is related to the impact of criminal court testimony on the abused child (Goodman et al., 1992; Whitcomb et al., 1991).

The various activities associated with professional intervention may affect the level of psychological distress. Multiple interviews by *different* personnel appear to increase symptoms (Tedesco & Schell, 1987), although multiple interviews with the *same* individual may not necessarily do so. Placement or separation per se is not always distressing (Berliner & Conte, 1995). The increased symptomatology noted in children who are taken into protective custody may be secondary to the lack of caretaker support that provoked placement (Runyan, Everson, Edelsohn, Hunter, & Coulter, 1988). Testifying in *juvenile* court has not been found to increase distress in child victims (Runyan et al., 1988). However, testimony in *criminal* court is associated with increased distress when it occurs more than once or is lengthy and harsh (Goodman et al., 1992; Whitcomb et al., 1991). The outcome of the case or whether the children received psychotherapy is not associated with the impact of testifying on psychological distress. However, children who are provided with a stress inoculation court preparation intervention have reduced psychological distress associated with providing court testimony (Sas, 1991).

Treatment Issues

Clinical Assessment

As previously stated, several studies using generic measures of distress have not demonstrated differences between non-clinical abused and nonabused children. Such instruments may not tap the specific effects of sexual abuse and thus overestimate the number of asymptomatic abuse victims. In response to this problem, investigators have attempted to identify abuse-specific effects by developing measures specifically designed to assess the impact of abuse. Briere (in press), for example, has developed the Trauma Symptoms Checklist for Children (TSCC), which taps into symptoms such as anger, dissociation, PTSD, and sexual concerns and has been shown to distinguish abused from nonabused children (e.g., Elliott & Briere, 1994). Other helpful abuse-

specific measures include Friedrich et al.'s (1992) Child Sexual Behavior Inventory, the Child Dissociative Checklist (Putnum, Helmers, & Trickett, 1993), the Children's Impact of Traumatic Events Scale (Wolfe, Wolfe, & LaRose, 1986), and the Children's Attribution and Perception Scale (Mannarino et al., 1994).

In addition, the use of generic psychological tests by clinicians examining *adult* sexual abuse survivors (e.g., Minnesota Multiphasic Personality Inventory [MMPI], Millon Clinical Multiaxial Inventory [MCMI], Rorschach) may underestimate the specific abuse-related distress of these individuals. Elliott (1993a), for example, found that neither the MMPI-2 nor the MCMI-II distinguish adult victims from nonvictims. However, the Trauma Symptom Inventory (Briere, 1995), a clinical instrument designed to assess traumatic impacts in adults, discriminated between the two groups on 8 of the 10 scales. These and similar data suggest that although measures of personality disturbance and generic psychological distress may not be particularly helpful in clarifying the symptom picture unique to victims of interpersonal violence, more specific measures such as the Belief Inventory—Revised (Jehu, 1988), the Impact of Events Scale (Horowitz, Wilner, & Alvarez, 1979), and the Trauma Symptom Inventory (Briere, 1995) appear to address the symptoms and concerns most relevant to sexual abuse treatment.

Treatment Issues With Children

It is widely accepted that treatment is indicated for most children who have been sexually victimized (Friedrich, 1990). Whether a child actually receives treatment, however, is affected by socioeconomic status and ethnicity (Haskett, Nowlan, Hutcheson, & Whitworth, 1991). Most children who are seen for treatment receive relatively few sessions (Gomes-Schwartz et al., 1990). Keller, Cicchinelli, and Gardner (1989) surveyed more than 400 programs and found that individual therapy is the most common form of therapy for sexually abused children, although group and family therapy also are employed frequently. Programs for sexually abused children often lack conceptual clarity about the specific purpose or expected outcomes of treatment (e.g., Kolko, 1987).

Empirical evaluation of treatment effectiveness is just beginning. Pre- and posttreatment studies reveal that children generally improve over the course of abuse-specific therapy (Bentovim, van Elberg, & Boston, 1988; Deblinger, McLeer, & Henry, 1990; Lanktree & Briere, 1995; Nelki & Watters, 1989). Without comparison groups, the improvement cannot be ascribed definitively to the treatment process, although Lanktree and Briere (1995) found that time in treatment accounted for the improvement when time from abuse to the onset of treatment was controlled. No controlled clinical trials have been published, but a review (Finkelhor & Berliner, 1995) finds that abuse-specific treatment appears to be effective when compared to no-treatment control groups. On the other hand, when two alternative treatments are compared, few significant differences emerge. Extensive clinical literature describes treatment approaches for sexually abused children. Friedrich (1990), Gil (1991), and James (1989) offer a theoretical framework for abuse-focused therapy and give examples of specific interventions. Case studies illustrate a variety of approaches to therapy with individual clients: cognitive-behavioral (Becker, Skinner, & Abel, 1982; Kolko, 1986), psychodynamic (Ellis, Piersma, & Grayson, 1990; Seinfeld, 1989; Van Leeuwen, 1988), and pharmacological (Famularo, Kinscherff, & Fenton, 1988). Friedrich (1991) has edited a volume of case studies by various authors encompassing a range of clinical situations.

Group therapy is the most specifically described therapeutic approach, with numerous published articles (e.g., Berman, 1990; Corder, Haizlip, & DeBoer, 1990; Furniss, Bingley-Miller, & Van Elburg, 1988; Mandell & Damon, 1989; Steward, Farquar, Dicharry, Glick, & Martin, 1986). Groups are usually theme oriented and characterized as supportive and psychoeducational. They are often time limited, especially for younger children. Topics frequently covered are feelings about the abuse and the offender, corrective information about abuse and offenders, education regarding sexuality, sexual abuse prevention material, preparation for court, and identification of a support system. In some cases, a concurrent parent support group is recommended (e.g., Damon & Waterman, 1986).

Specific treatment approaches for children with sexual behavior problems have been described by Gil and Johnson (1993), Cunningham and MacFarlane (1991), and Berliner and Rawlings (1991). All borrow from abuse-focused therapy, offender treatment, and standard interventions for child behavior problems and/or family dysfunction. The source of the behavior (especially unresolved victimization issues), the behavior itself, and the family context are addressed. The process of treatment may be as simple as educating parents to supervise and set appropriate limits. Typically, however, treatment is complex and requires intervention at many levels. The need for intervention targeted on specific behaviors is supported by the apparent unresponsiveness of sexual acting out to conventional abuse therapy.

Family therapy is strongly indicated because poor family functioning and family disruption are associated with increased risk for abuse, official response following abuse disclosure, and psychological harm to children. Negative parental reactions are related to initial impact, recovery over time, and the impact of the criminal justice process. Siblings also experience psychological distress in families in which there has been incest (DiPietro, 1987; Lipovsky, Saunders, & Murphy, 1989). Clinical literature often mentions the importance of enhancing parental support, usually through supportive, psychoeducational approaches in which the parent is provided with information about victimization and offenders and is helped to understand and empathize with the child's experience. However, little empirical data are available on family interventions. Winton (1990) reports on a positive evaluation of a parent support group. Approaches to reunification of offenders with the family have been described (Meinig & Bonner, 1990), although there has been no formal investigation of this type of therapeutic intervention.

Treatment Issues With Adults

Because of the complex array of symptoms evidenced by many adult survivors of sexual abuse, diagnosis and treatment of such individuals require careful attention to a variety of issues. Survivors in treatment may satisfy diagnostic criteria for several different forms of psychological disturbance (including various affective, dissociative, and somatization disorders), posttraumatic stress, and substance abuse or addiction (Pribor & Dinwiddle, 1992; Saunders, Villeponteaux, et al., 1992; Stein et al., 1988). As a result of this complexity, clinicians run the risk of either over- or underdiagnosing or of being distracted by the diagnosis per se. A case in point is the borderline personality disorder (BPD). The association between a childhood sexual abuse history and the diagnosis of BPD has received particular attention in the recent literature (Briere & Zaidi, 1989; Herman, Perry, & van der Kolk, 1989; Kroll, 1993) because many of the logical affective and interpersonal sequelae of chronic child abuse are contained in the diagnostic criteria for BPD. The excessive or reflexive use of this diagnosis with abuse survivors, however, demonstrates that the mere application of a diagnostic label is often not helpful without a contextual understanding of the specific dynamics and phenomenology of the childhood events that underlie it (Briere, 1992a; Kroll, 1993).

Despite the many abuse-related problems cited earlier and the prevalence of childhood sexual abuse among clinical groups, relatively few works elucidate abuse-specific treatment methodologies with adults (e.g., Briere, 1989; Courtois, 1988; Jehu, 1988; Maltz & Holman, 1987), and only a handful of studies report on the efficacy of a group treatment approach with adult survivors (e.g., Alexander, Neimeyer, & Follette, 1991; Follette, Alexander, & Follette, 1991). These treatment studies suggest that although there is significant benefit to an interpersonal group therapy approach in terms of reducing symptoms of depression and social anxiety, treatment effects are mitigated by the current social support system and education of the survivor. Such treatment may be most helpful as an adjunct to intensive individual therapy.

Although clinical outcome data are limited at this time, abuse-specific treatment is probably more helpful in the resolution of postabuse trauma than are therapies that overlook the existence and impact of childhood molestation. Because the known effects of childhood sexual victimization are so varied (e.g., posttraumatic symptoms, cognitive distortions, problems with self-development, and disturbed relatedness), abuse-focused therapy must respond to a wide range of clinical problems and employ a variety of treatment interventions rather than rely on a single therapeutic approach or philosophy.

Conclusion

Sexual abuse is a relatively common experience in the lives of children, and sexually abused children typically suffer psychological aftereffects. Of great concern is the fact that such experiences not only produce immediate difficulties but also constitute a significant risk factor for the development of subsequent health, psychiatric, and life-functioning difficulties. Important mediating variables have been identified, including characteristics of the abuse and support from the family. Prospective studies that follow children into adulthood would provide the best method for understanding the processes and experiences that mitigate or exacerbate abuse effects. In the absence of such research, intervention efforts should be designed not only to ameliorate current symptoms but also promote an emotional and cognitive resolution that may improve the likelihood of a positive outcome in later years.

References

Alexander, P. C. (1992). Application of attachment theory to the study of sexual abuse. *Journal of Consulting and Clinical Psychology, 60,* 185-195.

Alexander, P. C., Neimeyer, R. A., & Follette, V. M. (1991). Group therapy for women sexually abused as children: A controlled study and investigation of individual differences. *Journal of Interpersonal Violence, 6,* 218-231.

American Psychiatric Association. (1994). *Diagnostic and statistical manual IV.* Washington, DC: Author.

Basta, S. M., & Peterson, R. F. (1990). Perpetrator status and the personality characteristics of molested children. *Child Abuse & Neglect, 14,* 555-566.

Becker, J. V., Skinner, L. J., & Abel, G. G. (1982). Treatment of a four-year-old victim of incest. *American Journal of Family Therapy, 10,* 41-46.

Beitchman, J. H., Zucker, K. J., Hood, J. E., daCosta, G. A., & Ackman, D. (1991). A review of the short-term effects of child sexual abuse. *Child Abuse & Neglect, 15,* 537-556.

Bentovim, A., van Elberg, A., & Boston, P. (1988). The results of treatment. In A. Bentovim, A. Elton, J. Hildebrand, M. Tranter, & E. Vizard (Eds.), *Child sexual abuse within the family: Assessment and treatment* (pp. 252-268). London: Wright.

Berliner, L. (1991, June). Effects of sexual abuse on children. *Violence Update,* pp. 1-11.

Berliner, L., & Conte, J. R. (1990). The process of victimization: The victim's perspective. *Child Abuse & Neglect, 14,* 29-40.

Berliner, L., & Conte, J. R. (1995). The effects of disclosure and intervention on sexually abused children. *Child Abuse & Neglect, 19,* 371-384.

Berliner, L., & Rawlings, L. (1991). *A treatment manual: Children with sexual behavior problems* [Monograph]. (Available from Harborview Sexual Assault Center, Seattle, WA, supported by Office of Crime Victim Advocacy, DCD, State of Washington)

Berman, P. (1990). Group therapy techniques for sexually abused preteen girls. *Child Welfare, 69,* 239-252.

Boney-McCoy, S., & Finkelhor, D. (1995). The psychosocial sequelae of violent victimization in a national youth sample. *Journal of Consulting and Clinical Psychology, 63,* 726-736.

Boyer, D., & Fine, D. (1991). Sexual abuse as a factor in adolescent pregnancy and child maltreatment. *Family Planning Perspectives, 24,* 4-19.

Briere, J. (1989). *Therapy for adults molested as children: Beyond survival.* New York: Springer.

Briere, J. (1992a). *Child abuse trauma: Theory and treatment of the lasting effects.* Newbury Park, CA: Sage.

Briere, J. (1992b). Methodological issues in the study of sexual abuse effects. *Journal of Consulting and Clinical Psychology, 60,* 196-203.

Briere, J. (1995). *Trauma symptom inventory.* Odessa, FL: Psychological Assessment Resources.

Briere, J. (in press). *Trauma symptom checklist for children.* Odessa, FL: Psychological Assessment Resources.

Briere, J., & Conte, J. R. (1993). Self-reported amnesia for abuse in adults molested as children. *Journal of Traumatic Stress, 6,* 21-32.

Briere, J., & Elliott, D. M. (1993). Sexual abuse, family environment, and psychological symptoms: On the validity of statistical control. *Journal of Consulting and Clinical Psychology, 61,* 284-288.

Briere, J., & Runtz, M. (1987). Post-sexual abuse trauma: Data and implications for clinical practice. *Journal of Interpersonal Violence, 2,* 367-379.

Briere, J., & Runtz, M. (1993). Child sexual abuse: Long-term sequelae and implications for assessment. *Journal of Interpersonal Violence, 8,* 312-330.

Briere, J., Smiljanich, K., & Henschel, D. (1994). Sexual fantasies, gender, and molestation. *Child Abuse & Neglect, 18,* 131-177.

Briere, J., & Zaidi, L. Y. (1989). Sexual abuse histories and sequelae in female psychiatric emergency room patients. *American Journal of Psychiatry, 146,* 1602-1606.

Browne, A., & Finkelhor, D. (1986). Impact of child sexual abuse: A review of the research. *Psychological Bulletin, 99,* 66-77.

Cavaiola, A. A., & Schiff, M. (1989). Self-esteem in abused, chemically dependent adolescents. *Child Abuse & Neglect, 13,* 327-334.

Chu, J. A., & Dill, D. L. (1990). Dissociative symptoms in relation to childhood physical and sexual abuse. *American Journal of Psychiatry, 147,* 887-892.

Cohen, J., & Mannarino, A. P. (1988). Psychological symptoms in sexually abused girls. *Child Abuse & Neglect, 12,* 571-577.

Cole, P. M. & Putnum, F. W. (1992). Effect of incest on self and social functioning: A developmental psychopathology perspective. *Journal of Consulting and Clinical Psychology, 60,* 174-184.

Conte, J. R., & Schuerman, J. R. (1987). Factors associated with an increased impact of child sexual abuse. *Child Abuse & Neglect, 11,* 201-211.

Conte, J. R., Wolfe, S. R., & Smith, T. (1989). What sexual offenders tell us about prevention strategies. *Child Abuse & Neglect, 13,* 293-302.

Corder, B. F., Haizlip, T., & DeBoer, P. (1990). A pilot study for a structured, time-limited therapy group for sexually abused preadolescent victims. *Child Abuse & Neglect, 14,* 243-251.

Courtois, C. A. (1988). *Healing the incest wound: Adult survivors in therapy.* New York: Norton.

Cunningham, C., & MacFarlane, K. (1991). *When children molest children.* Orwell, VT: Safer Society Press.

Dadds, M., Smith, M., Weber, Y., & Robinson, A. (1991). An exploration of family and individual profiles following father daughter incest. *Child Abuse & Neglect, 5,* 575-586.

Damon, L., & Waterman, J. (1986). Parallel group treatment of children and their mothers. In K. MacFarlane & J. Waterman (Eds.), *Sexual abuse of young children* (pp. 244-298). New York: Guilford.

Deblinger, E., McLeer, S. V., Atkins, M. S., Ralphe, D. L. & Foa, E. (1989). Post-traumatic stress in sexually abused, physically abused, and nonabused children. *Child Abuse & Neglect, 13,* 403-408.

Deblinger, E., McLeer, M. D., & Henry, D. (1990). Cognitive behavioral treatment for sexually abused children suffering post-traumatic stress: Preliminary findings. *Journal of the American Academy of Child and Adolescent Psychiatry, 29,* 747-752.

DiPietro, S. B. (1987). The effects of intrafamilial child sexual abuse on the adjustment and attitudes of adolescents. *Violence and Victims, 2,* 59-78.

Donaldson, M. A., & Gardner, R., Jr. (1985). Diagnosis and treatment of traumatic stress among women after childhood incest. In C. R. Figley (Ed.), *Trauma and its wake: The study and treatment of post-traumatic stress disorder.* New York: Brunner/Mazel.

Einbender, A. J., & Friedrich, W. N. (1989). Psychological functioning and behavior of sexually abused girls. *Journal of Consulting and Clinical Psychology, 57,* 155-157.

Elliott, D. M. (1993a, October). *Assessing the psychological impact of recent violence in an inpatient setting.* Paper presented at the 1993 International Society for Traumatic Stress Studies, San Antonio, TX.

Elliott, D. M. (1993b, October). *Disclosing sexual abuse: Predictors and consequences.* Paper presented at the 1993 International Society for Traumatic Stress Studies, San Antonio, TX.

Elliott, D. M. (1994). Impaired object relations in professional women molested as children. *Psychotherapy, 31,* 79-86.

Elliott, D. M., & Briere, J. (1994). Forensic sexual abuse evaluations: Disclosures and symptomatology. *Behavioral Sciences and the Law, 12,* 261-277.

Elliott, D. M., & Briere, J. (1995). Posttraumatic stress associated with delayed recall of sexual abuse: A general population study. *Journal of Traumatic Stress Studies, 8,* 629-648.

Ellis, P. L., Piersma, H. L., & Grayson, C. E. (1990). Interrupting the reenactment cycle: Psychotherapy of a sexually traumatized boy. *American Journal of Psychotherapy, 44,* 525-535.

Everson, M. D., Hunter, W. M., Runyan, D. K., Edelsohn, G. A., & Coulter, M. L. (1989). Maternal support following disclosure of incest. *American Journal of Orthopsychiatry, 59,* 198-207.

Faller, K. C. (1989). The myths of the "collusive mother": Variability in the functioning of mothers of victims of intrafamilial sexual abuse. *Journal of Interpersonal Violence, 3,* 190-196.

Famularo, R., Kinscherff, R., & Fenton, T. (1988). Propranolol treatment for childhood post-traumatic stress disorder, acute type. *American Journal of Diseases of Children, 142,* 1244-1247.

Feldman, W., Feldman, E., Goodman, J. T., McGrath, P. J., Pless, R. P., Corsini, L., & Bennett, S. (1991). Is child sexual abuse really increasing in prevalence? Analysis of the evidence. *Pediatrics, 88,* 29-33.

Finkelhor, D. (1979). What's wrong with sex between adults and children? Ethics and the problem of sexual abuse. *American Journal of Orthopsychiatry, 49,* 692-697.

Finkelhor, D. (1990). Early and long-term effects of child sexual abuse: An update. *Professional Psychology, 21,* 325-330.

Finkelhor, D. (1994). Current information on the scope and nature of child sexual abuse. *The Future of Children, 4,* 31-53.

Finkelhor, D., & Baron, L. (1986). Risk factors for child sexual abuse. *Journal of Interpersonal Violence, 1,* 43-71.

Finkelhor, D., & Berliner, L. (1995). Research on the treatment of sexually abused children: A review and recommendations. *Journal of the American Academy of Child and Adolescent Psychiatry, 34,* 1408-1423.

Finkelhor, D., & Browne, A. (1985). The traumatic impact of child sexual abuse: A conceptualization. *American Journal of Orthopsychiatry, 55,* 530-541.

Finkelhor, D., Hotaling, G., Lewis, I. A., & Smith, C. (1990). Sexual abuse in a national survey of adult men and women: Prevalence, characteristics, and risk factors. *Child Abuse & Neglect, 14,* 19-28.

Finkelhor, D., & Russell, D. E. H. (1984). Women as perpetrators: Review of the evidence. In D. Finkelhor (Ed.), *Child sexual abuse: New theory and research* (pp. 171-185). New York: Free Press.

Finkelhor, D., Williams, L. M., & Burns, N. (1988). *Nursery crimes: Sexual abuse in day care.* Newbury Park, CA: Sage.

Follette, V. M., Alexander, P. C., & Follette, W. C. (1991). Individual predictors of outcome in group treatment for incest survivors. *Journal of Consulting and Clinical Psychology, 59,* 150-155.

Friedrich, W. N. (1990). *Psychotherapy of sexually abused children and their families.* New York: Norton.

Friedrich, W. N. (1991). *Casebook of sexual abuse treatment.* New York: Norton.

Friedrich, W. N. (1993). Sexual victimization and sexual behavior in children: A review of recent literature. *Child Abuse & Neglect, 17,* 59-66.

Friedrich, W. N., Beilke, R. L., & Urquiza, A. (1987). Children from sexually abusive families: A behavioral comparison. *Journal of Interpersonal Violence, 2,* 391-402.

Friedrich, W. N., Beilke, R. L., & Urquiza, A. J. (1988). Behavior problems in young sexually abused boys: A comparison study. *Journal of Interpersonal Violence, 3,* 21-28.

Friedrich, W. N., Grambsch, P., Broughton, D., Kuiper, J., & Beilke, R. L. (1991). Normative sexual behavior in children. *Pediatrics, 88,* 456-464.

Friedrich, W. N., Grambsch, P., Damon, L., Koverola, C., Hewitt, S. K., Lang, R. A., & Broughton, D. (1992). Child sexual behavior inventory: Normative and clinical comparisons. *Psychological Assessment, 4,* 303-311.

Friedrich, W. N., & Luecke, W. (1989). Young school-age sexually aggressive children. *Professional Psychology, 19,* 155-164.

Friedrich, W. N., & Reams, R. A. (1987). Course of psychological symptoms in sexually abused young children. *Psychotherapy, 24,* 160-170.

Furniss, T., Bingley-Miller, L., & Van Elburg, A. (1988). Goal oriented group treatment for sexually abused adolescent girls. *British Journal of Psychiatry, 152,* 97-106.

Gale, J., Thompson, R. J., Moran, T., & Sack, W. H. (1988). Sexual abuse in young children: Its clinical presentation and characteristic patterns. *Child Abuse & Neglect, 12,* 163-171.

German, D. E., Habernicht, D. J., & Futcher, W. G. (1990). Psychological profile of the female adolescent incest victim. *Child Abuse & Neglect, 14,* 429-438.

Gidycz, C. A., & Koss, M. P. (1989). The impact of adolescent sexual victimization: Standardized measures of anxiety, depression and behavioral deviancy. *Violence & Victims, 4*(2), 139-149.

Gil, E. (1991). *The healing power of play.* New York: Guilford.

Gil, E., & Johnson, T. C. (1993). *Sexualized children: Assessment and treatment of sexualized children and children who molest.* Rockville, MD: Launch.

Gold, E. R. (1986). Long-term effects of sexual victimization in childhood: An attributional approach. *Journal of Consulting and Clinical Psychology, 54,* 471-475.

Gomes-Schwartz, B., Horowitz, J., & Cardarelli, A. (1990). *Child sexual abuse: The initial effects.* Newbury Park, CA: Sage.

Goodman, G. S., Pyle-Taub, E. P., Jones, D. P. H., England, P., Port, L. K., Rudy, L., & Prado, L. (1992). Testifying in criminal court. *Monographs of the Society for Research in Child Development, 57* (Serial No. 229), 1-161.

Harter, S., Alexander, P. C., & Neimeyer, R. A. (1988). Long-term effects of incestuous child abuse in college women: Social adjustment, social cognition, and family characteristics. *Journal of Consulting and Clinical Psychology, 56,* 5-8.

Haskett, M. E., Nowlan, N. P., Hutcheson, J. S., & Whitworth, J. M. (1991). Factors associated with successful entry into therapy in child sexual abuse cases. *Child Abuse & Neglect, 15,* 467-476.

Herman, J. L. (1988). Considering sex offenders: A model of addiction. *Signs: Journal of Women in Culture and Society, 13,* 695-724.

Herman, J. L. (1992). *Trauma and recovery.* New York: Basic Books.

Herman, J. L., Perry, J. C., & van der Kolk, B. A. (1989). Childhood trauma in borderline personality disorder. *American Journal of Psychiatry, 146,* 490-495.

Herman, J. L., & Schatzow, E. (1987). Recovery and verification of memories of childhood sexual trauma. *Psychoanalytic Psychology, 4,* 490-494.

Hibbard, R. A., Ingersoll, G. M., & Orr, D. P. (1990). Behavior risk, emotional risk, and child abuse among adolescents in a nonclinical setting. *Pediatrics, 86,* 896-901.

Hoagwood, K., & Stewart, J. M. (1989). Sexually abused children's perceptions of family functioning. *Child and Adolescent Social Work, 6,* 139-149.

Horowitz, M. D., Wilner, N., & Alvarez, W. (1979). Impact of Events Scale: A measure of subjective stress. *Psychosomatic Medicine, 41,* 209-218.

Hotte, J. P., & Rafman, S. (1992). The specific effects of incest on prepubertal girls from dysfunctional families. *Child Abuse & Neglect, 16,* 273-283.

Hunter, J., Goodwin, D. W., & Wilson, R. J. (1992). Attributions of blame in child sexual abuse victims: An analysis of age and gender influences. *Journal of Child Sexual Abuse, 1,* 75-90.

Hunter, W. M., Coulter, M. L., Runyan, D. K., & Everson, M. D. (1990). Determinants of placement for sexually abused children. *Child Abuse & Neglect, 14,* 407-418.

James, B. (1989). *Treating traumatized children.* Lexington, MA: Lexington Books.

Jehu, D. (1988). *Beyond sexual abuse: Therapy with women who were childhood victims.* Chichester, UK: Wiley.

Johnson, B. K., & Kenkel, M. B. (1991). Stress, coping and adjustment in female adolescent incest victims. *Child Abuse & Neglect, 15,* 293-305.

Jones, D. P. H., & McGraw, J. M. (1987). Reliable and fictitious accounts of sexual abuse to children. *Journal of Interpersonal Violence, 2,* 27-45.

Keller, R. A., Cicchinelli, L. F., & Gardner, D. M. (1989). Characteristics of child sexual abuse treatment programs. *Child Abuse & Neglect, 13,* 361-368.

Kendall-Tackett, K. A., Williams, L. M., & Finkelhor, D. (1993). Impact of sexual abuse on children: A review and synthesis of recent empirical studies. *Psychological Bulletin, 113,* 164-180.

Kluft, R. P. (Ed.). (1985). *Childhood antecedents of multiple personality.* Washington, DC: American Psychiatric Press.

Kolko, D. J. (1986). Social-cognitive skills in training with a sexually abused and abusive child psychiatric patient: Training, generalization, and follow up. *Journal of Family Violence, 1,* 149-166.

Kolko, D. J. (1987). Treatment of child sexual abuse: Programs, progress, and prospects. *Journal of Family Violence, 2,* 303-318.

Kolko, D. J., Moser, J. T., & Weldy, S. R. (1988). Behavioral/emotional indicators of sexual abuse in psychiatric inpatients: A controlled comparison with physical abuse. *Child Abuse & Neglect, 12,* 529-541.

Kroll, J. (1993). *PTSD/borderlines in therapy: Finding the balance.* New York: Norton.

Lang, R. A., & Frenzel, R. R. (1988). How sex offenders lure children. *Annals of Sex Research, 1,* 303-317.

Lanktree, C., & Briere, J. (1995). Outcome of therapy for sexually abused children: A repeated measures study. *Child Abuse & Neglect, 19,* 1145-1155.

Lanktree, C., Briere, J., & Zaidi, L. (1991). Incidence and impact of sexual abuse in a child outpatient sample: The role of direct inquiry. *Child Abuse & Neglect, 15,* 447-453.

Lawson, L., & Chaffin, M. (1992). False negatives in sexual abuse disclosure interviews: Incidence and influence of caretakers' belief in abuse in cases of accidental abuse discovery by diagnosis of STD. *Journal of Interpersonal Violence, 7*(4), 532-542.

Leitenberg, H., Greenwald, E., & Cado, S. (1992). A retrospective study of long-term methods of coping with having been sexually abused during childhood. *Child Abuse & Neglect, 16,* 399-407.

Lew, M. (1988). *Victims no longer.* New York: Harper & Row.

Lipovsky, J. A., Saunders, B. E., & Murphy, S. M. (1989). Depression, anxiety, and behavior problems among victims of father-child sexual assault and nonabused siblings. *Journal of Interpersonal Violence, 4,* 452-468.

Madonna, P. G., Van Scoyk, S., & Jones, D. P. H. (1991). Family interactions within incest and nonincest families. *American Journal of Psychiatry, 148,* 46-49.

Maltz, W., & Holman, B. (1987). *Incest and sexuality: A guide to understanding and healing.* Lexington, MA: Lexington Books.

Mandell, J. G., & Damon, L. (1989). *Group treatment for sexually abused children.* New York: Guilford.

Mannarino, A. P., Cohen, J. A., & Berman, S. R. (1994). The Children's Attributions and Perceptions Scale: A new measure of sexual abuse-related factors. *Journal of Clinical Child Psychology, 23,* 204-211.

Mannarino, A. P., Cohen, J. A., & Gregor, M. (1989). Emotional and behavioral difficulties in sexually abused girls. *Journal of Interpersonal Violence, 4,* 437-451.

McLeer, S. V., Deblinger, E., Atkins, M. S., Ralphe, D. L., & Foa, E. (1988). Post-traumatic stress disorder in sexually abused children. *Journal of the American Academy of Child and Adolescent Psychiatry, 27,* 650-654.

McLeer, S. V., Deblinger, E., Henry, D., & Orvaschel, H. (1992). Sexually abused children at high risk for post-traumatic stress disorder. *Journal of the American Academy of Child Adolescent Psychiatry, 31,* 875-879.

Meinig, M., & Bonner, B. L. (1990, October). Intrafamilial sexual abuse: A structured approach to family intervention. *Violence Update,* pp. 1-11.

Meyers, J. E. B. (1992). *Legal issues in child abuse and neglect.* Newbury Park, CA: Sage.

Morrow, K. B. (1991). Attributions of female adolescent incest victims regarding their molestation. *Child Abuse & Neglect, 15,* 477-482.

National Center on Child Abuse and Neglect (NCCAN). (1993). *A report on the maltreatment of children with disabilities.* Washington, DC: Department of Health and Human Services.

Nelki, J. S., & Watters, J. (1989). A group for sexually abused young children: Unraveling the web. *Child Abuse & Neglect, 13,* 369-378.

Peters, S. D. (1988). Child sexual abuse and later psychological problems. In G. E. Wyatt & G. J. Powell (Eds.), *The lasting effects of child sexual abuse* (pp. 101-117). Newbury Park, CA: Sage.

Piran, N., Lerner, P., Garfinkel, P. E., Kennedy, S. H., & Brouillette, C. (1988). Personality disorders in anorectic patients. *International Journal of Eating Disorders, 7,* 589-599.

Pribor, E. F., & Dinwiddle, S. H. (1992). Psychiatric correlates of incest in childhood. *American Journal of Psychiatry, 149,* 52-56.

Putnum, F. W. (1990). Disturbance of "self" in victims of childhood sexual abuse. In P. R. Kluft (Ed.), *Incest-related syndromes of adult psychopathology* (pp. 113-132). Washington, DC: American Psychiatric Press.

Putnum, F. W., Helmers, K., & Trickett, P. K. (1993). Development, reliability, and validity of a child dissociation scale. *Child Abuse & Neglect, 17,* 731-741.

Rao, K., DiClemente, R. J., & Ponton, L. E. (1992). Child sexual abuse of Asians compared with other populations. *Journal of the American Academy of Child and Adolescent Psychiatry, 31,* 880-886.

Runyan, D. K., Everson, M. D., Edelsohn, G. A., Hunter, W. M., & Coulter, M. L. (1988). Impact of intervention on sexually abused children. *Journal of Pediatrics, 113,* 647-653.

Runyan, D. K., Hunter, W. M., & Everson, M. D. (1992). *Maternal support for child victims of sexual abuse: Determinants and implications* (Final report [Grant No. 90-CA-1368]). Washington, DC: National Center on Child Abuse and Neglect.

Russell, D. E. H. (1984). *Sexual exploitation: Rape, child sexual abuse, and workplace harassment.* Beverly Hills, CA: Sage.

Russell, D. E. H. (1986). *The secret trauma: Incest in the lives of girls and women.* New York: Basic Books.

Ryan, G. (1991). Juvenile sex offenders: Defining the population. In G. D. Ryan & S. L. Lane (Eds.), *Juvenile sexual offending: Causes, consequences and corrections.* Lexington, MA: Lexington Books.

Sas, L. (1991). *Reducing the system-induced trauma for child sexual abuse victims through court preparation, assessment, and follow-up* (Report No. 4555-1-125). Canada: National Welfare Grants Division, Health and Welfare.

Saunders, B. E., Kilpatrick, D. G., Resnick, H. S., Hanson, R. A., & Lipovsky, J. A. (1992, January). *Epidemiological characteristics of child sexual abuse: Results from Wave II of the National Women's Study.* Paper presented at the San Diego Conference on Responding to Child Maltreatment, San Diego.

Saunders, B. E., Villeponteaux, L. A., Lipovsky, J. A., & Kilpatrick, D. G. (1992). Child sexual assault as a risk factor for mental disorder among women: A community survey. *Journal of Interpersonal Violence, 7,* 189-204.

Sauzier, M. (1989). Disclosure of child sexual abuse: For better or worse. *Psychiatric Clinics of North America, 12,* 455-469.

Scott, R. L., & Stone, D. A. (1986). MMPI profile constellations in incest families. *Journal of Consulting and Clinical Psychology, 54,* 354-368.

Seinfeld, J. (1989). Therapy with a severely abused child: An object relations perspective. *Clinical Social Work Journal, 17,* 40-49.

Sgroi, S. M. (1982). *Handbook of clinical intervention in child sexual abuse.* Lexington, MA: Lexington Books.

Shapiro, J. P., Leifer, M., Martone, M. W., & Kassem, L. (1990). Multimethod assessment of depression in sexually abused girls. *Journal of Personality Assessment, 55,* 234-248.

Shapiro, J. P., Leifer, M., Martone, M. W., & Kassem, L. (1992). Cognitive functioning and social competence as predictors of maladjustment in sexually abused girls. *Journal of Interpersonal Violence, 7,* 156-164.

Shengold, L. (1989). *Soul murder: The effects of childhood abuse and deprivation.* New Haven, CT: Yale University Press.

Singer, M. I., Petchers, M. K., & Hussey, D. (1989). The relationship between sexual abuse and substance abuse among psychiatrically hospitalized adolescents. *Child Abuse & Neglect, 13,* 319-325.

Sirles, E., & Franke, P. J. (1989). Factors influencing mothers' reactions to intrafamilial sexual abuse. *Child Abuse & Neglect, 13,* 131-139.

Sorensen, S. B., Siegel, J. M., Golding, J. M., & Stein, J. A. (1991). Repeated sexual victimization. *Victims and Violence, 91,* 299-308.

Sorensen, T., & Snow, B. (1991). How children tell: The process of disclosure in child sexual abuse. *Child Welfare League of America, 70,* 3-15.

Spaccarelli, S. (1994). Stress appraisal and coping in child sexual abuse: A theoretical and empirical review. *Psychological Bulletin, 116,* 340-362.

Spaccarelli, S. (in press). Measuring abuse stress and negative cognitive appraisals in child sexual abuse: Validating data on two new scales. *Journal of Abnormal Child Psychology.*

Springs, F. E., & Friedrich, W. N. (1992). Health risk behaviors and medical sequelae of childhood sexual abuse. *Mayo Clinic Proceedings, 67,* 527-532.

Steiger, H., & Zanko, M. (1990). Sexual traumata among eating disordered, psychiatric, and normal female groups: Comparison of prevalences and defense styles. *Journal of Interpersonal Violence, 5,* 74-86.

Stein, J. A., Golding, J. M., Siegel, J. M., Burnam, M. A., & Sorensen, S. B. (1988). Long-term psychological sequelae of child sexual abuse: The Los Angeles Epidemiological Catchment Area Study. In G. E. Wyatt & G. J. Powell (Eds.), *The lasting effects of child sexual abuse* (pp. 135-154). Newbury Park, CA: Sage.

Steward, M. S., Farquar, L., Dicharry, D. C., Glick, D. R., & Martin, P. W. (1986). Group therapy: A treatment of choice for young victims of child abuse. *International Journal of Psychotherapy, 36,* 261-277.

Stovall, G., & Craig, R. J. (1990). Mental representations of physically and sexually abused latency-aged females. *Child Abuse & Neglect, 11,* 371-383.

Sullivan, E. J. (1988). Association between chemical dependency and sexual problems in nurses. *Journal of Interpersonal Violence, 3,* 326-330.

Summit, R. C. (1983). The child sexual abuse accommodation syndrome. *Child Abuse & Neglect, 7,* 177-193.

Tedesco, J. F., & Schnell, S. V. (1987). Children's reactions to sex abuse investigation and litigation. *Child Abuse & Neglect, 11,* 267-272.

Tharinger, D., Horton, C. B., & Millea, S. (1990). Sexual abuse and exploitation of children and adults with mental retardation and other handicaps. *Child Abuse & Neglect, 14,* 301-312.

Tong, L., Oates, K., & McDowell, M. (1986). Personality development following sexual abuse. *Child Abuse & Neglect, 11,* 371-383.

Urquiza, A., & Crowley, C. (1986, May). *Sex differences in the survivors of childhood sexual abuse.* Paper presented at the Fourth National Conference on the Sexual Victimization of Children, New Orleans, LA.

van der Kolk, B. A., & Kadish, W. (1987). Amnesia, dissociation, and the return of the repressed. In B. A. van der Kolk (Ed.), *Psychological trauma.* Washington, DC: American Psychiatric Press.

van der Kolk, B. A., Perry, J. C., & Herman, J. L. (1991). Childhood origins of self-destructive behavior. *American Journal of Psychiatry, 148,* 1665-1671.

Van Leeuwen, K. (1988). Resistances in the treatment of a sexually molested six-year-old girl. *International Review of Psychoanalysis, 15,* 149-156.

Walsh, B. W., & Rosen, P. (1988). *Self-mutilation: Theory, research, and treatment.* New York: Guilford.

Whitcomb, D., Runyan, D. K., De Vos, E., Hunter, W. M., Cross, T. P., Everson, M. D., Peeler, N. A., Porter, C. Q., Toth, P. A., & Cropper, C. (1991). *Child victim as witness research and development program* (Executive summary [Grant No. 87-MC-CX-0026]). Washington, DC: U.S. Department of Justice, Office of Juvenile Justice and Delinquency Prevention.

White, S., Halpin, B. M., Strom, G. A., & Santelli, G. (1988). Behavioral comparisons of young sexually abused, neglected, and nonreferred children. *Journal of Clinical Child Psychology, 17,* 53-61.

Williams, L. (1994). Recall of childhood trauma: A prospective study of women's memories of child sexual abuse. *Journal of Consulting and Clinical Psychology, 62,* 1167-1176.

Winton, M. A. (1990). An evaluation of a support group for parents who have a sexually abused child. *Child Abuse & Neglect, 14,* 397-406.

Wolfe, V. V., Gentile, C., & Wolfe, D. A. (1989). The impact of sexual abuse on children: A PTSD formulation. *Behavior Therapy, 20,* 215-228.

Wolfe, V. V., Wolfe, D. A., & LaRose, L. (1986). *The Children's Impact of Traumatic Events Scale.* Unpublished manuscript, University of Western Ontario.

Wozencraft, T., Wagner, W., & Pellegrin, A. (1991). Depression and suicidal ideation in sexually abused children. *Child Abuse & Neglect, 15,* 505-510.

Wyatt, G. E. (1985). The sexual abuse of Afro-American and white-American women in childhood. *Child Abuse & Neglect, 9,* 507-519.

4

Psychological Maltreatment

STUART N. HART

MARLA R. BRASSARD

HENRY C. KARLSON

There are two major forms of child abuse and neglect: physical and psychological. Sexual abuse is a combination of the two, often primarily psychological in the nature of its acts and consequences. Psychological maltreatment is embedded in all other forms of child maltreatment, and it exists in its own discreet forms. Recent research suggests that it is the strongest influencer and best predictor of the developmental outcomes of other forms of child abuse and neglect (Claussen & Crittenden, 1991; Vissing, Straus, Gelles, & Harrop, 1991).

Psychological maltreatment has been given relatively little serious attention in the past two decades of state and national concern for child abuse and neglect. There are many reasons for this, including problems of inadequate definitions, failure to establish cause-and-effect relationships, and the difficulty of clarifying the cumulated impact of psychological maltreatment.

Fortunately, interest in the topic of psychological maltreatment has grown in our society in general, and increased attention has been given to it recently in research and practice (Baily & Baily, 1986; Brassard, Germain, & Hart, 1987; Briere, 1992; Briere & Runtz, 1988; Claussen & Crittenden, 1991; Crittenden, Claussen, & Sugarman, 1994; Garbarino, Guttman, & Seeley, 1986; Hart & Brassard,

1986, 1987a, 1990; McGee & Wolfe, 1991; O'Hagan, 1993). Genuine progress has accrued through this increase in attention. Where relevant, recent developments in knowledge will be highlighted and integrated in the sections of this chapter that include the following: Definitions, Incidence and Prevalence, Evidence of Impact on Children, Theoretical Models, the Law and Psychological Maltreatment, Implications for Intervention, and Research Agenda.

Definitions

The term *psychological maltreatment* is used throughout this chapter. This term is preferred to others, such as *emotional abuse and neglect*, because it denotes a category that is sufficiently broad to include all of the important cognitive and affective dimensions of maltreatment. The term *psychological maltreatment* is given meaning primarily by the definitions of its acts and the substantiation of its occurrence. The acts of psychological maltreatment must be recognizable and objectively verifiable if the individual clinician, child protective services (CPS) team, or legal establishment is to deal with it effectively. Substantiation depends on valid and practical operational definitions.

The establishment of operational definitions has been the major impediment to progress in dealing with this problem. At a generic level, many experts have considered psychological maltreatment to embody the repeated pattern of behavior that conveys to children that they are worthless, unloved, unwanted, only of value in meeting another's needs, or seriously threatened with physical or psychological violence (Brassard, Hart, & Hardy, 1991). A stronger generic conceptual base was developed by the International Conference on Psychological Abuse of Children and Youth (Proceedings, 1983):

> Psychological maltreatment of children and youth consists of acts of omission and commission which are judged on the basis of a combination of community standards and professional expertise to be psychologically damaging. Such acts are committed by individuals, singly or collectively, who by their characteristics (e.g., age, status, knowledge, organizational form) are in a position of differential power that

renders a child vulnerable. Such acts damage immediately or ultimately the behavioral, cognitive, affective, or physical functioning of the child. Examples of psychological maltreatment include acts of rejecting, terrorizing, isolating, exploiting, and missocializing.

Recent research has produced the most advanced developmental stage of work toward operational definitions. The following five categories, derived from research and expert opinion, have been articulated (Hart & Brassard, 1991): (a) spurning, (b) terrorizing, (c) isolating, (d) exploiting/corrupting, and (e) denying emotional responsiveness. A sixth category—mental health, medical, and educational neglect—derived from the five major categories and traditionally included among child maltreatment categories has been added. Table 4.1 includes these categories and clarifying definitional and subcategory information.

Psychological maltreatment can be differentiated into these distinct subcategories and distinguished from appropriate parenting by multidimensional scaling of parenting practices. The five main categories of psychological maltreatment presented earlier and in Table 4.1 represent the accumulation of research and perspectives of leaders in this field and are recommended for application in efforts to advance the state of knowledge and practice (Egeland, 1991).

Conceptual Issues

The articles devoted to conceptual issues in a recent edition of *Development and Psychopathology* ("Psychological Maltreatment," 1991) explored the following conceptual issues.

Separation of acts of psychological maltreatment from associated consequences. In general, it is agreed that operational definitions must deal thoroughly with the acts or discovery dimensions of psychological maltreatment separate from any consequences they may produce. It will be noted that Hart and Brassard's (1991) operational definitions do just this. However, those working with psychological maltreatment issues recognize that standards of evidence used in decision making about cases, particularly from a legal perspective, require that cause-and-effect

TABLE 4.1 Psychological Maltreatment Forms

SIX MAJOR TYPES OF PSYCHOLOGICAL MALTREATMENT ARE DESCRIBED BELOW AND FURTHER CLARIFIED BY IDENTIFICATION OF SUBCATEGORIES.

A repeated pattern or extreme incident(s) of the conditions described in this table constitute psychological maltreatment. Such conditions convey the message that the child is worthless, flawed, unloved, endangered, or only valuable in meeting someone else's needs.

SPURNING (Hostile Rejecting/Degrading) includes verbal and nonverbal caregiver acts that reject and degrade a child. SPURNING includes the following:
- Belittling, degrading, and other nonphysical forms of overtly hostile or rejecting treatment
- Shaming and/or ridiculing the child for showing normal emotions such as affection, grief, or sorrow
- Consistently singling out one child to criticize and punish, to perform most of the household chores, or to receive fewer rewards
- Public humiliation

TERRORIZING includes caregiver behavior that threatens or is likely to physically hurt, kill, abandon, or place the child or child's loved ones or objects in recognizably dangerous situations. TERRORIZING includes the following:
- Placing a child in unpredictable or chaotic circumstances
- Placing a child in recognizably dangerous situations
- Setting rigid or unrealistic expectations with the threat of loss, harm, or danger if they are not met
- Threatening or perpetrating violence against the child
- Threatening or perpetrating violence against a child's loved ones or objects

ISOLATING includes caregiver acts that consistently deny the child opportunities to meet needs for interacting or communicating with peers or adults inside or outside the home. ISOLATING includes the following:
- Confining the child or placing unreasonable limitations on the child's freedom of movement within his or her environment
- Placing unreasonable limitations or restrictions on social interactions with peers or adults in the community

EXPLOITING/CORRUPTING includes caregiver acts that encourage the child to develop inappropriate behaviors (self-destructive, antisocial, criminal, deviant, or other maladaptive behaviors). EXPLOITING/CORRUPTING includes the following:
- Modeling, permitting, or encouraging antisocial behavior (e.g., prostitution, performance in pornographic media, initiation of criminal activities, substance abuse, violence to or corruption of others)
- Modeling, permitting, or encouraging developmentally inappropriate behavior (e.g., parentification, infantalization, living the parent's unfulfilled dreams)
- Encouraging or coercing abandonment of developmentally appropriate autonomy through extreme overinvolvement, intrusiveness, and/or dominance (e.g., allowing little or no opportunity or support for child's views, feelings, and wishes; micromanaging child's life)
- Restricting or interfering with cognitive development

DENYING EMOTIONAL RESPONSIVENESS (Ignoring) includes caregiver acts that ignore the child's attempts and needs to interact (failing to express affection, caring, and love for the child) and show no emotion in interactions with the child. DENYING EMOTIONAL RESPONSIVENESS includes the following:
- Being detached and uninvolved through either incapacity or lack of motivation
- Interacting only when absolutely necessary
- Failing to express affection, caring, and love for the child

MENTAL HEALTH, MEDICAL, AND EDUCATIONAL NEGLECT includes unwarranted caregiver acts that ignore, refuse to allow, or fail to provide the necessary treatment for the mental health, medical, and educational problems or needs of the child. MENTAL HEALTH, MEDICAL, AND EDUCATIONAL NEGLECT includes the following:
- Ignoring the need for, failing, or refusing to allow or provide treatment for serious emotional/behavioral problems or needs of the child
- Ignoring the need for, failing, or refusing to allow or provide treatment for serious physical health problems or needs of the child
- Ignoring the need for, failing, or refusing to allow or provide treatment for services for serious educational problems or needs of the child

SOURCE: Office for the Study of the Psychological Rights of the Child, Indiana University, Purdue University at Indianapolis, 902 West New York Street, Indianapolis, IN 46202-5155.

relationships between acts and consequences be established either as (a) existing in a particular case or (b) strongly predictable, based on previous research that has established that connection.

Concentration on psychological dimensions of maltreatment separate from its physical correlates. The argument relevant to this point is that psychological maltreatment never will be clarified sufficiently or dealt with in practice until it is established in its own right as a primary factor. Accepting this, it must be recognized that psychological dimensions of maltreatment often are related to physical abuse and physical damage inextricably. Terrorizing, for example, frequently is embedded in acts of physical violence and may produce ulcers; denying emotional responsiveness acts may be associated with malnutrition and produce retarded physical and intellectual development (Corson & Davidson, 1987; Egeland & Erickson, 1987; Erickson & Egeland, 1987; Hart, Germain, & Brassard, 1987; Montagu, 1970). These relationships should not be ignored in practice or research but should be explored fully.

Consideration of both direct and indirect forms of psychological maltreatment. We join others (Eron & Huesmann, 1987; Jones & Jones, 1987; Reschly & Graham-Clay, 1987; Telzrow, 1987) in arguing that psychological maltreatment exists in indirect forms that also must be given consideration in addition to direct forms. Children may be terrorized by a threat of violence directed toward them or toward a loved one under conditions that they observe (Hughes, 1992). Children may be maltreated by being directly encouraged to lie, cheat, steal, use drugs, or become involved in deviant sexual activity or by observing these behaviors on the part of powerful role models.

The need for multiple broad and narrow definitions. Legal definitions should focus narrowly on the salient and severe aspects of psychological maltreatment. This is especially true for definitions to be applied in case determinations by CPS, used in the processing of such cases by the legal establishment, and incorporated in the mandatory intervention practices of society. A more comprehensive definitional set, incorporating the full breadth of qualitative and quantitative dimensions of psychological maltreatment, deserves

theoretical and research exploration and application in prescriptive interventions that range beyond mandatory to voluntary participation by perpetrators and victims.

In the practice domain, psychological maltreatment has relevance in criminal cases in which a person has been the victim and/or perpetrator of psychological maltreatment and in CPS cases, child custody cases, and civil suits in which a child or the child's advocates are seeking redress for maltreatment.

In addition, consideration must be given to where psychological maltreatment falls along a continuum of poor to good parenting practices. Crittenden and Hart (1989) and others (see "Psychological Maltreatment," 1991) have recommended that the term *psychological maltreatment* and the research and coercive intervention directed toward it should be reserved for the most salient, extreme, and severe forms of psychologically damaging or limiting care and interactions. From this perspective, psychological maltreatment falls at the extreme negative end of a continuum of psychological aspects of child rearing or interpersonal behaviors. Concentration on this point in the continuum is likely to receive approval from both expert and lay publics and is supported by the recognized vulnerability of children to psychological maltreatment (see Egeland & Erickson, 1987; Finkelhor & Dziuba-Leatherman, 1994). Psychological maltreatment that falls on the less serious end of the continuum would be properly labeled inappropriate, inadequate, or misdirected child rearing and would be the subject of voluntary preventative and educational intervention strategies as well as research.

Mediating variables. Attention must be given to mediating variables that influence the likelihood that one will perpetrate specific forms and levels of psychological maltreatment or that one will be a victim subject to or surviving negative consequences. Developmental variables require consideration, particularly with regard to the types of maltreatment likely to be directed toward individuals and the relative vulnerability to negative consequences of various types at particular developmental stages. For example, denying emotional responsiveness may have its greatest impact for the infant and toddler stages when the child needs the sensitive, loving caretaking necessary to produce basic trust in the human environment. Differential vulnerability to types of maltreatment (including psychological abuse and neglect) by developmental periods and gender has been demonstrated in adolescents in one recent study (Wolfe & McGee, 1994).

Ecological variables require attention at the intraindividual level and across dyadic interpersonal relationships, intimate family or subgroup relationships, and community and societal network levels. For example, the severity of acts of psychological maltreatment may be strong when several members of, or the family as a whole, spurn the victim and greater yet when the child's subjective perspective and society's reactions magnify the significance of those spurning behaviors.

Finally, presently available data suggest that the negative power of psychological maltreatment may be mediated by the degree to which counterbalancing positive interpersonal behavior directed at the victim is expressed by the perpetrator and others (Hart & Brassard, 1991; Schaeffer & Lewis, 1988-1989). Therefore, information about both positive and negative interpersonal behavior may be required to make a judgment about the level of severity or endangerment produced by psychological maltreatment.

Incidence and Prevalence

The true incidence or prevalence levels of psychological maltreatment are not known. In part, this is because it is difficult to discern the rate of child abuse and neglect in general. Because of its complexity, psychological maltreatment is even harder to quantify. Nevertheless, psychological maltreatment has been recognized as the primary abuse in approximately 11% of the 2 million cases of child maltreatment reported in the years 1986-1987 to the American Humane Association (1988, 1989) and 7% of the nearly 3 million cases reported for 1992 to the National Committee for the Prevention of Child Abuse (McCurdy & Daro, 1993).

The 1986 national incidence study of the National Center on Child Abuse and Neglect (NCCAN, 1988) identified 211,100 cases of emotional abuse and 223,100 cases of emotional neglect. There were age differences: Reports of emotional abuse in children ages birth to 2 were significantly below those reported for children ages 6 and older; 3- to 5-year-olds were reported as emotionally abused at lower levels than children aged 12 years and older. Although not significant, there also was a tendency for the same age-related trends to occur with emotional neglect. The risk for emotional neglect appeared to climb gradually throughout the age spectrums. There were no sex differences in reported emotional abuse or neglect. Interesting gender differences were found: Girls were just as likely to be emotionally abused as they were likely to be sexually abused; boys were likely to experience emotional abuse at a rate twice that of sexual abuse. Family income was related to the incidents of abuse and neglect, although not to same extent as with physical neglect. Reporting of emotional abuse was nearly 5 times more frequent for the lower-income group than for the higher-income group, and emotional neglect was 4.5 times more frequent among children from lower-income families. No racial or ethnic differences were reported. The NCCAN study established psychological maltreatment as occurring at a substantially higher level when cases were counted both under the conditions of extant and predicted harm.

In general, it is accepted that only a small percentage of child maltreatment cases come to the attention of authorities, and this is particularly true for psychological maltreatment (see Claussen & Crittenden, 1991; Egeland & Erickson, 1987, for supportive evidence).

Unless it co-occurs with other forms of severe abuse, cases of psychological maltreatment are likely to be unreported.

Unless it co-occurs with other forms of severe abuse, cases of psychological maltreatment are likely to be unreported. If reported, they are less likely to be screened into CPS, less likely to go to court, and less likely to receive serious interventions (Melton & Davidson, 1987).

A recent study by Vissing et al. (1991) sheds light on the prevalence of psychological maltreatment. These researchers used the Conflict Tactics Scale, developed to study family violence, in a nationally representative telephone survey of 3,346 families with children between the ages of birth and 18. In this study, parents were asked the degree to which nine different types of conflict resolution had been used by them, including verbal/symbolic aggression (e.g., sulking, refusing to talk to a child, berating a child). They reported that two thirds of U.S. children are abused verbally, with the frequency of incidents averaging 12.6 times per year.

Arguably, psychological maltreatment occurs at levels equal to or beyond the approximately 3 million cases of child abuse and neglect assumed to be occurring in recent years (McCurdy & Daro, 1993): It is embedded in all other forms of child maltreatment, and it exists in its own discrete forms that are the least likely to be reported. An additional factor supporting this argument is that the majority of child abuse and neglect cases reported are for perpetrators and victims at the lowest socioeconomic levels of our society. The authors speculate that perpetration of psychological maltreatment is related differently to socioeconomic status, and at higher socioeconomic status levels, where verbal and other psychological competencies are the mechanisms of choice to control and punish others, psychological maltreatment is as likely or more likely to occur than physical abuse.

Evidence of Impact on Children

Based on theories of child development and child psychopathology, psychological maltreatment is likely to produce maladaptive deviancy in intra- and interpersonal characteristics, retard and distort development and functioning, and lead to withdrawal and aggression. The review of expert opinions, clinical cases, and empirical research literature presented to the International Conference on Psychological Abuse of Children and Youth (Proceedings, 1983) provided support for all these assumptions in the following list of negative child development conditions associated with psychological maltreatment:

> Poor appetite, guilt, lying, stealing, enuresis, encopresis, low self-esteem, emotional instability, reduced emotional responsiveness, inability to become independent, incompetence and/or underachievement, inability to trust others, depression, autistic behavior, misuse of drugs, prostitution,

failure to thrive, withdrawal behaviors sometimes leading to suicide, aggression sometimes leading to homicide, and tendencies to maltreat others.

Although all these conditions eventually may be proven to be consequences of psychological maltreatment, strong empirical support for relationships presently exists for a much more limited set. One or more research studies has established relationships between psychological maltreatment and problems of (a) attachment, (b) social competence and social adjustment, (c) behavior, (d) cognitive ability and problem solving, and (e) educational achievement. Table 4.2 identifies these studies, their basic findings, and the developmental periods studied.

Attachment. A number of well-done studies have documented that, at least in lower socioeconomic groups, maltreated children are significantly more likely to form insecure attachment relationships with their mothers or other primary caregivers than are demographically matched comparison groups (see Cicchetti, 1989, for a review). Estimates of these insecure anxious attachments range from 70% to 100%. Egeland and Sroufe (1991) identified a group of children receiving psychologically unavailable caregiving but no other identifiable forms of maltreatment. Every child in this group developed an avoidant attachment with his or her caregiver (Egeland, 1991). The home environments of these maltreated children included emotional and physical rejection, hostile attempts at behavior management, verbal and emotional assault, or an absence of a synchronist interactional style between caregiver and child (Crittenden & Ainsworth, 1989). Security of attachment had indications for later development. Insecurely attached children developed negative views of themselves and their caregivers, based on their experiences in that relationship, and they may have been more prone to academic and behavior problems.

Social competence and social adjustment. Psychologically maltreated children, in comparison with demographically matched controls, have significantly lower levels of social competence and social adjustment, based on parent and teacher ratings (Brassard, Hart, & Hardy, 1993; Claussen & Crittenden, 1991; Erickson, Egeland, & Pianta, 1989; Hart & Brassard, 1991;

TABLE 4.2 Impact of Psychological Maltreatment on Children: Summary of Research

Area	Level	Qualities	References
Problems in learning		Significantly more academic problems; more psychological maltreatment, lower cognitive and educational performance; more observation of spousal violence, lower cognitive skills	Erickson, Egeland, & Pianta, 1989; Hart & Brassard, 1991; Hughes, 1992
Problems in relationships	Preschool/school	Significantly more aggression	Erickson et al., 1989
		Psychological maltreatment by mother predicts "no friends"	Hart & Brassard, 1991
	Adolescents	More social problems	Claussen & Crittenden, 1991
		More problems with peers	Vissing et al., 1991
Unusual behaviors and feelings	Infants	Attachment disorders—not seeking comfort when distressed or not benefiting from parent's presence when distressed	Cicchetti, 1989; Crittenden & Ainsworth, 1989; Egeland, 1991; Egeland & Sroufe, 1991; Erickson & Egeland, 1987; Erickson et al., 1989
	Preschool	Attacking peers in distress	Main & George, 1985
	School	Significantly more disruptive behavior in classroom	Erickson et al., 1989; Hart & Brassard, 1991
	All ages	Significantly more behavioral problems	Vissing et al., 1991; Wolfe & McGee, 1994
	Adolescents	Significantly more anti-social behaviorewis	Lewis, 1990, 1992
Unhappiness or depression		*Reduced emotional responsiveness; low self-esteem or negative self-concept	Fischoff, Whitten, & Petit, 1979; Krugman & Krugman, 1984; McCarthy, 1979; Rohner & Rohner, 1980; Shengold, 1979
		*Depression; suicide; emotional instability/maladjustment	Hyman, 1985; Krugman & Krugman, 1984; Laury & Meerloo, 1967; Moore, 1974; Shengold, 1979
Fears and physical symptoms	Infants	*Failure to thrive	Brook, 1980; Bullard, Glasser, Heagarty, & Pivchik, 1967; Egeland & Sroufe, 1981; Gardner, 1972; Powell, Brasel, & Blizzard, 1967
	Preschool and later	*Poor appetite; encopresis/enuresis; increase in somatic symptoms	Hughes, 1992; Hyman, 1985; Leonard, Rhymes, & Solnit, 1966; McCarthy, 1979; Pemberton & Benady, 1973; Spitz, 1946

NOTE: *Studies with lesser support.

Vissing et al., 1991). These findings hold from the preschool years through adolescence and have been found in studies varying in definitions of psychological maltreatment, measures of psychological maltreatment, and sample selection procedures.

Behavior problems. Psychologically maltreated children have significantly more behavioral problems than demographically matched peers. Teacher, professional, and parent ratings have been the primary sources for this conclusion.

Cognitive ability and problem solving. Only one study has found a significant difference in cognitive ability and problem solving in psychologically maltreated children. Egeland and his colleagues (Egeland & Erickson, 1987; Erickson & Egeland, 1987; Erickson et al., 1989) found that children whose mothers were psychologically unavailable showed "a notable decline in competence during the early years of life" (p. 665). At 9 months of age, this group had a mean score of 120 on the Baily Scale of Infant Development. However, by the age of 24 months, their mean score had dropped to 84. Some of these children had been physically abused as well. Those who had not been physically abused had their scores drop from 118 to 87. At 42 months of age, they lacked creativity on a barrier box task and lacked persistence and enthusiasm for the tasks given them. By preschool they were showing many behavioral problems, including self-abusive behavior, nervous signs, and other indicators of developing psychopathology (Egeland, Sroufe, & Erickson, 1983). Hart and Brassard (1991) found that psychologically maltreated children from a disadvantaged group were significantly more likely to show school-related problems in ability and academic achievement.

Educational achievement. The educational achievement in psychologically maltreated early school-age children has been found to be lower than that of demographically matched peers in highly disadvantaged samples (Erickson & Egeland, 1987; Hart & Brassard, 1991).

The essential role of psychological maltreatment, as a contributor to the consequences of all forms of child abuse and neglect, is further supported by a study done by Claussen and Crittenden (1991).

They used an unselected sample of 176 physically abusive and neglectful families among CPS cases and recruited a demographic control sample of 175 families. In addition, they recruited 37 family clinical controls. They found high rates of psychological maltreatment in all samples, and when they controlled for the degree of physical abuse and neglect in the CPS sample, they found that it was the degree of psychological maltreatment, rather than the degree of physical injury, that predicted the psychosocial and behavioral problems in children. The stability with which the degree of psychological maltreatment predicted behavioral and psychosocial problems also held for the two comparison groups.

Additional evidence of the pervading negative consequences of psychological maltreatment is provided in DeLozier's (1982) examination of 18 working-class Los Angeles mothers who physically assaulted their children and 18 matched controls. DeLozier investigated the mothers' childhood histories and gave them a separation anxiety test. This test depicts either a child leaving his or her parents or parents leaving their child. The abusive mothers were very sensitive to any type of separation depicted on the test, even commonplace forms such as saying goodbye when a mother would go to the store, and they responded with high levels of anxiety or anger in their stories. Their responses included a yearning for care but an expectation of rejection of any attempts to solicit it. Based on their responses, 12 of the 18 abusive mothers were classified as having an anxious attachment, as opposed to 2 of the control group mothers. DeLozier thought she would find a high incidence of separation from parents in the abusive women's childhood or a high level of actual violence from parents. Instead of actual abandonment and violence, she found significantly more repeated threats to abandon, beat, maim, or kill and uncertainty as to the availability of caregivers from the abusive mothers' parents. Only 7 of 18 abusive mothers reported that they could turn to their own mothers for help when in distress, whereas all of the control group mothers reported they could turn to their own mothers for help.

A final area strongly suggestive of the negative impact of psychological maltreatment, not only on the primary victim but also on those who interact with the victim, is the work being done to clarify relationships between child maltreatment and the perpetration of antisocial acts. These acts include violence, sometimes resulting in homicide by the victims of psychological maltreatment. Lewis (1990, 1992) have found maltreated children to be disproportionately represented at high levels within adolescent and young adult populations who have committed violent crimes. They speculate that maltreatment increases the likelihood of becoming violent, particularly when associated with certain mediating conditions (e.g., learning problems, signs of neurological dysfunctioning). Mones (1991) has made a careful study of children who have killed their parents and has found their backgrounds to be pervaded by maltreatment, particularly psychological maltreatment.

Taken together, these data suggest that the degree of psychological abuse, not the degree of physical abuse and neglect, is related to the impact on children's social competence, psychological well-being, and mastery of their environment.

Theoretical Models

Several theoretical models have relevance for psychological maltreatment. The authors take the position, shared by others (Barnett, Manly, & Cicchetti, 1991; Gil, 1987; Hart & Brassard, 1987a, 1987b), that the basic human needs theory has the greatest heuristic and explanatory power for the core dimensions of psychological maltreatment. It is readily seen that the psychological maltreatment described herein is in direct opposition to the fulfillment of basic needs as described by Maslow (1970): physiological needs, safety needs, love and belonging needs, and esteem needs. By virtue of its opposition to these basic needs, psychological maltreatment has the power to produce maladaptive deviancies (Hart & Brassard, 1987a).

Numerous other theoretical models are complementary or supplementary to the basic human needs model in clarifying the nature of psychological maltreatment. The organizational, coercion, and prisoner of war models are good examples. The organizational model clarifies the influence psychological maltreat-

ment can have because of the developmental issues experienced in predictable stage sequence by children in their interactions with the social world (Cicchetti & Braunwald, 1984; Erickson, Sroufe, & Egeland, 1985; Sroufe, 1979). The coercion model establishes the importance of recognizing that interpersonal relations involve interactions and that the significance of psychological maltreatment factors often increases through the escalating psychological maltreatment behaviors embedded in extended interactions (Patterson, 1982, 1986). The prisoner of war model aids in understanding the extreme vulnerability inherent in the subjective view of a child who has no one to blame and no historical nor present resources to draw on to deal with an extended pattern of psychological maltreatment (Benedek, 1985; Turgi & Hart, 1988). In addition, the psychosemantic model includes all the dimensions and mediating factors of the causes and effects of psychological maltreatment through its comprehensive inclusion of system interactions across developmental and ecological factors (Tzeng, Jackson, & Karlson, 1991).

The Law and Psychological Maltreatment

Psychological maltreatment unconnected with physical abuse/neglect or sexual abuse rarely leads to government intervention. One reason that psychological maltreatment has received so little attention from our legal system is the lack of a specific set of guidelines to be used in determining when a parent has crossed a line separating legal, if ineffective, parenting from psychological maltreatment. Parents have a fundamental right to raise their children without undue interference by the state (*Quilloin v. Walcott*, 1978). A judge may not merely substitute his or her judgment for that of the parent. Courts may not dictate to parents how to raise their children without showing that the parents' methods seriously impair or threaten the children's physical or mental well-being (*In re E. M. Bartholomew County, Department of Public Welfare*, 1991). Where specific guidelines exist, however, both legislators and courts have been very active in supporting children and in protecting children from conduct that could lead to psychological or emotional harm. This is best illustrated by the manner in which our legal system has dealt with child sexual abuse.

Laws prohibiting sexual conduct with children are found in the penal codes of every state. Although early criminal codes dealt only with incest, or sexual intercourse before the age of consent, modern codes are much more comprehensive. Analysis of criminal prosecutions arising from sexual conduct with children discloses that the vast majority of prosecutions involve sexual conduct that results in little, if any, long-lasting physical injury to the child victim. Justification for the prohibitions is not found in fear of physical injury; it is found in the belief that such conduct creates a great risk of psychological harm (see *New York v. Ferber,* 1982; *Osborne v. Ohio,* 1990).

Society has criminalized nonphysically injurious sexual conduct that poses a risk of mental harm to children.

Society has criminalized nonphysically injurious sexual conduct that poses a risk of mental harm to children. Why, then, has society not criminalized other conduct equally psychologically harmful? In general, conduct is criminalized only when three conditions can be met: (a) The conduct to be criminalized must be susceptible of *reasonably specific description and identification.* (b) The conduct must be shown to be the *reasonably proximate cause* of harm that the community seeks to prevent. (c) Harm caused by the conduct *must not be outweighed by the benefit arising from it.* When conduct is considered immoral, it may be criminalized even though proof that it also causes harm may not be great. However, conduct that is considered moral or proper only will be criminalized when exceptionally strong evidence is produced that it causes serious harm. We believe that all forms of sexual conduct with children meet the conditions necessary for criminalization. Critical to this belief is society's moral rejection of the conduct. Other conduct that is psychologically or emotionally harmful to the children will be subjected to greater regulation and criminalization

when our culture's moral rejection of that behavior is established.

Implications for Intervention

The knowledge of intervention practices and effects for child maltreatment suggests that our current approach to CPS needs to be rethought. Much of the research on intervention programs with maltreating families suggests that these families are difficult to treat and that often our efforts are unsuccessful. Cohn and Daro (1987) reviewed the findings of four multiyear evaluation studies, funded by the NCCAN, on the effectiveness of interventions with maltreating families. The majority of these interventions were model demonstration projects using a casework, family support approach. The authors' conclusions are discouraging, because they stated that "child abuse and neglect continue despite early, thoughtful, and often costly intervention" (p. 440).

Programs demonstrating the most success focused on improved parental functioning with parents charged with sexual abuse. These programs used interventions such as lay counseling and parent evaluation. Much success was reported in interventions with children. However, treatment of children did not seem to affect clinicians' ratings of the likelihood of future abuse. Relatively ineffective were programs that attempted to halt or reduce the likelihood of continuing abuse with the most severe cases of physical abuse and neglect and emotional maltreatment. Summarizing across these programs, 33% or more parents continued to maltreat during intervention, and more than 50% were rated by staff as likely to abuse following termination of the program. Because staff ratings were used as the measure of treatment success, these are likely to be overestimates of the effectiveness of these programs.

The current child protective system is set up to respond to what is viewed to be acute distress in families as opposed to chronic, long-term problems. Its coercive approach appears to do best at providing social sanctions for those who physically hit or sexually abuse their children. Our experience with the goals of the CPS program shows that efforts to improve the emotional climate or the quality of relationships within the family are not part of treatment goals or used as indications of treatment success.

This situation has led some researchers to question whether psychological maltreatment cases should be added to CPS caseloads, given the difficulty the overwhelmed CPS system has addressing the needs of physically and sexually maltreating families (Claussen & Crittenden, 1991). In most cases, a preventative and mental health approach specifically designed for at-risk and psychologically maltreating families would be more desirable. At some time in their lives, most individuals have been both perpetrators and victims of psychologically harmful treatment. However, for most the experience causes no lasting harm because it is at low levels of frequency, intensity, and duration. Some families have stressful interactions within and without the family and demonstrate inadequate or misguided parenting but do not physically or sexually maltreat their children. For these families, preventive, educational, and mental health approaches are preferable to coercive CPS intervention. However, when psychological maltreatment of high frequency, intensity, and duration or developmental salience occurs and is predicted to produce serious harm to the child, mandatory societal intervention may be justified. This is particularly true when perpetrators resist offered help.

Implications for Psychological Treatment of Victims and Their Families

Because psychological maltreatment may be relatively common in families not referred to CPS (Claussen & Crittenden, 1991; Vissing et al., 1991), we strongly endorse an approach that (a) combines prevention with treatment, (b) is universally available and thus not stigmatizing, (c) continues throughout the developmental period, and (d) if coercive societal intervention is required, employs an approach that is supported empirically. Specifically, we favor national home visitors, school-based mental health and health services for children and their families, and a CPS system that is client data driven, such as Lutzger's (1984) ecobehavioral model. Regardless of the service source or model employed, services should stress the provision of continuous, meaningful relationships; help with problems the families identify as important; support family

strengths; and provide the amount and intensity of contact that the family needs.

Given the lack of effectiveness of most approaches to treating child maltreatment and psychological maltreatment, in particular, it is imperative for interventions to focus on early prevention. The U.S. Advisory Board on Child Abuse and Neglect (1990) has recommended that the federal government implement a national universal voluntary home visitor program for children during the neonatal period (Krugman, 1993). The purpose of such a program is to prevent child abuse by providing help before a child is abused through services designed to enhance family interactions and give families someone to call if they are in trouble. The evidence in support of the home visitor model comes from widespread, popular use of the model in Europe and six randomized trials in this country of home visitor programs designed to prevent child maltreatment. Although none of the six programs demonstrated significant decreases in CPS-confirmed cases of maltreatment, three showed benefits for some participants in decreased maltreatment, improved parenting, or in decreased use of medical facilities such as emergency room visits that are associated with abuse and neglect (Olds & Kitzman, 1993). In their review of home visiting programs, Olds and Kitzman concluded that effective preventive home visitor programs must contain key components: a comprehensive, multiproblem service approach; well-trained visitors; and long-term involvement (at least birth to 1 year) with a child and family. They argue, and we agree, that the problems faced by at-risk families are so overwhelming that adopting this approach before it is fine-tuned empirically is a risk we must take.

The two home visitor programs that had the most promising preventive effects in reducing child maltreatment followed families from the program through at least the child's first year (Hardy & Street, 1989; Olds, Henderson, Chamberlain, & Tatelbaum, 1986). However, the lack of difference in reported maltreatment rates after the intervention ended in the second study led authors to suggest that families at highest risk for maltreatment be followed until children are enrolled in preschool or public school (Olds & Kitzman, 1993). We would go further to suggest that the schools should be prepared to pick up where home visiting leaves off.

Schools should play a central role in preventing psychological maltreatment through school-based family services for children and families.

Schools should play a central role in preventing psychological maltreatment through school-based family services for children and families. Schools already are involved actively in dealing with abused and neglected children, even though the children come to educators' attention through other problems. For example, maltreated children are overrepresented among special education students, pregnant teenagers, children at risk for dropping out, and children engaged in substance abuse and violence. Schools already have become a significant and, in many cases, the most used provider of mental health services for children (Knitzer, 1989; Nadar, Ray, & Brink, 1981; Zahner, Pawelkiewicz, DeFrancesco, & Adnopoz, 1992). Under the current system, fragmented programs have been developed within and without the school to address these students' needs without focusing on their underlying common human needs.

A number of compelling reasons for making schools central to prevention and treatment efforts include the following: (a) Schools already have trained staff members who are skilled in home-family-community collaboration, including school social workers, school psychologists, school guidance counselors, and school nurses. (b) Virtually all children attend school, where they are observed by staff who have developed internalized norms of what is normal and what is deviant behavior in children and adolescents. (c) School-based services are more acceptable to families and more accessible to children, and schools have better leverage in getting parents involved. (d) Schools are therapeutic environments in that they promote achievement and attainment of prosocial development in children, even when mental health problems, illness, and family pathology are present. (e) School personnel are the most reliable source of compensatory relationships in role models for children who otherwise do not have good relationships or positive role models in their lives.

The effectiveness of both the home visiting and school prevention and treatment efforts may be enhanced if we attend to key aspects of successful treatment with high-risk families. First, the effectiveness of our interventions is heavily influenced by the degree to which an intervener is able to build and maintain a relationship with high-risk and maltreating families (Lyons-Ruth, Botein, & Bruenbaum, 1984; Wieder, Poisson, Lourie, & Greenspan, 1988). Maximizing continuity of care and reducing the number of individuals involved with the families is also helpful.

Second, treatment effectiveness is enhanced when families are offered help with the problems that they have identified. Lutzger (1984) offered CPS families treatment programs that the parents found helpful, such as weight reduction and smoking cessation, as incentives to engage in programs that CPS wanted, such as improved child management skills and household hygiene. Goldstein, Keller, and Erne (1985) reported that allowing adjudicated teenagers and their families to choose which skills to focus on was a powerful incentive in getting them to work on prosocial skills and anger replacement training activities. Greenspan and his colleagues (Greenspan et al., 1987; Wieder et al., 1988) found that when parents were offered a variety of services and allowed to choose only those they found appropriate, the types of services they requested changed over time. For instance, some of their most at-risk families would only accept child care services and help with negotiating social service systems during the first year of a program. However, when families had good experiences with an agency in regard to some of these concrete services, many of them opted to take advantage of therapeutic services at a later time. Program designers could not predict, on the basis of risk indicators, which families would eventually choose to become most involved in their program and which would benefit the most.

Third, long-term treatment also is indicated by the research literature on maltreatment. Egeland, Jacobvitz, and Sroufe (1988), in their longitudinal sample, examined women who had been severely physically abused as children and compared those who abused their own children with those who were providing adequate care. They found that those who had broken the cycle of abuse had either had a supportive adult who loved them during their childhood or had extensive therapy of at least 1 year or more during their childhood. None of the mothers who had been abused and who also abused their own children had been in a therapeutic relationship, although three of them had a supportive, loving adult when they were a child. Without exception, those who broke the cycle were aware of the effects of the abuse on them and seemed to have changed their perception of themselves and of what could be involved in a good relationship. Most of them were in continuing, stable, nonabusive relationships with a partner, and none of them currently were being battered. Members of the group that continued the cycle appeared to lack understanding of the psychological complexities of their children or of their relationship with their children, and none were in a supportive continuing relationship with a partner.

A number of research studies have shown that there is a "dose effect" in relation to psychotherapy or services to families. Heinicke, Beckworth, and Thompson (1988); Seitz, Rosenbaum, and Apfel (1985); and Wieder et al. (1988) have shown that with at-risk families, contacts of more than 10 sessions were related to significantly greater treatment effectiveness than contacts of fewer than 10 sessions. The two effective home visitor programs mentioned previously found that the families who benefited most received the most visits from nurses (Hardy & Street, 1989; Olds et al., 1986). Longer sessions facilitate trust between practitioners and the families and do not make parents permanently dependent but rather more self-reliant. As Seitz et al. stated,

> Just as independence in children is fostered by appropriately meeting their legitimate early dependency needs, it may be that addressing the problems of troubled new parents increases the likelihood that their family will later be able to function independently as well. (p. 390)

Research Agenda

We suggest the following priorities for a research agenda on psychological maltreatment:

1. *The interactions, relationships with, and contributions of psychological maltreatment to other forms of child abuse and neglect should be specifically addressed in ongoing and new research projects.* The psychological meaning embedded in other forms of abuse and neglect and the psychological maltreatment associated with other maltreatment conditions may be the primary mediating variables producing maltreatment acts and their consequences (Hart, 1992). If so, it is essential to pursue this research goal as recommended by Crittenden and Hart (1989).

2. *Decision-making guidelines* for psychological maltreatment case determinations and interventions need to be field-developed for applications by CPS and the legal establishment. We recommend that this be done by one or more community or state CPS units in collaboration with researchers. The Hart and Brassard categories and subcategories presented previously in this chapter could be established as the major categories for information gathering and be accompanied by decision-making guides in regard to the chronicity, frequency, and intensity factors necessary to judge level of severity and endangerment. The decision-making guides for categorizing maltreatment and for determining level of severity and endangerment should be developed cooperatively by researchers and representatives of the CPS system.

Psychological maltreatment data should be gathered for cases that involve primarily other forms of child abuse and neglect. These data could be immediately useful in developing designs for prescriptive intervention and ultimately useful in analyzing an accumulation of case histories to determine the salience of psychological maltreatment data to overall case determination and disposition. Psychological maltreatment data gathered on cases that do not include other forms of child maltreatment could be applied in case determinations and dispositions in which the nature of psychological maltreatment was sufficiently salient and severe to be susceptible to effective case management.

3. Both *laboratory and field investigation* should determine the relative efficiency and efficacy of gathering and applying psychological maltreatment evidence through direct observation of natural conditions reported by credible witnesses, observation of interpersonal behavior under simulated or contrived con-

ditions (e.g., videotaped parent-child interaction in carrying out a standardized cooperative task), and self-report information (e.g., responses to questionnaires and interviews).

4. The *mediating variables* that influence the likelihood of perpetrating a particular act and the form and severity of the act perpetrated should be identified and investigated. The positive interactions of perpetrators and children also should be investigated to gain a more holistic understanding of the interpersonal context in which the maltreatment occurs.

5. Child maltreatment data should be gathered nationally on a yearly basis, using a reliable and valid definitional and coding system. Local, state, and national systems of data gathering should *apply the advanced definitions* of psychological maltreatment described at the beginning of this chapter.

6. Psychological maltreatment incidence data should be gathered that allow researchers to examine the forms and levels of severity, broken down by *victim socioeconomic status, sex, age, and developmental stage.*

7. The field would benefit from a more fully developed theoretical model that explains what makes verbal assaults, threats, and psychological unavailability so damaging to children.

8. The impact of pure (nonphysical or sexual) forms of psychological maltreatment of children at different developmental stages should be investigated along with the unique effect of psychological maltreatment when it coexists with other forms of abuse and neglect.

9. Once we have a better understanding of how to assess and explain the nature of psychological maltreatment, research should then focus on its prevention and treatment.

Conclusion

The good intentions and resources so far applied by society to understand and combat child abuse and neglect have produced disappointing results. In many ways, the history of child maltreatment work is analogous to the story of the man who looks for his lost keys under the streetlight where vision is good, though the keys were lost some distance away beside the road in the dark. Physical and sexual maltreatment have appeared relatively clear, concrete, and dramatic and have been the major focus of concern and action in child abuse and neglect work. Psychological maltreatment, with its somewhat shadowy forms and consequences, has received relatively little attention. The case made here is that psychological maltreatment is the core construct and key to understanding the dynamics of all child maltreatment. It not only exists in its own discrete forms, but it also is embedded in or associated with all other forms of maltreatment and appears to be the strongest influencer and best predictor of their developmental consequences. If genuine progress is to be made in reducing child abuse and neglect, the existing psychological maltreatment knowledge base must be applied in correction and prevention programs and expanded through further research.

References

American Humane Association. (1988). *Highlights of official child abuse and neglect reporting 1986.* Denver, CO: Author.

American Humane Association. (1989). *Highlights of official child abuse and neglect reporting 1987.* Denver, CO: Author.

Baily, F. T., & Baily, W. H. (1986). *Operational definitions of child emotional maltreatment.* Augusta: Maine Department of Social Services.

Barnett, D., Manly, J. T., & Cicchetti, D. (1991). Continuing toward an operational definition of psychological maltreatment. *Development and Psychopathology, 3,* 19-29.

Benedek, E. P. (1985). Children and psychic trauma: A brief review of contemporary thinking. In S. Eth & R. S. Pynoos (Eds.), *Posttraumatic stress disorder in children* (pp. 1-16). Washington, DC: American Psychiatric Association.

Brassard, M. R., Germain, R., & Hart, S. N. (Eds.). (1987). *Psychological maltreatment of children and youth.* Elmsford, NY: Pergamon.

Brassard, M. R., Hart, S. N., & Hardy, D. (1991). Psychological and emotional abuse of children. In R. T. Ammerman & M. Hersen (Eds.), *Case studies in family violence* (pp. 255-270). New York: Plenum.

Brassard, M. R., Hart, S. N., & Hardy, D. (1993). The psychological maltreatment rating scales. *Child Abuse & Neglect, 17,* 715-729.

Briere, J. (1992). *Child abuse trauma: Theory and treatment of the lasting effects.* Newbury Park, CA: Sage.

Briere, J., & Runtz, M. (1988). Multivariate correlates of childhood psychological and physical maltreatment among university women. *Child Abuse & Neglect, 12,* 331-341.

Brook, C. G. D. (1980). Short stature. *Practitioner, 244,* 131-138.

Bullard, D. M., Glasser, H. H., Heagarty, M. C., & Pivchik, E. C. (1967). Failure to thrive in the "neglected" child. *American Journal of Orthopsychiatry, 37,* 680-690.

Cicchetti, D. (1989). How research on child maltreatment has informed the study of child development: Perspectives from developmental psychopathology. In D. Cicchetti & V. Carlson (Eds.), *Child maltreatment: Theory and research on the causes and consequences of child abuse and neglect* (pp. 377-431). New York: Cambridge University Press.

Cicchetti, D., & Braunwald, K. G. (1984). An organizational approach to the study of emotional development in maltreated infants. *Infant Mental Health Journal, 5,* 172-183.

Claussen, A. H., & Crittenden, P. M. (1991). Physical and psychological maltreatment: Relations among types of maltreatment. *Child Abuse & Neglect, 15,* 5-18.

Cohn, A., & Daro, D. (1987). Is treatment too late: What ten years of evaluation research tell us. *Child Abuse & Neglect, 11,* 433-442.

Corson, J., & Davidson, H. (1987). Emotional abuse and the law. In M. R. Brassard, R. Germain, & S. N. Hart (Eds.), *Psychological maltreatment of children and youth* (pp. 185-202). Elmsford, NY: Pergamon.

Crittenden, P., & Ainsworth, M. (1989). Child maltreatment and attachment theory. In D. Cicchetti & V. Carlson (Eds.), *Child maltreatment: Theory and research on the causes and consequences of child abuse and neglect* (pp. 432-463). New York: Cambridge University Press.

Crittenden, P., Claussen, A., & Sugarman, D. (1994). Physical and psychological maltreatment in middle childhood and adolescence. *Development and Psychopathology, 6*(1), 145-164.

Crittenden, P., & Hart, S. (1989). *Report and recommendations to NCCAN regarding psychological maltreatment research.* Washington, DC: National Center on Child Abuse and Neglect.

DeLozier, P. P. (1982). Attachment theory and child abuse. In M. Parkes & J. Stevenson-Hinde (Eds.), *The place of attachment in human behavior* (pp. 95-117). New York: Basic Books.

Egeland, B. (1991). From data to definition. *Development and Psychopathology, 3,* 37-43.

Egeland, B., & Erickson, M. (1987). Psychologically unavailable caregiving. In M. R. Brassard, R. Germain, & S. N. Hart (Eds.), *Psychological maltreatment of children and youth* (pp. 110-120). Elmsford, NY: Pergamon.

Egeland, B., Jacobvitz, J., & Sroufe, L. A. (1988). Breaking the cycle of abuse. *Child Development, 59,* 1080-1088.

Egeland, B., & Sroufe, L. A. (1991). Attachment and early maltreatment. *Child Development, 52,* 44-52.

Egeland, B., Sroufe, L. A., & Erickson, M. (1983). The developmental consequences of different patterns of maltreatment. *Child Abuse & Neglect, 7,* 459-469.

Erickson, M., & Egeland, B. (1987). A developmental view of the psychological consequences of maltreatment. *School Psychology Review, 16,* 156-168.

Erickson, M. F., Egeland, B., & Pianta, R. (1989). The effects of maltreatment on the development of young children. In D. Cicchetti & V. Carlson (Eds.), *Child maltreatment: Theory and research on the causes and consequences of child abuse and neglect* (pp. 647-684). New York: Cambridge University Press.

Erickson, M. F., Sroufe, L. A., & Egeland, B. (1985). The relationship between quality of attachment and behavior problems in preschool in a high-risk sample. *Monographs of the Society for Research in Child Development, 50*(1-2), 147-166.

Eron, L. D., & Huesmann, R. (1987). Television as a source of maltreatment of children. *School Psychology Review, 16,* 195-202.

Finkelhor, D., & Dziuba-Leatherman, J. (1994). Victimization of children. *American Psychologist, 49,* 173-183.

Fischoff, J. K., Whitten, D. F., & Petit, M. G. (1979). A psychiatric study of mothers of infants with growth failure secondary to maternal deprivation. *Journal of Pediatrics, 79,* 209-215.

Garbarino, J., Guttman, E., & Seeley, J. (1986). *The psychologically battered child: Strategies for identification, assessment and intervention.* San Francisco: Jossey-Bass.

Gardner, L. I. (1972). Deprivation dwarfism. *Scientific American, 227,* 76-82.

Gil, D. (1987). Maltreatment as a function of the structure of social systems. In M. R. Brassard, R. Germain, & S. N. Hart (Eds.), *Psychological maltreatment of children and youth* (pp. 159-170). Elmsford, NY: Pergamon.

Goldstein, A., Keller, H., & Erne, D. (1985). *Changing the abusive parent.* Champaign, IL: Research Press.

Greenspan, S. I., Wieder, S., Nover, R. A., Lieberman, A. F., Lourie, R. S., & Robinson, M. E. (Eds.). (1987). *Infants in multi-risk families: Case studies in preventive intervention.* Madison, CT: International Universities Press.

Hardy, J., & Street, R. (1989). Family support and parenting education in the home: An effective extension of clinic-based preventative health care services for poor children. *Journal of Pediatrics, 115,* 927-931.

Hart, S. N. (1992, August). *Psychological meaning and maltreatment factors relevant to consequences and treatment* (Provided to the National Research Panel, Subpanel on Consequences and Treatment, Panel on Research on Child Abuse and Neglect, National Academy of Sciences, Washington, DC). Source: Indiana University—Purdue University at Indianapolis, Office for the Study of the Psychological Rights of the Child.

Hart, S. N., & Brassard, M. (1986). *Developing and validating operationally defined measures of emotional maltreatment: A multimodal study of the relationships between caretaker behaviors and child characteristics across three developmental levels* (Grant No. DHHS 90CA1216). Washington, DC: Department of Health and Human Services and the National Center on Child Abuse and Neglect.

Hart, S. N., & Brassard, M. R. (1987a). A major threat to children's mental health: Psychological maltreatment. *American Psychologist, 42,* 160-165.

Hart, S. N., & Brassard, M. R. (1987b). Psychological maltreatment: Integration and summary. In M. R. Brassard, R. Germain, & S. N. Hart (Eds.), *Psychological maltreatment of children and youth* (pp. 254-266). Elmsford, NY: Pergamon.

Hart, S. N., & Brassard, M. R. (1990). Psychological maltreatment of children. In R. T. Ammerman & M. Hersen (Eds.), *Treatment of family violence* (pp. 77-112). New York: John Wiley.

Hart, S. N., & Brassard, M. R. (1991). Psychological maltreatment: Progress achieved. *Development and Psychopathology, 3,* 61-70.

Hart, S. N., Germain, R., & Brassard, M. (1987). The challenge: To better understand and combat psychological maltreatment of children and youth. In M. R. Brassard, R. Germain, & S. N. Hart (Eds.), *Psychological maltreatment of children and youth* (pp. 3-24). Elmsford, NY: Pergamon.

Heinicke, C., Beckworth, B., & Thompson, A. (1988). Early intervention in the family system: A framework and review. *Infant Mental Health Journal, 9,* 111-141.

Hughes, H. M. (1992). Impact of spouse abuse on children of battered women. *Violence Update, 2,* 8-11.

Hyman, I. (1985, August). *Psychological abuse in the schools: A school psychologist's perspective.* Paper presented at the annual meeting of the American Psychological Association, Los Angeles.

In re E. M. Bartholomew County, Department of Public Welfare, 581 N. E. 2d 948 (Ind. App. 1991). *et seq.* (Burns 1985).

Jones, R. L., & Jones, J. M. (1987). Racism as psychological maltreatment. In M. R. Brassard, R. Germain, & S. N. Hart (Eds.), *Psychological maltreatment of children and youth* (pp. 146-158). Elmsford, NY: Pergamon.

Knitzer, J. (1989). *Collaborations between child welfare and mental health: Emerging patterns and challenges.* New York: Bank Street College of Education.

Krugman, R. D. (1993). Universal home visiting: A recommendation from the U. S. Advisory Board on Child Abuse and Neglect. *The Future of Children, 3,* 184-191.

Krugman, R. D., & Krugman M. K. (1984). Emotional abuse in the classroom. *American Journal of Diseases of Children, 138,* 284-286.

Laury, G. V., & Meerloo, J. A. M. (1967). Mental cruelty and child abuse. *Psychiatric Quarterly, 41,* 203-254.

Leonard, M. F., Rhymes, J. P., & Solnit, A. J. (1966). Failure to thrive in infants. *American Journal of Diseases of Children, 111,* 600-612.

Lewis, D. O. (1990). Neuropsychiatric and experiential correlates of violent juvenile delinquency. *Neuropsychology Review, 1,* 125-136.

Lewis, D. O. (1992). From abuse to violence: Psychophysiological consequences of maltreatment. *Journal of the American Academy of Child and Adolescent Psychiatry, 31,* 383-389.

Lutzger, J. R. (1984). Project 12-ways: Treating child abuse and neglect from an eco-behavioral perspective. In R. F. Dangel & R. A. Polster (Eds.), *Parent training* (pp. 260-297). New York: Guilford.

Lyons-Ruth, K., Botein, S., & Bruenbaum, H. U. (1984). Reaching the hard to reach: Serving isolated and depressed mothers with infants in the community. In B. Cohler & J. Musick (Eds.), *Intervention with psychiatrically disabled parents and their young children* (New Directions for Mental Health Series, Vol. 24, pp. 95-122). San Francisco: Jossey-Bass.

Main, M., & George, C. (1985). Responses of abused and disadvantaged toddlers to distress in agemates: A study in the day care setting. *Developmental Psychology, 21,* 407-412.

Maslow, A. (1970). *A theory of human motivation.* New York: Harper & Row.

McCarthy, D. (1979). Recognition of signs of emotional deprivation: A form of child abuse. *Child Abuse & Neglect, 3,* 423-428.

McCurdy, K., & Daro, D. (1993, April). *Current trends in child abuse reporting and fatalities: The results of the 1992 annual fifty-state survey* (Working paper 808). Chicago: National Committee for the Prevention of Child Abuse.

McGee, R. A., & Wolfe, D. A. (1991). Psychological maltreatment: Toward an operational definition. *Development and Psychopathology, 3,* 3-18.

Melton, G., & Davidson, H. (1987). Child protection and society: When should the state intervene? *American Psychologist, 42,* 172-175.

Mones, P. A. (1991). *When a child kills: Abused children who kill their parents.* New York: Pocket Books.

Montagu, A. (1970). A scientist looks at love. *Phi Delta Kappan,* 463-467.

Moore, J. G. (1974). Yo-yo children. *Nursing Times, 70,* 1888-1889.

Nadar, R., Ray, L., & Brink, S. (1981). The new morbidity: The use of school and community health care for behavioral, educational and social family problems. *Pediatrics, 67,* 53-60.

National Center on Child Abuse and Neglect (NCCAN). (1988). *Study findings: Study of national incidence and prevalence of child abuse and neglect: 1988.* Washington, DC: Author.

New York v. Ferber, 458 U. S. 747, 756-757 (1982).

O'Hagan, K. (1993). *Emotional and psychological abuse of children.* Buffalo, NY: University of Toronto Press.

Olds, D., Henderson, C., Chamberlain, R., & Tatelbaum, R. (1986). Preventing child abuse and neglect: A randomization trial of home visitation. *Pediatrics, 78,* 65-78.

Olds, D., & Kitzman, H. (1993). Review of research on home visiting for pregnant women and parents of young children. *The Future of Children: Home Visiting, 3*(3), 53-92.

Osborne v. Ohio, 495 U.S. 103 (1990).

Patterson, G. R. (1982). *Coercive family process.* Eugene, OR: Castalia.

Patterson, G. R. (1986). Performance models for antisocial boys. *American Psychologist, 41,* 432-444.

Pemberton, D. A., & Benady, D. R. (1973). Consciously rejected children. *British Journal of Psychiatry, 123,* 575-578.

Powell, G. F., Brasel, J. A., & Blizzard, R. M. (1967). Emotional deprivation and growth retardation simulating idiopathic hypopituitarism. *New England Journal of Medicine, 276,* 1271-1278.

Proceedings summary of the International Conference on Psychological Abuse of Children and Youth. (1983, August). Indianapolis: Indiana University, Office for the Study of the Psychological Rights of the Child.

Psychological maltreatment definitional issues. (1991). *Development and Psychopathology, 3.*

Quilloin v. Walcott, 434 U. S. 246, 255 (1978).

Reschly, D. J., & Graham-Clay, S. (1987). Psychological abuse from prejudice and cultural bias. In M. R. Brassard, R. Germain, & S. N. Hart (Eds.), *Psychological maltreatment of children and youth* (pp. 137-145). Elmsford, NY: Pergamon.

Rohner, R. P., & Rohner, E. C. (1980). Antecedents and consequences of parental rejection: A theory of emotional abuse. *Child Abuse & Neglect, 4,* 189-198.

Schaeffer, S., & Lewis, M. (1988-1989). Social behavior of maltreated children: A naturalistic study of day care. *Annual Report No. 12: Research and Clinical Center for Child Development* (pp. 79-117). Sapporo, Japan: Hokkaido University, Faculty of Education.

Seitz, V., Rosenbaum, L. K., & Apfel, N. H. (1985). Effects of family support intervention: A ten-year follow-up. *Child Development, 56,* 376-391.

Shengold, L. (1979). Child abuse and deprivation: Soul murder. *Journal of the American Psychoanalytic Association, 27,* 533-599.

Spitz, R. A. (1946). Anaclitic depression. *Psychoanalytic Study of the Child, 2,* 313-342.

Sroufe, L. A. (1979). The coherence of individual development. *American Psychologist, 34,* 834-841.

Telzrow, C. (1987). Influence by negative and limiting models. In M. R. Brassard, R. Germain, & S. N. Hart (Eds.), *Psychological maltreatment of children and youth* (pp. 121-136). Elmsford, NY: Pergamon.

Turgi, P., & Hart, S. N. (1988). Psychological maltreatment: Meaning and prevention. In O. C. S. Tzeng & J. J. Jacobsen (Eds.), *Sourcebook for child abuse and neglect* (pp. 287-317). Springfield, IL: Charles C Thomas.

Tzeng, O., Jackson, J., & Karlson, H. (1991). *Theories of child abuse and neglect.* (pp. 173-185). New York: Prager.

U.S. Advisory Board on Child Abuse and Neglect. (1990). *First report of the U.S. Advisory Board on Child Abuse and Neglect.* Washington, DC: Department of Health and Human Services and the National Center on Child Abuse and Neglect.

Vissing, Y. M., Straus, M. A., Gelles, R. J., & Harrop, J. W. (1991). Verbal aggression by parents and psychosocial problems of children. *Child Abuse & Neglect, 15,* 223-238.

Wieder, S., Poisson, S., Lourie, R., & Greenspan, S. (1988). Enduring gains: A five-year follow-up report on the Clinical Infant Development Program. *Zero to Three, 8,* 6-12.

Wolfe, D., & McGee, R. (1994). Dimensions of child maltreatment and their relationship to adolescent adjustment. *Development and Psychopathology, 6*(1), 165-182.

Zahner, G., Pawelkiewicz, W., DeFrancesco, J., & Adnopoz, J. (1992). Children's mental health service needs and utilization patterns in an urban community: An epidemiological assessment. *Journal of the American Academy of Child and Adolescent Psychiatry, 31*(5), 951-960.

5

Ritualistic Abuse of Children

SUSAN J. KELLEY

Reports of ritualistic abuse have received considerable attention in the past decade. Ritualistic abuse has been reported to occur in a variety of settings, including day care centers (Finkelhor, Williams, & Burns, 1988; Kelley, 1989, 1990; Waterman, Kelly, McCord, & Oliveri, 1993), neighborhood and community settings (Jonker & Jonker-Bakker, 1991; Snow & Sorensen, 1990), and within nuclear and extended families (Valente, 1992; Young, Sachs, Braun, & Watkins, 1991). Highly publicized cases have been reported in the United States, Canada, England, Australia, and the Netherlands.

Ritualistic abuse is currently one of the more controversial areas in the field of child maltreatment. Much debate occurs over its existence, prevalence, and the veracity of child victims' and adult survivors' accounts.

This chapter focuses on definitional issues, the prevalence of reported cases of ritualistic abuse, and characteristics and impact of ritualistic abuse. Current con-

troversies surrounding ritualistic abuse will also be explored.

Definitional Issues

A major problem in attempting to understand the phenomenon of what has been termed *ritualistic abuse* is that there is not one agreed-on definition of ritualistic abuse. Finkelhor et al. (1988) define ritualistic abuse as

> abuse which occurs in a context linked to some symbols or group activities that have a religious, magical, or supernatural connotation, and where the invocation of these symbols or activities, repeated over time, is used to frighten and intimidate the children. (p. 59)

Faller (1990) uses the term ritualistic abuse in cases "where the sexual abuse is part of some rite that appears to have significance related to a type of religion, satanism, witchcraft, or other cult practice" (p. 197).

Lloyd (1991) has defined ritualistic child abuse more broadly as

> the intentional physical abuse, sexual abuse or psychological abuse of a child by a person responsible for the child's welfare when such abuse is repeated and/or stylized and is typified by such other acts as cruelty to animals, or threats of harm to the child, other persons and animals. (p. 123)

This latter definition has the advantage of focusing on the nature of the abusive acts rather than the abusers' possible motivation, which is often difficult to determine.

Others consider the term ritualistic abuse problematic. Lanning (1991) prefers the term *multidimensional sex ring* to ritualistic abuse because he believes the term ritualistic abuse is "confusing, misleading, and counterproductive." Jones (1991) recommends that professionals be more concerned with the extent to which physical and psychological abuse accompanies child sexual abuse without invoking the new term of ritualistic abuse.

Prevalence

Reliable estimates of the extent of ritualistic abuse are difficult to ascertain for several reasons. First, as previously discussed, there is not an agreed-on definition of ritualistic abuse, nor is there agreement that the phenomenon warrants a special term or label such as *ritualistic*. Child protection and law enforcement agencies do not categorize cases systematically according to whether there

are ritualistic aspects to the abuse because, in most states, the phenomenon has not been defined specifically and prohibited by law. Another factor that prevents reliable reporting is that children often are too terrified initially to disclose the ritualistic components of the abuse (Kelley, Brant, & Waterman, 1993). The ritualistic aspects of the abuse often are disclosed months or years after the child has revealed the sexually abusive acts and often after an investigation has been completed or therapy has been terminated. Another major obstacle to determining the extent of ritualistic abuse is the skepticism with which allegations of ritualistic abuse are met.

The more horrible and bizarre the child's allegation, the less likely the child victim will be believed.

The more horrible and bizarre the child's allegation, the less likely the child victim will be believed. However, despite these issues, three studies shed some light on how often allegations of ritualistic abuse occur.

In a national study of sexual abuse of children in day care centers, Finkelhor et al. (1988) found that 13% of the 1,639 sexually abused children in their sample reported ritualistic elements. Reports of ritualistic abuse occurred in 66% of multiple-perpetrator cases, compared to 5% of single-perpetrator cases.

Goodman, Bottoms, and Shaver (1994) conducted a project funded by the National Center on Child Abuse and Neglect (NCCAN) to determine the characteristics and sources of allegations of ritualistic child abuse in the United States. They conducted a series of studies, including (a) a stratified random sample survey of clinical psychologists, social workers, and psychiatrists; (b) a random survey sample of county-level district attorneys' offices, social services agencies, and law enforcement agencies; (c) a comparison of the subset of cases from the survey of mental health professionals in which repressed memories of abuse were alleged with cases in which repressed memory was not an issue; (d) a study of children's knowledge of satanic abuse; and (e) an examination of religion-related cases. Examples of religion-related abuse included abuse by clergy, corporal punishment with the purpose of "beating the devil" out of children, and withholding medical care.

Findings from the survey of mental health professionals indicated that 31% of respondents had encountered a ritualistic abuse or religion-based case. Most respondents had encountered only one or two such cases. However, a very small proportion (1.4%) reported they had encountered more than 100 cases. Thirteen percent had encountered adult survivor cases of ritualistic abuse, and 11% had encountered child cases of ritualistic abuse.

Adult ritualistic cases were more likely than child ritualistic cases to involve allegations of extreme forms of abuse, such as murder. Adult ritualistic cases also involved the highest number of victims and perpetrators. Child cases of abuse were more likely than adult cases to be disclosed to professionals, family members, or neighbors and be linked to corroborative evidence. Adult cases were more likely to be disclosed in therapy. This pattern held for both ritualistic cases and religion-related cases.

Child cases typically involved more evidence of ritualistic or religion-related elements than did adult cases. There was no significant difference between ritualistic and religion-related abuse with respect to evidence of the ritualistic or religion-related elements. Child cases were more likely to involve evidence of abuse or harm to the victim than adult cases. No significant difference in evidence of abuse or harm was found between child ritualistic and religion-related abuse cases. The results obtained regarding evidence need to be interpreted with caution, given that much of what the respondents considered to be corroborative evidence is open to a variety of interpretations.

In regard to clinicians' confidence in their clients' claims of abuse, results indicated that respondents overwhelmingly believed both the allegations of abuse and the ritualistic or religious elements of the abuse.

Goodman and colleagues (1994) reported that hard evidence for satanic ritualistic abuse cases, especially those involving large cults, was scant to nonexistent. However, evidence for lone perpetrators or very small groups of perpetrators, who abuse children in ways that include sa-

tanic themes, was uncovered, although such abuse was considered to be infrequent. The researchers concluded that, in general, the ritualistic cases with the most convincing evidence did not fit the satanic ritualistic abuse stereotype.

A subset of cases from the survey of mental health professionals was used to compare claims of repressed memory of ritualistic and religion-based cases to cases in which repressed memory was not an issue. Findings indicated that repressed memory cases were more likely to be ritualistic abuse cases than nonrepressed memory cases. Reports of repressed memory of ritualistic abuse made by adult survivors were found to be particularly extreme, especially when victims reported being both a victim and a perpetrator. Although repressed memory cases involved more evidence for abuse than nonrepressed memory cases, they produced no more evidence for ritualistic and religion-related aspects of the abuse than nonrepressed memory cases.

Results of the survey of prosecutors, child protective services agencies, and law enforcement agencies revealed that 23% of respondents had encountered at least one case of ritualistic or religion-related child abuse. Consistent with the findings from the survey of mental health professionals, the majority of those who had encountered cases of ritualistic or religion-related abuse had encountered only one or two cases, with a small proportion (2.2%) indicating they had encountered more than 100 cases. Few differences were found in legal outcomes between ritualistic and religion-related cases, with the exception of a higher confession rate among perpetrators of religion-related cases. The conviction rate in ritualistic cases was almost as high as in religion-related cases. This finding is surprising, given that the religion-related cases had a higher rate of perpetrator confessions.

Findings from the agency survey indicated that ritualistic abuse cases were more likely to produce physical evidence than religion-related cases. The most commonly reported physical evidence included satanic symbols, books, artifacts, and paraphernalia. Other physical evidence included tattoos, scars, film, photos, ritualistic dolls, masks, and costumes. Although respondents indicated a higher acceptance of the validity of allegations of religion-related abuse than of ritualistic abuse, respondents overwhelmingly believed both the ritualistic abuse and religion-related allegations.

Research on Characteristics of Ritualistic Abuse

Four studies conducted to date that have systematically examined reports of child victims and adult survivors of alleged ritualistic abuse will be described briefly and then compared for similarities in findings.

Kelley (1989) conducted a study of abuse of children in day care centers to compare characteristics and impact of abuse between children who reported sexual abuse and those who reported ritualistic sexual abuse. The sample was made up of 32 children who were sexually abused, 35 children who were sexually abused and who also reported ritualistic abuse, and a comparison group of 67 nonabused children.

Reports of ritualistic abuse were associated with more victims per day care center, more offenders per child, and more extensive and severe abuse. Children in the ritualistic abuse group reported more episodes of sexual abuse per child than children in the sexual abuse group.

Allegations of sexual abuse for all subjects in both abuse groups were substantiated by the child protective agency responsible for investigating the charges of sexual abuse. Criminal charges were brought against the abusers in 92% of cases. When criminal charges were filed, 80% resulted in convictions of one or more offenders at the day care center. Consistent with the findings of Goodman et al. (1994), no significant differences were found in conviction rates between ritualistic sexual abuse cases and nonritualistic sexual abuse cases. It is important to note, however, that the offenses prosecuted were sexual abuse, not ritualistic abuse. Thus, the high conviction rate in the ritualistic abuse group does not confirm ritualistic elements of the abuse.

Waterman et al. (1993), in the most extensive study conducted to date on the effects of reported ritualistic abuse, compared behavioral functioning and emotional status in a sample of 82 children describing ritualistic abuse in day care, 15 children sexually abused in day care, and a comparison group of 37 nonabused

children. Children in the sexual abuse group reported sexual abuse by a single perpetrator in contrast to children in the ritualistic abuse group, who reported abuse by multiple perpetrators.

Snow and Sorensen (1990) studied a sample of 39 children, aged 4 to 17 years, who reported ritualistic abuse. The abuse involved both intrafamilial and extrafamilial perpetrators in five different neighborhood settings. Slightly more than half of the victims were female. Subjects reported sexual abuse, violent threats, and multiple perpetrators and multiple victims. Women, as well as men, were identified as perpetrators in each of the five neighborhoods. Two adults from two different neighborhoods were tried and convicted criminally. Five adolescents from two other neighborhoods were charged with sexual abuse. Two of these juveniles pleaded guilty and three were acquitted.

Young et al. (1991) conducted a study involving 37 adult dissociative disorder patients who reported intrafamilial, transgenerational ritualistic abuse in childhood. The psychiatric sequelae exhibited by the majority of subjects in Young et al.'s (1991) sample included severe posttraumatic stress disorder, dissociative states with satanic overtones, survivor guilt, bizarre self-abuse, sexualization of sadistic impulses, unusual fears, and substance abuse.

Abuse Allegations

Allegations of ritualistic abuse typically involve reports of (a) forced sexual activity (Bottoms, Shaver, & Goodman, 1991; Finkelhor et al., 1988; Jonker & Jonker-Bakker, 1991; Kelley, 1989; Snow & Sorensen, 1990; Waterman et al., 1993; Young et al., 1991); (b) physical abuse or torture (Finkelhor et al., 1988; Jonker & Jonker-Bakker, 1991; Kelley, 1989; Snow & Sorensen, 1990; Young et al., 1991); (c) ingestion of blood, semen, or excrement (Finkelhor et al., 1988; Jonker & Jonker-Bakker, 1991; Kelley, 1989; Snow & Sorensen, 1990; Young et al., 1991); (d) ingestion of drugs (Kelley, 1989; Snow & Sorensen, 1990; Young et al., 1991); (e) threats of violence or death (Finkelhor et al., 1988; Kelley, 1989; Snow & Sorensen, 1990; Waterman et al., 1993; Young et al., 1991); (f) threats with supernatural powers (Finkelhor et al., 1988; Kelley,

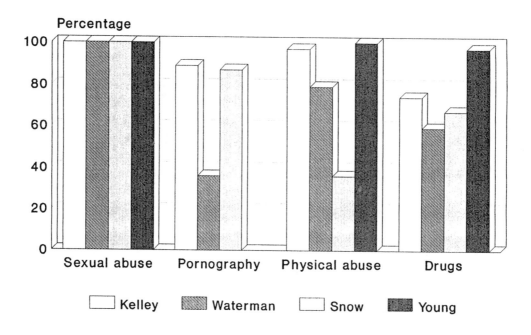

Figure 5.1. Ritualistic Abuse Allegations

1989; Snow & Sorensen, 1990; Waterman et al., 1993); (g) satanic reference or paraphernalia (Bottoms et al., 1991; Finkelhor et al., 1988; Kelley, 1989; Snow & Sorensen, 1990; Waterman et al., 1993; Young et al., 1991); (h) witnessing animal mutilations (Finkelhor et al., 1988; Kelley, 1989; Snow & Sorensen, 1990; Waterman et al., 1993; Young et al., 1991); and (i) killing of adults and children (Bottoms et al., 1991; Snow & Sorensen, 1990; Young et al., 1991).

Figures 5.1 through 5.3 compare the characteristics of ritualistic abuse allegations among the four studies previously described (Kelley, 1989; Snow & Sorensen, 1990; Waterman et al., 1993; Young et al., 1991). Figure 5.1 indicates that in these four studies, all subjects reported being sexually abused. The taking of pornographic pictures or movies was reported by the majority of subjects in Kelley's and Snow's samples. Many subjects in Waterman's study reported being shown pornography. (Young's study did not report pornography as a variable.) Despite allegations of the production of pornography in ritualistic abuse cases, law enforcement agencies have been unsuccessful in locating pornography depicting satanic ritualistic abuse of children.

A large proportion of subjects in each of the studies reported physical abuse, sometimes involving torture. The majority of subjects in each of the four studies

reported being given some type of drug or chemical substance that altered their level of consciousness. If indeed drugs were used, they may have been given to children for a variety of reasons. The use of drugs could be used to make children drowsy and therefore less resistant to abusive acts, distort children's perceptions of what has transpired so they are unable to later recall and relate the abusive episodes in a coherent manner, or render the child unconscious so that the child could be abused without memory of the event or be transported easily to another site.

The vast majority of subjects reported terrorizing acts or threats (Figures 5.2 and 5.3). Some children reported being made to lie down in coffins and pretend they were dead. In the three studies that examined death threats as a variable (Kelley, 1989; Waterman et al., 1993; Young et al., 1991), the vast majority of subjects reported threats that they would be killed if they ever disclosed the abuse. In many instances, they were told repeatedly that their parents, siblings, or pets would be killed.

Threats with supernatural or magical powers were reported by the majority of subjects in the three studies that reported this as a variable (Kelley, 1989; Snow & Sorensen, 1990; Waterman et al., 1993; Young et al., 1991). The most frequent threats were harm by a demon or mon-

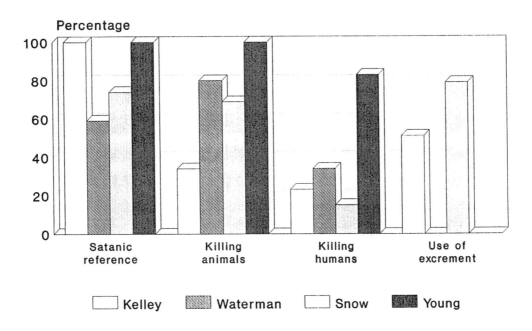

Figure 5.2. Ritualistic Abuse Allegations

ster. Threats of harm by the devil were also common.

As can be noted in Figure 5.2, although the majority of reports of ritualistic abuse involved satanic reference, not all did. It is important to note that the researchers did not describe clear criteria for what constitutes "satanic" reference. Animal killings or sacrifice were reported in each of the studies, with Young's sample of adult survivors reporting the highest rate. The majority of reports of killing of animals involved small animals, including rabbits, cats, and dogs. Often, the animals were tortured before being killed. Some children reported animals being set on fire. In many instances, it appears that the killing of animals was used to intimidate children and ensure their silence. Children who described animal killings frequently reported perpetrators saying to them, "This is what will happen to you if you ever tell."

It can be noted that murder reports were more common in the accounts of adults reporting childhood ritualistic abuse (Young et al., 1991) than in studies involving disclosures during childhood. Of those reporting homicides, reports of infant murders were more common than reports of adult murders. Reports of homicides tend to be the most troubling of accounts given by self-identified victims of ritualistic abuse and raise significant issues about credibility and verifiabil-ity because law enforcement agencies consistently have been unable to verify murders associated with reports of ritualistic abuse. One possibility is that these reported murders are staged events with the objective of terrorizing child victims to prevent disclosure.

In the three studies (Kelley, 1989; Snow & Sorensen, 1990; Waterman et al., 1993) that examined use of excrement or bodily fluids as a variable, the majority described being made to touch or ingest excrement or bodily fluids.

Impact

Researchers consistently have found that reports of ritualistic abuse are associated with greater impact than sexual abuse. Kelley (1989) used the Child Behavior Checklist (CBCL; Achenbach & Edelbrock, 1983) to measure impact of abuse in day care. Children in the ritualistic abuse group scored significantly higher than the sexual abuse group on total behavior problems and on internalizing behaviors. Children in the ritualistic abuse group (91%) were more likely than children in the sexual abuse group (80%) to report persistent fears related to their victimization.

Waterman et al. (1993) used multiple measures and informants to identify any

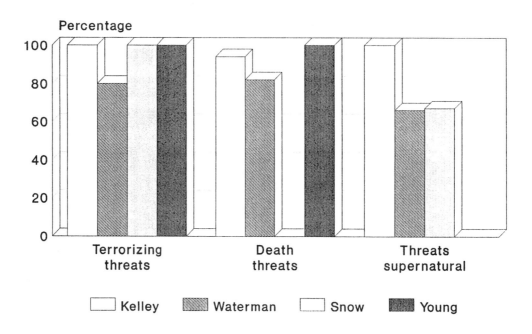

Figure 5.3. Ritualistic Abuse Allegations

differences in impact between sexual abuse and ritualistic abuse. They compared 15 children identified as ritually abused to 15 matched sexually abused children. Parents rated children in the ritualistic abuse group significantly higher than children in the sexual abuse group on total behavior problems and internalizing behaviors on the CBCL. Therapists reported that 80% of children in the ritualistic abuse group met the criteria for posttraumatic stress disorder (PTSD) compared to 36% of children in the sexual abuse group. At the end of therapy, or current time if the child was still in treatment, therapists reported that the children in the ritualistic abuse group were functioning at a lower level and were more symptomatic than children in the sexual abuse group, as measured by the Children's Global Assessment Scale and the Brief Psychiatric Rating Scale.

The children completed several measures and projective tests. On the Harter Self-Perception Profile, children reporting ritualistic abuse reported lower global self-worth and viewed themselves as less attractive than the sexually abused children. They also reported more negative responses on attitudes toward self and attitudes toward school on the Incomplete Sentences Test. And on the Draw-A-Person Test, the ritualistic abuse group scored higher in emotional indicators, suggesting greater emotional distur-

bances in the ritually abused children than in the sexually abused children.

Finkelhor et al. (1988) reported greater symptomatology in children reporting ritualistic abuse compared to children in the sexual abuse group. In adults, increased psychopathology also is associated with adults with childhood reports of ritualistic abuse. In a sample of adult survivors of childhood sexual abuse, Briere (1988) found that ritualistic and bizarre abuse reports in childhood were associated with increased symptomatology in adulthood.

Victim and Offender Characteristics

Reports of ritualistic abuse tend to involve almost equal numbers of males and females as victims (Kelley, 1989; Snow & Sorensen, 1990; Waterman et al., 1993). Females were disproportionately named as perpetrators in cases of ritualistic abuse when compared to nonritualistic cases of sexual abuse (Kelley, 1989; Snow & Sorensen, 1990; Waterman et al., 1993). Cases of ritualistic abuse typically involved multiple perpetrators and multiple victims (Finkelhor et al., 1988; Jonker & Jonker-Bakker, 1991; Kelley, 1989; Snow & Sorensen, 1990; Waterman et al., 1993), which makes these cases more complicated to investigate and prosecute.

Summary

The studies conducted to date on ritualistic abuse are modest in number, have methodological limitations, and findings that are subject to multiple interpretations. Given these limitations, caution must be used in interpreting findings and drawing conclusions.

The available research indicates that allegations of ritualistic abuse share many of the same features and characteristics; however, adult reports tend to be much more extreme. Reports of ritualistic abuse consistently are associated with increased impact on victims (Briere, 1988; Finkelhor et al., 1988; Kelley, 1989; Waterman et al., 1993). The similarities in allegations and the increased severity in symptomatology found in these studies do not, of course, prove that accounts of ritualistic abuse are valid. However, these findings do suggest that one of many possible viewpoints to be considered and further explored is that these children were indeed abused in brutal and bizarre fashions.

But how can the implausible allegations made in some of these cases be explained? One possibility is that some of the most incredible ritualistic abuse allegations are distortions of something else (Summit, 1993). During the abusive episodes, children may perceive events and related details incorrectly and may later recall from memory these inaccurate perceptions. The repeated and extreme nature of ritualistic abuse is thought to activate extreme psychological defenses, including denial and dissociation (Kelley et al., 1993). Children may be disoriented at the time of abuse due to ingestion of drugs or alcohol, which compromises future recall. In some instances, children may exaggerate or falsify accounts. Terr (1988) has suggested that some young children appear to cope with overwhelming, noxious past memories by elaborating on them when they recall and relate them at a future date. Another possibility, proposed by some observers, is that reports of ritualistic abuse are influenced intentionally or unintentionally during suggestive or coercive interviewing by therapists and parents. Findings of a laboratory-based study conducted by Goodman et al. (1994) indicated that although children possessed stereotypic knowledge about the devil and crime, they did not demonstrate knowledge of satanic activity associated with child sexual abuse. The researchers concluded that it is unlikely that children invent stories of satanic sexual abuse on their own. Until further data are available, each possibility needs to be considered. It is unlikely that any single possibility explains all reports of ritualistic abuse.

A question that has yet to be answered is, What could be the possible motivation of individuals who use rituals in conjunction with sexual abuse of children? The existence of a large-scale network of satanic cults whose primary interest is the sexual abuse of children is clearly *not* supported by empirical findings (Goodman et al., 1994) or law enforcement officials (Lanning, 1991). The possibility does exist that adults who sexually abuse children in conjunction with satanic-like practices are not satanists but instead use satanic-like rituals and symbols simply to scare and intimidate children. In addition, it is often difficult to distinguish genuine satanic activity from activities that might be classified more accurately as bizarre sexual behavior, neo-Nazi rituals, and idiosyncratic mental aberrations (Langone & Blood, 1990). Therefore, although some cases of ritualistic abuse contain satanic-like activities, it is difficult to determine from children's accounts whether perpetrators actually were engaged in some form of satanic worship or merely used satanic symbols and invoked the name of Satan to scare child victims. Offenders also might use bizarre rituals, costumes, and occult paraphernalia because they know that children who disclose the bizarre, ritualistic components of their abuse often are discredited.

It is often reported that the level of skepticism by which professionals approach accounts of ritualistic abuse varies by the discipline of the professional (Langone & Blood, 1990; Lanning, 1991). Because the role of law enforcement is to discover pertinent facts that will withstand the adversarial inquiry of the judicial system, law enforcement officials are often more doubtful of ritualistic abuse allegations than mental health professionals. Some believe that therapists, on the other hand, have less need for skepticism and more need for empathy (Langone & Blood, 1990). Thus, ritualistic abuse allegations raise ethical dilemmas for therapists. Although most would agree that therapists should empathize with a client's emotional trauma, should therapists believe or be skeptical of the more bizarre, incredulous claims?

Further research is needed to examine systematically allegations in ritualistic abuse cases, patterns of disclosure, presence and quality of corroborating evidence, offender characteristics, and the influence of therapists and parents on children's disclosures. Faller (1994) recommends a multidisciplinary research approach using teams of professionals from mental health, sociology, religion, anthropology, and law enforcement, which would allow for diverse perspectives on findings and systematic collection of confirming and disconfirming information.

In summary, ritualistic abuse of children continues to be an area with more questions than answers. First and fore- most is a need for greater clarity of the definition of ritualistic abuse. Or, as some have suggested, should the term be abandoned altogether in favor of more accurate, descriptive terms to describe atypical abuse? Researchers, professionals, and the media need to use a dispassionate approach in examining the complexities of these cases. Individuals who exaggerate the scope and extent of the problem of ritualistic abuse distract attention from other, more prevalent forms of child abuse. Skeptics who totally discount claims of ritualistic abuse may also be performing a disservice to the field. Although the allegations in ritualistic abuse cases are not always completely believable, it does not follow that the entirety of what children report is false. As the issues continue to be debated, professionals should not lose sight of the needs of these traumatized children and their families.

References

Achenbach, T. M., & Edelbrock, C. S. (1983). *The child behavior checklist manual.* Burlington: The University of Vermont.

Bottoms, B. L., Shaver, P., & Goodman, G. S. (1991, August). *Profile of ritualistic and religion-related abuse allegations reported to clinical psychologists in the United States.* Paper presented at the 99th annual convention of the American Psychological Association, San Francisco.

Briere, J. (1988). The long-term clinical correlates of childhood sexual victimization. *Annals of New York Academy of Sciences, 528,* 327-334.

Goodman, G. S., Bottoms, B. L., & Shaver, P. R. (1994). *Characteristics and sources of allegations of ritualistic child abuse* (Executive summary of the final report to the National Center on Child Abuse and Neglect [Grant No. 90CA1405]). Washington, DC: National Center on Child Abuse and Neglect.

Faller, K. C. (1990). *Understanding child sexual maltreatment.* Newbury Park, CA: Sage.

Faller, K. C. (1994). Ritual abuse: A review of research. *APSAC Advisor, 7(1), 19-27.*

Finkelhor, D., Williams, L., & Burns, N. (1988). *Nursery crimes: Sexual abuse in day care.* Newbury Park, CA: Sage.

Jones, D. P. H. (1991). Ritualism and child sexual abuse. *Child Abuse & Neglect, 15,* 163-170.

Jonker, F., & Jonker-Bakker, P. (1991). Experiences with ritualistic child sexual abuse: A case study from the Netherlands. *Child Abuse & Neglect, 15,* 191-196.

Kelley, S. J. (1989). Stress responses of children to sexual abuse and ritualistic abuse in day care centers. *Journal of Interpersonal Violence, 4(4),* 502-513.

Kelley, S. J. (1990). Parental stress response to sexual abuse and ritualistic abuse of children in day care centers. *Nursing Research, 39(1),* 25-29.

Kelley, S. J., Brant, R., & Waterman, J. (1993). Sexual abuse of children in day care centers. *Child Abuse & Neglect, 17,* 71-89.

Langone, M. D., & Blood, L. O. (1990). *Satanism and occult related violence: What you should know.* Weston, MA: American Family Foundation.

Lanning, K. V. (1991). Ritual abuse: A law enforcement view or perspective. *Child Abuse & Neglect, 15,* 171-173.

Lloyd, D. (1991). Ritual child abuse: Understanding the controversies. *Cultic Studies Journal, 8(2)* 122-133.

Snow, B., & Sorensen, T. (1990). Ritualistic child abuse in a neighborhood setting. *Journal of Interpersonal Violence, 5(4),* 474-487.

Summit, R. C. (1993). Epilogue: Uses and abuses of research: Cross-currents of community exploitation. In J. Waterman, R. J. Kelly, J. McCord, & M. K. Oliveri (Eds.), *Behind playground walls: Sexual abuse in day care* (pp. 261-277). New York: Guilford.

Terr, L. (1988). What happens to early memories of trauma? A study of twenty children under age five at the time of documented traumatic events. *Journal of the American Academy of Child and Adolescent Psychiatry, 27,* 96-104.

Valente, S. M. (1992). The challenge of ritual abuse. *Journal of Child and Adolescent Psychiatric and Mental Health Nursing, 5*(2), 37-46.

Waterman, J., Kelly, R. J., McCord, J., & Oliveri, M. K. (Eds.). (1993). *Behind playground walls: Sexual abuse in day care.* New York: Guilford.

Young, W. C., Sachs, R. G., Braun, B. G., & Watkins, R. T. (1991). Patients reporting ritual abuse in childhood: A clinical syndrome: Report of 37 cases. *Child Abuse & Neglect, 15,* 181-189.

PART TWO

Psychosocial Treatment

If Part One provides a bird's-eye view of the behaviors that concern professionals in the field of child maltreatment, Part Two provides a closer look at the state of the art of psychosocial interventions with those involved in child maltreatment—as victims, perpetrators, or family members.

In Chapter 6 on psychotherapy with abused children, psychologist William N. Friedrich sounds a refrain that is repeated in each of the chapters that follow: Although clinical practice should be driven by theory and research findings, research into treatment efficacy with these children and families is in its infancy. Regrettably, the treatment of people affected by child abuse and neglect is often atheoretical and based on a variety of generic techniques. One of the strongest lessons of Part Two is the need for rigorous treatment outcome studies, for mutually respectful collaborations between researchers and clinicians to make such studies possible, and for persistent efforts to disseminate the resultant knowledge through publications and training. It is hoped that the next edition of *The APSAC Handbook on Child Maltreatment* will reflect significant gains in all of these areas.

Friedrich offers a treatment model for physically and sexually abused children that integrates theory and research on attachment, the regulation of behavior and emotion, and the development of self-concept. The fact that the abused child exists in a family context is a basic consideration that must inform theory and intervention, Friedrich stresses. He identifies specific treatment approaches for individual, group, and family therapy that derive from each of the three elements of his integrated model.

In Chapter 7, Mark Chaffin, Barbara L. Bonner, Karen Boyd Worley, and Louanne Lawson write about abuse-focused therapy (AFT) with adolescents. Drawing on a wide variety of behavioral, cognitive, systemic, and reconstructive or dynamic therapy techniques, AFT frames abuse sequelae as understandable adaptations to abnormal experience. Although AFT applies to all age groups, these authors discuss its uses within the developmental context of adolescence. They note that disclosures of abuse by angry adolescents should not be dismissed; anger is a common motivation for disclosure in this age group. They also note that adolescents' avoidance—their ambivalence and reluctance to seek help—is associated with greater symptomatology and should not be the sole basis for the decision about whether or not to intervene. The authors discuss assessment, testing, initial interviews, treatment planning, and treatment settings. Further research, they urge, should be aimed not just toward the question, "Does treatment help?" but toward the question, "What kind of treatment helps with what patients in what settings and circumstances?"

In Chapter 8 on psychotherapy with adult survivors of child maltreatment, John Briere articulates a self-trauma model (STM) that integrates within a developmental perspective aspects of four psychotherapeutic approaches: trauma, self-psychology, cognitive psychology, and behavior therapy. Like AFT, STM assumes that much of abuse-related "pathology" and dysfunction are solutions in the making, albeit ones intrinsically more focused on survival than recovery. Briere offers suggestions regarding the correct focus, pace, and intensity of psychotherapy, cautioning that therapists can undershoot the therapeutic "window," wasting time and resources, or overshoot, overwhelming the client. Because therapist errors can be harmful to the client, Briere focuses on feedback in the form of client behavior that can signal therapeutic errors. Briere points out that client behaviors often labeled *resistance* may be appropriate survival responses to therapist process errors. As the client's advocate and the therapist's coach, Briere stresses that therapist behavior determines client perceptions—and reality—regarding whether therapy is, ultimately, safe as well as growth producing.

Patricia M. Crittenden focuses on child maltreatment as a family problem in Chapter 9. In addition to the child and perpetrator typically identified in the report, the family includes nonoffending parents or partners, siblings, grandparents who may be abusive, and unborn children of abusers. This chapter focuses on available research with families involved in six types of maltreatment: physical abuse, physical neglect, abuse and neglect, sexual abuse, psychological abuse, and marginal maltreatment. Crittenden notes that much more is known about physical abuse and neglect than about the other types of maltreatment, for all of which theoretical approaches only are beginning to move beyond the descriptive level to true hypothesis testing. For families in each condition, Crittenden reviews the state of knowledge and theory, applications to treatment, and recommendations for further research. Treatment planning can be clarified, Crittenden maintains, if families are viewed as problem-solving, resource-allocating units: How able are they to assess their own state, seek services to meet their own needs, and change in accord with their needs? Crittenden proposes a four-point scale of family functioning and discusses implications for intervention with families at different points on the scale.

In Chapter 10, William D. Murphy and Timothy A. Smith focus on the individual again—in this case, the sex offender. The authors continue the efforts of many researchers and practitioners to debunk the prevalent assumption that victims typically become offenders. In fact, it appears that only 20% to 30% of offenders were victims themselves, compared to an estimated 10% to 15% of the male population at large. The vast majority of victims do not become offenders; the etiology of offending behavior is more complex and elusive than that theory suggests.

Murphy and Smith point out that the main rationale for treating sex offenders is to reduce recidivism. Unfortunately, outcome research is plagued by methodological problems, making it difficult to say at this time whether or not sex offender treatment is effective. Given the great heterogeneity of sex offenders, the question Chaffin and colleagues ask about treatment of victims—What kind of treatment helps with what patients in what settings and circumstances?—is the appropriate question to ask of sex offender treatment as well. Although unable to state with confidence that treatment reduces recidivism, the authors suggest that other benefits might accrue from treatment: Offenders in treatment may be monitored more closely than offenders not in treatment, and more victims—and offenders—might come forward if they felt the offender would receive treatment rather than incarceration. Like the authors of other chapters in this part, Murphy and Smith offer solid suggestions for future research.

—T.R.

6

An Integrated Model of Psychotherapy for Abused Children

WILLIAM N. FRIEDRICH

Special Issues in Psychotherapy With Children

Clinical practice should be driven by theory and research findings. However, the treatment of abused children is often atheoretical and consists of a variety of generic treatment techniques. In addition, research into treatment efficacy with abused children only now is emerging (Deblinger, McLeer, & Henry, 1990; Friedrich, Luecke, Beilke, & Place, 1992; Hiebert-Murphy, DeLuca, & Runtz, 1992; Lanktree & Briere, 1995).

Although two conceptualizations, the posttraumatic stress disorder (PTSD) model (McLeer, Deblinger, Atkins, Foa, & Ralphe, 1988) and the traumagenic factors model (Finkelhor & Browne, 1985) help define the impact of abuse on children, only the former directly lends itself to treatment practice. The PTSD model emphasizes the traumatic nature of abuse and a fairly constant set of behavioral and cognitive effects, including numbing, intrusive thoughts, hyperarousal, and avoidance of triggering events. Treatment techniques derived from the PTSD formulation include anxiety reduction techniques and cognitive restructuring. Evidence supports that this approach is useful in reducing anxiety in sexually abused children (Berliner, 1991; Deblinger et al., 1990).

The traumagenic factors model identifies a broad range of potential treatment targets, but it has less direct relevance to treatment practices. Sexual abuse is thought to be deleterious as a result of four traumagenic factors: betrayal, stigmatization, powerlessness, and traumatic sexualization. Each of these traumagenic factors has an impact on both overt behavior and internal cognitions. Although this model is extremely helpful in identifying possible treatment needs, it does not suggest interventions.

There is overlap between the PTSD model and the traumagenic factors model. Both accept the traumatic nature of abuse, and each suggests a wide range of possible acute and long-term sequelae. Each of these conceptualizations is relevant as well to both sexual and physical abuse, although traumatic sexualization, from the traumagenic factors model, is unique to sexual abuse.

Another problem with the above conceptualizations is their focus on the individual victim. Theory that appreciates both *individual impact* and *family context* truly is needed to guide the treatment of abused children. Based on these issues and concerns, this chapter outlines an integrated model for psychotherapy with abused children.

The Need for a Treatment Model

The abused child exists in a family context. Although some clinical literature exists regarding parents' PTSD-like reactions to their child's sexual abuse (Uherek, 1991), the PTSD model has primarily an individual focus. Research increasingly points to family variables (e.g., support for the child) as being associated with the effect of abuse as well as specific features of the abuse itself (Friedrich, Beilke, & Urquiza, 1987). This is also true for long-term consequences of physical abuse, where moderator variables, including individual, family, and environmental factors, are important (Malinosky-Rummell & Hansen, 1993). Thus, individually based models, such as the traumagenic factors model and the PTSD model, are not sufficient either to understand the

impact of child abuse or guide the type of broad-based treatment that is needed.

Currently, the majority of abused children do not receive treatment, and those who do may be seen by therapists who (a) may not appreciate the unique and differential impacts of physical and sexual abuse, (b) have little broad-based clinical training and are not aware of a wide variety of empirically validated treatment techniques, and (c) have little idea of how and what to treat and follow approaches that are too brief (or even traumagenic) and often are not directed at the system the child is living in.

These impressions suggest the need for treatment that is contextual and derived from theoretical formulations that are more unifying and empirically validated than either of the two models mentioned earlier. Needed theoretical formulations should include specific and effective treatment techniques—both those unique to sexual and physical abuse and those that are widely applicable.

Although many of the examples used in this chapter are particularly germane to sexual abuse, I believe that much of the theory and techniques discussed in this chapter are applicable to physical abuse as well. Sexually abusive and physically abusive families share some of the same features of inattention to children's needs and a multigenerational history of poor parenting. As a result, the treatment challenges can be significant, and a planful, sensitive approach clearly is needed.

An Integrated, Contextual Model

The integrated model outlined in the rest of this chapter borrows from attachment theory (Alexander, 1992), behavior/emotion regulation (Dodge & Garber, 1991), and self-perception/concept (Harter, 1988; Meichenbaum, 1974). The effects of abuse are reflected in each of these three broad domains. Treatment approaches specific to individual, group, and family treatment can be derived from this model.

This integrated model subsumes both the traumagenic factors and PTSD models and provides an additional developmental and family context. For example, the traumagenic factor of betrayal (Finkelhor & Browne, 1985) has both psychological and behavioral impacts (e.g., distrust of others, impaired ability to form close relationships). These effects also are pertinent to attachment theory. Stigmatization and powerlessness have behavioral and psychological sequelae (e.g., reduced self-efficacy, distorted view of self) that are related directly to the child's self-perception. Finally, the traumatic nature of child abuse affects children's ability to regulate their emotions, thoughts, and behaviors, leading to some of the specific symptoms outlined in the PTSD model.

The remainder of this chapter will outline the relevance of the three elements of this integrated model—attachment, dysregulation, and self-perception—identify specific treatment approaches that follow from each of these elements, and apply each approach to individual, group, and family therapy.

Attachment

The concept of attachment is a central element in almost all contemporary theories of child psychopathology and child treatment (Ainsworth, 1989). For example, children's prosocial inclinations are governed primarily by the quality of their relationships with their parents. This has implications for the emergence of peer relationships, aggression, and social skills.

According to Bowlby (1969), attachment is a biologically based bond with a caregiver. Attachment behavior, which ensures the child proximity with the caregiver, is most apparent during periods of early childhood distress. However, it also relates to reciprocal and mutual relationships across the life span.

An important aspect of Bowlby's theory is his concept of the internal working model, a mental construction that forms the basis of the personality. Early experiences with the attachment figure allow the children to develop expectations about their role in relationships (e.g., worthy vs. unworthy) and other's roles in relationships (e.g., caring vs. uncaring). Because the development of this internal working model is so tied to the relationship, the child learns caregiving while receiving care.

Applying attachment theory to the onset and outcome of abuse necessitates examining the interactions of the whole family, a natural and logical focus of any trauma. Developmental psychologists ar-

gue strongly the need to view family relations as part of an interrelated system, with each member affecting the others (Sroufe, Jacobvitz, Mangelsdorf, DeAngelo, & Ward, 1985).

Children's attachment behavior can be sorted into four categories. The first and healthiest category is *secure* attachment. In addition, there are three types of insecure attachment: *resistant, avoidant,* and *disorganized* (Alexander, 1992). Securely attached children have an internal working model of caregivers as consistent, supportive in times of stress, attuned to their needs, and reciprocal. Insecurely attached children operate from the assumption that interpersonal relationships are characterized by different levels of unpredictability, the absence of reciprocity, and punitiveness. For example, the avoidantly attached child eventually may adopt a self-protective stance and hold back from caregivers, including therapists. The child who exhibits a disorganized pattern of attachment is inconsistent in dealing with relationships (e.g., simultaneously approaching and avoiding others). Given the frequent history of abuse in parents of abused children (Friedrich, 1991b), parents of children who exhibit disorganized attachment are thought to be characterized themselves by unresolved trauma (Main & Cassidy, 1988).

Harsh and abusive treatment by caregivers can inhibit the development of prosocial responses in children. Main and George (1985) found that physically abused preschoolers did not show responses of concern, sadness, or empathy when a peer was distressed. And physically abused children were consistently more aggressive in their social interactions, although there was between-child variability (George & Main, 1979).

There is evidence that sexual abuse is experienced by the child victim as betrayal. This is true not only in the perpetrator-child relationship but is also reflective of a preexisting, impaired level of attachment with one or more caregivers.

In general, child abuse of all types occurs in the context of reduced income, a chaotic and frequently disrupted lifestyle, and emotional deprivation (Friedrich, 1990). Thus, it is essential for the therapist to respect the child's entire history of victimization, including neglect.

Alexander (1992) has identified three organizing themes, pertaining to attachment, that have been observed in abusive and neglectful families, including sexually abusive families. The first theme is *rejection,* which is most often associated with subsequent avoidant attachment in the

---

In general, child abuse of all types occurs in the context of reduced income, a chaotic and frequently disrupted lifestyle, and emotional deprivation.

---

child. Parents' earlier attachment affects their subsequent attachment to their own child. For example, male children in the sexually abusive family may be rejected because of their representation as potential abusers by the mother, and female children may be rejected because of the intimacy threat that they represent to the abusive father. Another critical consequence of rejection is that preoccupied or dismissive parents selectively attune to the child's positive and negative expressions. Children learn that those affective experiences (e.g., distress) "fall outside the realm of shareable experience and [as a result they] deny or disavow such feelings" (Alexander, 1992, p. 188).

A second organizing theme outlined by Alexander (1992) pertains to the *parentification and role reversal* process that has been documented empirically in sexually abusive families (Levang, 1989). Children who have been elevated into a parental position may be more vulnerable to abuse and less likely to receive the support they need, both before and after the trauma.

The final organizing theme pertains to the *multigenerational transmission* of fear and unresolved trauma evident in families with a history of abuse. Thus, insecure attachment in the parents, as a result of their own abuse experiences, will precede insecure attachment in the child. This is consistent with evidence on risk factors contributing to sexual abuse (Friedrich, 1990).

The above themes pertain to preexisting attachment. However, the very act of abuse and the response of significant others to the disclosure of abuse may result in a sudden change in attachment. This may be true of a child with a previous history of reasonably secure attachment.

Although there are no studies specifically on the attachment behavior of sexually abused children, a great deal of research demonstrates the high frequency of insecure attachment in physically abused or neglected children (Egeland, Sroufe, & Erickson, 1983). The attachment model helps the therapist to appreciate (a) the origin and diversity of relationships between children and their parents, (b) the influence the internal working model plays on the formation of the treatment relationships and all other social relationships, and (c) the need to improve attachment relationships if the therapist is to alter basic assumptions children have about themselves.

Symptoms Reflecting Impaired Attachment

One advantage of theory is the potential for specificity in treatment goals. Potential targets of treatment include boundary problems, poor social skills, the recapitulation of victim or victimizing behavior in relationships, distrust of others, and the sexualizing of relationships. In addition, the relationship of insecure attachment to future psychopathology emphasizes the need to repair attachment problems within the family.

In the next three sections, attachment-related treatment suggestions are made in the areas of individual, group, and family therapy. (See Appendix A for a brief, selective synopsis of techniques in these areas.)

Individual Treatment Techniques Derived From Attachment Theory

Formation of a therapeutic alliance is the first application of attachment theory and is critical in all three modes of treatment—individual, group, and family. Literature on treatment effectiveness routinely finds the therapeutic relationship to be of critical importance (Strupp & Binder, 1984). The quality of the therapist-patient relationship may be central and more important than specific therapeutic techniques or approaches. From the beginning it is the therapist's duty to determine how best to maximize the quality of the therapist-patient attachment relationship.

The therapist has the greatest control over factors that facilitate an alliance with the child. Therapists must ask themselves the question, How can I best use myself as a therapeutic instrument that maximizes the child's ability to develop a good attachment relationship, not only with me but also with their current parents and caregivers? Such factors as the sex of the therapist, the emotional and behavioral style of the therapist, the ethnic match between child and therapist, and the therapist's current level of internal emotional resources should be considered.

The therapist must avoid practices that interfere with acceptance by the child. Sexualized, aggressive, and physically unattractive children can elicit rejection from the therapist. At times, therapists can feel they have "lost control" of the therapy process and are playing out a script from a prior relationship the child has had with a caregiver. This illustrates the power of the internal working model of the child and the need for the therapist to provide a corrective experience.

Children's attachment histories will dictate their interactions with the therapist. For example, boundaryless children (those with disorganized attachment) will need therapists who are clear in their own boundaries so that they can tolerate and gradually alter the child's dependency, physical proximity-seeking, and variability. On the other hand, a resistant child with a physical abuse history may expect aggression and work to provoke it. This child presents a challenge to the therapist, who will need to work differently with either this or an avoidant child than with the boundaryless child. The avoidant child may be very slow in forming an alliance, always anticipating rejection, and hypersensitive to therapist unavailability.

The sooner both therapist and child have a sense of "we-ness," or a dyad, the better. Therapists can start by being "fully present" and emotionally available in the session. Consultations with school personnel and occasional phone calls to the child can be important, along with small gifts to the child. Pictures of the therapist and child create a visual symbol of connection and can be given to the child brought into sessions. Therapeutic triangulation allows the therapist-child dyad to ally with one another and be against a third party (e.g., a nonfamilial perpetrator), thus pushing the treatment alliance along (Friedrich, 1990). Finally, a sense of connection may be facilitated by closer attention to ethnic and gender matching of child and therapist.

If a child continues to be victimized at home, he or she will not feel safe and cannot turn his or her emotional energies to the formation of a therapeutic relationship.

It is important early on in the therapy process to help children feel they have a "secure base" in their home and that their parent supports their disclosure of abuse.

It is important early on in the therapy process to help children feel they have a "secure base" in their home and that their parent supports their disclosure of abuse. Unsupervised visitation by an abusive parent, foster placement that is nonsupportive, and other factors or combination of factors may contribute to this absence of safety. One technique useful in helping to create a sense of safety in the child is to include the nonoffending parent early on in the therapy process for the purpose of giving children permission to talk about their victimization.

Group Treatment Techniques Derived From Attachment Theory

It is important that the child identify with the group and its members. Although disclosure creates a sense of universality (Yalom, 1975) and also can foster a sense of connection, children who have few social skills are likely to find the group experience a rejecting one. Screening is critical to ensure a good mix of children, particularly if the group process is expected to be important.

The creation of a group identity develops a sense of group attachment. This can be facilitated in a number of ways (e.g., members may select a name for the group that implies a common bond). The use of cotherapists is also important so that the availability of potential attachments is higher.

We sometimes forget that victims have directly experienced unemphatic behavior from the offender and consequently are more likely to behave in a nonreciprocal, unempathic manner themselves. Group treatment provides an excellent setting in which to begin to address this often-neglected treatment need of victims.

Family Treatment Techniques Derived From Attachment Theory

Egeland and Erickson (1983) describe psychologically unavailable caregiving, which in my experience describes a common subset of families of abused children. It is characterized by the absence of a reciprocal child-parent relationship and parental ambivalence toward the child. Some of the goals they describe for intervention include helping the parent understand the child's behavior and become better perspective takers to respond more effectively to the child's signals, providing peer support to the parent, meeting the parent's emotional needs, and assisting parents to learn how parental needs influence their perceptions of the child. Egeland and Erickson (1983) state that this approach must go beyond traditional psychological services and actively bring parents and children together.

These suggestions fit directly with the "constructionistic" approach to family therapy, which focuses on constructing a new set of perceptions, a new reality, or a new set of stories regarding the child and family (White, 1989). Rather than allowing the family to persist in its view of the problem or residing "inside" the child, White (1989) actively "externalizes" the problem. For example, the family of the encopretic child would look for those times the child is "successful" at preventing the encopresis from "sneaking up on her." In addition, the therapist should highlight positive aspects of the child's behavior (Selvini-Palazzolli, Boscolo, Cecchin, & Prata, 1978). In my own practice, I sometimes have had the impression that the family therapist actively must "market" the child to the parent (Friedrich, 1991a).

Involvement of offending parents in their own therapy at this critical time is also important and can result in these parents becoming less rejecting and having more attuned attachment "prospects" for the child. Parallel group treatment for nonoffending parents is also useful at this point (Mandell & Damon, 1989).

Egeland and Erickson (1983) mention that insecurely attached infants move toward secure attachment when mothers make friends with other adults and feel supported.

Finally, attachment is in part a function of reciprocity and acceptance. For families who feel misunderstood and for whom sessions in the therapist's office are foreign, home visits not only can facilitate a more accurate therapist perception of the family but also may impart a sense of acceptance and validation to the family that adds to the developing therapy alliance.

Regulation and Dysregulation

Children must face the core tasks of modulating arousal, developing the ability to maintain a psychological homeostasis, and differentiating the expression of a broad range of positive and negative affect. Maltreatment of all types interferes with this developing capacity of self-regulation, not only of feelings but also of thoughts and behaviors (Cicchetti, Ganiban, & Barnett, 1991).

Maltreatment is dysregulating for several reasons. Not only are there traumatic features of the abuse, but the abusive family itself is characterized by numerous other potentially dysregulating stressors, including marital conflict, frequent moves and losses, and higher levels of unpredictability and chaos. This is true for physically abusive (Malinosky-Rummell & Hansen, 1993) as well as incestuous and nonincestuous families (Kendall-Tackett, Williams, & Finkelhor, 1993). Given the heterogeneity of maltreatment, for many children, the major contributors to dysregulation are nonabuse specific.

Katz and Gottman (1991) have operationalized emotion regulation "as consisting of children's ability to (1) inhibit inappropriate behavior related to strong negative or positive affect, (2) self-soothe any physiological arousal the strong affect has induced, (3) focus attention, and (4) organize themselves for coordinated action in the service of an external goal" (p. 130). The authors go on to talk about a child's ability to coordinate play and manage conflict as being directly related to their ability to make friends. This relates directly to the attachment discussed earlier and indicates the linkage between these theoretical constructs.

Cicchetti and his colleagues (1991) argued that the development of emotional regulation in the child involves both physiological (e.g., central nervous system functioning) and psychological levels (e.g., growing cognitive and representational skills). In addition to these first two levels of intraorganismic factors, there are factors outside of the child (e.g., parental response to the child's affect, parental socialization of affective displays).

Research on how maltreated children differentiate and respond to affect is critical. How a child responds to strong feelings is part of self-regulation. Cicchetti et al. (1991) refer to four patterns of affect differentiation/response in children that presumably depend on caregiver experiences: (a) developmentally and affectively retarded, (b) depressed, (c) ambivalent and affectively labile, and (d) angry. For example, neglected children may fall into the first pattern more often, with physically abused children more often in the fourth pattern.

There is evidence also that prolonged abuse is related to physiological alterations. Putnam (1991) has found consistently elevated cortisol levels in sexually abused girls when contrasted with closely matched, socioeconomically disadvantaged girls. The presence of PTSD symptoms in sexually abused children also reflects the dysregulating and overwhelming aspects of victimization and has been found in a significant minority of clinical cases (McLeer et al., 1988).

Behaviorally, dysregulation in abused children is reflected in greater sleep problems in very young sexually abused children (Hewitt & Friedrich, 1991) and more aggressive behavior in physically abused children (Walker, Bonner, & Kaufman, 1988). There is also evidence that attention deficit hyperactivity disorder (ADHD)-like symptoms are related to overstimulating types of parental interaction in the first 42 months of life (i.e., failure to soothe, maternal seductive behavior, frequent disruptions, etc.) (Sroufe, 1989). There is certainly a reason to find parallels to the above forms of parental interaction in the lives of sexually and physically abused children.

The attachment-related internal working model, referred to earlier, also carries with it "rules for the perception, display, and regulation of emotion" (Cicchetti et al., 1991, p. 31). Thus, when an abused child idealizes or is not given an opportunity to be honest about an abusive parent, a core of anger and hurt is sealed over, thus preventing the learning of new ways of dealing with painful affect. A related phenomenon is the abuse-related hypervigilance discussed in Chapter 8, this volume.

A legitimate question for both therapists and parents of abused children is whether the therapy itself, particularly the disclosure of abuse, is dysregulating to the child by virtue of its negative and upsetting nature. My perspective is that a child who is not given the opportunity to disclose or who is having a hard time disclosing uses the maladaptive technique of avoidance. Because the opportunity to disclose in a new setting and alter one's cognitions about the abuse is important, therapists should develop ways to allow the disclosure to proceed in a manner that does not create further dysregulation in the child.

Symptoms Reflecting Dysregulation

Again, theory can identify specific treatment targets, beginning with affective disruption, such as anxiety, and its related problems, sleep problems, and behavioral regression. In addition, victimized children may not have learned self-soothing behaviors and therefore may live in a heightened state of arousal, resulting in somatic symptoms. Other manifestations are inattentiveness or overactivity in class, akin to ADHD symptoms (Sroufe, 1989). In addition, sexualized behavior can add to the child feeling out of control. This problem should be addressed specifically in therapy.

The following discussion focuses on individual, group, and family therapy techniques designed to correct the dysregulatory affects of abuse on feelings, thoughts, and behaviors. (See Appendix A for a brief synopsis of relevant techniques.)

Individual Treatment Techniques Derived From Dysregulation Theory

The therapist must remember that the child will not naturally associate uncovering painful aspects of abuse with an opportunity for support and feeling in control. This underscores the need for structure and predictability in the therapy process. This can prevent regression or decompensation in the child. When that happens, the therapist may be paired with this distress and be viewed by the child as negative and abusive.

Strategies to provide structure and predictability include a clear definition of the therapy process and the need for disclosure. Children can even schedule formally when and how they want to talk about their victimization experiences. The therapist and the child may also develop a word or phrase for the abuse that makes it easier to discuss.

Therapy with children can sometimes be psychoeducational and involve the use of didactic information (e.g., safety and sexual education). Psychoeducational techniques are not as dysregulating and may be more useful to extremely reactive children. It is also possible for the therapist to partition the session into working portions and play portions, with children provided an agreed-on amount of time to work on issues, followed by another period in which they are feeling less threatened. A part of the play portion can be placed at the end of the session to give the child a chance to reorganize and restabilize.

Other therapists have talked about "as-if" approaches to therapy (Friedrich, 1991a). Children may never acknowledge having been molested directly, but they may talk to the therapist as if they had been or give the therapist advice for working with a similarly aged child who had a similar abuse experience. This particular technique underscores the need for the child to be given some element of control in the therapy.

It is in this area of therapy that some of the most empirically validated techniques are available from the cognitive behavioral area (Meichenbaum, 1974). These are best described as anxiety reduction techniques. Using relaxation training and self-hypnosis instruction, the child can be assisted to develop a repertoire of strategies ranging from thought stopping to anxiety management strategies that are useful in a variety of settings.

It is important that the therapy become a reliable and predictable process for the child. This can prevent emotional and behavioral "spillover" from the therapy to the home and school situation, with the result that the child is ostracized. Other elements of the therapy process that can be difficult for the child to manage include the gender of the therapist, particularly when the therapist is the same sex as the child's perpetrator. However, at this time, nothing in the literature supports any particular therapist-child gender match.

Group Treatment Techniques Derived From Dysregulation Theory

Children should be screened for their appropriateness for group treatment, because group therapy can be overwhelming and thus dysregulating. We should not view group therapy as automatic for every sexually abused child nor as a panacea for every child. Children who have a history of poor peer relationships and frequent victimization may need to be involved either in individual or pair therapy (Selman & Schultz, 1990) before being involved in group treatment.

Here again, didactic and structured techniques lend themselves to preventing dysregulation in the group setting. The use of structured treatment modules, in which the child has the opportunity to work through a relevant segment (e.g., talking about feelings related to the abuse) and has a sense of closure by the end of it can add a great deal to the child's sense of resolution and feeling in control.

There has been discussion of gender differences in group treatment, with boys presenting as more disruptive and prone to acting out and feeling dysregulated (Friedrich, Berliner, Urquiza, & Beilke, 1988). The clinical literature also supports this finding, suggesting that greater attention to regulation of affect and behavior be given to treatment groups for boy victims.

Family Treatment Techniques Derived From Dysregulation Theory

In the same way that individual therapy can be confusing and dysregulating to the child, family therapy can have the same effect on the child and family combination that is being seen by the therapist. Therapists must learn to help the families they see realize the purpose of therapy and focus on specific behavioral targets that provide the family with both a measure of success and an opportunity to learn to be more consistent with the child. Again, a psychoeducational component to the family therapy, mixed with liberal amounts of support, will be useful (Trepper & Barrett, 1989).

For physically abusive families, one form of dysregulation is aggressive behavior. Therapists should attend to issues of anger management and self-control and suggest alternatives to physical punishment (Walker et al., 1988).

An approach to therapy that provides the necessary structure to prevent dysregulation is the use of the Goal Attainment Scaling system as described in Friedrich (1990) for families of sexually abused children. With this goal-setting strategy, families are helped to identify a number of specific goals that have levels of accomplishment (e.g., acceptable level of outcome, optimal level of outcome). The family then can focus on these goals. A number of goals can be agreed on, with some related to attachment and others to dysregulation and self-perception. Dysregulation-based goals may include anger management for parents, the creation of predictable opportunities for family interaction, and learning more consistent parenting approaches.

The prescription of rituals, which can be regularly scheduled events in the family, also can go a long way toward increasing a sense of structure and order within the family. These rituals should be targeted around eating and bedtime, two naturally occurring occasions when families can become dysregulated. Empirical support for the use of rituals comes from research on the multigenerational transmission of alcoholism within families (Steinglass, 1987).

Finally, if family members do not feel safe from further victimization, the family setting itself is upsetting and potentially dysregulating to the child. Toward this end, the creation of a sense of safety in each family member is critical. The therapist must help family members realize different ways that they are potentially victimizing to each other or excitatory in one way or the other. Examples of the latter include family nudity, overt family sexuality, and other potential reminders to the child of sexuality or vulnerability.

Self-Perception

Children's understanding of their self-attributes and emotions follows a developmental course and should focus on both cognitive and affective processes (Harter, 1988).

There are a number of developmental shifts in the child's self-understanding, beginning with descriptions of one's physical self, which transitions to the active self, then to the social self, and finally the psychological self, the latter containing one's emotions and cognitions. Recent findings of increased somatic symptoms in sexually abused children may be related to a heightened focus on the physical self in the young abused child (Friedrich & Schafer, 1995).

A critical component of self-perception is the accuracy with which the child views the self. Young children are highly egocentric, and their self-assumptions often reflect wishes rather than accurate self-perceptions. Harter (1988) points out that environmental changes produce inaccuracies in the judgment of one's abilities. Presumably, abuse could count as an environmental change. In addition, she writes that children who consistently view themselves inaccurately, either by over- or underestimating their competence, expose themselves to less challenging problems. For example, they may engage in avoidant coping.

There are some significant clinical implications for this finding. Supportive therapists who want to inflate an abused child's self-esteem should concentrate on the accuracy of the self-perception, not necessarily on the optimism of the perception. In fact, Harter (1988) states that "a strategy . . . undoubtedly doomed to failure involves . . . categorically asserting . . . 'you are not dumb, you know, you really are quite smart' " (p. 135).

Numerous contributors to inaccurate self-perception exist in the world of the maltreated child. Examples of these inaccuracies include all-or-none thinking, overgeneralizations, and shifts from one extreme self-perception to the other. Although these phenomena are seen in normal, nonabused children as well, the likelihood is that in the presence of increased stress and reduced support, an abused child is likely to remain stuck at an immature level of self-perception.

Harter (1977) presents several clinical examples of all-or-none thinking (e.g., "all dumb") and her approach to its resolution (i.e., increase the accuracy of self-perception). Her approach is developmentally sensitive in that it takes into consideration how children think about feelings. In addition, it focuses not only on cognition but also on conflicting emotions.

Another phenomenon in the area of self-perception pertains to stability, or conservation of self, across settings or in the face of contradictions. Children will vary in whether changes are attributed to internal versus external forces, with internally focused children and adolescents not as likely to be bothered by these fluctuations (Harter, 1988). Because maltreatment is an external force, it takes a significant effort for the child to not blame him- or herself.

Despite the centrality of self-perception in the establishment of the self, it may come as a surprise to child therapists that children have little interest in self-examination. Because children are so deeply embedded in the family matrix, they most naturally will externalize their problems. The therapist may find it more useful working to alter the environmental influences on self-development (e.g., poor attachment) rather than help the child develop insight. Harter (1988) goes so far as to suggest that there are developmental reasons for the use of more didactic techniques and fewer attempts at insight with children. This suggestion supports the types of group interventions suggested in Mandell and Damon (1989).

In addition to the interpersonally related self-perception described earlier, it is also useful to consider an intrapsychic self. The intrapsychic self is manifested by the presence of defense mechanisms and its own sense of what constitutes intimate relationships (e.g., object relations), thus bringing us back again to the concept of attachment, albeit on an intrapsychic level. Winnicott's (1965) term *false self* is apt with many abused children who are precociously mature superficially but feel empty internally. Although seen more often in adolescents and adults, this can be seen in children as well.

Symptoms Reflecting Problems With the Self

Issues of self-perception are less tangible, and specific symptoms may not be as overt, particularly with younger children. Gender differences frequently will be evident as well, with girls reporting more depression (Zahn-Waxler, Cole, & Barrett, 1992). As mentioned earlier, somatic symptoms may reflect the abused child being fixated at the physical self. However, disadvantaged children of all ages may have more than the usual difficulties identifying their feelings or talking about how they feel about themselves. Thus, a symptom focus may be less important than creating a therapy context in which the child can develop a greater sense of both efficacy and a capacity to talk about thoughts and feelings.

The next portion of this chapter focuses on individual, group, and family therapy approaches that facilitate the development of an accurate self-perception. (See Appendix A for a brief synopsis of relevant techniques.)

Individual Therapy Approaches Derived From Self-Perception Theory

Techniques that are derived from this perspective can be distilled into those that help children correct the immature and inaccurate self-perceptions that they hold. First among these is learning how to understand feelings. This can be facilitated through feeling exercises, the use of a feelings list, and related techniques.

Another approach emphasizes the need for the therapist first to understand the children's view of themselves and their world, before the therapist provides blanket reassurances about the child's worth as an individual. These communications directed at the child may be confusing and unbelievable to children and may undermine their sense of connection to the therapist. For example, a child who had physiological arousal to the victimization and appreciated some of the support that came from the abuser may not understand the therapist's focus on the negative aspects of the abuse, particularly at the initial stage of treatment.

Harter (1977) has described an excellent technique to deal with the "good-bad" extremes that the victimized child frequently engages in. This technique is strongly recommended for work with abused children so that they can make progressive approximations to a more accurate perception of themselves as having a combination of positive, neutral, and negative features.

It is also important in this area to increase a child's sense of efficacy. An example of this would be to "contract with the child for competency" (e.g., putting the sexually reactive child "in charge of his penis"). Cognitive approaches that address the physically abused child's self-defeating cognitions are also useful in enhancing a child's sense of mastery and competency (Meichenbaum, 1974).

For older children, particularly those who have some mastery of their feelings, it is also useful to "externalize the problem," which borrows from Michael White's (1989) constructionistic approach to therapy. Children are egocentric and assume blame for numerous things that happen to them. This is true for sexually abused children, who view themselves as bad, duplicitious, and guilty of the abuse. Reassurances to the child of their goodness are not helpful. However, if you help the child learn how to talk about the problem as "outside of them" and "sneaking up on them when they are unaware," they can learn to view themselves as having the potential for a more active role in keeping negative feelings outside of them. They also can learn to cope better with those times in which they are vulnerable to feeling poorly about themselves.

In addition, a maltreated child can be self-critical, creating the potential for depression and a reduced self-efficacy.

Older latency and adolescent victims can be aided in the development of a "personal fable" regarding some unique aspect that helps in their overcoming the abuse.

Older latency and adolescent victims can be aided in the development of a "personal fable" regarding some unique aspect that helps in their overcoming the

abuse. This can be done in a cognitive therapy format, complete with a blackboard to facilitate the child's visual perception of the important concept that thoughts create feelings and direct behavior. For example, Cunningham and MacFarlane (1990) have written about the role of "vulture thoughts" in the thinking of sexually aggressive children.

Finally, in keeping with Harter's (1988) finding, the therapist would do well to avoid focusing on insight in the child and concentrate on a developmentally simpler task (i.e., accuracy of self-perception).

Group Therapy Approaches Derived From Self-Perception Theory

The universality present in group therapy helps not only with attachment, which was described earlier, but also helps children view themselves more accurately (Yalom, 1975). Sullivan (1953) has written that our self-perception is constructed in part based on our understanding of other people's perceptions of us. Group therapy provides an excellent opportunity for peer perspectives to be incorporated into one's sense of self. In addition, the group format allows children to hear feedback from other people about gains they have made. Finally, by the use of structured treatment modules, children can realize that they are working gradually through the victimization, achieving closure, and, it is hoped, improving their sense of self-efficacy.

Family Therapy Techniques Derived From Self-Perception Theory

Abusive parents who have been victimized in the past and who now have a child whom they have abused will most likely view themselves as inept. Countering that perspective will be very difficult, but family therapy is an appropriate arena to confront that parental perception. This may be done by empowering parents and allowing them to see their effectiveness with small, easily attainable goals that are set in terms of their ability to parent their child in a less angry and nonvictimizing manner.

Some of the same all-or-nothing thinking that children have about themselves will be found in parents regarding their perceptions of their child. Parents can be encouraged to externalize their negative projections of the child (White, 1989). For example, parents do not always hate their child, although their abusive behavior suggests that. However, there are times when their "dislike for the child gets the better of them." Discussion between the parent and the child about these specific instances can go a long way toward developing a more positive sense of connection between the parent and the child.

Need for Research

A recent review of the impact of sexual abuse (Kendall-Tackett et al., 1993) decried the atheoretical approach to assessing abuse impact. The theoretical model suggested in this chapter combines a number of developmentally sensitive theories that can guide both the assessment and treatment of sexually and physically abused children and their families. However, child treatment clinicians seem to view outcome research as daunting. Shirk (1988) wrote that an average of only one child therapy outcome study has been published annually for the past 30 years, an enormous contrast with the adult treatment literature. What little published research exists on the treatment of sexually abused children suggests that it can be effective in the short-term for anxiety and depression (Lanktree & Briere, 1995) and requires significantly longer periods of time for the externalizing problems of aggression and sexual acting out (Friedrich et al., 1992; Lanktree & Briere, 1995). PTSD symptoms also lend themselves to treatment with a cognitive behavioral approach (Deblinger et al., 1990). These findings need to be replicated, and the treated children need to be followed for longer periods, preferably over a developmental transition (e.g., from childhood into adolescence) to determine long-term efficacy.

In addition, the efficacy of group treatment needs to be documented (Hiebert-Murphy et al., 1992). Directive therapy, including disclosure of victimization, is also strongly suggested by many clinicians

(Friedrich, 1990), but its treatment value is being demonstrated only now. We also need to know whether child treatment can be helpful with children who are in foster care, whose parents are not in treatment, or whose parental relationship faces termination. Finally, it may be that changing external factors (e.g., poverty, maternal depression, use of physical punishment) are as important to the child's long-term adjustment as any "internal" changes the child makes. However, we do not know that. These big questions must be answered before we can ask more narrow questions about the utility of specific techniques.

Conclusion

Therapists owe it to the children they treat to do at least the following: (a) assess the presence of behavioral problems, using standard measures and pretreatment immediately after treatment and 3 to 6 months later; (b) document the interventions used in therapy; (c) document the amount of therapy and whether the abuse was discussed; (d) invite other clinicians to collaborate to expand sample size and types of interventions; and (e) share findings. Not only will this inform the practice, but it can guide the treatment of other abused children as well.

In addition, the theories and associated techniques identified in this chapter have the added advantage of targeting specific symptoms presented by abused children. An equally valid approach to determine treatment effectiveness is Goal Attainment Scaling, discussed specifically for sexually abused children in Friedrich (1990). This approach can be used to determine therapy outcome for a diverse group of abused children with a broad range of presenting complaints. For example, treatment goals can be established in each of the domains suggested (e.g., an attachment-related goal of more positive interactions with their child, a dysregulation-related goal of no physical punishment, and a self-perception goal of improved school achievement by the child). Goal Attainment Scaling can enhance treatment and enable the therapist to measure outcome empirically.

Appendix A

Synopsis of Selected Treatment Techniques

I. Attachment

    A. Individual Therapy
1. Acceptance
2. Alliance formation
3. Correcting the internal working model
4. Creating safety

    B. Group Therapy
1. Developing cohesion
2. Maintaining boundaries
3. Creating safety
4. Developing empathy

    C. Family Therapy
1. Positive connotation
2. Identifying similarities among family members
3. Creating rapid treatment gains
4. Goal setting
5. Home visits

II. Dysregulation

    A. Individual Therapy
1. Explaining the process of therapy
2. Establishing specific goals
3. Modulating treatment intensity
4. Teaching self-soothing techniques
5. Using psychoeducational approaches
6. Using cognitive behavioral strategies for PTSD and anxiety

    B. Group Therapy
1. Creating safety
2. Reducing agitation
3. Practicing boundaries
4. Interrupting victims/victimizer dynamics

    C. Family Therapy
1. Creating safety
2. Reducing sexualized behavior
3. Behaviorally based family therapy
4. Goal setting

III. Self-Theory

    A. Individual Therapy
1. Identifying and processing feelings
2. Contracting for competency
3. Externalizing the problem
4. Confronting all-or-nothing thinking
5. Correcting inappropriate cognitions

    B. Group Therapy
1. Respecting the child's developmental level
2. Using pair therapy

    C. Family Therapy
1. Normalizing unacceptable feelings
2. Examining the parenting process
3. Exploring parents' projections
4. Examining parents feeling betrayed
5. Creating new stories about the child

References

Ainsworth, M. D. S. (1989). Attachments beyond infancy. *American Psychologist, 44,* 709-716.

Alexander, P. C. (1992). Application of attachment theory to the study of sexual abuse. *Journal of Consulting and Clinical Psychology, 60,* 185-195.

Berliner, L. (1991). Therapy with victimized children and their families. *New Directions for Mental Health Services, 51,* 29-46.

Bowlby, J. (1969). *Attachment and loss: Vol. 1. Attachment.* New York: Basic Books.

Cicchetti, D., Ganiban, J., & Barnett, D. (1991). Contributions from the study of high risk populations to understanding the development of emotion regulation. In J. Garber & K. A. Dodge (Eds.), *The development of emotion regulation and dysregulation* (pp. 15-48). New York: Cambridge University Press.

Cunningham, C., & MacFarlane, K. (1990). *When children molest children.* Orwell, VT: Safer Society Press.

Deblinger, E., McLeer, S., & Henry, D. (1990). Cognitive behavioral treatment for sexually abused children suffering post-traumatic stress: Preliminary findings. *Journal of the American Academy of Child and Adolescent Psychiatry, 29,* 747-752.

Dodge, K., & Garber, J. (1991). Domains of emotion regulation. In J. Garber & K. A. Dodge (Eds.), *The development of emotion regulation and dysregulation* (pp. 3-11). New York: Cambridge University Press.

Egeland, B., & Erickson, M. F. (1983, August). *Psychologically unavailable caregiving: The effects on development of young children and the implications for intervention.* Paper presented at the International Conference on Psychological Abuse, Indianapolis, IN.

Egeland, B., Sroufe, L. A., & Erickson, M. (1983). The developmental consequence of different patterns of maltreatment. *Child Abuse & Neglect, 7,* 459-469.

Finkelhor, D., & Browne, A. (1985). The traumatic impact of child sexual abuse: A conceptualization. *American Journal of Orthopsychiatry, 55,* 530-541.

Friedrich, W. N. (1990). *Psychotherapy of sexually abused children and their families.* New York: Norton.

Friedrich, W. N. (1991a). *Casebook of sexual abuse treatment.* New York: Norton.

Friedrich, W. N. (1991b). Mothers of sexually abused children: An MMPI study. *Journal of Clinical Psychology, 47,* 778-783.

Friedrich, W. N., Beilke, R. L., & Urquiza, A. J. (1987). Children from sexually abusive families: A behavioral comparison. *Journal of Interpersonal Violence, 2,* 391-402.

Friedrich, W. N., Berliner, L., Urquiza, A. J., & Beilke, R. L. (1988). Brief diagnostic group treatment of sexually abused boys. *Journal of Interpersonal Violence, 3,* 331-343.

Friedrich, W. N., Luecke, W. J., Beilke, R. L., & Place, V. (1992). Psychotherapy outcome of sexually abused boys: An agency study. *Journal of Interpersonal Violence, 7,* 396-409.

Friedrich, W. N., & Schafer, L. C. (1995). Somatization in sexually abused children. *Journal of Pediatric Psychology, 20,* 661-670.

George, C., & Main, M. (1979). Social interactions of young abused children: Approach, avoidance, and aggression. *Child Development, 50,* 306-318.

Harter, S. (1977). A cognitive-developmental approach to children's expression of conflicting feelings and a technique to facilitate such expression in play therapy. *Journal of Consulting and Clinical Psychology, 45,* 417-432.

Harter, S. (1988). Developmental and dynamic changes in the nature of the self-concept. In S. R. Shirk (Ed.), *Cognitive development and child psychotherapy* (pp. 119-160). New York: Plenum.

Hewitt, S. K., & Friedrich, W. N. (1991). Effects of probable sexual abuse on preschool children. In M. Q. Patton (Ed.), *Family sexual abuse* (pp. 54-74). Newbury Park, CA: Sage.

Hiebert-Murphy, D., DeLuca, R., & Runtz, M. (1992). Group treatment for sexually abused girls: Evaluating outcome. *Families in Society, 73,* 205-213.

Katz, L. F., & Gottman, J. M. (1991). Marital discord and child outcomes: A social-psychophysiological approach. In J. Garber & K. A. Dodge (Eds.), *The development of emotion regulation and dysregulation* (pp. 129-155). New York: Cambridge University Press.

Kendall-Tackett, K. A., Williams, L. M., & Finkelhor, D. (1993). Impact of sexual abuse on children: A review and synthesis of recent empirical studies. *Psychological Bulletin, 113,* 164-180.

Lanktree, C., & Briere, J. (1995). Outcome of therapy for sexually abused children: A repeated measures study. *Child Abuse & Neglect, 19,* 1145-1155.

Levang, C. A. (1989). Interactional communication patterns in father/daughter incest families. *Journal of Psychology and Human Sexuality, 1,* 53-68.

Main, M., & Cassidy, J. (1988). Categories of response to reunion with the parent at age 6: Predictable from infant attachment classifications and stable over a 1-month period. *Developmental Psychology, 24,* 415-426.

Main, M., & George, C. (1985). Responses of abused and disadvantaged toddlers to distress in age mates: A study in the day care setting. *Developmental Psychology, 21,* 407-412.

Malinosky-Rummell, R., & Hansen, D. J. (1993). Long-term consequences of childhood physical abuse. *Psychological Bulletin, 114,* 68-79.

Mandell, J. G., & Damon, L. (1989). *Group treatment for sexually abused children.* New York: Guilford.

McLeer, S., Deblinger, E., Atkins, M., Foa, E., & Ralphe, D. (1988). Post-traumatic stress disorder in sexually abused children. *Journal of American Academy of Child and Adolescent Psychiatry, 27,* 650-654.

Meichenbaum, D. (1974). Self-instructional methods. In F. H. Kaufer & A. P. Goldstein (Eds.), *Helping people change.* Elmsford, NY: Pergamon.

Putnam, F. (1991, October). *Behavioral and psychophysiological correlates of sexual abuse.* Paper presented at the annual meeting of the American Academy of Child and Adolescent Psychiatry, San Francisco.

Selman, R. L., & Schultz, L. H. (1990). *Making a friend in youth.* Chicago: University of Chicago Press.

Selvini-Palazzolli, M., Boscolo, L., Cecchin, G., & Prata, G. (1978). *Paradox and counter paradox.* New York: Aronson.

Shirk, S. R. (Ed.). (1988). *Cognitive development and child psychotherapy.* New York: Plenum.

Sroufe, L. A. (1989). Pathways to adaptation and maladaptation: Psychopathology as developmental deviation. In D. Cicchetti (Ed.), *The emergence of a discipline: Rochester symposium on developmental psychopathology* (Vol. 1, pp. 13-40). Hillsdale, NJ: Lawrence Erlbaum.

Sroufe, L. A., Jacobvitz, D., Mangelsdorf, S., DeAngelo, E., & Ward, M. J. (1985). Generational boundary dissolution between mothers and their preschool children: A relationship's systems approach. *Child Development, 56,* 317-325.

Steinglass, P. (1987). *The alcoholic family.* New York: Basic Books.

Strupp, H. H., & Binder, J. L. (1984). *Psychotherapy in a new key.* New York: Basic Books.

Sullivan, H. S. (1953). *The interpersonal theory of psychiatry.* New York: Norton.

Trepper, T. S., & Barrett, M. J. (1989). *Systemic treatment of incest.* New York: Brunner/Mazel.

Uherek, A. M. (1991). Treatment of a ritually abused preschooler. In W. N. Friedrich (Ed.), *Casebook of sexual abuse treatment* (pp. 70-92). New York: Norton.

Walker, C. E., Bonner, B. L., & Kaufman, K. L. (1988). *The physically and sexually abused child: Evaluation and treatment.* Elmsford, NY: Pergamon.

White, M. (1989). *Selected papers.* Adelaide, Australia: Dulwich Center.

Winnicott, D. W. (1965). *Maturational processes and the facilitating environment.* New York: International Universities Press.

Yalom, I. (1975). *The theory and practice of group psychotherapy* (2nd ed.). New York: Basic Books.

Zahn-Waxler, C., Cole, P. M., & Barrett, K. C. (1992). Guilt and empathy: Sex differences and implications for the development of depression. In J. Garber & K. A. Dodge (Eds.), *The development of emotion regulation and dysregulation* (pp. 243-272). New York: Cambridge University Press.

7

Treating Abused Adolescents

MARK CHAFFIN

BARBARA L. BONNER

KAREN BOYD WORLEY

LOUANNE LAWSON

One of the ironies in the field of psychotherapy is that we have produced almost no empirical studies and comparatively limited clinical literature on the treatment of abuse sequelae in young men and women. This is true even though we have been treating abuse sequelae for almost a hundred years. The problem is that we have not always identified them as such until recently. Although the history of what we now know as psychotherapy began with a clear focus on trauma, especially sexual abuse-related trauma (Breuer & Freud, 1895/1955), this perspective was not to endure, and the day soon passed when therapeutic practice was guided by the stories of young patients disclosing histories of childhood seduction or maltreatment. Later, no doubt for complex reasons, this "naive" position of believing patients gave way to increasingly intricate intrapsychic formulations that localized the origin of symptoms in the vicissitudes of unconscious fantasy and erotic development, minimizing the importance of real trauma in human misery (Freud, 1905). Many of us trained in this tradition can recall the day in which the "technically correct" response to a disclosure of childhood incest in psychotherapy was to respond with neutrality to the question of whether or not the memories were "real" and focus instead on the Oedipal implications presumed to underlie the associated distress.

What was termed *traumatic neurosis*[1] still remained recognized as a legitimate entity, albeit usually limited to unusual and bizarre traumatic experiences in adult life, such as major disasters or military combat. In classic psychoanalytic theory, traumatic neurosis was seen as one of the simplest and most straightforward disorders to understand and treat (Fenichel, 1945), not requiring the invocation of complicated intrapsychic motivational complexes aside from the simple need of clients to protect themselves from the overwhelming emotions understandably brought on by the trauma. When faced with so many of the difficulties experienced by young men and women that we now suspect bear a direct relationship to abuse trauma (depression, anxiety, dissociation, self-injurious behavior, substance abuse, acting out, etc.), perhaps we did not look for the "simpler" answer of trauma because we already had so many other explanations for these patterns without needing any specific reference to the unpleasant reality of child abuse (Briere, 1989).

Abuse-Focused Therapy

As appreciation of the reality and frequency of abuse has grown, clinicians increasingly have begun to inquire into its occurrence in the histories of adolescent patients, finding that the simple act of asking about sexual abuse, for example, can result in a four- to fivefold increase in its clinical identification (31% vs. 7%; Lanktree, Briere, & Zaidi, 1991). Incidence rates for identification of harm due to maltreatment increase with age, resulting in a substantial number of identified abused teens entering either clinical or child protective services (CPS) systems annually (NIS-II, 1988).

Currently, a core tenet of modern approaches to treating significantly abused children, adolescents, or adults is that treatment should be abuse focused. Emerging largely within the past 10 to 15 years, the field of abuse-focused therapy (AFT) has produced several book-length works that define the current state of the art and differentiate AFT from previous approaches (Briere, 1989, 1992; Friedrich, 1990; Gil, 1991; Hunter, 1990; Meiselman, 1990). AFT is not affiliated with any particular theoretical perspective on the larger issues of human psychology—personality, development, cognition, and learning—and has yet to develop fully its own generally accepted treatment theory or model. Nor is it associated with any particular set of techniques or approaches. Indeed, AFT borrows from a wide variety of behavioral, cognitive, systemic, and reconstructive or dynamic therapy techniques.

The common threads are predominantly philosophical, rooted in the perspective that abuse is a form of victimization by the powerful against the relatively powerless, and that abuse sequelae are readily understandable if not expected and "normal" adaptations to an abnormal experience. This perspective, as well as the typical symptom presentation of abused adolescents and young adults, increasingly has led the field in the direction of diagnostic and treatment conceptualizations based on full or partial posttraumatic stress disorder (PTSD), emphasizing the trauma of abuse rather than an endogenous disorder residing within the victim (Coons, Bowman, Pellow, & Schneider, 1989; Deblinger, 1991; McCormack, Burgess, & Hartman, 1988). In addition, because a variety of cognitive and behavioral techniques have been applied successfully to the treatment of PTSD in nonabused clients, AFT is able to borrow many of these techniques to target directly some of the more disruptive abuse sequelae such as severe anxiety, hyperarousal, and avoidance symptoms (Deblinger, McLeer, & Henry, 1990; Lipovsky, 1991).

Also, as its name implies, abuse-focused therapy devotes considerable emphasis to describing, exploring, and comprehending the abuse itself as it is phenomenologically experienced by victims. This is important for constructing an understanding of problematic emotional, cognitive, and interpersonal patterns as outgrowths of the abuse experience. Rooted in a victimization perspective, AFT suggests the construction of an alternate "story" of the abuse from that characteristically produced by the abuse experience itself. Abused adolescents commonly present as laboring under beliefs about their own internalized stigmatization, powerlessness, and shame (Finkelhor, 1988; Finkelhor & Browne, 1985). As one adolescent girl put it when asked to write how sexual abuse had affected her life, "I have felt so bad about myself. . . . What kind of person lets their father molest them?" By implicitly separating the problem from the person, externalizing and objectifying it, AFT invites the young abuse survivor to author a new version of events, one offering a sense of personal agency, empowerment, and efficacy (Adams-Wescott & Isenbart, 1990; White, 1989).

Related to abuse-focused treatment are other perspectives explicitly recognizing the critical role of severe trauma in development of core aspects of the self, personality, and intrapersonal and interpersonal schemata (i.e., basic templates for interpersonal and intrapersonal interchanges). These related approaches emphasize the impact of severe trauma on the development of core personality functions, such as affect modulation, attachment, or development, of a well-integrated versus fragmented self-structure (see Chapter 6, this volume, for a discussion of many of these issues).

There are common threads of AFT across abuse type and population age. However, before addressing specific issues and approaches for adolescents, it is important to review briefly the developmental status and tasks of adolescence, for it is within this developmental context that the experience of both abuse and therapy is interpreted and constructed by the teenager.

Adolescence

Although the concept of adolescence as a discrete stage in the human life span has been described as a 20th-century invention (Aries, 1962), it seems that the adults' complaints about the prevailing stereotype of adolescent turmoil and trouble have been legion throughout the ages. As Shakespeare wrote, "I would there were no age between ten and three and twenty, or that youth would sleep out the rest; for there is nothing in the between but getting wenches with child, wronging the ancientry, stealing, fight-

ing" (A Winter's Tale, Act II, Scene 3). This perception of adolescence as a time of Sturm und Drang is held widely among both the general populace and mental health professionals (Levine, 1987; Offer, Ostrov, & Howard, 1981). The picture is one of moodiness, identity confusion, and rebelliousness in which "what takes place is a steady drumfire of impulse and desire pressing against . . . the ego. . . . The stress of the time may be considerable and the evidence of an ego under pressure is pervasive" (Noshpitz & King, 1991, p. 372).

Certainly one might get this impression from experiences limited to a mental health clinic or a courtroom, where the modal referral is for behavior problems, but how well does the stereotype fit what we know about adolescents in the general population? Two recent reviews summarizing a decade of research have concurred that the majority of adolescents (around 80%) appear to manage the transition from childhood to adulthood fairly smoothly, maintaining a positive self-image and coping well (Offer & Boxer, 1991; Petersen, 1988). The stereotype of adolescent turmoil is more appropriately a description of an at-risk youngster whose problems will likely continue into adulthood (Jessor & Jessor, 1977).

Physical/sexual development. Puberty signals the entrance into adolescence, although the age at which this occurs can vary considerably. Most data suggest that puberty has been beginning earlier and earlier over the past century and is somewhat earlier for girls than for boys, although the amount of growth is greater for boys (Tanner, 1981). Although clear physical changes and increased sexual interest occur during puberty, the view that raging hormones impinge markedly on behavior is not justified completely. Most of the psychological impact of puberty is interwoven with social or cultural standards. For example, boys have been found to report increased feelings of attractiveness during puberty, but girls express more dislike for their bodies, particularly regarding the more public aspects of their development such as breasts, increased height, and loss of "thinness" (Crockett & Petersen, 1987; Petersen, 1988).

Adultlike sexuality, sexual identity issues, and romantic pairing make their debut during adolescence, and accommodating these physically derived psychological and social changes is a major developmental task of the period. Romantic intimacy, dating, and decisions (some would say preoccupations) over sexual activity quickly come to occupy a major part of the adolescent's concerns. By age 18, the majority of adolescents have experienced intercourse, more so and earlier for boys than for girls, for African Americans than for Caucasians, and for sexually abused than for nonabused girls (Hayes, 1987; Wyatt, 1988). Unfortunately, most initial and later adolescent experiences with intercourse in this country are unplanned and unprotected, putting young men and women at risk for unwanted pregnancies and diseases, including HIV (Brooks-Gunn & Furstenberg, 1989).

Changes in dependency status. Adolescence also is characterized by increasing role competency, emphasis on peer relations, and independence from parental and adult control. The latter is often a regular focus of negotiation, if not conflict. Peer groups increase in size, complexity, and emotional intimacy as increasing amounts of time are spent in contact with close friends, sharing thoughts, feelings, and activities (Petersen, 1988). Although this implies a different sort of relationship to family and parents than the dependency and relative exclusivity of earlier years, it would be a mistake to equate individuation or autonomy with freedom from parental attachments and influences. Rather, it appears that although most adolescents in Western cultures adhere to peer or idiosyncratic standards in dress, music, and other matters of fashion, they continue to hold fundamentally similar core values and beliefs with their parents (Kandel & Lesser, 1972). Within different cultural groups, moving away from dependency may be manifested differently. For example, whereas the majority American culture may value increased individualism and pursuit of individual goals among adolescents, other cultures may be more group or family oriented and value adolescents taking increasingly contributory or responsible roles within the group.

Parents' ability to adjust adequately to their adolescent's movements away from dependency appears to play a crucial role in determining the direction and character of this process.

> **Greater adolescent autonomy has been associated with having parents who are authoritative and who combine context-specific limit setting and negotiation with an enabling, caring, and supportive attitude.**

Greater adolescent autonomy has been associated with having parents who are authoritative, as opposed to authoritarian or restrictive, and who combine context-specific limit setting and negotiation with an enabling, caring, and supportive attitude (Powers, Hauser, & Kilner, 1989). Unfortunately, parental styles that support autonomy are likely to be far from the experience of many abused adolescents, due to psychologically neglectful or abusive parenting styles that frequently coexist with physical and sexual abuse (Claussen & Crittenden, 1991; Hart & Brassard, 1990).

Cognitive development. Cognitive abilities, particularly the ability to think abstractly and introspectively, increase significantly during adolescence. Most teens develop the capacity to see things from the perspective of others, paradoxically combined with a heightened self-consciousness and egocentrism that diminish as adolescence progresses (Enright, Lapsley, & Shukla, 1979). Increased cognitive and self-reflexive abilities and the ability to be sensitive to the plight of others can combine to produce an often philosophical and socially conscious perspective on life and questions of identity and social justice.

Perhaps as a result of moving increasingly away from dependent status, the overall pattern of adolescent victimization (including maltreatment) changes relative to younger children. For example, adolescents are far less likely than younger children to be victims of family abductions or physical neglect. As children grow older, victimization patterns become more like those of adults—indeed, even more so. For example, adolescents are more likely to be victims of rape, robbery, or assault than either younger children or the adult population as a whole (Finkelhor & Dzuiba-Leatherman, 1994). Adolescents may be abused physically, sexually, psychologically, or in any combination. Although the types of abuse may not always be discrete, each will be addressed separately.

Sexual Abuse

Sexually abused adolescents can enter abuse-focused treatment for ongoing and recently disclosed abuse or for abuse that occurred several years earlier and either has come to light recently or is assumed to be related to emerging present difficulties. Little effort has been devoted to teasing out the differences, if any, among these presentations, particularly as they might influence treatment. Aside from safety needs, however, we cannot routinely assume that simply because abuse occurred long ago that the treatment need is less. Delayed and chronic PTSD symptoms have been reported in adult survivors (Gelinas, 1983; Murphy et al., 1988), often precipitated or exacerbated by a developmental change or life event involving sexuality. Adolescence certainly qualifies.

Although adolescents, compared to younger children, have had an opportunity to be abused more often and over a longer time, thereby resulting in greater damage, the relationships between number of events, age at onset, and duration of abuse are complex and not entirely clear. Although some studies have found that pubescent or postpubescent onset is associated with greater symptomatology (Murphy et al., 1988; Sedney & Brooks, 1984; Sirles, Smith, & Kusama, 1989), others have reported the opposite, with early abuse resulting in more profound later problems (Russell, 1986). Still others have found that children for whom onset occurs in the 7 to 13 age range are most vulnerable (Gomes-Schwartz, Horowitz, & Sauzier, 1985). One possibility, which is particularly plausible from a developmental point of view, is that abuse effects are mediated, in part, by the developmental phases through which the abuse persists (Browne & Finkelhor, 1986) and the corresponding number and nature of developmental tasks that could be compromised.

In any case, there do appear to be differences in the types of abuse effects experienced by adolescents compared to younger children, which are relevant to understanding the wide variety of ways in which sexually abused adolescents may present. A recent review suggests that, in contrast to their preschool and school-age counterparts who are more likely to present with atypical sexualized behavior problems and preoccupations, sexually abused adolescents present more often with low self-esteem, depression, and suicidal ideation or behavior (Beitchman, Zucker, Hood, daCosta, & Akman, 1991). Adolescents are also more likely to disclose their abuse actively than accidentally, with disclosure commonly motivated by anger (Sorensen & Snow, 1991). Consequently, adolescents presenting with nonspecific psychological symptoms and angry accusations of abuse should not be dismissed because they either fail to fit some supposed abuse syndrome or their disclosures are seen as vindictive or malicious. The high prevalence of sexual abuse among early adolescents who attempt suicide suggests that suicidality be assessed carefully (Runtz & Briere, 1986), and inquiry into abuse may be prudent among adolescent suicide attemptors. Adolescent "acting out" behaviors such as school problems, conflicts with authority, early sexual behavior, and eating disorders also have been associated with abuse in teenaged girls (Hibbard, Ingersoll, & Orr, 1990; Runtz & Briere, 1986), although abused teens show lower problem levels than general adolescent psychiatric populations (Gomes-Schwartz, Horowitz, & Cardarelli, 1990).

Assessment

Is treatment needed? Although not all teenagers who have been sexually abused require treatment, it is not clear how to determine who does not, even among those exhibiting very limited or moderate symptoms. Victims may seek to avoid dealing with the reality and implications of their abuse, vacillating between intrusive thoughts about the abuse and periods of avoidance and denial (Shapiro & Dominiak, 1990). Avoidant adolescents will not welcome the therapeutic invitation to recall that which they are actively trying to forget or may interpret the referral as simply another exposure of their most embarrassing secrets and further stigmatization. Many tell us, "Look, there's nothing wrong with me, I just want to forget about it—OK?" This can be compounded by the fact that the youngster's abuser often "escapes" without having to submit to treatment at all, reinforcing a sense of unfairness and implicit blame in his or her referral for therapy.

Although the experience of having to tell strangers repeatedly about the abuse can be deleterious (Tedesco & Schnell, 1987), passively encouraging teenaged abuse victims to rely on avoidant coping mechanisms is also risky. A recent study found that denial and emotional suppression were the most common coping mechanisms used by adult survivors from a community sample. Paradoxically, although rated as helpful by survivors, these avoidant coping mechanisms actually were associated with poorer psychosocial adjustment (Leitenberg, Greenwald, & Cado, 1992). Among adolescent incest victims, avoidant coping strategies such as wishful thinking, detachment, distancing, or denial have been found to be associated with higher symptom levels (Johnson & Kenkel, 1991).

In the absence of longitudinal data, however, it is difficult to determine whether avoidant coping styles actively contribute to a poorer resolution of abuse issues and consequently greater distress, as many trauma theorists suspect, or whether greater distress "requires" using more pronounced and "primitive" coping strategies to safeguard psychological integrity. In either case, the available evidence suggests that we cannot afford to neglect the needs of abused adolescents solely on the basis of their ambivalence or reluctance to seek help.

The initial interview. Sensitive assessment of the adolescent who has been sexually abused must bear these points in mind. Consistent with an abuse focus, the initial interview should respect the youngster's boundaries and possible reluctance about therapy and grant some sense of control over discussion of sensitive material. Often, it is sufficient to give some choice over how much detail will be talked about while holding out for the possibility that talking about this difficult topic may become less anxiety provoking in the future. In addition, it is important to convey respect for the prevailing coping efforts and devote some time to detail-

ing how well the adolescent has coped with the experience to date, rather than opening the assessment with an exploration of symptoms or problems. The initial interview also can serve as a doorway into focusing on the teenager's strengths by depathologizing the mental status interview and separating the self from the problem. For example, it may be useful to frame questions with a statement to the effect that, "I've talked with a lot of people your age who have been through sexual abuse about the effects it has had on them. Everyone's different, but I want to find out if some of the things that have bothered some other people have bothered you. I'd also like to find out what sorts of things you've done that seem to help the most."

In addition to obtaining the usual historical and mental status information, it is important to inquire into a range of abuse-specific effects and correlates, including (a) a history of additional abuse, rape, or violent assault experiences beyond the referral report; (b) PTSD symptoms, including dissociation, avoidance, numbing, intrusive thoughts, or flashbacks; (c) triggers for fearfulness and anxiety; (d) relationship issues, including those with adults and peers of the same gender as the abuser; (e) sleep disturbances, including nightmares; (f) depression; (g) suicidal or self-injurious tendencies; (h) sexual behavior; (i) substance use/abuse or eating problems; and (j) difficulties with memory or other unusual experiences potentially suggestive of a dissociative disorder.

Clinicians also should assess the youngster's social support network and ongoing stressors.

> *Particularly critical are the belief and support of the nonoffending parent(s), which have been demonstrated to be the most powerful predictors of recovery.*

Particularly critical are the belief and support of the nonoffending parent(s), which have been demonstrated to be the most powerful predictors of recovery (Everson, Hunter, Runyan, Edelsohn, & Coulter, 1989; Wyatt & Mickey, 1987). Social stressors may arise from the tendency for many adolescents to be exquisitely sensitive to the possibility that peers and schoolmates might discover the abuse and view them as responsible, disgraced, or stigmatized. Among teenaged girls, many guard their reputations with the fear that they might be labeled as "sluts," a term for which there appears to be no masculine equivalent. Boys may fear homophobic stigmatization and loss of their masculine status, leading to reluctance to having their abuse known to others (Faller, 1991; Porter, 1986; Rew & Esparza, 1990). Developmentally, it is important that adolescents learn to turn to their peers and experience intimacy and support without betrayal, a task that can be difficult if the youngster fears stigmatization. Clinical experience suggests that the presence of even a single trusted peer confidante can be helpful. Additional stressors complicating the abuse may include court involvement, pressures from family members, or repeated, unwanted "advice." Court involvement can be more stressful for adolescents than younger children, particularly if they are without parental support and required to testify multiple times under harsh cross-examination (Lipovsky, 1992).

Assessing attributions. Bright preteens or middle- to late-phase adolescents are usually capable of abstract and introspective thought required to discuss their own attributions about the abuse (Celano, 1992; Offer & Boxer, 1991). Attribution theory holds that abuse effects are mediated not so much by the objective characteristics of the abuse as by how we subjectively explain it to ourselves. Attributions are the internal "theory" we articulate about what caused and maintained the problem. In general, it is assumed that self-blaming (internal attribution) leads to depression and greater distress. Morrow (1991), for example, found that adolescent incest victims who tended toward internal attributions experienced more depression and lower self-esteem.

However, the relationship between attributions and outcome may be complex. Celano (1992) has suggested that internal attributions may be particularly damaging only when they refer to *characterological* (or global-stable) aspects of oneself rather than *situational* or behavioral aspects. Likewise, external attributions that are global-stable may lead to fearfulness or feelings that one is helpless in a world of ubiquitous danger and seem-

ingly random and unavoidable victimization. Thus, it may be important for these adolescents to maintain some perception that they have the ability, at least in some situations, to control what happens to them.

This suggests that we should resist the temptation to challenge all internal attributions reflexively, particularly at the time of assessment. Here, it is more important to lay the groundwork for exploration of the adolescent's attributions, rather than attempt to change them. Efforts to press the point that "it wasn't your fault" may risk functionally prohibiting future disclosure and discussion. In our culture, adolescent sexual abuse victims are viewed as more causally and morally responsible for their abuse than are younger children, particularly if the assault was not violently forceful of if they responded passively (Collings & Payne, 1991). Developmentally already sensitive to any social exposure of "flaws," adolescents may be keenly aware of the stigma that could await them on revealing reasons for their internal attributions. It is preferable for the clinician to accept the internal attributions and explore them nonjudgmentally before beginning to suggest that there may be other ways of thinking about what happened.

Psychological testing. Consistent with the notable lack of empirical data on treatment outcome or standardized assessment and triage, many treatment programs make minimal use of standardized assessment tools, either as pretreatment, progress, or outcome measures (Friedrich, 1990). Although there is no "profile" to be found in psychological testing that is typical or indicative of sexual abuse (APSAC, 1990), testing can be useful in providing a broad range of information about how the teenager copes, the extent of current symptoms or discomfort, what resources are present, and what problems may lie ahead. The results can serve as a useful baseline against which treatment progress can be assessed and documented. Again, consistent with an abuse-focused philosophy, clinicians should make every effort to depathologize the testing experience implicitly and emphasize determination of victims' strengths and resources, as well as their problems.

A testing protocol should be comprehensive and targeted to assess typical effects of sexual abuse. A multitarget, multimethod, and multisource approach provides the most reliable results. First, it is important to use both a variety of general measures as well as abuse-specific instruments to cover a range of target areas. General areas include cognitive/ intellectual screening, family organization, personality style, coping style, and behavioral/emotional symptomatic status. Any number of valid and reliable instruments are available for these purposes and have been described in greater detail elsewhere (Bonner, Kaufman, Harbeck, & Brassard, 1992; Friedrich, 1990). Second, it is important that instruments be selected that use multiple methods and sources of information. For example, findings have suggested that depression may be minimized on self-report instruments completed by sexually abused girls compared with that measured by either parental report or a projective instrument such as the Rorschach (Shapiro, Leifer, Martone, & Kassem, 1990). Conversely, assessment relying on parental report instruments alone may be biased if the parent holds an overly negative perception of the teenager or is unable to separate the teenager's abuse experience from his or her own. In addition to self-report, parent report, and projective measures, teacher report and observational methods should be included when possible.

Only recently have researchers begun to develop measures to assess abuse-specific issues in sexually abused children and adults. Even less attention has been devoted to instruments specifically for teenagers. The Children's Fears Related to Victimization Scale (Wolfe & Wolfe, 1988) and the Children's Impact of Traumatic Events Scale—Revised (CITES-R) (Wolfe & Gentile, 1991) are self-report and structured interview instruments for children. The CITES-R was developed specifically to assess posttraumatic stress-related symptoms among sexually abused children. The most recent version, based on a factor analytic study of the original CITES, is made up of 78 items falling into 11 scales along four dimensions: PTSD (intrusive thoughts, avoidance, hyperarousal, sexual anxiety), social reactions (negative reactions from others and social support), abuse attributions (self-blame and guilt, empowerment, vulnerability and dangerous world), and eroticism. The questionnaire can be administered verbally and requires approximately 15 minutes. The Trauma Symptom Checklist for Children (TSCC)

(Briere, in press), for ages 8 through 16, is a self-report instrument with scales reflecting anxiety, depression, posttraumatic stress, sexual concerns, dissociation, and anger symptoms. The TSCC has been demonstrated to possess adequate reliability, validity, and sensitivity to changes across the course of treatment (Evans, Briere, Boggiano, & Barrett, 1994; Lanktree & Briere, 1995). Much of the data for both instruments come from child or mixed child and adolescent populations. Abuse-specific instruments share many similarities in target areas with abuse-focused therapy, making them particularly well-suited to assess progress and document treatment outcome.

Treatment

Initial treatment plan. Friedrich (1990) has emphasized the importance of viewing sexually abused children and adolescents as a heterogeneous population with correspondingly diverse treatment needs.

There is no "one size fits all" treatment model or protocol, and we should be skeptical of either self-help or professionally led programs that suggest otherwise.

There is no "one size fits all" treatment model or protocol, and we should be skeptical of either self-help or professionally led programs that suggest otherwise. It is important to recognize both the common and the idiosyncratic aspects of each case and approach treatment accordingly. By the end of assessment, the clinician should be far better prepared to suggest an individualized treatment plan and have some idea of the teenager's problem areas, strengths, and current family and social status. The first questions to be addressed are the following: (a) Is the adolescent currently in a safe and appropriate environment? (b) What is the least restrictive appropriate setting for treatment? (c) Are there any acute difficulties that require immediate relief?

Although not formally the responsibility of treatment professionals, safety issues cannot be ignored in assessment and treatment. Oftentimes, teenagers may not report additional abusers or continued exposure to their reported abuser until they reach the treatment setting. The therapist may be the first to find out about changes in status that place the youngster at risk or identify oversights in the child protection and legal systems. Although therapists do not have the authority to intervene directly in these situations, it is critical that they assume an advocacy role when necessary and work closely with CPS, courts, and law enforcement to ensure adequate protection. A youngster who is exposed to ongoing abuse, undue pressure from family members or the abuser, or the threat of further abuse or retaliation may be unlikely to talk even in therapy.

Residential or inpatient treatment may be required in some cases. Because hospitalization can be disruptive to important peer relations and schooling, adolescents should be hospitalized no longer than their need for stabilization warrants and then transitioned into an outpatient setting. A history of abuse alone is never sufficient reason for hospitalization. In our experience, the most common reason for hospitalization among sexually abused teenagers is a high suicide risk and/or a serious attempt. Additional reasons might include any of the following problems *if* they are judged to be sufficiently severe: drug or alcohol addiction, self-mutilation, eating disorders, dissociative disorders, PTSD symptoms, or psychosis. It is important to recognize that intense emotion, catharsis, and often dramatic symptoms can follow disclosure of abuse directly, and these should not be mistaken for psychotic decompensation or squelched by hospitalization simply because the therapist may be unprepared for or uncomfortable with their intensity (Briere, 1989; Gelinas, 1983).

Early in therapy, it is important to address any acutely painful abuse sequelae such as panic attacks, sleeping problems, severe anxiety, or fearfulness. These symptoms often are experienced as *ego-dystonic*. In other words, they are not felt to be part of the self, and victims would gladly be rid of them if they could. In addition to its face value, it is important to target these symptoms immediately for other reasons. First, AFT implicitly runs the risk of becoming experienced as aversive due to the repeated pairing of "coming to therapy" with "being reminded of things that make me feel bad." The experience of finding relief early on in treatment can, in effect, immunize against later frustrations. This can set a collaborative tone of "help that feels like help," ultimately benefiting the therapeutic alliance.

A number of behavioral or cognitive/ behavioral techniques can be employed in obtaining some relief. These include relaxation training, distraction and self-control techniques, or exposure procedures such as systematic desensitization or stress inoculation training (Lipovsky, 1991). Short-term use of psychoactive medications cautiously may be considered when symptom relief is critical or when psychological remedies have been exhausted. Ideally, medication should be supervised by a psychiatrist who is well-versed in abuse issues and abuse-focused therapy, include the teenager in the decision-making process if at all possible, and be adequately titrated to provide relief without completely numbing the affect and cognitive acuity needed to work through the trauma.

Educative therapies. Given their abstractive and intellectual capacities, teenagers are able to understand complex and detailed didactic information. Discussions, readings, and handouts can be particularly useful tools for validating the victimization experience and normalizing many of the effects, such as PTSD symptoms (Lipovsky, 1991). Educative approaches are also appropriate for gaining a general explanation for why someone would commit sexual abuse (Berliner & Wheeler, 1987), a persistent question among adolescents that requires more than a perfunctory answer.

If the therapist does not have access to information about the youngster's offender or familiarity with the literature on offenders, one option is to invite a "guest expert" to answer questions and provide information.

If the therapist does not have access to information about the youngster's offender or familiarity with the literature on offenders, one option is to invite a "guest expert" in this area into a session to answer questions and provide information. Alternately, therapists may be involved in work with both a victim and his or her offender, thereby being suited to address these issues (Chaffin, 1994).

In-depth sex education is widely recommended for adolescents who have been sexually abused (Cornman, 1989; Furniss, Bingley-Miller, & Van Elburg, 1988; Meiselman, 1990) to neutralize anxiety, provide a language for discussing sexuality, facilitate a healthy body image, and correct any misconceptions about sexuality that may have been conveyed by the abuse or abuser. This should include abstract principles of appropriate sexual or courtship behavior (e.g., mutual consent; caring relationship; appropriate age, power, familial status; consistency with personal religious and moral values). Clinically, some adolescents who have been abused, and many offenders for that matter, make few stable or well-thought-out distinctions among types of sexual behavior, alternately feeling that it is either "all bad and forbidden" or "anything goes." Making clear and internally elaborated distinctions not only helps youngsters to cognitively separate their abuse-related sexual experiences from their normal sexuality but will hopefully reduce the risk of victims becoming victimizers (Ryan, 1989).

Therapists should not be misled by the occasional pseudomature or "worldly" presentation of some youngsters into thinking that their sexual information is either accurate or consistent with healthy self-protection. Because of the increased risk for revictimization (Beitchman et al., 1992) or unwanted pregnancy, it is also important to include information on rape, date rape, recognizing and responding to unwanted advances, identifying signs of sexually dangerous situations, contraception, and preventing sexually transmitted diseases. Educational interventions also can be helpful in preparing teenagers for their role in legal proceedings, explaining the confusing mix of roles among participants in "the system" and the general purpose and process of therapy, including their "job" as clients. It has been our experience that all these areas can be fraught with confusion and misinformation but respond well to an educative approach.

Group psychotherapy. Although no studies have examined its relative efficacy among adolescents, group therapy widely is endorsed as a treatment of choice for this age group (Blick & Porter, 1983; Cornman, 1989; Furniss et al., 1988; Gagliano, 1987; Goodwin & Talwar, 1989; Meiselman, 1990). Groups offer the advantage of harnessing the powerful influence of peer interactions and relationships that are already accented during this developmental stage. Oftentimes, teenagers will accept comments or interpretations from peers that would be rejected out of hand if they were offered by the adult therapist. Groups offer other intrinsic advantages: (a) Group norms can have a powerful socializing impact (Phelan, 1987); (b) members can vicariously benefit from the work of others, taking advantage of individual differences; (c) group therapy offers the opportunity to withdraw and listen without having to be "on the spot" throughout a session, thereby avoiding much of the silent "resistance" sometimes seen in individual work with teenagers; (d) the empowering and humanly meaningful experience of helping others is shared and not limited to the therapist; (e) support, normalization, and validation of experiences are readily available; (f) interpersonal styles, social skills, and change can be observed and implemented *in vivo;* (g) the sense of isolation and "differentness" can be diminished; and (h) in those cases in which parental or family support will never be adequate realistically, groups can provide a context for youngsters to learn to rely on peers as an alternate family.

However, group therapy is not appropriate for all abused adolescents. Although blanket referrals of adolescents to support or therapy groups is sometimes practiced, this is not recommended. Teenagers with severe depression, psychosis, or serious developmental delays, for example, not only may be overwhelmed or ostracized in a group but may disrupt the progress of others. Groups may not be appropriate for youngsters who do not have some ability to tolerate limits and control impulses or who are psychologically fragile or too acutely in crisis. Likewise, severely shy or antagonistic youngsters may not fare well. This is why screening and assessment are not luxuries but basics that cannot be ignored. With questionable candidates, it is preferable to spend some time in individual therapy preparing for the group than to risk a "failure" necessitating removal from the group with consequent individual as well as group disruption. Despite this caution, it has been our experience that the vast majority of teenagers who have been sexually abused are good candidates for group therapy and should participate if a group is available and assessment does not reveal any contraindications.

Abuse-focused groups can differ in duration (short-term vs. long-term), format (structured vs. unstructured), composition (coeducational vs. single gender), therapists (single vs. cotherapy; mixed vs. single gender) and membership (open-ended vs. closed). There is no accepted algorithm for selecting among these choices, which leaves the matter to be determined by clinical judgment. The clinician must weigh the exigencies of the particular client population, overall treatment program, and talents of available therapists in deriving a format. Our perspective is that shorter-term groups work well as an adjunct to individual therapy and when the format involves a set structure, closed membership, and more supportive and educative content. Where group is the core of the treatment program, however, there are advantages to longer-term, open-ended groups with looser structure and a more process-oriented format.

Our experience has been that teenagers will not tolerate too much structure for too long and eventually will usurp any efforts to constrain the topic of conversation or disallow time for freeform discussion of their day-to-day concerns. Nonetheless, even process-oriented group formats seem to benefit from some general boundaries (e.g., "We're mainly here to deal with sexual abuse") and a few established rituals or routines (Blick & Porter, 1983). These may be more important early in a group's life. Among adult survivors, less experienced patients have been found to do better in structured groups, but more experienced patients seem to benefit from a less structured format (Alexander, Neimeyer, & Follette, 1991). A format we have found useful is to allow group members to define their own structure by selecting or requesting topics for structured sessions while generally maintaining a moderately unstructured framework. Our experience has been that the group almost inevitably selects significant abuse-related topics for structured sessions and occasionally ones that require some creativity from the therapists (e.g., a session on the question of what

boys want or inviting a successful adult survivor as a guest speaker to talk about coping with the effects of abuse in later life).

There are, as yet, no data from which to evaluate the efficacy of group therapy with adolescents. Particularly lacking are studies making adequate between-treatment or treatment/no-treatment comparisons. One study of adult survivors found that group treatment, irrespective of format, was superior to a waiting list control, and treatment gains were maintained at a 6-month follow-up (Alexander, Neimeyer, Follette, Moore, & Harter, 1989). Although supporting the contention that group therapy can ameliorate abuse effects among adults, we can only speculate about its relevance to adolescents.

Individual therapy. The combination of individual therapy and group therapy often is seen as the optimal approach to treating an adolescent who has been sexually abused. However, it is not always possible to provide both, and some decision may need to be made regarding which modality is primary and which is adjunctive. There is no model for making this decision and no empirical data on which to base a determination, leaving us again in the domain of clinical judgment, therapist ability or availability, and the exigencies of workload and need. When there is a shortage of staff time and many referrals, using group treatment as a primary approach and individual therapy as supplementary is practical. In settings in which there are rarely enough teenagers to make up a relatively homogeneous group (e.g., a rural mental health clinic), using individual therapy as the primary modality might be preferred. Individual therapy complements group therapy by allowing greater privacy and time to focus on the unique needs of each youngster.

Like group therapies, individual therapies vary in duration and format. Deblinger et al. (1990) have described a structured, short-term, cognitive/behavioral treatment for sexually abused children with PTSD, using parallel modules for children and their nonabusing parent. Coping skills, modeling, gradual exposure, education, and prevention were used to target specific PTSD-related symptoms. Patients showed significant decreases from baseline in anxiety, depression, and behavior problems. Similar treatment approaches involving anxiety reduction techniques, stress inoculation therapy, exploration of attributions, cognitive restructuring, and problem-solving techniques have been described as useful clinically (Berliner & Wheeler, 1987; Saunders, 1992).

Longer-term and less structured individual therapies also are used for adolescents. Some treatment outcome data for sexually abused children suggest that longer-term treatment may be required in many cases before reduction in some categories of pathological symptomatology is seen (Lanktree & Briere, 1995). However, no data specifically on adolescents or the use of clear control or comparison groups have been reported currently. Among one group of hearing impaired adolescents with sexual abuse histories, those receiving long-term individual treatment fared better than a treatment refusal group (Sullivan, Scanlan, Brookhouser, Schulte, & Knutson, 1992). No published studies are available to date that draw comparisons between long-term and short-term approaches or different treatment models. Essentially nothing is known empirically regarding any number of critical questions. For example, it remains unclear whether lengthy, reconstructive treatment targeting in-depth issues offers any advantage over symptomatically focused treatment for either short- or long-term outcomes. The question of whether abuse sequelae in adulthood can be averted by treatment in childhood or adolescence is unanswered. Is it better to attempt to resolve all sexual abuse issues at the time of abuse or periodically when developmentally triggered difficulties emerge?

In the absence of answers to these and other questions, and given the vast need and limited treatment resources available for these patients, it is difficult to endorse a blanket recommendation for long-term, in-depth individual therapy for sexually abused adolescents. However, given the extreme symptoms that can be present in some cases (e.g., self-mutilation, severe depression, dissociative disorders), intensive individual treatment is imperative for at least some abused teenagers. Intensive individual work with adolescent patients manifesting these sorts of serious abuse sequelae can make heavy demands on the therapist, both personally and professionally. Dynamic or relationship-based trauma therapy is a highly intimate interaction between two people that is not readily reduced to discrete techniques or procedures. Therapists working regularly with these youngsters may experience vicarious traumatization (McCann & Pearlman, 1990) and must withstand sometimes being the object of intense emotional needs, rage, ambivalent attachments, projections, or distortions.

Therapists must be alert to the risks of overidentification with their patients, losing their perspective and impairing their ability to work with parents (abusive and nonabusive) or others in the system.

Therapists must be alert to the risks of overidentification with their patients, losing their perspective and impairing their ability to work with parents (abusive and nonabusive) or others in the system. Sexualized behaviors, either as a probe of trustworthiness or as the currency of affection, can test the mettle of even the most experienced therapist.

Remaining compassionate and objective without withdrawing, retaliating, defending, rejecting, reenacting abuse, or exploiting is not always easy but is critical in working through these processes. Regular consultation, either from peers or a formal supervisor, can be a welcome asset. For therapists whose own abuse issues are not well-resolved, who are uncomfortable with intimacy or intense emotion, or who tend to be caught repeatedly in interpersonal dilemmas with clients, personal therapy may be a responsible choice before continuing to see these youngsters in intensive individual therapy.

Acute inpatient treatment. In general, sexually abused adolescents are admitted to inpatient psychiatric facilities for the same reasons nonabused teenagers are: suicide attempts, uncontrolled substance abuse, or severe behavioral problems (Emslie & Rosenfeld, 1983). Unfortunately, some are admitted inappropriately simply on the basis of their history as abuse victims and the emotional upset that may accompany disclosure. Estimates of how many hospitalized teens have been abused vary. One survey of 110 inpatient facilities found histories of *detected* abuse in 48% of the girls and 16% of the boys (Kohan, Polthier, & Norbeck, 1986). Forty-two percent of teenaged boys and 71% to 90% of teenaged girls in inpatient substance abuse treatment report histories of childhood sexual abuse (Rohsenow, Corbett, & Devine, 1988). Findings suggest that for more than two thirds of physically and sexually abused teens in residential substance abuse treatment, their abuse has not been previously reported (Cavaiola & Schiff, 1988). Abuse status is not always known prior to admission, and it is common for disclosure to first occur during a hospitalization for what might be identified retrospectively as abuse sequelae. In these circumstances, investigation and treatment are simultaneous, and care must be taken that one does not interfere with or contaminate the other.

The key to minimizing these problems is for all involved to know and remain within their respective roles. This requires that the therapist work quickly to inform and cooperate with CPS at the earliest sign of disclosure. Having established joint CPS/hospital protocols for managing disclosures can be useful. The first goal, of course, is to ensure that all necessary steps have been taken to protect against further abuse prior to discharge, which is not always a simple matter, given decreasing length of hospital stays and the fact that disclosure may occur late in a hospitalization. Until a safety plan is in place, the young person cannot be discharged without risk.

In an acute inpatient setting, it is important to set limited and realistically achievable treatment goals because of the short amount of time available for treatment, often around 2 to 3 weeks. Working through abuse trauma and its associated defenses is not feasible. The goal within this time is to assist the teenager in instituting or reinstituting effective coping. Two goals that can be addressed during an acute hospitalization are developing a feeling of personal safety and increased self-control (Hartman & Burgess, 1988). To restore some feeling of predictability and safety, the inpatient unit must maintain a reliable structure and provide calm, unintrusive nurturance and support, even in the face of decompensation and disruptive behavior. Once the young person *is* safe and *feels* safe, treatment can fo-

cus on self-regulation and problem-solving strategies to help restore behavioral and emotional self-control. Structured teenage survivors groups can provide support, normalization, and information (Sturkie, 1983). Daily individual therapy can use any of the cognitive/behavioral techniques described earlier. In some cases, parent-child sessions can help ensure that adequate support is maintained outside the hospital.

Once a safety plan is in place and adequate self-control achieved, it is usually time for discharge. If possible, the hospital should be involved in developing a multidisciplinary or multiagency plan through a formal joint conference or liaison person to ensure that gains are maintained and appropriate follow-up treatment for the adolescent and family is instituted.

Treatment compliance. Unfortunately, not all teenagers who have been sexually abused or their parents will comply with recommendations for needed treatment. The reasons for this are no doubt complex and as yet not well-articulated, although trauma avoidance for both teenagers and their parents probably plays some role. In incest cases, some authoritative mandate for treatment to occur usually is thought to be necessary (Chaffin, 1992; Ryan, 1986). Haskett and colleagues found that approximately 35% of sexually abused children and adolescents failed their initial appointment (Haskett, Nowlan, Hutcheson, & Whitworth, 1991). African American children were more likely to fail the appointment than Caucasians (41% vs. 17%), consistent with the literature reflecting a trend that people of color will use informal helpers (e.g., ministers, neighbors, family) during times of crisis rather than the professional mental health system (Chatters, Taylor, & Neighbors, 1989; Neighbors, 1984). Consequently, it is critical that professional treatment delivery systems for abused teenagers and their families become more culturally competent and culturally relevant to meet the needs of broad and diverse groups of people.

Physical Abuse

Physical abuse among adolescents is underrecognized for several reasons. Compared with younger children, teenagers are seen as less helpless or vulnerable and more able to defend themselves against attack. Much like battered spouses, battered teenagers are perceived as "imperfect victims" capable of obtaining outside help if they really needed or wanted it, or whose abuse is seen as a mutual struggle for power and control rather than a victimization (Bonner et al., 1992). A survey of the literature suggests that between 25% and 47% of all physically abused children are teenagers, and adolescent abuse is more likely to involve female victims and male abusers than their younger counterparts (Doueck, Ishisaka, Sweany, & Gilchrist, 1987). Often self-reporting their own abuse, battered teenagers are more likely to have their complaints substantiated, although overall reporting rates are the lowest for any age group (Garbarino & Gilliam, 1980).

Like their sexually abused counterparts, physically abused teenagers make internal attributions about their abuse or may feel that they "deserved it" (Doueck et al., 1987). Others are likely to agree. Based on stereotypes of adolescence as a time of trouble and turmoil, a parent's physically assaultive behavior may be seen as justifiable discipline or reaction to unbearable teenage provocations. An adolescent in trouble at home is more likely to come to the attention of the juvenile justice system than the child protection system (Fisher & Berdie, 1978; Garbarino & Gilliam, 1980). Indeed, these youngsters' behavior often invites their being identified as the problem. Physical abuse histories are associated with court involvement, ungovernable behaviors, juvenile delinquency, substance abuse, and mental disorders (Bonner et al., 1992).

Much as with the onset of sexual abuse, physical abuse can begin in either adolescence or childhood. Seventy-five percent of the adolescent victims in one study were abused and neglected children grown older (Berdie, Berdie, Wexler, & Fisher, 1983). Many of their families have extensive histories of CPS involvement. Pelcovitz and colleagues have identified three onset patterns (Pelcovitz, Kaplan, Samit, Krieger, & Cornelius, 1984). In addition to childhood onset, two adolescent onset types are described, one involving parental rigidity and harshness increasingly challenged by the adolescent's strivings for independence and autonomy, and the other characterized by enmeshed and permissive parents whose long-sup-

pressed anger explodes as separation conflicts escalate. Adolescent onset abuse was described as carrying the more favorable prognosis.

Assessment

Lacking any abuse-focused or specific instruments or procedures, assessment recommendations follow along the same general lines described for sexual abuse. It is important to obtain a clear history and mental status, with special emphasis on the potential sequelae of physical abuse (Graziano & Mills, 1992; Kolko, 1992). As previously described, assessment should involve multiple target areas, including both general and abuse-specific targets, multiple assessment methodologies, and multiple sources of information. Target areas specifically relevant to physical abuse include (a) self-control and impulsivity, (b) aggressive behavior, (c) social skills and sensitivity, (d) cognitive skills and academic performance, (e) depression, (f) affective expression (other than anger), (g) history of delinquency, and (h) presence of PTSD-related symptoms. A variety of published psychological testing instruments are available that are appropriate for inclusion in a broad-based assessment and are described at length elsewhere (Bonner et al., 1992).

Treatment

Although both short- and long-term sequelae of physical child abuse have been identified, treatment approaches in general have been limited to intervention focused on parents or caregivers rather than the youngster's individual needs (Fantuzzo, 1990; Williams, 1983). However, without some attempt to repair the physical, cognitive, and emotional effects of the abuse, these teenagers remain at risk. Graziano and Mills (1992) argue that although treating abused children is only a "partial solution" (p. 217) to the problem of abuse, it is one needing increased emphasis, particularly in light of the availability of a variety of demonstrably effective treatment approaches for many of the types of behaviors and emotional problems commonly seen among physically abused teenagers.

Mann and Borduin (1991) reviewed psychotherapy outcome studies conducted between 1978 and 1988 on adolescents, mainly with externalizing behavior problems. Positive short-term outcomes were noted with social skills and assertiveness training, cognitive self-instructional techniques, and problem-solving training, although longer-term outcomes remained unclear. The evaluation of systemic family therapy noted that positive outcomes tended to be maintained over extended periods of time, suggesting that involvement of parents may be critical for successfully treating these sorts of problems. One well-researched approach, multisystemic therapy, has had excellent results for adolescents with delinquent behavior problems (Henggeler & Borduin, 1990).

Not all teenagers who have been physically abused fit the picture of an angry, aggressive, or violent youngster. Among a community sample, physical abuse alone has been found to be associated with an approximately doubled risk for eating disorders and sleep disturbances, greater than tripled risk for considering or attempting suicide, and an elevenfold increase in risk for sexual abuse (Hibbard et al., 1990). Farber and Joseph (1985) have described six different patterns of adjustment among physically abused adolescents, including depression, anxiety, emotional-thought disturbances, and helplessness-dependency, in addition to the more commonly mentioned externalizing sorts of behaviors. These more internalizing problems accounted for a full two thirds of their categorized subjects.

Unfortunately, AFT has yet to identify significantly the interplay of abuse dynamics, effects, and treatment approaches for physical abuse victims comparable to the relatively rich clinical literature available on sexual abuse. In the absence of this, symptomatically focused treatment within a context of the general philosophical and interpretative framework of AFT is suggested for these adolescents. Clinicians are encouraged to (a) draw from as varied a repertoire of clinical approaches as possible to meet the teenager's particular treatment needs, (b) use treatment approaches that are consistent with the adolescent's overall cognitive abilities, and (c) select techniques that have demonstrated effectiveness in ameliorating the target symptoms.

Treatment compliance. Most adolescents are at least partially dependent on their parents for transportation to and from treatment. Because parents themselves show high attrition rates in treatment, consideration should be given to methods of encouraging parental compliance. Available evidence supports the utility of court mandates for maintaining abusive parents' involvement (Irueste-Montes & Montes, 1988; Wolfe, Aragona, Kaufman, & Sandler, 1980). In addition, providers can strive to schedule sessions to coincide with those for parents, offer services at convenient times, and encourage parental input and involvement in their teenager's treatment.

Psychological Abuse

Claussen and Crittenden (1991) studied psychological maltreatment in a sample of physically abused and nonabused children, finding that where there was physical abuse, psychological abuse was invariably present and associated with detrimental effects. Some have argued that because its effects are largely psychological, sexual abuse can also be viewed as a form of psychological abuse (Brassard & McNeill, 1987). Psychological abuse also can exist in isolation from other types of abuse, although these cases seem to rarely enter the child protection system. In either case, psychological maltreatment appears to be associated with poor outcomes for children.

Studies of psychological maltreatment among adolescents are few, and the literature on treatment interventions for psychological abuse is largely limited to describing work with abusive parents whose children are young (Bonner et al., 1992). Nonetheless, clinical experience suggests that teenagers often internalize the rejecting, belittling, or threatening aspects of their parents and may experience a variety of both internalizing and externalizing problems. Depression, aggression, conduct disorders, substance abuse, and relationship dysfunction are among the potential consequences (Hart, Germain, & Brassard, 1987).

Assessment

Psychological, abuse-specific instruments for adolescents are virtually nonexistent. Consequently, assessment must focus on obtaining a broad-based picture of the youngster, with particular emphasis on the more likely abuse sequelae. Parent report information should be interpreted cautiously due to potential tendencies to present the youngster in an overly negative light and compared to information obtained from teachers, peers, or others, if available. Direct observation of parent-child interaction, when possible, is recommended.

Treatment

Much like their parents, psychologically abused teenagers need assistance in learning new models of relating and communicating with others. Group therapy, communication skills training, or other socially based treatments may be helpful. In addition, cognitive techniques may be useful in addressing the internalized cognitions and self-definitions associated with depression and low self-efficacy expectations (DeRubeis & Beck, 1988). For some, the individualized attention and the long-term stable and supportive relationship of intensive individual therapy may be required.

Future Directions

Treatment Outcome

Throughout this chapter, we have commented on the glaring absence of outcome data in this field, despite the massive and growing numbers of children and adolescents receiving services. We know far more about the efficacy of programs for treating sexual offenders than we do about programs for treating sexually abused children or adolescents. This is ironic, considering that there are always far more victims than offenders in treatment. Beyond answering the overly global question—Does treatment help?—lie more complex questions about what sorts of treatments help with what sorts of youngsters in what sorts of settings and circumstances. We need to know how cultural factors affect treatment outcomes. We need to know if various approaches are differentially effective depending on abuse-related factors or developmental phase. Also, the questions raised earlier in this chapter regarding long-term versus short-term treatment and intensive versus periodic approaches remain unad-

dressed. Finkelhor and colleagues (Finkelhor, Hotaling, & Yllö, 1988) and Friedrich (1991) have outlined a number of specific research questions for the field. These are not simply esoteric intellectual questions: They are fundamental pieces of knowledge that are necessary to articulate any coherent response to child maltreatment. Answering these questions will require not only collaborative efforts between clinicians and researchers but also a real commitment on the part of public policymakers to fund far more research and provide a far more coordinated federal research management system for this field (Melton & Flood, 1994).

Treatment as Prevention

Despite widespread evidence that abused adolescents are at higher risk for becoming abusive parents, sometimes even before their own abuse or their adolescence ends, there has been little investigation of the impact of treatment interventions on this process.

Although no controlled data are available on the process, tentative findings have suggested that participation in psychotherapy may be one of many factors that distinguish those who break from those who repeat the cycle.

Although no controlled data are available on the process, tentative findings have suggested that participation in psychotherapy may be one of many factors that distinguish those who break from those who repeat the cycle (Egeland, 1993). It is not clear, however, what components of treatment may be responsible for this effect. To maximize any effect on intergenerational transmission of abuse rates, victim treatment may need to directly address "abuser issues," such as child-rearing skills, appropriate versus inappropriate sexual behavior, anger management, and conflict resolution skills (Burgess et al., 1991; Ryan, 1989). Although this is not to suggest that treatment of abused adolescents should acquire an either explicitly or implicitly

accusatory tone regarding these young- ventions with abused adolescents in an ac-
sters' future parental behavior, ignoring cepting and supportive way may require
the issue of teenagers' risk in their future modifying and integrating aspects of
roles as parents is not wise. Recognizing abuser treatment into our treatment of
this risk and incorporating it into inter- victims.

Note

1. Traumatic neurosis today would generally be termed *posttraumatic stress disorder.*

References

Adams-Wescott, J., & Isenbart, D. (1990). *Using rituals to empower family members who have experienced child sexual abuse.* Unpublished manuscript, Family and Children's Services, Inc., Tulsa, OK.

Alexander, P., Neimeyer, R., & Follette, V. (1991). Group therapy for women sexually abused as children: A controlled study and investigation of individual differences. *Journal of Interpersonal Violence, 6,* 218-231.

Alexander, P., Neimeyer, R., Follette, V., Moore, M., & Harter, S. (1989). A comparison of group treatments of women sexually abused as children. *Journal of Consulting and Clinical Psychology, 57,* 479-483.

American Professional Society on the Abuse of Children (APSAC). (1990). *Guidelines for psychosocial evaluation of suspected sexual abuse in young children.* Chicago: Author.

Aries, P. (1962). *Centuries of childhood: A social history on family life.* New York: Random House.

Beitchman, J., Zucker, K., Hood, J., daCosta, G., & Akman, D. (1991). Short-term effects of child sexual abuse. *Child Abuse & Neglect, 15,* 537-556.

Beitchman, J., Zucker, K., Hood, J., daCosta, G., Akman, D., & Cassavia, E. (1992). A review of the long-term effects of child sexual abuse. *Child Abuse & Neglect, 16,* 101-118.

Berdie, J., Berdie, M., Wexler, S., & Fisher, B. (1983). *An empirical study of families involved in adolescent maltreatment.* San Francisco: URSA Institute.

Berliner, L., & Wheeler J. (1987). Treating the effects of sexual abuse on children. *Journal of Interpersonal Violence, 2,* 415-434.

Blick, L., & Porter, F. (1983). Group therapy with female adolescent incest victims. In S. Sgroi (Ed.), *Handbook of clinical intervention in child sexual abuse* (pp. 147-175). Lexington, MA: Lexington Books.

Bonner, B., Kaufman, K., Harbeck, C., & Brassard, M. (1992). Child maltreatment. In C. E. Walker & M. C. Roberts (Eds.), *Handbook of clinical child psychology* (pp. 967-1008). New York: John Wiley.

Brassard, M., & McNeill, L. (1987). Child sexual abuse. In M. Brassard, R. Bermain, & S. Hart (Eds.), *Psychological maltreatment of children and youth* (pp. 89-100). Elmsford, NY: Pergamon.

Breuer, J., & Freud, S. (1955). Studies in hysteria. In J. Strachey (Ed. & Trans.), *Standard edition of the complete works of Sigmund Freud* (Vol 2, pp. 1-310). London: Hogarth. (Original publication 1895)

Briere, J. (1989). *Therapy for adults molested as children: Beyond survival.* New York: Springer.

Briere, J. (1992). *Child abuse trauma: Theory and treatment of the lasting effects.* Newbury Park, CA: Sage.

Briere, J. (in press). *Trauma symptom checklist for children.* Odessa, FL: Psychological Assessment Resources.

Briere, J., & Runtz, M. (1986). Suicidal thoughts and behaviors in former sexual abuse victims. *Canadian Journal of Behavioral Sciences, 18,* 413-423.

Brooks-Gunn, J., & Furstenberg, F. (1989). Adolescent sexual behavior. *American Psychologist, 44,* 249-257.

Browne, A., & Finkelhor, D. (1986). Impact of child sexual abuse: A review of the research. *Psychological Bulletin, 99,* 66-77.

Burgess, A., Hartman, C., Grant, C., Clover, C., Snyder, W., & King, L. (1991). Drawing a connection from victim to victimizer. *Journal of Psychosocial Nursing, 29,* 9-14.

Cavaiola, A., & Schiff, M. (1988). Behavioral sequelae of physical and/or sexual abuse in adolescents. *Child Abuse & Neglect, 12,* 181-188.

Celano, M. (1992). A developmental model of victims' internal attributions of responsibility for sexual abuse. *Journal of Interpersonal Violence, 7,* 57-69.

Chaffin, M. (1992). Factors associated with treatment compliance and progress among intrafamilial sexual abusers. *Child Abuse & Neglect, 16,* 251-264.

Chaffin, M. (1994). Treating both the victim and the offender in sexual abuse: Can one therapist do both? *Violence Update, 4,* 3, 8.

Chatters, L., Taylor, R., & Neighbors, H. (1989). Size of informal helper network mobilized during a serious personal problem among black Americans. *Journal of Marriage and the Family, 51,* 667-676.

Claussen, A. H., & Crittenden, P. M. (1991). Physical and psychological maltreatment: Relations among types of maltreatment. *Child Abuse & Neglect, 15,* 5-18.

Collings, S., & Payne, M. (1991). Attribution of causal and moral responsibility to victims of father-daughter incest: An exploratory examination of five factors. *Child Abuse & Neglect, 15,* 513-521.

Coons, P., Bowman, E., Pellow, T., & Schneider, P. (1989). Post-traumatic aspects of the treatment of victims of sexual abuse and incest. *Psychiatric Clinics of North America, 12,* 325-335.

Cornman, B. (1989). Group treatment for female adolescent sexual abuse victims. *Issues in Mental Health Nursing, 10,* 261-271.

Crockett, L., & Petersen, A. (1987). Pubertal status and psychosocial development: Findings from the early adolescence study. In R. Lerner & T. Foch (Eds.), *Biological-psychosocial interactions in early adolescence: A life-span perspective.* Hillsdale, NJ: Lawrence Erlbaum.

Deblinger, E. (1991). Diagnosis of posttraumatic stress disorder in childhood. *Violence Update,* 2(1), 9-11.

Deblinger, E., McLeer, S., & Henry, D. (1990). Cognitive behavioral treatment for sexually abused children suffering post-traumatic stress: Preliminary findings. *Journal of the American Academy of Child and Adolescent Psychiatry, 29,* 747-752.

DeRubeis, R., & Beck, A. (1988). Cognitive therapy. In K. Dobson (Ed.), *Handbook of cognitive-behavioral therapies* (pp. 273-307). New York: Guilford.

Doueck, H., Ishisaka, A., Sweany, S., & Gilchrist, L. (1987). Adolescent maltreatment: Themes from the empirical literature. *Journal of Interpersonal Violence, 2,* 139-153.

Egeland, B. (1993). A history of abuse is a major risk factor for abusing the next generation. In R. Gelles & D. Loseke (Eds.), *Current controversies on family violence* (pp. 197-208). Newbury Park, CA: Sage.

Emslie, G., & Rosenfeld, A. (1983). Incest reported by children and adolescents hospitalized for severe psychiatric problems. *American Journal of Psychiatry, 140,* 708-711.

Enright, R., Lapsley, D., & Shukla, D. (1979). Adolescent egocentrism in early and late adolescence. *Adolescence, 14,* 687-696.

Evans, J., Briere, J., Boggiano, A., & Barrett, M. (1994, January). *Reliability and validity of the trauma symptom checklist for children in a normal child sample.* Paper presented at the San Diego Conference on Responding to Child Maltreatment, San Diego.

Everson, M. D., Hunter, W. M., Runyan, D. K., Edelsohn, G. A., & Coulter, M. L. (1989). Maternal support following disclosure of incest. *American Journal of Orthopsychiatry, 59,* 197-207.

Faller, K. (1991). Treatment of boy victims of sexual abuse. *APSAC Advisor, 4*(4), 7-8.

Fantuzzo, J. (1990). Behavioral treatment of the victims of child abuse and neglect. *Behavior Modification, 14,* 316-339.

Farber, E., & Joseph, J. (1985). The maltreated adolescent: Patterns of physical abuse. *Child Abuse & Neglect, 9,* 201-206.

Fenichel, O. (1945). *The psychoanalytic theory of neurosis.* New York: Norton.

Finkelhor, D. (1988). The trauma of child sexual abuse: Two models. In G. Wyatt & G. Powell (Eds.), *Lasting effects of child sexual abuse* (pp. 61-82). Newbury Park, CA: Sage.

Finkelhor, D., & Browne, A. (1985). The traumatic impact of childhood sexual abuse: A conceptualization. *American Journal of Orthopsychiatry, 55,* 530-541.

Finkelhor, D., & Dzuiba-Leatherman, J. (1994). Victimization of children. *American Psychologist, 49,* 173-184.

Finkelhor, D., Hotaling, G., & Yllö, K. (1988). *Stopping family violence: Research priorities for the coming decade.* Newbury Park, CA: Sage.

Fisher, B., & Berdie, J. (1978). Adolescent abuse and neglect: Issues of incidence, intervention, and service delivery. *Child Abuse & Neglect, 2,* 178-192.

Freud, S. (1905). Fragment of an analysis of a case of hysteria. In J. Strachey (Ed. & Trans.), *Standard edition of the complete works of Sigmund Freud* (Vol. 7, pp. 1-122). London: Hogarth.

Friedrich, W. (1990). *Psychotherapy of sexually abused children and their families.* New York: Norton.

Friedrich, W. (1991). Child victims: Promising techniques and programs in the treatment of child sexual abuse. *APSAC Advisor, 4*(2), 5-6.

Furniss, T., Bingley-Miller, L., & Van Elburg, A. (1988). Goal-oriented group treatment for sexually abused adolescent girls. *British Journal of Psychiatry, 152,* 97-106.

Gagliano, C. (1987). Group treatment for sexually abused girls. *Social Casework, 68,* 102-108.

Garbarino, J., & Gilliam, G. (1980). *Understanding abusive families.* Lexington, MA: Lexington Books.

Gelinas, D. (1983). The persisting negative effects of incest. *Psychiatry, 46,* 312-332.

Gil, E. (1991). *The healing power of play: Working with abused children.* New York: Guilford.

Gomes-Schwartz, B., Horowitz, J., & Cardarelli, A. (1990). *Child sexual abuse: The initial effects.* Newbury Park, CA: Sage.

Gomes-Schwartz, B., Horowitz, J., & Sauzier, M. (1985). Severity of emotional distress among sexually abused preschool, school-age, and adolescent children. *Hospital and Community Psychiatry, 36,* 503-508.

Goodwin, J., & Talwar, N. (1989). Group psychotherapy for victims of incest. *Psychiatric Clinics of North America, 12,* 279-293.

Graziano, A., & Mills, J. (1992). Treatment for abused children: When is a partial solution acceptable? *Child Abuse & Neglect, 16,* 217-228.

Hart, S., & Brassard, M. (1990). Psychological maltreatment of children. In R. Ammerman & M. Hersen (Eds.), *Treatment of family violence* (pp. 77-112). New York: John Wiley.

Hart, S., Germain, R., & Brassard, M. (1987). The challenge: To better understand and combat psychological maltreatment of children and youth. In M. Brassard, R. Germain, & S. Hart (Eds.), *Psychological maltreatment of children and youth* (pp. 3-25). Elmsford, NY: Pergamon.

Hartman, C., & Burgess, A. (1988). Information processing of trauma: Case application of a model. *Journal of Interpersonal Violence, 3,* 443-457.

Hayes, C. (1987). *Risking the future: Adolescent sexuality, pregnancy, and childbearing.* Washington, DC: National Academy Press.

Haskett, M. E., Nowlan, N. P., Hutcheson, J. S., & Whitworth, J. M. (1991). Factors associated with successful entry into therapy in child sexual abuse cases. *Child Abuse & Neglect, 15,* 467-476.

Henggeler, S. W., & Borduin, C. M. (1990). *Treatment of delinquent behavior: Family therapy and beyond: A multisystemic approach to treating the behavior problems of children and adolescents.* Pacific Grove, CA: Brooks/Cole.

Hibbard, R., Ingersoll, G., & Orr, D. (1990). Behavioral risk, emotional risk, and child abuse among adolescents in a nonclinical setting. *Pediatrics, 86,* 896-901.

Hunter, M. (1990). *The sexually abused male: Vol. 2. Application of treatment strategies.* Lexington, MA: Lexington Books.

Irueste-Montes, A., & Montes, F. (1988). Court-ordered vs. voluntary treatment of abusive and neglectful parents. *Child Abuse & Neglect, 12,* 33-39.

Jessor, R., & Jessor, L. (1977). *Problem behavior and psychological development.* New York: Academic Press.

Johnson, B., & Kenkel, M. (1991). Stress, coping and adjustment in female adolescent incest victims. *Child Abuse & Neglect, 15,* 293-305.

Kandel, D., & Lesser, G. (1972). *Youth in two worlds.* San Francisco: Jossey-Bass.

Kohan, M., Polthier, P., & Norbeck, J. (1986). Hospitalized children with history of sexual abuse: Incidence and care issues. *American Journal of Orthopsychiatry, 57,* 258-264.

Kolko, D. (1992). Characteristics of child victims of physical violence: Research findings and clinical implications. *Journal of Interpersonal Violence, 7,* 244-276.

Lanktree, C., & Briere, J. (1995). Outcome of therapy for sexually abused children: A repeated measures study. *Child Abuse & Neglect, 19,* 1145-1155.

Lanktree, C., Briere, J., & Zaidi, L. (1991). Incidence and impact of sexual abuse in a child outpatient sample: The role of direct inquiry. *Child Abuse & Neglect, 15,* 447-453.

Leitenberg, H., Greenwald, E., & Cado, S. (1992). A retrospective study of long-term methods of coping with having been sexually abused during childhood. *Child Abuse & Neglect, 16,* 399-407.

Levine, S. (1987). The myths and needs of contemporary youth. *Adolescent Psychiatry, 14,* 48-62.

Lipovsky, J. (1991). Posttraumatic stress disorder in children. *Family and Community Health, 14,* 42-51.

Lipovsky, J. (1992, February). *Research in action: Children in court.* Paper presented at the Eighth Annual National Symposium on Child Sexual Abuse, Huntsville, AL.

Mann, B., & Borduin, C. (1991). A critical review of psychotherapy outcome studies with adolescents: 1978-1988. *Adolescence, 26,* 505-540.

McCann, L., & Pearlman, L. (1990). Vicarious traumatization: A framework for understanding the psychological effects of working with victims. *Journal of Traumatic Stress, 3,* 131-149.

McCormack, A., Burgess, A., & Hartman, C. (1988). Familial abuse and post-traumatic stress disorder. *Journal of Traumatic Stress, 1,* 231-242.

Meiselman, K. (1990). *Resolving the trauma of incest: Reintegration therapy with survivors.* San Francisco: Jossey-Bass.

Melton, G., & Flood, M. (1994). Research policy and child maltreatment: Developing the scientific foundation for effective protection of children. *Child Abuse & Neglect, 18,* 1-28.

Morrow, K. (1991). Attributions of female adolescent incest victims regarding their molestation. *Child Abuse & Neglect, 15,* 477-483.

Murphy, S., Kilpatrick, D., Amick-McMullan, A., Veronen, L., Paduhovich, J., Best, C., Villeponteaux, L., & Saunders, B. (1988). Current psychological functioning of child sexual assault survivors. *Journal of Interpersonal Violence, 3,* 55-79.

Neighbors, H. (1984). Professional help use among black Americans: Implications for unmet need. *American Journal of Community Psychology, 12,* 551-565.

NIS-II study findings: Study of national incidence and prevalence of child abuse and neglect. (1988). Washington, DC: U.S. Department of Health and Human Services—National Center on Child Abuse and Neglect.

Noshpitz, J., & King, R. (1991). *Pathways of growth: Essentials of child psychiatry: Vol I. Normal development.* New York: John Wiley.

Offer, D., & Boxer, A. (1991). Normal adolescent development: Empirical research findings. In M. Lewis (Ed.), *Child and adolescent psychiatry: A comprehensive textbook.* Baltimore, MD: Williams and Wilkins.

Offer, D., Ostrov, E., & Howard, K. (1981). The mental health professional's concept of the normal adolescent. *Archives of General Psychiatry, 38,* 149-152.

Pelcovitz, D., Kaplan, S., Samit, C., Krieger, R., & Cornelius, P. (1984). Adolescent abuse: Family structure and implications for treatment. *Journal of the American Academy of Child Psychiatry, 23,* 85-90.

Petersen, A. (1988). Adolescent development. *Annual Review of Psychology, 39,* 583-607.

Phelan, P. (1987). Incest: Socialization within a treatment program. *American Journal of Orthopsychiatry, 57,* 84-92.

Porter, E. (1986). *Treating the young male victim of sexual assault: Issues and intervention strategies.* Syracuse, NY: Safer Society Press.

Powers, S., Hauser, S., & Kilner, L. (1989). Adolescent mental health. *American Psychologist, 44,* 200-208.

Rew, L., & Esparza, D. (1990). Barriers to disclosure among sexually abused male children: Implications for nursing practice. *Journal of Child and Adolescent Psychiatric and Mental Health Nursing, 3,* 120-127.

Rohsenow, D., Corbett, R., & Devine, D. (1988). Molested as children: A hidden contribution to substance abuse? *Journal of Substance Abuse Treatment, 5,* 13-18.

Runtz, M., & Briere, J. (1986). Adolescent "acting-out" and childhood history of sexual abuse. *Journal of Interpersonal Violence, 1,* 326-334.

Russell, D. (1986). *The secret trauma: Incest in the lives of girls and women.* New York: Basic Books.

Ryan, G. (1989). Victim to victimizer: Rethinking victim treatment. *Journal of Interpersonal Violence, 4,* 325-341.

Ryan, T. (1986). Problems, errors and opportunities in the treatment of father-daughter incest. *Journal of Interpersonal Violence, 1,* 113-124.

Saunders, B. (1992, March). *Treatment of child sexual assault: A family systems-multicomponent approach.* Paper presented at the annual meeting of the South Carolina Chapter of the National Association of Social Workers, Columbia, SC.

Sedney, M., & Brooks, B. (1984). Factors associated with a history of childhood sexual experience in a nonclinical female population. *Journal of the American Academy of Child Psychiatry, 23,* 215-218.

Shapiro, J., Leifer, M., Martone, M., & Kassem, L. (1990). Multimethod assessment of depression in sexually abused girls. *Journal of Personality Assessment, 55,* 234-248.

Shapiro, S., & Dominiak, G. (1990). Common psychological defenses seen in the treatment of sexually abused adolescents. *American Journal of Psychotherapy, 44,* 68-74.

Sirles, F., Smith, J., & Kusama, H. (1989). Psychiatric status of intrafamilial child sexual abuse victims. *Journal of the American Academy of Child and Adolescent Psychiatry, 28,* 225-229.

Sorensen, T., & Snow, B. (1991). How children tell: The process of disclosure in child sexual abuse. *Child Welfare, 70,* 3-15.

Sturkie, K. (1983). Structured group treatment for sexually abused children. *Health and Social Work, 8,* 299-308.

Sullivan, P. M., Scanlan, J. M., Brookhouser, P. E., Schulte, L., & Knutson, J. (1992). The effects of psychotherapy on behavior problems of sexually abused deaf children. *Child Abuse & Neglect, 16,* 297-307.

Tanner, J. (1981). *A history of the study of human growth.* Cambridge, MA: Harvard University Press.

Tedesco, J., & Schnell, S. (1987). Children's reactions to sex abuse investigation and litigation. *Child Abuse & Neglect, 11,* 267-272.

White, M. (1989, Summer). The externalizing of the problem. *Dulwich Centre Newsletter,* pp. 1-20.

Williams, G. (1983). Child abuse reconsidered: The urgency of authentic prevention. *Journal of Clinical Child Psychology, 12,* 312-319.

Wolfe, D., Aragona, J., Kaufman, K., & Sandler, J. (1980). The importance of adjudication in the treatment of child abuse: Some preliminary findings. *Child Abuse & Neglect, 4,* 127-135.

Wolfe, V., & Gentile, C. (1991). *The children's impact of traumatic events scale—Revised (CITES-R).* (Available from the authors at the Department of Psychology, Children's Hospital of Western Ontario, 800 Commissioners Rd., E. London, Ontario, N6A4G5 Canada)

Wolfe, V., & Wolfe, D. (1988). The sexually abused child. In E. Mash & L. Terdal (Eds.), *Behavioral assessment of childhood disorders* (2nd ed., pp. 670-714). New York: Guilford.

Wyatt, G. (1988). The relationship between child sexual abuse and adolescent sexual functioning in Afro-American and white American women. *Annals of the New York Academy of Sciences, 528,* 111-122.

Wyatt, G., & Mickey, M. (1987). Ameliorating the effects of child sexual abuse: An exploratory study of support by parents and others. *Journal of Interpersonal Violence, 2,* 403-414.

8

A Self-Trauma Model for Treating Adult Survivors of Severe Child Abuse

JOHN BRIERE

This chapter presents a general theoretical model of symptom development and a subsequent therapeutic focus for adults severely abused as children. Most of this material can be found in the extant therapy or trauma literature, except for some newer hypotheses regarding the role of intrusive experiences and emotional discharge.

The perspective presented in this chapter, hereafter referred to as the self-trauma model, integrates aspects of four general psychotherapeutic approaches (trauma, self-psychology, cognitive, and behavior therapy) within a developmental perspective. It assumes that major[1] childhood abuse and neglect often disrupt child development and produce later symptomatology in several different ways: (a) by altering early childhood attachment dynamics, (b) through the effects of early posttraumatic stress on subsequent development, (c) by motivating the development of (necessarily) primitive coping strategies, and (d) by distorting the child's cognitive understanding of self, others, and the future.

This chapter describes the therapeutic implications of the self-trauma model in terms of therapeutic process and the specific content and goals of abuse-relevant psychotherapy. Because abuse-focused theory and intervention are still at a relatively early stage of development, this chapter, out of necessity, will rely less on empirical data and more on clinical hypotheses than is true of most other chapters in this book. Finally, it should be noted that the long-term psychological effects of severe childhood abuse are often complex and frequently include difficulties beyond the trauma and self-disturbance addressed in this chapter. For additional information on abuse effects and treatment approaches, the reader is referred to recent books by Briere (1992), Courtois (1988), Davies and Frawley (1994), Jehu (1988), Meiselman (1990), and Salter (1995), as well as chapters by Berliner and Elliott (Chapter 3, this volume), Briere and Runtz (1991), Courtois (1991), Meiselman (1994), and Neumann (1994).

Theory of Symptom Development

A central theoretical tenet of modern trauma therapy concerns the individual's need to accommodate traumatic distress through the application of internal resources. The extent to which a given stimulus or event is perceived as traumatic is thought to be a function of the degree to which it challenges the ability of the individual to "handle" it through internal coping strategies, generally referred to as self-resources and capacities (McCann & Pearlman, 1990). Self-trauma theory hypothesizes that the relative failure of internal capacities to resolve overwhelming trauma produces a psychological imbalance that, in turn, triggers intrusive posttraumatic responses such as flashbacks, nightmares, and other "reexperiencing" phenomena. In contradistinction to more classical pathology models, the self-trauma model suggests that these intrusive responses are not merely symptoms of dysfunction but rather are biological mechanisms evolved to serve an important psychological function—that of reducing the internal impact of trauma to the point that it eventually can

be accommodated by existing self-capacities.

Self-Functions and Capacities

Although a variety of self-capacities and resources have been posited (e.g., see McCann & Pearlman's [1990] innovative constructivist self-development theory), three are most related to the individual's response to aversive events: identity, boundary, and affect regulation.

Identity refers to a consistent sense of personal existence, of an internal locus of conscious awareness. A strong sense of personal identity is helpful in the face of potentially traumatic events because it allows the individual to respond from a secure internal base, wherein challenging stimuli can be readily organized and contextualized without excessive confusion or disorientation (Hamilton, 1988). Individuals whose sense of identity is less stable, or who "lose track" of themselves in the face of upsetting events, easily may become overwhelmed; they may become less internally organized and may fragment at those times when awareness of their own needs, perspectives, entitlements, and goals are most necessary.

Boundary is closely related to identity, in that it refers to an individual's awareness of the demarcation between self and others. People said to have poor or weak boundaries have difficulty knowing where their identities, needs, and perspectives end and others' begin, such that they either allow others to intrude on them or they inappropriately transgress on others (Elliott, 1994). An absence of boundaries, when confronted with a stressor, can reduce the individual's ability to negotiate interpersonal interactions, leading to, for example, difficulties in self-other discrimination, effective help seeking, and self-assertion in the face of victimization. In addition, the boundary-impaired victim of a traumatic assault may be less aware of his or her rights to safety, leading to inappropriate acceptance of being victimized.

The third self-function described here, that of *affect regulation,* has been viewed as quite important to the individual's management of potentially traumatic experiences (Briere, 1992; Linehan, 1993; Chapter 6, this volume). Affect regulation may be divided into two subfunctions: affect modulation and affect tolerance. The first refers to the individual's ability to engage in internal activities that in some way allow him or her to reduce or change negative affective states (Linehan, 1993; McCann & Pearlman, 1990). Activities thought to assist in affect modulation include self-soothing, positive self-talk, placing upsetting events in perspective, and self-distraction. Affect tolerance, on the other hand, refers to the individual's relative ability to experience sustained negative affects without having to resort to external activities that distract or soothe, or avoidance through the use of psychoactive substances. For example, people with good affect tolerance may be able to experience considerable frustration, anxiety, or anger without engaging in tension reduction behaviors (Briere, 1992) such as aggression, self-mutilatory activities, sexual "acting out," or self-destructiveness.

Normal development of self-functions. The self-functions described earlier are thought to arise from normal childhood development, primarily in the first years of life (Cole & Putnam, 1992). Identity and boundary awareness, for example, appear to unfold in the context of normal parent-child attachment experiences (Alexander, 1992). As the child interacts in the context of one or more consistent, loving, and supportive caretakers, a sense of self in contradistinction to "other" develops. This sense of self incorporates the sustained and reliable positive responses of the caregiver, typically leading to self-esteem, self-efficacy, and a view of others and the interpersonal environment as essentially benign. In combination, these and related processes result in a sense of internal stability: a secure psychological base from which to interact with the world (Bowlby, 1982).

As the child develops in a generally positive (or at least "good enough") environment, he or she nevertheless encounters a variety of surmountable obstacles or challenges—ranging from diaper rash to small frustrations to momentarily unavailable caretakers. In the context of sustained external security, the child learns to deal with the associated uncomfortable (but not overwhelming) internal states through trial and error, slowly building a progressively more sophisticated set of internal coping strategies as he or she grows and confronts increasingly more challenging and stressful experiences. At the same time, because the associated discomfort does not exceed the child's grow-

ing internal resources, he or she is able to become more and more at home with some level of distress and is able to tolerate greater levels of emotional pain. This growing affective competence is thought to be self-sustaining: As the individual becomes better able to modulate and tolerate distress or dysphoria, such discomfort becomes less destabilizing, and the individual is able to seek more challenging and complex interactions with the environment without being derailed by concomitant increases in stress and anxiety.

Effects of Abuse and Neglect on Self-Functions

Because the development of self-capacities and self-functions occurs during childhood, child abuse or neglect is an unfortunately potent source of later self-difficulties (Cole & Putnam, 1992; Elliott, 1994). For ease of explication, such maltreatment and its impacts of self-development will be divided into two categories: acts of omission and acts of commission.

Acts of omission. Most typically, child maltreatment in this category consists of child neglect. In general, psychological neglect of children refers to sustained parental nonresponsiveness and psychological unavailability, such that the child is deprived of the normal psychological stimulation and support described in Chapter 1 of this volume. One of the most obvious impacts of child neglect is its tendency to decrease the extent to which secure parent-child attachment can occur. As a result, the child may not be as likely to encounter social experiences that teach self-confidence, self-efficacy, complex social skills, and regulated affective responses to manageable interpersonal challenges.

In addition to the obvious effects of parental nonavailability on intra- and interpersonal learning, neglect is thought to produce acute psychological distress (Bowlby, 1988). Because children are social beings with profound biopsychological needs for contact comfort, nurturance, and love, sustained psychological neglect can result in painful core feelings of deprivation and abandonment. This pain, in turn, may affect the child's development in many of the same ways described below for caretaker acts of commission. Also present may be a growing sense of psychological emptiness and neediness and a general tendency later in life to be especially sensitive to the possibility of abandonment, rejection, or isolation.

Acts of commission. In contrast to acts of omission, acts of commission involve actual abusive behaviors directed toward the child. These acts can produce long-standing difficulties in self-functioning and can directly stimulate trauma-related symptoms (Pynoos, 1993; Chapter 6, this volume). As opposed to acts of omission, acts of commission during early childhood are injurious by virtue of their ability to disrupt normal development, produce intrusive reexperiencing, and motivate primitive avoidance strategies.

Implicit in the normal attachment process is the child's growing sense of safety and security—a base from which he or she can remain maximally "open" to experience and from which he or she can explore intra- and interpersonal environments and develop increasingly sophisticated self-skills (Bowlby, 1988). In the case of child abuse, however, safety is diminished or disappears altogether.

> *Faced with parental violence, the child may develop an avoidant style of relating, wherein he or she psychologically attenuates or avoids attachment interactions with a given abusive caretaker.*

Faced with parental violence, the child may develop an avoidant style of relating, wherein he or she psychologically attenuates or avoids attachment interactions with a given abusive caretaker. Although this defense protects the child from pain, to some extent, and further distorted environmental input, it also tends to reduce his or her responsivity to any positive attachment stimuli that might be available in the environment.[2] This response, in turn, further deprives the child of normal attachment-related learning and development, reinforces avoidance as a primary response style, and may partially replicate the self-difficulties associated with neglect-related attachment deprivation.

It is likely that one of the primary ways in which the child avoids is through disso-

ciation. A defensive alteration in the normal links between thoughts, feelings, and memory (Briere, 1992), dissociation can be called on to reduce distress by decreasing awareness of upsetting events and by numbing or attenuating perception of painful internal states (Putnam, 1985). Thus, the child dissociatively may exclude complete awareness of negative events in an attempt to survive relatively uncontrollable childhood trauma and may divert or suppress normal (probably biological) attachment responses. As noted earlier, this is likely to generalize in severe cases to the point that it reduces the amount of normal attachment-specific learning and development that can occur. However, except for the most profound cases, this dissociation is less than continual or complete. As a result, some abuse-related material continues to be internalized rather than deflected or compartmentalized, presenting later as negative views of self, others, and the environment.

Beyond its impacts on attachment, dissociation during early abuse would seemingly reduce opportunities for learning how to tolerate painful affect without avoidance. Dissociation is also likely to preclude the need to develop other, more complex and conscious affect regulation skills. In the words of one survivor in treatment, "I spaced out [during] most of my childhood. I was never around to learn regular ways of dealing with hassles." This forced reliance on dissociation during early childhood thus motivates the continued need for dissociation and other primitive avoidance strategies later in life.

Finally, child abuse distorts the victim's perceptions and understanding of self. As described by various writers (e.g., Janoff-Bulman, 1992; Jehu, 1988; Peterson & Seligman, 1983), abuse may teach the child that he or she is helpless (i.e., to avoid the abuse), inadequate (i.e., to mount a successful defense), and loathsome (i.e., to deserve such maltreatment)—lessons the individual will continue to apply later in life. A chaotic and painful childhood also may easily inform the child regarding what to expect of relationships, persons in authority, and vulnerability (Brown, 1988). It is in this regard that attachment dynamics provide an unfortunately direct channel through which parental abuse can become internalized as enduring negative cognitive schemata.

Psychological Trauma

Intrusive symptoms. Beyond its impacts on self-development, the violence of child abuse can produce posttraumatic intrusive symptoms. The self-trauma model posits, as noted in the beginning of this chapter, that the flashbacks, nightmares, rumination, and other intrusive symptoms of posttraumatic stress are triggered when traumatic experience stresses the individual by challenging the self's capacities to "handle" or integrate such stimuli. This may occur as a result of preexisting, inadequate self-capacities or in the face of extreme trauma regardless of self-resources.

Given that overwhelming stressors commonly produce repetitive, intrusive experiences, an important question is what psychological purpose, if any, such painful and disruptive phenomena might serve. Integrating Horowitz's (1976, 1986) ideas with behavioral exposure models and Rachman's (1980) notion of emotional processing, I propose that posttraumatic intrusion is an inborn, self-healing activity. Specifically, symptoms such as flashbacks, intrusive thoughts, nightmares, and even rumination in some instances may represent the mind's automatic attempt to desensitize and integrate affectively laden material by repeatedly exposing itself to small, moderately distressing fragments of an otherwise overwhelming trauma (e.g., brief sensations, visions, repetitive thoughts, or incomplete autobiographic memories of the event). From this perspective, flashbacks and related intrusive experiences, as well as avoidant symptoms such as numbing and cognitive disengagement, represent the mind's desensitization and processing activities more than they reflect underlying pathology per se.

This view of repetitive intrusion as a desensitization device is in many ways similar to Horowitz's (1976, 1986) cognitive stress response theory. Horowitz, however, suggests that posttraumatic intrusions represent the mind's ongoing attempt to integrate traumatic material into a preexisting cognitive schemata that did not include the trauma or its implications. Horowitz hypothesizes that the traumatized individual automatically cycles through periods of intrusion and avoidance in an attempt to process and accommodate new trauma-related material cognitively.

Although acknowledging the importance of gradual accommodation of cognitively unacceptable material, self-trauma theory suggests that these cycles also represent (perhaps more directly) the stepwise exposure and consolidation associated with an inborn form of systematic desensitization of *affect*. In this regard, many traumatic memories appear to be too anxiety producing to be accommodated cognitively prior to some reduction in their stress-producing capacity (Foa & Riggs, 1993) and therefore must be at least partially desensitized before the equally important cognitive processes Horowitz suggests can occur.

The self-trauma model of intrusion as a desensitization function is also similar to Rachman's (1980) notion of *emotional processing*. According to Rachman,

> Emotional processing is regarded as a process whereby emotional disturbances are absorbed, and decline to the extent that other experiences and behavior can proceed without disruption. . . . If an emotional disturbance is *not* absorbed satisfactorily, some signs become evident. These signs are likely to recur intermittently. . . . The central, indispensable index of unsatisfactory emotional processing is the persistence or return of intrusive signs of emotional activity (such as obsessions, nightmares, pressure of talk, phobias, [and] inappropriate expressions of emotion). (p. 51)

Although Rachman was silent on *how* emotional disturbances are absorbed, he did offer the important insight that unprocessed material of a traumatic or upsetting nature is likely to return as repetitive, intrusive symptoms and that this repetition occurs until more complete emotional (not just cognitive) processing takes place.

Unfortunately, some survivors of severe child maltreatment (and later adult traumas) are not able to desensitize and accommodate trauma entirely through intrusive reexperiencing of affects, memories, or cognitions alone and hence present with chronic posttraumatic stress. This may occur because the severity of the trauma and/or the extent of impaired self-capacities motivate excessive use of cognitive and emotional avoidance strategies (Rachman, 1980). However, the presence of excessive dissociation or other avoidance responses lessens the survivor's self-exposure to traumatic material—and the availability of the associated anxious arousal to habituation—and thus reduces the efficacy of the intrusion-desensitization process (see Koss & Harvey, 1991; Resick & Schnicke, 1993, for related perspectives). In support of this notion, it appears that individuals who tend to avoid cognitive access to traumatic material suffer more psychological distress than do those with less avoidant tendencies (Wirtz & Harrell, 1987). Furthermore, research suggests that suppression of emotional processing in the face of stress is associated with reduced psychological and physical health (Pennebaker, 1989; Wegner, Shortt, Blake, & Page, 1990). This seeming competition between two relatively automatic trauma-related processes, intrusion and avoidance, will be considered in the upcoming treatment section.

Summary of the Self-Trauma Model

In summary, the self-trauma model proposes that early and severe child maltreatment interrupts normal child development and the usual acquisition of self-skills—primarily by disrupting parent-child attachment and by producing enough internal distress to motivate dissociation, tension reduction activities, and other avoidance responses. This impairment in self-functioning places the individual at risk for being easily overwhelmed by current and later trauma-related affects, thereby leading to further dissociation and other methods of avoidance in adolescence and adulthood. In this way, impaired self-functioning leads to reliance on avoidance strategies that, in turn, preclude the development of further self-capacities. This negative cycle is exacerbated by the concomitant need of the traumatized individual to desensitize and accommodate trauma by repetitively reexperiencing fragments of the original traumatic event—a process that presents as intrusive symptomatology and that can affect self-functioning negatively.

Unfortunately, if the individual is dissociated sufficiently, this intrusion-desensitization process will not include enough direct exposure to upsetting material to reduce the survivor's trauma level. As a result, the individual will continue to have (ineffectual) flashbacks and other intrusive symptoms indefinitely and will continue to rely on avoidance responses such as dissociation, tension reduction, or sub-

stance abuse. This process may lead the abuse survivor in therapy to present as chronically dissociated, besieged by overwhelming yet unending intrusive symptomatology, and as having "characterological" difficulties associated with identity, boundary, and affect regulation difficulties.

Treatment Implications of the Self-Trauma Model

The etiological model presented here has a number of implications for the treatment of adults severely abused as children. These include suggestions regarding (a) the correct focus, pace, and intensity of psychotherapy; (b) how one might intervene in the self- and cognitive difficulties of abuse survivors; and (c) possible approaches to the resolution of the chronic posttraumatic symptomatology found in this population.

Treatment Process Issues and the Therapeutic Window

A major implication of the self-trauma model is that many untreated adult survivors of severe childhood abuse may spend considerable time and energy balancing trauma-related distress and intrusion with avoidance mechanisms. In other words, the survivor whose trauma generally exceeds his or her internal affect regulation capacities continually is forced to invoke dissociation, tension reduction behaviors, and other avoidance responses to maintain internal equilibrium (Briere, 1992). In the absence of such mechanisms, the individual is likely to become overwhelmed by anxiety and other negative affects. As a result, avoidance defenses are viewed as necessary survival responses by some clients, and overly enthusiastic or heavy-handed attempts by the therapist to "take them away" may be seen as potential threats to the client's internal equilibrium (Meiselman, 1990). For this reason, the psychotherapeutic process must proceed slowly and carefully, both to avoid overwhelming the client and to keep from stimulating further avoidance responses that otherwise would impede further therapeutic progress.

I have found it useful to frame the process of effective psychotherapy in terms of a *therapeutic window*. This window refers to that psychological "place" during treatment wherein appropriate therapeutic interventions are cast. Such interventions are neither so nondemanding as to be useless nor so evocative or powerful that the client's delicate balance between trauma and avoidance is tipped toward the former.

Interventions correctly pitched into the therapeutic window challenge and motivate psychological growth, accommodation, and desensitization but do not overwhelm internal protective systems and thereby motivate unwanted avoidance responses.

In other words, interventions correctly pitched into the therapeutic window challenge and motivate psychological growth, accommodation, and desensitization but do not overwhelm internal protective systems and thereby motivate unwanted avoidance responses.

Interventions that undershoot the therapeutic window either (a) completely and consistently avoid traumatic material, including any exploration of childhood trauma, or (b) are focused solely on support and validation in a client who could, in fact, tolerate some processing of a traumatic experience or affect. Undershooting interventions is rarely dangerous; it can, however, waste time and resources when more effective therapeutic interventions might be possible.

Overshooting the window occurs when interventions provide too much intensity or focus on material that requires additional processing before it can be addressed safely. In addition, interventions that are too fast paced may overshoot the window because they do not allow the client to accommodate and otherwise process previously activated material adequately before adding new, potentially stressful stimuli. When therapy consistently overshoots the window, the survivor must engage in avoidance maneuvers to keep from being overwhelmed and, in some cases, actually hurt by the therapy process. Most often, the client will in-

crease his or her level of dissociation during the session (Cornell & Olio, 1991) or will interrupt the focus or pace of therapy through arguments, by "not getting" obvious therapeutic points, or by radically changing the subject of the session. Although these behaviors are often labeled as resistance by the therapist, they are, in fact, appropriate survival responses to therapist process errors. The client's need for such avoidance strategies can complicate the therapeutic dynamic and may impede therapy by decreasing her or his exposure to effective treatment components.

In the worst situation, therapeutic interventions that exceed the window can harm the survivor. This occurs when the process errors are too numerous and severe to be balanced or neutralized by client avoidance, or when the client is so impaired in the self-domain or so cowed by the therapist that he or she cannot use self-protective defenses. In such instances, the survivor may become flooded with intrusive stimuli, may "fragment" to the point where he or she appears to be functioning at a primitive (or even psychotic) level, or may become sufficiently overwhelmed that more extreme dissociative behaviors emerge. Furthermore, in an attempt to restore a self-trauma equilibrium, she or he may have to engage in avoidance activities such as self-mutilation or excessive substance abuse after an overstimulating session. Although these states and responses may not be permanent, they are stigmatizing or disheartening for many clients and may lead them to quit treatment or become especially defensive during subsequent sessions.

In contrast, effective therapy provides sufficient safety and containment so that the client does not have to overrely on avoidance strategies. By carefully titrating therapeutic challenge and attendant distress so that neither exceeds the survivor's internal capacities, treatment in the therapeutic window allows the client to go where he or she may not have gone before without being injured in the process. As is described in the "Intervening in Abuse-Related Trauma Symptoms" section, this sense of safety and concomitant lower level of avoidance is an absolute prerequisite to the successful desensitization of posttraumatic stress.

I have found that, at minimum, three aspects of the therapeutic process should be considered in effective (window-centered) abuse-focused psychotherapy: (a) exploration versus consolidation, (b) intensity control, and (c) goal sequence. Each represents the therapist's attempt to find the appropriate point between support and opportunity for growth, with the assumption that, when in doubt, the former is always preferable to the latter.

Exploration versus consolidation. This aspect of the therapeutic process occurs on a continuum, with one end anchored in interventions devoted to greater awareness of potentially threatening (but therapeutically important) material and the other constrained to interventions that support and solidify previous progress or provide a secure base from which the survivor can operate without fear. This continuum is in many ways similar to McCann and Pearlman's (1990) notion of the differential functions of "supportive" versus "uncovering" interventions.

Exploratory interventions typically invite the client to examine or reexperience material related to his or her traumatic history. For some abuse survivors, exploration may not involve as much consideration of cognitive material, per se, as a testing of the waters in the affective domain. For example, an exploratory intervention might involve asking the client to approach the possibility of using less cognitive avoidance or dissociation when describing a previously described painful subject. The key here is that the survivor—in the context of relative safety—attempts to do something new, whether it be thinking of something previously not considered completely or feeling something previously not experienced fully.

Consolidation, on the other hand, is less concerned with exposure or processing than it is with safety and foundation. Consolidative interventions focus the client on potential imbalances between trauma and self at a given moment and invite the client to shore up the latter. An important issue here is that the survivor is not being asked merely to avoid existing traumatic states but rather to anchor him- or herself more fully in such a way as to strengthen faltering self-capacities. Interventions in this domain may involve, in one instance, "grounding" the agitated client in the "here and now." In another, it may involve reminding the client who is attempting to move too fast of how far he or she has come and of the need to honor his or her needs for safety.

The decision to explore or consolidate at any given moment reflects the therapist's assessment of which direction the client's balance between stresses and resources is tilting. The overwhelmed client, for example, typically requires less exploration and more consolidation, whereas the stable client may benefit most from the opposite. Furthermore, this assessment of the client's internal state may vary from moment to moment: At one point exploration may be indicated, whereas at another consolidation may be required. From the therapeutic window perspective, exploration moves the client toward the outer edge of the window, where emotional processing and new insights may occur, whereas consolidation moves toward the inner edge, where safety is more predominant.

Intensity control. Intensity control refers to the therapist's awareness of and access to the relative level of affect occurring within the session. Most generally, it is recommended that intensity be highest at around midsession, whereas the beginning and end of the session should be at the lowest intensity. At the onset of the session, the therapist should be respectful of the client's need to enter the therapeutic domain of trauma and self-work gradually, whereas by the end of the session the client should be de-aroused sufficiently so that she or he can reenter the outside world without difficulty. In addition, the relative safety of the session may encourage some clients to become more aroused affectively than they normally would outside of the therapeutic environment. As a result, it is the therapist's responsibility to leave the client in as calm an affective state as is possible—ideally no more than the arousal level present initially—lest the client be left with more affective tension than he or she can tolerate.

Beyond the time-oriented aspects of intensity control, the therapist should appreciate what some have referred to as the survivor's dread of affect (e.g., Krystal, 1978). For those severely abused as children, there may be a fear that extreme anger will lead to violent behavior and that extreme sadness will result in self-destructiveness (Briere, 1989). For others, immersion in extreme abuse-related fear may seem to signal that childhood trauma is about to happen all over again (Krystal, 1978). Some survivors with major self-difficulties unconsciously fear that extreme affect will engulf them or destroy their sanity. For such individuals, intensity control is a mandatory aspect of good therapy.

From the perspective offered in this chapter, intense affect during treatment may push the survivor toward the outer edge of the window, whereas less intensity will represent movement toward the inner (safer) edge. The need for the client, at some point, to feel seemingly dangerous feelings—not to dissociate them—during abuse-focused treatment requires the therapist to titrate the level of affect the client experiences carefully, at least to the extent this is under the therapist's control. The goal is for the client to neither feel too little (i.e., dissociate or otherwise avoid to the point that pain cannot be processed) nor feel too much (become so flooded with previously avoided affect that he or she overwhelms available self-resources).

> *The goal is for the client to neither feel too little (i.e., dissociate or otherwise avoid to the point that pain cannot be processed) nor feel too much (become so flooded with previously avoided affect that he or she overwhelms available self-resources).*

Goal sequence. As noted by various authors (Courtois, 1991; Linehan, 1993; McCann & Pearlman, 1990), therapy for severe abuse-related difficulties generally should proceed in a stepwise fashion, with early therapeutic attention paid more to the development of self-resources and coping skills than to trauma per se. This notion of "self before trauma" takes into account the fact that those interventions most helpful in working through major traumatic stress may overwhelm the client who lacks sufficient internal resources (Linehan, 1993). Specifically, the process of remembering and processing traumatic experiences affectively requires basic levels of affect tolerance and regulation skills. In the relative absence of such self-resources, the processing of traumatic material easily can exceed the therapeutic window and lead to fragmentation, increased dissociation, and later involvement in tension reduction activities—an outcome that is, sadly, not un-

common when the therapist is undertrained or inexperienced in trauma therapy.

Because of the need for adequate self-skills prior to intensive trauma work, the choice of therapeutic goals for a client must rely on detailed psychological assessment. Whether done with the assistance of psychological tests that tap both self- and trauma domains (e.g., the Trauma Symptom Inventory) (Briere, 1995) or solely through careful attention to self- and trauma dynamics during early sessions, the therapist must determine if a given client has sufficient self-functioning to tolerate relatively quick progression to trauma-focused interventions or whether she or he requires extended therapeutic attention to identity, boundary, and affect regulation before significant trauma work can be undertaken (Linehan, 1993).

Unfortunately, due to the complex relationship between self-capacities and traumatic stress, assessment of readiness to do trauma work cannot be determined solely at one point in time and then assumed thereafter. Indeed, self-functioning may appear sufficiently early in treatment, only to emerge as far less substantial later in therapy. For example, as therapy successfully reduces dissociative symptomatology, it may become clear that what originally appeared to be good affect regulation actually represents the effects of dissociative avoidance of painful affect. Alternatively, a client who initially had superficially intact self-functioning may later experience a reduction in self-capacities as he or she addresses especially traumatic material. Although some of this fragmentation may be amenable to careful attention to the therapeutic window, it is also true that intense reexperiencing of traumatic events can reduce self-functioning temporarily (Linehan, 1993). Given these potential scenarios, it is strongly recommended that the therapist continue to evaluate the client's current self-functioning and trauma level throughout treatment so that he or she can adjust the type, focus, or intensity of intervention when necessary.

Intervening in Impaired Self-Functioning

As noted earlier, the availability and quality of self-resources are typically major determinants of the level of symptomatology and response to treatment. Self-resources are so important to traumatic stress and therapeutic intervention that, as mentioned, some clients may require extensive "self-work" before any significant trauma-focused interventions can occur. For others, there may be sufficient self-skills available to allow some trauma-based interventions, yet continued attention to the development of further self-resources will be required. In a relatively small number of clinical abuse survivors, self-issues may not require any significant intervention, and desensitization of traumatic material may occur more quickly (Linehan, 1993). Even in the latter case, however, it is possible that the processing of an especially painful traumatic memory may overwhelm normally sufficient self-capacities briefly, thereby requiring some (typically temporary) self-level interventions.

Safety and support. Because, for many survivors, the earliest hazard to the development of self-resources was the experience of danger and lack of support or protection, these issues must receive continuing attention in abuse-focused psychotherapy. In the absence of continual and reliable safety and support during treatment, the survivor is unlikely to reduce his or her reliance on avoidance defenses, nor attempt the necessary work of forming an open relationship with the psychotherapist. Because early neglect and/or abuse may have led to the development of an ambivalent or avoidant attachment pattern (Alexander, 1992), the client is, in some sense, being asked to go against lifelong learning and become dangerously vulnerable to a powerful figure. That he or she is willing to do so at all in such cases is testament to the investment and bravery that many abuse survivors bring to therapy.

Obviously, given the above, the clinician must work very hard to provide an environment in which the survivor can "let in" therapeutic nurturance and support. Just as the chronically avoidant child may reject a loving foster parent, the survivor of severe abuse may use similar defenses that, at least initially, preclude a working relationship with his or her therapist. As many clinicians will attest, there is no shortcut to the process of developing trust in such instances. Instead, the clinician must provide ongoing, reliable data to the survivor that he or she is not in danger—not from physical or sexual assaults, nor from rejection, domination, intrusion, or abandonment (Courtois, 1988; Meiselman, 1990; Salter, 1995).

Some therapists will agree to these principles but nevertheless unconsciously violate them. For instance, a clinician may spend considerable time reassuring the client that he or she is safe and supportive, yet at other times implicitly criticize, pathologize, or intrude on the survivor (Salter, 1995). Examples of such behavior are frequent interruptions, excessive clinical interpretations, ill-conceived confrontations, uninvited probing, and various forms of boundary violations. Or, the therapist may violate the principles of good therapeutic process outlined earlier (e.g., pacing, intensity control), thereby communicating to the client that therapy is not, in fact, a safe place nor a process under the client's control. Such therapists may present in clinical consultation with complaints of client resistance or untreatable pathology, not realizing that their behavior in therapy is motivating (or at least not lessening the need for) the client's responses.

In my experience, the therapist goes on record from the early moments of the intake interview to the last treatment session. Has his or her behavior shown that vulnerability is possible without injury, criticism, or rejection? Does the client have any evidence that the clinician is prone to potentially abusive, neglectful, or boundary violating behavior? Is it, ultimately, safe in the consultation room? These questions, constantly evaluated, form the base from which the abuse survivor will (or will not) respond to treatment interventions. When the answers consistently support the notion of safety, the survivor is more likely to "open up" and attempt new behaviors and experiences (Meiselman, 1990).

Beyond providing a secure base from which the client can explore his or her internal and interpersonal environment, therapeutic safety and support ideally provide a curative example of relationship per se. Long-term interactions in a safe therapeutic relationship can rework previous assumptions about the value of self in relation to others, such that the client begins to approximate a sense of personal validity. In addition, by receiving continuous support from the therapist, the client has the opportunity to internalize the possibility of benevolent others and of situations for whom avoidance and defense are less required.

Facilitating self-awareness and positive identity. In the context of sustained and reliable support and acceptance, the survivor has the opportunity to engage in the relative luxury of introspection. Looking inward may have been punished by the survivor's early environment in at least two ways: It took attention away from hypervigilance and therefore safety, and greater internal awareness meant, by definition, greater pain (Briere, 1989). As a result, many untreated survivors of severe abuse are surprisingly unaware of their internal processes and may, in fact, appear to have very little self-knowledge. This may present, for example, as reports of not being able to predict one's own behavior in various situations or of having little insight regarding the abuse or its effects. Some survivors refer to this knowledge gap as evidence of being "dumb" or "stupid": It is, of course, not a matter of intelligence but rather of motivated avoidance and the psychological costs of survival-based externality.

By facilitating self-exploration, abuse-focused therapy may allow the survivor to become more acquainted with self and thus gain a greater sense of personal identity.

By facilitating self-exploration, abuse-focused therapy may allow the survivor to become more acquainted with self and thus gain a greater sense of personal identity. Increased self-awareness especially may be fostered by "Socratic therapy" (Briere, 1992), wherein clients are asked many open-ended questions throughout the course of treatment. These include multiple, gentle questions about, for example, the clients' early (preabuse) perceptions and experiences, the options that were and were not available to them at the time of the abuse, their feelings and reactions during and after victimization experiences, and their current thoughts, feelings, and self-assessments. As opposed to the overuse of therapeutic interpretations or blanket reassurances, Socratic interventions not only support the survivor's acquisition of a growing body of information regarding self but also teach the techniques of self-exploration and self-examination.

In the process of self-exploration, many opportunities arise for the reworking of cognitive distortions and negative self-perceptions. These distortions typically involve harsh self-judgments of having caused, encouraged, or deserved the abuse (Jehu, Gazan, & Klassen, 1984/1985), as well as those broader self-esteem problems typically associated with child maltreatment. By exploring with the survivor the inadequate information and logical errors associated with such beliefs and self-perceptions, the therapist can assist in the development of a more positive model of self. The reader is referred to Janoff-Bulman (1992), Jehu (1988), and Resick and Schnicke (1993) for further information on interventions helpful with the cognitive sequelae of interpersonal victimization.

Self-other and boundary issues. As noted earlier, many survivors of severe childhood sexual abuse have difficulty distinguishing the boundary between self and others. This problem is thought to arise both from attachment disruption, wherein the child is deprived of the opportunity to learn normal self-other behaviors, and from early intrusion by the abuser into the child's bodily space (McCann & Pearlman, 1990).

Effective abuse-focused therapy addresses both of these bases. The clinician is careful to honor the client's dignity, rights, and psychological integrity—even if the survivor is unaware of his or her entitlement to such treatment. Over time, the therapist's consistent regard for the client's rights to safety and freedom from intrusion can be internalized by the client as evidence of his or her physical and psychological boundaries. Some of this learning process is cognitive—during the client's recounting of his or her child abuse history and later adult experiences of violation or exploitation, the therapist actively reinforces the survivor's previous and current entitlement to integrity and self-determinism. Other aspects of this process are intrinsic—as he or she is treated with respect by the therapist and slowly develops a growing sense of personal identity, the survivor begins to *assume* that he or she has outside limits and that these boundaries should not be violated by others.

At the same time that the demarcation of his or her own boundaries is being demonstrated and learned, the survivor in therapy may be exposed to important lessons regarding the boundaries of others. This may occur as the client impinges on the therapist, typically through inappropriate questions, requests, or behavior. As the therapist firmly (and, it is hoped, adroitly) repels such intrusions, he or she both teaches about the needs and rights of others to boundary integrity and models for the survivor appropriate limit-setting strategies the survivor can use in his or her own life (Elliott & Briere, 1995). In this way, the interpersonal give-and-take of psychotherapy tends to replicate some of the lessons the survivor would have learned in childhood if it were possible.

Affect modulation and affect tolerance. Because affect tolerance and modulation are such important issues for adults severely abused as children, the self-trauma model addresses these issues in as many ways as possible. It stresses two general pathways to the development of affective competence: the acquisition of an affect regulation repertoire and the strengthening of inborn but underdeveloped affective capacities.

Skills training in this area is well-outlined by Linehan (1993) in her outstanding treatise on the cognitive behavioral treatment of borderline personality disorder. She notes that distress tolerance and emotional regulation are both internal behaviors that can be taught during therapy. Among the specific skills directly taught by Linehan's dialectical behavior therapy (DBT) for distress tolerance are distraction, self-soothing, "improving the moment" (e.g., through relaxation), and thinking of the "pros and cons" of behavior (p. 148). In the area of emotional regulation skills, Linehan teaches the survivor to (a) identify and label affect, (b) identify obstacles to changing emotions, (c) reduce vulnerability to hyperemotionality through decreased stress, (d) increase the frequency of positive emotional events, and (e) develop the ability to experience emotions without judging or rejecting them (pp. 147-148).

Self-trauma theory makes use of these skills training approaches, although it generally avoids the formally programmatic aspects of DBT. Linehan's (1993) model, which has been shown in outcome research to be effective for borderline personality disorder, stresses a central issue: Affect dysregulation does not reflect a structural, psychological defect (as suggested by some neoanalytic theories and

approaches) as much as skills deficits arising from distorted or disrupted childhood development.

Affect regulation and tolerance also are learned implicitly during self-trauma therapy. Because, as outlined in the next section, trauma-focused interventions involve the repeated evocation and resolution of distressing but nonoverwhelming affect, such treatment slowly teaches the survivor to become more "at home" with some level of distress and to develop whatever skills necessary to deescalate moderate levels of emotional arousal. This growing ability to move in and out of strong affective states, in turn, fosters an increased sense of emotional control and reduced fear of affect. The reader is referred to McCann and Pearlman (1990, pp. 144-153) for further information on the development and strengthening of affect regulation capacities.

Intervening in Abuse-Related Trauma Symptoms

Assuming that the client either has sufficient self-skills or that these self-functions have been strengthened sufficiently, the treatment of trauma symptoms is relatively straightforward. There are at least three major steps in this process, although they may recur in different orders at various points in treatment: identification of traumatic (i.e., abuse-related) events, gradual reexposure to the affect and stimuli associated with a memory of the abuse while keeping avoidance responses minimal, and emotional discharge and cognitive processing.

Identification of traumatic events. In order for traumatic material to be processed in treatment, it must be identified as such. Although this seems an obvious step, it is more difficult to implement in some cases than might be expected. The survivor's avoidance of abuse-related material may lead either to conscious reluctance to think about or speak of upsetting abuse incidents (denial and suppression) or to less conscious dissociation of such events. In the former case, the survivor may believe that a detailed description of the abuse would be more painful than he or she is willing to endure or that exploration of the abuse would overwhelm his or her self-resources. Dissociation of abuse material, on the other hand, may present as incomplete or absent recall of the events in question.[3]

Whether denial or dissociation, avoidance of abuse-related material by an abuse survivor should be respected, because it indicates his or her judgment that exploration in that area would exceed the therapeutic window. The role of the therapist at such junctures is not to overpower the client's defenses or in any way convince him or her that abuse occurred, but rather to provide the conditions (e.g., safety, support, and a trustworthy environment) whereby avoidance is less necessary. Because this latter step can require significant time and skill, specific enumeration and description of abusive events are far from a simple matter.

Gradual exposure to abuse-related material. If, at some point, there is sufficient abuse material available to the treatment process, the next step in the treatment of abuse-related trauma is careful, graduated exposure to various aspects of the abuse memory. According to Abueg and Fairbank (1992), exposure treatment can be defined as "repeated or extended exposure, either in vivo or in imagination, to objectively harmless but feared stimuli for the purpose of reducing anxiety" (p. 127). As noted earlier, the goal of exposure techniques in the current context is somewhat more ambitious than solely eradicating irrational anxiety. Instead, the intended outcome includes the reduction of intrusive (and, secondarily, avoidant) symptomatology associated with unresolved traumatic events.

The exposure approach suggested here for abuse trauma is a form of systematic desensitization (Wolpe, 1958), wherein the survivor is asked to recall nonoverwhelming but painful abuse-specific experiences in the context of a safe, therapeutic environment. The exposure is graduated according to the intensity of the recalled abuse, with less upsetting memories being recalled, verbalized, and desensitized before more upsetting ones are considered. It should be noted that this form of exposure is self-administered: The client is asked to recall painful material, as opposed to a "fear hierarchy" approach in which the client is presented with a series of gradually more upsetting or frightening stimuli. The use of exposure or desensitization procedures appears to be effective in the treatment of various types of trauma survivors, including rape victims (e.g., Foa,

Rothbaum, Riggs, & Murdock, 1991; Frank & Stewart, 1983) and war veterans (e.g., Bowen & Lambert, 1986; Keane et al., 1989).

In contrast to more strictly behavioral interventions, the self-trauma approach does not adhere to a strict, preplanned series of exposure activities. This is because the survivor's ability to tolerate exposure may be quite compromised and may vary considerably from session to session as a function of outside life stressors; level of support from friends, relatives, and others; and the "place" in the therapeutic window that the therapy occupies at any given moment. Regarding the last point, the client may be sufficiently stressed by previous therapeutic events or aspects of the therapeutic relationship (e.g., restimulated attachment dynamics; Elliott & Briere, 1995) that his or her ability to handle any further stressful material is limited. Further exposure at such times usually leads to avoidance responses or even to some level of fragmentation. Instead of exposure, the focus of therapy should become consolidation, arousal reduction, and the shoring up of self-resources as indicated in the earlier "process" section of this chapter. In addition, if previous exposure has led to enduring feelings of revulsion, self-hatred, or helplessness, the client may require interventions that interrupt or contradict cognitive distortions before he or she can move on to more exposure.

As noted by McCann and Pearlman (1990), exposure to abuse memories is complicated by the fact that there are probably at least two different coding systems to address: verbal and sensorimotor (van der Kolk & Fisler, 1995). The former is more narrative and autobiographical, whereas the latter involves the encoding and recovery of sensations and affects. McCann and Pearlman note that material from both systems must be desensitized—the first by repeatedly exploring the factual aspects of the event (e.g., who, what, where, and when) and the second by recollection of the physical sensations and affects associated with the abuse. In my experience, exposure to verbal memories is considerably less overwhelming for most survivors than processing of sensory memories, and therefore the former usually should be addressed before the latter.

As indicated earlier, for abuse-focused therapy to work well, there should be as little avoidance as possible during the session. Specifically, the client should be encouraged to stay as "present" as he or she can during the detailed recall of abuse memories, so that exposure, per se, is maximized. The very dissociated survivor may have little true exposure to abuse material during treatment—despite what may be detailed verbal renditions of a given memory. Of course, the therapist must keep the therapeutic window in mind and not interrupt survivor dissociation that is, in fact, appropriate in the face of therapeutic overstimulation. This might occur, for example, when the therapist requires or allows client access to memories whose affective characteristics exceed the survivor's self-resources. On the other hand, it is not uncommon for dissociative responses to become so overlearned that they automatically (but unnecessarily) emerge during exposure to stress. In this case, some level of reduced dissociation during treatment is not only safe but frequently imperative for significant desensitization to occur.

Emotional and cognitive processing. The last component of abuse-focused desensitization of traumatic memories involves the emotional and cognitive activity that must occur during self-exposure to traumatic memories. This is an important step because, without such processing, exposure may result only in reexperienced pain, not resolution (Rachman, 1980). In other words, therapeutic interventions that focus solely on the narration of abuse-related memories will not necessarily produce symptom relief. Two aspects of abuse-related emotional processing are relevant to the self-trauma model: facilitation of emotional discharge and titration of level of affect.

Classic exposure therapy is not concerned especially with catharsis or emotional release during therapy. Instead, it tends to involve one of two approaches. In the first approach, *exposure alone,* the client is exposed repeatedly to a stimulus (e.g., a tape recording or detailed description of a battle or assault) that triggers conditioned emotional responses (e.g., fear) until the emotional response fades away (habituates) for lack of reinforcement (i.e., because there is, in fact, no current danger). In the second approach, *exposure and relaxation* (i.e., the classic systematic desensitization paradigm), the traumatic stimulus is experienced during low autonomic arousal and thus is less able to produce anxiety (see Marmar, Foy, Kagan, & Pynoos, 1993;

Rothblum & Foa, 1992, for descriptions of these approaches).

Although repeated client descriptions of abuse memories during therapy alone often result in some habituation and counterconditioning of painful emotional responses (i.e., via the experienced safety of the therapy office), self-trauma therapy also capitalizes on the positive effects of emotional release. Specifically, I propose that the inherent biological "reason" for crying (and perhaps other forms of emotional discharge) in response to upsetting events may be that such release engenders a relatively positive emotional experience. This more positive state can then inhibit and countercondition the fear and related affects initially associated with the trauma. In other words, the lay suggestion that someone "have a good cry" or "get it off of your chest" may reflect support for ventilation and other emotional activities that naturally desensitize posttraumatic dysphoria. From this perspective, just as traditional systematic desensitization pairs a formerly distressing stimulus to a relaxed (anxiety-incompatible) state and thereby neutralizes the original anxious response over time, repeated emotional catharsis during nondissociated exposure to painful memories involves the experience of traumatic stimuli in the context of those relatively positive internal states associated with emotional release. Thus, a "good cry" is good because, in the absence of significant dissociation, it tends to countercondition traumatic stress.

Although appropriate emotional expression may facilitate the counterconditioning of abuse-related trauma, such activity is not equivalent to the recently rediscovered notion of *abreaction* of chronic abuse trauma. These more dramatic procedures often involve pressure on the client to engage in extreme emotional discharge, often in the context of a hypnotic state. Unfortunately, such techniques run the risk of greatly exceeding the therapeutic window, with resultant flooding of painful affects. In addition, by their very nature, such interventions encourage dissociated emotional release—a phenomenon that, although easily accomplished by many survivors, is unlikely to be helpful therapeutically. As noted by Cornell and Olio (1991), "[Abreactive] techniques may appear to deepen affect and produce dramatic results in the session, but they may not result in the client's sustained understanding of, or connection to, their experience of abuse" (p. 62).

At the same time that the client is encouraged to remember and feel, he or she also is asked to think. For example, the client might explore the circumstances of the abuse, the basis for his or her reactions, and the dynamics operating in the abuser. This process is likely to alter the survivor's internal schema so that the abuse experience can be integrated cognitively, as described by Horowitz (1976). Resick and Schnicke (1993), for example, note that "prolonged exposure activates the memory structure but does not provide corrective information regarding misattributions or other maladaptive beliefs" (p. 17). They recommend their cognitive processing therapy (CPT) to address these latter targets. Resick and Schnicke's book on this approach is recommended to the reader, because it fully outlines this component of trauma recovery.

Together, emotional discharge and cognitive processing change considerably the original associations to traumatic abuse; the first by counterconditioning distress and the second by providing insight and altering the cognitive matrix in which the abuse was embedded. In this way, the survivor who remembers his or her abuse (both narratively and through intrusive reexperiencing), who cries or rages about it, and who repetitively talks and ruminates about it is engaging in a natural healing response. This process may occur best during therapy, where the clinician can provide a safe and organized structure for the unfolding of each component and can be counted on to keep the processing well within the therapeutic window. As noted earlier, the survivor's existing self-resources will determine how much exposure and processing can occur, without overwhelming the survivor and stimulating avoidance responses.

Access to Previously Unavailable Material

Taken together, the self-trauma approach outlined in this chapter allows the therapist to address the impaired self-functioning, cognitive distortions, and posttraumatic stress found in some adults who were severely abused as children. The serial desensitization of painful memories is likely to slowly reduce the survivor's

overall level of posttraumatic stress—a condition that eventually lessens the general level of dissociation required by the survivor for internal stability. This process also increases self-resources: As noted earlier, progressive exposure to nonoverwhelming distress is likely to increase affect regulation skills and affect tolerance. As a result, successful ongoing treatment allows the survivor to confront increasingly more painful memories without exceeding the survivor's (now greater) self-capacities.

Decreasing stress levels and increasing self-resources can lead to a relatively self-sustaining process: As the need to avoid painful material lessens with treatment, memories previously too overwhelming to address become more available for processing. As this new material is, in turn, desensitized and accommodated cognitively, self-capacity is further improved and the overall stress level is further reduced—thereby permitting access to (and processing of) even more unavailable material. Ultimately, treatment ends when traumatic material is desensitized and integrated and self-resources are learned and strengthened sufficiently so that the survivor no longer experiences significant intrusive, avoidant, or dysphoric symptoms.

This progressive function of self-trauma therapy removes the need for any so-called memory recovery techniques.

This progressive function of self-trauma therapy removes the need for any so-called memory recovery techniques. Instead of relying on hypnosis or drug-assisted interviews, for example, to increase access to unavailable material, self-trauma therapy allows these memories to emerge naturally as a function of the survivor's reduced need for avoidance. Whereas authoritarian memory recovery techniques might easily exceed the therapeutic window and flood the survivor with destabilizing memories and affects,[4] the self-trauma dynamic only allows access to dissociated material when, by definition, the therapeutic window has not been exceeded.

The self-trauma model reverses an assumption held by those who advocate aggressive memory retrieval: It holds that clients do not get better when they remember more, but rather that they may remember more as they get better.

Conclusions

This chapter has presented the self-trauma model, a synthesis of current dynamic, cognitive, and behavioral approaches that have been found helpful in the treatment of severe abuse trauma. This model suggests that postabuse "symptomatology" generally reflects the survivor's adaptive attempts to maintain internal stability in the face of potentially overwhelming abuse-related pain. It further suggests that many of these symptoms are, in actuality, inborn self-healing procedures that only fail when overwhelming stress or inadequate internal resources motivate the hyperdevelopment of avoidance responses.

I have argued in this chapter that successful treatment for abuse-related distress and dysfunction should not seek to impose alien techniques and perspectives on the survivor but rather should help the client to do better what he or she is already attempting to do. Thus, like the survivor, the therapist should be concerned with balancing challenge with resource and growth with safety. The natural healing aspects of intrusion and avoidance are not countered in treatment but instead are refined to the point that they are maximally helpful and can be abandoned once successful.

In this way, the self-trauma model is ultimately optimistic; it assumes that much of abuse-related "pathology" and dysfunction are solutions in the making, albeit ones intrinsically more focused on survival than recovery. At the same time, unfortunately, the "bottom line" of abuse-focused therapy is that in order to reduce posttraumatic pain and fear, both must be confronted and experienced repeatedly. As therapists, we must not forget what we are asking of our clients in this regard, lest we lose track of the courage and strength that they inevitably must bring to the process.

Notes

1. This discussion is limited to childhood abuse experiences that were especially severe and that require clinical intervention. Less severe abuse experiences may or may not result in significant psychological difficulties and thus the treatment methodology outlined here may or may not apply.

2. Foster parents often report a similar dynamic when caring for a child who was previously abused elsewhere. In the words of one foster mother, "We had so much love to give her, and she needed love so badly. But she wouldn't let us in."

3. Although this issue is a source of controversy, with some individuals claiming that psychological amnesia for childhood abuse is impossible (e.g., Loftus, 1993; Ofshe & Watters, 1993), the last three editions of the American Psychiatric Association's diagnostic manual (*DSM-III, DSM-III-R, DSM-IV*) and recent research (e.g., see Berliner & Elliott, Chapter 3, this volume) suggest that dissociative amnesia for traumatic events is not especially rare.

4. Other problems potentially associated with the use of such techniques will not be addressed in this chapter due to space limitations, including capitalization on suggestibility and the possibility that such activities occasionally may motivate the development of less accurate (and thus less overwhelming) memories as an avoidance/distraction device.

References

Abueg, F. R., & Fairbanks, J. A. (1992). Behavioral treatment of posttraumatic stress disorder and co-occurring substance abuse. In P. A. Saigh (Ed.), *Posttraumatic stress disorder: A behavioral approach to assessment and treatment* (pp. 111-146). Needham Heights, MA: Allyn & Bacon.

Alexander, P. C. (1992). Effect of incest on self and social functioning: A developmental psychopathology perspective. *Journal of Consulting and Clinical Psychology, 60,* 185-195.

Bowen, G. R., & Lambert, J. A. (1986). Systematic desensitization therapy with post-traumatic stress disorder cases. In C. R. Figley (Ed.), *Trauma and its wake* (Vol. 2). New York: Brunner/Mazel.

Bowlby, J. (1982). *Attachment and loss: Vol. 1. Attachment* (2nd ed.). New York: Basic Books.

Bowlby, J. (1988). *A secure base: Parent-child attachment and healthy human development.* New York: Basic Books.

Briere, J. (1989). *Therapy for adults molested as children: Beyond survival.* New York: Springer.

Briere, J. (1992). *Child abuse trauma: Theory and treatment of the lasting effects.* Newbury Park, CA: Sage.

Briere, J. (1995). *Trauma symptom inventory professional manual.* Odessa, FL: Psychological Assessment Resources.

Briere, J., & Runtz, M. (1991). The long-term effects of sexual abuse: A review and synthesis. In J. Briere (Ed.), *Treating victims of child sexual abuse* (pp. 3-14). San Francisco: Jossey-Bass.

Brown, S. (1988). *Treating adult children of alcoholics: A developmental perspective.* New York: John Wiley.

Cole, P. M., & Putnam, F. W. (1992). Effect of incest on self and social functioning: A developmental psychopathology perspective. *Journal of Consulting and Clinical Psychology, 60,* 174-184.

Cornell, W. F., & Olio, K. A. (1991). Integrating affect in treatment with adult survivors of physical and sexual abuse. *American Journal of Orthopsychiatry, 61,* 59-69.

Courtois, C. A. (1988). *Healing the incest wound: Adult survivors in therapy.* New York: Norton.

Courtois, C. A. (1991). Theory, sequencing, and strategy in treating adult survivors. In J. Briere (Ed.), *Treating victims of child sexual abuse* (pp. 47-60). San Francisco: Jossey-Bass.

Davies, J. M., & Frawley, M. G. (1994). *Treating the adult survivor of childhood sexual abuse: A psychoanalytic perspective.* New York: Basic Books.

Elliott, D. M. (1994). Impaired object relationships in professional women molested as children. *Psychotherapy, 31,* 79-86.

Elliott, D. M., & Briere, J. (1995). Transference and countertransference. In C. Classen (Ed.), *Treating women molested in childhood* (pp. 187-226). San Francisco: Jossey-Bass.

Foa, E. B., & Riggs, D. S. (1993). Posttraumatic stress disorder and rape. In R. S. Pynoos (Ed.), *Posttraumatic stress disorder: A clinical review* (pp. 133-163). Lutherville, MD: Sindran.

Foa, E. B., Rothbaum, B. O., Riggs, D. S., & Murdock, T. B. (1991). Treatment of posttraumatic disorder in rape victims: A comparison between cognitive-behavioral procedures and counseling. *Journal of Consulting and Clinical Psychology, 59,* 715-723.

Frank, E., & Stewart, B. D. (1983). Depressive symptoms in rape victims: A revisit. *Journal of Affective Disorders, 7,* 77-85.

Hamilton, N. G. (1988). *Self and others: Object relations theory in practice.* Northvale, NJ: Jason Aronson.

Horowitz, M. J. (1976). *Stress response syndromes.* Northvale, NJ: Jason Aronson.

Horowitz, M. J. (1986). Stress-response syndromes: A review of posttraumatic and adjustment disorders. *Hospital and Community Psychiatry, 37,* 241-249.

Janoff-Bulman, B. (1992). *Shattered assumptions: Towards a new psychology of trauma.* New York: Free Press.

Jehu, D. (1988). *Beyond sexual abuse: Therapy with women who were childhood victims.* Chichester, UK: Wiley.

Jehu, D., Gazan, M., & Klassen, C. (1984/1985). Common therapeutic targets among women who were sexually abused in childhood. *Journal of Social Work and Human Sexuality, 3,* 25-45.

Koss, M. P., & Harvey, M. R. (1991). *The rape victim: Clinical and community interventions* (2nd ed.). Newbury Park, CA: Sage.

Keane, T. M., Fairbank, J. A., Caddell, J. M., Zimering, R. T., Taylor, K. L., & Mora, C. A. (1989). Clinical evaluation of a measure to assess combat exposure. *Psychological Assessment: A Journal of Consulting and Clinical Psychology, 1,* 53-55.

Krystal, H. (1978). Trauma and effects. *Psychoanalytic Study of the Child, 33,* 81-116.

Linehan, M. M. (1993). *Cognitive-behavioral treatment of borderline personality disorder.* New York: Guilford.

Loftus, E. F. (1993). The reality of repressed memories. *American Psychologist, 48,* 518-537.

Marmar, C. R., Foy, D., Kagan, B., & Pynoos, R. S. (1993). An integrated approach for treating posttraumatic stress. In R. S. Pynoos (Ed.), *Posttraumatic stress disorder: A clinical review* (pp. 99-132). Lutherville, MD: Sindran.

McCann, I. L., & Pearlman, L. A. (1990). *Psychological trauma and the adult survivor: Theory, therapy, and transformation.* New York: Brunner/Mazel.

Meiselman, K. C. (1990). *Resolving the trauma of incest: Reintegration therapy with survivors.* San Francisco: Jossey-Bass.

Meiselman, K. C. (1994). Treating survivors of child sexual abuse: A strategy for reintegration. In J. Briere (Ed.), *Assessing and treating victims of violence* (pp. 91-100). San Francisco: Jossey-Bass.

Neumann, D. A. (1994). Long-term correlates of childhood sexual abuse in adult survivors. In J. Briere (Ed.), *Assessing and treating victims of violence* (pp. 29-38). San Francisco: Jossey-Bass.

Ofshe, R., & Watters, E. (1993). Making monsters. *Society, 30,* 4-16.

Pennebaker, J. W. (1989). Confession, inhibition, and disease. In L. Berkowitz (Ed.), *Advances in experimental social psychology* (Vol. 22, pp. 211-244). New York: Academic Press.

Peterson, C., & Seligman, M. E. P. (1983). Learned helplessness and victimization. *Journal of Social Issues, 39,* 103-116.

Putnam, F. W. (1985). Dissociation as a response to extreme trauma. In R. P. Kluft (Ed.), *Childhood antecedents of multiple personality* (pp. 65-97). Washington, DC: American Psychiatric Press.

Pynoos, R. S. (1993). Traumatic stress and developmental psychopathology in children and adolescents. In R. S. Pynoos (Ed.), *Posttraumatic stress disorder: A clinical review* (pp. 65-98). Lutherville, MD: Sindran.

Rachman, S. (1980). Emotional processing. *Behavior, Research, and Therapy, 18,* 51-60.

Resick, P. A., & Schnicke, M. K. (1993). *Cognitive processing therapy for rape victims: A treatment manual.* Newbury Park, CA: Sage.

Rothblum, B. O., & Foa, E. B. (1992). Cognitive-behavioral treatment of posttraumtic stress disorder. In P. A. Saigh (Ed.), *Posttraumatic stress disorder: A behavioral approach to assessment and treatment* (pp. 85-110). Needham Heights, MA: Allyn & Bacon.

Salter, A. C. (1995). *Transforming trauma: A guide to understanding and treating adult survivors of child sexual abuse.* Thousand Oaks, CA: Sage.

Van der Kolk, B. A., & Fisler, R. (1995). Dissociation and the fragmentary nature of traumatic memories: Overview and exploratory study. *Journal of Traumatic Stress, 8,* 505-525.

Wegner, D. M., Shortt, J. W., Blake, A. W., & Page, M. S. (1990). The suppression of excited thought. *Journal of Personality and Social Psychology, 55,* 882-892.

Wirtz, P., & Harrell, A. (1987). Effects of post-assault exposure to attack-similar stimuli on long-term recovery of victims. *Journal of Consulting and Clinical Psychology, 55,* 10-16.

Wolpe, J. (1958). *Psychotherapy by reciprocal inhibition.* Stanford, CA: Stanford University Press.

9

Research on Maltreating Families

Implications for Intervention

PATRICIA M. CRITTENDEN

Maltreatment is a family problem. Although reported instances generally involve only one parent and child, these instances are embedded in the functioning of families. For example, nonreported spouses or partners often permit the maltreatment; moreover, in many cases, the partners also abuse one another. Siblings of reported children often witness the maltreatment, and many, on other occasions, are mistreated as well. Furthermore, in most cases, the parents were maltreated in their own childhood by their parents. Finally, some reported children will, in their adulthood, maltreat their children and spouses. Because maltreatment is a family problem, it should be understood, prevented, and treated in the context of families.

Research on families with different types of maltreatment varies in breadth and sophistication. For established areas of inquiry, such as physical abuse, much is known with considerable certainty. For less fully investigated topics—for example, physical neglect—much is known but the paucity of studies and the methodological limitations of the studies reduce the certainty and breadth of understanding. For the most recently identified areas—for example, psychological maltreatment and sexual abuse—the re-

search is more limited. Considered as a whole, the research on families with maltreatment reflects developmental trends in methods and theories from (a) clinical studies presenting evidence that a condition exists, to (b) studies comparing subjects with the condition to subjects without the condition to determine specificity of the symptoms associated with the condition, to (c) studies testing theoretically based hypotheses, to (d) studies using multiple comparison groups to partial variance among possible causal conditions (see Jean-Gilles & Crittenden, 1990, for an example of this design).

This chapter focuses on research regarding families experiencing six types of maltreatment: physical abuse, physical neglect, abuse and neglect, sexual abuse, psychological maltreatment, and marginal maltreatment. The perspective is that the breadth and certainty of our knowledge are tied to the sophistication of methods and theories. For families with each condition, the state of knowledge and theory, recommendations for further research, and applications to treatment are offered.

Families With Physical Child Abuse

The earliest reports of child abuse were predominately clinical reports. That is, researchers described cases of child abuse in terms of their salient features. These features became the basis for *battered child syndrome* (Kempe, Silverman, Steele, Droegemueller, & Silver, 1962). Although identification of syndromes is typical of early work in an area, with further development of theory and more sophisticated studies that test hypotheses using methodological controls, aspects of the syndrome come to be seen as common to a range of conditions (e.g., various types of trauma) or as limited to only a subset of cases with the condition (e.g., acting out behavior). In place of a syndrome, sets of developmental pathways emerge that reflect the interaction of salient aspects of experience and environment on the development of affected children. Among aspects of the environment relevant to physical abuse, the family consistently is identified as being of critical importance.

Family characteristics. Families in which there is physical abuse are in many ways typical of other low-income families. That is, they have relatively young parents, with relatively little education, and larger than usual numbers of closely spaced children (Maden & Wrench, 1977; National Center on Child Abuse and Neglect, 1978; Parke & Collmer, 1977). They also tend to have unstable relationships, with many mothers being unmarried, divorced, or separated. In addition, many families with abuse depend in part or entirely on

public resources for economic support. Finally, most abusive parents were abused or neglected in their own childhood (Jayaratne, 1977; Kaufman & Zigler, 1987).

Families with physical child abuse also resemble families with other forms of violence (Emery, 1989; Wolfe & Mosk, 1983). Often, there is spousal and sibling violence as well as abuse of other children (Jean-Gilles & Crittenden, 1990). In addition, abusive parents have difficulty maintaining supportive relationships with friends and relatives (Crittenden, 1985b; Garbarino & Sherman, 1980).

Distorted relationships as a critical cause of child abuse. One approach to integrating this information is to consider *critical causes*—that is, the cause that explains or affects most of the other correlated conditions (Crittenden & Ainsworth, 1989). For child abuse, the evidence suggests that distorted patterns of interpersonal relationships may underlie abusing parents' problems with their own parents, with partners, with children, with friends and relatives, and even with employers and coworkers. If so, understanding how members of abusive families initiate and manage relationships may be critical both for understanding family functioning and also for organizing treatment.

Studies show that abusive families interact less frequently than nonviolent controls, are more negative, and often cover hostility with falsely pleasant behavior.

Studies show that abusive families interact less frequently than nonviolent controls, are more negative, and often cover hostility with falsely pleasant behavior (Bousha & Twentyman, 1984; Burgess & Conger, 1978; Crittenden, 1981, 1985a, 1985b; Dietrich, Starr, & Weisfeld, 1983; Kavanagh, Youngblade, Reid, & Fagot, 1988). Moreover, family members may shift style of interaction in different relationships—that is, abused children may be compliant with teachers and yet bully peers, and abusive mothers may be aggressive with their infants but submissive to partners (Crittenden, 1988a, 1992d; George & Main, 1979; Lynch & Cicchetti, 1991).

Relationships between family members reflect the negative quality of daily interactions: Children are attached insecurely, and mothers and partners have anxious relationships with their parents and with each other (Crittenden, Partridge, & Claussen, 1991; Egeland & Sroufe, 1981; Gaensbauer & Harmon, 1982; Lynch & Cicchetti, 1991; Lyons-Ruth, Connell, & Zoll, 1989). Current work suggests that information about relationships actually is perceived and processed differently by individuals who have lived in violent families than by those who have not (Crittenden, 1988b, 1993; Frodi & Lamb, 1980; Frodi & Smetna, 1984; Main & Goldwyn, 1984; Rieder & Cicchetti, 1989). Specifically, the work of Crittenden and of Frodi and her colleagues suggests that members of abusive families may respond more negatively than normative controls to aversive communications while concurrently attributing negative intent to positive communications. Crittenden's finding that hostility and aggression often underlie abusers' smiles and apparently playful or affectionate behavior may explain the process whereby children (and the adults they become) come to distrust and misuse ordinary communicative signals. See Crittenden (1995) for an expansion of this idea.

Representations of relationships. One way to understand shifts in behavior is to infer the nature of individuals' representations of themselves, others, and relationships (Bowlby, 1980). Three types of representations have been described: (a) procedural, based on familiar sensorimotor response patterns; (b) semantic, based on generalized verbal knowledge, and (c) episodic, based on remembered experiences. Crittenden has proposed that, in their daily behavior (i.e., based on procedural representations), members of violent families behave as if they believed that important resources (e.g., love, attention, money) were in short supply and were allocated on the basis of power (Crittenden, 1988a). Thus, in a relationship in which one perceives oneself to be powerful, aggressive behavior would function to retain one's own resources as well as to obtain some of the other person's resources. For example, an abusive mother might respond angrily to her crying infant because she has perceived her baby as trying to monopolize her attention. On

the other hand, when she perceives herself to be "down one," she might become compliant and use misleading behavior to retain her own resources and possibly cajole resources from the other.

Semantic representations are thought to be used for problem solving when procedural representations have not been effective (Crittenden, 1992d). Because semantic representations are drawn from what one is told by parents, teachers, and others, they would not necessarily match procedural representations. Indeed, the more upsetting one's prior experience, the more likely that procedural and semantic representations would be kept separate and unintegrated (Bowlby, 1980; Crittenden, 1990; Tulving, 1985). For violent families, representations inferred from behavior would not be expected to match individuals' verbalized beliefs and knowledge regarding child rearing (Azar, Robinson, Hekimian, & Twentyman, 1984; Crittenden, 1992d). Instead, verbal explanations would reflect what parents had been told and now themselves believe. Thus, violent parents might discuss their child-rearing style and values in a normative manner without awareness of the conflict with their actual behavior.

Finally, behavior when individuals are aroused emotionally would be based on episodic representations that reflect prior experiences when the individual has been strongly aroused by the same emotions.

The pain, distress, shame, and feelings of helpless rage associated with experiences of abuse may create mental barriers to reliving these unresolvable agonies; such barriers can prevent individuals from recalling them.

The pain, distress, shame, and feelings of helpless rage associated with experiences of abuse may create mental barriers to reliving these unresolvable agonies; such barriers can prevent individuals from recalling them (Bowlby, 1980; Crittenden, 1992d; Crittenden, Lang, Claussen, & Partridge, 1992). The outcome may be both inexplicable shifts in behavior and failure of individuals to learn to control their behavior when highly aroused.

Developmental pathways. A second perspective, that of developmental pathways, focuses on variation (Bowlby, 1988). Not all families with abuse are identical, nor are they static over time. Studies that identify developmental pathways and the conditions associated with those pathways are useful for understanding the adaptive value of children's behavior. This approach conceptualizes abused children as actively seeking ways of adapting to their world rather than solely as being victims of it.

Two patterns of adaptation to abuse have been reported (Crittenden, 1992b). One involves fear, inhibition, and compliance (Crittenden & DiLalla, 1988; Lynch & Roberts, 1982; Ounsted, Oppenheimer, & Lindsay, 1975). Some children learn in infancy to inhibit displays of negative affect that anger caregivers; in doing so, they take responsibility for regulating parental behavior. Later, many learn to portray falsely positive affect and comply with even the most unreasonable parental demands. Such compulsively compliant children become very skilled at interpreting social signals, covering their true feelings, and meeting the demands of others. They also experience pervasive but unacknowledged anger and fear.

The second pattern typifies children who use coercive behavior to limit parental aggression. Such children become increasingly disruptive, uncontrollable, and, in some cases, delinquent (Patterson, 1982; Reidy, 1977; Wolfe, 1985). By refusing to accept responsibility for managing others' behavior, focusing instead on their own anger and the injustice of their circumstances, they attempt to intimidate others into placating them (Crittenden, 1994). This pattern relieves them of guilt and protects them psychologically from internalized anger. The price, however, is failure to (a) learn prosocial behavior, (b) use internal regulatory strategies, and (c) recognize and modify their contribution to relationships. These, in turn, increase the probability that others will be angered by them (even to the point of violence) and will, ultimately, fulfill their expectation of rejection and mistreatment (Patterson, 1982). In sum, it appears that although both patterns of adaptation reduce the risk of parental violence, each exacts a toll on the development of children who use it.

Suggestions for research. In the context of what is already known about physically abusing families, three areas of investigation are most important. First, more information is needed about developmental pathways, both for individual family members and for families as a whole. This is particularly true for school-aged children and adolescents on whom there are relatively few studies. Of particular importance is identifying variables associated with the selection of and shifts in developmental pathways. A second important focus is the mental process that results in the distortions of child rearing that typify abusers. In particular, a focus on differential patterns of (a) affect regulation and communication of affect and (b) patterns of mental access to information is recommended. Third, patterns of spousal relationship and regulation of family organization warrant further investigation. These three recommendations are related and should be integrated.

Implications for intervention. Most parents who physically abuse children possess both developmental information and the ability to articulate appropriate approaches to child rearing (Kravitz & Driscoll, 1983). Nevertheless, this information does not appear to guide their behavior in stressful circumstances. In fact, information can be misapplied by emotionally aroused parents as, for example, when parents place small children in isolating and extended time-out conditions. Consequently, parent education may be of little value and may even be harmful in some cases by giving parents new weapons to misuse while concurrently increasing their feelings of competence and authority.

Instead, intervention should focus on (a) "curbing" dangerous parental behavior, (b) teaching coping strategies that create affective distance of the parent from the conflict, and, ultimately, (c) focusing on patterns of miscommunication, particularly affective miscommunication, that may instigate bouts of violence. However, if the research suggesting that there is more than one type of abusive family is accurate, then we must presume that more than one type of intervention is needed. Moreover, as with pharmacological treatment, applying the wrong intervention to a family may be harmful. Such an approach will require individualized combinations of limit setting and supportive relations but can be implemented in group settings (Crittenden, 1991).

Families With Physical Child Neglect

The study of neglectful families has followed a different course from the study of physical child abuse. Instead of being supported by national outrage, the study of child neglect has been the province of a relatively small number of investigators. These investigators recognized the threat to children of a condition that produced few injuries and fewer cases that could be construed, in adversarial terms, as parental attack on innocent children.

One of the most obvious features of neglectful families is that everyone is neglected.

Indeed, one of the most obvious features of neglectful families is that everyone is neglected (Crittenden, 1992a; Lally, 1984; Polansky, Borgman, & DeSaix, 1972; Wolock & Horowitz, 1984). In these families, there is not even the appearance of winners or of the misuse of strength; there are only losers and pervasive incompetence. In the context of societal neglect, less research has been undertaken. With fewer empirical findings and limited success of intervention (Daro, 1988), development of theory has lagged behind theory relevant to physical child abuse. Nevertheless, there are interesting hypotheses for testing in future research as well as initiatives in the development of theory.

Characteristics of families that neglect children. Child neglect is even more closely tied to poverty than physical child abuse. Indeed, most neglectful families depend on public assistance for their basic life needs. In addition, neglectful families tend to be large, have relatively few adults, and are structured around the mother and her children (Crittenden, 1988a; Nelson, Saunders, & Landsman, 1990; Polansky, Hally, & Polansky, 1975). Men often bear a tangential relationship to neglectful families; although some are married, most are boyfriends functioning

temporarily as family members. Maternal grandmothers, on the other hand, often function in permanent parental roles. Geographic instability appears related to urbanization, with neglectful families in rural areas remaining stable but isolated and neglectful families in cities moving frequently as a result of income and interpersonal difficulties. The only stable social network for most neglectful families consists of relatives who are as impoverished as the neglectful parents and who often reinforce the parents' limited understanding of parental roles (Crittenden, 1985b; Gaudin, Wodarski, Arkinson, & Avery, 1990-1991; Polansky, Ammons, & Gaudin, 1985).

Neglect, in most cases, is an integral and pervasive aspect of the family's functioning. In this way, neglect resembles mental retardation and depression. Indeed, although most maltreating parents have less education than nonmaltreating parents, neglectful parents have the least education, with many functioning in the mildly retarded range (Polansky et al., 1972). Moreover, most appear depressed, although few are evaluated formally for depression. Consequently, it is probable that mental retardation and depression interact with physical neglect, although the nature and extent of the interaction are unclear at present. Nevertheless, identifying psychological constraints on intellectual performance and mood would be useful for developing successful treatments for neglectful families.

Critical causes of neglect. Because there has been substantially less research on neglect than on abuse, theories regarding its causes are less developed. Three perspectives have been offered; these theories differ in the emphasis placed on causal conditions, although they are not incompatible.

One perspective is sociological; neglect is seen as being caused primarily by inadequate distribution of resources, particularly among minority groups (Wolock & Horowitz, 1979). The second focuses on the nature of interaction among members of neglectful families and identifies lack of responsiveness as reflecting, in the microcosm, the process of neglect (Crittenden, 1988a). Crittenden's (1993) recent application of the information-processing theory to parental neglect expands this line of thinking. Finally, the third focuses on the immaturity of neglectful parent (Heap, 1991; Polansky,

Chalmers, Williams, & Buttenweiser, 1981; Polansky, Gaudin, Ammons, & Davis, 1985). Each of these perspectives adds useful information, with the second and third having much in common. To date, however, studies that differentiate among them have not been carried out.

Psychological unavailability. Interactions among members of neglectful families differ from interactions in both normative and violent families in several ways. First, there is much less interaction among family members in neglectful families than in any other type of family (Burgess & Conger, 1978; Crittenden, 1981, 1985a, 1985b; Crittenden & Bonvillian, 1984; Deitrich et al., 1983). Moreover, the interaction that does occur tends to be brief, lifeless, and, especially with older children, negative. The effect on children is the perception of parents as psychologically unavailable (Egeland & Erickson, 1987).

Psychological unavailability has been associated with greater developmental problems than the hostility and anger of abuse or even the deprivation of physical neglect.

Psychological unavailability has been associated with greater developmental problems than the hostility and anger of abuse or even the deprivation of physical neglect (Claussen & Crittenden, 1991; Crittenden, Claussen, & Sugarman, 1994; Egeland, Sroufe, & Erickson, 1983).

Applying the notion of internal representational models to neglect suggests that both neglectful parents and their children have models of powerlessness (Crittenden, 1988a). They not only see themselves as powerless, but they perceive everyone else to be powerless. Because they believe everyone is powerless, they believe that effort to achieve goals is futile. Even accepting an offer of a reward for certain kinds of effort (e.g., better housing as a result of filling out applications) appears useless if one believes that no one has the power to make things happen. Luck and fate (e.g., "If it is meant to be, it will happen") become the primary explanatory mechanisms. Such beliefs are associated with lethargy and depres-

sion (Seligman, 1975) and are precisely the beliefs fostered by the vacuous family experiences of neglectful families.

In sum, neglectful families appear to experience very attenuated interpersonal relationships. Men are distanced from the mother-child core of the family, interaction and affective involvement between adults and children are minimal, and relationships with friends are limited in quantity and intensity. On the other hand, there is an element of enmeshment in neglectful families, with multigeneration family units blending and maintaining proximity, continuity, and functional unity over time (Nelson et al., 1990).

Developmental pathways. Infants who experience neglect become listless, apathetic, and developmentally delayed. As they become more passive, they offer less impetus to their parents to engage them in activity. Thus, an interactive cycle of progressively less stimulation is created.

For children, however, maturation creates possibilities for change. Specifically, when neglected infants achieve locomotion, some respond with tremendous activity (Crittenden, 1992b). They seem frantic in their seeking of stimulation. Nevertheless, this stimulation often has little impact on their cognitive development because they do not attend to the effects of their behavior. Instead, they behave in ways typical of hyperactive children with attention deficits (Aragona & Eyberg, 1981). For other neglected children, however, the passivity and depression of early infancy remain unchanged.

For families, the developmental progression begins with unresponsive and withdrawn parents who fail to learn how to cope with infant behavior as it emerges. Instead, they face increasing numbers of children (each with different developmental needs). Without either the usual resources of adults for dealing with problems or the learned competencies of parents who developed parenting skills by responding to their growing children, neglectful parents are completely unable to comprehend or manage the demands of their maturing families. The outcome is chaos: families with little structure, few rules, and family members without learned self-control. In this context, neglectful parents often respond with outbursts of anger and frustration when the situation becomes overwhelming (see the "Families With Both Physical Abuse and Physical Neglect" section, below). Unlike discipline-related abuse, however, the violence in neglectful families is unpredictable and unfocused. Consequently, it leaves children with few options for predicting and accommodating parental behavior.

Recommendations for research. In the most troublesome cases, neglect is endemic and chronic. It is also most prevalent in contexts in which preventive and rehabilitative services are most limited. Future research should differentiate the role of poverty from characteristics of the families themselves (e.g., experiences of powerlessness and/or verbal attributions of powerlessness). In addition, approaches to prevention and treatment that focus on the unique needs of neglectful families are needed. Finally, careful developmental work is needed to understand the contributions to neglect of mental retardation and depression.

Implications for treatment. Many individuals in neglectful families function like mildly retarded individuals. Thus, it is unlikely that they can respond easily to interventions that require rapid changes or substantial cognitive involvement. Moreover, multiple interventions delivered concurrently are likely to overwhelm their limited social competency.

Instead, it seems appropriate that the community takes responsibility for some of the needs of neglectful families (e.g., housing, intellectual stimulation of young children, and school attendance of older children). Treatment should focus on the meaningfulness of behavior (i.e., teaching all members of neglectful families to expect outcomes, especially rewards, for effort on their part). Until the cycle of failure to learn cause-and-effect relations is broken, other efforts to create change are likely to fail. Finally, the limited social competencies of neglectful parents suggest that only a very few individuals should deliver services, and their relationship to the family should be long and intensive (see Crittenden, 1991; Gaudin, in press).

Families With Both Physical Abuse and Physical Neglect

Most families that maltreat children experience forms of both abuse and neglect. Very few studies, however, differentiate this group from others; consequently, less is known about the unique characteristics of families who both abuse and neglect their children than about families in which the conditions are separate.

In the absence of more complete information, both descriptions above can be applied to these families. An important aspect of this combination, however, may be the manner in which hostile interference and unavailability are integrated. In some families, it is clear what will arouse withdrawn parents from lethargy to angry involvement. In such cases, children will be able to make reasonable predictions about the effects of their behavior and thus organize their behavior protectively.

In other cases, parental oscillation between these two states is unpredictable. In such cases, children will not be able to discern relations between their own behavior and parental responses. Not only is their situation dangerous, it is uncontrollable and unpredictable. Unfortunately, children are likely to respond with frozen wariness. This not only stifles their development, but it is also likely to further aggravate hurt, angry, and withdrawn parents, thus exacerbating and continuing the pattern of family functioning.

Families With Sexual Abuse

The literature on sexually abusing families is less developed than that on families with physical abuse or physical neglect. Until recently, most studies of sexual abuse were clinical descriptions of psychopathological symptoms. Even now, primary focuses are prevalence, symptoms, and effects. In other words, studies focus on establishing the importance and extent of the problem.

Those studies that focus directly on the familial environment explore clinically derived hypotheses regarding such constructs as the structure, patterns of communication, and power/control imbalance within families with a sexually abused child. Nevertheless these studies are, in general, methodologically weak (Haugaard & Reppucci, 1988; Reppucci & Haugaard, 1993). For example, many use very small samples (e.g., Levang, 1988, 1989) or retrospective measures.

Others select samples and comparison groups of convenience that are biased in ways that do not reflect the population of sexually abused children and their families (e.g., children in residential treatment centers) (Hoagwood, 1990), college students, men in court processes (Lang, Langevin, Van Santen, Billingsley, & Wright, 1990), men who admit the sexual abuse and accept treatment (Smith & Saunders, 1994), and women in treatment for childhood experiences of incest.

Most of these studies use general self-report measures that are easy to administer but that have not proven to be powerful in other areas of psychology. Indeed, the contradictory nature of the results reported in studies using such measures may be due, in part, to the lack of relation between the name of the construct to be measured (e.g., dominance, enmeshment) and what actually is measured. Unfortunately, the few studies that use more time-consuming observational measures are hampered by unreasonably small samples and the lack of blind observers (e.g., Hoagwood, 1990).

Finally, most test univariate hypotheses in which sexual abuse is presumed to account for any observed effects. As Briere and Elliott (1993) point out, multivariate theories, methodologies, and statistics are all needed. Ironically, one of the few studies that collected data on other forms of maltreatment in sexually abusing families did not report the relative impact of these experiences on the functioning of family members. Finally, there is still a tendency to treat sexual abuse as a unique syndrome rather than to integrate it into the body of developmental and clinical literature.

In light of these limitations, it is not surprising that the outcomes are often meager and contradictory. One of the clearest hypotheses—that of male perpetrators expressing power, dominance, and control through sexual behavior— has not been supported (Levang, 1988). Other studies have found differences in family structure, but the nature of the differences is unclear. In one study, mothers appear to be excluded from family involvement (Levang, 1988), but in another, the estranged individuals are nonabused siblings (Saunders, Lipovsky, & Hanson, 1994). Similarly, there is some evidence that incestuous families are enmeshed, but this is not supported by self-report measures (Smith & Saunders,

1994) or receives only inferential support (Saunders et al., 1994).

Saunders's conclusion that there may not be a single sexual abuse syndrome fits both the variations in findings across studies and the direction of research in the area of physical abuse. Pursuing both this hypothesis and the notion of multiple, correlated causal variables (i.e., systemically organized sets of causal conditions) permits speculation that two opposite family processes might account for the higher than usual occurrence of sexual abuse. In one pattern, intrafamilial boundaries would be blurred (Finkelhor, 1986; Sgroi, 1982), family members would experience anxiety about relationships and fear of abandonment by loved ones (Finkelhor, 1986; Herman & Hirschman, 1981), conflict and dissatisfaction would characterize relationships (Lang et al., 1990), and members would perceive one another as intimidatingly dominant and themselves as yielding, compliant, and victimized (Finkelhor, 1986; Lang et al., 1990). Based on similar patterns of dyadic functioning in the attachment literature (i.e., the Type-C coercive pattern) (Crittenden, 1995), such families would both seek closeness and find intimacy uncomfortable (Finkelhor, 1986; Lang et al., 1990). High levels of anxiety would be expressed both directly (Smith & Saunders, 1994) and as relatively volatile shifts among feelings of desire for comfort, fear, and anger (Lang et al., 1990). These mixed feelings would lead to lack of clarity as to why family members behaved as they did, including the reasons for the sexual abuse (Lang et al., 1990). In these families, sexual activity with both spouse and children would reflect an unsoothable anxiety about relationships but not sexual dysfunction (Lang et al., 1990). Other efforts to regulate anxiety and intensely volatile feelings would be expected to include alcohol or drug use; such usage would also lower sexual inhibition (Finkelhor, 1986; Langevin & Lang, 1988). Sexually abusing men in families with this pattern would be likely to admit to the behavior but would claim that the child invited and enjoyed it and express remorse and the intent to desist in the future. They would be likely to do whatever was necessary to maintain contact with other family members.

In the case of the other possible pattern, a Type-A defended pattern, family members would be relatively disengaged

(Harter, Alexander, & Neimeyer, 1988), fearful of showing feelings (especially negative or tender feelings), rigid with regard to acceptable behavior (Saunders et al., 1994), and fearful of closeness. The spousal relationship in such families might be one of distance, withdrawal, and rejection (Saunders et al., 1994). Sexual abuse in such families might reflect a desperate attempt at a relationship in a manner that allows neurological, reflexive engagement in a masculine domain (i.e., sex) while, nevertheless, allowing the participants to remain psychologically distant and unavailable. If such a pattern exists, it would be likely that the perpetrators would highly condemn such behavior and, like victimized children who forget the traumatizing incident, the perpetrators might forget or deny their participation. To professionals, they would appear as incalitrant, denying men who are willing to accept separation from their families rather than admit their behavior and accept treatment.

Regardless of the number or nature of the individual and family patterns associated with child sexual abuse, several conclusions can be drawn. First, there is no evidence of a single "child sexual abuse syndrome" found in most adults or children in sexually abusive families. Second, child sexual abuse, especially incestuous abuse, appears to be quite frequent, with estimates ranging from 1:10 to 1:4 female children, depending on definition and method of estimation (Finkelhor, 1986; Reppucci & Haugaard, 1993). Third, with such a high frequency, sexual behavior might be considered more as a common variant of human behavior than abnormal behavior; this might facilitate application of knowledge of normal behavior to cases of child sexual abuse. In support of this suggestion is the well-replicated finding that perpetrators of child sexual behavior do not suffer from inflated levels of psychopathology and are, indeed, normal in most ways (Finkelhor, 1986). Of particular importance is the role of gender (i.e., biology) and gender stereotypes (i.e., culture) on sexual behavior. Fourth, child sexual abuse is not solely a function of distortions in the perpetrator; instead, it is tied to aspects of communities, families, and children themselves (Hoagwood, 1990). These, in turn, may leave some families and their children vulnerable to repeated abuse even when the original perpetrator is removed. Finally, the effects of child sexual abuse on children's development vary greatly, from no discernible effects to a range of widely disparate outcomes.

Given the relatively unsophisticated state of research in sexual abuse as well as the contradictory findings, practitioners should exercise caution in interpreting findings of individual studies; this is especially important, given the emotional and political impact of sexual abuse. Under current conditions of public and professional outrage over sexual abuse, it can be especially difficult to differentiate empirical information from theories, hypotheses, and beliefs (Finkelhor, 1986).

Recognizing these limitations, the current literature suggests the need to study *families* in which there is sexual abuse. Specifically, a number of studies suggests problems in the developmental history of sexually abusing men (Finkelhor, 1986), maternal functioning (Everson, Hunter, Runyan, Edelsohn, & Coulter, 1989; Goodwin, McCarthy, & DiVasto, 1981), and the social-emotional development of sexually abused children. Furthermore, the data show that familial sexual abuse is not distributed randomly among all possible adult-child dyads (Hoagwood, 1990). Rather, male relative/daughter incest is the most common form, with father/daughter, father/son, mother/son, and mother/daughter incest showing descending frequencies (Finkelhor, 1986).

Suggestions for research. Given the relatively undeveloped state of the literature on sexual abuse and the intensely political arena in which it will be received, several directions for research are especially important. First, sound descriptive studies of family functioning are needed; these should use standard methodological controls to protect the validity of the data and results. Research on sexual abuse is hampered particularly by the absence of widely accepted theory and empirical information regarding normal development and expression of sexuality among humans. Although such work is most properly within the domain of developmental psychology, the importance of sexual abuse highlights the need for a normative basis from which to understand aberrations of sexual behavior.

Second, studies using systemic theories (i.e., social ecology, family systems, attachment, communication, and social learning theory with feedback loops) may illuminate perplexing areas of our current understanding. The use of systemic theories is especially advantageous because these theories focus on the functioning of complexly interactive organizations (such as human beings and families), without imposing assumptions of blame or victimization on the observations. These interpretative features might best be applied in the arenas of politics, law, and religion, *after* sound descriptive data have been generated.

Third, future studies should devote more effort to operationalizing central constructs. Of particular importance is the use of multimethod designs that include a variety of data-gathering procedures, especially observational measures, in contrast to excessive dependence on self-report scales.

Fourth, future studies should consider aspects of sexual abuse that can be conceptualized in more universal terms. For example, coercion, intimacy, violence, and falsification of affective displays are all relevant to sexual abuse. Much is known about these conditions in families in which sexual abuse is not the focal issue. These findings could be informative regarding the functioning of families with sexual abuse.

Finally, given the findings that suggest one quarter of females may have experienced sexual abuse, often in a familial context, more consideration should be given to the prevalence among males of sexually abusive behavior. Although at present sexual abuse is treated as deviance, statistically it may turn out to be fairly common. If so, the distinction between deviant and unacceptable will become important, as will consideration of the causes of such frequent occurrence of an unacceptable behavior. (A parallel to this is physical punishment, which is very common among parents but increasingly unacceptable.)

Implications for treatment. Most treatment of sexual abuse is directed at either the child or the perpetrator; family treatment is very rare. Although many clinicians strenuously would oppose "subjecting" the child to further contact with the sexually abusive adult, the implications of the limited research on sexually abusive families and the more substantial literature on families and maltreating families more generally suggests that all family members are affected by and participate in the family process, which includes sexual abuse. Of course, participation in a family process does not imply responsibil-

ity for, or even knowledge of, that process. It does imply that one's behavior is modified as a result of it and that modification often enables the process to persist. In the case of familial sexual abuse, the child, siblings, and the other parent all learn to relate in the context of a sexual relation between parent and child. There is clear evidence that this affects sexually abused girls' behavior by making them more sexual and more vulnerable to future sexual abuse by other men. It is probable that other family members also are affected. Family treatment that enables all family members to learn more healthy ways of interacting and maintaining closeness both could heal the family (an important support to humans throughout their lives) and increase the children's potential of moving forward into healthy marital relationships with appropriate parenting of their own children. In addition, abused children may learn in the family and confirm in some sorts of treatment that they are victims—that is, they are unable to protect themselves. This self-definition will serve them very poorly in the future. Family treatment that enables them to participate actively in the restructuring of family relationships might prove to be a more empowering process than anger, accusations, and separation from family members.

Families With Psychological Maltreatment

Psychological maltreatment has only received attention recently (Garrison, 1987). Moreover, even that attention has not had the priority of the focus on physical and sexual abuse. Consequently, far less is known about the nature of families with psychological maltreatment. This is unfortunate because psychological maltreatment appears to be the "active ingredient" in other types of maltreatment (Brassard, Germain, & Hart, 1987; Claussen & Crittenden, 1991; Crittenden et al., 1994; Garbarino, Guttman, & Seely, 1986; Hart & Brassard, 1987; Jean-Gilles & Crittenden, 1990). That is, the evidence suggests that the presence and severity of psychological maltreatment affect outcomes to children more than do the presence and severity of physical maltreatment (Crittenden et al., 1994; Kavanagh, 1982; Navarre, 1987).

Characteristics of psychologically maltreating families. Most studies of psychological maltreatment focus on defining and assessing psychological maltreatment; few have attended to the effects of psychological maltreatment as differentiated from the effects of physical abuse or neglect (cf. Claussen & Crittenden, 1991). In this context, it is not surprising that studies of families with psychological maltreatment have not been undertaken.

On the other hand, it is apparent that the great majority of cases of physical maltreatment have psychological components. Consequently, what has been said above with regard to specific types of maltreatment can be applied to psychologically maltreating families in which there is physical abuse and/or neglect.

The functioning of psychologically maltreating families that have not been reported for physical maltreatment is less well investigated. In fact, it is not clear who these families are. They may include middle-income families with both physical and psychological maltreatment who, because of biases protecting middle-income families, are not reported. They may also include families who enter the mental health treatment system rather than the child protection system. In addition, there may be many families who, under the stress of family crises, such as divorce, death, relocation, and unemployment, temporarily psychologically maltreat their children. That such families exist in sufficient numbers to warrant investigation is suggested by Crittenden and her colleagues' findings of 11% to 13% of unreported psychological maltreatment of at least mild severity in a community control sample (Claussen & Crittenden, 1991; Crittenden et al., 1994).

Recommendations for research. The primary issues needing research in the area of psychological maltreatment are more basic than those for physical abuse and neglect. Consensus needs to be achieved regarding the definition and assessment of psychological maltreatment. This information then can be used to determine which groups are at risk and which institutional structures (e.g., mental health treatment, child protection, the courts) can best respond to the issue. Moreover, only when cases of psychological maltreatment can be identified with consistency can meaningful studies of family functioning be undertaken.

Implications for treatment. Two approaches need to be taken for the treatment of psychological maltreatment. The first involves case management and treatment for families already referred to protective services for physical maltreatment. For these families, it is critical that current means of assessing psychological maltreatment (cf. Baily & Baily, 1986; Cicchetti & Barnett, 1991; Claussen & Crittenden, 1991) be applied at once and integrated into the treatment planning process. This information will probably reduce judgments regarding severity in some cases, but in other cases that currently are being given little attention, judgments of severity would increase, implying an increased need for resources. In addition, there is a need for family-level interventions (e.g., family therapy or counseling). In other words, enough already is known about psychological maltreatment to improve services to families that are currently in the child protection system.

On the other hand, there is too little information on unreported cases of psychological maltreatment to determine where they should be directed or what services should be provided. Without such information, a rush to expand the child protection system to include them might be counterproductive for both the families already being managed by this overwhelmed system and the families to be added. In this context, development of prevention, family support, and mental health services to meet the needs of psychologically maltreating families is recommended.

Families With Marginal Maltreatment

Half of all families reported for maltreatment do not, after investigation, receive protective services. In most cases, however, there is evidence of child-rearing problems that are not severe enough to warrant mandated protective services. These families are considered here under the label of marginal maltreatment.

Family characteristics. Marginally maltreating families are not a homogeneous group. Instead, they consist of mildly abusing, abusing and neglecting, and neglecting families as well as severely maltreating families in the process of recovering and formerly adequate families whose situation is deteriorating. Such a heterogeneous group obviously has families that are similar to other groups of maltreating and adequate families. Nevertheless, a few characteristics do seem to typify marginally maltreating families. The most prominent is their crisis orientation.

Like other maltreating families, marginally maltreating families are typified by low income, limited education, large numbers of children, and family instability. Unlike many families with substantiated maltreatment, however, marginally maltreating families seem to lurch from crisis to crisis. Every time problems surface, it is unclear whether they will survive or be overwhelmed by the problems. Indeed, the group is at high risk for parenting failure.

Nevertheless, most crises are resolved sufficiently for the family to function with at least minimum adequacy. On the basis of current research, the source of this resilience only can be conjectured but is of considerable importance for this group of families as well as for more disturbed families.

Representational models as critical causes. The range of problems typifying marginally maltreating families highlights the need for parsimony in theory. Again, quality of relationships may function as a "critical cause." Marginally maltreating families may be troubled by both distancing from, and preoccupation with, family relationships; that is, if family relationships are conceptualized on a continuum from uninvolved to overinvolved, marginally maltreating families may oscillate from underinvolved to overinvolved. Unlike more seriously dysfunctional families, who tend to deny problems even when faced with obvious dysfunction, marginally maltreating families may deny the daily assortment of troubles as well as some past traumas, but only until the problem reaches crisis proportions. When action must be taken to prevent disaster, marginally maltreating families suddenly may become preoccupied with the problem to the exclusion of other concerns.

Behaviorally, this would appear as sudden support of family members (even those whom one has threatened to abandon) in the context of angry preoccupation with efforts to stave off the impending disaster. This approach, in its early (dismissing/disengaged) stages would protect family members from being constantly aware of, and aroused by, threats to their unity. In later (preoccupied/enmeshed) stages, it would protect families from disintegration. This bimodal approach, however, would also preclude constructive action to resolve difficulties and prevent future problems, thus leaving families enmeshed in troubled relationships about which they could not communicate fruitfully.

Recommendations for research. Research on marginally maltreating families is needed across a wide range of topics. Studies of families with unsubstantiated reports should identify the proportion that is deteriorating in functioning as opposed to those that are improving or remaining stable. Given the hypothesis of interpersonal relationships as critical causes, researchers should explore the quality of relations associated with family deficiencies (e.g., school, work, and agency relationships). More focused studies of family functioning could test the hypothesis of oscillation from underinvolved to overinvolved and the presence of anxious relationships (i.e., parent-child, parent-parent).

Implications for intervention. Although the multiple problems of these families suggest the need to deliver an array of services, it is possible that doing so would be counterproductive. Indeed, the families' chaotic situation and anxious relationships suggest the need to establish one or two long-term, stable, professional relationships and to organize interventions sequentially so as not to demand too much change too soon (i.e., to avoid destabilizing the family). These suggestions are expanded at greater length below and in Crittenden (1991).

Assessment and Treatment Planning

This chapter offers an integration of the literature on families that maltreat children. Type of maltreatment was found to be a useful basis on which to distinguish among patterns of family dynamics. These patterns, however, should be applied with care. No family fully fits any one pattern, and some maltreating families fit none of them. Moreover, the pattern of any specific family may not fit the type of maltreatment with which the pattern is usually associated. The point is that the patterns are prototypical guides, not structures into which families can be forced.

The intent in describing these patterns is to highlight important aspects of family dynamics.

The intent in describing these patterns is to highlight important aspects of family dynamics. Knowledge of these dynamics is important both for assessment and for treatment. It is hoped that recognition of the systemic interrelatedness of family functioning will broaden the assessment process to all family members and encourage family-based treatment planning and service delivery.

One approach is to consider families' level of functioning from the perspective of *how* services are used (Crittenden, 1992c). Traditionally, assessment is used to identify *what* families need and match appropriate services to those needs. This can, however, result in supplying too many or inappropriate services to families. This, in turn, not only reduces the effectiveness of intervention, but it also wastes valuable resources.

For example, treatment plans for multiproblem families usually involve an array of services to address the families' many needs. Families, however, are left to manage complex service schedules, establish relationships with the many professionals delivering the services, and integrate the various changes implied by the services into the functioning of their families. Most multiproblem families are not capable of such organization, planning, networking, and integration. In some cases, rapid change itself threatens tenuous family bonds. Under such conditions, many families break up by having the adults separate or by having children removed to foster care. Others refuse to comply by moving or passively failing to respond (Crittenden, 1987).

These problems can be avoided if families are considered from the perspective of their ability to assess their own state, to seek services to meet their own needs,

and to change in accordance with their needs. From this perspective, families are viewed as problem-solving, resource-allocating units. Because all families experience problems, and all families must adjust to the development of their members, problems alone are not informative of family functioning. Of interest here is families' ability to respond adaptively to problems. The application of a scale of family functioning might be helpful (Crittenden, 1992c).

Independent and adequate families adequately assess the needs of family members, gather resources to meet those needs, and integrate necessary changes into the family's functioning.

Other families are best described as *vulnerable to crisis*. In general, these families are capable of independent and adequate functioning but, in the light of some current problem, temporarily need help in organizing a response. Families experiencing divorce, giving birth to a handicapped child, or experiencing nonfamilial assault on one of their children may become vulnerable to crisis. Such families need several months of assistance before they are able to regain their balance and manage their own affairs.

Multiproblem families tend to be restorable or supportable. *Restorable* families are potentially independent and adequate but typically require 2 to 5 years of carefully managed service provision to become capable of independent functioning.

Supportable families, on the other hand, are sufficiently limited that they cannot be expected to make essential changes quickly enough to meet the developmental needs of their children. With assistance through ongoing services, however, they can be sustained as family units. Examples of supportable families would be families with retarded or chronically depressed parents.

A small number of families are unable to rear their children with even minimal adequacy, regardless of what services are offered. These families are *inadequate* and should have their children moved to permanent placements immediately.

Application of this type of assessment to families offers a new dimension to planning. Rather than simply identifying deficiencies, this approach considers strengths and families' ability to participate in the process of assessment and provision of resources. Using it could prevent short-term, preventive, and crisis services from being offered to "restorable" and "supportable" families (who are unlikely to benefit from them), thus making these services available to "vulnerable to crisis" families. In addition, such an approach would highlight the need for appropriate services to more troubled families. Finally, application of these ideas could lead to more successful treatment (see Crittenden, 1991, for a fuller discussion of these ideas).

Conclusion

The literature on the functioning of families with maltreated children varies considerably by type of maltreatment. Because more research has been directed toward physical abuse, well-delineated patterns can be described in the context of sophisticated theories. For neglect, there is less research but enough to have comparative studies and several theoretical perspectives that await testing and integration. For physical abuse and neglect, the role of poverty is critical to defining the extent of the problem.

Until economic policies are enacted that assist families, it is unrealistic to expect that family-level intervention will be sufficient to end the problems of child abuse and neglect (Crittenden, 1993). The literature in the areas of sexual abuse, psychological maltreatment, and marginal maltreatment is far less complete or well controlled. Consequently, conclusions regarding families experiencing those problems are much less certain. Moreover, theoretical approaches are only beginning to move beyond the descriptive level to true hypothesis testing.

Finally, the implications for treatment of the research have been considered. The descriptions of family patterns suggest aspects of family functioning that might be incorporated into current assessment procedures. In addition, both suggestions relate to each type of maltreatment, and a suggestion for evaluating families in terms of level of family functioning has been offered. Together, these approaches indicate the need for family-level assessment and intervention and for differential treatment for different types of families.

References

Aragona, J., & Eyberg, S. (1981). Neglected children: Mothers' report of child behavior problems and observed verbal behavior. *Child Development, 52,* 596-602.

Azar, S., Robinson, D., Hekimian, E., & Twentyman, C. (1984). Unrealistic expectations and problem-solving ability in maltreating and comparison mothers. *Journal of Consulting and Clinical Psychology, 52,* 687-691.

Baily, T. F., & Baily, W. F. (1986). *Operational definitions of child emotional maltreatment: Final report.* Augusta: Maine Department of Social Services, EM Project, Bureau of Social Services.

Bousha, D., & Twentyman, C. (1984). Mother-child interactional style in abuse, neglect, and control groups: Naturalistic observations in the home. *Journal of Abnormal Psychology, 93,* 106-114.

Bowlby, J. (1980). *Attachment and loss: Vol. 3. Loss, sadness and depression.* New York: Basic Books.

Bowlby, J. (1988). *A secure base: Clinical applications of attachment theory.* London: Tavistock/ Routledge.

Brassard, M., Germain, R., & Hart, S. (Eds.). (1987). *Psychological maltreatment of children and youth.* Elmsford, NY: Pergamon.

Briere, J., & Elliott, D. M. (1993). Sexual abuse, family environment, and psychological symptoms: On validity of statistical control. *Journal of Consulting and Clinical Psychology, 3*(2), 284-288.

Burgess, R. L., & Conger, R. D. (1978). Family interaction in abusive, neglectful, and normal families. *Child Development, 49,* 1163-1173.

Cicchetti, D., & Barnett, D. (1991). Toward the development of a scientific nosology of child maltreatment. In D. Cicchetti & W. Grove (Eds.), *Thinking clearly about psychology: Essays in honor of Paul E. Meehl* (pp. 346-377). Minneapolis: University of Minnesota Press.

Claussen, A. H., & Crittenden, P. M. (1991). Physical and psychological maltreatment: Relations among types of maltreatment. *Child Abuse & Neglect, 15,* 5-18.

Crittenden, P. M. (1981). Abusing, neglecting, problematic, and adequate dyads: Differentiating by patterns of interaction. *Merrill-Palmer Quarterly, 27,* 1-18.

Crittenden, P. M. (1985a). Maltreated infants: Vulnerability and resilience. *Journal of Child Psychology and Psychiatry, 26,* 85-96.

Crittenden, P. M. (1985b). Social networks, quality of parenting, and child development. *Child Development, 56,* 1299-1313.

Crittenden, P. M. (1987). Non-organic failure-to-thrive: Deprivation or distortion? *Infant Mental Health Journal, 8,* 51-64.

Crittenden, P. M. (1988a). Family and dyadic patterns of functioning in maltreating families. In K. Browne, C. Davies, & P. Stratton (Eds.), *Early prediction and prevention of child abuse* (pp. 161-189). London: Wiley.

Crittenden, P. M. (1988b). Relationships at risk. In J. Belsky & T. Nezworski (Eds.), *Clinical implications of attachment* (pp. 136-174). Hillsdale, NJ: Lawrence Erlbaum.

Crittenden, P. M. (1990). Internal representational models of attachment relationships. *Infant Mental Health, 11,* 259-277.

Crittenden, P. M. (1991). Treatment of child abuse and neglect. *Human systems, 2,* 161-179.

Crittenden, P. M. (1992a). *Child neglect.* Chicago: National Committee for the Prevention of Child Abuse.

Crittenden, P. M. (1992b). Children's strategies for coping with adverse home environments. *Child Abuse & Neglect, 16,* 329-343.

Crittenden, P. M. (1992c). The social ecology of treatment: Case study of a service system for maltreated children. *American Journal of Orthopsychiatry, 62,* 22-34.

Crittenden, P. M. (1992d). Treatment of anxious attachment in infancy and early childhood. *Development & Psychopathology, 4,* 575-602.

Crittenden, P. M. (1993). An information processing perspective on the behavior of neglectful parents. *Criminal Justice and Behavior, 20,* 27-48.

Crittenden, P. M. (1994). Peering into the black box: An exploratory treatise on the development of self in young children. In D. Cicchetti & S. Toth (Eds.), *Rochester symposium on developmental psychopathology: Vol. 5. The self and its disorders* (pp. 79-148). Rochester, NY: University of Rochester Press.

Crittenden, P. M. (1995). Attachment and psychopathology. In S. Goldberg, R. Muir, & J. Kerr (Eds.), *Attachment theory: Social, developmental, and clinical perspectives* (pp. 367-406). Hillsdale, NJ: Analytic Press.

Crittenden, P. M., & Ainsworth, M. D. S. (1989). Child maltreatment and attachment theory. In D. Cicchetti & V. Carlson (Eds.), *Child maltreatment: Theory and research on the causes and consequences of child abuse and neglect* (pp. 432-463). New York: Cambridge University Press.

Crittenden, P. M., & Bonvillian, J. D. (1984). The effect of maternal risk status on maternal sensitivity to infant cues. *American Journal of Orthopsychiatry, 54,* 250-262.

Crittenden, P. M., Claussen, A. H., & Sugarman, D. B. (1994). Physical and psychological maltreatment in middle childhood and adolescence. *Development and Psychopathology, 6,* 145-164.

Crittenden, P. M., & DiLalla, D. (1988). Compulsive compliance: The development of an inhibitory coping strategy in infancy. *Journal of Abnormal Child Psychology, 16,* 585-599.

Crittenden, P. M., Lang, C., Claussen, A. H., & Partridge, M. (1992, September). *Relations among mothers' procedural, semantic, and episodic models of attachment relationships.* Paper presented at the Fifth European Conference on Developmental Psychology, Sevilla, Spain.

Crittenden, P. M., Partridge, M. F., & Claussen, A. H. (1991). Family patterns of relationship in normative and dysfunctional families. *Development and Psychopathology, 3,* 491-512.

Daro, D. (1988). *Confronting child abuse.* New York: Free Press.

Deitrich, K. N., Starr, R., & Weisfeld, G. E. (1983). Infant maltreatment: Caretaker-infant interaction and developmental consequences at different levels of parenting failure. *Pediatrics, 72,* 532-540.

Egeland, B., & Erickson, M. (1987). Psychologically unavailable caregiving. In M. R. Brassard, R. Germain, & S. N. Hart (Eds.), *Psychological maltreatment of children and youth* (pp. 110-120). Elmsford, NY: Pergamon.

Egeland, B., & Sroufe, L. A. (1981). Attachment and early maltreatment. *Child Development, 52,* 44-52.

Egeland, B., Sroufe, A., & Erickson, M. (1983). The developmental consequences of different types of maltreatment. *Child Abuse & Neglect, 7,* 459-469.

Emery, R. E. (1989). Family violence. *American Psychologist, 44,* 321-328.

Everson, M. D., Hunter, W. M., Runyan, D. K., Edelsohn, G. A., & Coulter, M. L. (1989). Maternal support following disclosure of incest. *American Journal of Orthopsychiatry, 59,* 197-297.

Finkelhor, D. (1986). *A sourcebook on child sexual abuse.* Newbury Park, CA: Sage.

Frodi, A., & Smetna, J. (1984). Abused, neglected, and nonmaltreated preschoolers' ability to discriminate emotions in others: The effects of I.Q. *Child Abuse & Neglect, 8,* 459-465.

Frodi, A. M., & Lamb, M. E. (1980). Child abusers' responses to infant smiles and cries. *Child Development, 51,* 238-241.

Gaensbauer, T. J., & Harmon, R. J. (1982). Attachment behavior in abused/neglected and premature infants: Implications for the concept of attachment. In R. N. Emde & R. J. Harmon (Eds.), *The development of attachment and affiliative systems* (pp. 263-280). New York: Plenum.

Garbarino, J., & Sherman, D. (1980). High-risk neighborhoods and high-risk families: The human ecology of child maltreatment. *Child Development, 51,* 188-198.

Garbarino, J., Guttman, E., & Seely, J. W. (1986). *The psychologically battered child.* San Francisco: Jossey-Bass.

Garrison, E. G. (1987). Psychological maltreatment of children: An emerging focus for inquiry and concern. *American Psychologist, 42*(2), 157-159.

Gaudin, J. (in press). *Child neglect: Guidelines for intervention* (User manual series). Washington, DC: National Center on Child Abuse and Neglect.

Gaudin, J., Wodarski, J., Arkinson, M., & Avery, L. (1990-1991). Remedying child neglect: Effectiveness of social network interventions. *Journal of Applied Social Sciences, 15,* 97-123.

George, C., & Main, M. (1979). Social interactions of young abused children. *Child Development, 50,* 306-318.

Goodwin, J., McCarthy, T., & DiVasto, P. (1981). Prior incest in mothers of abused children. *Child Abuse & Neglect, 5,* 87-96.

Hart, S. N., & Brassard, M. R. (1987). A major threat to children's mental health: Psychological maltreatment. *American Psychologist, 42*(2), 160-165.

Harter, S., Alexander, P. C., & Neimeyer, R. A. (1988). Long-term effects of incestuous child abuse in college women: Social adjustment, social cognition, and family characteristics. *Journal of Consulting and Clinical Psychology, 56,* 5-8.

Haugaard, J. J., & Reppucci, N. D. (1988). *The sexual abuse of children: A comprehensive guide to current knowledge and intervention strategies.* San Francisco: Jossey-Bass.

Heap, K. K. (1991). A predictive and follow-up study of abusive and neglectful families by case analysis. *Child Abuse & Neglect, 15,* 261-273.

Herman, J., & Hirschman, J. (1981). Families at risk for father-daughter incest. *American Journal of Psychiatry, 138,* 967-970.

Hoagwood, K. (1990). Parental functioning and child sexual abuse. *Child and Adolescent Social Work, 7*(5), 377-387.

Jayaratne, S. (1977). Child abusers as parents and children: A review. *Social Work, 22,* 5-9.

Jean-Gilles, M., & Crittenden, P. M. (1990). Maltreating families: A look at siblings. *Family Relations,* 323-329.

Kaufman, J., & Zigler, E. (1987). Do abused children become abusive parents? *American Journal of Orthopsychiatry, 57,* 186-191.

Kavanagh, C. (1982). Emotional abuse and mental injury. *Journal of the American Academy of Psychiatry, 21,* 171-177.

Kavanagh, K. A., Youngblade, L., Reid, J. B., & Fagot, B. I. (1988). Interactions between children and abusive versus control parents. *Journal of Clinical and Child Psychology, 17*(2), 137-142.

Kempe, C. H., Silverman, F. N., Steele, B. B., Droegemueller, W., & Silver, H. K. (1962). The battered child syndrome. *Journal of the American Medical Association, 181,* 17-24.

Kravitz, R. I., & Driscoll, J. M. (1983). Expectations for child development among abusing and non-abusing parents. *American Journal of Orthopsychiatry, 53,* 336-344.

Lally, J. R. (1984). Three views of child neglect: Expanding visions of preventive intervention. *Child Abuse & Neglect, 8,* 243-254.

Lang, R. A., Langevin, R., Van Santen, V., Billingsley, D., & Wright, P. (1990). Marital relations in incest offenders. *Journal of Sex and Marital Therapy, 16,* 214-229.

Langevin, R., & Lang, R. A. (1988). *Incest: The offender, victim, and family.* Toronto: Juniper.

Levang, C. A. (1988). Interactional communication patterns in father-daughter incest patterns. *Journal of Psychology and Human Sexuality, 1,* 53-68.

Levang, C. A. (1989). Father-daughter incest families. *Contemporary Family Therapy: An International Journal, 11,* 28-44.

Lynch, M., & Cicchetti, D. (1991). Patterns of relatedness in maltreated and non-maltreated children: Connections among multiple representational models. *Development and Psychopathology, 3,* 207-226.

Lynch, M. A., & Roberts, J. (1982). *Consequences of child abuse.* London: Academic Press.

Lyons-Ruth, K., & Connell, D. B., & Zoll, D. (1989). Patterns of behavior among infants at risk for abuse: Relations with infant attachment behavior and infant development at 12 months of age. In D. Cicchetti & V. Carlson (Eds.), *Handbook of child maltreatment* (pp. 464-494). New York: Cambridge University Press.

Maden, M. F., & Wrench, D. F. (1977). Significant findings in child abuse research. *Victimology, 2,* 196-225.

Main, M., & Goldwyn, R. (1984). Predicting rejection of her infant from mother's representation of her own experience: Implications for the abused-abusing intergenerational cycle. *Child Abuse & Neglect, 8,* 203-217.

National Center on Child Abuse and Neglect. (1978). *1977 analysis of child abuse and neglect research* (Publication No. 017-091-11223-1). Washington, DC: Government Printing Office.

Navarre, E. L. (1987). Psychological maltreatment: The core component of child abuse. In M. R. Brassard, R. B. Germain, & S. N. Hart (Eds.), *Psychological maltreatment of children and youth.* Elmsford, NY: Pergamon.

Nelson, K., Saunders, E., & Landsman, M. (1990). *Chronic neglect in perspective: A study of chronically neglecting families in a large metropolitan county.* Oakdale: University of Iowa School of Social Work, National Resource Center on Family-Based Services.

Ounsted, C., Oppenheimer, R., & Lindsay, J. (1975). The psychopathology and psychotherapy of the family: Aspects of bonding failure. In A. Franklin (Ed.), *Concerning child abuse* (pp. 30-40). Edinburgh, UK: Churchill Livingston.

Parke, R. D., & Collmer, W. C. (1977). Child abuse: An interdisciplinary analysis. In E. M. Hetherington (Ed.), *Review of child development research* (Vol. 5, pp. 509-590). Chicago: University of Chicago Press.

Patterson, G. R. (1982). *Coercive families.* Eugene, OR: Castalia.

Polansky, N. A., Ammons, P. W., & Gaudin, J. (1985). Loneliness and isolation in child neglect. *Social Casework, 66,* 38-47.

Polansky, N. A., Borgman, R. D., & DeSaix, C. (1972). *Roots of futility.* San Francisco: Jossey-Bass.

Polansky, N. A., Chalmers, M. A., Williams, D. P., & Buttenweiser, E. W. (1981). *Damaged parents: An anatomy of neglect.* Chicago: University of Chicago Press.

Polansky, N. A., Gaudin, J., Ammons, P., & Davis, K. (1985). The psychological ecology of the neglectful mother. *Child Abuse & Neglect, 9,* 265-275.

Polansky, N. A., Hally, C., & Polansky, N. F. (1975). *Profile of neglect: A survey of the state of the knowledge of child neglect.* Washington, DC: Department of Health, Education, and Welfare.

Reidy, T. J. (1977). The aggressive characteristics of abused and neglected children. *Journal of Clinical Psychology, 33,* 1140-1145.

Reppucci, N. D., & Haugaard, J. J. (1993). Problems with child sexual abuse programs. In R. Gelles & D. Loseke (Eds.), *Current controversies in domestic violence* (pp. 306-322). Newbury Park, CA: Sage.

Rieder, C., & Cicchetti, D. (1989). An organizational perspective on cognitive control functioning and cognitive-affective balance in maltreated children. *Developmental Psychology, 25,* 482-493.

Saunders, B. E., Lipovsky, J. A., & Hanson, R. F. (1994). *Couple and familial characteristics of father-child incest families.* Unpublished manuscript, Medical University of South Carolina, Charleston.

Seligman, M. E. P. (1975). *Helplessness: On depression, development, and death.* San Francisco: Freeman.

Sgroi, S. M. (1982). *Handbook of clinical intervention in child sexual abuse.* Lexington, MA: Lexington Books.

Smith, D. W., & Saunders, B. E. (1994). *Personality characteristics of father/perpetrator and non-offending mothers in incest families: Individual and dyadic analyses.* Unpublished manuscript, Medical University of South Carolina, Charleston.

Tulving, E. (1985). How many memory systems are there? *American Psychologist, 40,* 385-398.

Wolfe, D. A. (1985). Child-abusive parents: An empirical review and analysis. *Psychological Bulletin, 97,* 462-482.

Wolfe, D. A., & Mosk, M. D. (1983). Behavioral comparisons of children from abusive and distressed families. *Journal of Consulting and Clinical Psychology, 51,* 702-708.

Wolock, I., & Horowitz, B. (1979). Child maltreatment and material deprivation among AFDC-recipient families. *Social Service Review, 53,* 175-194.

Wolock, I., & Horowitz, B. (1984). Child maltreatment as a social problem: The neglect of neglect. *American Journal of Orthopsychiatry, 54,* 530-543.

10

Sex Offenders Against Children

Empirical and Clinical Issues

WILLIAM D. MURPHY

TIMOTHY A. SMITH

This chapter will focus on one piece of the puzzle: the offenders. We will review existing clinical and theoretical literature and briefly discuss selected clinical issues.

Given the complexity of the literature, it is impossible to review all pertinent information in this chapter. Notably absent from this chapter are anthropological and cross-cultural studies and studies of pornography. These important areas, however, have been reviewed recently and thoroughly by others (Mrazek, 1981; Murrin & Laws, 1990; Quinsey, 1986; Stermac, Segal, & Gillis, 1990).

Empirical Foundation

Rationale for treating sex offenders. The primary rationale for treating offenders usually is considered to be the reduction of future reoffenses and therefore the reduction of the number of victims. How-

ever, outcome research, which is difficult in the mental health field in general, is particularly problematic in criminal populations in which reoffense rate or recidivism is considered the "bottom-line measure" (Furby, Weinrott, & Blackshaw, 1989). The numerous methodological problems with research in this area have been outlined by Furby et al. (1989). For example, official arrest records significantly underestimate true reoffense rates. Data from Abel and his colleagues (Abel et al., 1987) and Weinrott and Saylor (1991) indicate that offenders self-report many more victims than are known officially.

Furby et al. (1989) reviewed approximately 55 studies of recidivism with sex offenders. The studies vary considerably in types of offenders studied, length of follow-up, and definition of recidivism. In many of the studies, differential rates for child molesters were not provided. Not surprisingly, given the variability in the studies, recidivism rates varied from 0 to more than 50%, and of the studies reviewed, there was no clear trend for treated offenders to have lower recidivism rates than untreated offenders. However, in many cases, there was not random assignment, and treated and untreated offenders may have varied on a number of variables besides seeking treatment. Also, as Furby et al. (1989) point out, the treatment of sex offenders has evolved considerably over the past 10 years, and many of the studies reviewed were not studies of current treatment approaches.

Recent reviews focusing on more contemporary cognitive behavioral treatments (Marshall & Barbaree, 1990; Marshall, Jones, Ward, Johnson, & Barbaree, 1991) suggest more positive outcomes. Data from outpatient programs indicate recidivism rates ranging from 0 to 17.9% across studies and across types of child molesters. Marshall and Barbaree (1988), using official and unofficial records of follow-up ranging from 12 to 117 months, found recidivism rates of 8% for incest offenders, 13.9% for offenders against male children, and 17.9% for offenders against female children. Untreated cases showed recidivism rates of approximately 21% for incest offenders and 42.9% for both groups of offenders against nonrelated children. As one would expect, the longer the follow-up, the greater the reoffense rate. Of the 24 treated cases followed over 4 years, the recidivism rate was 25%, but for the 20 untreated cases followed over 4 years, the rate was 60%. Pithers and Cumming (1989) found a 3% recidivism rate among 137 child molesters followed for 6 years. This study of incarcerated offenders involved those who had gone through a relapse prevention program and had a very coordinated and intensive aftercare program. It appears that the more comprehensive behavioral programs show promise of reducing recidivism, although more comprehensive outcome studies are needed.

It is also possible that treatment per se is less important than the fact that the offenders in treatment are monitored more closely than offenders not in treatment. This close monitoring in incarcerated samples may provide more information for release decisions, and therefore more

dangerous offenders may be less likely to be released. In an outpatient setting, close monitoring may allow the identification of offenders who appear close to relapse so that the parole or probation system may intervene appropriately before actual offenses occur. This issue, although complex, seldom is investigated in outcome studies.

Another set of issues not usually discussed in the literature is whether the availability of offender treatment allows the child protective services system and legal system more flexibility in dealing with the problem of sexual abuse. For example, is it possible that more victims would come forward if they felt the offender would receive treatment rather than incarceration? Does the availability of treatment make it more likely that offenders would confess rather than deny their offenses, therefore not subjecting victims to the potential traumatic aspects of the legal system? This is not to imply that the legal system has to be traumatic for victims, nor does this negate the fact that for some victims, punishment of the offender may be therapeutic. However, the lack of offender treatment could reduce the options available to the criminal justice and child protective services systems in dealing with certain cases.

Of course, treatment should not be pitted against punishment. The two are not mutually exclusive, and the availability of offender treatment is desirable for all the reasons cited above.

Onset and specificity. Until recently, the common myth was that pedophilia was an adult disorder and that paraphiliacs were fairly specific in their preferred victims. However, data by Abel and his colleagues, with a group of offenders promised confidentiality, have called this notion into question (Abel, Becker, Cunningham-Rathner, Mittelman, & Rouleau, 1988; Abel et al., 1987; Abel & Rouleau, 1990).

Abel and Rouleau (1990) report that more than 50% of their offenders with multiple paraphilias had the onset of their deviant interest by age 18. Similar data have been reported by Groth, Longo, and McFadin (1982), who found the age of onset for a group of 83 rapists and 54 child molesters to be 16. Hindman (1988) reported that close to 70% of her sample of offenders began their offense patterns in adolescence. Thomas (1982) also reports that approximately 50% of victims identify their offenders as adolescents. Marshall, Barbaree, and Eccles (1991) report somewhat lower rates of onset in adolescents. Abel et al. (1988) also reported that the majority of offenders had multiple paraphilias, and this included even the incest cases. Similarly, Weinrott and Saylor (1991), using a prison sample and a self-administered offender interview, found high rates of multiple paraphilias and high rates of general criminality even among the pedophilic samples.

Current data suggest that offenders against children have an early onset, and many do not limit their offenses to one type of victim.

Current data suggest that offenders against children have an early onset, and many do not limit their offenses to one type of victim. In addition, among incarcerated offenders, the level of general criminality may be high. From a theoretical standpoint, models that attempt to explain "child molesting" also should be able to account for those offenders with multiple paraphilias and general criminal behavior. From a clinical standpoint, therapists should be aware that offenders against children may have other paraphilias and must target them for treatment. This may be especially relevant to the "incest case," in which the perpetrator may have a long history of a variety of paraphilic behaviors.

Personality and psychopathology. Attempts to find specific personality characteristics or specific types of psychopathology in sex offenders have appeared repeatedly in the literature. Much of the literature is of limited value because of the use of nonstandardized instruments or scoring techniques, inadequate control groups, and the mixing of a variety of paraphiliacs in the same group (Levin & Stava, 1987; Murphy & Stalgaitis, 1987).

Another common problem in such studies is the use of group data that may suggest more homogeneous patterns of personality types than actually exist. This error frequently is found in the interpretation of research using the Minnesota Multiphasic Personality Inventory (MMPI) with sex offenders. A number of studies found elevations on Scale 4 (psycho-

pathic deviance on the MMPI), and at times Scale 9 (hypomania) also was elevated (Langevin, Paitich, Freeman, Mann, & Handy, 1978; Panton, 1979; Swenson & Grimes, 1969). Also frequently observed were elevations on Scales 4 and 8 (schizophrenia) (Anderson & Kunce, 1979; Armentrout & Hauer, 1978; Quinsey, Arnold, & Pruesse, 1980).

Although such studies suggest certain consistencies, large-scale studies that look at the frequency of specific profiles indicate the difficulties of generalizing from mean profiles (Ericksen, Luxenburg, Walbek, & Seely, 1987; Hall, Maiuro, Vitaliano, & Proctor, 1986). These studies, with 498 and 408 subjects, respectively, found the 4-8 mean profile described earlier. However, it occurred in only 13% of the child molesters in the Ericksen et al. study and 7% of those in the Hall et al. study. In both studies, almost every possible two-point MMPI code was represented, including normal profiles. Furthermore, it does not appear that these profiles are specific to sex offenders. Quinsey et al. (1980) found similar mean profiles in a variety of forensic psychiatric populations.

The search for the typical child molester personality profile has not been successful. What the data do suggest, however, is that sex offenders against children present with a variety of personality styles and with a wide range of concomitant psychopathology. Clinically, personality assessment may still have a role in the overall assessment of patients because certain personality profiles may affect the treatment process. For example, the patients who demonstrate antisocial or borderline personality traits may raise different issues in treatment than those with dependent or avoidant patterns. These issues—that is, the impact of personality and psychopathology on the treatment process—are probably more relevant than the continued search for a specific offender profile.

Sexual arousal/sexual preference. Along with studies of personality and psychopathology, the most frequently investigated area is the physiological assessment of sexual arousal through either circumferential or volumetric penile erection measures. There have been numerous reviews that focus on the instrumentation and the operation of laboratories (Farrell, 1992; Laws & Osborn, 1983) and the critical reviews of the empirical studies (Barbaree, 1990; McConaghy, 1989; Murphy & Barbaree, 1988; Murphy, Haynes, & Worley, 1991; Murphy & Peters, 1992; Simon & Schouten, 1991).

Since the early studies of Freund (1965, 1967a, 1967b), sufficient evidence has accumulated that erectile responses to child stimuli in the laboratory situation reliably differentiate pedophiles from nonpedophiles on a group basis (see Murphy & Peters, 1992, for a review). However, this is not the case for incestuous child molesters. Quinsey, Chaplin, and Carrigan (1979); Frenzel and Lang (1989); Lang, Black, Frenzel, and Checkley (1988); and Marshall, Barbaree, and Christophe (1986) all indicate that incest offenders respond more as nonoffenders than they do as nonincestuous child molesters. Abel, Becker, Murphy, and Flanagan (1981), in a small sample using audiotaped stimuli, did not find differences between incestuous and nonincestuous offenders. Murphy, Haynes, Stalgaitis, and Flanagan (1986) replicated Abel's data with audiotapes, but with slide stimuli the incestuous offenders did not show deviant patterns. The weight of evidence indicates that the incest offenders more typically respond as nonoffenders in the laboratory.

A second problem with erection data is the problem similar to the MMPI data reviewed—that is, group data may not describe the individual accurately. Murphy et al. (1986) found that 75% of heterosexual pedophiles, 78% of homosexual pedophiles, 42% of the incest cases, and 62% of mixed cases of incest and nonincest offenders could be classified correctly using an index of the ratio of deviant to nondeviant penile arousal. However, others have found even lower rates of classification using various criteria. Marshall et al. (1986) were able to correctly classify 60% of their pedophile patients and 82% of normals using penile erection measures. Frenzel and Lang (1989) found that 42% to 50% of the various groups of pedophiles in their studies showed clear pedophilic arousal patterns.

A third problem is the use of technology with nonadmitters. Only 55% of the nonadmitters could be correctly classified by Freund and Blanchard (1989), and in a second study, Freund and Watson (1991) reported sensitivity—that is, accurately identified pedophiles—ranging from 44% to more than 80% in identifying nonadmitters (those denying their of-

fense), depending on factors such as sex, age, and number of victims. However, 14% to 26% of the patients were eliminated from the analysis for low responding or documented faking. If these subjects were included as misses, then accuracy would have been decreased further.

In summary, although sexual arousal measures may be more accurate at classifying offenders than any other measure, there is still a large error rate, and there are situations in which the measures may be of little help, such as with incestuous offenders and nonadmitters. The assessment of penile sexual arousal is an important clinical and research tool, but its limitations need to be appreciated. The technique may be useful for monitoring treatment in those with deviant arousal and at times can be used to confront subjects who deny their offense. However, little information can be gained from offenders who fail to respond in the laboratory, and the technique cannot be used to make statements regarding whether an individual fits certain profiles (Murphy & Peters, 1992).

Social competence. The clinical literature is replete with descriptions of child molesters as nonassertive, passive, shy, and inhibited. Most comprehensive clinical programs include various forms of social competency training as a component of treatment (Knopp, 1984). However, empirical studies in this area are limited. They have been reviewed recently by Stermac et al. (1990). Segal and Marshall (1985) found that child molesters were lower in assertiveness on a self-report inventory than rapists, incarcerated nonsex offenders, and high and low socioeconomic status (SES) community controls. However, no differences were found for child molesters on an assertive role-play, on a heterosocial measure, or on an attitudes toward women scale. Overall, the major differences observed in that study were that high SES subjects tended to be more socially competent than other groups.

Overholser and Beck (1986) found a trend ($p < .08$) for child molesters to be lower on self-report measures of assertiveness than rapists, nonsex offenders, and community controls. Segal and Marshall (1985) provided further evidence that child molesters may have difficulties in heterosocial skills and assertiveness skills, although findings were not consistent across different measures. Of interest was that child molesters rated themselves lower in social skills following a behavioral role-play assessment, even though judges and confederates did not necessarily rate them lower than control groups (except for the high SES control group). Similarly, Segal and Marshall (1985) found that child molesters were poorer at evaluating and predicting their performance than other sex offenders or community controls. Both child molesters and rapists were less skilled in social interactions than community controls. A recent unpublished study (Barbaree, Marshall, & Connor [1988], cited in the Stermac et al. [1990] review on problem-solving skills) found that child molesters were able to recognize a problem and could generate solutions but tended to choose inadequate solutions.

Offenders who can project blame on others and find excuses for their behavior are blocked from truly recognizing the impact their behavior has on victims.

Although studies in this area are limited, some findings have clinical significance and suggest future research directions. It is not clear that child molesters, who most clearly match the low SES subjects in low socioeconomic status, are deficient in the behavioral aspects of social skills, even though there is a trend for child molesters to score lower on self-report measures of social skills. There is also a tendency for child molesters to rate their skills lower and show poor judgment in choosing solutions to problems. These limited data suggest a need to focus not only on the behavioral aspects of social competencies but also on the offenders' perceptions of their skills and their ability to choose appropriate responses in social situations.

Cognitive distortions. Cognitive distortions in the sex offender generally refers to the excuses, minimizations, justifications, and rationalizations offenders use to describe their behavior. The focus on these kinds of variables recognizes that denial is not a yes or no phenomenon but is rather a continuum. Between the two extremes, patients vary considerably on the level of responsibility they take for their behavior. Also inherent in the discussion of cognitive distortions is the issue of victim empathy.

Offenders who can project blame on others and find excuses for their behavior basically are blocked from truly recognizing the impact their behavior has on victims.

Despite the theoretical importance of cognitive distortions, there has been limited research on cognitive characteristics of child molesters. Murphy (1990) provides a theoretical model of cognitive distortions based on Bandura's (1977) social learning model. Murphy suggests that distortions employed by offenders can be categorized under specific cognitive processes, such as justifying reprehensible conduct ("It was sex education"), misperceiving consequences ("The child didn't suffer"), or devaluing or attributing blame to the victim ("She was a very seductive child").

Similarly, Pollock and Hashmall (1991) selected 250 explanatory statements from the clinical records of 86 child molesters. These explanatory statements were used to develop an excuse syntax presented in a series of branching statements that can be used to describe the offender's level of denial. This syntax moves from

1. Denial of fact ("Nothing happened.")
2. Denial of responsibility ("Something happened but it wasn't my idea.")
3. Denial of sexual intent ("Something happened and it was my idea, but it wasn't sexual.")
4. Denial of wrongfulness ("Something happened and it was my idea, and it was sexual but it wasn't wrong.")
5. Denial of self-determination ("Something happened and it was my idea, and it was sexual and it was wrong, but there were extenuating factors.") (p. 57)

Abel et al. (1989) found that the Abel and Becker Cognition Scale separated child molesters from other types of offenders, and this was replicated by Stermac and Segal (1987). This scale measured the excuses offenders use to justify their behavior. Stermac and Segal also developed a number of offense vignettes that varied on level of sexual contact and the child's response to sexual contact. Ratings of these vignettes suggested that, compared to offenders who raped adults and nonoffenders, offenders against children saw the abuse as more beneficial to the child, saw the child as more responsible, and perceived the adult as less responsible.

With the importance cognitive factors have been given in offender treatment and the increasing presence of a cognitive focus in psychology and mental health in general, it is unfortunate that so little empirical literature exists. It is hoped that as the importance of cognitive distortions is recognized, we will see an increase in empirical investigation equal to the other areas, such as deviant sexual arousal.

Family Dysfunction

The role of family functioning within the child sexual abuse area has received significant clinical attention but little empirical investigation. Various theories speculate on issues such as family isolation, enmeshment among family members, the mother's collusion in the abuse, marital and sexual discord between the adult partners, the daughter assuming the mother's role, role confusion, and lack of clear sexual boundaries (Alexander, 1985; Cooper & Cormier, 1982; Finkelhor, 1978; Mrazek & Bentovim, 1981; Trepper & Barrett, 1986). Conte (1985) has raised concerns about much of this literature. The first and most important problem is that there is limited empirical literature to support the clinical observations generally derived from small sample case studies. Second, most theorizing regarding family dysfunction assumes a fundamental difference between intrafamily and extrafamily child sexual offending. Data by Abel and his colleagues suggest that such distinctions are not as clear as once thought. Third, although the patterns described earlier may be observed in some incestuous families, they are not observed in all families and also may be observed in nonincestuous families seeking treatment for other issues. Also not considered at times is the extent to which the incest itself is causative of family dysfunction rather than the dysfunction causing the incest. An analogy might be the family in which one of the members has a chronic, debilitating illness, and the family develops what appears to be dysfunctional patterns in coping with this illness.

Although family dysfunction may not be causative, family treatment may still be a necessary part of treatment. For whatever reasons, some families presenting for treatment are dysfunctional and are not healthy for children, regardless of whether this dysfunction is related directly to the abuse. In addition, if families are to be reunited, then families have to learn how to live with an incest offender, which in and of itself may require changes in roles within the family. Finally, the way the family functions may affect treatment significantly. The rigid, enmeshed family may require different treatment interventions and may have a different impact on the offender's treatment than the very chaotic family system.

Biological Factors

The investigation of biological dysfunctions in pedophilias has received limited attention compared to the "biological explosion" in other areas of psychopathology, such as affective and anxiety disorders. There have been case reports (Regestein & Reich, 1978) of the onset of pedophilia after cognitive impairment. Berlin (1983) described a variety of biological abnormalities in a group of 34 paraphilic patients who presented for treatment. These included endocrine, chromosome, and cortical abnormalities. It is not clear how selective this group of patients was or what percentage of the overall population seen in the clinic that this group represented.

Hucker and Bain (1990), in a review of literature related to androgen hormones, found little consistent empirical support for hormone abnormalities in child molesters, at least for abnormalities in levels of a single hormone. However, there may be more promise in endocrine challenge tests rather than in monitoring of individual hormone levels. For example, Gaffney and Berlin (1984) found that luteinizing hormone levels in pedophiles rose significantly higher after administration of a gonadotropin-releasing hormone than in nonpedophiles. Langevin, Wortzman, Wright, and Handy (1989) and Langevin, Wortzman, Dickey, Wright, and Handy (1988) provide preliminary data suggesting impairment on neuropsychological testing in pedophiles. Although in both studies pedophiles evidenced some dysfunction, there were inconsistencies in terms of specific test patterns across studies.

At this point, the investigation of biological dysfunctions is in its infancy, and the role of endocrine and neurological factors in pedophilia is unclear. A major difficulty in this area, as with other areas, is the heterogeneity of the population of child molesters. Until we are better able to diagnosis and subtype offenders against children, it is likely that inconsistencies across studies will continue, based on variations in the population studied.

Offenders as Victims

The victim to victimizer theory of sexual abuse receives repeated mention in the professional and popular literatures. It appears that in the mind of the public, and unfortunately in the minds of some professionals, all offenders are victims, and being a victim is a direct cause of sexual abuse. However, what little empirical data exist fail to support this.

The current estimate is that 10% to 15% of the male population are victimized as children (Finkelhor, Hotaling, Lewis, & Smith, 1990; Peters, Wyatt, & Finkelhor, 1986). It is highly unlikely that 10% of the male population become sex offenders. Therefore, it appears that the vast majority of victims of sexual abuse do not become offenders. Similarly, although females are victimized at even a higher rate than males, very few become offenders.

Examination of the percentage of offenders themselves who are also victims casts doubt on the role prior victimization has in the etiology of sex offending.

Examination of the percentage of offenders themselves who are also victims casts doubt on the role prior victimization has in the etiology of sex offending. Hanson and Slater (1988), in a review of 18 studies that reported rate of victimizations among offenders, found rates from 0 to about 70%. Of relevance, however, was that as the sample size increased, the rate tended to stabilize between 20% and 30%, and only in the small sample size studies was the variability in rates observed.

Hindman (1988), in a quasi-experimental study of offenders, reported that prior to requiring polygraph examinations, 67% reported they had been victims, but after subjects were informed that they would have to undergo polygraph examination, only 29% indicated they were abused. Similarly, Freund, Watson, and Dickey (1990) reported rates of prior victimization ranging between approximately 20% and 29% of a group of three types of offenders against children, versus rates of approximately 11% to 14% in three separate control groups.

Overall, the empirical data suggest that around 30% of child molesters report having been sexually abused as children. Though higher than the general population, this is not at all as high as is sometimes suggested by the literature. However, offenders who are victims may be different. Hanson (1990) and Langevin et al. (1989) found that history of sexual abuse was associated with higher levels of overall sexual deviancy, increased psychological disturbances, and increased likelihood of coming from more dysfunctional families. Therefore, the empirical literature does not support a strong link between victimization and offending, but there is at least tentative evidence that suggests that those offenders who were victims have a number of coexisting problems that may affect treatment.

Conceptual models and classification systems. The previous section has attempted to review a number of factors on a variable-by-variable basis. As we have attempted to show, no one characteristic is found in all offenders. There have been attempts to develop theoretical models or clinical classification systems to account for the heterogeneity in this population. Some systems have been based on clinical observation, others have been informed by the empirical literature, and at times the theories have directed empirical research. As the field matures, we hope to see more theoretical integration of the empirical literature and more empirical studies to test and refine conceptual formulations.

There has been a tradition in the field to divide offenders on the basis of victim characteristics or victim choice. There has been much discussion of intrafamilial (incest cases) versus extrafamilial (true pedophiles) offenders, and these have been subdivided further in terms of whether the victims were male or female.

The *DSM-IV* definition of pedophila is derived from this traditional way of viewing offenders. Early recidivism studies (Frisbee & Dondis, 1965) suggest some utility in this approach, in that incest cases had the lowest level of recidivism, offenders against males had the highest level, and offenders against unrelated females had an intermediate level. Also, the intrafamilial versus the extrafamilial distinction has had heuristic value in spurring a clinical and theoretical focus on family issues.

Although a useful starting point, more current data raise some questions about the utility of the above system. Marshall and Barbaree (1990), reviewing more recent recidivism studies using cognitive-behavioral approaches, failed to find a traditional distinction in recidivistic rates between offenders with male and female targets, although incest cases were found to have lower recidivism rates. A second problem is that data by Abel et al. (1987) and by Weinrott and Saylor (1991) reviewed previously suggest that offenders are not as exclusive in their choice of victims as once thought.

Implicit in the preceding notion is that offenders vary in the degree of preoccupation with or sexual attraction to children. This has led to a focus on this distinction, regardless of the relationship of the victim to the offender or the victim's gender. A number of investigators have described two-group classification systems, such as fixated versus regressed (Groth, Hobson, & Gary, 1982) or preferential versus situational offenders (Howells, 1981). Problems with the above solutions are that they focus on only one aspect of child molestation—that is, the degree of attraction to children—but ignore other possible motivators. In addition, Simon, Sales, Kaszniak, and Kahn (1992), in testing Groth's fixated versus regressed classification system, found a unimodal and continuous distribution rather than the bimodal distribution suggested. Clinically, there are offenders who do fit the extremes of this distribution, but many seem to fall somewhere in between.

Not always recognized as a theoretical model, but one that has guided a great deal of empirical research, is a cognitive-behavioral model of sex offenders (Conte, 1985; Laws, 1989; Marques, Day, Nelson, & Miner, 1989; Marshall & Barbaree, 1988; Murphy & Stalgaitis, 1987; Pithers, 1990). In general, the model includes (a) degree of deviant arousal, (b) degree of nondeviant arousal, (c) social competence, (d) cognitive distortions, (e) victim empathy, (f) general sexual functioning, and (g) identification of high-risk situations. The model has served as a guide for many of the treatment programs in this country. However, many of the areas suggested as relevant to treatment have not been tested empirically. The relationship of individual areas (or their interaction) to recidivism is unknown. In addition, except for the excellent review by Laws and Marshall (1990), there has been little speculation on how variables in this model might be related to the etiology or maintenance of offending.

Another important contribution to organizing existing empirical literature has been Finkelhor's four-factor model (Finkelhor, 1984). Finkelhor has organized the current theories and empirical data related to pedophilia into four basic factors: (a) emotional congruence (the nonsexual and emotional needs met through molestation of children), (b) sexual arousal (degree of sexual attraction to children), (c) blockage (factors that interfere with the development of appropriate adult relationships), and (d) disinhibitions (factors that allow an individual to overcome the internal and social inhibitions to child molestation). This model includes two levels of explanation of each of the above factors: the individual level (i.e., sexual attraction developed by conditioning and modeling) and the social-cultural level (i.e., sexualization of children through the mass media).

A somewhat related model, the quadripartite model, has been proposed by Hall and Hirschman (1992). This model focuses on four motivational precursors: (a) sexual arousal, (b) cognitive distortions, (c) affective dyscontrol, and (d) developmentally related personality problems. Hall and Hirschman feel that these four factors may allow classification of offenders and may be useful in developing new approaches to assessment and treatment. However, like other models, the clinical utility and validity of this model await empirical testing.

One of the most systematic approaches to developing a classification system for child molesters has been described by Knight, Prentky, and their colleagues (Knight, 1989; Knight, Carter, & Prentky, 1989; Knight & Prentky, 1990; Prentky, Knight, Rosenberg, & Lee, 1989). This

TABLE 10.1 Recommended Areas of Assessment of Sex Offenders Against Children

Offender specific:

    Denial
    Details of offense
    Cognitive distortions/Victim empathy
    Risk factors/Sexual abuse cycle
    Sexual arousal pattern

General:

    IQ
    Personality/Psychopathology
    Social competence
    Marital/Family functioning
    Alcohol/Drug usage
    Sexual functioning/Dysfunctioning
    Criminal history
    Personal abuse history

TABLE 10.2 Commonly Used Standardized Instruments

Otis Quick Scoring Mental Ability Test

Minnesota Multiphasic Personality Inventory

Millon Clinical Multiaxial Inventory

State-Trait Anger Expression Inventory

Interpersonal Behavior Survey

Multiphasic Sex Inventory

Burt Scales

Clarke Sexual History Questionnaire

Derogatis Sexual Functioning Inventory

Family Adaptation and Cohesion Scale

Psychophysiological Assessment of Sexual Arousal

Abel and Becker Card Sort

system, developed over a number of years with multiple refinements at the Massachusetts Treatment Center, follows a dual, deductive/rational and inductive/empirical strategy for developing taxonomic systems. This two-axis system of classification is complex but accounts for a number of variables, such as (a) degree of fixation, (b) social competence, (c) amount of contact with the child, (d) meaning of the contact (sexual and social vs. sexual only), (e) degree of physical injury, and (f) degree of sadism. This system is beginning to undergo external validation and generalization, and current data suggest that the system is reliable. Data also are beginning to suggest that different subtypes may have different developmental histories (Prentky et al., 1989).

The above discussion is not meant to be a detailed analysis of all of the taxonomic and conceptual systems available but only highlights the most frequently cited ones. The systems vary in their clinical usefulness at this time, but these models are likely to guide future research.

Clinical Implications

This final section will be a brief review of clinical implications and clinical approaches to patients. This section is not "a cookbook" of "how to do offender treatment" but is a brief discussion of relevant clinical issues.

Assessment. The empirical literature suggests that sex offenders against children are heterogeneous. Therefore, comprehensive assessment of offenders is necessary to pinpoint problems for any one individual. Although programs differ in specific assessment modalities, most programs focus on the problem areas outlined in Table 10.1. Table 10.2 provides a sample list of standardized testing instruments used in a number of programs (see also Pithers, Martin, & Cumming [1989]). Table 10.2 is not meant to suggest that every program uses every instrument, but these are representative of the types of instruments employed. The instruments are meant to assess the areas outlined in Table 10.1—those that are sex offender specific and those that are more general.

Comprehensive assessment of sex offenders requires multiple information or data sources. Five primary sources of data are used in most programs: (a) detailed histories from the offender, (b) detailed histories from significant others, (c) official reports, (d) standardized tests, and (e) some method of assessing sexual arousal patterns. A number of programs also use a polygraph exam as a further validity check on the offender's history. A major error in offender assessment is an overreliance on one source of information. Many times, this source is the often-biased report of the offender him- or herself. The overall goal of the assessment of an offender is to get as clear a picture as possible of each of the areas outlined in Table 10.1. The methods of assessment are meant to be redundant, with each instrument used as a check on the others.

As important as the method of assessment and the specific instruments employed is the recognition of the differential validity of offender assessment, depending on the use of the evaluation. Offender assessment approaches are most valid for outlining treatment needs. A comprehensive assessment can specify specific risk situations, excesses or deficits, and arousal patterns that can be targeted for treatment. In treatment planning, it is probably appropriate for clinicians to interpret their data "liberally," because overtreating or treating offenders in an area in which they truly do not have a problem is less of a risk than it is a failure to treat or target some area for treatment that could increase community safety.

Another valid use of offender assessment is to monitor treatment effectiveness. Periodically repeating certain assessment instruments, such as social skills instruments or sexual arousal assessments, can alert the clinician to whether treatment is changing target behaviors. However, the clinician needs to be aware that the most valid and reliable data probably indicate no change. One can better trust lack of change as being an indication that treatment is not working than one can trust that changes in these target behaviors indicate that treatment is working. There are numerous reasons for patients to bias responding during treatment, such as pleasing the therapist and trying to look good so they can return home.

> *It is extremely important when assessing change within treatment that multiple sources of data be used and that offenders be confronted about any discrepancies.*

It is extremely important when assessing change within treatment that multiple sources of data be used and that offenders be confronted about any discrepancies.

Initial assessment data are also useful for determining patients' ability to be treated safely in the community. However, the clinician needs to be aware that there is little literature directly relating specific assessment approaches to recidivism. Clinicians should be careful in how data are used to make statements regarding community safety. Assessments of community safety have less to do with specific test instruments than they do with the facts of the offense and the offenders' general history. Factors such as number of victims, compulsiveness of the behavior, violence in the offense, and offenders' general criminal history should weigh as heavily as test scores in decisions to place patients in community settings. Clinicians also must be aware that the ability to treat safely in the community involves a number of issues outside of the offender. Issues such as a cooperative significant other and parole/probation counselors who are well-trained in supervising sex offenders significantly influence the ability to treat safely in the community.

Because of these issues, the first author of this chapter takes the position that it is not the assessing clinician's task to state whether someone should or should not be incarcerated. The purpose of the evaluation should be to specify treatment needs, as well as the type of environmental controls necessary for treatment to occur safely, and, within the limits of current data, to state the risk the clinician sees if treatment is to occur in the community. It is the province of the judicial system—weighing the facts of the offense, the offender evaluation, victim impact, impact on victim's family, and impact on society—to determine the appropriate disposition of the offender. Those who evaluate offenders recognize that they must cooperate with and be part of the comprehensive system that attempts to reduce victimization. However, those involved in offender assessment and treatment also must be aware of what their role is in this system and not confuse that role with that of the judge and jury.

The above are those areas in which offender assessment is appropriate, but in certain areas, the use of assessment data is highly inappropriate. The assessment of the accused individuals to determine whether they have committed a specific act or fit the profile of a child molester (Murphy & Peters, 1992; Peters & Murphy, 1992) is not supported by the current literature. Offenders are a heterogeneous group and have different diagnoses and a variety of problem areas. There is no one profile, and the use of offender assessment for the purpose of determining profiles or determining guilt or innocence currently is not supported by the research literature.

Treatment Considerations

Most modern treatment programs operate from a relapse prevention/ cognitive behavioral framework. Therefore, most programs include the following offender-specific treatment components:

1. Confronting denial
2. Identifying risk factors
3. Decreasing cognitive distortions
4. Increasing victim empathy
5. Increasing social competency
6. Decreasing deviant arousal
7. Where appropriate, addressing offender's personal victimization

Those programs that specifically deal with incest cases also usually employ family and marital therapy as adjuncts to treatment. Most programs, either directly or through the use of other community resources, address more general psychological or psychiatric problems such as severe psychiatric disorders and alcohol and drug abuse.

Most programs use a group therapy format, employing individual therapy either as a standard addition to the group treatment or as an adjunctive treatment. Although the use of group treatment with offenders has become the recommended treatment modality, there is no clear evidence at this point suggesting that this is the most effective modality. Group treatments are, however, most cost effective. Also, clinical experience suggests that it is probably easier to confront denial and distortions in a group setting, where confrontation comes from other offenders, rather than in the individual therapy situation, where confrontation has to come from the therapist. Also, there are probably advantages to male/female cotherapy teams, so that appropriate modeling can occur between the male and female therapists, and offenders can learn to relate more appropriately to females. However, there is no empirical evidence to suggest that this is necessary, and in many small programs this luxury cannot be afforded.

Specifics of these modalities have been well-reviewed previously (Barbaree, 1991; Knopp, 1984; Laws, 1989; Marques et al., 1989; Marshall & Barbaree, 1988; Murphy, 1990; Murphy et al., 1991; Murphy & Stalgaitis, 1987; Pithers, 1990; Pithers, Martin, & Cumming, 1989), and patient workbooks to assist in treatment are available (Bays & Freeman-Longo, 1989; Free-man-Longo & Bays, 1988; Freeman-Longo & Hildebran, 1990). In addition, various resource materials are available through Safer Society Press (Safer Society Press, Shoreham Depot Road, RR1, Box 24-B, Orwell, VT 05760-9756). Therefore, in this section, we will focus on more general clinical issues in dealing with offenders that are not always addressed in any detail in the literature that describes treatment techniques.

Assumptions underlying offender treatment guide approaches to treatment. Two of these assumptions are that "there is no cure," and the clinician who assumes responsibility for treating offenders also assumes some responsibility for community safety. Many offenders entering treatment, even those motivated, make the assumption that treatment will find the cause of their offending and "fix it" so that life can return to "normal." Although part of this might relate to offender resistance and denial, it also probably relates to societal attitudes toward the "doctor" or "healer," whose job is to eradicate "diseases." Many patients with chronic disorders, be they medical or psychological, are resistant to the need for lifelong adaptation, and sex offenders are no different. From the beginning of treatment, the therapist must confront this offender assumption, and the offender needs to be made aware of the lifelong risk of sex offending, the lack of a cure, and the need for significant changes in lifestyle.

Another issue arising out of this assumption is that treatment must extend outside the therapist's office. Optimal treatment requires close monitoring in the community by probation or parole personnel and/or significant others who are aware of risk factors and who are willing to coordinate their monitoring with the treatment provider. Treatment providers must educate those responsible for monitoring, and offenders must be willing to waive confidentiality and accept that their behavior cannot be kept between themselves and the therapist.

In addition, offenders must be willing and the therapist must insist on specific lifestyle changes to reduce the risk of reoffending. Therefore, offenders will need to move out of the home if children are present and change occupations or avocational activities if they place them in continuous contact or give them authority over children. Offenders must be willing to change the type of television shows they watch, avoid places where children congregate, and so on. It is unlikely that treatment will be successful if therapists do not spend as much time with these environmental issues as they do with teaching coping skills and reducing deviant arousal.

A final issue arising out of these assumptions is that the therapist must know "when to say when." In traditional mental health treatment, patients who miss appointments and fail to do homework assignments will be interpreted as resistant, and such resistance becomes a focus of treatment. Although the treatment of sex offenders must also address issues around resistance, therapists do not have the luxury of doing long-term therapy around resistance issues. Offenders not cooperating with treatment are at risk to hurt others. Therefore, patients who continually resist the requirements of treatment must be dropped from treatment and returned to the legal system for further disposition.

Most offenders, as the section on cognitive distortions indicated, enter treatment with some level of denial. However, those offenders in total denial represent significant problems for the treatment provider. Programs vary in their approach to offenders in total denial. Many refuse to accept such patients, but others provide special time-limited groups to break through denial. Barbaree (1991) has devised a structured approach to deal with denial. However, in addition to techniques, there are more general issues that need to be addressed in dealing with denial.

There are many motivations for offenders to maintain denial, and they all do not have to do with the offender being "untreatable." Offenders are asked to discuss in detail very personal sexual behavior that is difficult for most patients, even those who are not offenders. In addition, they are asked to describe very socially unacceptable behavior and may believe that the therapist will display a negative reaction to disclosures. In many jurisdictions, by detailing their behavior, offenders increase their risk of incarceration, of losing their job and their source of support for their family, and, in many instances, increase their risk of losing family and friends. Although we agree, as do most offender therapists, that they should have considered these consequences before offending, this does not change the fact that these motivators operate to maintain offender denial. The clinician needs to address these and other motivators to de-

nial as part of the process of overcoming that denial.

Current treatment techniques are difficult, if not impossible, to apply to offenders who do not admit to what they have done. Therapists will have extreme difficulty identifying risk factors, confronting distortions, applying behavioral approaches to deviant arousal, monitoring urges and fantasies, and monitoring risk factors in the community if the offender does not admit to the offense.

Therapists must also be careful not to accept total responsibility for "making offenders admit." The therapists' task is to apply what techniques are available to assist offenders in admitting their offenses for treatment purposes. Offenders who continue in denial are not appropriate for treatment and probably cannot benefit from current treatment modalities.

It is the task of the criminal justice system, not the mental health system, to determine disposition of those who cannot benefit from current treatment.

It is the task of the criminal justice system, not the mental health system, to determine disposition of those who cannot benefit from current treatment. As noted, although therapists must work closely with the criminal justice and child protective service systems, they do not replace these systems and cannot assume responsibility for what the criminal justice system does or does not do.

The nature of offender treatment changes the patient and therapist relationship compared to traditional approaches. Therapists are in the role of the treater but also serve as one of the monitors of the offender's behavior for other systems. As such, therapists are likely to be more directive, set more limits, and dictate more specific changes in the offender's lifestyle than in more traditional therapeutic relationships. Therapists are likely to be more confrontive and less likely to allow patients to develop "insight" on their own through traditional therapeutic techniques. Because of the power many offenders see the therapist as having (e.g., determine whether they are incarcerated, whether they return to their family, etc.), they many times are fearful and distrusting of a therapist. The therapist must be willing to recognize these issues and address them in treatment. Although suspiciousness and difficulty dealing with authority may be part of offenders' overall pathology, some of their feelings are probably based in reality because of the nature of offender treatment.

Although the therapist many times does not have the amount of control in the offender's life as the offender perceives, they generally do have more power and authority than in the typical therapeutic situation. The therapist must be aware of this and not abuse this power and authority. Confrontation in offender treatment should not be an opportunity for therapists to vent their anger. Confrontation is the willingness of the therapist to hold the offender responsible within treatment and to set clear limits and expectations. It is not necessary that this be done in a hostile or threatening manner. Offender therapists are in a unique position to model appropriate use of authority to individuals who have abused authority. Offender therapists must be willing to confront, set limits, and terminate noncompliant patients. However, they also must communicate to offenders that control over their behavior is possible and that therapists are willing to be allies in helping them learn such control.

Conclusions

This chapter has reviewed the empirical literature on the evaluation and treatment of sex offenders. This literature has expanded dramatically over the past 20 years, and although there are many unknowns at this time, significant progress has been made in our understanding of offenders. The field is beginning to see the development of more comprehensive theoretical models that will guide our research and clinical practice in the future. There has also been the development of a number of clinical techniques that are specific to offenders and which preliminary evidence suggests are helpful. Further research on the efficacy of treatment approaches is needed. Those who treat offenders must be cognizant of both the limitations and advances of existing knowledge. Child sexual abuse remains a major public health problem, and it is important that those involved in offender research, evaluation, and treatment continue to make contributions toward reducing this problem.

References

Abel, G. G., Becker, J. V., Cunningham-Rathner, J., Mittelman, M. S., & Rouleau, J. L. (1988). Multiple paraphilic diagnoses among sex offenders. *Bulletin of the American Academy of Psychiatry and the Law, 16,* 153-168.

Abel, G. G., Becker, J. V., Mittelman, M. S., Cunningham-Rathner, J., Rouleau, J. L., & Murphy, W. D. (1987). Self-report sex crimes of nonincarcerated paraphiliacs. *Journal of Interpersonal Violence, 2,* 3-25.

Abel, G. G., Becker, J. V., Murphy, W. D., & Flanagan, B. (1981). Identifying dangerous child molesters. In R. B. Stuart (Ed.), *Violent behavior: Social learning approaches to prediction, management, and treatment* (pp. 116-137). New York: Brunner/Mazel.

Abel, G. G., Gore, D. K., Holland, C. L., Camp, N., Becker, J. V., & Rathner, J. (1989). The measurement of the cognitive distortions of child molesters. *Annals of Sex Research, 2,* 135-152.

Abel, G. G., & Rouleau, J. L. (1990). The nature and extent of sexual assault. In W. L. Marshall, D. R. Laws, & H. E. Barbaree (Eds.), *Handbook of sexual assault: Issues, theories, and treatment of the offender* (pp. 9-21). New York: Plenum.

Alexander, P. (1985). A systems theory conceptualization of incest. *Family Process, 24,* 79-88.

Anderson, W. P., & Kunce, J. T. (1979). Sex offenders: Three personality types. *Journal of Clinical Psychology, 35,* 671-676.

Armentrout, J. A., & Hauer, A. L. (1978). MMPIs of rapists of adults, rapists of children, and non-rapist sex offenders. *Journal of Clinical Psychology, 34,* 330-332.

Bandura, A. (1977). *Social learning theory.* Englewood Cliffs, NJ: Prentice Hall.

Barbaree, H. E. (1990). Stimulus control of sexual arousal: Its role in sexual assault. In W. L. Marshall, D. R. Laws, & H. E. Barbaree (Eds.), *Handbook of sexual assault: Issues, theories, and treatment of the offender* (pp. 115-142). New York: Plenum.

Barbaree, H. E. (1991). Denial and minimization among sex offenders: Assessment and treatment outcome. *Forum on Corrections Research, 3,* 30-33.

Barbaree, H. E., Marshall, W. L., & Connor, J. (1988). *The social problem-solving of child molesters.* Unpublished manuscript, Queen's University, Kingston, Ontario, Canada.

Bays, L., & Freeman-Longo, R. E. (1989). *Why did I do it again? Understanding my cycle of problem behaviors.* Orwell, VT: Safer Society Press.

Berlin, F. S. (1983). Sex offenders: A biomedical perspective and a status report on biomedical treatment. In J. G. Greer & I. R. Stuart (Eds.), *The sexual aggressor: Current perspectives on treatment* (pp. 83-123). New York: Van Nostrand Reinhold.

Conte, J. R. (1985). Clinical dimensions of adult sexual abuse of children analysis. *Behavioral Sciences and the Law, 3,* 341-354.

Cooper, I., & Cormier, B. M. (1982). Inter-generational transmission of incest. *Canadian Journal of Psychiatry, 27,* 231-235.

Ericksen, W. D., Luxenburg, M. G., Walbek, N. H., & Seely, R. K. (1987). Frequency of MMPI two-point code types among sex offenders. *Journal of Consulting and Clinical Psychology, 55,* 566-570.

Farrell, W. R. (1992). Instrumentation and methodological issues in the assessment of sexual arousal. In W. O'Donohue & J. H. Geer (Eds.), *The sexual abuse of children: Clinical issues* (Vol. 2, pp. 188-231). Hillsdale, NJ: Lawrence Erlbaum.

Finkelhor, D. (1978). Psychological, cultural and family factors in incest and family sexual abuse. *Journal of Marriage and Family Counseling, 4,* 41-49.

Finkelhor, D. (1984). *Child sexual abuse.* New York: Free Press.

Finkelhor, D., Hotaling, G., Lewis, I. A., & Smith, C. (1990). Sexual abuse in a national study of adult men and women: Prevalence, characteristics, and risk factors. *Child Abuse & Neglect, 14,* 19-28.

Freeman-Longo, R. E., & Bays, L. (1988). *Who am I and why am I in treatment?* Orwell, VT: Safer Society Press.

Freeman-Longo, R. E., & Hildebran, D. D. (1990). *How can I stop? Breaking my deviant cycle.* Orwell, VT: Safer Society Press.

Frenzel, R. R., & Lang, R. A. (1989). Identifying sexual preferences in intrafamilial and extrafamilial child sexual abusers. *Annals of Sex Research, 2,* 255-275.

Freund, K. (1965). Diagnosing heterosexual pedophilia by means of a test for sexual interest. *Behavior Research and Therapy, 3,* 229-234.

Freund, K. (1967a). Diagnosing homo- or heterosexuality and erotic age-preference by means of a psychophysiological test. *Behavior Research and Therapy, 5,* 209-228.

Freund, K. (1967b). Erotic preference in pedophilia. *Behavior Research and Therapy, 5,* 339-348.

Freund, K., & Blanchard, R. (1989). Phallometric diagnosis of pedophilia. *Journal of Consulting and Clinical Psychology, 57,* 100-105.

Freund, K., & Watson, R. J. (1991). Assessment of the sensitivity and specificity of a phallometric test: An update of phallometric diagnosis of pedophilia. *Psychological Assessment: A Journal of Consulting and Clinical Psychology, 3,* 254-260.

Freund, K., Watson, R., & Dickey, R. (1990). Does sexual abuse in childhood cause pedophilia: An exploratory study. *Archives of Sexual Behavior, 19,* 557-568.

Frisbee, L. V., & Dondis, E. H. (1965). *Recidivism among treated sex offenders* (California Mental Health Research Monograph No. 5). Sacramento, CA: Department of Mental Health.

Furby, L., Weinrott, M. R., & Blackshaw, L. (1989). Sex offender recidivism: A review. *Psychological Bulletin, 105,* 3-30.

Gaffney, G. R., & Berlin, F. S. (1984). Is there hypothalamic-pituitary-gonadal dysfunction in pedophiles? *British Journal of Psychiatry, 145,* 657-660.

Groth, A. N., Hobson, W., & Gary, T. (1982). The child molester: Clinical observations. In J. Conte & D. Shore (Eds.), *Social work and child sexual abuse* (pp. 129-144). New York: Haworth.

Groth, A. N., Longo, R. E., & McFadin, J. B. (1982). Undetected recidivism among rapists and child molesters. *Crime and Delinquency, 28,* 450-458.

Hall, G. C. N., & Hirschman, R. (1992). Sexual aggression against children: A conceptual perspective of etiology. *Criminal Justice and Behavior, 19,* 8-23.

Hall, G. C. N., Maiuro, R. D., Vitaliano, P. P., & Proctor, W. D. (1986). The utility of the MMPI with men who have sexually assaulted children. *Journal of Consulting and Clinical Psychology, 54,* 493-496.

Hanson, R. K. (1990). Characteristics of sex offenders who were sexually abused as children. In R. Langevin (Ed.), *Sex offenders and their victims* (pp. 77-85). Oakville, Ontario: Juniper.

Hanson, R. K., & Slater, S. (1988). Sexual victimization in the history of sexual abusers: A review. *Annals of Sex Research, 1,* 485-499.

Hindman, J. (1988). New insight into adult and juvenile sexual offenders. *Community Safety Quarterly, 1,* 3.

Howells, K. (1981). Adult sexual interest in children: Considerations relevant to theories of etiology. In M. Cook & K. Howells (Eds.), *Adult sexual interest in children* (pp. 55-94). London: Academic Press.

Hucker, S. J., & Bain, J. (1990). Androgenic hormones and sexual assault. In W. L. Marshall, D. R. Laws, & H. E. Barbaree (Eds.), *Handbook of sexual assault: Issues, theories, and treatment of the offender* (pp. 93-102). New York: Plenum.

Knight, R. A. (1989). An assessment of the concurrent validity of a child molester typology. *Journal of Interpersonal Violence, 4,* 131-150.

Knight, R. A., Carter, D. L., & Prentky, R. A. (1989). A system for the classification of child molesters: Reliability and application. *Journal of Interpersonal Violence, 1,* 3-23.

Knight, R. A., & Prentky, R. A. (1990). Classifying sexual offenders: The development and corroboration of taxonomic models. In W. L. Marshall, D. R. Laws, & H. E. Barbaree (Eds.), *Handbook of sexual assault: Issues, theories, and treatment of the offender* (pp. 23-51). New York: Plenum.

Knopp, F. H. (1984). *Retraining adult sex offenders: Methods and models.* Syracuse, NY: Safer Press.

Lang, R. A., Black, E. L., Frenzel, R. R., & Checkley, K. L. (1988). Aggression and erotic attraction toward children in incestuous and pedophilic men. *Annals of Sex Research, 1,* 417-441.

Langevin, R., Paitich, D., Freeman, R., Mann, K., & Handy, L. (1978). Personality characteristics and sexual anomalies in males. *Canadian Journal of Behavioral Science, 10,* 222-238.

Langevin, R., Wortzman, G., Dickey, R., Wright, P., & Handy, L. (1988). Neuropsychological impairment in incest offenders. *Annals of Sex Research, 1,* 401-416.

Langevin, R., Wortzman, G., Wright, P., & Handy, L. (1989). Studies of brain damage and dysfunction in sex offenders. *Annals of Sex Research, 2,* 163-179.

Laws, D. R. (Ed.). (1989). *Relapse prevention with sex offenders.* New York: Guilford.

Laws, D. R., & Marshall, W. L. (1990). A conditioning theory of the etiology and maintenance of deviant sexual preference and behavior. In W. L. Marshall, D. R. Laws, & H. E. Barbaree (Eds.), *Handbook of sexual assault: Issues, theories, and treatment of the offender* (pp. 209-229). New York: Plenum.

Laws, D. R., & Osborn, C. A. (1983). How to build and operate a behavioral laboratory to evaluate and treat sexual deviance. In J. G. Greer & I. R. Stuart (Eds.), *The sexual aggressor: Current perspectives on treatment* (pp. 293-335). New York: Van Nostrand Reinhold.

Levin, S. M., & Stava, L. (1987). Personality characteristics of sex offenders: A review. *Archives of Sexual Behavior, 16,* 57-79.

Marques, J. K., Day, D. M., Nelson, C., & Miner, M. H. (1989). The sex offender treatment and evaluation project: California's relapse prevention program. In D. R. Laws (Ed.), *Relapse prevention with sex offenders* (pp. 247-267). New York: Guilford.

Marshall, W. L., & Barbaree, H. E. (1988). The long-term evaluation of a behavioral treatment program for child molesters. *Behavior Research and Therapy, 26,* 499-511.

Marshall, W. L., & Barbaree, H. E. (1990). An integrated theory of the etiology of sexual offending. In W. L. Marshall, D. R. Laws, & H. E. Barbaree (Eds.), *Handbook of sexual assault: Issues, theories, and treatment of the offender* (pp. 257-275). New York: Plenum.

Marshall, W. L., Barbaree, H. E., & Christophe, D. (1986). Sexual offenders against children: Sexual preferences for age of victims and type of behavior. *Canadian Journal of Behavioral Science, 18,* 424-439.

Marshall, W. L., Barbaree, H. E., & Eccles, A. (1991). Early onset and deviant sexuality in child molesters. *Journal of Interpersonal Violence, 6,* 323-335.

Marshall, W. L., Jones, R., Ward, T., Johnson, P., & Barbaree, H. E. (1991). Treatment outcome with sex offenders. *Psychology Review, 11,* 465-485.

McConaghy, N. (1989). Validity and ethics of penile circumference measures of sexual arousal: A critical review. *Archives of Sexual Behavior, 18,* 357-369.

Mrazek, P. B. (1981). Definition and recognition of sexual child abuse: Historical and cultural perspectives. In P. B. Mrazek & C. H. Kempe (Eds.), *Sexually abused children and their families* (pp. 5-16). Oxford, UK: Pergamon.

Mrazek, P. B., & Bentovim, A. (1981). Incest and the dysfunctional family system. In P. B. Mrazek & C. H. Kempe (Eds.), *Sexually abused children and their families* (pp. 167-178). Oxford, UK: Pergamon.

Murphy, W. D. (1990). Assessment and modification of cognitive distortions in sex offenders. In W. L. Marshall, D. R. Laws, & H. E. Barbaree (Eds.), *Handbook of sexual assault: Issues, theories, and treatment of the offender* (pp. 331-342). New York: Plenum.

Murphy, W. D., & Barbaree, H. E. (1988). *Assessments of sexual offenders by measures of erectile response: Psychometric properties and decision making* (Monograph Order No. 86M0506500501D). Rockville, MD: National Institutes of Health.

Murphy, W. D., Haynes, M. R., Stalgaitis, S. J., & Flanagan, B. (1986). Differential sexual responding among four groups of sexual offenders against children. *Journal of Psychopathology and Behavioral Assessment, 8,* 339-353.

Murphy, W. D., Haynes, M. R., & Worley, P. J. (1991). Assessment of adult sexual interest. In C. R. Hollin & K. Howells (Eds.), *Clinical approaches to sex offenders and their victims* (pp. 77-92). West Sussex, UK: Wiley.

Murphy, W. D., & Peters, J. M. (1992). Profiling child sexual abusers: Psychological considerations. *Criminal Justice and Behavior, 19,* 24-37.

Murphy, W. D., & Stalgaitis, S. J. (1987). Assessment and treatment considerations for sexual offenders against children: Behavioral and social learning approaches. In J. R. McNamara & M. A. Appel (Eds.), *Critical issues, developments, and trends in professional psychology* (Vol. 3, pp. 177-210). New York: Praeger.

Murrin, M. R., & Laws, D. R. (1990). The influence of pornography on sexual crimes. In W. L. Marshall, D. R. Laws, & H. E. Barbaree (Eds.), *Handbook of sexual assault: Issues, theories, and treatment of the offender* (pp. 73-91). New York: Plenum.

Overholser, C., & Beck, S. (1986). Multimethod assessment of rapists, child molesters, and three control groups on behavioral and psychological measures. *Journal of Consulting and Clinical Psychology, 54,* 682-687.

Panton, J. H. (1979). MMPI profile configurations associated with incestuous and non-incestuous child molesting. *Psychological Reports, 45,* 335-338.

Peters, J. M., & Murphy, W. D. (1992). Profiling child sexual abusers: Legal considerations. *Criminal Justice and Behavior, 19,* 38-53.

Peters, S. D., Wyatt, G. E., & Finkelhor, D. (1986). Prevalence. In D. Finkelhor (Ed.), *A sourcebook on child sexual abuse* (pp. 15-59). Newbury Park, CA: Sage.

Pithers, W. D. (1990). Relapse prevention with sexual aggressors: A method for maintaining therapeutic gain and enhancing external supervision. In W. L. Marshall, D. R. Laws, & H. E. Barbaree (Eds.), *Handbook of sexual assault: Issues, theories, and treatment of the offender* (pp. 363-385). New York: Plenum.

Pithers, W. D., & Cumming, G. F. (1989). Can relapses be prevented? Initial outcome data from the Vermont Treatment Program for Sexual Aggressors. In D. R. Laws (Ed.), *Relapse prevention with sex offenders* (pp. 313-325). New York: Guilford.

Pithers, W. D., Martin, G. R., & Cumming, G. F. (1989). Vermont treatment program for sexual aggressors. In D. R. Laws (Ed.), *Relapse prevention with sex offenders* (pp. 292-310). New York: Guilford.

Pollock, N. L., & Hashmall, J. M. (1991). The excuses of child molesters. *Behavioral Sciences and the Law, 9,* 53-59.

Prentky, R. A., Knight, R. A., Rosenberg, R., & Lee, A. (1989). A path analytic approach to the validation of a taxonomic system for classifying child molesters. *Journal of Quantitative Criminology, 5,* 231-257.

Quinsey, V. L. (1986). Men who have sex with children. In D. N. Weistub (Ed.), *Law and mental health: International perspectives* (Vol. 2, pp. 140-172). Elmsford, NY: Pergamon.

Quinsey, V. L., Arnold, L. S., & Pruesse, M. G. (1980). MMPI profiles of men referred for a pretrial psychiatric assessment as a function of offense type. *Journal of Clinical Psychology, 36,* 410-417.

Quinsey, V. L., Chaplin, T. C., & Carrigan, W. F. (1979). Sexual preferences among incestuous and nonincestuous child molesters. *Behavior Therapy, 10,* 562-565.

Regestein, Q. R., & Reich, P. (1978). Pedophilia occurring after onset of cognitive impairment. *Journal of Nervous and Mental Disease, 166,* 794-798.

Segal, Z. V., & Marshall, W. L. (1985). Heterosexual social skills in a population of rapists and child molesters. *Journal of Consulting and Clinical Psychology, 53,* 55-63.

Simon, L. M. J., Sales, B., Kaszniak, A., & Kahn, M. (1992). Characteristics of child molesters: Implications for the fixated-regressed dichotomy. *Journal of Interpersonal Violence, 7,* 211-225.

Simon, W. T., & Schouten, P. G. W. (1991). Plethysmography in the assessment and treatment of sexual deviance: An overview. *Archives of Sexual Behavior, 20,* 75-91.

Stermac, L. E., & Segal, Z. V. (1987). Adult sexual contact with children: An examination of cognitive factors. *Behavior Therapy, 20,* 573-584.

Stermac, L. E., Segal, Z. V., & Gillis, R. (1990). Social and cultural factors in sexual assault. In W. L. Marshall, D. R. Laws, & H. E. Barbaree (Eds.), *Handbook of sexual assault: Issues, theories, and treatment of the offender* (pp. 143-159). New York: Plenum.

Swenson, W. M., & Grimes, B. P. (1969). Characteristics of sex offenders admitted to a Minnesota state hospital for pre-sentence psychiatric investigation. *Psychiatric Quarterly Supplement, 34,* 110-123.

Thomas, J. N. (1982). Juvenile sex offenders: Physician and parent communication. *Pediatric Annals, 11,* 807-812.

Trepper, T. S., & Barrett, M. J. (1986). *Treating incest: A multimodal systems perspective.* New York: Haworth.

Weinrott, M. R., & Saylor, M. (1991). Self-report of crimes committed by sex offenders. *Journal of Interpersonal Violence, 6,* 286-300.

PART THREE

Medical Aspects

Differential diagnosis and medical management of neglect, physical abuse, and sexual abuse are the topics of chapters in Part Three.

In Chapter 11, Carole Jenny notes that many medical personnel are not trained to diagnose child sexual abuse and might avoid the issue because of discomfort. The diagnosis of child sexual abuse is difficult, Jenny stresses, because it is rarely made through obvious physical signs. Most sexual abuse does not leave physical evidence, and even dramatic physical evidence can resolve completely over time. Complicating the physician's task, Jenny points out, is that genital anomalies formerly thought to be associated with child sexual abuse have been found in a high percentage of girls presumably not sexually abused. Among the opportunities medical personnel have to diagnose sexual abuse are regular physical exams and exams for sexually transmitted diseases, pregnancies, and psychological conditions. Jenny discusses each of these opportunities and gives concrete advice about the level of detail needed for the medical record, which is a very important legal document in child abuse cases.

In Chapter 12, Charles F. Johnson also stresses the importance of the medical record. In one study, emergency room doctors' charts were reviewed and found to include information about a complete exam only 22.3% of the time. Physicians failed to note such facts as where the injury occurred, the existence of previous injuries, results of a chart review, and size, color, and age of the injury. Because as many as 10% of children seen in emergency rooms are victims of abuse, it is critical that physicians be able to distinguish accidental from inflicted injury. Johnson reviews distinguishing characteristics of accidental and inflicted burns, bruises, fractures, lacerations, and other injuries sustained by children. Johnson points out how easy it is for practitioners to be blind to (or conversely, more likely to suspect) possible perpetrators because of stereotypes regarding age, sex, race, socioeconomic status, nationality, and other factors. Johnson notes the questions that need to be asked of all caretakers giving histories. Charts for *all* injuries, Johnson argues, should contain the following statement: "This injury is/is not compatible with the history given and the child's development." Because misdiagnosing accidental injury as abuse, or abuse as accidental injury, can have grave medical and legal consequences, Johnson calls for staffings of all individuals participating in the investigation, including nurses, physicians, emergency medicine technicians, laboratory technicians, and radiologists, to reduce the likelihood of error in diagnosis.

In Chapter 13, Howard Dubowitz and Maureen Black argue for a broad definition of neglect that focuses on the impact on the child rather than on parental actions. This definition, they argue, implicates not just parents but society—communities, legislators, landlords, and others—as responsible for both the causes and solutions to neglect. The authors point out that, although most poor families are not neglectful, poverty is more strongly linked to neglect than to any other form of child maltreatment. Poverty exposes one in five U.S. children to inferior schooling, malnutrition, illnesses, little recreation, violence, and environmental hazards such as exposure to lead. Dubowitz and Black argue that medical practitioners should be both technical experts and advocates: against laws allowing religious exemptions for medical neglect (on the books in 44 states) and for laws that mandate safe physical environments for children and families and for community programs and resources that produce such environments.

—T.R.

11

Medical Issues in Sexual Abuse

CAROLE JENNY

Medical practitioners play an important role in the diagnosis and treatment of child sexual abuse. Physicians and nurses are in a good position to detect early signs of sexual abuse during physical examinations of children and during interactions with children and members of their family.

Unfortunately, medical personnel are not always trained in diagnosing child sexual abuse. This may account for the reluctance many feel in identifying and reporting sexual abuse. However, with modest training, doctors, nurses, and other members of the health care team can become more alert to this problem and more comfortable in initiating steps to resolve it. As professionals committed to the well-being of their patients, health care providers have a duty to identify sexually abused children and ensure their well-being.

There are many ways in which medical professionals are called on to help in the diagnosis, treatment, and prosecution of child sexual abuse. In this chapter, I review the most important ways that medical professionals are involved in this area.

Roles for Health Care Professionals

Because most children obtain well-baby care during the first 5 years of their lives, medical personnel usually have regular and repeated contact with young children. For children who are not in pre-school, clinic visits may provide the only opportunity for an adult outside of the family to interact with the child. Therefore, the clinic is an important setting for *primary identification* of child abuse. Screening for child abuse should be a regular feature of well-child visits.

Pediatricians, family practitioners, nurse practitioners, physician's assistants, and nurses all have had extensive experience in *interviewing* children. Medical practitioners should include questions in the medical interview that would alert practitioners to the likelihood of sexual abuse.

A properly conducted medical interview will yield information that would not otherwise be disclosed outside the family.

A properly conducted medical interview will yield information that would not otherwise be disclosed outside the family.

Children who are sexually abused are often characterized by physical signs and symptoms that are revealed during *physical examinations*. For example, there may be unusual bruising of the genital area. Evidence of findings such as this can provide powerful corroboration of a child's account of sexual abuse. The documentation of an injury is an important part of the role of the medical practitioner.

During medical examinations of children, physicians may identify *sexually transmitted diseases*. All the sexually transmitted diseases that affect adults also can be transmitted to children. These diseases can affect children's physical and psychological health, the health of their reproductive systems, and can even threaten their lives.

The sexual abuse or assault of adolescent girls may result in pregnancies. Although most adolescent pregnancies are not the result of sexual assault, the medical practitioner should be alert to this possibility.

Particularly in an emergency care setting, the practitioner may see a child who has been sexually assaulted in the hours or days prior to the visit. In these cases, the medical exam may provide forensic specimens for analysis to confirm abuse or to help identify the abuser.

Medical practitioners may diagnose and treat *psychological or psychosomatic conditions resulting from abuse*. Sexual abuse can lead to other physical and psychological illnesses. Depression, dissociative states, posttraumatic stress disorder, and sexual behavior disorders can be recognized by medical practitioners. Psychosomatic disorders such as enuresis, encopresis, and chronic pain syndromes can be diagnosed and treated.

Physicians, nurses, and other medical personnel should keep accurate records of all their contacts and examinations with children who potentially may be abused. A complete and accurate medical record is an important way of documenting verbal and physical evidence of abuse. These records should include photographs and/or drawings of the child and other physical evidence. In most states, a child's statements recorded in the medical record are presentable in court under rules governing exceptions to hearsay.

Primary Identification of Abused Children

The diagnosis of sexual abuse in the medical setting can be difficult; it is rarely made because of obvious physical signs.

Occasionally, the parent or child presents with a complaint of abuse, but more likely the diagnosis is "masked," and children will present with behavioral disturbances, physical illness caused by abuse, or psychosomatic or emotional problems related to abuse (Hunter, Kilstrom, & Loda, 1985; Krugman, 1986; Massie & Johnson, 1989). Table 11.1 lists common presenting complaints in cases of sexual abuse. It is important to recognize that all of these complaints also are found in nonabused children. None of these complaints are diagnostic of abuse. An understanding of the effect of base rates is important for weighing the significance of any of these symptoms (see Chapter 17, this volume).

TABLE 11.1 Common Presenting Complaints of Sexually Abused Children and Adolescents
in the Medical Setting

Physical signs and symptoms:

Genital discharge, bleeding	Genital skin lesions
Genital pruritis (itching)	Genital or urethral trauma
Pregnancy, including pregnancy with genetic	Sexually transmitted diseases: typical, atypical, or
disorders	disseminated
Other genital infections	Short stature
Recurrent urinary tract infections	Muscle weakness
Abdominal pain	Enuresis and/or encopresis
Migraine headache	Numbing of body parts
Fatigue or exhaustion	Seizures
Sleep disturbance	Appetite disturbance
Drug overdose	

Psychosomatic disorders:

Diffuse somatic complaints	Abdominal pain
Anorexia	Hysterical or conversion reactions

Sexual problems:

Sexualized play	Promiscuity or prostitution
Sexual perpetration to others	Sexual self-abuse
Sexual revictimization	Sexual dysfunction
Excessive masturbation	Fear of intimacy

Social and behavioral problems:

School adjustment problems	Family conflicts
Taking on parental roles	Neurotic or conduct disorders
Phobias, avoidance behavior	Social withdrawal
Temper tantrums	Aggressive behavior
Truancy or runaway behavior	Substance abuse
Self-mutilating behavior	Impulsive behavior
Suicidal ideation, gestures, or attempts	

Other psychological problems:

Excessive guilt	Anxiety
Irritability	Depression
Feelings of helplessness	Self-hate, self-blame
Low self-esteem	Mistrust
Amnesia	Hyperalertness
Fear of criticism or praise	Terrified of rejection
Rage	Flashbacks
Obsessive ideas	Dissociation
Identity diffusion	Multiple personalities
Altered states of consciousness	

Other:

Asymptomatic sibling of a victim	Association with a known offender (Schmitt, 1982a)

SOURCES: From Hunter et al. (1985), Krugman (1986), and Massie and Johnson (1989).

With greater public awareness of sexual abuse, medical practitioners often are confronted by parents who are concerned about abuse even if no objective evidence is present. It can be difficult to know when to reassure parents, when to interview and assess the child, when to refer to a medical subspecialist for evaluation, when to refer for psychotherapy, or when to report to child protection authorities. The American Academy of Pediatrics has published general guidelines for reporting suspected abuse based on available evidence (see Table 11.2).

TABLE 11.2 Guidelines for Making the Decision to Report Sexual Abuse

History	Physical	Laboratory	Level of Concern About Abuse	Action
None	Normal examination	None	None	None
Behavioral changes	Normal examination	None	Low (worry)	+/– report;[a] follow closely (possible mental health referral)
None	Nonspecific findings	None	Low (worry)	+/– report;[a] follow closely
Nonspecific history by child or history by parent only	Nonspecific findings	None	Possible (suspect)	+/– report;[a] follow closely
None	Specific findings	None	Probable	Report
Clear statement	Normal examination	None	Probable	Report
None	Normal examination, nonspecific or specific findings	Positive culture for gonorrhea; positive serologic test for syphilis; presence of semen, sperm, acid phosphatase	Definite	Report
Behavioral changes	Nonspecific changes	Other sexually transmitted diseases	Probable	Report

Data Available spans: History, Physical, Laboratory. Response spans: Level of Concern About Abuse, Action.

SOURCE: American Academy of Pediatrics Committee on Child Abuse and Neglect (1991).
a. A report may or may not be indicated. The decision to report should be based on discussion with local or regional experts and/or child protective service agencies.

Once the diagnosis of abuse is suspected, reporting is mandatory throughout the United States.

Interviewing

The type and extent of the medical interview of abused children depend on many factors. When multidisciplinary forensic interviewing teams are available, children ideally will need to relate the details of their abuse on only one occasion. In many communities, this type of interview team does not exist, and the medical practitioner examining the child may be the most experienced interviewer at hand.

An extensive interview may be indicated if the child is giving an initial, spontaneous disclosure to the practitioner. It is not helpful to tell a child who has just told you about sexual abuse that you do not want to know any details about the abuse. A unique opportunity to obtain important information may be lost if the child becomes reluctant to talk at a later date or in a different setting. Some children will relate details of abuse spontaneously during a physical examination. A child may be more likely to talk about abuse to a medical practitioner who has had a relationship with him or her over time rather than talk to a stranger about abuse.

The child's response to the interview will depend on the child's cognitive, emotional, and behavioral development; the

TABLE 11.3 Guidelines for a Medical Interview With the Caretakers of a Sexually Abused Child

Interview the child's caretakers about suspected abuse:

1. Elicit details of concerning incidents or behaviors. Ask about past episodes of sexual abuse.
2. Determine relationships in family constellation (genogram).
3. Screen for history of other types of abuse or neglect and history of family violence or inappropriate sexuality.
4. Obtain a list of agencies and people involved in investigation or treatment.
5. Obtain developmental history, including level of functioning in school and quality of peer relationships.
6. Obtain menstrual history, if indicated.
7. Ask about behavioral symptoms, depression, or posttraumatic stress disorder.
8. Take a history of physical problems related to abuse, including vaginal and anal pain, bleeding, discharge, or inflammation; enuresis or encopresis; chronic pain syndromes; sexually transmitted diseases; and pregnancy.
9. Obtain child's past medical history, growth history, and diet history and ask about immunization status, allergies, and medications.
10. Take a family illness history.
11. Screen for risk factors for sexually transmitted diseases in the perpetrator, including drug use, sexual preference, promiscuity, and history of known sexually transmitted diseases.

nature of the sexual assault experienced; and the response received after previous disclosure. Tasks for the interviewer are to establish rapport; ask open-ended, non-leading questions rather than "yes-no" questions; ask about pain, bleeding, or other physical symptoms; and give the child a chance to ask questions.

Table 11.3 provides a list of subjects to cover when interviewing the caretakers of a child who has been sexually abused.

Physical Examinations

When abuse is suspected, the physical examination of the child should be done with maximum sensitivity to the child's feelings of vulnerability and embarrassment. The examination will be less stressful if the examiner prepares the child by explaining procedures, uses drapes to protect the child's modesty, and uses distraction techniques during the examination. A child should not be physically forced to be examined. Sedation can be used in cases in which the child is unable to cooperate.

Genital and anal examinations can be accomplished with the child supine in a frog-leg position or prone in a knee-chest position (Herman-Giddens & Frothingham, 1987). The labia are separated with gentle lateral traction or with traction toward the examiner. An excellent light source is needed to see internal structures, and magnification is also helpful.

The physical examination for sexual abuse often is entirely normal, even in cases of proven abuse (Muram, 1989). The absence of trauma does not mean that abuse did not occur. Gross trauma to the genital or anal tract generally is not difficult to diagnose (Pokorny, Pokorny, & Kramer, 1992), but healed or subtle trauma may be more problematic. Recent studies of genital and anal anatomy in normal, nonabused children have elucidated a wide range of normal findings previously attributed to abuse (Emans, Woods, Flagg, & Freeman, 1987; Gardner, 1992a; McCann, Voris, Simon, & Wells, 1989; McCann, Wells, Simon, & Voris, 1990).

The diameter of the hymenal opening previously has been used as a diagnostic criterion for abuse. More recent studies have shown this to be undependable (Paradise, 1989). Factors affecting hymenal and anal diameter include the examination position (McCann, Voris, Simon, & Wells, 1990) and the degree of relaxation of the child. The anal diameter is also affected by the presence of stool in the ampulla. Hymenal diameter may increase with age and with the onset of pubertal development.

A high percentage of children with well-documented abuse will have normal physical examinations.

A high percentage of children with well-documented abuse will have normal physical examinations (Muram, 1989). Many types of abuse, such as fondling or oral-genital contact, will not cause anal, genital, or oral trauma. Other types of trauma may heal completely (Finkel, 1989). As children develop during puberty, even dramatic physical signs of abuse may resolve.

Sexually Transmitted Diseases

The presence of sexually transmitted diseases and microorganisms in children may or may not be diagnostic of sexual abuse. The epidemiology, diagnosis, and modes of transmission of sexually transmitted diseases in children differ from adults for several reasons. Physicians should be aware of the biological differences in children's genital tracts that affect infectivity of organisms. They also need to differentiate sexual acquisition of organisms from perinatal transmission carefully. Finally, screening procedures need to reflect the fact that the sensitivity and specificity of diagnostic tests for sexually transmitted microorganisms used in adults may not be adequate for use in children.

A variety of pathogenic organisms may be sexually transmitted from adult to child:

Neisseria gonorrhoeae. Gonorrhea infections outside the immediate neonatal period can be attributed to sexual abuse. The organism is very fastidious and unlikely to be transmitted through casual contact (Neinstein, Goldenring, & Carpenter, 1984). *Neisseria gonorrhoeae* can be misidentified using rapid diagnostic tests (Whittington, Rice, Biddle, & Knapp, 1988). The use of at least two different confirmatory tests is indicated in cases of childhood gonorrhea.

Neisseria gonorrhoeae has been shown to be sensitive to a single-dose therapy with cefixime in adults (Handsfield et al., 1991). This offers a simple treatment for children that avoids an intramuscular injection. Because the effectiveness of this treatment in children has not been proven, follow-up cultures for "test of cure" are imperative if this therapeutic regimen is used.

Chlamydia trachomatis. Chlamydia trachomatis can be acquired perinatally and carried by the child without symptoms after birth. The longest documented cases remained asymptomatic for 12.5 months after birth in the anus and 12.2 months in the vagina (Bell et al., 1992). Infections after the second year of life and/or symptomatic infections are more likely to be sexually acquired.

Rapid diagnostic tests for *C. trachomatis* are neither sensitive nor specific for infections in children. Taking a culture of the organism is the only acceptable diagnostic method when sexual abuse is suspected (Hammerschlag, Rettig, & Shields, 1988; Hauger et al., 1988; Porder, Sanchez, Roblin, McHugh, & Hammerschlag, 1989).

Trichomonas vaginalis. Trichomonal vaginal infections in children are likely to be caused by sexual abuse (Jones, Yamauchi, & Lambert, 1985). Diagnosis by saline wet preparation of vaginal fluids may miss trichomonal infections (Krieger et al., 1988).

Herpes simplex virus. Genital herpes virus infections can be difficult to differentiate from other genital infections and conditions by clinical appearance (Nahmias, Dowdle, Zuher, Josey, & Luce, 1968). Cultures can be helpful if positive and viral typing is available. Type-specific serologic assays for antibodies are most useful in documenting infection (Koutsky et al., 1992).

The presence of Type-I herpes genital infection does not rule out sexual abuse. Both Type-I and Type-II infections can be transmitted by sexual contact (Gardner & Jones, 1984; Kaplan, Fleisher, Paradise, & Friedman, 1984).

Bacterial vaginosis. Bacterial vaginosis (a mixed-gram negative infection associated with *Gardnerella vaginalis*) is found more commonly in sexually abused girls than in controls (Gardner, 1992b). The presence of bacterial vaginosis or *Gardnerella vaginalis* is not diagnostic for abuse.

Human papillomavirus infections. Genital and anal warts are caused by infections with human papillomavirus. In adults, anal or genital warts are sexually transmitted. Fomite transmission is not likely (Koutsky, Galloway, & Holmes, 1988). In infants and toddlers, perinatal acquisition of the wart virus is well-documented (Fletcher, 1991). Many cases of genital and anal warts in children have been shown to be sexually acquired. Most cases of genital and anal warts in children are caused by one of the types of human papillomavirus known to cause sexually transmitted condylomata acuminata in adults rather than by the virus types that cause common nongenital skin warts (Davis & Emans, 1989; Gutman, St. Claire, Herman-Giddens, Johnston, & Phelps, 1992; Hanson, Glasson, McCrossin, & Rogers, 1989).

Recent reports of the ubiquitousness of the wart virus (Jenison et al., 1990) have raised questions about the mode of transmission of genital and anal warts in children. Differences between children and adults that would affect modes of transmission might include the difference between genital and anal skin in children and in adults and differences in the clinical presentation of primary viral infections versus reinfections.

Although caution is advised in interpreting the implications of genital or anal warts, in every case occurring outside the neonatal period, sexual abuse should be considered as a possible etiology (Gutman, Herman-Giddens, & Phelps, 1993).

Syphilis. Infections with *Treponema pallidum* have been documented in sexually abused children (Starling, 1994). Syphilis should be considered proof of sexual abuse unless it is shown to be acquired congenitally. The clinical diagnosis of syphilis in children may be missed. Most medical practitioners have a low "index of suspicion," and syphilitic rashes and lesions can mimic other common childhood diseases.

Human immunodeficiency virus (HIV). HIV infection can be a horrifying result of sexual abuse. Cases have been reported of children contracting acquired immunodeficiency syndrome (AIDS) from sexual abuse (Gellert, Durfee, & Berkowitz, 1990). A history of sexual abuse in childhood has been found to be a "risk factor" for HIV infection in adults (Zierler et al., 1991).

The necessity of screening for sexually transmitted diseases has been debated. The Centers for Disease Control recommends culturing sexually abused children for *Neisseria gonorrhoeae* from three orifices and *Chlamydia trachomatis* from the genitals and anus, as well as a wet mount and gram stain of vaginal secretions and storage of a serum sample for further analysis, if necessary. In addition, they recommend serologies for syphilis, hepatitis B, and human immunodeficiency virus 12 weeks postassault (Centers for Disease Control, 1993).

This regimen is very expensive and may not be well-tolerated by younger children. When deciding what tests for sexually transmitted diseases are to be done, the following factors should be considered (Sirotnak, 1994):

■ How likely is it that abuse has occurred? What type of sexual contact is alleged? (Sexually transmitted diseases are more likely to be transmitted after contact with the offender's penis or vagina than after fondling or contact with the offender's mouth.)
■ What are the risk factors for sexually transmitted diseases in the offender's history? If the offender is known to be promiscuous, a frequenter of prostitutes, a man known to have sex with other men, or an intravenous drug user, screening for sexually transmitted diseases definitely would be indicated.
■ Is the child symptomatic? In any case where sexual abuse is suspected and the child has symptoms of sexually transmitted diseases, screening should be done.
■ Does the child have one proven sexually transmitted disease? If a child has one sexually transmitted disease, complete screening for other diseases is indicated.
■ Does the child live in a high-risk geographic area? Sexually transmitted diseases are much more prevalent in some communities than in others. If the child lives in an area where disease rates are high, screening is more likely to yield positive results.

The ideal work-up for sexually transmitted diseases when abuse is suspected may vary, depending on the above factors, the cost of pursuing unlikely diagnoses, and the ability of the child to cooperate with and tolerate testing.

Prevention, Diagnosis, and Management of Pregnancy

Pregnancy resulting from abuse or rape can be emotionally devastating to an adolescent girl. The incidence and risk of such pregnancies are not known. If an acute sexual assault is immediately reported, effective medication for the prevention of pregnancy can be offered. The most frequently used regimen is the following: Ovral (norgestrel, 0.5 mg. and ethinyl estradiol, 0.05 mg.), two tablets by mouth within 72 hours of sexual intercourse. Repeat the same dose (two tablets) 12 hours after the first dose.

This medication may cause nausea and vomiting. Antiemetic medications can be prescribed to control side effects. After a single episode of unprotected intercourse followed by combined estro-progestin prophylaxis, the pregnancy rate is estimated to be 1.8% (Fasoli, Parazzini, Cecchetti, & La Vecchia, 1992).

If pregnancy occurs after postcoital contraception, the possibility of harm to the fetus cannot be ruled out. However, the risk of fetal malformation is probably less than would be encountered if the mother took birth control pills early in pregnancy (Yuzpe & Kubba, 1989). Because the medication is 98% effective in preventing pregnancy, the risk of fetal damage is very unlikely. It is important, however, to rule out a preexisting pregnancy before using the medication by obtaining a serum pregnancy test. If the serum pregnancy test is negative, it should be repeated weekly until the test is positive or until menstruation occurs.

When a pregnancy is the result of incest, the likelihood of serious genetic disease in the offspring is greatly increased (Thompson, McInnes, & Huntington, 1991). In matings of first-degree relatives (father/daughter or brother/sister), the chance of serious malformations and/or mental retardation in the offspring has been found to be 50% to 69% (Baird & McGillivray, 1982). In matings of second-degree relatives (brother/half sister, uncle/niece) the chance of malformed and/or mentally retarded offspring is half that of first-degree relative matings. In matings of cousins, the risk is one fourth that of first-degree matings.

When pregnancy results from incest, abuse, or assault, options for management include abortion, term pregnancy leading to adoption, or term pregnancy without placement. In any case, psychological counseling for the pregnant adolescent is imperative.

Recent studies have shown that a history of sexual abuse can increase the risk and complications of adolescent pregnancy. Pregnant teens have been shown to have a high prevalence of sexual abuse histories (Boyer & Fine, 1992; McCullough & Scherman, 1991; Stevens-Simon, Kaplan, & McAnarney, 1992). In addition, pregnant teens with a history of abuse are more likely to abuse drugs and alcohol, are less likely to use contraception, and had their first intercourse at a younger age than pregnant teens without a history of abuse. Teens with a history of abuse may be at a higher risk for complications of pregnancy, including preterm labor and bleeding early in pregnancy (Stevens-Simon & Reichert, 1994) than adolescents without a history of abuse. Abused teens also are more likely than nonabused teens to try to conceive purposefully (Rainey, Stevens-Simon, & Kaplan, 1992). Medical practitioners caring for adolescent abuse victims should provide information and counseling on pregnancy prevention, contraception, and sexuality to these "high-risk" young people.

Collection of Forensic Evidence

Good forensic examinations of acutely sexually assaulted children and adolescents can facilitate effective police investigation of these crimes. Most physicians do not receive training in forensic examinations of sexual assault victims. Thus, many opportunities to collect important evidence are missed.

Any facility offering medical care to victims of sexual assault should use a sexual assault examination protocol to guide evidence collection. Forensic examinations usually are indicated if the victim is seen within 72 hours of the assault. Any evidence collected should be processed, labeled, and stored carefully to ensure its integrity and quality (Jenny, 1992; Kanda, Thomas, & Lloyd, 1985).

Forensic examinations can be traumatic for young children. If multiple swabs and tests are to be collected, the use of sedation or anesthesia should be considered. The value of collecting good forensic evidence should be compared to the emotional cost of the procedure to the child or to the risk of sedation.

Psychological and Psychosomatic Sequela

The medical evaluation of abused children includes an assessment of the child's general physical and mental health. Abuse is a stressful experience for a child, often leading to health problems. Abused children are sometimes neglected as well. A health assessment can uncover untreated illnesses, risk factors for future illnesses, psychological problems such as depression or dissociation, or psychosomatic problems.

Psychosomatic diseases and conditions associated with abuse include enuresis and encopresis, chronic pain, and eating disorders.

Enuresis and encopresis. Many children experience urinary tract or anal inflammation and pain after episodes of abuse. This can lead to urinary incontinence, fecal impaction, or fecal soiling. Behavioral problems and the inability to deal with psychologically charged body areas cause persistence of the enuresis and encopresis.

Eneuretic and encopretic children often are ridiculed by peers and punished by adults. The child gets into a downward spiral of shame and denial, leading to further bowel and bladder dysfunction. Although the treatment of enuresis and encopresis is difficult in children dealing with abuse issues, medical diagnosis and management can decrease the child's feelings of guilt and stigma (Levine, 1982; Schmitt, 1982a, 1982b).

Chronic pain syndromes. Abused children and adult survivors of sexual abuse often express their emotional discomfort in physical symptoms. In children, chronic abdominal pain, headaches, and anal or genital pain may be related to abuse (Barsky, Wool, Barnett, & Cleary, 1994; Krugman, 1990). The symptoms of discomfort are not feigned but result from a somatic response to stress and psychological pain. Treatment of psychosomatic pain syndromes includes ruling out pathologic causes of pain, reassurance of the patient, effective pain control without overreliance on pain medications, and referral for psychotherapy.

Eating disorders. Anorexia nervosa and obesity have been correlated with sexual abuse histories in adults, although the data are less convincing for bulimia nervosa (Pope & Hudson, 1992). Similar data are not available for children, but many sexually abused children present with poor appetite or obesity. It is difficult to sort out psychological factors, environmental factors, and body habitus, but an evaluation of nutritional status is indicated when abused children present with abnormal growth.

Accurate Medical Record

In child abuse cases, the medical record is a legal document. Careful recording of the children's histories can help protect both victims and the accused. In what follows, I summarize guidelines for the preparation of the medical record:

- When recording history, note the source. Is the child reporting abuse, or is it another person telling you what the child said? Write legibly or dictate the record. If dictating, read the finished record carefully for accuracy of transcription.
- Use direct quotes from the child. Include in the history what questions you asked to elicit the child's response and record details such as the child's affect, developmental level, and use of language. Use careful descriptors of physical examination findings, both normal and abnormal.
- Photographs of physical findings are helpful in abuse cases. If a camera is not available, careful drawings by the examiner should be done, particularly if trauma or abnormalities exist.

Summary

Medical practitioners perform essential services in the evaluation and treatment of abuse victims. Training in the management of abuse cases should be part of every primary care physician's education. The competent medical practitioner functions as a member of the larger team of professionals protecting children and their families.

References

American Academy of Pediatrics Committee on Child Abuse and Neglect. (1991). Guidelines for the evaluation of sexual abuse of children. *Pediatrics, 87,* 254-260.

Baird, P. A., & McGillivray, B. (1982). Children of incest. *Journal of Pediatrics, 101,* 854-857.

Barsky, A. J., Wool, C., Barnett, M. C., & Cleary, P. D. (1994). Histories of childhood trauma in adult hypochondriacal patients. *American Journal of Psychiatry, 151,* 397-401.

Bell, T. A., Stamm, W. E., Wang, S. P., Kuo, C. C., Holmes, K. K., & Grayston, J. T. (1992). Chronic chlamydia trachomatis infections in infants. *Journal of the American Medical Association, 15,* 400-402.

Boyer, D., & Fine, D. (1992). Sexual abuse as a factor in adolescent pregnancy and child maltreatment. *Family Planning Perspectives, 24,* 4-11.

Centers for Disease Control. (1993). 1993 sexually transmitted diseases treatment guidelines. *MMWR Morbid Mortal Weekly Report, 42*(RR-14), 1-102.

Davis, A. J., & Emans, S. J. (1989). Human papilloma virus infection in the pediatric and adolescent patient. *Journal of Pediatrics, 115,* 1-9.

Emans, S. J., Woods, E. R., Flagg, N. T., & Freeman, A. (1987). Genital findings in sexually abused, symptomatic and asymptomatic girls. *Pediatrics, 79,* 778-785.

Fasoli, M., Parazzini, F., Cecchetti, G., & La Vecchia, C. (1992). Post-coital contraception: An overview of published studies. *Contraception, 39,* 459-468.

Finkel, M. A. (1989). Anogenital trauma in sexually abused children. *Pediatrics, 84,* 317-322.

Fletcher, J. L., Jr. (1991). Perinatal transmission of human papillomavirus. *American Family Physician, 43,* 143-148.

Gardner, J. J. (1992a). A descriptive study of the genital variation in healthy, nonabused premenarcheal girls. *Journal of Pediatrics, 120,* 251-257.

Gardner, J. J. (1992b). Comparison of the vaginal flora in sexually abused and nonabused girls. *Journal of Pediatrics, 120,* 872-877.

Gardner, M., & Jones, J. J. (1984). Genital herpes acquired by sexual abuse of children. *Journal of Pediatrics, 104,* 243-244.

Gellert, G. A., Durfee, M. J., & Berkowitz, C. D. (1990). Developing guidelines for HIV antibody testing among victims of pediatric sexual abuse. *Child Abuse & Neglect, 14,* 9-17.

Gutman, L. T., Herman-Giddens, M. E., & Phelps, W. C. (1993). Transmission of human genital papillomavirus disease: Comparison of data from adults and children. *Pediatrics, 91,* 31-38.

Gutman, L. T., St. Claire, K., Herman-Giddens, M. E., Johnston, W. W., & Phelps, W. C. (1992). Evaluation of sexually abused and nonabused young girls for intravaginal human papillomavirus infection. *American Journal of Diseases of Children, 146,* 694-699.

Hammerschlag, M. R., Rettig, P. J., & Shields, M. E. (1988). False positive results with the use of chlamydial antigen detection tests in the evaluation of suspected sexual abuse in children. *Pediatric Infectious Disease Journal, 7,* 11-14.

Handsfield, H. H., McCormack, W. M., Hook, E. W., Douglas, J. M., Covino, J. M., Verdon, M. S., Reichart, C. A., Ehret, J. M., & the Gonorrhea Treatment Study Group. (1991). A comparison of single dose cefixime with ceftriaxone as treatment for uncomplicated gonorrhea. *New England Journal of Medicine, 325,* 1337-1341.

Hanson, R. M., Glasson, M., McCrossin, I., & Rogers, M. (1989). Anogenital warts in childhood. *Child Abuse & Neglect, 13,* 225-233.

Hauger, S. B., Brown, S. J., Agre, F., Sahraie, F., Ortiz, R., & Ellner, P. (1988). Failure of direct fluorescent antibody staining to detect chlamydia trachomatis from genital tract sites of prepubertal children at risk for sexual abuse. *Pediatric Infectious Disease Journal, 7,* 660-661.

Herman-Giddens, M. E., & Frothingham, T. E. (1987). Prepubertal female genitalia: Examination for evidence of sexual abuse. *Pediatrics, 80,* 203-208.

Hunter, R. S., Kilstrom, N., & Loda, F. (1985). Sexually abused children: Identifying masked presentation in a medical setting. *Child Abuse & Neglect, 9,* 17-25.

Jenison, S. A., Yu, X. P., Valentine, J. M., Koutsky, L. A., Christiansen, A. E., Beckmann, A. M., & Galloway, D. A. (1990). Evidence of prevalent genital-type human papillomavirus infections in adults and children. *Journal of Infectious Diseases, 162,* 60-69.

Jenny, C. (1992). The physician as medical detective. In A. H. Heger, S. J. Emans, C. Jenny, & D. A. Stuart (Eds.), *Evaluation of the sexually abused child: A medical testbook and photographic atlas* (pp. 51-62). New York: Oxford University Press.

Jones, J. G., Yamauchi, T., & Lambert, B. (1985). Trichomonas vaginalis infestation in sexually abused girls. *American Journal of Diseases of Children, 139,* 846-847.

Kanda, M., Thomas, J. N., & Lloyd, D. W. (1985). The role of forensic evidence in child abuse and neglect. *American Journal of Forensic Medical Pathology, 6,* 7-15.

Kaplan, K. M., Fleisher, G. R., Paradise, J. E., & Friedman, H. N. (1984). Social relevance of genital herpes simplex in children. *American Journal of Diseases of Children, 138,* 872-874.

Koutsky, L. A., Galloway, D. A., & Holmes, K. K. (1988). Epidemiology of genital human papillomavirus infection. *Epidemiologic Reviews, 10,* 122-163.

Koutsky, L. A., Stevens, C. E., Holmes, K. K., Ashley, R. L., Kiviat, N. B., Critchlow, C. W., & Corey, L. (1992). Underdiagnosis of genital herpes by current clinical and viral-isolation procedures. *New England Journal of Medicine, 326,* 1533-1539.

Krieger, J. N., Tam, M. R., Stevens, C. E., Nielsen, I. O., Hale, J., Kiviat, N. B., & Holmes, K. K. (1988). Diagnosis of trichomoniasis: Comparison of conventional wet mount examination with cytologic studies, cultures and monoclonal antibody staining of direct specimens *Journal of the American Medical Association, 259,* 1223-1227.

Krugman, R. D. (1986). Recognition of sexual abuse in children. *Pediatrics in Review, 8,* 25-30.

Krugman, R. D. (1990). Physical indicators of child sexual abuse. *Review of Psychiatry, 10,* 336-344.

Levine, M. D. (1982). Encopresis: Its potentiation, evaluation, and alleviation. *Pediatric Clinics of North America, 29,* 315-330.

Massie, M. E., & Johnson, S. M. (1989). The importance of recognizing a history of sexual abuse in female adolescents. *Journal of Adolescent Health Care, 10,* 184-191.

McCann, J., Voris, J., Simon, M., & Wells, R. (1989). Perianal finding in prepubertal children selected for non abuse: A descriptive study. *Child Abuse & Neglect, 13,* 179-193.

McCann, J., Voris, J., Simon, M., & Wells, R. (1990). Comparison of genital examination techniques in prepubertal girls. *Pediatrics, 85,* 182-187.

McCann, J., Wells, R., Simon, M., & Vorris, J. (1990). Genital findings in prepubertal girls selected for nonabuse: A descriptive study. *Pediatrics, 86,* 428-439.

McCullough, M., & Scherman, A. (1991). Adolescent pregnancy: Contributing factors and strategies for prevention. *Adolescence, 26,* 809-816.

Muram, D. (1989). Child sexual abuse: Relationship between sexual acts and genital findings. *Child Abuse & Neglect, 13,* 211-216.

Nahmias, A. J., Dowdle, W. R., Zuher, M. N., Josey, W. E., & Luce, C. F. (1968). Genital infection with herpesvirus hominis types 1 and 2 in children. *Pediatrics, 42,* 659-665.

Neinstein, L. S., Goldenring, J., & Carpenter, S. (1984). Nonsexual transmission of sexually transmitted diseases: An infrequent occurrence. *Pediatrics, 74,* 67-76.

Paradise, J. E. (1989). Predictive accuracy and the diagnosis of sexual abuse: A big issue about a little tissue. *Child Abuse & Neglect, 13,* 169-176.

Pokorny, S. F., Pokorny, W. J., & Kramer, W. (1992). Acute genital injury in the prepubertal girl. *American Journal of Obstetrical Gynecology, 166,* 1461-1466.

Pope, H. G., & Hudson, J. I. (1992). Is childhood sexual abuse a risk factor for bulimia nervosa? *American Journal of Psychiatry, 149,* 455-463.

Porder, K., Sanchez, N., Roblin, P. M., McHugh, M., & Hammerschlag, M. R. (1989). Lack of specificity of chlamydiazyme for detection of vaginal chlamydial infection in prepubertal girls. *Pediatric Infectious Disease Journal, 8,* 358-360.

Rainey, D. Y., Stevens-Simon, C., & Kaplan, D. W. (1992). Adolescents trying to conceive: An association with child sexual abuse? [Abstract] *American Journal of Diseases of Children, 146,* 487.

Schmitt, B. D. (1982a). Daytime wetting (diurnal enuresis). *Pediatric Clinics of North America, 29,* 9-20.

Schmitt, B. D. (1982b). Nocturnal enuresis: An update on treatment. *Pediatric Clinics of North America, 29,* 21-36.

Sirotnak, A. P. (1994). Testing sexually abused children for sexually transmitted diseases: Whom to test, when to test, and why? *Pediatric Annals, 23,* 370-374.

Starling, S. P. (1994). Syphilis in infants and young children. *Pediatric Annals, 23,* 334-340.

Stevens-Simon, C., Kaplan, D. W., & McAnarney, E. R. (1992). Prenatal risk assessment for adolescents [Abstract]. *Journal of Adolescent Health, 13,* 44.

Stevens-Simon, C., & Reichert, S. (1994). Sexual abuse, adolescent pregnancy, and child abuse: A developmental approach to an intergenerational cycle. *Archives of Pediatric Adolescent Medicine, 148,* 23-27.

Thompson, M. W., McInnes, R. R., & Huntington, H. F. (1991). *Genetics in medicine* (5th ed.). Philadelphia: W. B. Saunders.

Whittington, W. L., Rice, R. J., Biddle, J. W., & Knapp, J. S. (1988). Incorrect identification of neisseria gonohorrhoeae from infants and children. *Pediatric Infectious Disease Journal, 7,* 3-10.

Yuzpe, A., & Kubba, A. (1989). Postcoital contraception. In M. Filshie & J. Guillebaud (Eds.), *Contraception: Science and practice* (pp. 126-143). Boston: Butterworth and Co.

Zierler, S., Feingold, L., Laufer, D., Velentgas P., Kantrowitz-Gordon, I., & Mayer, K. (1991). Adult survivors of childhood sexual abuse and subsequent risk of HIV infection. *American Journal of Public Health, 81,* 572-575.

12

Physical Abuse

Accidental Versus
Intentional Trauma in Children

CHARLES F. JOHNSON

Accidents and Child Abuse: Common Childhood Experiences

Children suffer a wide variety of injuries. In 1967, it was estimated that 1,750,000 children aged less than 1 year sustained an injury from a fall (Kravitz, Driessen, Gomberg, & Korach, 1969), and approximately 15,000,000 children of all ages were injured annually in the United States (Izant & Hubay, 1966). One study has found that 10% of children seen in an emergency department have been abused (Holter & Friedman, 1968). Determining which children have suffered nonaccidental injury and should be reported to proper authorities requires diligence. A wise approach is to routinely determine the cause of all injuries.

Tissue and Trauma

Because state laws require all professionals dealing with children to report suspect abuse, they must become familiar with the manifestations of accidental and nonaccidental trauma. Tissues have a limited repertory of responses to trauma. Although a variety of orderly and complex activities take place at the microscopic and biochemical levels, relatively few *observable* changes take place when the integrity of a tissue has been disrupted by heat, force, infection, or chemical insult. The visible manifestations of tissue trauma depend on (a) the amount and vectors of force delivered to the tissue (Spivak, 1992), (b) concentration of a caustic substance, (c) time of exposure, (d) temperature of a hot agent, and (e) how and where these are distributed on and into the body. Darker skin color may hide the consequences of mild trauma. What appears to be easy bruising may be the normal manifestations of trauma to a fair-skinned child. Underlying fat and muscle may dissipate the force of a blow. The shape of an instrument also may dissipate or concentrate the force of a blow. For example, a blow from a large, flat surface may dilate superficial blood vessels. This results in a visible and temporary

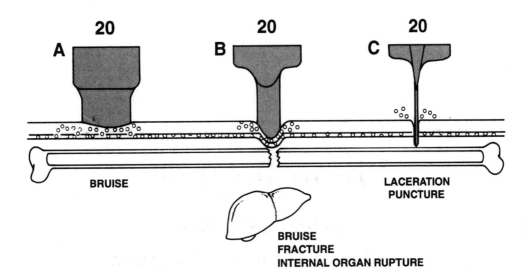

Figure 12.1. Concentration of Force and Injury Consequences

erythema or redness (see Figure 12.1A). With more force to the same area, small blood vessels under the skin will rupture. Having escaped the blood vessels, the red blood cells are seen as a prolonged discoloration or bruise. The time of appearance of a bruise may be delayed if the trauma is to deeper tissues, such as that of the buttocks or thighs (Wilson, 1977).

If unyielding bone is close to the surface, the skin is more likely to be crushed between the striking object and the bone, with more visible and extensive tissue damage. For example, a blunt blow to the hand is more likely to cause bruising than a blow to the buttocks or thighs. Thick tissue of the buttocks and thighs may dissipate and conceal the consequences of certain injuries. The pelvic bones and femurs lie deep below the surface and are difficult to fracture, but hand bones are superficial and easily fractured.

A blow of similar force to the same body area from a smaller object is likely to cause more concentrated, serious, and deeper damage (see Figure 12.1B). Underlying and inflexible bone is more likely to be fractured. If the blow is to the chest, the relatively flexible ribs may escape damage; however, if the blow is low on the right side of the chest, the underlying liver can be ruptured. If the blow is to the midabdomen, the part of the duodenum that is bound to the back of the abdomen against the spine is not free to move and may be crushed against the spine. If the object striking the body is narrow or pointed, the force is concentrated further; the skin and underlying tissue are lacerated or punctured. Little bruising may be seen because blood cells are not trapped in the skin, but they escape to the skin surface as bleeding (see Figure 12.1C). This type of trauma results from electric cords, switches, picks, screwdrivers, nails, knives, and bullets.

The above descriptions are qualitative. It is not ethically possible to research the force that is required to cause a specific injury to the tissues of children. Surveys have been conducted to analyze the consequences of falls from windows and fire escapes (Barlow, Niemirska, & Gandhi, 1983; Sieben, Leavitt, & French, 1971; Smith, Burrington, & Woolf, 1975), from beds in hospitals (Helfer, Slovis, & Black, 1977; Lyons & Oates, 1993), from elevated surfaces and down stairs in homes (Joffe & Ludwig, 1988), and from observed falls in playgrounds. A fall from a 36- to 48-inch height may fracture the skull, clavicle, or femur, but no central nervous system damage is seen (Helfer et al., 1977). Falls from greater heights are not associated with injury necessarily (Lehman & Schonfeld, 1993; Smith et al., 1975). In one study of infants and children, 14 died who fell four or more stories, but 47 others survived with few permanent sequela (Barlow et al., 1983). The determination of the cause of an injury requires familiarity with the manifestations and locations of *common* accidental and nonaccidental injuries of children, the common objects that injure children (Johnson & Showers, 1985), and the pattern of healing of bruises (Wilson, 1977), fractures (Swischuk, 1992), and burns.

Caretakers' Responses to Injuries

If caretakers could be depended on to give an accurate and truthful history, there would be no need to evaluate the truth of their explanations for a child's injury.

Children may be too young, frightened, or intimidated to give an accurate or truthful history of an injury.

Children may be too young, frightened, or intimidated to give an accurate or truthful history of an injury. Although caretakers readily have admitted to spanking or slapping their children, it is unlikely that perpetrators of a serious intentional injury readily will admit their role.

In accidental injuries, caretakers may not have witnessed the injury. In this instance, it is necessary to apply the term *unexplained injury*. This circumstance may raise concern about appropriate supervision or safety neglect (Johnson & Coury, 1992). In their efforts to escape culpability and ire, caretakers who accidentally injure a child may concoct a story that is improbable or impossible and thereby create suspicion of intentional injury. For example, the caretaker may blame the child or a sibling when neither is developmentally able to have caused the injury. When the true details finally are related, the explanation may seem defensive and therefore false.

A caretaker's delay in seeking help for an injury is considered a risk factor for abuse. The delay may be the result of ignorance, failure to comprehend the seriousness of the injury, lack of transportation, or fear of reprisal. A burn may progress from first-degree erythema at bedtime to a vesiculated (blistered) second-degree burn by morning.

Professional Attitudes and Practices: Reporting of Suspected Abuse

Professionals who believe that certain caretakers are unlikely perpetrators of physical abuse because of age, sex, race, or socioeconomic status may neglect to consider the possibility (Morris, Johnson, & Clasen, 1985). A young child with a history of previous or severe abuse, whose parents are perceived as lazy, angry, and poor, is more likely to be reported (Zellman, 1992).

The physician's examinations or medical records may be incomplete in cases of injury to children. The records of emergency department physicians in a hospital for children have been studied to determine if they routinely ask and record the answers to basic questions that can help determine the cause of an injury. Missing information included where the injury occurred, notation of previous injuries, chart review, and size, color, and age of the injury (Johnson, Apollo, Joseph, & Corbitt, 1986). A complete examination was recorded only 22.3% of the time.

When interpreting injury, knowledge about normal child development is necessary; however, some children may be capable of physical activity that is beyond what is expected. It may be necessary to question noninvolved adults about the child's capabilities. For example, accidents to children in strollers are common. The speed with which perambulating children in a stroller can travel and the trunk support given by the stroller seat may facilitate accidents expected to occur only in an older child (Johnson, Erickson, & Caniano, 1990).

What Constitutes Reportable Abuse?

Despite state mandates, professionals continue to fail to report suspected abuse (Finkelhor & Zellman, 1991). Physicians asked to rate the appropriateness of various types of child discipline also were asked if they would report those actions that they considered to be inappropriate discipline (Morris, Johnson, & Clasen, 1985). There were disparities about what constituted appropriate discipline. Instances of inappropriate discipline were not considered uniformly reportable as abuse until the consequences were seri-

---

CHILDREN'S HOSPITAL, COLUMBUS, OHIO

An injury caused by a parent, guardian, or custodian caretaker—for any reason, including injury resulting from reaction to an unwanted behavior—is child abuse and must be reported to proper authorities. Temporary redness of the hand or buttocks from a caretaker's hand may not be abuse. Temporary redness or more severe injury to any other anatomic area is child abuse.

Physical discipline should not be used on children who are under 12 months of age or abnormal developmentally, emotionally, or physically. Tissue damage includes bruises, burns, tears, punctures, fractures, ruptures of organs, and disruption of functions. The injury may be caused by impact, penetration, heat, a caustic substance, or a chemical or drug. The use of an instrument on any body part is child abuse.

Figure 12.2. Children's Hospital Definition of Abuse

ous. Other reasons why general pediatricians and practitioners fail to consider abuse and fail to report included seriousness of the injury, familiarity with the family, presence of other injuries, single versus repeated injury, affect or attitude of the caretakers, personal experience, child's affect, legal requirements, trust of social and legal agencies, and legal and economic consequences. In order to remove the influence of individual and cultural experiences and biases about what constitutes acceptable discipline, as well as the propensity to avoid reporting, Children's Hospital, in Columbus, Ohio, has established a narrow definition of child abuse (Figure 12.2).

This definition is not the same as the laws relating to child abuse in the state of Ohio, nor does it reflect the conclusions in individual courtrooms in Ohio. It indicates what actions professionals in an institution caring for children should report as physical abuse. The definition does not condone any form of corporal punishment.

The History of the Injury From the Child

Children routinely should be asked about the cause of any injuries they suffer. This practice will (a) increase the opportunities for children to tell about the causes of their injuries, (b) improve the professional's techniques for questioning children of various ages about trauma, (c) increase the interviewer's knowledge about the manifestations of various types of injury in children, and (d) teach children and their caretakers that it is likely and proper for adults to be concerned about children's injuries.

Medical and Social History

The presence of risk factors involving the child, the caretaker, and the injury (Dubowitz, Hampton, Bithoney, & Newberger, 1987; Johnson, 1983) increases concerns that an injury is not accidental (Table 12.1).

Social factors associated with risk for abuse may begin in the past history of the parent with inadequate or no preparation for pregnancy, drug use (Taylor et al., 1991), and lack of child-rearing and accident prevention knowledge (Johnson, Loxterkamp, & Albanese, 1982; Showers & Johnson, 1985). Other risk factors or recent stresses include illness, divorce, death in the family, and loss of employment (Johnson & Cohn, 1990). Many of the social risk factors for nonaccidental injuries are the same for accidental injuries (Bourguet & McArtor, 1989; Dubowitz et al., 1987; Gregg & Elmer, 1969). Caretakers, under stress, may not be able to provide for the safety of their children. Despite evidence of a variety of risk factors, no perpetrator profile has been validated adequately (Milner & Chilamkurti, 1991).

TABLE 12.1 Risk Factors Associated With Physical Abuse

Factors in the child: premature, twin, chronic illness, delayed development, retarded, hyperactive, seen as different, previous severe injury, poor health care, unkempt.

Factors in the caretaker: unplanned or unwanted pregnancy, single parent, young parent, closely spaced children, abused as child, stressed, substance abuse, isolated, limited support system, limited knowledge of child rearing and child development, known to child protective services, chronic or acute illness, emotional disturbance, developmentally delayed, lack of empathy, lack of control.

Factors in the injury(ies): no history, not in keeping with history, different histories, different ages, different types of injuries, symmetrical, geometric, silhouette of object, outline of object, mirror or bilateral, not in keeping with child's development, delay in seeking attention, protected area (genitalia, buttocks), nonleading surface (back, back of legs, ears, neck, underarms), nonexploratory surface (top of hands), bands, tattoos.

Obtaining a detailed social history for every injured child is impractical; however, knowledge of high-risk factors may increase suspicion and depth of investigation. When an injury appears to be nonaccidental, it is essential to obtain a detailed past medical and social history to guide approaches to management. The charts of children with injuries who are seen in the emergency room should be reviewed for records of previous injuries (Olney, 1988).

The question "What caused this mark here?" should be directed to the communicating child and parent for all injuries. The answers to the question should include details about what object(s) caused the injury or came in contact with the child. If the history given is that the child fell, it is important to know the distance involved and the characteristics of the surface(s) contacted. When the injury is highly suggestive of abuse, additional questions must be asked to determine (a) when the injury occurred; (b) where the injury occurred; (c) who witnessed the injury; (d) the child's developmental abilities for rolling, crawling, reaching, grasping, turning faucets and door handles, climbing, walking, running, and riding; and (e) clothing worn by the child. This information should be recorded carefully. The record *for all injuries* should include the following statement: "This injury is/is not compatible with the history given and the child's development."

Examination of the Injury

Complete examination requires determination of the location, size, shape, and age of all external and internal injuries.

Bruises are the most common injury to the skin of children who are abused and seen in a hospital setting (Johnson & Showers, 1985). Bruises are also common in nonaccidental injuries. Accidental bruises occur on surfaces over bones that are close to the surface and "the leading edges" of the body as the child interacts with the environment (Figure 12.3). The location of the injury may be incompatible with an accident. Bilateral accidental injuries are uncommon (Lasing & Buchan, 1976).

To determine if the age of a bruise is in keeping with the history given, one must determine the color of the bruise. Bruises go through a series of color changes as the blood cells ruptured from the vessel walls disintegrate and undergo chemical transformations (Wilson, 1977). The *exact* number of days that have transpired cannot be determined, especially if the bruise is deep; however, red or blue, yellow, green, and brown bruises on the body are of different ages and therefore not due to a single incident. Yellow-, green-, and brown-colored bruises are not from injuries that occurred in the previous 1 or 2 days and suggest delay in seeking attention for injuries.

The shape of a bruise will present as a silhouette or outline of the shape of the object that caused it (Figure 12.4).

The marks from a slap to the cheeks or buttocks appear as an outline of the hand, as if the fingers have pressed the blood from underlying vessels to vessels underlying the periphery of the fingers where the vessels subsequently rupture. If the perpetrator is right handed, the marks are expected on the left cheek of the child and the outline of the fingers is angled toward the ear. Because the face is

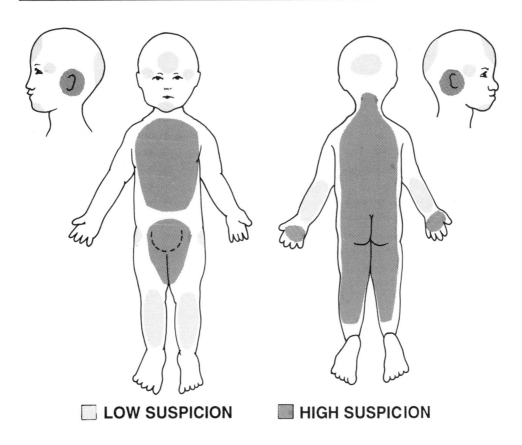

☐ LOW SUSPICION   ■ HIGH SUSPICION

Figure 12.3. Bruises and Abuse: Bruise Location in Accidental and Nonaccidental Injury

a common target for discipline and is in proximity to delicate structures such as the eyes, eardrums, and brain, slap marks on the face should be recognized by all individuals dealing with children and should be considered pathognomonic for child abuse (Photo 12.1).

Although the hand (22%) and belt strap (23%) were found to be the most common objects to cause injury to the abused child seen in a hospital setting, a variety of other instruments or objects may be used (see Table 12.2) (Showers & Johnson, 1984).

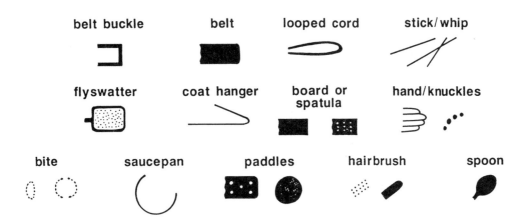

Figure 12.4. Marks From Instruments

SOURCE: Johnson (1990). Reprinted by permission of W. B. Saunders.

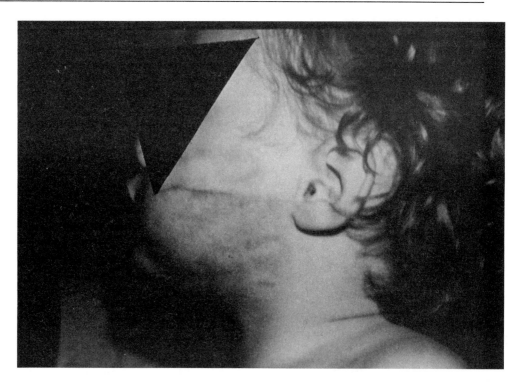

Photo 12.1. Slap Mark

Extremities may be bound by a cord to restrain a child during a beating or sexual abuse (Johnson, Kaufman, & Callendar, 1990). Human bite marks have elliptical or oval patterns. Teeth marks can be matched against dental impressions from suspected perpetrators (Wagner, 1986).

Culture also may influence the choice of an instrument. The use of electrical cords to inflict punishment has been reported to be more common among black families (Showers & Bandman, 1986).

It would appear that the choice of object is more likely to be a matter of convenience and availability. Poor families are more likely to live in homes with limited numbers of electric outlets, making extension cords more available. Not all serious internal injuries have external markers; the child who is thrown against a soft surface, such as a bed, may have extensive brain damage and no external marks. This act (Table 12.2) is a common cause of injuries of children seen in a hospital setting (Johnson & Showers, 1985).

The Laboratory and X-Rays

Parents may claim that their child bruises more readily than normal. It is important to rule out this possibility by performing clotting studies, including a prothrombin time (PT), partial thromboplastin time (PTT), a platelet count, and a complete blood count. It is possible that the child with a bleeding problem, such as hemophilia, may be abused (Johnson & Coury, 1988).

A skeletal survey should be considered in the evaluation of children under 2 years of age who have unusual bruises or other signs of abuse. In addition, because newly fractured bones, especially ribs (Spivak, 1992), may not be seen on a bone survey, a bone scan should be considered (Merten, Radkowski, & Leonidas, 1983). Skull fractures may not be seen on bone scans (Howard, Barron, & Smith, 1990). Follow-up x-rays may reveal fractures that were not seen on the original survey but become more visible as the result of callus formation during healing.

When the abdomen has been injured, a transaminase should be ordered to rule out trauma to the liver (Coant, Kornberg, Brody, & Edwards-Holmes, 1992). Although creatine phosphokinase (CPK) elevations are seen in damage to the muscle or brain, there are no standards for using the laboratory results to quantitate severity or date the injury in children. Fractionation of the CPK will determine

TABLE 12.2 Primary Injury by Cause Among 616 Children Reported for Physical Abuse by Children's Hospital of Columbus, Ohio, 1980-1982[a]

Known Cause of Injury	Frequency	Percentage
Belt or strap	124	23
Hand open (choken, grabbed, pinched, or slapped)	120	22
Fist	60	11
Propelled (thrown, dropped, pushed, pulled, or dragged)	41	8
Other (e.g., hit by toy, telephone, kitchen fork, bottle, household item, etc.; shot with gun; or dunked in ice water, etc.)	41	8
Switch or stick	33	6
Paddle or board	32	6
Cord	19	4
Hot liquid	17	3
Foot	11	2
Grid, heater, or stove	11	2
Cigarette	8	1
Shoe	5	1
Knife	4	1
Mouth	4	1
Shaking	3	< 1
Iron	3	< 1

SOURCE: Adapted from Johnson and Showers (1985).
a. Cause unknown = 157 (23% of total).

if the source is muscle or brain tissue. The computerized tomography (CT) scan and magnetic resonance imagery (MRI), used in the evaluation of head trauma, are also of value in investigating trauma to the lungs or abdominal organs in crushing injuries. Because head injuries are reported in 10% to 44% of abused children (Alexander, Kao, & Ellerbroek, 1989), a head CT scan or MRI has been recommended for all children under 2 years of age with external signs of abuse, especially if there is a past history of abuse (Alexander et al., 1990). On the other hand, a child with a normal neurological examination and a normal head circumference is unlikely to have significant injury on a CT scan or MRI of the head.

Unusual injuries, especially when they appear in a series, may be a manifestation of Munchausen syndrome by proxy (MSBP) (Meadow, 1977, 1984). In MSBP, an adult, typically the mother, (a) fabricates a disease by indicating nonexistent or subjective symptoms; (b) creates wounds with instruments, including the hands or the mouth, hot liquids, or caustic substances; (c) creates objective signs of disease such as vomiting, seizures, respiratory arrest, bleeding problems, and diarrhea; or (d) alters laboratory specimens (Rosenberg, 1987).

The child in Photo 12.2 presented to the hospital on several occasions with pairs of vesicles scattered over the body.

The lesions would heal in the hospital, only to reappear at home. The symmetry of the lesions was unusual and suggestive of nonaccidental trauma. When the mother was confronted, she admitted to burning the child with the heated tongs of a cooking fork. The symptoms of MSBP do not necessarily stop when the child is admitted to the hospital. The parent may continue to cause the symptoms if he or she has access to the child. Careful observation and, when appropriate, the use of hidden videocameras will help establish the diagnosis. The parent, when confronted, may deny his or her actions or attempt to incriminate the nursing or medical staff.

The evaluation of possible MSBP requires careful collection and analysis of data from all sources that have served the child. It is imperative to recognize the possibility of MSBP before the child suffers iatrogenic trauma as the result of laboratory and surgical efforts to uncover the cause of unusual symptoms. Once diagnosed, separation of the child from the parent is necessary if the child is to escape permanent injury or death.

Bruised Brains and Babies Who Are Shaken or Thrown

The highest morbidity and mortality from child abuse are caused by central

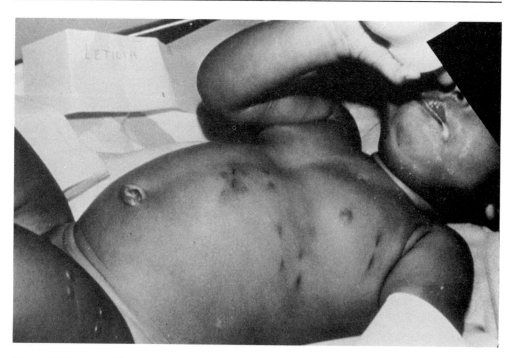

Photo 12.2. Paired Blisters From a Hot Cooking Fork

nervous system injuries (Caniano, Beaver, & Boles, 1986). The term *shaken baby syndrome* (SBS) has been applied to acceleration-deceleration injuries to the brains of infants that result from vigorous shaking. These infants, generally less than 1 year of age, present with seizures, failure to thrive, vomiting associated with lethargy or drowsiness, hypothermia, bradycardia, hypotension, respiratory irregularities, coma, or death (Spaide, Swengel, Scharre, & Mein, 1990). The common histories given are that the infant (a) spontaneously stopped breathing, and marks about the face are explained as the results of slapping the child to initiate respiration; (b) went to sleep and could not be aroused; (c) was dropped by a sibling; and (d) rolled from an elevated surface to the floor. The condition also can result if the infant is thrown against an object or surface.

When babies are shaken, their relatively large and poorly supported head whips back and forth—hence the term *whiplash shaken baby syndrome,* which was originally coined by Caffey (1972, 1974). As the head moves back and forth, the brain moves in the opposite direction. Brain tissue is sheared, and blood vessels are ruptured. A spinal tap will reveal fresh bleeding if the injury is recent. Physicians who obtain a bloody tap when investi-

gating central nervous system problems in young children should not conclude that the bleeding was iatrogenic (Apollo, 1978). The term *tin ear syndrome* has been applied to a variant of SBS in which there is unilateral ear bruising, ipsilateral cerebral edema with obliteration of basilar cisterns, and hemorrhagic retinopathy (Hanigan, Peterson, & Njus, 1987).

The diagnosis of SBS is made by CT scan or MRI and eye examination. Other causes of brain hemorrhage, such as arteriovenous malformation or aneurysm, and trauma resulting from resuscitation usually can be excluded. Skull fractures generally are not present. CT scan or MRI reveals hemorrhages in the brain. MRI has been shown to be the better technique for demonstrating cortical contusions, subdural hematomas, and shearing injuries, but CT scan is superior in detecting subarachnoid hemorrhage (Alexander et al., 1989). Eye-ground examination reveals retinal hemorrhage in 50% to 80% of cases (Levin, 1990). Although retinal hemorrhage should suggest the diagnosis of shaken baby syndrome, other causes have been described. For example, retinal hemorrhages are seen in 40% of newborns after vaginal delivery (Smith, Alexander, Jurisch, Sato, & Kao, 1992), although these hemorrhages clear in 2 weeks.

Follow-up laboratory, hearing, vision, and developmental studies are necessary because the full extent of brain injury may not be apparent for several months. Developmental assessments should be videotaped for presentation in court to aid in demonstrating the extent of functional central nervous system damage. The coroner should be notified if an abused child's condition is deteriorating so that a properly detailed autopsy can be performed. In addition, it is helpful if the coroner is provided with a written or verbal summary of the case in addition to a copy of the hospital record. The police and social service agencies may be impatient for a definitive diagnosis. It is appropriate to suggest firmly that they remove any children remaining in the home, until a suspicion of shaken baby syndrome can be verified.

Other Injuries to the Face and Head

When the face is the target of intentional trauma, careful examination of the mouth (Tate, 1971), eyes (Levin, 1990), and ears (Manning, Casselbrant, & Lammers, 1990) is necessary. A blow to the face or a fall may fracture teeth or put them through the lips. The shape of the bruise overlying the mouth may be consistent with a blow from a hand. The eardrum may be ruptured by a blow to the ear from a hand or object (Obiako, 1987). The frenulum between the tongue and base of the mouth or from the lips to the jaw may be torn as the result of force feeding. The nasal septum may be eroded by intentional trauma (Grace & Grace, 1987). Because the internal structures of the eye may be injured when the face is struck, an ophthalmoscopic examination is necessary when a child suffers a black eye or shiner.

Bruised Abdomens and Internal Injuries in Child Abuse

Marks on the outside of the body routinely should raise the question of what anatomic structures lie inside that may have been damaged by force (see Figure 12.1B). A blow that results in trauma to the internal abdominal organs may have serious repercussions for the child with consequent bowel evisceration (Press,

Grant, Thompson, & Milles, 1991), organ contusion, or rupture (Grosfeld & Ballantine, 1976; McCort & Vaudagna, 1964; Philipart, 1977; Vasundhara, 1990).

In one study, abdominal or lower thoracic visceral injury was found in 14 of 69 children (20.3%) suffering blunt trauma suspected as being due to child abuse. The abdominal organs injured included liver (5), spleen (3), kidney, adrenal glands, pancreas, and duodenum. Thoracic injuries included pulmonary contusion or laceration in two children. Four of the children died (Sivit, Taylor, & Eichelberger, 1989). Traumatic pancreatitis has resulted from intentional injury to the abdomen; CT scan is recommended in suspected abdominal trauma, with ultrasound as a supplemental diagnostic tool. Knuckle marks from a blow to the abdomen by a fist will appear as a row of three or four circular bruises whose diameter approximates that of the metacarpal-phalangeal joints of an adult (Figure 12.4).

Misdiagnosis of Child Abuse

Any injury that results from accidental contact with an object also can result from the object being wielded carelessly or intentionally by an assailant. In addition, a variety of metabolic (Hurwitz & Castells, 1987) infectious diseases, hematologic bleeding disorders (Brown & Melinkovich, 1986; Johnson & Coury, 1988; McRae, Ferguson, & Lederman, 1973; O'Hare & Eden, 1984), allergic skin reactions (Adler & Kane-Nussen, 1983), and birthmarks may be mistaken for child abuse (Table 12.3).

Cigarette burns may be difficult to distinguish from a similar-sized lesion of impetigo on the face or hand (Raimer, Raimer, & Hebeler, 1981). The primary lesion of impetigo is a pustule; autoinoculation from scratching will spread the lesions of impetigo, and when surfaces contact each other, such as between the buttocks, underarms, or thighs, "kissing" lesions may result. Mongolian spots, present at birth, are more likely to be seen on the buttocks of dark-skinned infants. The spots, which are slate-blue color, may appear on any body surface and can be confused with bruises; however, Mongolian spots will not clear over a few weeks.

Children may discolor their skin with various pigments temporarily, or they

TABLE 12.3 Conditions That May Mimic Child Abuse Injuries

SKIN CONDITIONS

Coagulopathies
    Congenital:
        Hemophilia
    Acquired:
        Vitamin K deficiency
            liver disease
            binding by resins
            malnutrition
    Toxic:
        Salicylate poisoning
Other vascular-hematologic conditions
    Schonlein-Henoch purpura
    Platelet aggregation disorders
    Disseminated intravascular coagulation
    Blood dyscrasias
Connective tissue disorders
    Type-I Ehlers-Danlos syndrome
Chromosomal disorders
Birthmarks
    Stork bites (bruises, pinchmarks)
    Mongolian spots (bruises)
    Pigmented nevi (bruises)
    Strawberry hemangiomas
Infectious diseases
    Chicken pox scars (cigarette burns)
    Impetigo (cigarette burns)
    Monilia (burn)
    Scalded skin syndrome (burn)
    Purpura fulminans of meningococcemia
    Endocarditis
Hypersensitivity vasculitis
    Stephens-Johnson syndrome
    Hives
    Phytophotodermatitis (burn)
Self-inflicted or factitial injury
    Sucker-bites/hickies (pinchmarks)
    Bruise, burn, puncture
    Banding
    Self-stimulation in retarded child
    Cornelia de Lange syndrome
    Lesch-Nyhan syndrome
    Familial disautonomia
Self-inflicted skin coloration
    Tattoo
    Paint, crayons, dyes
Neglect/accident
    Car restraint belt buckle burn (geometric burn)
Folk medicine practices
    Cia Gao/coin rubbing (linear bruise or burn)
    Moxibustion (burn)
    Cupping (geometric burn)

Parasite
    Pediculosis (maculae ceruleae mimic bruises)
    Crab louse (maculae ceruleae mimic bruises)

SKIN CONDITIONS (continued)

Miscellaneous
    Lichen sclerosis (in genital area may suggest
        trauma)
    Valsalva (bilateral ecchymosis of eyes)
    Forceful vomiting or coughing (petechial
        lesions on face)

FRACTURES

Congenital
    Osteogenesis imperfecta (old and new fractures)
    Chromosomal disorders
    Schmid-like metaphyseal chondrodysplasia
        (corner fractures)
    Wilson's disease (rib fractures)
Infectious
    Syphilis
Accidental
    Fatigue fracture from exercise
Iatrogenic
    Cardiopulmonary resuscitation
    Restraint
    Physical therapy
Acquired
    Vitamin C or D deficiency
    Prostaglandin use in newborn (subperiosteal
        hemorrhage)

RETINAL HEMORRHAGES

Folk medicine practices
    Caida de Mollera/fallen fontanel
Normal birth[a]
Coagulopathies[a]
Blood dyscrasias[a]
Infectious[a]
    Meningitis
    Endocarditis
Miscellaneous
    Severe hypertension
    CPR (Purtscher retinopathy) (very rare)
    Accidental (very, very rare)

SHAKEN BABY SYNDROME

Congenital anomalies
    Arterio-venous fistula
    Ruptured aneurism
Coagulopathies
    Hemophilia[b]

a. These are possible causes of retinal hemorrhage in children under 3 years of age.
b. Children with any acute or chronic disease also may be abused.

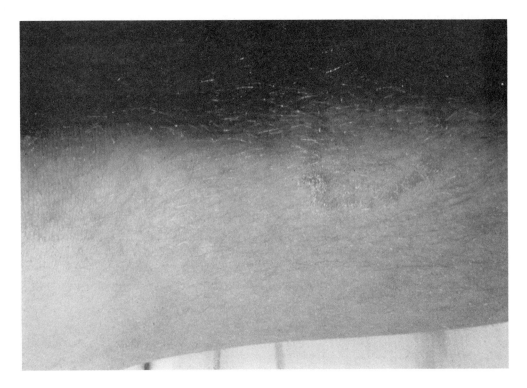

Photo 12.3. Tirea Corporus (Ringworm)

may tattoo themselves with pigments or objects permanently. A tattoo by a caretaker may be considered a form of abuse. Self-mutilation is most likely to involve the hands in retarded or emotionally disturbed children (Putnam & Stein, 1985). Accidental and self-mutilation may be seen when sensation is lost in the Cornelia-DeLange syndrome, familial dysautonomia, and Lesch-Nyhan syndrome. Banding, with the possible consequence of amputation or circular scarring, of a digit or the penis may be accidental or intentional (Johnson, 1988). Ringworm may simulate a human bite (Photo 12.3).

Because injuries to the skin may heal as scars, the examination of a child should include an inquiry into the etiology of any scars.

Professionals who are uncertain about the cause of a mark on a child or internal injuries should seek consultation from individuals experienced in child abuse or trauma investigation. A staff that involves all professionals participating in the investigation—including nurses, physicians, emergency medicine technicians, laboratory technicians, and radiologists—can reduce the likelihood for error. The group can clarify the etiology of an unusual injury and increase credibility and understanding of a report to protective agencies and the police.

Fractures in Child Abuse

The consequences of force to a bone will depend on the bone's location and resiliency. Growing children suffer types of fractures that are not seen in adults. The growing portion of the bone is an anatomically distinct area from the bone shaft. *Epiphyseal-metaphyseal* fractures in infants are highly suspect for child abuse (Carty, 1993; Swischuk, 1992). This may also occur in cases of Schmid-like metaphyseal chondrodysplasia (Kleinman, 1991) and in children with decreased or absent pain sensation (Swischuk, 1981). Healing epiphyseal-metaphyseal fractures may mimic scurvy, leukemia, or congenital syphilis. Spiral fractures, in which a bone is fixed at one end and twisted at the other, are unusual in small children but not restricted to intentional injury (Mellick & Reesor, 1990). If a history of accidental fixation and twisting is not obtained, one should consider the likelihood that one end of the extremity was held and the other end twisted. Direct blows to an extremity are most likely to

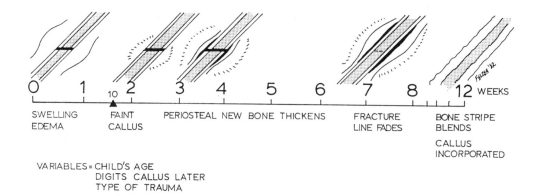

VARIABLES = CHILD'S AGE
            DIGITS CALLUS LATER
            TYPE OF TRAUMA

Figure 12.5. Dating Longbone Fractures

fracture the shaft of the bone; however, it is difficult to fracture the relatively resilient ribs, even during cardiopulmonary resuscitation (Feldman & Brewer, 1984). Rib fractures of infants, which can occur when the chest is squeezed or crushed by a caretaker's hands or feet, are highly suggestive of intentional injury (Leonidas, 1983). Other fractures with a high specificity for abuse include scapular fractures, vertebral fractures or subluxations, finger injuries in nonambulating children, bilateral fractures, and complex skull fractures (Carty, 1993).

In considering the cause of a fracture, it must be ascertained if the mass and speed of the child were sufficient to result in a fracture. It is possible to fracture the clavicle, skull, or humerus in a fall from 36 inches or more (Helfer, Slovis, & Black, 1977). Fractures of the ribs, skull, clavicles, cervical spine, and extremities can occur during birth (Rizzolo, 1989). In children less than 2 years of age, multiple, complex, depressed, wide, or growing skull fractures; fractures that involve more than a single cranial bone; and fractures of skull bones other than the parietal bone are more likely to be due to abuse (Hobbs, 1984; Meservy, Towbin, McLaurin, Myers, & Ball, 1987). It is important to recognize that 50% of all intracranial injuries are not associated with skull fractures (Merten, Osborne, Radkowski, & Leonidas, 1984). If a child falls onto a small object, thereby concentrating the force on a small area, deeper injury, including a fracture, is more likely. One would expect obvious tissue damage overlying a fracture caused by a fall (Figure 12.1B).

Fractures heal in a regular sequence (Swischuk, 1981). Dating the age of a fracture, like that of a bruise, is necessary to determine the credibility of the injury history. The first radiological signs of healing appear as a callus in 10 to 14 days (Figure 12.5) (Swischuk, 1981). As with any tissue, this timing may be modified by individual variations, the specific bone(s) involved, and the existence of repetitive injuries. Early peak and late time ranges have been described, with the earliest periosteal new bone formation visible at 4 days and late appearance at 21 days (O'Connor & Cohen, 1987).

If an infant who is more than 2 weeks old presents with a fracture that shows no signs of healing, it is *unlikely* that this was due to an injury at birth. Fractures that show various stages of healing at one point in time are not compatible with a single injury. Children with osteogenesis imperfecta (Gahagen & Rimsza, 1991), a genetic disease with several types and manifestations, have bones that fracture easily. In Type II, the fractures may appear at birth. Blue sclerae, a common finding in Type I, may not be obvious, especially in fair-skinned children. The diagnosis can be made definitively by analysis of Type-I collagen obtained by biopsy. Not all cases of multiple fractures of differing ages will require this analysis.

Trauma Resulting From Folk Medicine Practice

In an effort to treat illness, the caretaker may resort to a variety of home or

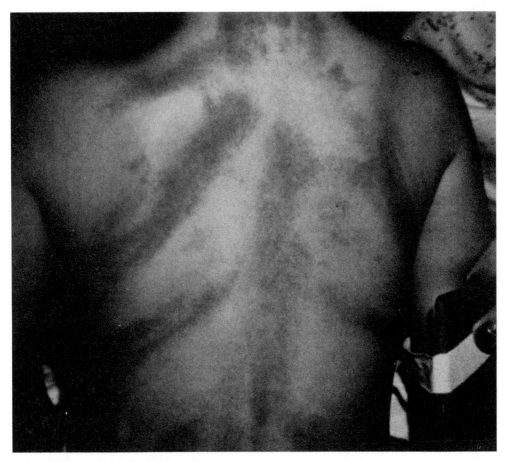

Photo 12.4. *Cia Gao*—A Folk Medicine Practice
SOURCE: Johnson (1990). Reprinted by permission of W. B. Saunders.

folk remedies. Although the merits of chicken soup are familiar to most people in the United States, other folk practices may not be readily recognized. If folk practices leave a mark, they are likely to be mistaken for child abuse. For example, in *Cia Gao* (Gellis & Feingold, 1976; Yeatman, 1976, 1980), a folk medicine practice among certain East Asians, the skin is rubbed with a spoon or coin that may be dipped in heated oil. The skin of the area is reddened in a linear pattern. On the chest, the marks follow the directions of the ribs (Photo 12.4).

The injury is intentional, and visible trauma results. The parents readily will describe what they have done. Their intent, although of no proven medical benefit, is not to vent anger or influence the child's behavior but to elicit a cure. Treatment should be guided toward ensuring that prescribed "Western medicine" is given to the child.

Physicians should familiarize themselves with the folk practices of immigrants to their communities. The practice of *Caida de Mollera* (fallen fontanelle) may be used by Hispanics. In an attempt to treat diarrhea and vomiting in which the anterior fontanelle has sunken from dehydration, the child is held upside down. Retinal hemorrhages, which may result, mimic those resulting from shaken baby syndrome (Guarnaschelli, Lee, & Pitts, 1972). A lack of professional sensitivity to these issues may result in families avoiding the medical system. It may be as difficult to change these behaviors among immigrants as it is to modify unnecessary or controversial practices performed in this country, such as ritual or routine circumcision (Herrera, Cochran, Herrera, & Wallace, 1983; "Task Force on Circumcision," 1989).

If a healing practice is performed by a "recognized religious organization," the

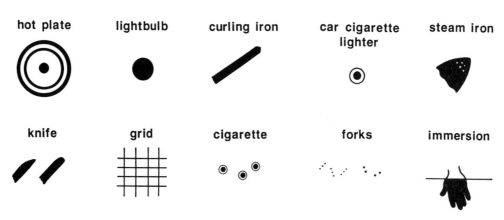

Figure 12.6. Marks From Burns
SOURCE: Johnson (1990). Reprinted by permission of W. B. Saunders.

state laws defining child abuse and neglect may not allow an abuse report to be processed or acted on. Parents who repeatedly fail to follow medical advice that has been accompanied by adequate instruction and that endangers the child should be reported for medical neglect (Johnson & Coury, 1992). The deaths of children from medical neglect that result from religious belief have been used to challenge the religious exemption laws.

Thermal Injuries in Child Abuse

Any instrument that is capable of containing or generating heat can be applied to the child's skin. A hot object will imprint the skin with its mark. Underlying structures, such as bony prominences, can distort the shape of the mark (Figure 12.6).

If a child is immersed in hot water, all body surfaces in contact with the water will be burned except for areas that are protected by flexion. For example, when a child is placed in hot water feet first, legs may be flexed onto the abdomen, and the skin in the antecubital fossa, groin, and abdominal folds will be spared from heat injury. Because the palm and sole skin are thicker than other areas of skin, these surfaces may not be burned as severely, and the resulting burn pattern may suggest that hot water was poured on the top of the hand or foot. A stocking or glove-like pattern, without evidence of burns from splashing, should suggest an immersion burn. The degree of injury depends on the temperature of the object, the amount of time the object remains on the skin, and the peculiarities of children's skin on various parts of the body. Caretakers may not be aware of the short amount of time required to inflict a first- or second-degree burn on a child. Studies of adults have indicated that if water temperature is 64 degrees Centigrade (147 degrees Fahrenheit), a 1-second contact will result in a second- or third-degree burn (Moritz & Henriques, 1947) (Table 12.4). Burns from hot grease generally are more severe than burns from hot water. Water cannot be heated beyond 100 degrees Centigrade (220 degrees Fahrenheit).

Hot water heater thermostats may be set at dangerously high temperatures. Parents living in rental units may not be able to change the hot water heater thermostat. Intentional immersion burns usually occur during the toilet training ages of 6 to 24 months. Inexperienced parents may begin toilet training as early as 6 months (Johnson et al., 1982). Diaper changing, which takes place in the bathroom where hot water is accessible, may provide the opportunity to "teach the baby not to mess the diaper." Alternatively, hot water is run, and the child is placed in the water to be cleansed, without the water temperature being tested. The caretaker may cover for the accident by blaming the child or a sibling, creating a history that is incompatible with the burn.

In determining the feasibility of the history of a burn, it is important to visit

TABLE 12.4 Time Required for Water to Cause First- or Second-Degree Burns on Human Skin

Water Temperature (°C/°F)	Time of Exposure (seconds)
52 (125.6)	70
54 (129.2)	30
56 (132.8)	14
58 (136.4)	6
60 (140.0)	3
62 (143.6)	1.6
64 (147.2)	1

SOURCE: Johnson (1990). Reprinted by permission of W. B. Saunders.

the accident site and measure water temperature, height and style of control knobs, tub depth, tub sill height, and location of spouts. These measurements can be compared to the child's height and reach measurements and motor capacity. Turning a round faucet is considered to be possible after 24 months of age. The height of the sill of the tub may preclude feet first entry into water. Small children entering a tub will generally slide in sideways or head first. In addition, one would expect a child who enters hot water, at any angle, to move and splash as they attempt to escape. When the cause of an immersion burn cannot be diagnosed as intentional, filing for safety neglect is necessary. A home safety inspection should be performed with education in accident prevention. Accident risk factors, commonly shared with child abuse, should be ascertained and appropriate services offered.

Determining the cause of burns from hot irons is especially perplexing. If the palm of the hand is involved, an exploratory or self-inflicted burn is probable. Burns to the dorsum of the hand or to multiple body surfaces decrease the likelihood of an accident. Iron burns may involve the curved edge of the iron or the flat surface. Steam holes may be seen in the burn pattern. Hot irons or hot liquids may be pulled into strollers by young infants (Johnson et al., 1990).

Accidental splash burns from containers on tables or stoves are most severe on the upper body and under insulated clothing; the burn pattern "feathers" as the hot liquid runs down the body and cools. A plastic diaper may spare the diaper area in a splash burn or contain the hot water in a pour burn.

Cigarette burns can occur when the child explores the ignited end or runs into it. Burns that are complete circles, indicating prolonged contact, on the dorsum of the hand or on other protected surfaces, suggest an intentional burn. Flame burns are likely to be more serious and accidental; however, thumbs may be burned with cigarette lighters in response to thumb sucking, and children may be held over flames. Two children who were placed in a microwave oven sustained third-degree burns. In one, the pattern involved the abdomen, thorax, and left thigh, with circumferential burns on the left hand and right foot. Another suffered second- and third-degree burns to the midback. The burn location was influenced by proximity to the microwave emitting device (Alexander, Surrell, & Cohle, 1987).

Children Who Die: Child Abuse or Accident?

Children who die in the hospital are likely to have an autopsy to confirm the cause of death. Children who die from child abuse in the community may be signed out as sudden infant death syndrome or death due to accidental cause. When the cause of death is uncertain, it is required by law that the coroner be notified and imperative that an autopsy be performed. The examination of the child who has died from unknown causes should be as detailed and extensive as the child who has survived trauma and include external and internal examination, with radiological studies and toxicology screening by the coroner (Norman, Newman, Smialek, & Horembala, 1984). The police department routinely should investigate the death scene and interview the caretakers and witnesses. If abuse is indicated, it is important that the welfare agency be notified immediately to obtain a court order to protect other children who may be at risk in the home. Active surveillance of infant deaths, with review of the child abuse registry, has been recommended as a way to monitor the success of efforts to prevent child abuse fatalities (Schloesser, Pierpont, & Poertner, 1992).

Summary

A high degree of skepticism, as well as knowledge of the many ways child abuse can be manifested, is necessary if children are to be protected from further abuse through reports to the law enforcement and social service systems.

Reporting should be guided by an ethical and moral responsibility to serve children rather than personal bias, economics, state mandates, or fear of court or legal actions. The training required in child abuse recognition and reporting (Dubowitz, 1988; Johnson, 1989) should begin in undergraduate school and continue throughout the professional's career. Familiarity with the training and language of the various professionals involved in serving the needs of abused children and the sharing of information about diagnosis, treatment, and outcome are necessary for continued improvement in the motivation of mandated reporters to investigate, report, and appear in court to testify in cases of abuse. It is imperative that future parents, parents, caretakers, and vulnerable infants and children be screened and flagged for abuse risk so that prevention services can be offered (Alvarez, Doris, & Larson, 1988; Caldwell, Bogat, & Davidson, 1988; Dubowitz, 1989; Fischler, 1985; Zuravin, 1989).

References

Adler, R., & Kane-Nussen, B. (1983). Erythema multiform: Confusion with child battering syndrome. *Pediatrics, 72,* 718-720.

Alexander, R. C., Surrell, J. A., & Cohle, S. D. (1987). Microwave oven burns to children: An unusual manifestation of child abuse. *Pediatrics, 79,* 255-260.

Alexander, R., Kao, S. C. S., & Ellerbroek, C. J. (1989). Head injury in child abuse: Evaluation with MR imaging. *Radiology, 17*(3), 653-657.

Alexander, R., Altemeier, W. A., O'Connor, S., Crabbe, L., Sato, Y., Smith, W., & Bennett, T. (1990, January). Serial abuse in children who are shaken. *American Journal of Diseases of Children, 144,* 58-60.

Alvarez, W. F., Doris J., & Larson, O. (1988, August). Children of migrant farm families are at high risk for maltreatment: New York state study. *American Journal of Public Health, 78*(8), 934-936.

Apollo, J. O. (1978). Bloody cerebrospinal fluid: Traumatic tap or child abuse? *Pediatric Emergency Care, 3,* 93-95.

Barlow, B., Niemirska, M., & Gandhi, R. P. (1983). Ten years of experience with falls from a height in children. *Journal of Pediatric Surgery, 18,* 509-511.

Bourguet, C. C., & McArtor, R. E. (1989, May). Unintentional injuries. *American Journal of Diseases of Children, 143,* 556-559.

Brown, J., & Melinkovich P. (1986). Shoenlein-Henoch purpura misdiagnosed as suspected child abuse: A case report and literature review. *Journal of the American Medical Association, 256,* 617-618.

Caffey, J. (1972). On the theory and practice of shaking infants. *American Journal of Diseases of Children, 124,* 161.

Caffey, J. (1974). The whiplash shaken infant syndrome: Manual shaking by the extremities with whiplash induced intracranial and intraocular bleedings, linked with residual permanent brain damage and mental retardation. *Pediatrics, 54,* 396.

Caldwell, R. A., Bogat, G. A., & Davidson, W. S. (1988). The assessment of child abuse potential and the prevention of child abuse and neglect. *American Journal of Community Psychology, 16,* 609-624.

Caniano, D. A., Beaver, B. L., & Boles, E. T. (1986). An update on surgical management in 256 cases. *Annals of Surgery, 203,* 219-224.

Carty, H. M. (1993). Fractures caused by child abuse. *Journal of Bone and Joint Surgery, 75,* 849-857.

Coant, P. N., Kornberg, A. E., Brody, A. S., Edwards-Holmes, K. (1992). Markers for occult liver injury in cases of physical abuse in children. *Pediatrics, 89,* 274-278.

Dubowitz, H. (1988). Child abuse programs and pediatric residency training. *Pediatrics, 82*(suppl), 477-480.

Dubowitz, H. (1989). Prevention of child maltreatment: What is known. *Pediatrics, 83,* 570-577.

Dubowitz, H., Hampton, R. L., Bithoney, W. G., & Newberger, E. H. (1987). Inflicted and non-inflicted injuries: Differences in child and familial characteristics. *American Journal of Orthopsychiatry, 57,* 525-535.

Feldman, K. W., & Brewer, D. K. (1984). Child abuse, cardiopulmonary resuscitation, and rib fractures. *Pediatrics, 73*(3), 339-342.

Finkelhor, D., & Zellman, G. L. (1991). Flexible reporting options for skilled child abuse professionals. *Child Abuse & Neglect, 15,* 335-341.

Fischler, R. S. (1985). Child abuse and neglect in American Indian communities. *Child Abuse & Neglect, 9,* 99-106.

Gahagan, S., & Rimsza, M. E. (1991). Child abuse or osteogenesis imperfecta: How can we tell? *Pediatrics, 88,* 987-992.

Gellis, S., & Feingold, M. (1976). Cao gio: Psuedobattering in Vietnamese children. *American Journal of Diseases of Children, 130,* 857-858.

Grace, A., & Grace, S. (1987). Child abuse within the ear, nose & throat. *Journal of Otolaryngology, 16,* 111.

Gregg, G. S., & Elmer, E. (1969). Infant injuries: Accident or abuse? *Pediatrics, 44,* 434-439.

Grosfeld, J. L., & Ballantine, T. V. (1976). Surgical aspects of child abuse (Trauma-X). *Pediatrics, 5,* 106-120.

Guarnaschelli, J., Lee, J., & Pitts, F. W. (1972). Fallen fontanelle (Caida de Mollera): A variant of the battered child syndrome. *Journal of the American Medical Association, 222,* 1545.

Hanigan, W. C., Peterson, R. A., & Njus, G. (1987). Tin ear syndrome. *Pediatrics, 80,* 618-622.

Helfer, R. E., Slovis, T. L., & Black, M. (1977). Injuries resulting when small children fall out of bed. *Pediatrics, 60,* 533-535.

Herrera, A. J., Cochran, B., Herrera, A., & Wallace, B. (1983). Parental information and circumcisions in highly motivated couples with higher education. *Pediatrics, 71,* 233-234.

Hobbs, C. J. (1984). Skull fracture and the diagnosis of abuse. *Archives of Disease in Childhood, 59,* 246-252.

Holter, J. C., & Friedman, S. B. (1968). Child abuse: Early case finding in the emergency department. *Pediatrics, 42,* 128-138.

Howard, J. L., Barron, B. J., & Smith, G. G. (1990). Bone scintigraphy in the evaluation of extraskeletal injuries from child abuse. *Radio Graphics, 10,* 67-81.

Hurwitz, A., & Castells, S. (1987). Misdiagnosed child abuse and metabolic disorders. *Pediatric Nursing, 13,* 33-36.

Izant, R. J., & Hubay, C. (1966). The annual injury of 15,000,000 children: A limited study of childhood accidental injury and death. *Journal of Trauma, 6,* 65-74.

Joffe, M., & Ludwig, S. (1988). Stairway injuries in children. *Pediatrics, 82,* 457-461.

Johnson, C. F. (1983). Sudden infant death syndrome vs. child abuse: The teenage connection. *Journal of Pedodontics, 7,* 196-208.

Johnson, C. F. (1988). Constricting bands: Manifestations of possible child abuse. *Clinical Pediatrics, 27,* 439-444.

Johnson, C. F. (1989). Residency and child abuse [Letter to the editor]. *Pediatrics, 83,* 805-806.

Johnson, C. F. (1990). Inflicted injury versus accidental injury. *Pediatric Clinics of North America, 37,* 791-814.

Johnson, C. F., Apollo J., Joseph, J. A., & Corbitt, T. (1986). Child abuse diagnosis and the emergency department chart. *Pediatric Emergency Care, 2,* 6-9.

Johnson, C. F., & Cohn, D. S. (1990). The stress of child abuse and other family violence. In L. E. Arnold (Ed.), *Childhood stress* (pp. 268-295). New York: John Wiley.

Johnson, C. F., & Coury, D. L. (1988). Bruising and hemophilia: Accident or child abuse? *Child Abuse & Neglect, 12,* 409-415.

Johnson, C. F., & Coury, D. L. (1992). Child neglect: General concepts and medical neglect in child abuse. In S. Ludwig & A. E. Kornberg (Eds.), *Child abuse: A medical reference* (2nd ed., pp. 321-331). New York: Churchill Livingstone.

Johnson, C. F., Erickson, K. A., & Caniano, D. (1990). Walker-related burns in infants and toddlers. *Pediatric Emergency Care, 6,* 58-61.

Johnson, C. F., Kaufman, K. L., & Callendar, C. (1990). The hand as a target organ in child abuse. *Clinical Pediatrics, 29,* 66-72.

Johnson, C. F., Loxterkamp, D., & Albanese, M. (1982, May). Effect of high school students' knowledge of child development and child health on approaches to child discipline. *Pediatrics, 69,* 559-563.

Johnson, C. F., & Showers, J. (1985). Injury variables in child abuse. *Child Abuse & Neglect, 9,* 207-215.

Kleinman, P. K. (1991). Schmid-like metaphyseal chondro-dysplasia simulating child abuse. *American Journal of Radiology, 156,* 576-578.

Kravitz, H., Driessen, G., Gomberg, R., & Korach, A. (1969). Accidental falls from elevated surfaces in infants from birth to one year of age. *Pediatrics, 44,* 869-876.

Lasing, S. A., & Buchan, A. R. (1976). Bilateral injuries in childhood: An alerting sign? *British Medical Journal, 2,* 940-941.

Lehman, D., & Schonfeld, N. (1993). Falls from heights: A problem not just in the northeast. *Pediatrics, 92,* 121-24.

Leonidas, J. C. (1983). Skeletal trauma in the child abuse syndrome. *Pediatrics Annual, 12,* 875-881.

Levin, A. V. (1990). Ocular manifestations of child abuse. *Pediatric Ophthamology, 3*(2), 249-264.

Lyons, T., & Oates, R. K. (1993, July). Falling out of bed: A relatively benign occurrence. *Pediatrics, 92,* 125-127.

Manning, S. C., Casselbrant, M., & Lammers, D. (1990). Otolaryngolic manifestations of child abuse. *International Journal of Pediatric Otorhinolaryngology, 20,* 7-16.

McCort, J., & Vaudagna, J. (1964). Visceral injuries in battered children. *Radiology, 88,* 424-428.

McRae, K. N., Ferguson, C. A., & Lederman, R. S. (1973). The battered child syndrome. *Canadian Medical Association Journal, 108,* 859-860.

Meadow, R. (1977). Munchausen syndrome by proxy: The hinterland of child abuse. *Lancett, 2,* 343-345.

Meadow, R. (1984). Factitious illness: The hinterland of child abuse. *Recent Advances in Pediatrics, 7,* 217-232.

Mellick, L. B., & Reesor, K. (1990, May). Spiral tibial fractures of children: A commonly accidental spiral long bone fracture. *American Journal of Emergency Medicine, 8*(3), 234-237.

Merten, D. F., Osborne, D. R. S., Radkowski, M. A., & Leonidas, J. L. (1984). Craniocerebral trauma in the child abuse syndrome: Radiological observations. *Pediatric Radiology, 14,* 272-277.

Merten, D. F., Radkowski, M. A., & Leonidas, J. C. (1983). The abused child: A radiological reappraisal. *Radiology, 146,* 377-381.

Meservy, C. J., Towbin, R., McLaurin, R. L., Myers, P. A., & Ball, W. (1987). Radiographic characteristics of skull fractures resulting from child abuse. *American Journal of Neuroradiology, 8,* 455-457.

Milner, J. S., & Chilamkurti, C. (1991). Physical child abuse perpetrator characteristics: A review of the literature. *Journal of Interpersonal Violence, 6,* 345-366.

Moritz, A. R., & Henriques, F. C. (1947). Studies of thermal injury: Pathology and pathogenesis of cutaneous burns experimental study. *American Journal of Pathology, 23,* 915-941.

Morris, J. L., Johnson, C. F., & Clasen, M. (1985). To report or not to report: Physicians' attitudes toward discipline and child abuse. *American Journal of Diseases of Children, 139,* 194-197.

Norman, M. G., Newman, D. E., Smialek, J. E., & Horembala, E. J. (1984, Winter). The postmortem examination on the abused child. *Perspectives in Pediatric Pathology, 8,* 313-342.

Obiako, M. N. (1987). Eardrum perforation as evidence of child abuse. *Child Abuse & Neglect, 11,* 149-151.

O'Connor, J. F., & Cohen, J. (1987). Dating fractures. In P. K. Kleinman (Ed.), *Diagnostic imaging of child abuse* (pp. 103-113). Baltimore, MD: Williams and Wilkins.

O'Hare, A. E., & Eden, B. (1984). Bleeding disorders and nonaccidental injury. *Archives of Diseases in Childhood, 50,* 860-864.

Olney, D. B. (1988). Patterns of presentation of abused children to the accident and emergency department. *Archives of Emergency Medicine, 5,* 228-232.

Philipart, A. I. (1977). Blunt abdominal trauma in childhood. *Surgical Clinics of North America, 57,* 151-163.

Press, S., Grant, P., Thompson, V. T., & Milles, K. L. (1991). Small bowel evisceration. *Pediatrics, 88,* 807-809.

Putnam, N., & Stein, M. (1985). Self-inflicted injuries in childhood: A review and diagnostic approach. *Clinical Pediatrics, 24,* 514-518.

Raimer, B. G., Raimer, S. S., & Hebeler, J. R. (1981). Cutaneous signs of child abuse. *Journal of the American Academy of Dermatology, 5,* 203-214.

Rizzolo, P. J. (1989). Neonatal rib fracture: Birth trauma or child abuse? *Journal of Family Practice, 29,* 561-563.

Rosenberg, D. (1987). Web of deceit: A literature review of Munchausen syndrome by proxy. *Child Abuse & Neglect, 11,* 547-563.

Schloesser, P., Pierpont, J., & Poertner, J. (1992). Active surveillance of child abuse fatalities. *Child Abuse & Neglect, 16*(1), 3-10.

Showers, J., & Bandman, R. L. (1986). Scarring for life: Abuse with electric cords. *Child Abuse & Neglect, 10,* 25-31.

Showers, J., & Johnson, C. F. (1984). Students' knowledge of child health and development: Effects on approaches to discipline. *Journal of School Health, 54*(3), 122-125.

Showers, J., & Johnson, C. F. (1985). Child development, child health and child rearing knowledge among urban adolescents. *Health Education, 16,* 37-41.

Sieben, R. L., Leavitt, J. D., & French, J. H. (1971). Falls as childhood accidents: An increasing urban risk. *Pediatrics, 47,* 886-892.

Sivit, C. J., Taylor, G. A., & Eichelberger, M. R. (1989). Visceral injury in battered children: A changing perspective. *Radiology, 173,* 659-661.

Smith, M. D., Burrington, J. D., & Woolf, A. D. (1975). Injuries in children sustained in free falls: An analysis of 66 cases. *Journal of Trauma, 15,* 987-991.

Smith, W. L., Alexander, R. C., Jurisch, F. G., Sato, Y., & Kao, S. C. S. (1992). Magnetic resonance imaging evaluation of neonates with retinal hemorrhage. *Pediatrics, 89,* 332-333.

Spaide, R. F., Swengel, R. M., Scharre, D. W., & Mein, C. E. (1990, April). Shaken baby syndrome. *American Family Physician, 41,* 1145-1152.

Spivak, B. S. (1992). Biomechanics of nonaccidental trauma in child abuse. In S. Ludwig & A. E. Kornberg (Eds.), *Child abuse: A medical reference* (2nd ed., pp. 61-78). New York: Churchill Livingstone.

Swischuk, L. E. (1981). Radiology of the skeletal system in child abuse and neglect. In N. S. Ellerstein (Ed.), *Child abuse and neglect: A medical reference* (pp. 253-273). New York: John Wiley.

Swischuk, L. E. (1992). Radiologic signs of skeletal trauma. In S. Ludwig & A. E. Kornberg (Eds.), *Child abuse and neglect: A medical reference* (2nd ed., pp. 151-174). New York: Churchill Livingstone.

Task force on circumcision: Report of the task force on circumcision. (1989). *Pediatrics, 84,* 388-391.

Tate, R. J. (1971). Facial injuries associated with the battered child syndrome. *British Journal of Oral Surgery, 9,* 41-45.

Taylor, C. G., Norman, D. K., Murphy, M. J., Jellinek, M., Quinn, D., Poitrast, F. G., & Goshko, M. (1991). Diagnosed intellectual and emotional impairment among parents who seriously mistreat their children. *Child Abuse & Neglect, 15,* 389-401.

Vasundhara, T. (1990, November). Pancreatic fracture secondary to child abuse: The role of computed tomography in its diagnosis. *Clinical Pediatrics, 29*(11), 667-668.

Wagner, G. (1986). Bitemark identification in child abuse cases. *Pediatric Dentistry, 8,* 96-100.

Wilson, E. F. (1977). Estimation of the age of cutaneous contusions in child abuse. *Pediatrics, 60,* 750-752.

Yeatman, G. W. (1976). Psuedobattering in Vietnamese children. *Pediatrics, 58,* 617-618.

Yeatman, G. W. (1980). Cao gio (coin rubbing): Vietnamese attitudes toward health care. *Journal of the American Medical Association, 244,* 2748-2749.

Zellman, G. L. (1992). The impact of case characteristics on child abuse reporting decisions. *Child Abuse & Neglect, 16,* 57-74.

Zuravin, A. J. (1989). The ecology of child abuse and neglect: Review of the literature and presentation of data. *Violence Victims, 4,* 101-120.

13

Medical Neglect

HOWARD DUBOWITZ
MAUREEN BLACK

Health care providers and others have focused on child physical and sexual abuse but have overlooked child neglect (Wolock & Horowitz, 1984). There are several reasons why child neglect has not been given the attention it deserves (Dubowitz, 1994). The typically vague definitions of neglect have made it an amorphous phenomenon; many are understandably unclear about what constitutes neglect. The strong association between child neglect and poverty (Giavannoni & Becerra, 1979) has evoked a sense of hopelessness and helplessness among professionals, deterring them from becoming involved in this complex issue. In addition, neglect does not evoke the feelings of horror and outrage associated with abuse. However, more than half the reports for child maltreatment made in the United States each year are for neglect (U.S. Department of Health and Human Services [DHHS], 1988), and the morbidity and mortality associated with child neglect are substantial (Daro & McCurdy, 1992).

AUTHORS' NOTE: Parts of this chapter are adapted with permission from Dubowitz, H., & Black, M. (1994), "Child Neglect," in R. Reece (Ed.), *Child Abuse: Medical Diagnosis and Management.* Malvern, PA: Lea & Febiger. This work was partially supported by a grant (90CA1401/01) from the National Center on Child Abuse and Neglect to study child neglect.

This chapter largely concerns one major form of child neglect: medical neglect. In the following sections, we discuss (a) a conceptual definition of medical neglect, (b) incidence data, (c) etiology, (d) major manifestations, and (e) general principles for evaluation and intervention.

Defining Medical Neglect

Medical neglect can be conceptualized as a situation in which a child's clear medical need is not met. This relatively broad definition of neglect focuses on important unmet needs of children, not on parental omissions in care (Dubowitz, Black, Starr, & Zuravin, 1993). A "clear" medical need is one that a layperson could reasonably be expected to recognize as requiring professional health care *and* to act on by seeking such care. Many minor health problems (e.g., colds, diaper rash) are treated reasonably by parents and do not meet the standard of clear medical need.

A definition based on a child's unmet needs does not include the issues of cause(s) or contributory factor(s). From a child's perspective, not receiving necessary care is neglect, regardless of the reasons why such care is not provided. The causes, however, *are* important when considering how to best intervene and ensure the child's well-being.

There is no single cause of child neglect. Belsky (1980) has proposed an ecological model in which multiple interacting factors contribute to medical neglect (and other forms of child maltreatment). This model is illustrated by a case of a toddler with a chronic, toxic blood lead level. This child is experiencing medical neglect in that he is not being protected from this hazard, nor is he receiving satisfactory treatment. Contributory factors may include the parents' unwillingness to allow treatment, a landlord's refusal to have the home deleaded, a city's inability to ensure an adequate lead abatement program, and society's limited investment in low-income housing. An understanding of a neglectful situation demands an appreciation of the contributory factors to plan the optimal interventions. But regardless of which contributory factors are responsible, the child with the high lead level experiences neglect.

This broad definition of medical neglect differs from the narrow focus of federal and state laws, which limit neglect to omissions in care by a parent or primary caregiver (Office of Human Development Services, 1987). Child protective services (CPS) accordingly confines its involvement to this narrow view. The Second National Incidence Study of Child Abuse and Neglect defined two forms of medical neglect as follows: "Delay in health care" is the failure to seek timely and appropriate medical care for a serious health problem that any reasonable layperson would have recognized as needing professional medical attention; "refusal of health care" is the failure to provide or allow needed care in accordance with recommendations of a competent health care professional for a physical injury, illness, medical condition, or impairment (U.S. DHHS, 1988).

The broad definition has advantages over the narrow one. By comprehensively examining the role of *all* the contributory factors, the broad definition should lead to more varied and appropriate interventions. Potentially, this broad approach should be more effective in preventing or ameliorating neglectful situations. The suggested broad definition of medical neglect still requires clarification of the parental role, and parental omissions in care remain a concern. Parents do bear responsibility for the care of their children. But professionals, community agencies, and social policies also influence the health of children and therefore share this responsibility.

There is considerable variation in cases of medical neglect, in terms of the type of neglect, contributory factors, chronicity, and severity of harm. Some situations involve parents' inability to care for a child; others involve their refusal to seek professional care, lack of access to health care, or exposure to harmful environmental conditions (e.g., asbestos). These different situations require varied interventions, tailored to meet the needs of the individual child and family. In many circumstances, parent education and support are sufficient.

In some cases, referral to CPS is indicated, and for a small minority of cases prosecution is appropriate. At times, public health strategies or changes in social policies and programs are needed. A number of issues are relevant to conceptualizing child neglect: actual versus potential harm, severity of harm, and frequency and chronicity of the incidents or behavior.

Actual versus potential harm. Does there need to be *actual* harm to a child before assessing a situation as neglectful, or is the *risk* of harm sufficient? Most states' laws follow federal guidelines and include potential harm in their definitions of child abuse and neglect. Most CPS agencies, however, overwhelmed by the number of reports, have tended to prioritize the more "serious" cases, and actual harm obviously is viewed as more serious than potential harm. Consequently, cases involving only mild or moderate potential harm often are screened out or not substantiated.

If the purpose of defining neglect is to ensure the health and well-being of children, a focus on actual harm seems too little, too late.

If the purpose of defining neglect is to ensure the health and well-being of children, a focus on actual harm seems too little, too late. It is important to include potential harm in defining medical neglect. Many untreated conditions might not have immediate consequences but may lead to later physical or psychological harm. A concern with potential harm also should draw attention to the need for preventive interventions.

Severity. With regard to potential harm, some risks entail only minor consequences, and others might be life-threatening. Missing a follow-up appointment for a child with an ear infection is very different from not seeking care for a severely dehydrated infant with frequent vomiting and diarrhea. The more severe the actual or potential harm, the more serious the consideration of neglect. The potential long-term medical and psychological ramifications should be considered.

Frequency/chronicity. Neglect usually is inferred when the condition is chronic or there is a pattern of omissions in care. A dilemma arises of how to consider single or rare incidents that harm or endanger children. Even a single incident can have devastating results, such as failure to obtain prompt medical care after a child has

suffered a serious head injury. Although there is a tendency to consider single lapses in care as "only human," even one incident may constitute neglect. The intervention, however, might be different if there is a persistent pattern of neglect.

In many instances, omissions in care are unlikely to be harmful unless they are recurrent. For example, there may be serious risks for a child who repeatedly does not get his anticonvulsant medication, but not if this happens occasionally. Only if the child's health is clearly in jeopardy is neglect an issue.

In summary, we propose a conceptual definition of medical neglect, focusing on critical needs of children that are not being met. In addition to actual harm, potential harm is of concern, although in the latter circumstance CPS often becomes involved only if severe harm is at issue. Neglect is more likely to be inferred if there is actual harm. Actual or potential harm that is relatively severe is apt to be considered more seriously. Although chronic or recurrent neglectful situations are especially worrisome, a single exposure to harmful conditions also may constitute neglect, particularly if severe harm is involved.

Incidence Data

Child neglect frequently is not detected or reported to CPS (U.S. DHHS, 1988), making estimating its incidence or prevalence quite difficult. The best attempt was made in the 2nd National Incidence Study in 1986-1987 (NIS-II) (U.S. DHHS, 1988). In addition to reports made to CPS, professionals in the community (e.g., physicians, workers in child care centers, teachers) served as sentinels to identify cases that met the study definitions. For example, social workers, nurses, and pediatricians working in selected health care facilities were informed about the study and asked to record each case they encountered over a 3-month period. The distribution of different types of neglect is presented in Table 13.1. Children were classified in all categories that applied.

Physical neglect is by far the most common type. Medical neglect can be construed broadly to include unmet mental health needs. Similar definitions to those described earlier were developed by NIS-II for psychological care. "Refusal of

TABLE 13.1 Incidence of Child Neglect in the United States in 1986

Category	Number of Children	Rate per 1,000 Children
Physical neglect	507,700	8.1
Emotional neglect	203,000	3.2
Educational neglect	285,900	4.5
Total neglect	917,200	14.6

psychological care" was the refusal to allow needed and available treatment for a child's emotional or behavioral impairment or problem in accordance with a competent professional recommendation. "Delay in psychological care" was the failure to seek or provide needed treatment for a child's emotional or behavioral impairment or problem that any reasonable layperson would have recognized as needing professional psychological attention (e.g., severe depression, suicide attempt). The incidence of these forms of neglect is shown in Table 13.2.

There are other forms of medical neglect, even though these typically are not seen in the same way as parental omissions in care. One example is the 16% of children without any medical insurance (National Center for Children in Poverty, 1991). In addition, there are the problems of underinsurance and limited access to health care if local providers do not accept patients on medical assistance. Children under 5 reported to be in poor health and living above the poverty level have been found to be two and a half times more likely to have seen a physician than those living below poverty (U.S. DHHS, 1989). Less access to health care is associated with less use of health care services, and, frequently, poor children in relatively poor health are most affected. Malnutrition, lead poisoning, increased injuries, and other health problems that often are associated with poverty can also be seen as forms of medical neglect.

Etiology

As mentioned earlier, there is no single cause of child neglect. Rather, multiple and interacting factors at the individual (parent and child), familial, community, and societal levels may contribute. For example, maternal depression alone might not lead to neglect. But a child with developmental delays living in poverty with a depressed mother and with few social supports is a very high-risk situation for neglect. Different neglectful situations may involve different contributory factors. Although no studies of the etiology of medical neglect are available, many of the risk factors for neglect in general also may apply to medical neglect. There have been few prospective studies of neglect; most of the research has been conducted on families already identified as neglectful. Therefore, much of the following section may represent characteristics and manifestations of neglect as well as contributory factors.

Parental characteristics. Maternal problems in emotional health, intellectual abilities, and substance abuse have been associated with child neglect. Emotional disturbances, including depression, frequently are found among mothers of neglected children (e.g., Polansky, Chalmers, Williams, & Buttenwieser, 1981; Zuravin, 1988). Neglecting mothers[1] have been described as bored, depressed, restless, lonely, and less satisfied with life compared to nonneglecting mothers (Wolock & Horowitz, 1979) and more hostile, impulsive, stressed, and less socialized than either abusive or nonmaltreating mothers (Friedrich, Tyler, & Clark, 1985). Intellectual impairment, including severe mental retardation and a lack of education, also have been associated with neglect (Kadushin, 1988; Martin & Walters, 1982; Wolock & Horowitz, 1979).

An increased prevalence of alcoholism (Martin & Walters, 1982) and drug addiction (Wolock & Horowitz, 1979) has been found among neglecting families. Jones (1987) reported rates of 28% and 25% for alcohol and drug abuse, respectively, in neglecting families.

Maternal drug use during pregnancy has become a pervasive problem; more than 10% of urine toxicology screens in newborns have been positive in both

TABLE 13.2 Incidence of Specific Forms of Neglect

Form of Neglect	Number of Children	Rate per 1,000 Children
Refusal of health care	69,000	1.1
Delay in health care	37,000	0.6
Refusal of psychological care	23,300	0.4
Delay in psychological care	24,800	0.4
Total	154,100	2.5

urban and suburban areas (Gomby & Shiono, 1991). Although most illicit drugs pose definite risks to the fetus and child, the magnitude of these risks and the long-term sequelae of drug exposure are still unclear (Zuckerman, 1991). In addition to the direct effects of drugs, the compromised caregiving abilities of drug-abusing parents are a major concern. It has been proposed, mostly unsuccessfully, in several states' legislatures that maternal drug use be considered a form of child, or fetal, neglect or abuse and be grounds for CPS involvement and even criminal prosecution. Many professionals in the field prefer a therapeutic approach, offering appropriate services to mothers and babies (Larson, 1991). Only when such a plan fails and the child remains at significant risk is CPS involvement considered.

Child characteristics. It is unclear whether children with various health problems are at increased risk for child abuse and neglect. Certain child characteristics may be stressful for parents, contributing to child maltreatment (Belsky, 1980). Research has, for example, found increased depression and stress in parents of chronically disabled children (Shapiro, 1983). Other studies have found increased rates of abuse and neglect among children with chronic disabilities; for example, cerebral palsy was found to be a risk factor for neglect (Diamond & Jaudes, 1983). But another study found no increase in maltreatment among 500 moderately to profoundly retarded children, 82% of whom had cerebral palsy (Benedict, White, Wulff, & Hall, 1990).

Several studies have found low birth weight or prematurity to be risk factors for abuse and neglect (e.g., Herrenkohl & Herrenkohl, 1981). Because these babies usually receive close pediatric follow-up as well as other interventions, however, increased rates of reported maltreatment may reflect closer surveillance. In addition, medical neglect might be expected to be more prevalent among children who require frequent health care, because their increased needs place them at risk for these needs not being met.

The preponderance of evidence suggests that child factors do not play a major causative role in child maltreatment (Ammerman, 1990), although the "goodness of fit" between child and parent characteristics does influence a child's vulnerability to maltreatment. Because clinical experience suggests that children with conditions that place special demands on parents or who substantially disappoint parental expectations might be a source of stress, such families may require extra support.

Family interactions. Problems in the parent-child relationship, including disturbances in attachment between mother and infant, have been found among neglecting families (Crittenden, 1985; Egeland, Sroufe, & Erickson, 1983). Several studies have described the poor nurturing qualities of neglectful mothers. Compared to abusive parents and controls, neglecting parents have been found to have the most negative interactions with their children (Aragona & Eyberg, 1981; Burgess & Conger, 1978). Neglectful parents made more requests of their children and were least responsive to requests from them.

Although both abusing and neglecting mothers may have unrealistic expectations of their young children compared to controls (Azar, Robinson, Hekemian, & Twentyman, 1984), a lack of knowledge concerning developmental milestones (e.g., at what age an infant should be able to sit) has not been associated with child maltreatment (Twentyman & Plotkin, 1982). Deficient problem-solving skills, poor parenting skills, and inadequate knowledge of children's needs have been associated with child neglect (Azar et al., 1984; Herrenkohl, Herrenkohl, & Egolf, 1983; Jones & McNeely, 1980).

In his work with neglected children, Kadushin (1988) described chaotic families with impulse-ridden mothers who repeatedly demonstrated poor planning. He further described the negative relationships many neglectful mothers had with the fathers of their children, particularly because "the fathers often have deserted or are incarcerated." Most of the research on child neglect and high-risk families focuses on mothers and ignores fathers. This bias probably reflects the greater accessibility of mothers and suggests that the frequently modest involvement of fathers in these families might contribute to neglect or be a form of neglect per se.

Neglect has been strongly associated with social isolation (Polansky, Ammons, & Gaudin, 1985; Polansky, Gaudin, Ammons, & Davis, 1985; Wolock & Horowitz, 1979). Single parenthood without support from a spouse, family members, or friends may pose a risk for neglect. In one large controlled study, neglecting mothers perceived themselves as isolated and as living in unfriendly neighborhoods (Polansky, Gaudin, et al., 1985). Indeed, their neighbors saw these mothers as deviant and avoided social contact with them.

Stress also has been associated with child maltreatment. One study found the highest level of stress—concerning unemployment, illness, eviction, and arrest—among neglecting families compared to abusive and control families (Gaines, Sangrund, Green, & Power, 1978). Lapp (1983) found stress to be frequent among parents reported to CPS for neglect, particularly regarding family relationships and financial and health problems.

Community/neighborhood. The community setting and its resources influence parent-child relationships and are strongly associated with child maltreatment (Garbarino & Crouter, 1978). A community with a rich array of services such as parenting groups, child care, and good public transportation enhances positive feelings about the neighborhood and the

ability of families to nurture and protect children. Informal support networks, safety, and recreational facilities also are important in supporting healthy family functioning.

A comparison of neighborhoods with low and high rates of child maltreatment found that families with the most needs tended to cluster together in areas with the least social services (Garbarino & Sherman, 1980). In addition to the role of personal histories, the authors attribute the formation of high-risk neighborhoods to political and economic forces. Families in a high-risk environment are less able to give and share and might be mistrustful of neighborly exchanges. In this way, a family's problems may be "compounded rather than ameliorated by the neighborhood context, dominated as it is by other needy families" (Garbarino & Sherman, 1980). In summary, communities can serve as valuable sources of support to families, or they may add to the stresses that families experience.

Society. Many factors at the broader societal level compromise the nurturing abilities of families and the health and well-being of children. In addition, these societal or institutional problems can be *directly* neglectful of children. A detailed description of these factors is beyond the scope of this chapter, but a few examples are illustrative.

The harmful effects of poverty on the health and development of children have been referred to earlier. In addition to its influence on family functioning, poverty directly threatens and harms the well-being of children (Klerman, 1991; Parker, Greer, & Zuckerman, 1988; Wise & Meyers, 1988). These families are the poorest of the poor, concluded one study of neglectful families (Giovannoni & Billingsley, 1970). Although poverty has been associated with all forms of child maltreatment, the contribution to neglect is particularly striking (American Humane Association, 1985). It should be noted, however, that most poor families are not neglectful.

For many children, living in poverty means being exposed to environmental hazards (e.g., lead, violence), inferior schooling, malnutrition, few recreational opportunities, and more illnesses with less access to health care. With one in five U.S. children living in poverty (National Center for Children in Poverty, 1991), it is probably the major contributor to neglect. Poverty may constitute neglect in and of itself. Of all the risk factors known to impair the health and well-being of children, poverty is very important.

The child welfare system, the very system intended to assist children needing care and protection, is another example of institutional neglect.

> If the nation had deliberately designed a system that would frustrate the professionals who staff it, anger the public who finance it, and abandon the children who depend on it, it could not have done a better job than the present child welfare system. (National Commission on Children, 1991)

Inadequately financed, with staff who often are undertrained and overwhelmed, and with poorly coordinated services, CPS often is unable to fulfill their mandate of protecting children. Not surprisingly, recent reports by the National Advisory Committee to the National Center on Child Abuse and Neglect (1991) and the National Center for Children in Poverty (1991) call for a drastic overhaul of the child welfare system.

Manifestations of Medical Neglect

Noncompliance With Medical Recommendations

Probably the most common form of medical neglect involves noncompliance with health care appointments or recommendations. For example, approximately half of adolescents have been estimated to be noncompliant with medical regimens (Litt & Cuskey, 1980). Another study found only 25% of parents of hyperactive children adhered to the treatment plan, and fewer than 10% of them consulted the physician before stopping medication (Firestone & Witt, 1982). Noncompliance is not restricted to patients. Studies of physicians rated their clinical performance as ranging between 48% and 72% below professional standards (Meichenbaum, 1989). The pervasiveness of noncompliance does not minimize its importance, but our understanding of and approach to this problem need to be considered in this context.

Many factors may contribute to noncompliance, particularly a lack of clear communication between the physician and family.

If the treatment plan is not clearly explained or is misunderstood, the importance of the treatment might not be appreciated.

If the treatment plan is not clearly explained or is misunderstood, the importance of the treatment might not be appreciated. Families may harbor concerns about potential side-effects. All these factors contribute to noncompliance and children not receiving necessary care. Even if parents understand the treatment plan, practical barriers may prevent its implementation. A child refusing to take a medication or a lack of funds to purchase the medication are commonly encountered problems. Perhaps the most common reason for noncompliance is the parent simply forgetting to give the medicine; remembering three or four daily doses can be a challenge in the course of a busy day. In addition, when symptoms have resolved and the child appears well, there is less imperative for completing the treatment course, unless specific instructions are given.

Problems in compliance also arise when the child and family do not share the pediatrician's concern. Obesity is one example. Families might not be sufficiently motivated to make the effort demanded to resolve a condition they do not regard as a problem. In the realm of mental health, there may be a discomfort with or lack of acceptance of psychotherapy. It is not surprising that a lack of concern or ambivalence leads to noncompliance.

Failure or Delay in Seeking Health Care

Parents or primary caregivers frequently decide on the appropriate care for minor ailments (e.g., a scrape, cold, constipation). As conditions become more complex or serious, the need for professional medical care increases, and parents are responsible for seeking such care. If necessary care is not sought and a child's health is jeopardized, this constitutes a form of neglect.

Various factors might explain why care was not sought; these factors need to be clarified in order to intervene effectively. Parents may think or hope their child's condition is improving or stabilizing, when instead there is deterioration. In many circumstances, the symptoms may be subtle or nonexistent (e.g., anemia); if laypersons cannot reasonably be expected to appreciate such problems, they should not be held responsible. Parents may not know that treatment exists for the problem (e.g., bed wetting). Finally, practical constraints, such as a lack of health insurance or transportation, may delay seeking health care.

Religiously Motivated Medical Neglect

Medical neglect might occur when parents actively refuse medical treatment, based on their belief that an alternative treatment is preferable or because the prescribed approach is prohibited by their religion. These situations involve parents' refusal to seek or allow medical care for children with serious conditions. Jehovah's Witnesses, with their prohibition of blood transfusions, routinely refuse surgery where the need for transfusions is anticipated.

Another example is the belief of the Christian Science Church in its own faith healers and its rejection of Western medicine. For example, a Boston jury found the Christian Science parents of 2½-year-old Robyn Twitchell guilty of negligent homicide (Skolnick, 1990), the 21st such conviction of Christian Science parents in the past decade. Robyn died of a medically untreated bowel obstruction, after vomiting fecal material and becoming comatose. Robyn received treatment consisting of "heartfelt yet disciplined prayer." The Twitchells were sentenced to 10 years' probation for failing to seek medical care that could have saved their child's life.

At what point should alternative approaches and beliefs not be tolerated? At what point does one declare that a child's crucial health care needs are not being met and that a neglectful situation exists? How do we balance a concern with civil liberties and respect for varying beliefs in a pluralistic society with an interest in protecting children? The principle of *parens patria* establishes the state's right and duty to protect the rights of its younger citizens; if a child's parents cannot or will not care for him or her, for any reason, then society and the state must do so. However, 44 states have religious exemptions from their child abuse statutes, stating, for example, "that a child is not to be deemed abused or neglected merely because he or she is receiving treatment by spiritual means, through prayer according to the tenets of a recognized religion" (American Academy of Pediatrics, 1988).

These exemptions have been based on the arguments of various religious groups that the U.S. Constitution guarantees the protection of religious practice. This interpretation of the Constitution is challenged by court rulings prohibiting parents from martyring their children based on parental beliefs (*Prince v. Massachusetts*, 1944) and from denying them essential medical care (*Jehovah's Witnesses of Washington v. King County Hospital*, 1967). The separation of church and state in the First Amendment does not sanction harming individuals in the practice of religion. The American Academy of Pediatrics has strongly opposed these religious exemptions, arguing that

> the opportunity to grow and develop safe from physical harm with the protection of our society is a fundamental right of every child. . . . The basic moral principles of justice and of protection of children as vulnerable citizens require that all parents and caretakers must be treated equally by the laws and regulations that have been enacted by State and Federal governments to protect children. (American Academy of Pediatrics, 1988)

Drug-Exposed Newborns

Several illicit drugs, such as cocaine, can harm the fetus and may be associated with long-term neurological and developmental sequelae. The issue is complicated by a host of legal, ethical, and pragmatic considerations. There is concern about infringing on a pregnant mother's rights concerning her own body. Because laws pertaining to child maltreatment typically concern a child and not a fetus, it has been argued successfully that the mother "gave" the child the drug after birth via the umbilical cord. In addition, the potential for harm meets most states' criteria for neglect, and a mother addicted to drugs poses a high-risk situation for neglect and probable harm.

A punitive approach toward pregnant women abusing drugs is controversial.

A punitive approach toward pregnant women abusing drugs is controversial. It is difficult to justify punishing a drug addict while there is a drastic shortage of treatment facilities. A punitive approach, or an approach that is perceived as punitive (e.g., referral to CPS), might deter women from obtaining prenatal care and drug treatment. These are a few of the issues that have led many to prefer a therapeutic approach, offering appropriate services to mothers and babies (Larson, 1991). The national debate continues, and there is currently no consensus on an approach to substance abuse by pregnant women.

Principles of Evaluation and Intervention

Medical neglect is often part of a larger picture of neglect, in which other major needs of children are not being met. In addition to specific issues pertaining to forms of medical neglect, general principles can help guide interventions in the area of child neglect.

Practitioners need to determine if a child is experiencing neglect. As discussed earlier, we propose that this determination be based on whether a child's crucial health care needs are being met, regardless of cause. Each situation requires an understanding of the specific harm or risks involved for a particular child. In some instances, the harm or risks to a child can be inferred from knowledge of the likely outcomes of certain conditions, such as high blood lead levels or inadequate physiotherapy following a burn.

Compliance is not always associated with optimal health. In addition, less than 100% adherence to treatment might still be adequate. For example, one study found children with streptococcal sore throats were cured with only 80% adherence to treatment (Olson, Zimmerman, & Reyes de la Rocha, 1985). Many in-

stances of noncompliance may involve no or little harm; for example, a child who is asymptomatic after an admission for pneumonia is unlikely to incur any harm if the follow-up appointment is not kept. Aside from immunizations, the benefits of child health supervision (i.e., regular checkups) have not been demonstrated (U.S. Congress, 1988); therefore, as long as immunizations are up to date, missing these appointments is not clearly harmful and should probably not be seen as neglect.

With regard to *neglect based on religious beliefs,* Fost (1988) has noted that "standard medical practice isn't always effective, and some conditions are helped by non-traditional approaches, but this should not be confused with life-threatening illnesses for which there is effective, established medical treatment." The refusal of medical treatment must be evaluated in light of potential benefits and potential harm. Bross (1982) has presented criteria for legal involvement in this form of medical neglect. These criteria are useful for assessing whether the circumstances constitute neglect and should be pursued vigorously:

1. *The treatment refused by the parents should have definite and substantial benefits over the alternative.* Therefore, if the treatment has only a modest chance of success or if there is a risk of major complications, neglect is probably *not* an issue.
2. *Not receiving the recommended treatment could result in serious harm.* Most cases that have been settled in court have involved the risk of death or severe impairment, although a number of court decisions have mandated treatment for less serious conditions.
3. *The child is likely to enjoy a "high quality" or "normal" life.* This reflects the court's reluctance to mandate treatment for severely handicapped and terminally ill children. Indeed, the Baby Doe law concerning treatment of severely impaired newborns has had little impact on the management of these cases.
4. In the case of older children (i.e., teenagers), *the child consents to treatment.* This criterion reflects the reasonable right of children to participate in decisions regarding their health.

If all the above criteria are met, a situation of medical neglect exists. The seriousness of the child's situation and the importance of the recommended treatment should be conveyed clearly and the parents' beliefs and concerns acknowledged respectfully. The legal route should be the last resort if clear neglect exists and attempts to provide adequate treatment have not succeeded.

Practitioners should evaluate the immediacy of harm or endangerment and the severity of the neglect, because the safety and well-being of a child are paramount. Immediacy hinges on the specific circumstances. A dehydrated infant faces immediate harm, whereas an inadequate diet in an older child entails longer-term risks. At times, medical care is resisted due to religious beliefs, and care is only sought at a very late stage when a child might be terminally ill. At that point, physicians should make every effort to provide necessary treatment, including court authorization for treatment if parents refuse permission.

The assessment of *severity* is based on the frequency and nature of prior and current incidents and their effect on the child, as well as possible future harm. As stated earlier, the more severe the child's condition, the more serious the neglect is likely to be judged.

Practitioners should develop a clear understanding of what is contributing to the neglectful situation. A comprehensive understanding is needed to help tailor the intervention to the specific needs of a child and family. The ecological model and contributory factors discussed in the "Etiology" section offer a useful guide to the individual parent, child, familial, community, and societal factors that need to be considered. In cases of noncompliance, it is important to clarify whether the treatment needs were understood and if so why the recommendations were not implemented. The parents' perception of the problem and the need for treatment also should be discussed.

An interdisciplinary approach is optimal for both evaluation and management (e.g., Berkowitz, 1984). It is often difficult for a single professional to evaluate and manage a case of child neglect. A social work assessment addresses resources within the family and the community. For hospitalized children, a primary nurse might have helpful observations of the child and family. A mental health evaluation can assess a child's developmental and emotional status and parents' abilities to nurture

and protect children. Teachers can report on school behavior and performance. Health care providers can review the medical record for prior conditions and observations as well as compliance with appointments and recommendations. Specific problems, such as failure to thrive, may call for nutritional or other consultation. Professionals need to work collaboratively to understand the situation fully and plan accordingly.

Intervention should begin with the least intrusive approach possible. Successful intervention requires working in collaboration with families. Positive rapport and mutual respect between professionals and families are critical components of effective interventions. Helping parents resolve a problem they identify as important to them can help establish rapport and trust.

Meichenbaum (1989) offers valuable guidance on how to enhance *compliance:* name the disorder and the medication, reassure that the treatment should work, review the medication schedule, anticipate problems contributing to noncompliance, check parents' comprehension, probe for any concerns, repeat critical points, and stress the importance of completing the treatment course. It is helpful to clarify what treatment recommendations were made and how they were conveyed to the parents and child.

When *religious beliefs* prevent treatment, it is most constructive to avoid a confrontation and attempt to negotiate an acceptable compromise. For example, surgery may be possible without the use of blood products. But in some life-threatening situations, court action to allow treatment may be necessary.

Practitioners should encourage the use of the family's natural and informal supports. Professionals need to consider possible support from family and friends and encourage their involvement. For example, by inviting fathers to pediatric visits, pediatricians may encourage fathers' involvement in child care. If a mother needs time for herself, she might request help with baby-sitting from extended family members. Community resources such as church or peer support groups (e.g., Family Support Centers, Parents Anonymous) can help address the social isolation often associated with child neglect.

Professionals should determine when it is necessary to report to CPS. Two principles guide professionals considering a report to CPS to help ensure adequate care. A report should be filed when the degree of actual or potential harm to the child transcends the threshold of serious concern and when less intrusive interventions have not succeeded.

Although most state laws require only the suspicion of neglect to make a report, many cases that do not appear to be serious are probably not reported, and, if they are, they might well be screened out or not substantiated by CPS. As suggested, less intrusive alternative strategies may be preferable. For example, if a mother is mixing the formula incorrectly, resulting in an infant's poor growth, teaching her how to prepare formula is more appropriate than a report to CPS.

There is enormous heterogeneity among neglectful situations, and CPS should be seen as one of several resources to strengthen families and protect children. The decision to report to CPS is a difficult one and should be made with an appreciation of the capabilities of the local agency and the resources available in the community.

Interventions should be based on existing knowledge and theory. Interventions known to be effective should be favored whenever possible. For example, because neglectful families often lack basic parenting skills, a behavioral approach may be preferable to insight-oriented psychotherapy. Similarly, if poverty is a major contributor to child neglect, the treatment plan also should address this fact. It is also important to review the effectiveness, or lack thereof, of interventions that have been implemented.

Interventions should target the underlying contributory factors, including parents' limitations and environmental stresses, while using available strengths and resources. Project 12-Ways (Lutzker & Rice, 1984) is an exemplary program providing a rich array of services, tailored to the needs of individual families. Serving mainly neglectful families in rural Illinois, the program includes training in parent skills, stress reduction, self- (impulse) control, money management, job-finding services, weight reduction and smoking cessation, marital counseling, and teaching parents to play with their children. The program has led to improved family functioning and decreased child maltreatment.

The needs of parents, children, and families should be considered. Effective programs focus on basic problem-solving skills and concrete family needs (Daro, 1988; Sudia, 1981), provide behavior management strategies, *and* address environmental factors (Gambrill, 1983). Parents may benefit from a therapeutic relationship that includes nurturance, support, empathy, encouragement to express feelings, and motivation to change behavior. Neglectful parents often require attention to their own emotional needs in order to adequately nurture their children. However, insight-oriented therapy that is abstract, verbal, time-consuming, and expensive may be inappropriate for most neglectful parents (Howing, Wodarski, Gaudin, & Kurtz, 1989). An evaluation of 19 demonstration programs for maltreating families found individual therapy to be less effective than family or group therapy (Daro, 1988).

Although a family-level approach generally is needed, *neglected children may require individual attention.* The focus of CPS largely has been on parents, and few maltreated children have received direct services (Daro, 1988). Treatment of neglected children may reduce the psychological harm and possibly the intergenerational transmission of neglectful parenting. There are few treatment programs specifically for neglected or maltreated children. Nevertheless, a number of interventions appear useful, including therapeutic day care for younger children and group therapy for older children and adolescents (Howing et al., 1989). It is important that parents be included in their children's treatment and that therapeutic strategies also be implemented at home.

Videka-Sherman (1988), in a review of the knowledge base for intervening in child neglect, described the need to build positive family experiences, "not just controlling or decreasing negative interaction." For example, neglectful parents need to learn how to play with their children. She also noted the need to be innovative and to look for resources in the home. Pots and pans can be used for play; basic play materials such as paper and crayons might need to be provided.

Interventions should be structured. Videka-Sherman (1988) emphasized the importance of structure in interventions. This structure includes clear guidelines as to which families receive what services, exactly how interventions should be implemented, and the development of proximal, intermediate, and distal goals.

Parents should participate in establishing goals, and goals should be reasonable and clearly identified, preferably in writing.

Intervention programs should employ home visitors. Home-based intervention enables an appreciation of the family's circumstances, facilitates rapport between practitioner and family, and allows guidance in the setting where recommendations need to be implemented. A randomized trial of nurse home visitors for high-risk mothers (low income, single, or adolescent) having their first baby improved families' functioning and reduced child maltreatment (Olds, Henderson, Chamberlain, & Tatelbaum, 1986). Although some studies have found parent aide or home visitor programs to be effective (e.g., Miller, Fein, Howe, Gaudio, & Bishop, 1985), other studies have not (Haynes, Cutler, Gray, & Kempe, 1984).

Interventions should be long-term. The problems in many neglectful situations are often multiple, deeply rooted, and chronic; seldom are there quick fixes. It is helpful for both professionals and families to recognize early on that long-term intervention is probably necessary. In most instances, treatment may be necessary for 12 to 18 months and, for some families, years. This time commitment raises a dilemma for public policy of how to best allocate limited resources. It has been suggested that if good efforts have been made for 18 months with little progress, an alternative plan should be considered (Daro, 1988).

More focus should be placed on prevention (Dubowitz, 1990). Prevention of child neglect requires efforts to enhance the nurturing abilities of families via education, training, and support. In addition, social policies (e.g., access to health care) and programs (e.g., removal of lead from the environment) and community resources (e.g., therapeutic day care) are needed to support families and children better.

Secondary prevention requires the identification of high-risk situations and intervention before neglect occurs (e.g., home visitors for high-risk parents with a new baby). Tertiary prevention or treatment involves interventions after neglect has occurred, with the goals of diminishing the harmful effects of neglect and preventing further neglect.

In cases of neglect due to religious beliefs, the future health of children in the family may be a concern. The court should mandate close monitoring of the children's health and appropriate health care.

Practitioners should act as advocates. Many factors at different levels contribute to child neglect. Advocates for children and families can help in a variety of ways. For example, explaining to a parent the safety needs of an increasingly mobile and curious toddler is one form of advocacy on behalf of the toddler. Helping a family obtain services is another form of advocacy, as is remaining involved with a family *after* a report to CPS is made. Finally, efforts to develop community programs and resources and to improve social policies and institutional practices concerning children and families are also valuable forms of advocacy. For example, child advocates should attempt to repeal the religious exemptions in state child abuse and neglect laws. The child's right to life and critical medical care reasonably supersedes a family's religious beliefs.

Ensuring adequate health and well-being of children is an enormous challenge. It is impossible for any one person to be active in all of the above issues, but it is critical that anyone concerned with the well-being of children help address at least some of these issues.

Note

1. The term *neglecting mothers* commonly is used in the existing literature. Because the proposed definition focuses on children's needs, *neglecting mothers* would become *mothers of neglected children.*

References

American Academy of Pediatrics, Committee on Bioethics. (1988). Religious exemptions from child abuse statutes. *Pediatrics, 81,* 169-171.

American Humane Association. (1985). *Highlights of official child abuse and neglect reporting.* Denver, CO: Author.

Ammerman, R. T. (1990). Predisposing child factors. In R. T. Ammerman & M. Hersen (Eds.), *Children at risk: An evaluation of factors contributing to child abuse and neglect* (pp. 199-221). New York: Plenum.

Aragona, J. A., & Eyberg, S. M. (1981). Neglected children: Mother's report of child behavior problems and observed verbal behavior. *Child Development, 52,* 596-602.

Azar, S., Robinson, D., Hekemian, E., & Twentyman, C. (1984). Unrealistic expectations and problem solving ability in maltreating and comparison mothers. *Journal of Consulting and Clinical Psychology, 52,* 687-691.

Belsky, J. (1980). Child maltreatment: An ecological integration. *American Psychologist, 35,* 320-335.

Benedict, M. I., White, R. B., Wulff, L. M., & Hall, B. J. (1990). Reported maltreatment in children with multiple disabilities. *Child Abuse & Neglect, 14,* 207-217.

Berkowitz, C. (1984). Comprehensive pediatric management of failure to thrive: An interdisciplinary approach. In D. Drotar (Ed.), *New directions in failure to thrive* (pp. 193-210). New York: Plenum.

Bross, D. C. (1982). Medical care neglect. *Child Abuse & Neglect, 6,* 375-381.

Burgess, R., & Conger, R. (1978). Family interaction in abusive, neglectful, and normal families. *Child Development, 49,* 1163-1173.

Crittenden, P. M. (1985). Maltreated infants: Vulnerability and resilience. *Journal of Child Psychology and Psychiatry, 26,* 85-96.

Daro, D. (1988). *Confronting child abuse: Research for effective program design.* New York: Free Press.

Daro, D., & McCurdy, K. (1992). *Current trends in child abuse fatalities and reporting: The results of the 1991 50 state survey.* Chicago: National Center for the Prevention of Child Abuse.

Diamond, L. J., & Jaudes, P. K. (1983). Child abuse and the cerebral palsied patient. *Developmental Medicine and Child Neurology, 25,* 169-174.

Dubowitz, H. (1990). The pediatrician's role in preventing child maltreatment. *Pediatric Clinics of North America, 37,* 989-1001.

Dubowitz, H. (1994). Neglecting the neglect of neglect. *Journal of Interpersonal Violence, 9*(4), 556-560.

Dubowitz, H., & Black, M. (1994). Child neglect. In R. Reece (Ed.), *Child abuse: Medical diagnosis and management.* Malvern, PA: Lea & Febiger.

Dubowitz, H., Black, M., Starr, R., & Zuravin, S. (1993). A conceptual definition of child neglect. *Criminal Justice and Psychology, 20*(1), 8-26.

Egeland, B., Sroufe, L. A., & Erickson, M. F. (1983). Developmental consequences of different patterns of maltreatment. *Child Abuse & Neglect, 7*(4), 456-469.

Firestone, P., & Witt, J. E. (1982). Characteristics of families completing and prematurely discontinuing a behavioral parent-training program. *General Pediatric Psychology, 7,* 209-222.

Fost, N. (1988, March 14). Loopholes permit child abuse. *Medical World News,* p. 99.

Friedrich, W. N., Tyler, J. D., & Clark, J. A. (1985). Personality and psychophysiological variables in abusive, neglectful, and low-income control mothers. *Journal of Nervous and Mental Disease, 173*(8), 449-460.

Gaines, R., Sangrund, A., Green, A. H., & Power, E. (1978). Etiological factors in child maltreatment: A multivariate study of abusing, neglecting, and normal mothers. *Journal of Abnormal Psychology, 87,* 531-540.

Gambrill, E. D. (1983). Behavioral interventions with child abuse and neglect. *Progress in Behavior Modification, 15,* 1-56.

Garbarino, J., & Crouter, A. (1978). Defining the community context of parent-child relations. *Child Development, 49,* 604-616.

Garbarino, J., & Sherman, D. (1980). High-risk neighborhoods and high-risk families: The human ecology of child maltreatment. *Child Development, 51*(1), 188-198.

Giovannoni, J. M., & Becerra, R. M. (1979). *Defining child abuse.* New York: Free Press.

Giovannoni, J. M., & Billingsley, A. (1970). Child neglect among the poor: A study of parental adequacy in families of three ethnic groups. *Child Welfare, 49.*

Gomby, D. S., & Shiono, P. H. (1991). Estimating the number of substance-exposed infants. In Center for the Future of Children (Ed.), *The future of children: Drug exposed infants.* Los Altos, CA: Editor.

Haynes, C. F., Cutler, C., Gray, J., & Kempe, R. S. (1984). Hospitalized cases of nonorganic failure to thrive: The scope of the problem and short-term lay health visitor intervention. *Child Abuse & Neglect, 8,* 229-242.

Herrenkohl, E. C., & Herrenkohl, R. C. (1981). Some antecedents and developmental consequences of child maltreatment. In R. Risley & D. Cicchetti (Eds.), *Developmental perspectives on child maltreatment* (pp. 57-76). San Francisco: Jossey-Bass.

Herrenkohl, R., Herrenkohl, E., & Egolf, B. (1983). Circumstances surrounding the occurrence of child maltreatment. *Journal of Consulting and Clinical Psychology, 51,* 424-431.

Howing, P., Wodarski, J., Gaudin, J., & Kurtz, P. D. (1989). Effective interventions to ameliorate the incidence of child maltreatment: The empirical base. *Social Work, 34,* 330-338.

Jehovah's Witnesses of Washington v. King County Hospital, 278 F. Supp. 488 (Washington, DC, 1967), *aff'd* per curiam 390 US 598 (1968).

Jones, J. M., & McNeely, R. L. (1980). Mothers who neglect and those who do not: A comparative study. *Social Casework, 61,* 559-567.

Jones, M. A. (1987). *Parental lack of supervision: Nature and consequence of a major child neglect problem.* Washington, DC: Child Welfare League of America.

Kadushin, A. (1988). Neglect in families. In E. W. Nunnally, C. S. Chilman, & F. M. Cox (Eds.), *Mental illness, delinquency, addictions, and neglect* (pp. 147-166). Newbury Park, CA: Sage.

Klerman, L. V. (1991). The health of poor children: Problems and programs. In A. C. Huston (Ed.), *Children in poverty: Child development and public policy* (pp. 79-104). New York: Cambridge University Press.

Lapp, J. (1983). A profile of officially reported child neglect. In C. M. Trainer (Ed.), *The dilemma of child neglect: Identification and treatment.* Denver, CO: American Humane Association.

Larson, C. S. (1991). Overview of state legislative and judicial responses. In Center for the Future of Children (Ed.), *The future of children: Drug exposed infants.* Los Altos, CA: Editor.

Litt, I. F., & Cuskey, W. R. (1980). Compliance with medical regimens during adolescence. *Pediatric Clinics of North America, 27,* 3-15.

Lutzker, J. R., & Rice, J. N. (1984). Project 12-Ways: Measuring outcome of a large in-home service for treatment and prevention of child abuse. *Child Abuse & Neglect, 8,* 519-524.

Martin, M., & Walters, S. (1982). Familial correlates of selected types of child abuse and neglect. *Journal of Marriage and the Family, 44,* 267-275.

Meichenbaum, D. (1989). Non-compliance. *Feelings and Their Medical Significance, 31*(2), 4-8.

Miller, K., Fein, E., Howe, G. W., Gaudio, C. T., & Bishop, G. (1985). A parent-aide program: Record-keeping, outcomes and costs. *Child Welfare, 64,* 407-419.

National Center on Child Abuse and Neglect. (1991). *Creating caring communities: Blueprint for effective federal policy on child abuse and neglect.* Washington, DC: U.S. Department of Health and Human Services.

National Center for Children in Poverty. (1991). *Child welfare reform.* New York: Columbia University School of Public Health.

National Commission on Children. (1991). *Beyond rhetoric: A new American agenda for children and families: Final report of the National Commission on Children.* Washington, DC: Government Printing Office.

Office of Human Development Services. (1987). *CFR S1340.2 definitions.* Washington, DC: U.S. Department of Health and Human Services.

Olds, D. L., Henderson, C. R., Chamberlain, R., & Tatelbaum, R. (1986). Preventing child abuse and neglect: A randomized trial of nurse home visitation. *Pediatrics, 78,* 65-78.

Olson, R. A., Zimmerman, J., & Reyes de la Rocha, S. (1985). Medical adherence in pediatric populations. In N. Arziener, D. Bendell, & C. E. Walker (Eds.), *Health psychology treatment and research issues.* New York: Plenum.

Parker, S., Greer, S., & Zuckerman, B. (1988). Double jeopardy: The impact of poverty on early child development. *Pediatric Clinics of North American, 35,* 1227-1240.

Polansky, N. A., Ammons, P. W., & Gaudin, J. M., Jr. (1985). Loneliness and isolation in child neglect. *Social Casework, 66*(1), 38-47.

Polansky, N. A., Gaudin, J. M., Jr., Ammons, P. W., & Davis, K. B. (1985). The psychological ecology of the neglectful mother. *Child Abuse & Neglect, 9,* 265-275.

Polansky, N., Chalmers, M. E., Williams, D., & Buttenwieser, E. (1981). *Damaged parents: An anatomy of child neglect.* Chicago: University of Chicago.

Prince v. Massachusetts, 3/21 U.S. 158 (1944).

Shapiro, J. (1983). Family reactions and coping strategies in response to the physically ill or handicapped child. *Social Science Medicine, 17,* 913-931.

Skolnick, A. (1990). Religious exemptions to child neglect laws, still being passed despite convictions of parents. *American Medical Association, 264,* 1226-1233.

Sudia, C. (1981). What services do abusive families need? In L. Pelton (Ed.), *The social context of child abuse and neglect.* New York: Human Sciences Press.

Szykula, S. P. A., & Fleischman, M. J. (1985). Reducing out-of-home placements of abused children: Two controlled field studies. *Child Abuse & Neglect, 9,* 277-283.

Twentyman, C., & Plotkin, R. (1982). Unrealistic expectations of parents who maltreat their children: An educational deficit that pertains to child development. *Journal of Clinical Psychology, 38,* 497-503.

U.S. Congress, Office of Technology Assessment. (1988). *Healthy children: Investing in the future* (OTA-H-345). Washington, DC: Government Printing Office.

U.S. Department of Health and Human Services (DHHS). (1988). *Study findings: Study of national incidence and prevalence of child abuse and neglect—1988.* Washington, DC: Government Printing Office.

U.S. Department of Health and Human Services, Office of Maternal and Child Health. (1989). *Child Health USA '89.* Washington, DC: Government Printing Office.

Videka-Sherman, L. (1988). Intervention for child neglect: The empirical knowledge base. In A. Cowan (Ed.), *Current research on child neglect.* Rockville, MD: Aspen Systems Corporation.

Wise, P. H., & Meyers A. (1988). Poverty and child health. *Pediatric Clinics of North America, 35,* 1169-1186.

Wolock, I., & Horowitz, H. (1979). Child maltreatment and maternal deprivation among AFDC recipient families. *Social Services Resource, 53,* 175-194.

Wolock, I., & Horowitz, H. (1984). Child maltreatment as a social problem: The neglect of neglect. *American Journal of Orthopsychiatry, 54,* 530-543.

Zuckerman, B. (1991). Drug-exposed infants: Understanding the medical risk. In Center for the Future of Children (Ed.), *The future of children: Drug exposed infants.* Los Altos, CA: Editor.

Zuravin, S. (1988). Child abuse, child neglect, and maternal depression: Is there a connection? In National Center on Child Abuse and Neglect (Ed.), *Child neglect monograph: Proceedings from a symposium.* Washington, DC: Clearinghouse on Child Abuse and Neglect Information.

PART FOUR

Legal Aspects

Legal issues in child maltreatment begin with the investigation. In Chapter 14, Kenneth V. Lanning, Supervisory Special Agent for the Federal Bureau of Investigation, and Bill Walsh, Lieutenant in the Dallas Police Department, cover many important technical areas in the investigation of sexual abuse and physical abuse, including conducting interviews and interrogations, eliminating possible sources of contagion in a victim's account, documenting victim and perpetrator behavior, identifying witnesses and accomplices, and collecting physical evidence. These authors offer an interesting argument *against* videotaping forensic interviews as standard practice. (David L. Chadwick makes the opposite case in Chapter 21.) In addition, they address some overarching issues. One of these is the underacknowledgment of the impact of feelings on investigators' work. The authors argue that officers must be aware and in control of these feelings to do their job well. Another issue is the clash between the law enforcement role of corroborating victims' accounts and the argument from some advocates that victims' accounts must be taken on faith. The authors argue strongly that everyone is served better if law enforcement officers remain skeptical and conservative in their search for corroborating evidence. Their chapter is an excellent road map to the sources of such evidence.

The uses of evidence in court is one of the topics addressed by Josephine A. Bulkley, Jane Nusbaum Feller, Paul Stern, and Rebecca Roe in Chapter 15, which focuses on child maltreatment and legal proceedings. This chapter reflects the history, progress, and current status of child abuse in the courts. Major sections include constitutional and legal rights in juvenile and criminal cases, civil laws and proceedings, criminal laws and prosecution, evidence, and legal innovations. We have come a long way in legal protections for children since the 1600s, when the child whose parents were criminally prosecuted for child maltreatment was sent first to the "poorhouse" and eventually into involuntary servitude or apprenticeship. Although the first juvenile court was established (in Illinois) in 1899, not until 1967 (with the *Gault* decision) was it ruled that children have constitutional due process rights, that the arbitrary benevolence of the juvenile court was not sufficient protection for the child's interests. Although many of the recent legal innovations aimed at reducing the emotional trauma experienced by children and addressing the difficulties in proving child abuse are under attack as unconstitutional, this chapter reflects the very significant progress of the past 15 years in making the world—and the courts—safer for children.

In Chapter 16, Karen J. Saywitz and Gail S. Goodman examine an issue of critical importance to both investigators and attorneys: interviewing children. Lanning and Walsh's key point about corroborating evidence is that only corroboration can keep trials from degenerating into swearing contests between adults and children. With or without corroborating evidence, the interview with the child is central to virtually every child sexual abuse case. The major goal of child interviewing, like the goal of legal innovations, is to improve our ability to protect children without compromising the rights of the accused. Saywitz and Goodman discuss the research on children's memory and suggestibility, children's ability to use language, and children's experience of the courtroom and then apply this research to practice. Among the specific techniques they discuss are the cognitive interview and narrative elaboration for eliciting more detailed and accurate reports from children and techniques for increasing children's resistance to suggestive questions. In a finding with relevance for courtroom procedure, children tend to be more fluent, confident, relaxed, and consistent when testifying on closed-circuit television, but jurors are more likely to distrust their testimony. Research strongly suggests that children of different ages require different interview techniques, and Saywitz and Goodman end by presenting specific guidelines for interviewing children of different age groups.

John E. B. Myers closes the legal section with Chapter 17, which focuses on the provision of expert testimony in both criminal and family court. Myers reviews the differences between substantive and rehabilitative evidence and the qualifications required of experts who provide each type. Myers offers as ground rules for any expert the "HELP" principles of honesty, evenhandedness, limits of expertise, and preparation. Myers also reviews the *Frye* and *Daubert* rules for assessing the admissibility of expert testimony based on scientific principles or techniques. Myers contends that more frequent application of the *Frye* rule would have the salutary effect of submitting theories offered as evidence in child abuse cases to more rigorous examination. Myers reviews the courtroom uses of several different syndromes in physical and sexual abuse. Judgments about the child's credibility or the guilt of a particular person are the province of the jury, Myers reminds us; his chapter provides excellent guidance for experts offering any admissible testimony.

—T.R.

14

Criminal Investigation
of Suspected Child Abuse

Section I:
Criminal Investigation of
Sexual Victimization of Children

KENNETH V. LANNING

Section II:
Criminal Investigation of
Physical Abuse and Neglect

BILL WALSH

This chapter provides an overview of law enforcement's role in the investigation of suspected child abuse. Section I, written by Kenneth Lanning, addresses the criminal investigation of childhood sexual abuse. Section II, written by Bill Walsh, focuses on the investigation of childhood physical abuse and neglect, including child fatalities.

The goal of this chapter is to describe the investigational process in language understandable to a multidisciplinary audience. It is not intended as a detailed, step-by-step investigative manual, nor does it offer rigid standards for investigation of child abuse cases. The material presented here may not be applicable to every case or circumstance. Many real-world constraints, including lack of time and personnel, make following all the steps discussed here impossible. In the interest of readability, children alleging abuse or who are suspected of being abused will sometimes be referred to as "victims," even though their victimization may not have been proven. This shorthand should not blur the fact that investigators are expected to maintain complete objectivity.

Section 1: Criminal Investigation of Sexual Victimization of Children

Kenneth V. Lanning

Overview

It commonly is accepted that child sexual abuse is a complex problem requiring the efforts and coordination of many agencies and disciplines. No one agency or discipline possesses the personnel, resources, training, skills, or legal mandate to deal effectively with every aspect of child maltreatment. In this context, law enforcement interacts with a variety of professions and agencies during the investigation process. For example, some offenders cross jurisdictional boundaries, and many violate a variety of laws when abusing children. This often will mean working with other local, state, and federal law enforcement agencies in multijurisdictional investigative teams and with prosecutors, social services, and victim assistance in multidisciplinary teams. This can be done as part of informal networking or as part of a formal task force.

The multidisciplinary approach not only is advantageous in avoiding duplication and making cases but is also in the best interests of the child victim. It may

minimize the number of interviews and court appearances and provide the victim with needed support. The team approach also can help investigators to deal with the stress and isolation of this work by providing peer support. The multidisciplinary approach is mandated statutorily or authorized in the majority of states and under federal law (U.S. Department of Justice, 1993).

Working together as part of a multidisciplinary team means coordination, not abdication. Each discipline performs a function.

Working together as part of a multidisciplinary team means coordination, not abdication. Each discipline performs a function for which it has specific resources, training, and experience. Although each discipline must understand how its role contributes to the team approach, it is equally important that it understands the respective responsibilities and limitations of that role. For example, child protection agencies usually cannot get involved in cases in which the alleged perpetrator is not a parent or caretaker.

The team approach is a two-way street. Just as medical and psychological professionals are charged with evaluating and treating the abused or neglected child, law enforcement investigators are responsible for conducting criminal investigations. Just as law enforcement officers need to be concerned that their investigation might further traumatize a child victim, therapists and physicians need to be concerned that their treatment techniques might hinder the investigation.

The Law Enforcement Perspective

The law enforcement perspective deals with criminal activity and legally defensible fact-finding. Therefore, the process must focus more on admissible evidence of *what* happened than on emotional belief that *something* happened, more on the accuracy than on the existence of re-

---

AUTHOR'S NOTE: The material in Section I of this chapter is the work of a federal employee done during government time and, therefore, is not covered under Sage copyright.

pressed memory, more on objective than on subjective reality, and more on neutral investigation than on child advocacy.

In their desire to convince society that child sexual abuse exists and children do not lie about it, some professionals interpret efforts to seek corroboration for alleged abuse as a sign of denial or disbelief. Corroboration, however, is essential. When the only evidence offered is the word of a child against the word of an adult, child sexual abuse can be difficult to prove in a court of law. Moreover, many factors combine to make testifying in court difficult and possibly traumatic for children (see Chapter 16, this volume, for a fuller discussion of this issue). Despite some recent advances that make such testimony easier for the child victim or witness, the primary objective of every law enforcement investigation of child sexual abuse and exploitation should be to prove a valid case without child victim testimony in court. More often than many investigators realize, there *is* corroborative evidence. It is not the job of law enforcement officers to believe a child or any other victim or witness. Instead, law enforcement must listen, assess and evaluate, and then attempt to corroborate any and all aspects of a victim's statement. Obviously, in a valid case, the best and easiest way to avoid child victim testimony in court is to build a case that is so strong that the offender pleads guilty. Failing that, most children can testify in court if necessary.

Emotion Versus Reason

Regardless of intelligence and education, and often despite evidence to the contrary, adults tend to believe what they want or need to believe. The more emotionally involved, the greater the need. The extremely sensitive and emotional nature of child sexual abuse makes this phenomenon a potential problem in these cases. Investigators must evaluate this tendency in other interveners and minimize it in themselves by trying to do their job in a rational, professional manner.

In order to be effective interviewers, investigators must be both aware of and in control of their own feelings and beliefs about victims and offenders of child sexual abuse. Americans tend to have stereotypical concepts of the innocence of children and the malevolence of those who sexually victimize them. Most investiga-

tors now know that a child molester can look like anyone else and may even be someone we know and like. The stereotype of the child victim as a completely innocent little girl, however, is still with us and is less likely to be discussed by lay people or professionals. In reality, child victims of sexual abuse and exploitation can be boys as well as girls, and not all victims are "angels" or even "little." The idea that some children might enjoy some sexual activity or behave like human beings and submit to sexual acts as a way of receiving attention, affection, and gifts is troubling for society and for many investigators.

Before beginning an interview, the investigator must understand that the victim may have many positive feelings for the offender and may even resent law enforcement intervention.

Before beginning an interview, the investigator must understand that the victim may have many positive feelings for the offender and may even resent law enforcement intervention. The investigator must be able to discuss a wide variety of sexual activities, understand the victim's terminology, and avoid being judgmental. Not being judgmental is much more difficult with a delinquent adolescent engaged in homosexual activity with a prominent clergyman than with a sweet 5-year-old girl abused by her "low-life" father. Investigators often nonverbally communicate their judgmental attitude through gestures, facial expressions, and body language. Many investigators do a poor job of interviewing children because deep down inside they really do not want to hear the answers.

Another emotion-related problem that occurs frequently during subject and suspect interviews is the inability of many investigators to control or conceal their anger and outrage at the offender's behavior. They want to spend as little time as possible with the offender. Occasionally, investigators have the opposite problem and are confused that they have sympathetic feelings for the offender. Many investigators also find it difficult to discuss deviant sexual behavior calmly, nonjudgmentally, and in detail with anyone, much less an alleged child molester.

An officer who gets too emotionally involved in a case is more likely to make mistakes and errors in judgment. He or she might wind up losing a case and allowing a child molester to go free because the defendant's rights were violated in some way. The officer is also less likely to interview and assess a child victim properly and objectively. Investigators must learn to recognize and control these feelings. If they cannot, they should not be assigned to child sexual abuse cases or, at least, not to the interview phase.

Maligned Investigator

Any law enforcement officer assigned to the investigation of child sexual abuse should be a volunteer, even if reluctant at first, who has been carefully selected and trained in this highly specialized work. This kind of work is not for everyone. Investigators must decide for themselves if they can deal with it. Just as important, the investigators working these cases must monitor themselves continually. The strong emotional reactions provoked by this work and the isolation and prejudice to which they may expose the investigator can make this work "toxic" psychologically and socially.

Police officers investigating the sexual victimization of children must learn to cope with the stigma within law enforcement attached to sex crime and child abuse investigation. Because there is so much ignorance about sex in general and deviant sexual behavior specifically, fellow officers frequently joke about sex crime and vice investigators. This phenomenon is often most problematic for officers working child sexual abuse cases, especially in medium or small departments. Investigators frequently become isolated from their peer group because fellow officers do not want to hear about child sexual abuse. This is a problem that supervisors as well as individual investigators must recognize and address. Investigators must be alert to the early warning signs of overexposure or stress. By using appropriate humor, limiting exposure, maintaining good physical fitness, nurturing and seeking peer support, and feeling a sense of self-accomplishment, the investigator can turn a job perceived as "dirty" into a rewarding assignment (Lanning & Hazelwood, 1988).

The "Big Picture" Approach

Law enforcement officers must recognize that the sexual victimization of children involves more than father-daughter incest. Types of cases investigated can range from one-on-one intrafamilial abuse to multioffender/multivictim extrafamilial sex rings and from stranger abduction to child prostitution (Lanning, 1992b). The child victim can range in age from birth to almost 18 years of age. Cases also may involve the interview and investigation of allegations from adult survivors reporting delayed memories of sexual abuse. Although this chapter cannot cover in detail the investigation of all types of cases, it can serve to alert investigators to the "big picture" approach to the sexual victimization of children. Rather than focusing only on one act by one offender against one victim on one day, investigators also must consider offender typologies, patterns of behavior, multiple acts, multiple victims, child pornography, proactive techniques, and so on.

The "big picture" approach starts with recognizing four basic but often ignored statements about child molesters:

1. Child molesters sometimes molest multiple victims.
2. Intrafamilial child molesters sometimes molest children outside their families.
3. Sex offenders against adults sometimes molest children.
4. Other criminals sometimes molest children.

These elements are not always present or even usually present; nevertheless their possibility must be incorporated into the investigative strategy. The neat categories of offenders and crime we like to create are, unfortunately, often ignored by offenders. A window peeper, an exhibitionist, or a rapist also can be a child molester. "Regular" criminals also can be child molesters. The first child molester put on the FBI "Ten Most-Wanted" list was arrested for burglarizing a service station. Although most professionals now recognize that an intrafamilial child molester might victimize children outside his or her family and that identifying other victims can be an effective way to corroborate an allegation by one victim, few seem to incorporate a search for additional victims into their investigative approaches.

In numerous cases, offenders have operated for many years after first being identified because no one took the "big picture" approach. Convicting a child molester who is a "pillar of the community" is almost impossible based only on the testimony of one confused 5-year-old or one delinquent adolescent. To stop the offender, law enforcement must be willing to evaluate the allegation, do background investigation, document patterns of behavior, review records, identify other acts and victims, and, as soon as possible, develop probable cause for a search warrant. Simply interviewing the child (or obtaining the results of someone else's interview), asking the offender if he did it, polygraphing him, and then closing the case does not constitute a thorough investigation and is certainly not consistent with the "big picture" approach.

The "big picture" investigative process consists of three phases: (a) interview, (b) assess and evaluate, and (c) corroborate. These three phases do not always happen in this sequence and even may occur simultaneously.

Interview

A detailed discussion of the latest research and techniques for interviewing children is contained in Chapter 16 of this book. Therefore, only the law enforcement perspective of child victim interviewing and some general guidelines will be discussed here.

Law Enforcement Role

For some, the criminal investigation of child sexual abuse has evolved into using newly acquired interviewing skills to get children to communicate and then believing whatever they say. For others, it has become letting someone else do the interview and then blindly accepting the interviewer's opinions and assessments. Law enforcement officers should take advantage of the skills and expertise of other disciplines in the interviewing process. If the primary purpose of an interview of a child is to gain investigative information, however, law enforcement must be involved actively. This involvement can range from actually doing the interview to carefully monitoring the process. Although there is nothing wrong with admitting shortcomings and seeking

help, law enforcement should *never* abdicate its control over the investigative interview.

The solution to the problem of poorly trained investigators is better training, not therapists and physicians independently conducting investigative interviews. Even if, for good reasons, an investigative interview is conducted by or with a social worker or therapist, law enforcement must be in control.

The Disclosure Continuum

Before applying interviewing research, training, and skills, investigators first must attempt to determine where the child is on the disclosure continuum. This determination is essential to developing a proper interview approach that maximizes the amount of legally defensible information and minimizes allegations of leading and suggestive questioning. The disclosure process is set forth as a continuum because there can be many variations, combinations, and changes in situations involving the disclosure status of child victims. Training material and presentations often fail to consider and emphasize the determination of this disclosure status prior to conducting a child victim interview.

1. At one end of the continuum are children who already have made voluntary and full disclosures to one or more people. These are generally the easiest children to interview. The child has made the decision to disclose and has done so at least once. It is, of course, important to determine the length of time between the abuse and the disclosure.

2. At another point along the continuum are children who have voluntarily decided to disclose but have made only incomplete or partial disclosures. For understandable reasons, some children fail to disclose, minimize, or even deny all or part of their victimization; however, not every child who discloses sexual abuse has more horrible details not yet revealed.

3. Further down the continuum are children whose abuse was discovered rather than disclosed. These interviews can be more difficult because the child has not decided to disclose and may not be ready to disclose. They also can be easier, however, because the investigator knows with some degree of certainty

that the child was abused. The interview can now focus more on determining additional details.

4. At the far end of the continuum are children whose abuse is only suspected. These may be the most difficult, complex, and sensitive interviews. The investigator must weigh a child's understandable reluctance to talk about sexual abuse against the possibility that the child was not abused. The need to protect the child must be balanced with concern about leading or suggestive questioning.

Establishing Rapport and Clarifying Terms

The interviewer's first task, with any age child, is to establish rapport. Investigators should ask primarily open-ended questions that encourage narrative responses. It is hoped that this will set the stage for more reliable responses to investigative questions that follow.

Part of developing rapport is to subtly communicate the message that the child victim is not at fault.

Part of developing rapport is to subtly communicate the message that the child victim is not at fault. Victims need to understand that they are not responsible even though they did not say no, did not fight, actively cooperated, did not tell, or even enjoyed the sexual activity. If they think they are going to be judged, some children may exaggerate their victimization by alleging threats and force that did not occur to make the crime more socially acceptable. When the victim comes to believe that the investigator understands, he or she is more likely to talk.

Although many of the same interview principles apply to the interview of adolescent victims, it can be far more difficult to develop rapport with a 13-year-old streetwise boy than with a sweet, little 5-year-old girl. The investigator must recognize and sometimes allow the victim to use face-saving scenarios when disclosing victimization. These face-saving devices are used most often by adolescents, who pose special challenges for the interviewer.

Another critical task early in the interview is to clarify the suspected victim's terminology for various body parts and sexual activities. If this clarification is not achieved early on, much misunderstanding can occur. Similarly, although it is just as important to find out exactly what the adolescent victim means by the terms he or she uses for sexual activity, terms such as "head job" and "rim job" are not so readily acceptable as the 5-year-old's "pee-pee" and "nina." The interview of an adolescent boy victim of sexual exploitation is extremely difficult at best. The stigma of homosexuality and the embarrassment over victimization greatly increase the likelihood that the victims will deny or misrepresent the sexual activity. The investigator must accept the fact that even if a victim discloses, the information is likely to be incomplete, minimizing his involvement and responsibility and, in some cases, exaggerating the offender's.

Videotaping

The taping of victim interviews was once thought to be the ultimate solution to many of the problems involving child victim interviews and testimony. Many legislatures rushed to pass special laws allowing it. Aside from the constitutional issues, *there are advantages and disadvantages to videotaping or audiotaping child victims' statements.*

The advantages include the following:

1. The potential ability to reduce the number of interviews.
2. The visual impact of a videotaped statement.
3. The ability to deal with recanting or changing statements.
4. The potential to induce a confession when played for an offender who truly cares for the child victim.

The disadvantages include the following:

1. The artificial setting created when people "play" to the camera instead of concentrating on communicating.
2. Determining which interviews to record and explaining variations between them.
3. Accounting for the tapes after the investigation. Copies are sometimes furnished with little control to defense attorneys and expert witnesses. Many are

played at training conferences without concealing the identity of victims.

4. Because there are conflicting criteria on how to conduct such an interview, each tape is subject to interpretation and criticism by "experts."

Many experts now feel that child victim interviews must be videotaped in order to be assessed and evaluated properly. Some judges and courts now require videotaping of child victim interviews. Many people in favor of videotaping argue, "If you are doing it right, what do you have to hide?" When you videotape a victim interview, however, you create a piece of evidence that did not previously exist, and that evidence can become the target of a great deal of highly subjective scrutiny. Every word, inflection, gesture, and movement become the focus of attention rather than whether or not the child was molested. Reliable information can be obtained even from highly imperfect interviews, but this fact can be lost in the scrutiny of the interview.

Although some of the disadvantages can be reduced if the tapes are made during the medical evaluation, it is my opinion that the disadvantages of taping generally outweigh the advantages.

Many experienced child sexual abuse prosecutors oppose the taping of child victim statements, although special circumstances may alter this opinion on a case-by-case basis.

Many experienced child sexual abuse prosecutors oppose the taping of child victim statements, although special circumstances may alter this opinion on a case-by-case basis. One such special situation might be the interview of children under the age of 7. Departments should be careful of written policies concerning taping. It is potentially embarrassing and damaging to have to admit in court that you usually tape such interviews but you didn't in this case. It is better to be able to say that you usually don't tape such interviews, but you did in a certain case because of some special circumstances. In this controversy over videotaping, investigators should be guided by their prosecutors' expertise and preferences, legal or

judicial requirements, and their own common sense.

General Rules and Cautions

Investigative interviews always should be conducted with an open mind and the assumption that there are multiple hypotheses or explanations for what is being described or alleged. Investigative interviews should emphasize open-ended, age-appropriate questions that are hoped to elicit narrative accounts of events. All investigative interaction with victims must be documented carefully and thoroughly.

The interview of an alleged or potential child victim as part of a criminal investigation always must be conducted as quickly as possible. It is important to interview as many potential victims as is legally and ethically possible. This is especially important in cases involving adolescent boy victims, most of whom will deny their victimization no matter what the investigator does. Unfortunately for victims, but fortunately for the investigative corroboration, men who victimize adolescent boys appear to be the most persistent and prolific of all child molesters (Abel et al., 1987). The small percentage of their victims who disclose still may constitute a significant number of victims.

The investigation of allegations of recent activity from multiple young children must begin quickly, with interviews of all potential victims being completed as soon as possible. The investigation of adult survivors' allegations of activity 10 or more years earlier presents other problems and should proceed, unless victims are at immediate risk, more deliberately with gradually increasing resources as corroborated facts warrant. Children rarely get the undivided attention of adults, even their parents, for a long period of time. Investigators must be cautious about subtly rewarding a child by allowing this attention to continue only in return for furnishing additional details. The investigator should make sure this necessary attention is unconditional.

Interviews of young children under age 6 are potentially problematic and should be done by investigators trained and experienced in such interviews. Because suggestibility is potentially a bigger problem in younger children, the assessment and evaluation phase is especially important in cases involving these young victims.

Assess and Evaluate

This part of the investigative process in child sexual abuse cases seems to have gotten lost. Is the victim describing events and activities that are consistent with law enforcement-documented criminal behavior, or are they more consistent with distorted media accounts and erroneous public perceptions of criminal behavior? Investigators should apply the "template of probability." Accounts of child sexual victimization that are more like books, television, and movies (e.g., big conspiracies, child sex slaves, organized pornography rings) and less like documented cases should be viewed with skepticism, but *thoroughly investigated.* Consider and investigate all possible explanations of events. It is the investigator's job, and the information learned will be invaluable in counteracting the defense attorneys when they raise alternative explanations.

The so-called "backlash" has had both a positive and negative impact on the investigation and prosecution of child sexual abuse cases. In a positive way, it has reminded criminal justice interveners of the need to do their jobs in a more professional, objective, and fact-finding manner. Most of the damage caused by the backlash actually is self-inflicted by well-intentioned child advocates. In a negative way, it has cast a shadow over the validity and reality of child sexual abuse and has influenced some to avoid properly pursuing cases.

For many years, the statement, "Children never lie about sexual abuse. If they have the details, it must have happened," almost never was questioned or debated at training conferences. During the 1970s, there was a successful crusade to eliminate laws requiring corroboration of child victim statements in child sexual abuse cases. It was believed that the way to convict child molesters was to have the child victims testify in court. If we believe them, the jury will believe them. Any challenge to this basic premise was viewed as a threat to the progress made and a denial that the problem existed. Both parts of this statement—"Children never lie about sexual abuse" and "If they have the details, it must have happened"—are receiving much-needed reexamination today—a process that is critical to the investigator's task of assessing and evaluating the alleged victim's statements.

"Children Never Lie"

I believe that children rarely lie about sexual abuse, if a lie is defined as a statement deliberately and maliciously intended to deceive. However, just because a child is not lying does not mean he or she is making an accurate statement. Children might be telling you what they have come to believe happened to them, even though it might not be literally true. Other than lying, there are many possible alternative explanations for why victims might allege things that do not seem to be accurate:

- The child might be exhibiting distortions in traumatic memory.
- The child's account might reflect normal childhood fears and fantasy.
- The child's account might reflect misperception and confusion caused by deliberate trickery or drugs used by perpetrators.
- The child's account might be affected by suggestions, assumptions, and misinterpretations of overzealous interveners.
- The child's account might reflect urban legends and shared cultural mythology.

Such factors, alone or in combination, can influence a child's account to be inaccurate without necessarily making it a "lie." Children are not adults in little bodies and do go through developmental stages that must be evaluated and understood. In many ways, however, children are no better and no worse than other victims or witnesses of a crime. They should not be automatically believed or automatically dismissed. Some of what victims allege may be true and accurate, some may be misperceived or distorted, some may be screened or symbolic, and some may be "contaminated" or false. The problem and challenge, especially for law enforcement, is to determine which is which. This can only be done through evaluation and active investigation.

The investigator must remember, however, that almost anything is possible. Just because an allegation sounds farfetched or bizarre does not mean it did not happen. The debate over the literal accuracy of grotesque allegations of ritual abuse has obscured the well-documented fact that there are child sex rings, bizarre paraphilias, and cruel sexual sadists. Even if only a portion of what these victims allege is factual, it still may constitute significant criminal activity.

"If They Have the Details, It Must Have Happened"

The second part of the basic statement also must be evaluated carefully. The details in question in some cases have little to do with sexual activity. Investigators must do more than attempt to determine how a child could have known about sex acts. Some cases involve determining how a child could have known about a wide variety of bizarre activity. Young, nonabused children usually might know little about sex, but they might know more than you realize about monsters, torture, kidnapping, and even murder.

Victims might supply details of sexual or other acts using information from sources other than their own direct victimization. Such sources must be evaluated carefully and may include the following:

Personal knowledge. The victim might have personal knowledge of the activity, but not as a result of the alleged victimization. The knowledge could have come from participating in cultural practices; viewing pornography, sex education, or other pertinent material; witnessing sexual activity in the home; or witnessing the sexual abuse of others. It also could have come from having been sexually or physically abused by someone other than the alleged offender(s) and in ways other than the alleged offense.

Other children or victims. Young children today interact socially more often and at a younger age than ever before. Many parents are unable to provide possibly simple explanations for their children's stories or allegations because they were not with the children when the explaining events occurred. They do not know what videotapes their children might have seen, what games they might have played, and what stories they might have been told or overheard. Some children are placed in day care centers for 8, 10, or 12 hours a day, starting as young as 6 weeks of age. The children share experiences by playing house, school, or doctor. Bodily functions such as urination and defecation are a focus of attention for these young children. To a certain extent, each child shares the experiences of all the other children. The possible effects of the interaction of such children prior to the disclosure of the alleged abuse must be evaluated.

Media. The amount of sexually explicit, bizarre, or violence-oriented material available to children in the modern world is overwhelming. This includes movies, videotapes, music, books, games, and CD-ROMs. Cable television, computers, and the home VCR make all this material readily available to even young children. There are numerous popular toys on the market with bizarre or violent themes.

Suggestions and leading questions. This problem is particularly important in cases involving children under the age of 6 and especially those stemming from custody/visitation disputes. This is not to suggest that custody/visitation disputes usually involve sex abuse allegations, but when they do and when the child in question is young, such cases can be very difficult to evaluate. It is my opinion that most suggestive, leading questioning of children by interveners is done inadvertently as part of a good-faith effort to learn the truth.

Not all interveners are in equal positions to potentially influence allegations by children. Parents and relatives are in the best position to subtly cause their young children to describe their victimization in a certain way. Children also might overhear their parents discussing the details of the case. They might be trying to prolong the rarely given undivided attention of an adult. Children often tell their parents what they believe their parents want or need to hear. In one case, a father gave the police a tape recording to "prove" that his child's statements were spontaneous disclosures and not the result of leading, suggestive questions. The tape recording indicated just the opposite. Why, then, did the father voluntarily give it to the police? Probably because he truly believed he was not influencing his child's statement—but he was.

Some victims have been subtly as well as overtly rewarded by usually well-meaning interveners for furnishing details. Some "details" of a child's allegation even might have originated as a result of interveners making assumptions about or misinterpreting what the victim actually said. The interveners then repeat and possibly embellish these assumptions and misinterpretations, and eventually the victims come to agree with or accept this "official" version of what happened.

Therapists also can be in a good position to influence the allegations of children and adult survivors. One therapist personally told me that the reason the police cannot find out about certain aspects of sexual abuse from child victims is because they do not know how to ask leading questions. Types and styles of verbal interaction useful in therapy might create significant problems in a criminal investigation. It should be noted, however, that when a therapist does a poor investigative interview as part of a criminal investigation, it is the fault of the criminal justice system that allowed it—not of the therapist who did it.

Misperception and confusion by the victim. In one case, a child's description of the apparently impossible act of walking through a wall turned out to be the very possible act of walking between the studs of an unfinished wall in a room under construction. In another case, pennies in the anus turned out to be copper foil-covered suppositories. The children might describe what they believe happened. It is not a lie, but neither is it an accurate account. It might be due to confusion deliberately caused by the offender or to misperception inadvertently caused by youthful inexperience.

Many young and some older children have little experience or frame of reference for accurately describing sexual activity. They might not understand the difference between "in" and "on" or the concept of "penetration." Drugs also might be used deliberately to confuse the victims and distort their perceptions.

Education and awareness programs. Some well-intentioned awareness and sex education programs designed to prevent child sex abuse and child abduction or provide children with information about human sexuality may, in fact, unrealistically increase fears and provide some of the details that children are telling interveners. The answer to this potential problem, however, is to evaluate the possibility, not to stop education and prevention programs.

Areas of Evaluation

As part of the assessment and evaluation of victim statements, it is important to determine how much time elapsed between the time the disclosure was first made and the time the incident was re-

ported to the police or social welfare. The longer the delay, the greater the potential for problems. The next step is to determine the number and purpose of all prior interviews of the victim concerning the allegations. The more interviews conducted before the investigative interview, the greater the potential difficulties. Problems also can be created by interviews conducted by various interveners after the investigative interview(s).

The investigator must closely and carefully evaluate events in the victim's life before, during, and after the alleged abuse. Events occurring before the alleged abuse to be evaluated might include the following:

1. Background of the victim
2. Abuse or drugs in the home
3. Pornography in the home
4. Play, television, computer, and VCR habits
5. Attitudes about sexuality in the home
6. Religious beliefs and training
7. Extent of sex education in the home
8. Cultural and subcultural attitudes and practices
9. Activities of siblings
10. Need or craving for attention
11. Childhood fears
12. Custody/visitation disputes
13. Victimization of or by family members
14. Interaction between victims

Events occurring during the alleged abuse to be evaluated include the following:

1. Use of fear or scare tactics
2. Degree of trauma
3. Use of magic, deception, or trickery
4. Use of rituals
5. Use of drugs
6. Use of pornography

Events occurring after the alleged abuse to be evaluated include the following:

1. Disclosure sequence
2. Background of prior interviewers
3. Background of parents
4. Comingling of victims
5. Type of therapy received

Contagion

As part of this phase, investigators also must evaluate possible contagion. Consistent statements obtained from different interviews and from multiple victims are powerful pieces of corroborative evidence—that is, as long as those statements were not "contaminated." Investigation must evaluate both pre- and postdisclosure contagion and both victim and intervener contagion carefully. Are the different victim statements consistent because they describe common experiences or events or because they reflect contamination or shared cultural mythology?

The sources of potential contagion are widespread. Victims can communicate with each other both prior to and after their disclosures. Interveners can communicate with each other and with victims. The team or cell concepts are attempts to deal with potential investigator contagion in multivictim cases. All the victims are not interviewed by the same individuals, and interviewers do not necessarily share information directly with each other (Lanning, 1992b).

Documenting existing contagion and eliminating additional contagion is crucial to the successful investigation and prosecution of many cases. There is no way, however, to erase or undo contagion. The best you can hope for is to identify and evaluate it and attempt to explain it. Mental health professionals requested to evaluate suspected victims must be selected carefully.

Once a case is contaminated and out of control, little can be done to salvage what might have been a prosecutable criminal violation. A few cases have even been lost on appeal after a conviction because of contamination problems.

In order to evaluate the contagion element, investigators must investigate these cases meticulously and aggressively. Whenever possible, personal visits should be made to all locations of alleged abuse and the victims' homes. Events prior to the alleged abuse must be evaluated carefully. Investigators might have to view television programs, movies, computer games, and videotapes seen by the victims. In some cases, it might be necessary to conduct a background investigation and evaluation of everyone who, officially or unofficially, interviewed the victims about the allegations prior to and after the investigative interview(s).

Investigators must be familiar with the information about sexual abuse of children being disseminated in magazines, books, television programs, conferences, and so on. Every alternative way that a victim could have learned about the details of the abuse must be explored, if for no other reason than to eliminate them and counter defense arguments. There may be validity to these contagion factors, however. They might explain some of the "unbelievable" aspects of the case and result in the successful prosecution of the substance of the case. Consistency of statements becomes more significant if contagion is identified or disproved by independent investigation.

Munchausen syndrome and Munchausen syndrome by proxy are complex and controversial issues in child abuse cases. No attempt will be made to discuss them in detail, but they are well-documented facts. Most of the literature about them focuses on their manifestation in the medical setting as false or self-inflicted illness or injury. They are also manifested in the criminal justice setting as false or self-inflicted crime victimization. If parents would poison their children to prove an illness, they might sexually abuse their children to prove a crime. These are the unpopular but documented realities of the world. Recognizing their existence does not mean that child sexual abuse and sexual assault are any less real and serious.

Summary of Evaluation and Assessment

As much as investigators might wish otherwise, there is no simple way to determine the accuracy of a victim's allegation. Investigators cannot rely on therapists, evaluation experts, or the polygraph as shortcuts to determining the facts. Many mental health professionals might be good at determining that something traumatic happened to a child, but determining exactly *what* happened is another matter. Most mental health professionals are now willing to admit that they are unable to determine, with certainty, the accuracy of victim statements in these cases. There is no test or statement analysis formula that absolutely will determine how a child was sexually abused. Although resources such as expert opinion, statement validity analysis, and the polygraph might be potentially useful as part of the evaluation process, none of them should ever be the sole criterion for pursuing or not pursuing an allegation of child sexual abuse. Law enforcement must proceed with the investigation and rely primarily on the corroboration process.

The criminal justice system must identify (or develop) and use fair and objective criteria for evaluating the accuracy of allegations of child sexual abuse and for filing charges against the accused. Just because it is possible does not mean it happened. The lack of corroborative evidence *is* significant when there should be corroborative evidence. Blindly believing everything in spite of a lack of logical evidence or simply ignoring the impossible or improbable and accepting the possible is *not* good enough. If some of what the victim describes is accurate, some misperceived, some distorted, and some contaminated, what is the court supposed to believe? Until we come up with better answers, the court should be asked to believe what a thorough investigation can corroborate, understanding that physical evidence is only one form of corroboration. In those cases in which there simply is no corroborative evidence, the court may have to make its decision based on carefully assessed and evaluated victim testimony and the elimination of alternative explanations.

Corroborate

As a general principle, valid cases tend to get better and false cases tend to get worse with investigation. The following techniques are offered as ways to corroborate allegations of child sexual abuse and avoid child victim testimony in court. If child victim testimony cannot be avoided, at least the victim will not bear the total burden of proof if these techniques are used. These techniques can, to varying degrees, be used in any child sexual abuse case. The amount of corroborative evidence available might depend on the type of case, type of sexual activity, and type of offender(s) involved. Corroboration might be more difficult in an isolated one-on-one case perpetrated by a situational child molester and easier in a sex ring case perpetrated by a preferential child molester (Lanning, 1992a).

Document Behavioral
Symptoms of Sexual Abuse

Because the behavioral symptoms of child sexual abuse are described elsewhere in this book, they will not be presented here in detail. Developmentally unusual sexual knowledge and behavior

seem to be the strongest symptoms. The documentation of these symptoms can be of assistance in corroborating child victim statements. It must be emphasized, however, that these are only symptoms, and their significance must be carefully evaluated in context by objective experts. Many behavioral symptoms of child sexual abuse are actually symptoms of trauma, stress, and anxiety that could be caused by other events in the child's life. Almost every behavioral indicator of sexual abuse can be seen in nonabused children (see Chapter 17, this volume, on expert testimony). Because of variables such as the type and length of abuse, the resiliency of the child victim, and society's response to the abuse, not all children react to being abused in the same way. Therefore, just as the presence of behavioral symptoms does not prove that a child was sexually abused, the absence of them does not prove that a child was not abused.

The use of expert witnesses to introduce this evidence into a court of law is a complex legal issue that is thoroughly discussed in Chapter 17. Mental health professionals, social workers, child protective service workers, and law enforcement investigators can be the source of such expert testimony regarding symptoms of sexual abuse. Experts might not be allowed to testify about the guilt and innocence of the accused but might be able to testify about credibility issues by explaining and offering opinions about the nature of the offense and the victim's behavior. The most commonly acceptable use of such expert testimony is to impeach defense experts and to rehabilitate prosecution witnesses after their credibility has been attacked by the defense. An expert might be able to testify concerning such symptoms to rebut defense allegations that the prosecution has no evidence other than the testimony of a child victim or that the child's disclosure is totally the result of leading and improper questioning.

These and other possible uses of expert testimony should be discussed with the prosecutor of each case. Even if not admissible in court, the symptoms of sexual abuse still can be useful as part of investigative corroboration, particularly when symptoms predate any disclosure. New and ongoing research reveals that sexually abused girls also may experience physiological changes and symptoms (DeBellis, Lefter, Trickett, & Putnam, 1994). The investigative and prosecutive significance of these findings is unknown at this time.

Document Patterns of Behavior

Two patterns of behavior should be documented: victim patterns and offender patterns.

Victim patterns. By far, the most important victim pattern of behavior to identify and document is the disclosure process. Investigators must verify through active investigation the exact nature and content of each disclosure, outcry, or statement made by the victim. Second-hand information about disclosure is not good enough. To whatever extent humanly possible, the investigator should determine exactly when, where, to whom, in precisely what words, and why the victim disclosed. A well-documented, convincing disclosure, especially a spontaneous one with no secondary gain, can be corroborative evidence.

The fact that a victim does not disclose the abuse for years or recants previous disclosures might be part of a pattern of behavior that in fact helps to corroborate sexual abuse. The documentation of the secrecy, the sequence of disclosures, the recantation of statements, the distortion of events, and so on can all be part of the corroboration process.

Offender patterns. There is one answer to the questions investigators most commonly ask about child molesters, such as "What is the best way to interview them?" "Do they collect child pornography?" "How many victims do they have?" "Can they be polygraphed?" "Can they be treated?" The answer to these questions is "It depends." It depends on what kind of child molester you have. Documenting offender patterns of behavior is one of the most important and most overlooked steps in the corroboration process. Investigators must make every reasonable effort to document offender patterns of behavior and attempt to determine the type of offender involved.

I have previously developed and published an investigative typology of child molesters that distinguishes between "preferential" and "situational" offenders (Lanning, 1992a). Situational child molesters have no true sexual preference for children but might molest them for a wide variety of situational reasons. In many cases, children might be targeted because they are weak, vulnerable, or available. Situational molesters' patterns of behavior are more likely to involve the concept of *method of operation* (MO) that is well-known to most police officers. MO is something done by offenders because it works and will help them get away with the crime. MO is fueled by thought and deliberation. Most offenders change and improve their MO over time and with experience.

"Preferential" child molesters (pedophiles), on the other hand, have a real sexual preference for children. Their sexual fantasies and erotic imagery focus on children. The patterns of behavior of preferential child molesters are more likely to involve the concept of sexual ritual that is less-known to most police officers. Sexual ritual is nothing more than repeatedly engaging in an act or series of acts in a certain manner because of a sexual need. To become aroused and/or gratified, a person must engage in the act in a certain way. Unlike the situational offender's MO, ritual is necessary to the offender but not to the successful commission of the crime. In fact, instead of facilitating the crime, it often increases the odds of identification, apprehension, and conviction. Ritual is fueled by erotic imagery and fantasy and can be bizarre in nature. Most offenders find it difficult to change and modify ritual, even when their experience tells them they should. Understanding sexual ritual is the key to investigating preferential child molesters.

You cannot hope to determine the type of child molester with whom you are dealing unless you have the most complete, detailed, and accurate information possible. The law enforcement investigator must understand that doing a background investigation on a suspected child molester means more than obtaining the date and place of birth and credit and criminal checks. School, juvenile, military, medical, employment, bank, and child abuse registry records can be valuable sources of information about an offender. Knowing the kind of offender with whom you are dealing can go a long way toward learning where and what kind of corroborative evidence might be found. It can be helpful in determining the existence and location of other victims and child pornography or erotica (Lanning, 1992a).

Because their molestation of children is part of a long-term persistent pattern of behavior, preferential child molesters are like human evidence machines. During their lifetime, they leave behind a string of victims and a collection of child pornography and erotica. Therefore, the preferential child molester is easier to convict if investigators understand how to recognize him and how he operates and if their departments give them the time and resources. It is obviously better to convict a child molester based on his or her past behavior. If all else fails, however, preferential child molesters usually can be convicted in the future based on their continuing molestation of children.

Identify Adult Witnesses and Suspects

Not all sexual abuse is "one-on-one." There are cases with multiple offenders and accomplices. One benefit of a multioffender case is that it increases the likelihood that there is a weak link in the group. Do not assume that accomplices will not cooperate with the investigation. The conspiracy model of building a case against one suspect and then using that suspect's testimony against others can be useful. Because of the need to protect potential child victims, however, the conspiracy model of investigation has limitations in child sexual abuse cases. You cannot knowingly allow children to be molested as you build your case by turning suspects. Corroboration of a child victim's statement with adult witness testimony, however, is an important and valuable technique.

Medical Evidence

Whenever possible, all children suspected of having been sexually victimized should be afforded a medical examination by a trained and competent physician. This examination is covered in detail in Chapter 12, this volume. The primary purpose of this examination is to assess potential injury and the need for treatment and to reassure the patient. A secondary purpose is to determine the presence of any corroborating evidence of acute or chronic trauma. The ability and willingness of medical doctors to corroborate child sexual abuse has improved greatly in recent years, primarily due to better training and the use of protocols, rape kits, the colposcope, toluidine blue dye, ultraviolet light photography, and other techniques.

When used with a camera, the colposcope can document the trauma without additional examinations of the child victim. Positive laboratory tests for sexually transmitted diseases can be valuable evidence, especially in cases involving very young children. Statements made to doctors by the child victim as part of the medical examination might be admissible in court without the child testifying.

Law enforcement investigators should be cautious of doctors who have been identified as child abuse crusaders or who always find—or never find—medical evidence of sexual abuse. Medical doctors should be objective scientists doing a professional examination. The exact cause of any anal or vaginal trauma needs to be evaluated carefully and scientifically. It also should be noted that many acts of child sexual abuse do not leave any physical injuries that can be identified by a medical examination. In addition, children's injuries can heal rapidly. Thus, lack of medical corroboration does not mean that a child was not sexually abused or that it cannot be proven in court.

Other Victims

The simple understanding and recognition that a child molester might have other victims is one of the most important steps in corroborating an allegation of child sexual abuse. There is strength in numbers. If an investigation uncovers one or two victims, each will probably have to testify in court. If an investigation uncovers multiple victims, the odds are that none of them will testify because there will not be a trial. With multiple victims, the only defense is to allege a flawed, leading investigation.

Because of the volume of crime and limited resources, many law enforcement agencies are unable to continue an investigation to find multiple victims. If that is the case, they must try to identify as many victims as possible. Other victims are sometimes identified through publicity about the case. Consistency of statements obtained from multiple victims, independently interviewed, can be powerful corroboration.

Search Warrants

The major law enforcement problem with the use of search warrants in child sexual abuse cases is that they are not obtained soon enough. In many cases, investigators have probable cause for a search warrant but don't know it. Because evidence can be moved or destroyed so quickly, search warrants should be obtained as soon as legally possible. Waiting too long and developing, in essence, too much probable cause also might subject investigative agencies to criticism or even lawsuits that this delay allowed additional victims to be molested. The value and significance of child erotica (pedophile paraphernalia) often is not recognized by investigators (Lanning, 1992a).

The expertise of an experienced investigator and well-documented behavior patterns of preferential offenders sometimes can be used to add to the probable cause, expand the scope of the search, or address the legal staleness problem of old information. Such "expert" search warrants should be used only when necessary and only when there is probable cause to believe the alleged offender fits the preferential pattern of behavior (Lanning, 1992a).

Physical Evidence

Physical evidence can be defined as any object that corroborates anything a child victim said, saw, tasted, smelled, drew, and so on. It can be used to prove offender identity and type and location of activity. It could be bed sheets, articles of clothing, sexual aids, lubricants, fingerprints, documents, and so on. It also could be an object or sign on the wall described by a victim. If the victim says the offender ejaculated on a door knob, ejaculate on the doorknob becomes physical evidence if found. If the victim says the offender kept condoms in the nightstand by his bed, they become physical evidence if found. A pornography magazine with the back page missing described by the victim is physical evidence. Satanic occult paraphernalia is evidence if it corroborates criminal activity described by the victim. Positive identification of a subject through DNA analysis of trace amounts of biological evidence left on a child or at a crime scene might result in a child victim not having to testify because the perpetrator pleads guilty.

Child Pornography and Child Erotica

Child pornography, especially that produced by the offender, is one of the most valuable pieces of corroborative evidence of child sexual abuse that any investigator can have. Many collectors of child pornography do not molest children, and many child molesters do not possess or collect child pornography. However, investigators should always be alert for it. Child pornography can be present in intrafamilial cases. Preferential child molesters, especially those operating child sex rings, almost always collect child pornography or child erotica. If situational child molesters possess child pornography, they usually have pictures of their own victims.

Today, child pornography most often is found in videotape format. In addition to viewing any homemade videotapes seized from the offenders, investigators also must listen to them carefully. The voices and sounds might reveal valuable corroborative or intelligence information. If necessary, photographic enhancement can be used to help identify individuals, locations, and dates on newspapers and magazines otherwise unrecognizable in the child pornography. In one case, a subject was identified from his fingerprint, which was visible in a recovered child pornography photograph. Increasingly, child pornography is being found on home computer hard drives and disks.

Child erotica can be defined as any material, relating to children, that serves a sexual purpose for a given individual (Lanning, 1992a). Some of the more common types of child erotica include drawings, fantasy writings, diaries, souvenirs, letters, books about children, psychological books on pedophilia, and ordinary photographs of children. It must be evaluated in the context in which it is found using good judgment and common sense. Child erotica is not as significant as child pornography, but it can be of value. It can help prove intent. It can be a source of intelligence information, identifying other offenders or victims. It can be used to deny bond if it indicates the offender is a risk to the community. Child erotica can be instrumental in influencing the offender to plead guilty, and it also can be used at the time of sentencing to demonstrate the full scope of the offender's activity. This is consistent with the "big picture" approach.

Computers

Investigators must be alert to the possibility that a child molester with the intelligence, economic means, or employment access might use a computer in a variety of ways as part of his sexual victimization of children. He might use it to organize information and correspondence about his activity; communicate with other child molesters or potential child victims; or store, transfer, and manipulate child pornography. Therefore, legally searching and seizing such a computer potentially could provide almost unbelievable amounts of corroborative evidence. Investigators need to be careful about evaluating computer communications. Because of perceived anonymity and immediate feedback, many child molesters greatly exaggerate their sexual exploits when communicating by computer. As computers become less expensive, more sophisticated, and easier to operate, the potential for this abuse will grow rapidly.

Consensual Monitoring

Consensual monitoring is a valuable but often underused investigative technique. It includes the use of body recorders and pretext phone calls. Because of the legal issues involved and variations in state laws, use of this technique should always be discussed with prosecutors and police department legal advisers.

It is important to remember that children are not small adults and must never be endangered by investigators. The use of this technique with child victims presents ethical issues as well as legal considerations. Pretext phone calls are more suitable than body recorders with child victims but are obviously not appropriate in all cases. They might not be suitable for use with very young victims. The use of this technique usually should be discussed with the parents of a victim who is a minor. The parent, however, might not be trusted to be discreet about the use of this technique or might even be a suspect in the investigation. Although there is the potential for further emotional trauma, many victims afterward describe an almost therapeutic sense of empowerment or return of control through their participation in pretext phone calls.

Investigators using the pretext phone call should ensure that they have a telephone number that cannot be traced to the police and that they have a method to verify the date and time of the calls. In addition to victims, investigators also can make such calls themselves by impersonating a wide variety of potentially involved

or concerned individuals. Sometimes victims or their relatives or friends do the monitoring and recording on their own. Investigators need to check appropriate laws concerning the legality of such citizen taping and the admissibility of the material obtained.

Consensual monitoring with body recorders is probably best reserved for use with undercover investigators and adult informants. Under no circumstance should an investigative agency produce a videotape or audiotape of the actual molestation of a child victim as part of an investigative technique. However, the victim might be used to introduce the undercover investigator to the subject.

Inappropriate responses obtained through consensual monitoring can be almost as damaging as outright admissions. When told by a victim over the phone that the police or a therapist wants to discuss the sexual relationship, "Let's talk about it later tonight" is not an appropriate response by a suspect.

Subject Confessions

Getting a subject to confess obviously can be an effective way to corroborate child sexual abuse and avoid child victim testimony in court. Unfortunately, many investigators put minimal effort into subject interviews. Simply asking an alleged perpetrator if he molested a child does not constitute a proper interview. Any criminal investigator needs effective interviewing skills. In view of the stakes involved, child sexual abuse investigators must do everything reasonably possible to improve their skills in this area. Entire books and chapters have been written about interview techniques and strategies (Macdonald & Michaud, 1987; Machovec, 1989; Rutledge, 1987). In this limited space, only a brief review of interviewing issues will be offered.

Investigators need to collect background information and develop an interview strategy before conducting a potentially very important discussion with the alleged offender. Many sexual offenders against children really want to discuss either their behavior or at least their rationalization for it. If treated with professionalism, empathy, and understanding, many of these offenders will make significant admissions. If the offender is allowed to rationalize or project some of the blame for his behavior onto someone or something else, he is more likely to confess. Most sex offenders will admit only that which has been discovered and that which they can rationalize. If you do not confront the subject with all your evidence, he might be more likely to minimize his acts rather than totally deny them. Many child molesters admit their acts but deny the intent. A tougher approach can always be tried if the soft approach does not work.

Investigators should consider noncustodial (i.e., no arrest), nonconfrontational interviews of the subject at home or work. Interviews during the execution of a search warrant also should be considered. Investigators should not overlook admissions made by the offender to wives, girlfriends, neighbors, friends, and even the media.

The polygraph and other lie detection devices can be valuable tools when used as part of the interview strategy by skilled interviewers. Their greatest value is in the subject's belief that they will determine the truth of any statement he makes. Once used, their value is limited by their lack of legal admissibility. The polygraph (or any lie detection device) should never be the sole criterion for discontinuing the investigation of child sexual abuse allegations.

Surveillance

Surveillance can be a time-consuming and expensive investigative technique. In some cases, it also can be a very effective technique. Time and expense can be reduced if the surveillance is not open-ended but is based on inside information about the subject's activity. One obvious problem, however, is what to do when the surveillance team comes to believe that a child is being victimized. How much reasonable suspicion or probable cause does an investigator on physical or electronic surveillance need to take action? If a suspected child molester simply goes into a residence with a child, does law enforcement have the right to intervene? What if the offender is simply paying the newspaper boy or watching television with a neighborhood child? These are important legal and ethical issues to consider when using this surveillance technique. In spite of these potential problems, surveillance is a valuable technique, especially in the investigation of child sex rings.

Creative Prosecution

Another effective way to avoid child victim testimony is to prosecute the offender for violations that might not require such testimony. This is limited only by the imagination and skill of the prosecutor. One effective technique, when appropriate, is to file federal or local child pornography charges, which usually do not require victims to testify. A combination of federal and state charges for different aspects of his criminal sexual behavior might convince the subject to plead guilty. Some offenders might plead guilty in order to do their time in the federal penitentiary. Because the sexual abuse of children sometimes involves the commission of other crimes, charges involving violations of child labor laws, involuntary servitude, bad checks, drugs, or perjury also can be filed. Valuable information also can be introduced in court without child victim testimony if the prosecutor is familiar with the use of out-of-court statements and the exceptions to the hearsay rule.

Proactive Approach

Because this book is available to the general public, specific details of proactive investigative techniques will not be set forth. In general, however, proactive investigation involves the use of surveillance, mail covers, undercover correspondence, "sting" operations, reverse "sting" operations, and so on. For example, when an offender who has been communicating with other offenders is arrested, investigators can assume his identity and continue the correspondence.

It is not necessary for each law enforcement agency to "reinvent the wheel." Federal law enforcement agencies such as the U.S. Postal Inspection Service, U.S. Customs, the FBI, and some state and local departments have been using these techniques for years. Because the production and distribution of child pornography and child prostitution frequently involve violations of federal law, the U.S. Postal Inspection Service, U.S. Customs, and the FBI all have intelligence information about such activity. It is recommended that any law enforcement agency about to begin the use of these proactive techniques contact nearby federal, state, and local law enforcement agencies to determine what is already being done. Many areas of the country have organized task forces on sexual abuse and exploitation of children. Law enforcement agencies must learn to work together in these proactive techniques, or else they may wind up "investigating" each other. Some child molesters also are actively trying to identify and learn about these proactive techniques.

The proactive approach also includes the analysis of records and documents obtained or seized from offenders during an investigation. In addition to possibly being used to convict these offenders, such material can contain valuable intelligence information about other offenders and victims. This material must be evaluated carefully in order not to overestimate or underestimate its significance.

Establish Communication With Parents

The importance and difficulty of this technique in extrafamilial cases cannot be overemphasized. An investigator must maintain ongoing communication with the parents of victims in these abuse cases. Not all parents react the same way to the alleged abuse of their children. Some are very supportive and cooperative. Others overreact and some even deny the victimization. Sometimes there is animosity and mistrust among parents with differing reactions.

Once the parents lose faith in the police or prosecutor and begin to interrogate their children and conduct their own investigation, the case might be lost forever. Parents from one case communicate the results of their "investigation" with each other, and some have even contacted the parents in other cases. Such parental activity, however understandable, is an obvious source of potential contamination.

> *Parents must be reminded that their child's credibility will be jeopardized when and if the information obtained turns out to be unsubstantiated or false.*

Parents must be reminded that their child's credibility will be jeopardized when and if the information obtained turns out to be unsubstantiated or false. To minimize this problem, within the limits of the law and without jeopardizing investigative techniques, parents must be told on a regular basis how the case is progressing. Parents also can be assigned constructive things to do (e.g., lobbying for new legislation, working on awareness and prevention programs) to channel their energy, concern, and guilt.

Conclusion

It is the job of the professional investigator to listen to all victims, assess and evaluate the relevant information, and conduct an appropriate investigation. Corroborative evidence exists more often than many investigators realize. Investigators should remember that not all childhood trauma is abuse, and not all child abuse is a crime. There can be great frustration when, after a thorough investigation, you are convinced that something traumatic happened to the child victim but do not know with any degree of certainty exactly what happened, when it happened, or who did it. That is sometimes the price we pay for a criminal justice system in which people are considered innocent until proven guilty beyond a reasonable doubt.

Appendix A

The Investigator's Basic Library

The following 10 publications are recommended for inclusion in the basic reference library of a law enforcement investigator of *sexual* victimization of children:

Bulkley, J., & Sandt, C. (Eds.). (1994). *A judicial primer on child sexual abuse.* Washington, DC: American Bar Association.

Center for the Future of Children. (Ed.). (1994). Sexual abuse of children [Special issue]. *The Future of Children, 4*(2).

Goodman, G. S., & Bottoms, B. L. (Eds.). (1993). *Child victims, child witnesses: Understanding and improving testimony.* New York: Guilford.

Heger, A., & Emans, S. J. (1992). *Evaluation of the sexually abused child: A medical textbook and photographic atlas.* New York: Oxford University Press.

Lanning, K. (1992). *Child molesters: A behavioral analysis.* Arlington, VA: National Center for Missing and Exploited Children.

Lanning, K. (1992). *Child sex rings: A behavioral analysis.* Arlington, VA: National Center for Missing and Exploited Children.

Myers, J. E. B. (1992). *Legal issues in child abuse and neglect.* Newbury Park, CA: Sage.

Pence, D., & Wilson, C. (1994). *Team investigation of child sexual abuse: The uneasy alliance.* Thousand Oaks, CA: Sage.

Walker, A. (1994). *Handbook on questioning children: A linguistic perspective.* Washington, DC: American Bar Association.

Yapko, M. (1994). *Suggestions of abuse: True and false memories of childhood sexual trauma.* New York: Simon & Schuster.

Section II: Criminal Investigation of Physical Abuse and Neglect

Bill Walsh

Overview

The purpose of this section is to provide an overview of the strategies, techniques, and practices involved in the investigation of physical child abuse and neglect. It will not, however, provide a detailed description of specific investigative techniques or protocols. This section also will describe some of the unique problems, challenges, and dynamics associated with these forms of maltreatment from a criminal investigation perspective.

Though critical, a willingness among the different disciplines involved in dealing with child maltreatment to work together will not ensure a successful investigation. It is essential that each discipline possess a basic understanding of the functions of their partner disciplines so that they can effectively cooperate and coordinate in their combined efforts. The goal of this section is to provide such an understanding of law enforcement's investigation of physical abuse and neglect.

A Multidisciplinary Approach

As noted earlier in this chapter, child abuse is a complex problem that requires a multiagency and multidisciplinary approach to intervention. This is as true for physical abuse and neglect as it is for sexual abuse. There is no one agency or discipline that possesses the personnel, resources, training, skills, or legal mandate to deal effectively with every aspect of child maltreatment. It is the law enforcement investigator's responsibility to conduct criminal investigations. Law enforcement personnel have the training, experience, and skills to conduct interviews, interrogations, and evidence collection. They also have the legal mandate to effect arrests, execute search warrants, and take children into protective custody. Although every discipline's role contributes to the overall success of the investigation, it must be understood by all that the ultimate responsibility for conducting the criminal investigation of suspected abuse and neglect belongs solely with law enforcement. The law enforcement investigator in turn must realize that, although necessary for success, engaging in a joint or multidisciplinary investigation does not mean that this responsibility for assuming the lead role in the criminal investigation can be delegated, transferred, or shared with anyone else. This does not mean that the investigator cannot rely on the expertise of other professionals in their respective fields. Actually, quite the opposite is true. Investigators must consider the information and opinions offered by other professionals to make fully informed decisions during the investigation.

The Challenges to Investigations

Physical Abuse and Neglect

Both physical abuse and neglect can be viewed as a continuum of acts or omissions from the most severe forms of maltreatment that are usually criminal in nature to those that do not justify or benefit by law enforcement intervention. For example, the act of striking a child with a paddle may qualify as legally acceptable corporal punishment in one set of circumstances and as physical abuse in another. In fact, many state laws permit the use of physical force to discipline children by parents or others acting in *loco parentis*. The problem for the investigator is when an act that was intended to discipline the child instead causes an injury. Many times, there is a thin line between physical discipline and physical abuse.

In incidents in which a child is injured or subjected to risk of injury or endangered as a result of a caretaker's neglect, the law enforcement investigator must evaluate the caretaker's conduct to see if it is a crime. The investigator, with input from other disciplines, must determine if the caretaker's behavior qualifies as poor parenting practice, neglectful parenting, or criminal neglect. This is often a complicated decision. In addition to being an intentional or reckless act, neglect also can be a failure to act on a caretaker's part. Because there is no published list of required parental responsibilities, the standard that must be applied is a community standard. An instance of neglect may be prosecuted in one jurisdiction but not in another. Neglect can be viewed further as chronic or acute incidents. Single episodes of neglect by a caretaker are sometimes only "human error," and everyone makes mistakes. A clear pattern of repeated reckless behavior or omissions in care is necessary for neglect. Being a lousy parent alone does not always qualify one for criminal sanctions.

When Is Maltreatment Criminal?

Physical abuse and neglect investigations for law enforcement are very different from those involving sexual abuse. Unlike incidents of sexual abuse in which all sexual contact between the child and the offender is illegal and requires legal intervention, no such bright line exists for every alleged incident of physical maltreatment or neglect. It is important that the criminal investigator carefully evaluate each reported incident to determine if the injury the child sustained was inflicted, was the result of an accident, or has some other acceptable explanation.

The second issue the investigator must consider is whether the maltreatment in question qualifies as a criminal act. The variables that must be examined include but are not limited to the following:

1. The child's
   - Age
   - Mental and physical developmental level
   - General state of health, including any disabilities
   - Injuries and long-term consequences of such injuries
   - Exposed risk of injury if no injury was sustained
   - History of prior occurrences

2. The caretaker's
   - Age
   - Mental and physical developmental level
   - General state of health, including any disabilities
   - Intent or knowledge of the consequences of their behavior
   - Explanation for the injuries
   - History of prior occurrences
   - Ability to care for the child—that is, maturity, financial situation, intelligence, and so on

In addition, the investigator must consider if there is any other reasonable explanations for the child's injury or condition other than maltreatment.

The Child as a Crime Victim

A child's physical and mental development makes him or her a perfect victim for those who choose to physically abuse or neglect him or her. The overwhelming majority of children who die from abuse and neglect are under 5 years old (Reece, 1994). These children are too young to attend school and may in turn be socially isolated. As a result, there are few occasions for other people to observe the child, recognize signs of suspected abuse, intervene, or report it to the proper authorities. In addition, because of their development level, they totally depend on their caretaker to be fed, changed, supervised, and receive medical care. They also are unable to tell anyone about their maltreatment.

Even when children are old enough to be interviewed in these cases, the interview, although important, does not play the same critical role as it does in sexual abuse cases. In the latter cases, the investigative interview of the child is the cornerstone and one of the most critical components of the investigation. In physical abuse and neglect cases, the child does not bear the major burden of providing testimony against his or her abuser. Clinical findings in the evaluations of burns, bruises, fractures, and head injuries, along with the explanations for the same provided by the caretaker, are routinely used to determine if the injuries are abuse related or have some other explanation.

Witnesses and Accomplices

Unlike other crimes investigated by law enforcement, the vast majority of physical abuse and neglect occur in the privacy of the perpetrator's home. Consequently, actual witnesses to the event are usually limited to members of the child's family. In most cases of physical abuse and neglect, if both caretakers are not involved actively in the abuse, the passive one will usually suspect, know about, or even tolerate the abuse. The investigator must evaluate the criminal culpability of this individual for the abuse. Should this person be charged as an accomplice? Should he or she be charged for failure to protect or failure to report? Is he or she more important to the case as a witness than a suspect? Most states do not recognize privileged communication between a husband and wife in child abuse cases. The legality and practicality of attempting to have one spouse testify against another is a matter that must be discussed with the prosecutor who will handle the case.

Involvement of Child Protective Services

Child abuse cases are very different from other crimes investigated by law enforcement because of the involvement of a child protective services (CPS) agency. In cases in which the abuse or neglect occurred at the hands of a family member or in a day care facility, there will usually be a civil or administrative investigation by staff members of a CPS or day care licensing agency. Investigators for both of these agencies usually have backgrounds in social work and child development but rarely have any law enforcement training. As the inquiry into the abuse allegation begins, the concurrent civil and criminal investigations being conducted will overlap and often complicate matters.

Investigators from law enforcement and CPS agencies have different training, policies, decision-making processes, and goals related to the investigation of child maltreatment. Cooperation and communication between law enforcement and CPS are critical but not always present in these situations. Primarily, CPS agencies have the goals of (a) protecting and ensuring the safety of children who have been mistreated or are at risk of the same, (b) providing services that will change the conditions that create future risk of maltreatment to the child, and (c) whenever possible, doing this while keeping the family intact. Law enforcement's goals are to (a) investigate alleged violations of the law, (b) identify the people who violated the law and collect evidence against them, and (c) arrest the party or parties so they can be tried for their crimes. Although these respective goals have been greatly oversimplified here, it is easy to see how conflict between the actions of the CPS worker and the law en-

---

Because the resources of both CPS and law enforcement are necessary for successful intervention into child abuse and neglect, it is helpful to have protocols that address different areas of responsibility.

---

forcement investigator may occur.

Because the resources of both CPS and law enforcement are necessary for successful intervention into child abuse and neglect, it is helpful to have protocols that address different areas of responsibility. These protocols should address the issue of timely cross-notification of allegations. Because most CPS agencies operate centralized telephone hotlines for the public's use in reporting abuse, it follows that CPS usually will be notified first of suspected reports of abuse and neglect. Unless this information is promptly shared with law enforcement, the subsequent criminal investigation may suffer.

As time elapses from the incident to the start of the investigation, important physical evidence may be moved, hidden, or destroyed. Furthermore, as time passes, medical evidence may be fully or partially lost or diminished in value. Reduced knowledge to the details of the abuse lessens the thoroughness of subsequent witness interviews and offender interrogations.

Protocols also should address decisions regarding where, when, and by whom interviews of children, witnesses, and offenders are conducted. Only by working together can the safety of the child and the respective goals of CPS and law enforcement be attained.

The Investigative Process

The investigator's role in potential physical abuse cases is to determine how it happened, if a crime occurred, and, if so, who is responsible. Investigators are first and foremost fact finders. They must use all their training, skills, and resources to obtain the answers to the questions who, what, where, when, how, and why. It is important that investigators maintain the proper balance of an open mind, healthy skepticism, and a resistance to jumping to conclusions. Just as important as identifying those who have injured or caused the death of a child, the investigator bears the equally important burden of ensuring that charges are not brought against people when no crime has occurred.

Interviews

Often in the most serious cases, the investigator's first involvement occurs when the child is taken to the hospital and notification to law enforcement is made. On arrival at the hospital, investigators should ensure that CPS has been contacted and begin to coordinate their response with them. Repetitive interviews of medical staff and the caretakers not only are inefficient but may prove counterproductive as well. The physician treating the child should be interviewed regarding not only the child's injuries and prognosis but also the possibility of abuse. The investigator must realize that additional tests and procedures will provide far more detailed and accurate information. In fatal cases, an autopsy must be performed.

If there are other medical staff, paramedics, or police officers who were at the home or involved in transporting or treating the child, they also should be interviewed. If they are unavailable, plans should be made to interview them as soon as possible. They should be asked about what they heard the caretakers say, what they observed, and any impressions or opinions they have. Caretakers often say things in the presence of paramedics that they would not say in front of police officers.

If more than one caretaker is present, each should be interviewed separately in a location that affords privacy. The investigator should have them verbally tell their story without challenging any inconsistencies or improbable explanations. It is advisable to have them reduce their account to writing in affidavit form. This locks them into their story and may prove invaluable if they later try to change it. It also may be used to prove that what they said does not correspond with the physical, medical, or forensic evidence. Any written statements given by the person being interviewed are done on an "Affidavit in Fact" form. At this time, a potential suspect may give an alibi that can be verified or disproved through the investigation.

It is important that nonlaw enforcement professionals promptly notify investigators when they suspect a child may have been abused. Unless it is necessary to obtain information to treat the child, medical personnel should refrain from confronting the caretakers if they offer inconsistent or implausible explanations for the child's injuries. The CPS worker, paramedic, and any other professional involved also must avoid such unnecessary encounters. These confrontations only serve to increase the caretakers' awareness that they are under suspicion and greatly reduce any chance the investigator may have in obtaining a confession from them.

Interrogation of Offenders

Interrogation of criminal suspects is one of the most important tools available to law enforcement in the investigation of any form of child abuse. Except for a videotape of the crime in progress, there is probably no evidence more powerful and useful in the criminal prosecution of offenders than their voluntary statement admitted into evidence against them (*Bruton v. United States*, 1968).

Investigators should view interrogations as a part of the entire criminal investigation, which includes the interview of the victim and other witnesses, the medical examination, record and background checks, search warrants, and so on. The law enforcement officer must adopt the strategy to investigate, interrogate, and then investigate some more. An interrogation that results in a voluntary statement, in which the suspects admit their guilt, may eliminate the need for a trial and for the child to testify. If investigators view their role as that of finding out what happened, interrogations are a powerful tool in doing that job.

Many offenders will confess their abuse of children if properly interrogated by trained investigators. Although this chapter does not discuss the interrogation of a child abuse suspect in detail, the following points are important for the investigator to consider.

1. Know the case and the suspect as thoroughly as possible before beginning the interrogation. What is the medical evidence? Have there been previous reports of abuse?
2. Time the suspect's arrest and/or interrogation; balance the need for proper preparation with the element of surprise.
3. Use themes that minimize the severity of the injury or type of abuse. One example is to highlight that the injuries the child received were not permanent or disfiguring.
4. Realize that even if suspects do not confess, they may give a preview of what their defense is going to be and also may identify any possible alibi witnesses.

Search Warrants

Search warrants are investigative tools that can be used to recover physical evidence from a location, vehicle, object, or person. In physical abuse cases, the implements used to inflict the child's injuries can be searched for and seized. Belts, extension cords, paddles, and curling irons commonly are used to abuse children. In addition, these items may serve as valuable pieces of demonstrative evidence in the prosecution of the offender. In cases in which a child has been scalded in a tub, search warrants can be useful in allowing an investigator the opportunity to examine and photograph the location where the injury occurred and search for possible evidence.

Some state laws provide that search warrants can be used for purposes of photographing an injured child. This could prove to be useful in those situations in which abuse is suspected and the caretakers are not being cooperative.

In child abuse cases, the chance of recovering evidence is greatest if attempts are made to obtain it early in the investigation. Ideally, this is done before suspects know they are under investigation. Any delays may allow suspects the opportunity to move, destroy, or alter evidence. Even if suspects are placed in jail, delays may allow them the time to contact someone who will do the same for them.

Crime Scene Considerations

In serious physical abuse and neglect cases, the investigator should always conduct a scene investigation. Depending on local policy and law, this may be accomplished with a "consent to search" signed by the person responsible for the property or a search warrant. Often the paramedics will transport the child to the hospital when there is any chance the child can be saved, sometimes even when it is evident the child has died. In this situation, both the hospital and the child's home should be treated as crime scenes. Important evidence, such as the child's clothing, may be found at the hospital. Normal crime scene procedures should be followed, including scale sketches and photographs of the scene.

Photo documentation of physically abused and neglected children is critical to the investigation. In some cases, especially burn injuries, it is advisable to have the injuries photographed on several different days so as to allow for documentation of the injuries prior to, during, and after treatment.

Fatal Child Maltreatment

Fatal incidents of child abuse occur relatively infrequently compared to natural and accidental deaths or adult homicides. Depending on the source, the estimates of the number of deaths related to abuse and neglect ranges from a low of 1,500 to a high of 3,000 per year in the United States. Investigations of deaths due to child abuse and neglect present the investigator with problems on both a technical and emotional level. In addition to the obstacles found in nonfatal forms of abuse (no witnesses, child's developmental level, etc.), they have issues associated with homicide cases (autopsies, cause and manner of death, etc.). The death of a child from maltreatment affects even the most seasoned investigators emotionally. This combination of factors results in complex investigations with their own unique set of problems and solutions.

Because fatal child abuse cases contain issues found in both child abuse and homicide cases, the question often asked is, Who should do the investigation—child abuse or homicide detectives? In most law enforcement agencies today, it is the latter. It is my opinion that these cases require more experience and expertise related to child abuse than they do to homicide. Detectives who work in child abuse know about children. They know about the battered child syndrome, shaken baby syndrome, head trauma, scald burns, child development, neglect, and sudden infant death syndrome (SIDS). They know how children are hurt and the excuses people will offer for their injuries. They know how to work jointly with CPS, a necessity whose importance cannot be underestimated in child abuse cases.

Fatal Child Maltreatment
Versus Homicide

Though fatal child abuse and homicide do share some common ground, there are important differences that the investigator must consider.

Fatal child abuse occurs in one of two ways. The first involves repeated abuse and/or neglect over a period of time. One or more persons may be involved or at least aware of the abuse. Examples are cases involving the battered child syndrome or neglect. The second category involves a single incident of assault on the child. This would include cases of shaken baby syndrome, drowning, and suffocation. The offender usually acts impulsively and alone in these cases.

The majority of fatal injuries occur in the privacy of the home at the hands of parents or caretakers. Usually, there are no witnesses to tell what happened or identify the person responsible. As a rule, these cases are highly circumstantial in nature. Prosecution may hinge on complex medical and forensic evidence or the suspect's confession.

Fatal child abuse does not involve traditional weapons. Hands, feet, violent shaking, slamming, scalding water, and neglect are commonly the cause of fatal injuries. There is no ballistic, DNA, or fingerprint evidence to identify the suspect. Crime scene processing must focus on less obvious items of physical evidence. These may include medicine, proof of missed doctor appointments, soiled diapers, or lack of baby formula. These findings may indicate the child was ill, neglected, had a toilet training problem, or was not properly fed.

The injuries that cause children to die are different from those found in most homicide cases. The majority of fatalities are the result of severe head trauma. These often involve closed-head injuries that are not apparent on external examination. Medical staff may treat the child for several hours or even days before the injuries are determined to be nonaccidental. In some cases, abuse may not be confirmed until an autopsy is performed.

Children also die of neglect, primarily through a caretaker's failure to provide adequate nourishment, medical care, or supervision. In some cases, even though the death may be ruled an accident by the medical examiner, the caretakers may be subject to criminal prosecution. An example of this would be a case of negligent supervision. If a child, too young to be reasonably left alone, died as a result of injuries sustained in a house fire, the parent may be culpable of failing to properly supervise that child and be charged with injury by omission. In neglect cases, the investigator is faced with the challenge of determining if the death resulted from an accident or from criminal negligence.

The Investigation of
Fatal Child Maltreatment

When a child dies of abuse, it is law enforcement's responsibility to determine what happened and what person or persons are responsible. Standard investigative techniques (i.e., witness interviews, search warrants, crime scene processing, background checks, and interrogation) must be used in these cases. Because most children die from causes not related to maltreatment (illness, disease, or accidents), investigators must balance thoroughness with sensitivity when investigating a child's death.

Fact Finding

When a child dies of fatal child abuse or neglect, the question facing the investigator often is, Who could have caused the injuries? It usually is more important to determine which people had the opportunity rather than which people had the motive. The investigator must learn as much about the child as possible. Information about the child relating to preexisting medical problems or illnesses, toilet training, or physical handicaps is important. The answers to these questions may indicate what triggered the fatal assault. It is advisable to obtain the child's medical records. This can be accomplished by asking the parents to sign a medical release form early in the investigation. It is important to remember that medical records may exist at other hospitals, schools, day care centers, and other agencies. It is also important to know as much as possible about the possible suspects. Do they have a history of violence? Have they abused the child before? How did other people view the relationship between them and the child?

Occasionally, family members may have witnessed the event or have their suspicions, but they are usually reluctant to cooperate. The investigation must then determine when the fatal injuries could have occurred and who the child was with during this time. This is complicated by the fact that the child may have been in contact with several people during the time frame the injuries may have been inflicted.

Summary

The investigation of physical abuse and neglect requires a team approach with the law enforcement investigator responsible for the criminal investigation. Investigators must use the knowledge and information that other disciplines can offer in making decisions related to the investigation. The standard law enforcement practices of interviewing witnesses, interrogating suspects, executing search warrants, and processing crime scenes must be used in these cases. Although it is the investigator's role to investigate criminal child maltreatment, it must be done with the goal of apprehending the guilty and exonerating the innocent.

References

Abel, G., Becker, J., Mittelman, M., Cunningham-Rathner, J., Rouleau, J., & Murphy, W. (1987). Self-reported sex crimes of nonincarcerated paraphiliacs. *Journal of Interpersonal Violence, 2*(1), 3-25.

DeBellis, M., Lefter, L., Trickett, P., & Putnam, F. (1994). Urinary catecholamine excretion in sexually abused girls. *Journal of the American Academy of Child and Adolescent Psychiatry, 33,* 320-327.

Bruton v. United States, 391 U.S. 123, 139 (1968).

Lanning, K. (1992a). *Child molesters: A behavioral analysis.* Arlington, VA: National Center for Missing and Exploited Children.

Lanning, K. (1992b). *Child sex rings: A behavioral analysis.* Arlington, VA: National Center for Missing and Exploited Children.

Lanning, K., & Hazelwood, R. (1988, September). The maligned investigator of criminal sexuality. *FBI Law Enforcement Bulletin,* pp. 1-10.

Macdonald, J., & Michaud, D. (1987). *The confession.* Denver, CO: Apache Press.

Machovec, F. (1989). *Interview and interrogation.* Springfield, IL: Charles C Thomas.

Reece, R. M. (Ed.). (1994). *Child abuse: Medical diagnosis and management.* Malvern, PA: Lea & Febiger.

Rutledge, D. (1987). *Criminal interrogation.* Sacramento, CA: Custom Publishing.

U.S. Department of Justice. (1993). *Joint investigations of child abuse: Report of a symposium.* Washington, DC: Author.

15

Child Abuse and Neglect Laws and Legal Proceedings

JOSEPHINE A. BULKLEY

JANE NUSBAUM FELLER

PAUL STERN

REBECCA ROE

History and Overview

Since the mid-1600s, adults in the United States have been prosecuted criminally for abusing children. In those days, criminal actions usually were brought against parents who punished their children in a clearly excessive or unreasonable manner, abandoned them, or deprived them of basic necessities. A child whose parent was so prosecuted often ended up in a public institution for the poor and eventually was forced into involuntary servitude or apprenticed.[1]

In the late 1800s, civil actions for child maltreatment began to arise. The 1874 case of "Little Mary Ellen" was the first documented civil child protection case.[2] The first statewide juvenile court system was established in Illinois in 1899. Almost

AUTHORS' NOTE: Mark Horwitz, a former law clerk with the Center on Children and the Law, American Bar Association, researched and wrote the "Prior Abusive Acts" section and assisted in research and other aspects of writing this chapter.

all the other states (except two) set up juvenile courts within the 30 years that followed. Although these new courts addressed child maltreatment, their focus was delinquency. They initially were created largely to "save" children accused of crimes through rehabilitation rather than punishment.

In the early 1900s, two legal doctrines governed civil child protection proceedings: *parens patriae* and "best interests of the child." The *parens patriae* doctrine views the government as having the authority to intervene and limit a parent's power in dealing with children when their physical or mental health is jeopardized.[3] The "best interests of the child" doctrine requires consideration of children's best interests when courts are deciding whether to remove them or return them home (although children may not be removed from parents simply because they might be better off elsewhere).

The nature of juvenile courts changed dramatically in 1967, when the U.S. Supreme Court decided in *In re Gault*[4] that the juvenile court was failing to meet children's needs in spite of its best intentions. The Supreme Court rejected the old view of juvenile court judges as benevolent caretakers with unlimited discretion to protect children. Instead, it held that children in delinquency cases have constitutional due process rights. The effects of the *Gault* decision reached beyond delinquency cases to increase procedural protections in all juvenile court actions. New laws and court decisions have continued to expand and redefine the rights of children and families in juvenile courts.[5]

Today, all states continue to make child abuse and neglect both civil and criminal offenses. Every state has laws that mandate reporting of suspected child maltreatment by certain people and authorize child protection and law enforcement agencies to investigate suspected child maltreatment. Juvenile court acts also have been enacted in all states authorizing such courts to intervene in child protection cases. Penal laws include criminal offenses for various forms of child maltreatment, and child abuse victims (or adults on behalf of victims) may file private civil actions seeking either financial compensation or protection orders under domestic violence statutes (i.e., court orders to prevent contact with the alleged abuser). Finally, child maltreatment may arise in a divorce or custody case.

Constitutional and Legal Rights in Juvenile and Criminal Cases

Parents and children have a "right" to family autonomy, privacy, or integrity, and courts have deemed it a constitutionally protected "fundamental" right.[6] This right includes not only parents' rights to raise their children as they see fit but also a family's right (which belongs to both parents and children) to remain together without state interference. Of course, this right is not absolute. A state may restrict the right to family integrity (e.g., by removing a child from the home), but only if it is justified by a "compelling state interest," such as the need to protect children from significant harm.[7]

Parents also have a due process right to be notified of any abuse or neglect proceeding that involves their child. This right applies not only to parents who actually care for and reside with their child but to those exercising visitation rights as well.[8] Exceptions to the general parental notice requirement are *emergency custody orders,* which may be made without advance notice to parents. However, within a few days of any emergency custody order, the parents should be notified and another hearing held to review the initial removal decision.

Other persons also may be entitled to notice of a child protection proceeding. In general, "putative" (i.e., unmarried, biological) fathers should be notified.[9] This protects any constitutional rights that arise out of their biological relationship with their children and preserves a possible option for child placement. Most important, notice to putative fathers ensures that the relationship between them and their children will be clarified early in the court process.[10]

Parents also have the right to a trial (i.e., a contested fact-finding hearing) in a civil child protection case. A defendant has a Sixth Amendment right to a jury trial in criminal cases, which can be waived only by the defendant, not the prosecutor. In civil child protection cases, however, parents are entitled to a jury trial in only a few states. In criminal cases, both the defendant (under the Sixth Amendment) and the public (under the First Amendment) have a constitutional right to "open" (public) trials. In civil child protection cases, on the other hand, the courtroom may be "closed" (although the press has been permitted in some states) and the court records kept confidential.[11]

The U.S. Supreme Court has interpreted the due process clause to mean that criminal defendants are presumed innocent, and the state has the burden of proving the defendant guilty "beyond a reasonable doubt."[12] Defendants also have the right to a fair trial and to be proven guilty by reliable and trustworthy evidence.[13] Criminal defendants have a Fourth Amendment right to be free from unreasonable searches and seizures and a Sixth Amendment right to obtain witnesses in their favor.

In addition, a defendant has a Sixth Amendment right to confront witnesses against him or her in criminal court. In some states, parents have a right of confrontation in juvenile court cases under the due process clause.[14]

Finally, a criminal defendant has a Sixth Amendment right to counsel, which for an indigent person has been interpreted as a right to have counsel appointed and paid for at public expense. Most states also give indigent parents a right to free court-appointed counsel in abuse or neglect cases. The U.S. Supreme Court held in *Lassiter v. Department of Social Services*[15] that parents have a constitutional right to a lawyer in at least some *termination of parental rights* cases, depending on the circumstances of the particular case.

As the *Gault* case mentioned earlier made clear, when a child is accused of a crime, he or she has a right to an attorney under the Constitution. However, when a child is the subject of an abuse or neglect proceeding or a termination of parental rights case, the child's right to a lawyer varies from state to state. Nearly every state requires that a lawyer, a guardian *ad litem*, or both, be appointed for a child in juvenile court proceedings. In fact, the federal Child Abuse and Neglect Prevention and Treatment Act conditions eligibility for federal funds on meeting these requirements. In some states, guardians *ad litem* are not required to be lawyers. Nonattorney guardians *ad litem* (called court-appointed special advocates [CASAs] in some states) may be professionals trained in other disciplines (such as social work or psychology) or nonprofessional citizen volunteers.

The type of representation a child receives varies, depending on the state. In addition, the duties performed by that representative vary from state to state. The guardian *ad litem* may perform a variety of roles, including those of independent investigator, advocate, and adviser to the child. If the same child is involved in more than one court proceeding (e.g., a child protection case and a criminal case), the guardian *ad litem* may also serve the important purpose of bridging the gap between the various courts. When both an attorney and a lay advocate are used, the two may work as a team to perform these various functions cooperatively.[16]

A guardian *ad litem* who is an attorney or who works with an attorney may face conflicting roles. As a lawyer, the guardian *ad litem* has an obligation to advocate zealously for the child's position. When representing a child as a guardian *ad litem,* however, the lawyer also may be required to investigate the facts objectively and advance his or her own view of what is in the child's best interests. For example, an abused child may insist to her guardian *ad litem* that she wants to return home to parents who, in the guardian *ad litem*'s opinion, still pose a serious threat to her.

Civil Laws and Proceedings

Reporting Statutes

Every state has a law requiring the reporting of suspected child maltreatment.[17] Although anyone in any state *may* report a suspicion of child abuse, reporting laws usually *mandate* reporting only for certain classes of people, primarily professionals who have regular contact with children. In *all* states, the following are required to report: physicians, nurses, dentists, emergency room personnel, coroners, medical examiners, mental health professionals, social workers, teachers, day care workers, and law enforcement personnel. Some states also mandate reporting by others, such as foster parents, clergy, attorneys, camp counselors, and film processors. In about 20 states, any person who suspects child abuse or neglect is required to report.[18]

In most states, legislation or common law prohibits doctors, lawyers, and therapists from disclosing confidential communications. Although this appears to conflict with such professionals' obligation to report child abuse and neglect, state reporting laws generally abrogate privileges for reporting purposes.

Mandated reporters need not have actual knowledge of child abuse or neglect. Reporting requirements provide that a report must be made if the mandated reporter suspects or has reason to believe that a child has been abused or neglected. In general, state reporting laws only apply to maltreatment by a parent, guardian, custodian, or "other person responsible for the child's care."

Depending on the state's law and judicial interpretation of that law, however, maltreatment by others who live in the child's home, such as paramours, siblings, and other relatives, often are required to be reported as well. Moreover, a number of states specifically have expanded their reporting laws to cover abuse occurring in out-of-home placements, such as foster homes, institutions, and day care.[19]

Reporting laws provide that when a mandated reporter reports child maltreatment in good faith, he or she is immune from civil or criminal liability.

Reporting laws provide that when a mandated reporter reports child maltreatment in good faith, he or she is immune from civil or criminal liability. Reporters who are not mandated to report also enjoy immunity in some states. As long as the report was not made maliciously, recklessly, or with gross negligence, the reporter cannot be sued successfully, for example, for libel, slander, invasion of privacy, or breach of confidentiality.

On the other hand, reporting statutes subject a mandated reporter who knowingly or intentionally fails to report suspected abuse or neglect to civil or criminal liability. Some states impose criminal liability even if the mandated reporter did not realize the child was abused when a reasonable person would have suspected the abuse. Failure to report is a misdemeanor in all states, although until recently, criminal prosecutions have been rare.

Mandated reporters also may be held civilly liable for failing to report, either under statute or common law. As with criminal liability, when civil liability is imposed by statute, the failure to report usually must have been knowing or willful. Common law causes of action for negligence per se, professional malpractice, and violation of a duty to warn third parties also have been permitted.[20]

Child Protection System and Juvenile Court Actions

Background

Juvenile court actions, which are governed by state statute, generally are only available for parental abuse and neglect, although child protective services (CPS) agencies may investigate some cases involving nonparents (e.g., day care workers). These actions are brought by county attorneys or CPS agencies to protect the child from further abuse, provide services and treatment to the family, and, where necessary, terminate parental rights and provide permanent placements for children abused and neglected by their parents. Juvenile courts also have the power to order psychological or psychiatric examinations of the child and, sometimes, the parents.

The juvenile court system always has placed special emphasis on the assistance of nonlegal professionals and continues to do so today. Although the judge may not be familiar with certain topics that arise in child maltreatment cases, he or she is still responsible for deciding matters that may affect a child's life forever. Accordingly, juvenile court judges often rely on agency caseworkers, private social workers, psychiatrists, psychologists, and physicians.

Juvenile court intervention has advantages and disadvantages. One author lists some of the problems:

■ Removal of the child, rather than the offender, from the home
■ Lack of specialized treatment in many child protective services agencies
■ Petitions filed inappropriately against (or the child removed inappropriately from) a nonabusive parent capable of protecting and obtaining treatment for the child
■ Lack of the same protections in criminal court for alleged abusers

- Risk of unnecessary intervention with families
- Long, indefinite, or multiple out-of-home placements
- Unnecessary removal of some children without adequate preventive services[21]

The juvenile court's benefits are its ability to protect the child quickly through its power to remove the child from the home, its access to services and treatment and ability to provide long-term monitoring, and its goal of helping the child and family rather than punishing the offender. Moreover, the court process may be less traumatic for the child and the abuse easier to prove because (a) there is a lower burden of proof (preponderance of the evidence), (b) there are somewhat relaxed evidentiary rules and constitutional requirements, (c) there is no jury or public trial, (d) the child may not have to testify, and (e) a guardian *ad litem* is appointed to represent the child.

The juvenile court, sometimes called children's court or family court, is not always distinct from adult courts. Although many states do have separate juvenile court systems, other states hold juvenile sessions in regular courts of general jurisdiction. In states without separate juvenile courts, judges are often less familiar with issues relating to child protection, and delays generally are more common because the juvenile cases must compete for court time with many other types of cases. However, in many of these states, child protection cases are given priority on court dockets, and judges will remain with child protection cases already assigned to them, even after they have finished the juvenile term.

Jurisdiction and Legal Definitions

Juvenile court statutes' definitions of abuse and neglect vary widely, although they share certain common underlying principles. As with reporting statutes, juvenile court acts authorize courts to intervene (i.e., give them "jurisdiction") where a child has been maltreated by a parent, guardian, custodian, or other person responsible for the child's care. *Abuse* generally includes endangering or intentionally injuring a child. Abuse does not always have to be physical; a child may be abused emotionally or psychologically if, for example, he or she has been belittled,

ridiculed, screamed at, or ignored regularly.

Neglect may include actual abandonment of the child or may be limited to the failure to provide for the child's basic needs (i.e., food, clothing, and shelter). Some states refer to neglect in general terms as "lack of parental care or control." Failure to provide a child with proper medical care, education, supervision, or emotional support also may be considered neglect. In some states, a parent's lifestyle might be the basis for a finding of neglect if the parent has failed to provide the child with adequate "moral" care (e.g., parental promiscuity or homosexuality).

Sexual abuse commonly is defined as sexual intercourse, oral and anal intercourse, and sexual contact with a child (some states refer to their criminal law definitions). *Sexual exploitation* covers children used in pornography or encouraged to engage in prostitution. A juvenile court also may have jurisdiction over a child due to "parental incapacity," sometimes even if the child has not yet been harmed. Children of very young parents, parents with mental or physical disabilities, or parents with substance abuse problems often are especially vulnerable to harm. The mere fact of such parental incapacity, however, will not give the court jurisdiction. Rather, the parent's disability must affect his or her capacity to care for the child to such an extent that the child is in need of protection.[22]

Juvenile Court Proceedings[23]

In general, CPS agencies initiate a civil child protection proceeding by filing a petition with the court. In emergencies, a child may be removed from home before a petition has been filed. In that case, a hearing must be held within a specified number of hours or days after the child's removal, depending on state law.

If the child has not yet been removed, the first hearing usually takes place after the petition has been filed. This initial hearing is given a variety of names in different states, such as "shelter care" hearing, "detention" hearing, or "temporary custody" hearing. Regardless of its name, this hearing generally serves the same purpose everywhere: *to determine whether the child should be placed outside his or her home temporarily depending on the ultimate disposition of the case.* If the child is already in emergency out-of-home care, this hearing is used to decide whether this temporary custody arrangement should be continued.

Once any pretrial conferences or settlement negotiations have been conducted and discovery[24] has been completed, the adjudicatory hearing or trial can begin. Based on the evidence presented at trial, *the judge must decide whether the child has been abused or neglected.* Increasingly, state laws or court rules require courts to complete these hearings within a given period of time from the filing of the petition or removal of a child from the home (e.g., 30 days). In some additional states, a judge's written factual determination, known as *findings of fact,* also must be made within a specific period of time.[25] The purpose of these requirements is to avoid delays in case resolution that may be harmful to the child.

If the judge determines that abuse or neglect has occurred, the trial will proceed to the disposition hearing. At this stage of the civil court process, *the judge decides who will have custody and control over the child and may, in some jurisdictions, have the authority to issue certain conditions on placement or instructions to the parties.* In most states, the court has the authority to require parents to participate in treatment and counseling or cooperate with agency caseworkers as conditions of keeping the family intact.[26] At the disposition hearing, witnesses may be presented and cross-examined, and written agency reports (with recommendations) may be submitted.

If the child is to be removed from the home at the disposition phase of the case, the judge should consider at the disposition hearing whether reasonable efforts have been made to prevent the removal. When a child already has been removed, a *reasonable efforts* determination should have been made previously at the emergency custody or shelter care hearing. In that situation, the judge at the disposition hearing should then make a finding as to whether reasonable efforts were made to reunify the family.[27]

This reasonable efforts determination is required by federal law (P.L. 96-272) in order for a state to receive federal financial support for the costs resulting from a child's removal from home into foster care.[28] In many states, reasonable efforts findings have been made mandatory under state law whenever a child is placed or continued in foster care.[29] The purpose

of this requirement is to encourage state and county agencies to provide parents with the services they need to improve their ability to care for their children and thus prevent or cut short the time that children spend in foster care.[30]

The judge has a number of dispositional options, usually delineated by state law. One option is to issue a protective supervision order, permitting a parent (even after an adjudication of abuse or neglect) to retain legal custody of his or her child under certain conditions and with supervision by the CPS agency. Sometimes a child welfare agency will be given legal custody of the child with the understanding that it will exercise its discretion as to whether the child may reside in the parent's home. With these options, the court will maintain authority over the parties involved or will delegate its supervisory powers to the agency. The court or agency then has a continuing responsibility to ensure the terms of the court's order are being met. The specific conditions of supervision may vary significantly from state to state.

Another option is for the court to order removal of the child from his or her home.[31] In some states, a court can only give custody to a social services agency, which will then place the child with a relative, foster family, group home, or residential institution. In other states, the court may give custody directly to a specific person, such as a relative, foster home, or institution.

Placement with a relative (also known as *kinship care*) has become increasingly common in recent years. A child who remains with his or her extended family generally experiences less disruption and trauma than if placed with strangers. Kinship care may also preserve important cultural and community ties that would otherwise be disturbed.[32]

In most states, the judge also may issue an order of protection or restraining order to control the conduct of the abuser or any other person who might harm the child or interfere with the disposition. For example, such orders could require that a certain person refrain from abusing the child, not enter the child's home, or even have no contact whatsoever with the child.

If the child is placed outside the home, parental visitation generally is permitted. Unless there is a good reason for these visits to be supervised, parent-child contact typically will be frequent and unsupervised. However, supervision may be necessary to protect the child or to observe the interaction between the parent and child.

The most drastic option that *may* be available to the judge at the disposition stage (depending on state law) is to terminate a parent's rights to his or her child permanently, making the child available for adoption. This option is not often available or used at the disposition stage, except in unusually severe and hopeless cases. In many states, parental rights may only be terminated by filing a *separate* petition after the disposition of the abuse or neglect petition. In this situation, a separate hearing is held. The grounds for terminating parental rights must be established at this separate hearing by "clear and convincing evidence."

When termination of parental rights is not appropriate (e.g., when a suitable relative may want to become the child's permanent caretaker, an older child does not want to be adopted, or a long-term foster parent does not want to adopt), the judge may order some type of permanent placement to ensure the child continuity and stability. Although in most cases adoption is preferable when a child cannot be returned home, alternatives such as guardianship and long-term foster care are available as choices to promote permanency.[33] Long-term foster care generally is used in cases in which the child has become integrated into his or her foster home and cannot be adopted for some reason. The foster parent may then agree to keep the child in that foster home until the child reaches the age of majority. Another dispositional alternative is guardianship or custody by a relative or former foster parent that authorizes broad decision-making powers with respect to the child.

Special Foster Care Issues

The federal Adoption and Child Welfare Assistance Act ("the Act"; P.L. 96-272) requires that a public child welfare agency case plan be developed for every foster child whose care is subsidized federally.[34] Each case plan must include a description of the child's placement and a scheme for providing services to the child, the biological parents, and the foster parents. The child's health and education needs must be addressed specifically in this plan.[35] In some states, the case plan must be submitted to and approved by the court.[36] The judge in those states should hold a hearing at which the plan may be accepted, rejected, or modified.

Every state requires courts, child welfare agency panels, or citizen review boards to hold periodic reviews to re-evaluate the child's circumstances if he or she has been placed in foster care. The purpose of these reviews is to ensure that a child's placement continues to meet his or her needs and to avoid the problem of "foster care drift" by planning for the child's future and setting deadlines and time tables.

In order for a state to receive certain federal funds under the Act, a child's case must be reviewed at least every 6 months after he or she is placed in foster care.[37] The Act also requires a hearing within at least 18 months from the child's placement into foster care, continuing at regular intervals, to establish a firm, permanent plan for the case (i.e., whether the child is to be returned home, continued in foster care for a specified period, placed for adoption, or continued in long-term foster care).[38] Even after the 18-month hearing, reviews of the child's case will continue to be held every 6 months for as long as an agency maintains custody or control over the child (usually until the child is returned home or adopted).[39]

Domestic Relations Proceedings

Unlike juvenile or criminal court actions, a domestic relations proceeding in a state's family or domestic relations court involves a dispute between two private parties. Thus, when a parent believes his or her child is being abused or neglected by the child's other parent (or by someone in the other parent's home), the parent may seek a variety of remedies from the domestic relations court. First, if the parents are married to each other, a divorce may be sought. Second, if the parents are in the process of a divorce or separation action, one parent may request that he or she be awarded sole custody of the child based on the child's allegations of abuse or neglect by the other parent. Once custody has been awarded, the judge normally will permit the noncustodial parent to have reasonable visitation periods with the child. The custodial parent may ask the judge to order that these visits be supervised (by a friend, relative, or appropriate private or public agency) or that visitation be denied entirely because of prior abuse or neglect by the noncustodial parent.

Third, if custody already has been determined by a prior court decision and visitation has been arranged, a parent may reapply to the domestic relations court for a modification of its previous order. Proof of parental child abuse may warrant a complete change in custody from one parent to the other, elimination of all visitation, or restriction of the present terms of visitation (e.g., supervised visits or elimination of overnight visits).

When child abuse arises in a domestic relations proceeding, a number of difficulties exist.

When child abuse arises in a domestic relations proceeding, a number of difficulties exist. First, the CPS agency or juvenile court and the domestic relations court may not communicate or coordinate cases, resulting in conflicting orders or lack of protection of the child because each system believes the other is addressing the problem. Second, domestic relations courts often have little experience or expertise in dealing with child abuse and neglect and generally are more concerned with protecting parental rights.

In addition, in recent years, there has been growing concern that *deliberately* false allegations of abuse or neglect, particularly sexual abuse, sometimes are made by parents in a divorce situation to gain the advantage in a custody or visitation dispute.[40] At this point, only limited studies have addressed this issue, and although some suggest a somewhat higher rate of untrue reports in divorce cases, none supports the claims of widespread allegations of fabrication of sexual abuse.[41] Any allegations of child maltreatment that arise during a custody struggle must be taken seriously, although they should be investigated with great care by using accepted interviewing techniques.

To date, the largest study regarding allegations of sexual abuse in custody and visitation cases was conducted by the Association of Family and Conciliation Courts (AFCC, 1988) and the American Bar Association (ABA).[42] AFCC's research found that allegations of sexual abuse were made in an extremely small percentage of divorce cases. Moreover, their research revealed that only a small percentage of cases involved deliberately false reports. Finally, AFCC also made recommendations to improve handling of these cases in the domestic relations and juvenile courts, including the following:

- Provide cross-training of professionals and judges regarding each system (e.g., mandates, roles, limits)
- Create a formal liaison or coordination between CPS/juvenile court and family court
- Develop formal policies to share information between family and juvenile courts
- Assign family court to an interdisciplinary team
- Provide training of family court judges and attorneys regarding child sexual abuse
- Transfer cases of abuse to juvenile court for adjudication regarding abuse
- Consolidate cases in one court (preferably juvenile court) or create a specialized "family court" for all family and juvenile matters
- Appoint lawyer or guardian *ad litem* for the child in all divorce cases involving abuse
- Have the court appoint experts and evaluate all parties[43]

Many domestic relations courts provide mediation services for families involved in custody-related disputes. Mediation may not be appropriate, however, in cases in which child abuse is alleged. If one of the parents also has been abused by his or her spouse, the imbalance of power between the parties may make productive mediation impossible. The nonabusing parent must be able to protect the child for mediation to be effective. Otherwise, a mediated resolution may place the child in greater danger than he or she already was. In addition, mediation of child abuse claims may be inadvisable because mediators often favor joint custody. If a mediator encourages joint custody under all circumstances, the result could be disastrous for the abused child.

Like specialized juvenile courts, many domestic relations courts have available to them mental health professionals to perform evaluations of families. These evaluators may be members of the court staff or private practitioners, and their degree of experience with child maltreatment varies widely among jurisdictions.

An evaluation involves a comprehensive assessment of the family (including, for example, visits to both parents' homes and interviews with the parents, the child, and any other source of information, such as teachers and guidance counselors), followed by a full report and recommendations to the court. If the judge requires it, psychological testing may also be conducted in the course of a court-ordered custody evaluation.

Domestic Violence Proceedings

As noted earlier, many states also have special domestic violence statutes that permit courts to issue protection orders for victims of family violence.[44] Although originally designed for use by battered spouses, many state statutes allow protection orders on behalf of an abused child.[45] Civil protection order proceedings have several benefits for abused children. For example, such actions provide a means of preventing further contact with the offender without the proof problems and other difficulties in the criminal justice system. Another benefit is that the nonoffending parent can obtain a protection order, whereas in the juvenile court he or she would be a party along with the perpetrator, despite his or her ability and desire to protect the child. Indeed, such an order may be in force even before the case is brought to the attention of CPS.

In addition, such proceedings are useful when the parents are separated or divorced and the child does not live in the same household as the alleged abuser. Furthermore, the nonabusive parent may be a victim of abuse along with the children, all of whom may benefit from a civil protection order. Finally, children, although not abused directly, may suffer significant emotional harm from witnessing the abuse of their parent.

A protection order is a court directive designed to prevent family violence by imposing certain restrictions or requirements on the abuser. A protection order may require that the abuser move out of the victim's home, refrain from abusing the victim, avoid all contact with the victim, participate in treatment or counseling, or pay the victim support. Not all of these remedies are available in every state. In many states, however, other remedies may be ordered as well. It is also not unusual for courts to have the authority to impose additional terms or conditions it deems necessary for the victim's protection.

Although protection orders are one important tool to prevent domestic violence, they present a number of enforcement problems. Once an order is violated, it may be too late to protect the victim. Any consequences an abuser may feel only will be experienced *after* the damage has been done. Moreover, studies have shown that law enforcement officers are often reluctant to become involved in "family matters" by enforcing protection orders.[46] This problem, however, has been addressed in a growing number of jurisdictions by requiring training for officers specifically in handling domestic calls.[47]

Civil Tort/Damages Actions

An increasingly popular form of legal action is a civil lawsuit (called a *tort* action) by child maltreatment victims seeking money damages (i.e., financial compensation) from the abuser.[48]

Such suits may be brought by an adult on behalf of a minor child against an individual perpetrator or against an institution that employs an alleged offender (e.g., day care centers, schools, and churches). *Adult survivors* (adults who were abused as children) also are bringing such suits more frequently.

A child may have a legal claim against his or her parent for physical or sexual abuse or even possibly for emotional abuse. Parents generally have a privilege to use "reasonable" physical force on their children as a form of discipline or punishment. If a parent's physical abuse is unreasonable, however, it may constitute the tort of *assault* or *battery*. When determining whether a punishment is reasonable, courts look at the conduct being punished, the child's age, the injury caused, and other relevant factors. Courts agree that physical punishment resulting in severe injury or death will result in tort liability.[49]

Sexual abuse of a child may be the basis of tort actions for assault and battery, intentional and negligent infliction of emotional distress, or an action based on violation of criminal sexual offense laws.[50] Children also have been permitted to sue their parents for emotional harm based on the tort of intentional infliction of emotional distress.[51]

In the past, civil lawsuits by victims of child abuse were precluded by the *parental tort immunity doctrine.*[52] Today, however, most states have abandoned this doctrine, which refused to allow actions between parents and children for negligent or intentional torts.[53] In addition, a state's statute of limitations has been a major barrier to adult sexual abuse victims seeking civil damages. Each state has a specific time period during which a legal claim must be filed, usually 2 to 3 years after the defendant's wrongful conduct. These legislatively created time limits (barring civil and criminal actions after the time period has expired) are called *statutes of limitations*. The two major purposes of the statutes of limitations are to prevent legal proceedings where the evidence is stale and encourage prompt resolution of grievances and discourage manipulative tactics to delay actions for the advantage of one party.

When the person bringing a lawsuit is a minor, states usually provide that the time period does not begin to run until he or she reaches the age of majority.[54] Even with this additional time to file a suit after a child becomes an adult, there has been growing recognition that adult survivors have been without a legal remedy for childhood sexual abuse because the statute of limitations has expired. This is because child sexual abuse victims (a) have been sworn to secrecy or threatened into silence, (b) are unaware that various psychological or physical symptoms were the result of their earlier abuse, or (c) have repressed or forgotten the abuse until "discovering" it many years later (sometimes by a triggering event or in treatment).

As a result, there has been a movement to extend the statute of limitations or "toll" (i.e., stop) its running because of the unique features of this problem. Moreover, those favoring the extension argue that the reasons for the statute of limitations do not apply in child abuse situations. The purpose (of the statute of limitations) of preventing stale evidence does not apply, because the statute is tolled anyway in most states until the child reaches the age of majority. Furthermore, the delay in bringing the action is not caused by manipulation but by the defendant's threats.

There have been two basic ways the statute of limitations has been extended or held not to apply in civil cases. First, courts have applied two legal doctrines called the *delayed discovery rule* and the *doctrine of equitable estoppel* in holding that the statute of limitations did not prevent the victim from seeking relief.[55] Second, there has been a legislative trend to enact special statutes extending the statute of limitations specifically for child abuse victims. Methods for extending the statute of limitations include (a) providing additional time for a victim to sue after reaching the age of majority[56] and (b) tolling the statute of limitations until the victim either "discovers" or remembers the abuse or "discovers" the injury was caused by the abuse.[57]

Criminal Laws and Prosecution

Background

Crimes involving child abuse are defined by state penal laws or criminal laws, although no two states in the nation have the same definitions of a crime. All states provide criminal penalties for sexual abuse of a child under age 16 or 17 without regard to force or coercion, because a child is deemed incapable of consenting.[58] All sexual acts involving children are prohibited, including vaginal, anal, and oral penetration or intercourse and sexual contact.

Over the past 15 years, states have reformed their sexual offense statutes, replacing a single statutory rape provision with two or three degrees of sex offenses.[59] Penalties are highest for sexual penetration and for offenses against young children (under age 11, 12, 13, or 14, depending on the state). Most states have lower penalties for sexual offenses against older children and either impose a misdemeanor penalty or no penalty for sexual acts between teenagers who are close in age (usually by prohibiting acts in which the perpetrator is a certain number of years older than the victim or is above a certain age). In addition, many states have increased penalties when the victim is related to or in a relationship with the perpetrator (e.g., teacher, day care employee).

Most states have criminal penalties specifically for physical or emotional abuse and neglect of a child by a parent or caretaker.[60] Physical abuse also may be prosecuted under a state's general assault and battery, murder, or manslaughter provisions.[61]

Unless severe injury or death results, physical abuse and neglect are much less frequently prosecuted than sexual abuse of children.

Unless severe injury or death results, physical abuse and neglect are much less frequently prosecuted than sexual abuse of children.[62] As discussed later, until recent years, child abuse and neglect committed by parents were thought to be handled better in the juvenile court and not prosecuted.[63] Many, however, now advocate full prosecution of both parents and nonparents for child abuse and neglect.[64]

Despite greater support for criminal prosecution of child abuse, prosecution carries with it a number of inherent difficulties. Constitutional guarantees, particularly those afforded defendants, apply in the criminal context, making such cases difficult to prove. Moreover, for a number of reasons discussed later, child abuse is especially difficult to prove in a criminal case.

In addition, as more cases of child abuse have entered the criminal justice system, many have noted its negative effects on the child and family.[65] Often, in its zealous pursuit of evidence and winning a conviction, the system has treated children insensitively. Children have been subjected to multiple interviews, long delays, insensitive questioning, testimony at pretrial hearings as well as direct and cross-examination at trial, and the need to face the defendant in court.

Criminal prosecution also may have deleterious effects on the family when the offender is a parent, by leading to a loss of employment and income or splitting up the family and to the incarceration of the parent (sometimes creating guilt on the child's part). Most important, if there is an acquittal, it may lead to parental reprisals and leave the child feeling completely hopeless. Moreover, adequate, affordable treatment is not available in many places for offenders; in many cases, offenders serve relatively little prison time, are released without having received treatment, and continue to represent a threat to children.

Why then prosecute? Several experienced child abuse prosecutors argue that criminal prosecutions

- Establish the innocence of child victims and the sole responsibility of abusers
- Validate victims' and society's sense of fairness
- Educate the community on child abuse and deter others from abusing children
- Secure treatment for offenders, reducing the likelihood of recidivism
- Label offenders with a criminal record[66]

Moreover, many states and local jurisdictions, in response to concerns about revictimization of children by the criminal justice system, have reformed their procedures and laws to make the system more sensitive to child witnesses.[67] Many states also have passed laws to reduce evidentiary barriers to proving child abuse.[68]

Although relatively little research has been done regarding the emotional effects of legal intervention on children, a few studies indicate that although certain procedures seem associated with increased distress,[69] in some circumstances, testifying and other procedures may not be harmful.[70] Some experts claim that many children, in fact, may be empowered by testifying.[71] It also has been argued that because so few cases go to trial, few children testify and therefore few children are traumatized by the trial process.[72]

Investigation

In most states, police agencies investigate child abuse by gathering statements and physical evidence and submitting the case to the prosecutor for a decision regarding the filing of criminal charges. Prosecutors' offices rarely have their own investigators on staff. In the area of child sexual abuse investigations, many prosecutors become more involved in the investigation than they do in a typical case involving other types of crime. Interagency agreements may provide prosecutors with opportunities to meet and interview the child at the outset to consider questions of the child's competency to testify and the child's ability to be a reliable and credible witness.

The focus of most investigations involving physical or sexual abuse of an older child is the child's statement and efforts to corroborate it. The investigator tries to interview and gather statements from everyone the child has told about the abuse. Every person in the chain of disclosure should be interviewed to obtain information about what the child said, the child's demeanor, any motive to fabricate displayed by the child, or inconsistencies in the child's statements.

Working from the child's statements, investigators look for corroborating evidence. Other potential child victims will be interviewed. Verification of a child's description of the location will be attempted. For instance, is the bedspread in the residence the color described by the child? Do the child's school records verify the child was absent from school at the time the child says the perpetrator kept him or her at home for purposes of abuse? Are the sexual magazines, aids, or videos the child described seeing located where described? These kinds of documentation can be obtained by consent of the suspect, or a search warrant may be obtained for the suspect's premises if probable cause exists to believe items that are evidence of a crime are located in a particular place.

Investigators usually work with the child's parents, guardians, or CPS agencies to see that a medical examination is conducted. In physical abuse cases, medical evidence of the abuse is critical, particularly in cases in which the child is an infant or nonverbal and therefore cannot be a witness. The doctor looks for bruises; abrasions; bone fractures; head, chest, or abdominal injuries; or burns that were inflicted intentionally. The physician must be able to differentiate between intentionally inflicted injuries, which often look different than accidental injuries, and those that are nonaccidental but caused by the use of reasonable discipline (consistent with the explanation given by the parent). Depending on the type of injury, the doctor arranges for photographs or x-rays to be taken of the injuries.

The physician also may identify the child as suffering from *the battered child syndrome* (defined originally as multiple injuries in different stages of healing caused by nonaccidental means in children under age 3),[73] for which x-rays also should be taken. The doctor may also find evidence of various forms of severe neglect, including malnutrition, medical neglect, and nonorganic failure to thrive.[74]

In sexual abuse cases, if the abuse has occurred recently (generally within about 72 hours of the exam), the physician swabs for evidence of seminal fluid or traces of hair.[75] These items are submitted by the investigator to the crime lab for analysis of possible scientific evidence. Often, however, this kind of evidence is not available because sexually abused children commonly delay in reporting, or the sexual abuse did not involve penetration or ejaculation.

In sexual abuse cases, the medical examination also assesses the presence of sexually transmitted diseases. The fact that a child has a sexually transmitted disease generally is corroborative of sexual abuse by someone. Occasionally, however, a child's sexually transmitted disease may be compared to a suspect's to narrow down strains of diseases and increase the reliability of the identification. In addition to possible acute evidence of sexual assault or the existence of a sexually transmitted disease, the physician looks for any number of conditions of the child's genitalia that may be corroborative of sexual activity, such as bruises, tears, lacerations, or swelling. Because many conditions heal or repair themselves rapidly, timely medical exams are important.

Depending on the age of the victim, information from parents, child care providers, teachers, mental health workers, and others also may be sought to show behavioral changes of the victim associated with victimization.

The investigator generally attempts to contact the suspect for his or her side of the story. Sometimes this conversation will take place after the defendant is arrested. Other times, the suspect is interviewed at home, at work, in an office, or in the police station. Policies regarding when and if to arrest the suspect vary from case to case and police agency to police agency.

In deciding whether to arrest a suspect, the investigator will consider the following: (a) the seriousness of the crime and the danger to the victim and others, (b) the likelihood the defendant will flee the jurisdiction if not incarcerated, (c) the cooperativeness of the suspect, and (d) whether an arrest will impede or facilitate obtaining a statement from the defendant. It is very important to lock the defendant into a story early, before he or she has an opportunity to study the evidence against him or her and devise a more persuasive explanation.

Charging, Plea Negotiations, and Disposition

Charging

In deciding to charge a criminal case, the prosecutor must analyze whether there is admissible evidence to present to a jury that proves a defendant violated the state's criminal statutes. In physical abuse cases, intent is an important element of proving the crime of physical abuse, which is discussed in detail elsewhere.[76]

Acts that may be described variously by other professionals as sexual abuse may not be a violation of the criminal law. For instance, an adult requiring his 13-year-old daughter to shower with him is certainly inappropriate grooming behavior. However, it may well not amount to a violation of a criminal statute.

The prosecutor must also decide whether the crime was committed within the statute of limitations. Most states have some limitation on how long after a crime has occurred a criminal action may be brought. The theory behind the statute of limitations is that at some point after the commission of a crime, the goals of the criminal justice system, punishment, and rehabilitation diminish. There is also a concern that evidence, in the form of memories or physical evidence, becomes less reliable with the passage of time.

Therefore, most states require that a crime be charged within a certain number of years (e.g., 3, 5, 7) of its commission. The running of the criminal statute of limitations dates from commission of the crime, not from recall of the event or reporting to the police. Many state legislatures and courts, however, have extended their criminal statutes of limitations in the area of child sexual abuse because of the phenomenon of delayed reporting or repressed memories.[77]

A number of constitutional guarantees apply in criminal proceedings, especially rights afforded the defendant under the U.S. Constitution and many state constitutions. The burden of proof is also the highest in a criminal case, requiring the prosecution to prove beyond a reason-able doubt that the defendant is guilty. These important tenets of the criminal law result in decisions not to initiate criminal proceedings, even though a prosecutor may think the accused is *probably* guilty. Nor should prosecutors file charges against people they *know* are guilty when significant evidence, such as a coerced confession, is likely to be inadmissible. Prosecutors vary in the quantum of proof they require to file charges.

The mechanism of charging a criminal violation varies among the states. Prosecutors in a majority of states are required to present evidence either to a judge at a preliminary hearing or at a grand jury for an independent determination of whether charges should proceed. In a few states, the prosecutor can file charges by simply filing an information or complaint and a supporting affidavit summarizing the evidence.

Plea Negotiations and Sentencing

Plea negotiations are guided largely by a state's sentencing structure. Sentencing schemes and penalties are again a function of state statute and vary widely. Maximum sentences around the country for sexual intercourse of a child range from death, life imprisonment, 60 years imprisonment, and 20 years imprisonment.[78] Some states establish mandatory minimum sentences for sexual intercourse with a child, under which a certain number of years must be served without the possibility of parole.

The array of possibilities at sentencing is wide (assuming the state does not have mandatory sentences). Some judges impose long prison terms. Some courts impose prison terms during which the offender may obtain treatment in the prison system. In some states, the defendant can receive probation with outpatient treatment, frequently coupled with some amount of jail time served in a local county facility. A few jurisdictions have deferred prosecution or diversion programs where charges are filed, but after several years, the charges may be dismissed on the defendant's successful completion of a treatment program and fulfillment of other conditions.

By creative use of treatment options, misdemeanor pleas, and deferred prosecutions, the prosecutor frequently can fashion a sentence that is both legal under state law and meets several seemingly conflicting goals of the criminal law. The major goals of sentencing are to punish, incapacitate, and rehabilitate the offender. The sentence is based on the nature of the offender, the desires of the victim, and the goal of accountability and proportionality in the disposition of criminal sentences.

Plea negotiations are driven by the prosecutor's ultimate sentencing goal. For a serious predatory offender, the prosecutor will try to negotiate a sentence that allows for the maximum period of incarceration. An obstacle to getting a maximum sentence plea is the strength of the case. If a case is weak on identification of the defendant, for instance, the prosecutor must assess the likelihood that the state will lose and the defendant immediately will walk the streets versus taking a plea to a lesser amount of incarceration. Conscientious prosecutors do not bargain for the sake of it or to reduce their caseload.

The victim's input on plea negotiations is important. In incest cases, the desire of the victim's family to have the abuse stop but ultimately to reunite is the most common reason for using a treatment option or even a deferred prosecution. Good sentencing schemes allow many options. It is incumbent on the prosecutor and the judge to have the best information available in deciding which option is appropriate. Key information includes, but is not limited to (a) severity of the offense, (b) offender's history of offending, (c) risk of reoffense in a community treatment program, (d) likelihood of the defendant's ability to complete treatment safely, and (e) the victim's interest in punishment versus rehabilitation.

Trial

Overview and Burden of Proof

In criminal cases, a prosecutor must prove a defendant guilty "beyond a reasonable doubt." Criminal cases are much harder to prove than cases brought in juvenile court or a civil suit in which there is a lower standard of proof—preponderance of the evidence. Moreover, child abuse and neglect cases are particularly difficult to prove. Eyewitness testimony generally is not available, and physical or medical evidence often is lacking, especially in sexual abuse cases. Finally, the child victim either may be too young to be a competent witness or may not be an effective or credible witness. When the child is unable to be a witness, other evidence becomes crucial. Even when the child testifies, however, many prosecutors believe that additional evidence to corroborate the child's testimony is necessary, at least to obtain a criminal conviction. Indeed, until the past decade, corroboration (or evidence in addition to the victim's testimony) was required by law to prosecute a sex offense case.

At trial, a prosecutor's typical child abuse case involves the following presentation of evidence: (a) the child's testimony as to the particular criminal charges; (b) testimony of lay witnesses regarding what they observed, what the child told them about the offense (hearsay), or the defendant's opportunity to commit the offense (by testifying that he or she saw the defendant and child together at the general time of the abuse); (c) expert testimony by a physician regarding medical evidence or an explanation of the lack of such evidence; (d) expert testimony by a mental health professional regarding psychological behaviors or other issues; and (e) other corroborative evidence (such as prior abusive acts of the defendant). Some of these evidentiary issues are discussed in greater detail in the next section, and expert testimony regarding medical or psychological evidence in child abuse cases is examined in Chapter 13, this volume.

Hearsay Evidence

Witnesses generally are required to appear personally at trial, under oath, and be subject to cross-examination before the trier of fact in order to observe the witness' demeanor, expose possible inaccuracies in the witness' testimony, and assess his or her sincerity. State statutes or court rules therefore prohibit a person from repeating in court what someone else said out of court in order to prove that out-of-court statement was true. Such out-of-court statements are considered inadmissible hearsay.[79]

In certain situations, however, such statements are considered sufficiently reliable to be admitted at trial because of the special circumstances under which they are made. Most states recognize approximately 25 exceptions to the rule against admitting hearsay evidence. The hearsay exceptions most frequently encountered in child abuse and neglect cases will be discussed here.

Excited Utterances or Spontaneous Declarations Hearsay Exception

Statements made by someone under the immediate stress of a startling event[80] are considered reliable because they are made *spontaneously or without time to reflect.*[81] The significant factor for courts in determining whether to admit a statement as an excited utterance is whether the speaker was under the stress of the moment when the statement was made.

Although traditionally the statement must be made nearly contemporaneously with the event, in child abuse cases, some courts have been liberal in admitting statements made long after the sexually abusive event (e.g., hours, days, weeks, or even months).[82] Other courts, however, have not admitted a child's statements made more than a few minutes after the experience under this exception.[83] Courts also have admitted as excited utterances statements made by children in response to direct questioning.[84]

Statements for Purposes of Medical Diagnosis or Treatment Hearsay Exception

When someone goes to a doctor for medical attention, it is presumed that the person will tell the doctor the truth about his or her ailments to be properly diagnosed and treated. Accordingly, courts have held that statements to doctors made for the purposes of making a diagnosis and providing treatment are sufficiently reliable and trustworthy to be repeated in court to prove that the statements are true; in many states, this exception also covers statements to all medical personnel, not just physicians.[85]

Because a doctor's primary role is to treat injuries, the identity of the person inflicting them traditionally has been deemed to be outside of this exception. Courts recently, however, have begun to recognize that more than the child's physical injuries must be treated in child abuse cases. As one court has observed, "The treating physician must be attentive to the emotional and psychological injuries which accompany child abuse."[86]

Thus, some courts permit doctors to repeat in court, as statements for the purpose of medical treatment, the child's identification of the person who abused him or her.

The medical diagnosis exception also has been used to admit children's statements to mental health professionals who are "diagnosing and treating" the child's psychological injuries. For example, in *State v. Nelson,* the court allowed a psychologist to repeat in court the statements made by a child about the abuse because the court indicated that the child believed she was seeing the psychologist as a part of treatment.[87] Other courts, however, have found that children, especially young children, do not have the understanding that psychological treatment will make them better, and so the motive of being truthful does not exist. Therefore, the child's statements do not qualify as statements for purposes of medical diagnosis or treatment.[88]

Residual Hearsay Exception

Some states have enacted a residual or *catch-all* exception to the rule against hearsay.[89] This exception permits the introduction of hearsay evidence that does not fall within an existing exception but has comparable *circumstantial degrees of trustworthiness.* A statement's admissibility under this exception depends on whether it is deemed sufficiently reliable, based on such factors as the child's young age, spontaneity, age-appropriate language, the detailed nature of the statement, and the likelihood a child of that age would have knowledge of such sexual details (see factors listed in next section).

Child Abuse Hearsay Exception

Many states (at least 28) have enacted special statutes that expand the use of hearsay in child abuse cases.[90] Typically, these statutes permit the introduction of statements made by a child under a specific age (in general, under 10 years old) describing acts of abuse under certain conditions. About half of these state statutes restrict the admissibility of the statements to those concerning sexual (as opposed to physical) abuse.

Most statutes first require either that the child testify or be found "unavailable" to testify, although about seven statutes do not require an unavailability showing. Most statutes also have a second requirement that the court find the statement to be reliable (some require reliability to be shown even if the child testifies, but others only require a reliability showing if the child is not available to testify). The statutes generally call for the judge to make a determination of the reliability of the statements outside the presence of the jury. The court will hear testimony about how the statements were obtained and under what circumstances, and they will rule on whether they are sufficiently trustworthy for a jury to consider.

In determining whether the statement is reliable, among the factors courts consider are the following:

- Whether there is a motive to lie
- Whether more than one person heard the statement
- The general character of the child
- The timing of the statement and the relationship between the child and the witness who heard the child's statement
- Whether the statement was spontaneous
- Cross-examination could not show the child's lack of knowledge
- The possibility that the child's recollection is faulty
- The circumstances surrounding the statement are such that there is no reason to suppose the child misrepresented the defendant's involvement[91]

Under some statutes, if the child is unavailable to testify, the state also must present some other independent corroboration of the abuse.[92] This might be supplied by medical evidence, a statement by the defendant, or expert testimony regarding the behavioral changes in the child suggestive of sexual abuse.[93]

To improve the likelihood that a child's hearsay statements are admissible, professionals working with abused children should document carefully all that the child says about the abuse. They also should document meticulously their own questions that generate responses from the child.

Admission of Hearsay and the Right of Confrontation

As noted earlier, all criminal defendants are entitled under the Sixth Amendment to be confronted with their accusers in court. When the child testifies at the trial, the defendant can exercise his or her right to confront and cross-examine the child physically. On the other hand, when a child does not appear as a witness, admission of the child's hearsay statements potentially conflicts with this right because the defendant has no opportunity to confront and cross-examine the child. In 1980, the Supreme Court indicated in *Ohio v. Roberts*[94] that the confrontation clause was violated by admission of hearsay when the declarant was absent at trial, unless (a) the state produced the declarant or showed the declarant was "unavailable" to testify, and (b) the statement possessed adequate indicia of reliability. "Unavailability" to testify may include physical unavailability, incompetency, lack of memory, or an unwillingness or inability to testify.

In *Roberts* and subsequent decisions, the Court has indicated that the reliability requirement is satisfied automatically if hearsay falls within a "firmly rooted" hearsay exception. In *White v. Illinois* (1992), the Court also decided that when the state offers hearsay that satisfies the excited utterances and medical diagnosis exceptions, and the child is not offered by the state as a witness, the prosecution is not required to prove the child is "unavailable" or unable to testify. Most important, *White* held that if a child's hearsay statements satisfy a "firmly rooted" hearsay exception, they also satisfy the confrontation clause, even if the child is unable to testify and the defendant therefore is unable to confront him or her. A child's statement that does not fall within a firmly rooted exception may be repeated at trial only if the child testifies or if the prosecution demonstrates that the statement has particularized guarantees of trustworthiness and the child is unavailable as a witness.

Expert Evidence

Although courts seek the introduction of evidence that is relevant and probative, they are careful to exclude evidence if its prejudicial impact on the defendant is deemed greater than its probative value. Consistent with this philosophy, lay witnesses generally are not permitted to testify about their opinions but instead are limited to their observations. In some circumstances, however, courts permit certain witnesses to offer opinions about the evidence.

If someone is sufficiently experienced, trained, educated, or skilled in a specific area of specialty, such that their opinions would be helpful to hear and consider, they may be allowed to testify about those opinions.[95] The expert witness in child abuse cases might be used to interpret medical evidence, provide psychological information to explain why children delay in disclosure or recant their original report of abuse, or reestablish a child victim's credibility after he or she has testified.[96] These issues are discussed more fully in Chapter 13.

A witness may be qualified as an expert based on practical experience alone.[97] The most significant factor is whether the jury will be helped by the testimony of the professional. An expert witness might be someone connected to the case who offers an explanation of what certain facts mean. For example, a medical doctor who testifies about injuries seen during an examination of a child may offer a professional opinion as to the specific cause of the injury. Instead of being restricted to testifying exclusively about the injuries observed, the doctor may be permitted to offer an opinion that the injuries were probably caused by shaking the child, consistent with shaken baby syndrome.

A qualified expert also may be permitted to testify for the purpose of educating the jury without having had any prior connection with the specific case. For example, in a case in which an allegation of sexual abuse went unreported for many months, a child psychologist may testify and explain why a delay in reporting abuse is not uncommon in child abuse cases in general.[98]

An expert generally may not offer an opinion that a child is a credible witness, a child was abused, or the defendant is guilty or innocent.[99] In making very clear the limitations of an expert in offering an opinion about the credibility of a child, one court noted,

We have said it before, and we will say it again, but this time with emphasis—we really mean it—no psychotherapist may render an opinion on whether a witness is credible in any trial conducted in this state. The assessment of credibility is for the trier of fact and not for psychotherapists.[100]

Moreover, giving an opinion that the child was abused invades the province of

the jury and constitutes an opinion about the outcome of the case. As one expert further notes, an opinion that a child was abused "misleads the trier of fact" because it "lacks a firm scientific foundation" and, although "useful for treatment planning . . . connotes a certainty that goes well beyond current knowledge."[101]

Similarly, it is improper for an expert to suggest that a defendant is guilty because he or she falls within the statistically probable class of offenders.[102] In all jurisdictions except California, an expert may not testify that a defendant either fits or does not fit within a "profile" of a typical child molester.[103]

Defendant's Prior Abusive Acts

Child abuse is often a recurring event. Admission into evidence of previous incidents of abuse, therefore, can be extremely useful in proving that a subsequent abusive act occurred.

Prior acts of abuse, however, cannot be admitted into evidence merely to establish that a defendant has a propensity to commit future abusive acts.

Prior acts of abuse, however, cannot be admitted into evidence merely to establish that a defendant has a propensity to commit future abusive acts.[104] This is a type of character evidence, which courts traditionally have excluded when introduced to establish that a defendant acted in conformity with his character on a particular occasion.[105]

An exception to this rule, however, permits admission of such evidence for reasons other than to establish that the defendant committed the act.[106] Under these theories, prior acts might be admissible to establish motive, plan, identity, intent, or lack of accident.[107] These exceptions are best understood not as delineating rules but rather as guidelines when courts are balancing the probative value of evidence with any undue prejudice caused by its introduction.[108]

In some jurisdictions, prior sexual offenses may be admitted to establish that a defendant has a propensity for becoming involved in illicit sexual relations, sometimes called a "lustful disposition" or "depraved sexual instinct."[109] Under this exception, prior acts may be used to establish that the defendant is predisposed to commit acts of sexual deviance or misconduct. Courts have reasoned that the privacy surrounding sexual offenses makes these cases extraordinarily difficult to prove, and high recidivism rates of sexual offenders make prior acts evidence highly probative.[110] The result is a potentially broad exception allowing the admission of evidence that establishes the disposition of the defendant as probative of whether he or she committed the alleged act, even though it generally is considered inadmissible character evidence. The exceptions initially were limited to prior acts between the parties currently before the court and later expanded to include prior acts with third parties.[111]

In 1992, Indiana abolished its depraved sexual instinct exception.[112] Rejecting the traditional rationales for the exception, the Indiana Supreme Court held that the Federal Rules of Evidence should apply. The Federal Rules of Evidence make no provision for the admission of a "lustful disposition," "depraved sexual instinct," or evidence establishing that the defendant has a propensity to commit acts of sexual misconduct.[113] Under the Federal Rules, the only exceptions are those noted above, although a proposed amendment would allow admission of prior sexual acts for any relevant purpose in child molestation cases.[114]

Abrogation of Privileged Communications[115]

Statements made to doctors, lawyers, social workers, and others in their professional capacity generally are considered "privileged" and cannot be disclosed in court, unless the patient or client consents to such disclosure. The purpose of this legal rule is to encourage those who seek professional assistance to communicate freely and openly with their service providers without fear of public exposure or legal repercussions.

The scope of these privileges and the particular professional relationships to which they apply vary. In some states, privileges are abrogated (eliminated) by statute in child protection proceedings. In addition, all states mandate reporting of suspected child abuse, even when the reporter's suspicion originates from privi-

leged communications (although lawyers are not usually mandated reporters).

Conversations between husbands and wives also generally are privileged, which sometimes prevents one spouse from testifying against another in most legal proceedings. In a case alleging child maltreatment, however, this privilege generally does not apply, thus permitting the non-offending parent to testify against his or her spouse. Any abuse or neglect is deemed to have destroyed the family harmony the privilege was designed to protect, and, moreover, the safety of a child is at stake.

Competency of Child Witnesses

Because the child is the sole or most important witness in a child abuse case, the child's testimony is critical to successful outcomes in the legal system. In general, adults are presumed competent to testify, although any witness may be disqualified if a judge finds that the person "is so bereft of his powers of observation, recordation, recollection and recount, as to be so untrustworthy as a witness as to make his testimony lack relevance."[116]

On the other hand, children generally under age 10, 12, or 14 (depending on the state) have been presumed *incompetent to testify* legally. Despite this so-called presumption of incompetency, however, there never has been a fixed or precise age below which children have been considered automatically incompetent.[117] Instead, courts have assessed a child's competency to testify on a case-by-case basis by questioning the child in a hearing called a *voir dire*.

Today, about one third of the states still require that a child below a certain age (generally 10, 12, or 14 years) must be questioned by the judge to determine his or her competency prior to testifying based on the following four factors: (a) the child's mental capacity at the time of the event to observe or receive accurate impressions of the event, (b) the child's memory to retain an independent recollection of the observations, (c) the child's ability to communicate his or her memory of the event and understand simple questions about the event, and (d) the child's understanding of the difference between truth and falsity and appreciation of the responsibility to tell the truth.[118] The child is qualified to testify if these criteria are satisfied.

More than one third of the states have adopted Rule 601 of the Federal Rules of

Evidence, which establishes a presumption of competency for all persons.[119] These new rules reverse the presumption of incompetency accorded certain witnesses merely because they were part of a particular group, including children or mentally ill or convicted persons. In addition, in some states, legislation has been passed in recent years establishing a presumption of competency specifically for child victims of abuse and neglect.[120]

In these states, children now are on the same footing as adults and presumed competent as witnesses. As with adults, therefore, inconsistencies, vagueness, or other problems only affect the child's credibility, not competency. Questioning of children in these states is no longer required unless "no trier of fact could reasonably believe that the prospective witness could have observed, communicated, remembered or told the truth with respect to the event in question."[121] As with adults, however, the presumption of competency is rebuttable if it is shown that a particular child cannot meet the competency criteria.

Many commentators have recommended abolishment of mandatory competency hearings for children.[122] This position is supported, in part, by psychological research over the past 10 years indicating that most children ages 4 and older can satisfy basic competency requirements.[123] This research is summarized in Chapter 16. Although the trend is to abolish mandatory competency hearings, even if a state still requires such a hearing, courts frequently permit younger children to testify, including 3- and 4-year-olds.[124]

Legal Innovations in Child Abuse Cases

Over the past 15 years, numerous innovative procedures and laws have been adopted throughout the country to improve the legal system's handling of child abuse and neglect cases. Aimed at reducing the emotional trauma children experience and addressing the difficulties in proving child abuse (especially in the criminal justice system), these reforms include the following:

- Establishment of interdisciplinary teams
- Coordination of juvenile and criminal court proceedings

- Provision of a special advocate for the child in criminal as well as juvenile court
- Preventing excessive interviews with children through joint interviews, videotaped interviews, or one-way mirrors
- Special sexual abuse prosecution units with the same prosecutor assigned to all stages of the case
- Methods to avoid a child's testimony at grand jury and preliminary hearings
- Alternatives to a child's testimony in open court at trial, such as one-way mirrors, screens to hide the defendant, closed-circuit television, videotaping, or closing the courtroom

Despite their popularity, certain reforms, particularly those involving trial procedure and evidence rules, have come under attack. These challenges have been based on lack of empirical support for their need or efficacy and their potential illegality or unconstitutionality.[125] Certain limits clearly now apply to the use of these reforms, and research is beginning to be conducted addressing whether they are needed and if they work.[126]

The U.S. Supreme Court has been receptive to the use of special approaches for child victims in the legal system, assuming that certain requirements are met. In a 1982 case, *Globe Newspaper Co. v. Superior Court*, the Supreme Court held that the First Amendment permits closure of the courtroom in a child sexual abuse criminal case during the child's testimony, but only on a case-by-case basis if the state can demonstrate that a particular child would be traumatized.[127] The Court in *Globe* struck down a Massachusetts statute mandating exclusion of the public in all child sex offense criminal proceedings.

In *Maryland v. Craig*, the Court held that use of closed-circuit television or other alternatives for a child's testimony outside the defendant's presence did not violate the defendant's Sixth Amendment right of confrontation. The Court indicated that

[if] the state makes an adequate showing of necessity, the state interest in protecting child witnesses from the trauma of testifying in a child abuse case is sufficiently important to justify the use of a special procedure that permits a child witness in such cases to testify at trial against a defendant in the absence of face-to-face confrontation with the defendant.[128]

In *Craig,* the Court allowed alternatives, however, only when (a) a case-specific finding of necessity is made; (b) the child's trauma is caused specifically by the defendant's presence, not by courtroom trauma; and (c) the emotional distress is more than "*de minimus, i.e., more than mere nervousness or excitement or some reluctance to testify.*"[129] The Supreme Court also held in *Kentucky v. Stincer* (decided in 1988) that a defendant does not have a Sixth Amendment right to be present at a hearing to determine a child's competency to testify.[130]

Finally, as discussed above in the hearsay section, in two recent child sexual abuse decisions, *Idaho v. Wright* (1990) and *White v. Illinois* (1992), the Supreme Court made it clear that even when a child does not testify at trial, the child's hearsay statements, if admissible under a firmly rooted hearsay exception (such as spontaneous declarations and statements for the purpose of medical diagnosis and treatment), automatically satisfy the confrontation clause of the Sixth Amendment.[131]

On the other hand, if a child's statements do not fall within firmly rooted exceptions (such as the residual and child abuse exceptions), *Wright* requires the prosecution to show that the statements possess "particularized guarantees of trustworthiness." *White,* however, left open whether the state must prove a child is "unavailable to testify" to satisfy the confrontation clause for exceptions that are not firmly rooted.

Conclusion

As this chapter has described, both civil and criminal laws and legal actions are available for dealing with child abuse and neglect in the United States. Since the late 1970s, the legal system, especially the criminal justice system, has taken cases of child maltreatment more seriously. Moreover, numerous books and articles have been written over the past 15 years to assist lawyers and judges in handling these often complex, difficult cases. This chapter represents an effort to synthesize the major legal issues in child maltreatment cases and provide extensive references for the reader to obtain more in-depth, detailed analysis of such issues.

Notes

1. Howard Davidson & Robert Horowitz (1984). Protection of children from family maltreatment. In R. Horowitz & H. Davidson (Eds.), *Legal rights of children.*

2. Based on allegations that the child's stepmother abused her, a petition was brought seeking the child's removal from home. The child was championed by the founder and president of the Society for the Prevention of Cruelty to Animals, who later established the New York Society for the Prevention of Cruelty to Children. Ultimately, the stepmother was prosecuted on criminal charges, and the child was placed in an institution.

3. Prince v. Massachusetts, 321 U.S. 158 (1944).

4. In re Gault 387 U.S. 1 (1967).

5. Jane Nusbaum Feller with Howard Davidson et al., *Working with the courts in child protection* (1992, p. 3). This manual was developed and produced for the National Center on Child Abuse and Neglect by the Circle, Inc., McLean, Virginia, under contract number HHS-105-88-1702.

6. Parham v. J.R., 442 U.S. 584 (1979); Wisconsin v. Yoder, 406 U.S. 205 (1972); Stanley v. Illinois, 405 U.S. 645 (1972); Griswold v. Connecticut, 381 U.S. 479 (1965); Prince v. Massachusetts, 321 U.S. 158 (1944); Pierce v. Society of Sisters, 268 U.S. 510 (1924); Meyer v. Nebraska, 262 U.S. 390 (1922).

7. *Id.*

8. Although locating a parent can sometimes be very difficult, a judge will require that sufficient efforts be made to notify each parent before proceeding without him or her. Even if a parent cannot be notified and the original proceeding takes place without him or her, the court has the power to grant a rehearing at that parent's request as long as he or she did not willfully refuse to attend in the first place.

Another protection of the parent's right to notice is the judge's option to make only preliminary findings without the parent present, which will become final later if that parent still fails to appear. Mark Hardin (1989), *Court rules to achieve permanency for foster children: Sample rules and commentary* (p. 49).

9. A relative or other person who has cared for the child also may be entitled to notice, even if that person never had custody of the child.

10. Hardin, *supra* note 8, at 51; Mark Hardin & Ann Shalleck, "Children living apart from their parents," in *Legal rights of children, supra* note 1, at 401.

11. Josephine Bulkley (1988), "Legal proceedings, reforms and emerging issues," *Behavioral Sciences and the Law, 6,* 153.

12. McCormick notes that the higher standard in criminal cases is based on society's judgment that "it is significantly worse for an innocent man to be found guilty of a crime than a guilty man to go free." McCormick on Evidence, Section 341, at 798 (1970).

The U.S. Supreme Court held in 1970 that the due process clause "protects the accused against conviction except upon proof beyond a reasonable doubt of every fact necessary to constitute the crime with which he is charged." In re Winship, 397 U.S. 358 (1970). This standard essentially means that a juror may have some doubt, but not a reasonable doubt. Thus, the defendant need not be found guilty beyond *all* doubt, but if a juror has a reasonable doubt, he or she must acquit.

13. See generally cases annotated in Congressional Research Service, Library of Congress, The Constitution of the United States of America, Analysis and Interpretation, 1444-46 (1973 & Supp. 1980).

14. John E. B. Myers (1987), *Child witness law and practice* (p. 325) and (p. 174, Cum. Supp. 1991).

15. 452 U.S. 18 (1981).

16. Howard Davidson, *Collaborative advocacy on behalf of children: Effective partnerships between CASA and the child's attorney* (Unpublished paper on file with the Center on Children and the Law, American Bar Association); Mark Hardin (1987), "Guardians ad litem for child victims in criminal proceedings," *Journal of Family Law, 25,* 687.

17. To be eligible for federal funds under the Child Abuse Prevention and Treatment Act, states must require reporting of all types of maltreatment. Reportable child maltreatment usually includes physical, sexual, and emotional abuse; neglect (e.g., medical, emotional, or educational); abandonment; sexual exploitation; and physical endangerment.

18. Douglas Besharov (1990), *Recognizing child abuse* (p. 23, Chart 3-1).

19. Davidson & Horowitz, *supra* note 1, at 290; Besharov, *supra* note 18, at 33.

20. Besharov, *supra* note 18, at 39.

21. Bulkley, *supra* note 11, at 160-161.

22. Davidson & Horowitz, *supra* note 1, at 283.

23. This section is adapted from Feller et al., *supra* note 5.

24. Before trial, parties in any civil court proceeding are permitted to conduct "discovery." This process is designed to assist in preparing for trial by providing access to a variety of information sources. In most states, the parties to a civil child protection case will be allowed access to agency records (although laws generally permit the name of the original report of abuse or neglect to be omitted). Under certain circumstances, some "sensitive" material in these records (e.g., the child's psychiatric evaluations or reports of his or her therapy sessions) may be considered confidential and not accessible if it is not directly relevant to whether maltreatment occurred.

25. Hardin, *supra* note 8, at 58.

26. Barbara Caulfield & Robert Horowitz (1987), *Child abuse and the law: A legal primer for social workers* (p. 9).

27. Debra Ratterman (1987), *Reasonable efforts: A manual for judges* (p. 18).

28. Public Law 96-272.

29. Ratterman, *supra* note 27, at 1.

30. *Id.* at 2.

31. If the child is to be removed and placed in substitute care, the dispositional order should specify the type, location, and degree of restrictiveness of placement as well as any other appropriate conditions for placement. Parental visitation or other contact with the child also should be addressed by the court.

32. See National Black Child Development Institute, Inc. (1989), *Who will care when parents can't?;* Marianne Takas (1990), *Protective placements with relatives: A theoretical framework for policy development* (p. 267) (Paper prepared for the Fifth National Conference on Children and the Law, American Bar Association, Center on Children and the Law).

The U.S. Supreme Court has held in *Miller v. Youakim* that a relative who is licensed, certified, or approved as a foster parent is entitled to the same federal foster care payments as other foster parents. 440 U.S. 125 (1979).

33. It is important to note that the availability and impact of these permanent placement options vary widely from state to state.

34. Public Law 96-272.

35. *Id.;* National Legal Resource Center for Child Advocacy and Protection, American Bar Association (1983), *Adoption Assistance and Child Welfare Act of 1980: An introduction for juvenile court judges.*

The distinction between a case plan and a predisposition report is an important one. The report is prepared by the agency after investigating the family and should explore all alternatives thoroughly to help the court arrive at its decision. A case plan, on the other hand, specifies what actions are required of all of the parties involved to modify the conditions causing the need for placement and when they are to be completed.

36. Hardin, *supra* note 8, at 73.

37. The 6-month review addresses whether the child's placement is still necessary and appropriate, whether the case plan is being properly and adequately followed, and whether a degree of progress has been made toward reunifying the family. A target date for the child's return home, adoption, or some other permanent placement must be set at these reviews. National Legal Resource Center, *supra* note 35, at 5.

38. The 18-month hearing, unlike the 6-month review, must be held by the court or a court-appointed or approved body. It also must be conducted with relative formality. *Id.* at 6-7.

39. *Id.* These federal rules for case review are only minimum requirements. Some states have more rigorous procedures than those required by federal law. For example, in some states the hearing to establish a permanent plan must be conducted within 12 months (rather than within 18 months).

40. See, for example, Lee Coleman & Patrick E. Clancy (1990, Fall), "False allegations of child sexual abuse: Why is it happening? What can we do?" *Criminal Justice,* p. 14; Richard Gardner (1987), *The parental alienation syndrome and the differentiation between fabricated and genuine sex abuse;* Elissa Benedek & Diane Schetky (1985), "Allegations of sexual abuse in child custody and visitation disputes," in *Emerging issues in child psychiatry and the law* (E. Benedek & D. Schetky, eds.).

41. For an excellent review of recent studies to date, see Kathleen Faller et al. (1993, Fall), "Research on false allegations of sexual abuse in divorce," APSAC Advisor, 6, 1; Kathleen Coulborn Faller (1991), "Possible explanations for child sexual abuse allegations in divorce," *American Journal of Orthopsychiatry, 61,* 86; Association of Family and Conciliation Courts (1988), *Final report: Sexual abuse allegations project;* David Jones & Ann Seig (1988), "Sexual abuse allegations in custody or visitation cases: A report of 20 cases," in *Sexual abuse allegations in custody and visitation cases* (p. 22) (B. Nicholson with J. Bulkley, eds.); Lucy Berliner, "Deciding whether a child has been abused," in *Sexual abuse allegations in custody and visitation cases* (p. 48); Frances Sink, "Studies of true and false allegations," in *Sexual abuse allegations in custody and visitation disputes* (p. 37); David Corwin et al. (1987), "Child sexual abuse and custody disputes: No easy answers," *Journal of Interpersonal Violence, 2,* 91.

42. Association of Family and Conciliation Courts (1988), *Final report: Sexual abuse allegations project.* The study involved 12 sites and 9,000 cases. The research indicated that less than 2% of the divorce cases included an allegation of sexual abuse.

43. *Id.* at 85-94.

44. John E. B. Myers et al. (1992, December), "Domestic violence prevention statutes," *Violence Update;* Peter Finn (1989), "Statutory authority in the use and enforcement of civil protection orders against domestic abuse," *Family Law Quarterly, 23,* 43.

45. Davidson & Horowitz, *supra* note 1, at 301; Josephine Bulkley, American Bar Association (1983), "Analysis of civil child protection statutes dealing with sexual abuse," in *Child sexual abuse and the law* (p. 81).

46. Peter Finn (1989), "Statutory authority and the use and enforcement of civil protection orders against domestic abuse," *Family Law Quarterly, 23,* 43.

47. *Id.*

48. Joseph Crnich & Kimberly Crnich (1992), *Shifting the burden of truth: Suing child sexual abusers—A legal guide for survivors and their supporters;* Leonard Karp & Cheryl L. Karp (1989), *Domestic torts: Family violence, conflict and sexual abuse* (p. 143).

49. Karp & Karp, *supra* note 48.

50. *Id.* at 177.

51. *Id.* at 139.

52. *Id.* at 140, 148.

53. *Id.*

54. Connecticut, Delaware, Florida, and Louisiana do not allow the statute of limitations to toll while a child is a minor. *Id.* at 150.

55. Josephine A. Bulkley & Mark J. Horwitz (1994), "Adults sexually abused as children: Legal actions and issues," *Behavioral Sciences and the Law, 21,* 65. Numerous law journal articles have analyzed the statute of limitations issue in child sexual abuse cases. See, for example, Ann Marie Hagen (1991), "Tolling the statute of limitations for adult survivors of childhood sexual abuse" [Comment], *Iowa Law Review, 76,* 355; Alan Rosenfeld (1990), "The statute of limitations barrier in childhood sexual abuse cases: The equitable estoppel remedy," *Harvard Women's Law Journal, 12,* 206; Melissa G. Salten (1984), "Statutes of limitations in civil incest suits: Preserving the victim's remedy" [Comment], *Harvard Women's Law Journal, 7,* 189; and others cited in Bulkley & Horwitz, at 68 n. 16. Some states have no statute of limitations for serious felonies, including child sexual abuse. *Id.*

56. *Id.*

57. *Id.;* Karp & Karp, *supra* note 48, at 151.

58. Tami Trost & Josephine Bulkley, American Bar Association (1993), *Child maltreatment: Summary and analysis of criminal statutes.*

59. Trost & Bulkley, *supra* note 58.

60. *Id.*

61. Douglas Besharov (1986), "Child abuse: Arrest and prosecution decisionmaking," *American Criminal Law Review, 24,* 315.

62. See Barbara E. Smith & Sharon Elstein, American Bar Association (1993), *The prosecution of child physical and sexual abuse cases: Final report.*

63. Lucy Berliner, "Commentary editor's introduction" (p. 106), Scott Harshbarger, "Prosecution is an appropriate response in child sexual abuse cases" (p. 108), and Eli Newberger, "Prosecution: A problematic approach to child abuse" (p. 112), *Journal of Interpersonal Violence, 2* (1987); Besharov, *supra* note 61, at 317-319; Kee MacFarlane & Josephine Bulkley (1982), "Treating child sexual abuse: An overview of current program models," *Journal of Human Sexuality & Social Work, 1,* 69.

64. James M. Peters et al. (1989), "Why prosecute child abuse?" *South Dakota Law Review, 34,* 649; Attorney General's Task Force on Family Violence, U.S. Department of Justice (1984, September), *Final report;* Lucy Berliner & Mary Kay Barbieri (1984), "The testimony of the child victim of sexual assault," *Journal of Social Issues, 40,* 125, 128.

For a comprehensive guide to handling child abuse prosecutions, see National Center for the Prosecution of Child Abuse (1988), *Investigation and prosecution of child abuse* (P. Toth & M. Whalen, eds.). See also John E. B. Myers (1992), *Legal issues in child abuse and neglect* at 9-25 for a summary of the criminal justice process likely to occur in a child abuse case.

65. Josephine Bulkley (1985), "Evidentiary and procedural trends in state legislation and other emerging legal issues in child sexual abuse cases," *Dick. L. Rev., 89,* 645; Lucy Berliner & Doris Stevens (1980), "Advocating for sexually abused children in the criminal justice system," in *Sexual abuse of children: Selected readings* (p. 47) (B. Jones & K. MacFarlane, eds.); Vincent DeFrancis (1969), *Protecting the child victim of sex crimes,* American Humane Association.

66. Peters et al., *supra* note 64, at 654. See also Bulkley, *supra* note 65; Harshbarger, *supra* note 63; Besharov, *supra* note 61; Berliner & Barbieri, *supra* note 64.

67. Debra Whitcomb (1992), *When the victim is a child* (2nd ed.); Josephine A. Bulkley (1992), "Major legal issues in child sexual abuse cases," *The Sexual Abuse of Children: Theory and Research, 1,* 139.

68. *Id.* These include adoption of special hearsay exceptions for children's statements of abuse, elimination of mandatory competency requirements for children, and use of psychological expert testimony to counter defense attacks on the child's credibility.

69. For a brief overview of recent studies regarding the impact of legal proceedings on children, see Gail Goodman et al. (1992), "The effects of criminal court testimony on child sexual assault victims," *Monographs of the Society for Research in Child Development,* at 1-15. A handful of studies have been conducted indicating that the following legal procedures are correlated with emotional trauma to children: (a) testimony in criminal court and testifying in front of the defendant and repeated testimony (Gail Goodman et al., *supra*); (b) harsh cross-examination of older children (Debra Whitcomb et al. [1991], *Executive summary: Child victim as witness research and development program,* prepared under grant No. 87-MC-CX-0026 from the Office of Juvenile Justice and Delinquency Prevention, Office of Justice Programs, U.S. Department of Justice); (c) delays (Nancy M. P. King et al. [1988], "Going to court: The experience of child victims of intrafamilial sexual abuse," *Journal of Health Politics, Policy & Law, 13,* 1; Desmond K. Runyan et al.

[1988], "Impact of legal intervention on sexually abused children," *Journal of Pediatrics, 113,* 647); and (d) investigative procedures such as multiple interviews (John F. Tedesco & Steven V. Schnell [1987], "Children's reactions to sex abuse investigation and litigation," *Child Abuse & Neglect, 11,* 26).

See also Brief of *Amicus Curiae,* American Psychological Association, *Maryland v. Craig,* 110 S.Ct. 3157 (1990) for a discussion of studies concerning the effects of stress on children and the effects on children and the accuracy of their testimony when testifying in the defendant's presence.

70. Cross-examination of young children was not found to be traumatic by Whitcomb et al., *supra* note 69. Another study indicated that testifying in *juvenile court* was not stressful for children. See Runyan et al., *supra* note 69.

71. Berliner & Barbieri, *supra* note 64; Gary Melton & Ross Thompson (1987), "Getting out of a rut: Detours to less-traveled paths in child-witness research," in *Children's eyewitness memory* (pp. 209, 222).

72. *Id.*

73. C. Henry Kempe et al. (1962), "The battered child syndrome," *Journal of the American Medical Association, 181,* 17.

74. See generally John E. B. Myers (1992), *Evidence in Child Abuse and Neglect Litigation, 1,* 167-189 for a discussion of evidence in neglect cases.

75. See Josephine Bulkley (1994), American Bar Association, "Key evidentiary issues in child sexual abuse cases," in *A judicial primer on child sexual abuse* (p. 63) (J. Bulkley & Claire Sandt, eds.); "Medical evidence in sexual abuse cases," in *Investigation and prosecution of child abuse, supra* note 62, at V-27; Myers, *supra* note 74, at 268-283, for a discussion of medical evidence in child sexual abuse cases. See also Jan Bays & David Chadwick (1993), "Medical diagnosis of the sexually abused child," *Child Abuse & Neglect, 17,* 91; Michael Durfee et al. (1988), "Medical evaluation," in *Sexual abuse of young children* (K. MacFarlane & J. Waterman, eds.); Allan De Jong & Mimi Rose (1986), "Frequency and significance of physical evidence in legally proven cases of child sexual abuse," *Journal of Pediatrics, 84,* 1022.

76. Besharov, *supra* note 61, at 348-353; Myers, *supra* note 74, at 189-205.

77. National Center for Prosecution of Child Abuse, American Prosecutors Research Institute (1991), *State legislation extending or removing the statutes of limitation for offenses against children.* See also Bulkley & Horwitz, *supra* note 55; Jessica E. Mindlin (1990) "Child sexual abuse and criminal statutes of limitation: A model for reform" [Comment], *Washington Law Review, 65,* 189; Dirga M. Bharam (1989), "Statute of limitations for child sexual abuse offenses: A time for reform utilizing the discovery rule" [Comment], *Journal of Criminal Law & Criminology, 80,* 842. See p. 279 *infra,* for a discussion regarding civil statutes of limitation in child abuse cases.

78. Trost & Bulkley, *supra* note 58.

79. Fed. R. Evid. 801. Most states have enacted rules of evidence similar to the Federal Rules. For this discussion only the Federal Rules will be cited. For a comprehensive and detailed discussion of hearsay and common hearsay exceptions in child abuse cases see Myers, *supra* note 74, § 7.

80. Fed. R. Evid. 803(2).

81. Charles McCormick (1972), *Handbook of the law* (2nd ed.), § 297.

82. See, for example, People v. Houghteling, 455 N.W.2d 440 (Mich. Ct. App. 1990; admitted statement made 19 to 20 hours after the abusive event); Vargas v. State, 362 S.E.2d 461 (Ga. Ct. App. 1987; admitting statement made 4 months after the abuse). See also Whitcomb, *supra* note 67; Myers, *supra* note 74, at 166-169.

In permitting the introduction of a 3-year-old's statements to his mother as well as a police detective about 12 hours after the abuse, one court explained the rationale for liberally applying the excited utterance exception in child abuse cases: "[There] is a clear judicial trend to liberalize the requirements for an excited utterance when applied to young children victimized by sexual assaults. . . . As a three-year-old, truly in the age of innocence, he lacked the motive or reflective capacities to prevaricate the circumstances of the attack. . . . [T]he immediacy of each communication, considered in light of the available opportunities to express himself, satisfies the requirement of spontaneity." State v. Wagner, 508 N.E.2d 164, 166-167 (Ohio Ct. App.).

83. See, for example, State v. Allen, 755 P.2d 1153 (Ariz. 1988; statement made 2 months after alleged molestation did not qualify as excited utterance); Mounce v. Commonwealth, 795 S.W.2d 375 (Ky. 1990; statements made 9 to 23 days after alleged abusive act too remote).

84. See, for example, State v. Mateer, 383 N.W.2d 533 (Iowa 1986); State v. Wallace, 524 N.E.2d 466 (Ohio 1988).

85. Fed. R. Evid. 803(4). See, for example, State v. Janda, 397 N.W.2d 59 (N.D. 1986; admitting statements to a nurse); State v. Verley, 809 P.2d 723 (Or. Ct. App. 1991; admitting

statements to a hospital social worker). But see State v. Harris, 808 P.2d 453 (Mont. 1991; refusing to extend exception beyond medical doctors).

See generally Myers, *supra* note 74, at 221-223; Robert Mosteller (1989), "Child sexual abuse and statements for the purposes of medical diagnosis and treatment," *North Carolina Law Review, 67,* 257, for a discussion of the medical diagnosis and treatment exception in child abuse cases.

86. State v. Butler, 766 P.2d 505 (Wa. Ct. App. 1989).

87. 406 N.W.2d 385 (Wis. 1987), *cert. denied,* 110 S. Ct. 835 (1990).

88. See Mosteller, *supra* note 85; Myers, *supra* note 74, at 221-223.

89. Fed. R. Evid. 803 (24) states:

> A statement not specifically covered by any of the following exceptions but having equivalent circumstantial guarantees of trustworthiness, if the court determines that: (A) the statement is offered as evidence of a material fact; (B) the statement is more probative on the point for which it is offered that any other evidence which the proponent can procure through reasonable efforts; and (C) the general purpose of these rules and the interests of justice will best be served by admission of the statement into evidence. [See also Myers, *supra* note 74, § 7.42.]

90. Whitcomb, *supra* note 67; Josephine Bulkley (1992), "Recent Supreme Court decisions ease child abuse prosecutions: Use of closed-circuit television and children's statements of abuse under the confrontation clause," *Nova Law Review, 16,* 687, 689-690.

91. Idaho v. Wright, 110 S. Ct. 3139 (1990); State v. Ryan, 691 P.2d 197 (Wa. 1984); Bulkley, *supra* note 65; Myers, *supra* note 74, § 7.43 & § 7.53.

92. *Id.* at 89-92. See Myers, *supra* note 74, at 270-272; Whitcomb, *supra* note 67.

93. See State v. Swan, 790 P.2d 610 (Wash. 1990), *cert. denied* 111 S. Ct. 752 (1991), for an extensive discussion of the types of evidence that can be used as corroboration.

94. Ohio v. Roberts, 448 U.S. 56 (1980). *Roberts* indicated that reliability may be inferred if a statement falls within a firmly rooted exception. This was upheld in *Idaho v. Wright,* 110 S. Ct. 3139 (1990), although the Supreme Court also held that statements offered under nonfirmly rooted exceptions, such as the residual exception, are presumptively *unreliable* unless the state proves they possess "particularized guarantees of trustworthiness."

95. Fed. R. Evid. 702.

96. For other discussions of these issues, see Bulkley, *supra* note 75; Myers, *supra* note 74, § 3 & § 4; Josephine Bulkley (1992), "The prosecution's use of social science expert testimony in child sexual abuse cases: National trends and recommendations," *Journal of Child Sexual Abuse, 1,* 73; John E. B. Myers et al. (1989), "Expert testimony in child sexual abuse litigation," *Nebraska Law Review, 68,* 1; Josephine A. Bulkley (1988), "Psychological expert testimony in child sexual abuse cases," in *Sexual abuse allegations in custody and visitation cases* (p. 191) (B. Nicholson with J. Bulkley, eds.).

97. See State v. Smith, 564 P.2d 1154 (Wash. 1977); Emmons v. State, 807 P.2d 718 (Nev. 1991); State v. Hollingsworth, 467 N.W.2d 555 (Wis. Ct. App. 1991; Milwaukee Dept. of Social Services caseworker qualified as an expert on parenting skills).

98. Delay in disclosing sexual abuse is one of five elements of the child sexual abuse accommodation syndrome described by Roland Summit (1983) in *Child Abuse & Neglect, 7,* 177.

99. See Myers et al., *supra* note 96; Bulkley, *supra* note 96.

100. State v. Milbradt, 756 P.2d 620 (Ore. 1988).

101. Gary Melton & Susan Limber (1989), "Psychologists' involvement in cases of child maltreatment: Limits of role and expertise," *American Psychologist, 44,* 1225, 1229.

102. See, for example, State v. Petrich, 683 P.2d 96 (Wash. 1983).

103. James Peters & William Murphy (1992), "Profiling child sexual abusers: Legal considerations," *Criminal Justice and Behavior, 19,* 38. The California exception is People v. Stoll, 783 P.2d 698 (Ca. 1986), which is criticized by Peters and Murphy.

104. McCormick, *supra* note 81, § 190, at 447. The Federal Rules of Evidence state that prior acts evidence "is not admissible to prove the character of a person in order to show that he acted in conformity therewith." Fed. R. Evid. 404(b).

For a more thorough discussion of prior acts evidence see Myers, *supra* note 74, § 6, at 1-78; Edward Imwinkelried, *Uncharged misconduct evidence* (1984 & 1992 Supp.); Chris Hutton (1989), "Commentary: Prior bad acts evidence in cases of sexual contact with a child," *South Dakota Law Review, 34,* 604; John E. B. Myers (1988), "Uncharged misconduct evidence in child abuse litigation," *1988 Utah Law Review,* p. 479; Amber Donner-Froelich (1985), "Other crimes evidence to prove the corpus delicti of a child sexual offense" [Comment], *University of Miami Law Review,* *40,* 217.

105. McCormick, *supra* note 81, § 190, at 447; Fed. R. Evid. 404(a). The prejudicial implication that a defendant might have committed an act merely because he or she is the type of person thought to commit such acts is generally found to outweigh any probative value of the evidence. Propensity evidence is admissible, however, if a defendant has placed his or her character into contention (i.e., by maintaining that he or she is not the type of person to commit such an act).

106. Prior acts include both prior convictions and past uncharged misconduct. The prior acts may have occurred with the same victim or with other victims of the defendant.

107. McCormick, *supra* note 81, § 190, at 448-452; Fed. R. Evid. 404(b).

108. McCormick, *supra* note 81, § 190, at 453.

109. Imwinkelried, *supra* note 104, at 36-52; State v. Ray, 806 P.2d 1220 (Wash. 1991; prior acts admissible to show lustful disposition of defendant); State v. McCarty, 392 S.E.2d 359 (N.C. 1990; prior act admissible to show unnatural lust of defendant).

110. Imwinkelried, *supra* note 104, at 37.

111. *Id.* at 37-38.

112. Lannan v. State, 600 N.E.2d 1334 (Ind. 1992).

113. In some jurisdictions that have adopted the Federal Rules, courts have held that the Rules prohibit use of the sexual deviance or misconduct disposition exceptions. See Imwinkelried, *supra* note 109, at 50; Lannan v. State, 600 N.E.2d 1334 (Ind. 1992); Getz v. State, 538 A.2d 726 (Del. 1988); State v. Zybach, 44 Crim. L. Rep. (BNA) 2091 (Or. Ct. App. 1988).

114. Rule 414. Evidence of Similar Crimes in Child Molestation Cases: (a) In a criminal case in which the defendant is accused of an offense of child molestation, evidence of the defendant's commission of another offense or offenses of child molestation is admissible and may be considered for its bearing on any matter to which it is relevant. 137 Cong. Rec. S3212 (daily ed. Mar. 13, 1991).

115. This section is adapted from Feller, *supra* note 5, at 40-41.

116. Michael Graham, *Handbook of federal evidence,* Section 601.2 (1981); Weinstein on Evidence, Section 601-610 (1985).

117. Wheeler v. United States, 159 U.S. 523 (1895); Myers, *supra* note 14, at 55 (1987); Gary B. Melton et al., "Competency of children to testify," in *Child sexual abuse and the law* (p. 125) (J. Bulkley, ed.).

118. Josephine A. Bulkley (1992, October), "Abolishment of mandatory competency tests for child witnesses," *ABA Juvenile & Child Welfare Law Reporter, 11,* 125; Whitcomb, *supra* note 67, at 55-57.

119. *Id.*

120. *Id.* at 57.

121. State v. Superior Court, 719 P. 2d 283 (Ariz. Ct. App. 1986).

122. Bulkley, *supra* note 11, at 166-172; Wigmore, *Evidence in trials at common law,* Section 509 (1979); McCormick, *supra* note 81, § 62-71; Gary Melton (1981), "Children's competency to testify," *Law and Human Behavior, 5,* 73; Josephine Bulkley, American Bar Association (1982), "Recommendations for improving legal intervention," in *Child sexual abuse cases;* Ross Eatman & Josephine Bulkley, American Bar Association (1986), *Protecting child victim/witnesses: Sample laws and materials.*

123. Melton & Thompson, *supra* note 71; Josephine A. Bulkley (1989), "The impact of new child witness research on child sexual abuse prosecutions," in *Perspectives on children's testimony* (p. 208) (S. Ceci, D. Ross, & M. Toglia, eds.); Karen Saywitz (1994), American Bar Association, "Children in court: Principles of child development for judicial application," in *A judicial primer on child sexual abuse* (pp. 15, 41) (J. Bulkley & C. Sandt, eds.).

124. Myers, *supra* note 14, at 54 (1987) & 4 (Cum. Suppl. 1991).

125. Melton & Thompson, *supra* note 71; "Symposium on child sexual abuse prosecutions: The current state of the art" (1985), *University of Miami Law Review, 40;* Bulkley, *supra* note 11; Bulkley, *supra* note 65.

126. See *infra* note 69.

127. 102 S. Ct. 2613 (1982).

128. 110 S. Ct. 3157, 3169 (1990).

129. *Id.*

130. 107 S. Ct. 2658 (1987).

131. White v. Illinois, 112 S. Ct. 736 (1992); Idaho v. Wright, 110 S. Ct. 3139 (1990).

16

Interviewing Children in and out of Court

Current Research and Practice Implications

KAREN J. SAYWITZ

GAIL S. GOODMAN

What do we know about children's abilities to provide accurate eyewitness testimony? Until recently, scientific data were surprisingly sparse. However, beginning in the mid-1980s, the study of child victim/witnesses began to grow at an astounding rate; now it is a worldwide endeavor. When Melton (1981) published one of the first modern reviews of psychological research on children's testimony, only one contemporary empirical study directly addressing children's eyewitness memory was cited. Today, entire books and journal issues are devoted to research on this topic (e.g., Dent & Flin, 1992; Goodman, 1984; Goodman & Bottoms, 1993; Perry & Wrightsman, 1991; Spencer & Flin, 1990). Important research currently is being undertaken not only in the United States but also in England (e.g., Davies & Noon, 1991), Scotland (Flin, 1993), New Zealand (e.g., Pipe, Gee, & Wilson, 1993), Australia (e.g., Brennan & Brennan, 1988; Bussey, Lee, & Grimbeek, 1993), Canada (e.g., Sas, Hurley, Austin, & Wolfe, 1991), and elsewhere.

There are several reasons why understanding children's testimony is important and worthy of investigation. For example, exploration of children's testimony provides us with new insights into memory development. But aside from

AUTHORS' NOTE: Support for the writing of this chapter was provided by grants from the National Center on Child Abuse and Neglect.

theoretical reasons, pressing practical issues motivate the study of child witnesses; these practical issues add urgency and consequence to research endeavors.

Perhaps the most salient of the practical reasons concerns reports of child sexual abuse. It is estimated that in 1990 in the United States alone, 434,066 children were foci of reports of sexual abuse (U.S. Department of Health and Human Services, 1992). A very large number of these cases are likely to involve interviews of children; the children's statements will influence whether they receive protection or whether the case is deemed unfounded. In addition, an unknown number of children are questioned each year more informally by parents, relatives, therapists, teachers, doctors, and others about suspicions of abuse. The results of these interviews also will determine the number of children who receive protection and strongly influence the number of cases that come to the attention of social service and legal authorities. The study of children's testimony concerns in large part the accuracy and completeness of children's reports during such interviews.

In addition, although children are questioned more often in forensic investigations than in court, children take the stand at times. When they do, their testimony can influence whether justice prevails. National statistics concerning the number of child sexual abuse victims who testify in criminal or family court do not exist, but relevant information is available, at least in regard to criminal court. Such information indicates considerable variability across jurisdictions in the number of child sexual abuse cases prosecuted and the number of children who testify. For example, Smith (1993) recently conducted a national telephone survey of 530 district attorneys' offices; she uncovered a large range (1 to 800; $M = 66$) in the number of child sexual assault cases prosecuted by each office.

Rogers (1980) followed 261 child sexual abuse cases reported to the police in the District of Columbia and discovered that few children testified at trial. However, corroboration laws in Washington, D.C. undoubtedly limited the number of child sexual abuse cases that went to trial and the number of cases in which children testified. When corroboration (e.g., physical evidence, an eyewitness) is required, fewer cases are prosecuted, and, for those brought to trial, the child vic-

tim's testimony is not as necessary. In contrast to the picture provided by Rogers's study, Sas et al. (1991) substantiated that 50% of the nearly 150 children involved in research on preparing children for court later testified either at trial or in some type of preliminary hearing. Again, however, variability appears to be the rule. In a study of child sexual assault prosecutions in eight jurisdictions around the United States, Gray (1993) found that in several jurisdictions, children usually testified at grand jury hearings or preliminary hearings, but in other jurisdictions they did not. Cases were more likely to go to trial if the child was 5 to 6 years of age than if the child was older or younger.

These studies remind us that children do testify in court at times and that even if a case never reaches the trial stage, children may be required to provide eyewitness reports during investigative interviews or during competency examinations, grand jury hearings, or preliminary hearings. A focus on the number of children who testify at trial underestimates the number of children who provide information in forensic interviews and who serve as witnesses in courts of law at pretrial stages. At least in some jurisdictions, a relatively large percentage of children involved as victim/witnesses in sexual assault prosecutions do take the stand, even in trials.

In sum, there are important theoretical and practical reasons to study children's testimony. Given the complexities and seriousness of child sexual abuse charges and the fact that the case may boil down to a child's word against an adult's, the accuracy of children's testimony and the best way to obtain children's statements become matters of substantial societal concern. When one considers that the term *children's testimony* applies as much to children who are interviewed in a forensic, social service, therapeutic, school, or family setting as to children who testify in court, the importance of the topic is magnified.

In this chapter, we provide readers with a survey of some of the recent findings from child-witness research. We also draw practical implications of the studies for professionals who interview and evaluate children in actual cases. Although our review is not comprehensive, we trust that it will provide readers with the flavor of current empirical work and inform readers of child witnesses' abilities and needs.

We first discuss research concerning children's memory and suggestibility, particularly as they relate to child sexual abuse investigations. We next consider children's communicative competence— that is, their language and communication abilities—as they relate to children's testimony. We turn then to the topic of children in court, focusing special attention on ways to improve the investigative and courtroom process for children. Finally, we discuss practical implications of current research.

Memory and Suggestibility

The ability to provide accurate testimony depends on being able to remember and communicate memories to others. Research consistently indicates that the amount of information a witness reports about an event generally increases with age (e.g., Goodman & Reed, 1986; Leippe, Romanczyk, & Manion, 1992; Marin, Holmes, Guth, & Kovac, 1979), and young children (e.g., preschoolers) are often more suggestible than older children and adults (Goodman & Aman, 1991). Nevertheless, even young children do not necessarily have poor memories, and they are not necessarily highly suggestible. Memory abilities and the ability to resist suggestion typically vary at any age, be it childhood or adulthood, depending on situational and personality factors. These abilities are not stable even within a particular person but instead can change depending on a number of factors, including (a) the type of event experienced, (b) the type of information to be recounted, (c) the conditions surrounding an interview, (d) the strength of the memory, (e) the language used, and (f) postevent influences. It is precisely because memory and suggestibility are such complex, variable processes that researchers have devoted so much time and energy to studying them.

One source of variability in a person's memory and suggestibility concerns the context in which he or she is questioned.

One source of variability in a person's memory and suggestibility concerns the

context in which he or she is questioned. For example, a context can provide physical reminders of an incident, as when a witness is brought back to the scene of the crime. A context also can provide a socioemotional milieu that can support or interfere with accurate and complete reporting of a child's memory. It is widely believed that children's abilities are more affected by contextual factors than are the abilities of adults (e.g., Donaldson, 1979). Partly because contextual factors can play a large role in influencing eyewitness accuracy, one cannot rely on age alone to judge a witness' report. Although 3-year-olds cannot be expected to reach the same intellectual heights as do adults, age differences often can be magnified or minimized, depending on the context of interviewing.

Free recall and open-ended questions. One robust finding from the research literature is that free recall (a narrative provided in response to an open-ended question, such as "What happened?") is typically the most accurate form of memory report (e.g., see Dent & Stephenson, 1979). When an interviewer asks a broad, open-ended question, the information provided by the witness must come mainly, if not completely, from the witness' own mind and, ideally, from the witness' own experience. One problem, however, is that such reports predictably are the most circumscribed, especially when young children are questioned. A rather frustrating form of circumscribed free recall is evidenced commonly by timid 2- or 3-year-olds: It is not atypical for a very young child to answer "Nothing" to the question "What happened?" even though the child can demonstrate memory of an incident when asked more specifically about it. Some young children will even respond "Nothing" when interviewed about very significant real-life events that clearly happened (e.g., the child almost died after attempted murder). The problem for the interviewer, then, is that it can be difficult to determine, based solely on young child's free recall, whether something major or inconsequential occurred.

Although open-ended questions typically are recommended at least for the initial interview queries, recent research indicates that open-ended questions can elicit very inaccurate reports from a small number of children. For example, in a study by Goodman and Aman (1991), one young boy who had played games with a man later reported a wild adventure story of how the man and he had played cowboys and Indians, how he had been tied up, and so on. In this case, the child appeared to make up a story, but errors in free recall also can occur when the "wrong" event (an event that actually occurred but is not of interest to the interviewer) is described by the child. The "wrong" event may be one of significance to the child, such as a particularly frightening or happy event in the child's life. Thus, although free recall is most likely to lead to an accurate, albeit limited, statement, it is not guaranteed to do so.

Moreover, recent research indicates another possible source of error in free recall reports. An accusatory context may lead to inaccuracies in free recall and spontaneous statements by some preschool children. For example, Tobey and Goodman (1992) found that a small percentage of 4-year-olds make inaccurate, spontaneous statements when led by a police officer to think that a baby-sitter did something wrong. The accusatory context led one child to make such spontaneous statements as "the baby-sitter might have had a gun" and to answer "yes" when asked if the baby-sitter was mean (even when he or she was not). Nevertheless, in this study, the accusatory context did not result in false reports of abuse, even when children were asked leading abuse-related questions.

A few recent studies also indicate that the free recall of young children can be distorted if repeatedly misleading questions are asked, especially if negative expectations about a person have been created in the child's mind (Clarke-Stewart, Thompson, & Lepore, 1989; Leichtman & Ceci, 1995). For example, Leichtman and Ceci (1995) gave preschool children a negative stereotype of a man (i.e., that he was clumsy through repeated suggestions). The man then came to the children's class for a few minutes, where he did nothing wrong. Once a week for 4 weeks, the children were given misleading questions about the man's behavior; finally, the children were interviewed. When asked a free recall question at the start of the interview, 46% of the 3- to 4-year-olds and 30% of the 5- to 6-year-olds inaccurately recalled that the man did clumsy things. When probed further, up to 72% of the 3- to 4-year-olds made errors. However, only 21% of the younger children and less than 10% of the 5-year-

olds made the same type of claims when gently challenged what they really had seen.

Note that this study involved children who were bystanders to a neutral event and that neither the questions asked nor the statements made by the children concerned acts of abuse. Moreover, there were no anticipated consequences for the children of being accurate or not. Nevertheless, the study does show that if young children are interviewed repeatedly with false suggestions in an accusatory context, false information might intrude into young children's free recall. The findings also could be interpreted to suggest that, for preschoolers who actually suffered abuse, repeated suggestions that abuse did not occur might result in recantation, even in free recall or response to open-ended questions.

Specific questions, leading questions, and suggestibility. Despite demonstrations that young children's free recall can be inaccurate at times, typically, young children's responses to open-ended questions provide accurate but overly succinct information rather than error-ridden information. How can one obtain more information from children? The obvious answer is to ask children specific or directive questions. The amount of information one obtains is increased when children are asked specifically about information of interest (e.g., "Did you go to Uncle Bob's house?") or when their memory is triggered by physical cues (e.g., a picture of the child's home or preschool). A cost of this form of more detailed questioning and cuing, however, is that inaccuracies may increase, too (Dent & Stephenson, 1979), although researchers typically have not reported whether the inaccuracies are for trivial details or more significant actions.

In any case, how easily inaccuracies are obtained from children when specific questions are asked is a controversial issue. Moreover, the relative costs versus benefits of asking children more specific questions, especially leading questions in regard to abuse, are still largely unknown. Complicating the issue further, legal and mental health professionals often use the terms *specific questions* and *leading questions* differently. Although mental health professionals might think of a question such as "Did you go to Uncle Bob's house?" or "What else did you do?" as specific but not leading, legal professionals might argue that such questions are leading. Many professionals would probably agree on what constitutes highly coercive, strongly leading interviewing of children and that such interviewing is to be avoided, but there are gray areas around which debate more reasonably centers.

Because children often say little in free recall and more specific questioning can be controversial, in an actual case, "to lead or not to lead" becomes a crucial question. Those who argue that specific questions should not be asked of children want to reduce errors of false report; however, errors of nonreporting of abuse—that is, errors of omission—also must be considered. A study by Saywitz, Goodman, Nicholas, and Moan (1991) indicated that, when not asked specific questions about genital touch, the occurrence of omission errors was high, but when the children were asked specific questions about genital touch, the occurrence of false reports was relatively low (at least when 5- and 7-year-old children were interviewed in a neutral context). Children who had experienced genital touch by a doctor during a medical examination omitted the fact that they had experienced vaginal and anal touch more than 60% of the time *unless* asked directly about it. On the other hand, for children who did not experience genital contact during the doctor examination, there was an 8% false-report rate when asked a leading, anatomically doll-aided question. These results indicate that 5- to 7-year-old children are not as prone to give false reports of abuse as formerly believed, even when a leading, anatomically doll-aided question is employed, although some children are more vulnerable than others to error. However, in a similar study, 2- and 3-year-olds were found to make a relatively high number of false reports (Bruck, Ceci, Francouer, & Renick, 1995). It should be noted that neither study included an accusatory context, highly leading questioning, or repeated interviews, all of which could have changed the results.

Asking children directive, possibly leading questions raises the issue of children's suggestibility. As mentioned above, suggestibility varies considerably across individuals and situations, even within a specific age group. Children, like adults, are more likely to give incorrect reports and to be more suggestible about peripheral or poorly retained information than about more salient, memorable informa-tion. Abusive genital contact is likely to be a fairly salient event for a child; therefore, children are likely to be less suggestible about such actions. Nevertheless, young children (e.g., 3-year-olds) appear to conform to suggestive questions relating to abuse more often than older children, at least under the types of situations often studied in child testimony research (e.g., Goodman & Aman, 1991). Perhaps young children do not yet fully realize the impropriety of most genital touch and thus are not as taken aback by such questions as older children seem to be. Even by age 4 or 5, many nonabused children show signs of surprise or embarrassment when asked whether a stranger removed the child's clothes or was naked. In addition, intimidation can add to young children's suggestibility about abuse-related events, and younger children appear to be more easily intimidated. A supportive context may be especially important in bolstering young children's resistance to suggestive misinformation about abuse (Goodman, Bottoms, Schwartz-Kenney, & Rudy, 1991).

Trauma and memory. Many would agree that sexual abuse can be a traumatic experience for a child, yet most studies of children's testimony do not concern the effects of trauma on memory. A number of researchers are now studying children's and adults' memories for stressful events. Whereas the psychological lore used to be that stress had a debilitating effect on memory (e.g., Loftus, 1979), and some researchers still adhere to that view (Ceci & Bruck, 1993), recent work supports the notion that core features of highly emotional events are retained in memory with particular durability, although peripheral details may or may not be as strongly encoded or retained (Christiansson, 1992).

Findings from several studies of children's memory for stressful events are consistent with the view that core features of stressful events are retained especially well in memory. For example, Goodman and her colleagues (Goodman, Hepps, & Reed, 1986; Goodman, Hirschman, Hepps, & Rudy, 1991) found that distress was associated with children's more complete recall and greater resistance to suggestion. Warren-Leubecker (1991) reported that children who were more upset about the space shuttle Challenger disaster retained the event better in memory than children who were less upset. Steward (1992) found that compared to children who were less distressed during painful medical procedures, children who were more upset reported a greater amount and more accurate information at a 6-month postevent interview, although some highly stressed children were particularly incorrect. On the other hand, some researchers (e.g., those who test children's memory for information not integral to the stressor) report decrements in memory (Bugental, Blue, Cortez, Fleck, & Rodriguez, 1992; Peters, 1991).

Thus, stressful events may be associated with particularly strong memories, but memories that are in certain ways inaccurate. In a series of fascinating clinical studies (Pynoos & Eth, 1984; Pynoos & Nader, 1988; Terr, 1991) concerning children's memories for such horrifying events as homicides of loved ones, kidnappings, and sniper attacks on schools, both accuracies and inaccuracies were noted. Moreover, certain children may remember stressful events more accurately than others. Important individual differences in children's processing of a stressful event are just beginning to be uncovered (Goodman, Batterman-Faunce, Quas, Riddlesberger, & Kuhn, 1994; Ornstein, Baker-Ward, Gordon, & Merritt, 1993). Emotional forces, as yet not fully understood, may affect memory for highly traumatic events. Further research clearly is needed.

In regard to trauma and memory, of considerable recent interest has been the topic of "repressed memories." Can a traumatic event, such as child sexual abuse or witnessing a murder, be inaccessible to consciousness for years, only for the memory to reemerge vividly later? Freud and others believed that traumatic memories can be so distressing that psychic forces keep such memories out of consciousness. But some authorities doubt that repressed memories for entire traumatic events are likely to exist and point instead to suggestive questioning as the basis for "repressed memory" reports (Loftus, 1992). In a recent study, adults were instructed to convince a relative that the relative had been lost in a shopping mall as a child (Pickell, in press). One fourth of the relatives were led to recall what may have been a false memory of being lost in a mall as a child. However, in an extension of this work, researchers could not create false memories of events that more closely resemble sexual abuse, such as childhood enemas (Pezdek, 1995). Hence, false memories of child-

hood abuse may be difficult to induce. Furthermore, there is preliminary evidence that incidents of childhood sexual abuse can be forgotten temporarily or even permanently. Briere and Conte (1993) interviewed 450 women and men with alleged histories of child sexual victimization. More than 50% of the sample stated that, at least at some point in childhood, they had experienced periods of partial to total amnesia for the sexual abuse. Feldman-Summers and Pope (1994) surveyed 500 psychologists regarding their memories of childhood abuse (physical and sexual). Forty percent of the participants who reported having experienced

Forty percent of the participants who reported having experienced some form of childhood abuse also reported that there was a period of time when they could not remember some or all of the abuse.

some form of childhood abuse also reported that there was a period of time when they could not remember some or all of the abuse. Of the participants who reported forgotten abuse, 47% reported that they found corroboration for the memory.

Linda Meyers Williams (1994) recently published data from interviews of women who as children were treated at a hospital emergency room in cases of sexual abuse. Approximately 38% of the women evidenced no memory for the earlier emergency room visit or for the sexual assault. Williams provides fascinating case examples, indicating that repressed memory for traumatic events can occur, especially if a child is under 7 years of age at the time of the trauma. Moreover, based on clinical study, Terr (1991) reported that memories of repeated traumas may become repressed, whereas one-time traumatic events tend to be retained with clarity; unfortunately, empirical support for this interesting proposal remains scant.

However, these data do not rule out the possible falsehood of some claims of child sexual abuse or other early traumas. For example, in one recent study, adults reported memories from the first year of life when pressured for details with repeated questioning while being instructed to visualize and focus on the event (Malinoski et al., 1995). Research on the well-established phenomenon of infantile amnesia indicates that it is unlikely that memories for events that occurred in the first year of life can become consciously accessible in adulthood (Usher & Neisser, 1993). Even in childhood, such memories become quickly lost to consciousness. For example, in a study of documented childhood traumatic events (including child sexual abuse), Terr (1988) found that when children were under the age of approximately 2.5 to 3 years at the time of the trauma, they did not have consciously accessible memories for it later. Instead, very early trauma was more likely to lead to personality change or behavioral memories that incorporated elements of the trauma. Thus, cases in which memories of abuse experienced in the first year of life are recovered may lead one to question the validity of the report. Overall, however, at present we do not know how to distinguish true from false reports of repressed memories or true from false claims of sexual abuse in general.

Perhaps the most controversial claims of repressed memory come in the form of allegations of ritualistic child abuse. Adults have reported such horrific childhood events as (a) being sexually abused by groups of satanists, (b) being impregnated and forced to have abortions so that satanists could use the fetuses in rituals, and (c) being required to murder other children. Often, such reports involve repressed memories that emerge in therapy; therapists have been likely to believe such reports, even in the absence of hard evidence (Bottoms, Shaver, & Goodman, in press). Although some individuals or even small groups may commit acts of abuse in the name of Satan, there is no evidence for a large satanic conspiracy of child abusers (Lanning, 1991). However, it is also possible, perhaps likely, that for some cases involving allegations of ritualistic abuse, there is truth to at least part of the report. In other words, some form of abuse may have occurred, even if the satanic components are false. A continuum exists from cases involving individual perpetrators in which evidence for abuse has been obtained to suspect (atypical) cases involving highly leading questioning of children and adults.

In summary, research indicates that even young children can under certain conditions provide accurate testimony, especially when interviewed in a supportive manner that does not involve highly suggestive accusatory contexts. However, young children can be expected on average to make more errors in their statements than adults do. Substantial individual differences exist at all ages. Children may have particularly vivid memories for traumatic events, such as invasive genital touch, but may need to be asked specifically about such touch to reveal that it occurred. False memories, misperceptions, and errors in reporting of traumatic events also can occur. Preschoolers are often more susceptible to error and pose greater challenges for interviewers in attempts to obtain accurate and complete reports.

Children's Communicative Competence

It is through the spoken word that children typically are required to express their memories. Even when a child's memory is accurate and strong, efforts to elicit reliable reports from children may be frustrated by developmental limitations on communication. Only gradually do children master articulation, vocabulary, grammar, and conversational rules of everyday speech. From birth to 10 years of age, children learn to discriminate and articulate sounds, comprehend increasingly more complicated questions, and produce increasingly more complex and intelligible responses. Hence, much of the difficulties posed by child witnesses can be a function of children misunderstanding adult questions and adults misinterpreting children's answers.

To learn to communicate, children rely on familiar adults to structure conversations. They depend on familiar environments to glean meaning from context. With age, children learn to communicate effectively, regardless of the familiarity of the listener or setting. Initially, language serves only a limited number of functions, such as identifying objects and locations. With maturation and experience, language comes to serve a wide array of functions, including the exchange of information via question-answering. In the forensic context, the exchange of information follows unique and unfamiliar rules for sociolinguistic interaction in an unfamiliar setting (Walker, 1993). Given these conditions, the communication demands of the system can be poorly matched to the child's stage of language development. Even older children may not communicate at their optimal level of functioning under such conditions. Recent studies have begun to examine children's abilities to communicate in the forensic setting. The linguistic complexity, vocabulary, and content of questions have been investigated as have children's comprehension skills.

Linguistic complexity. Recent studies suggest that many types of grammatical constructions are not mastered by young children but are replete in the conversation of the courtroom. In one study, children's abilities to repeat questions drawn from the transcripts of same-aged child witnesses were tested (Brennan & Brennan, 1988; Walker, 1993). Repetitions were categorized by the degree to which error in repetition (e.g., rephrasing) captured the sense of the original question. Results revealed children misunderstand many common courtroom question types. Such question types often are referred to as *legalese*. Legalese contains lengthy compound sentences fraught with independent and embedded clauses and grammatical constructions that are beyond the comprehension and memory of many children under 8 years of age. Serious miscommunications can result; for example, when children are asked abuse-related questions in legalese, error rates increase substantially (Carter, 1991).

Vocabulary. Other researchers have tested children's knowledge of legal terminology. Results suggest that children under 8 to 10 years of age misunderstand or fail to comprehend many legal terms commonly used with children in and out of court (Flin, Stevenson, & Davies, 1989; Saywitz, Jaenicke, & Camparo, 1990). For example, young children tend to make auditory discrimination errors, mistaking an unfamiliar legal term for a similar sounding familiar word—for example, interpreting jury as jewelry ("that stuff my mom wears around her neck and on her finger") or journey ("a trip") (Saywitz et al., 1990). They also make errors by assuming a familiar nonlegal definition is the operative definition in the forensic context. For example, children maintained that "a court is a place to play basketball," "a hearing is something you do

with your ears," and "charges are something you do with a credit card" (Saywitz et al., 1990). Word choice and grammatical construction are critical factors in eliciting accurate reports from children, whether in the courtroom or in an investigative interview.

Content. Researchers are beginning to examine children's abilities to respond to questions that contain particular content and thus require specific cognitive skills or learning experiences. For example, forensic questions often require witnesses to pinpoint time or location and estimate height or weight by using conventional systems of measurement (e.g., minutes, hours, dates, feet, inches, pounds). Studies suggest that these skills are learned gradually over the course of the elementary school years (Brigham, Vanverst, & Bothwell, 1986; Davies, Stevenson, & Flin, 1988; Friedman, 1982; Saywitz et al., 1991). As discussed later, children may try to answer questions that require skills they have not yet developed. For example, young witnesses might be asked the time or day of an occurrence before they have learned to tell time, skills typically mastered around 7 to 8 years of age (Freidman, 1982). The type of information requested in a question can be an important determinant of the accuracy of children's responses.

Comprehension. Children's abilities to monitor their comprehension and identify misunderstandings are taxed heavily in the forensic context. Recent studies suggest that children being questioned about a past event may try to answer questions they do not fully understand (Saywitz & Snyder, 1993). They respond to a part of the question that they understand, typically the beginning or the end of a lengthy question, knowing that it is their turn in the conversation. However, their response is not necessarily the answer to the intended question. They follow the everyday rules of being a "good" conversational partner instead of the unique sociolinguistic rules for exchanging evidentiary information.

Although preschoolers have been shown to recognize comprehension difficulties and implement strategies for resolving them, they do so mainly in naturalistic settings on simple, familiar, nonverbal tasks (Gallagher, 1981; Revelle, Wellman, & Karabenik, 1985). In contrast, when settings, tasks, and stimuli are complex, unfamiliar, and verbal, young children may not know when they have failed to understand. In such situations, they rarely request clarification from adults (Asher, 1976; Markman, 1977; Patterson, Massad, & Cosgrove, 1978). Because the forensic context typically represents a complex, unfamiliar situation that relies heavily on verbal exchange, children can be expected to display *comprehension monitoring* difficulties.

Currently, researchers are beginning to develop techniques for improving children's abilities to respond accurately to forensic questions (Bull, 1995; Fisher & McCauley, 1995; Saywitz, Geiselman, & Bornstein, 1992; Saywitz & Snyder, 1993). One recent study suggests that through instruction and preparation, children can be taught to indicate their lack of comprehension and ask for rephrasing of questions, thus improving the resulting accuracy of their reports (Saywitz & Snyder, 1993). After participating in a scripted school activity, 6- to 8-year-olds were interviewed with questions that varied in comprehensibility from easy to difficult. One group of children was instructed, prior to the interview, to tell the interviewer when they did not understand a question. Their interview responses were significantly more accurate than those of children in a control group who were given only motivating instructions to do their best. A third group of children was prepared for the interview with an intervention that involved practicing, with feedback, asking for rephrases of questions about a videotaped vignette they had viewed previously. Later, their reports of the school activity were significantly more accurate than those from children in the other two groups.

In summary, studies suggest that the quality of a child's report depends on the competence of the questioner to ask questions in language children can comprehend about concepts they can understand. It also depends on the child's ability to detect and cope with noncomprehension, a skill that may be enhanced through instruction and preparation.

Children in Court

Children's increased participation in legal settings has brought considerable public and legislative attention not only to children's eyewitness memory but also to children's emotional capability to withstand legal proceedings. Courtrooms are austere, formal settings capable of intimidating adults, not to mention children. What do children know about the legal system, how does participation in it affect them, and what can be done to aid children while still protecting the rights of the accused?

Children's Legal Knowledge

A flourish of research activity in the past 5 years has aimed to document children's expectations and fears of the legal system. Studies tend to show that children possess limited legal knowledge. They possess misunderstandings and unrealistic as well as realistic fears of the legal process (Cashmore & Bussey, 1990; Flin et al., 1989; Melton, Limber, Jacobs, & Oberlander, 1992; Saywitz, 1989; Warren-Leubecker, Tate, Hinton, & Ozbek, 1989). As might be expected, with age, children show increasing knowledge of legal terms. One might suspect this comes from greater exposure to legal concepts. Although that is undoubtedly true, developmental differences in legal knowledge are not just a matter of exposure. Two studies indicate that child witnesses who had been involved directly in the legal system showed less accurate knowledge and more confusion than agemates without legal experience (Melton et al., 1992; Saywitz, 1989). However, the studies did not control completely for potentially confounding effects of socioeconomic status or psychological dysfunction.

Studies have found that by 10 years of age, most children understand the basics of the investigative and judicial process. They grasp the functions of the various court personnel as well as rudimentary notions of legal representation and the adversarial process. Younger children, 4 to 7 years of age, are aware of court personnel, but their conceptualizations are based on observations of overt behavior (e.g., "The judge is there to sit at a high desk and bang the hammer. He wears a black gown; I don't know why."). They may not be aware that the judge is in charge of the courtroom. They have little conception of invisible abstractions, such as laws, rules of evidence, or trial procedures. Children under 10 years of age do not fully understand the decision-making role of the jury or judge, often assuming that jurors are mere spectators (Saywitz, 1989; Warren-Leubecker et al., 1989). On the other hand, children as young as 5 years of age understand the need to tell the truth in court (Cashmore & Bussey, 1990; Saywitz, 1989). Although younger children cite fear of punishment as the reason for telling the truth, older children understand the fact-finding purpose of the trial.

Many authors speculate that lack of knowledge can affect the quality of children's evidence adversely, because anxiety associated with fear of the unknown disrupts memory performance (Cashmore & Bussey, 1990; Flin, 1993; Melton & Thompson, 1987; Sas et al., 1991; Saywitz, 1989; Saywitz & Snyder, 1993). Studies have not yet shown a definitive link between lack of legal knowledge and poor memory performance in the forensic setting. Support for the hypothesis that fear disrupts memory performance comes from studies that concern eyewitness testimony when children are questioned in a courtroom (involving a simulated trial environment) compared to a school or a private room (Hill & Hill, 1987; Saywitz & Nathanson, 1993; Saywitz, Nathanson, Snyder, & Lamphear, 1993). These preliminary studies show impaired recall and greater physiological correlates of anxiety (heart rate variability) when children are questioned in a courtroom atmosphere. However, it is unclear from these studies if knowledge of courtroom procedures mediates the results.

Also germane are studies showing impaired performance on identification tasks associated with confrontational stress at the time of questioning (Dent, 1977; Peters, 1991).

It is also possible, however, that in actual trials, children who are more knowledgeable about the legal system will show greater anxiety than less knowledgeable agemates.

It is also possible, however, that in actual trials, children who are more knowledgeable about the legal system will show greater anxiety than less knowledgeable agemates because the former would know, for example, that an attempt would be made to discredit their testimony in court. Older children and girls have been found to express greater negativity about testifying than younger children and boys

(Goodman, Pyle-Taub, et al., 1992), and older children who experience harsh cross-examination in court fare less well emotionally (Whitcomb et al., 1992). Further research is needed to address the relation between legal knowledge, the stress of testifying, and eyewitness performance.

Fears of court expressed by both child witnesses and peers with little or no legal experience include fears of public speaking, losing self-control on the stand, and not being believed (Cashmore & Bussey, 1990; Sas et al., 1991; Saywitz & Nathanson, 1993). Children also express concern that as a witness they would have to prove their own innocence in court or be punished for making a mistake and even be sent to jail. In addition, child witnesses express fear of facing the accused in court, retaliation, and physical harm to self or loved ones, especially if threatened not to tell. In intrafamilial cases of abuse, children express fear of angering family members if negative consequences are anticipated, such as loss of income. Although many of these fears also are expressed by adult rape victims (Katz & Mazur, 1979), children's emotional immaturity is likely to make them more vulnerable than adults to these fears.

In summary, as might be expected, children are relatively naive about the intricacies of the legal system and even about common legal terms that are often used in court, and children have a number of fears about testifying. One could well question the adequacy of the courtroom as an ideal setting for obtaining complete and accurate testimony from children. Although the courtroom is also less than an ideal setting for adult victim/witnesses, children's emotional and cognitive immaturity places them at an even greater risk of adverse effects. Given that children may be required to become involved in legal investigations and testify, are there ways we can improve the current system? Are there ways we can help prepare children for the experience? Research concerning these questions will be discussed next.

Improving the Process

Researchers are investigating the efficacy of legal reforms thought to improve the investigative and judicial process (Whitcomb et al., 1992). The goal of these reforms is to elicit the most accurate information from children in the least stressful manner. The reforms include scientifically based techniques for interviewing children, special methods to prepare children for court, implementation of multidisciplinary interviewing teams, and use of innovative courtroom procedures, such as closed-circuit television. Below, we discuss the results of these initial efforts to improve the quality of children's testimony and reduce their stress.

Innovative questioning techniques. Many contemporary researchers are beginning to turn away from the documentation of children's deficits to the investigation of techniques that compensate for children's weaknesses and capitalize on their strengths. Recently, the *cognitive interview* has received considerable attention because of its potential as a possible means of obtaining detailed information from children in a nonleading format. The cognitive interview is a collection of memory enhancement techniques based on principles of cognitive psychology. It has been shown to elicit 35% more information from adults than standard police interviews (Geiselman & Fischer, 1989). The four basic retrieval aids that comprise the bulk of the cognitive interview are (a) mentally reconstructing the context at the time of the crime; (b) reporting even partial information, regardless of perceived importance; (c) recounting events in a variety of orders; and (d) reporting events from a variety of perspectives. In one study, these retrieval aids were modified and tested with 7- to 12-year-olds, resulting in a 26% improvement over standard police interviews and a 45% improvement when children were given practice using the retrieval aids prior to the interview (Saywitz et al., 1992).

Another new questioning technique, *narrative elaboration,* is designed to increase the detail and relevance of information children provide without the use of leading questions (Saywitz & Snyder, 1993; Saywitz et al., 1993). Before being asked to provide a narrative account of what happened, children are taught that their narrative should include a high level of detail regarding the following categories of information: (a) participants, (b) setting, (c) actions, and (d) conversation/affective states. Each category is represented by a simple drawing on a card (e.g., Participants: The *Who* card depicts a

stick figure; Setting: The *Where* card depicts a simple house and yard). First, children practice using the cards to remind themselves to include details from each category while retelling routine events (e.g., what they did yesterday). Then, they are asked to describe the event under investigation and use the cards to trigger recall of detail for each category. In one study, 6- to 11-year-olds trained in this technique provided 53% more accurate information in a narrative report of a past school activity than did children in a control group who received no intervention.

Although research on cognitive interview and narrative elaboration techniques indicates promise, these techniques remain to be tested on preschoolers, on reports of traumatic events or events children are hesitant to report, or over long delays.

Preparing children for court. Preparation is one of many factors that can influence children's testimony and their subjective experience of the process (see Spencer & Flin, 1990). Attorneys who prepare children for court typically include a tour of the courtroom and perhaps a cursory review of the facts of the case. Although preliminary studies suggest a tour of the courtroom is indeed beneficial for children in reducing anxiety (Goodman, Sachsenmaier, et al., 1992), these steps alone are not sufficient to prepare children for the communicative, cognitive, and emotional challenges witnesses face (Saywitz & Snyder, 1993). Moreover, young children's limited knowledge of the legal system leaves them ill-equipped to understand the context and function of their testimony. They possess a limited repertoire of coping strategies to prevent anxiety from interfering with ability to testify optimally.

Recently, court schools designed to prepare children for the judicial process have appeared around the country. Some are operated by the public law offices of the prosecutor or juvenile counsel and are sanctioned by the judicial administration. Others are operated by outside social service or mental health agencies. Typically, the content is focused on educating children about courtroom personnel and their functions. Sometimes, programs include anxiety reduction techniques as well. The degree to which the facts of individual cases are discussed during court school sessions seems to vary widely. However, some programs prepare children in groups and prohibit discussion of individual cases to avoid contamination of testimony.

By and large, the efficacy of such programs has not been tested empirically. Because there is little systematic evaluation of these programs, it is difficult to determine which, if any, of the components of these programs actually improve children's performances and reduce stress. Also, there is insufficient evidence that such efforts are free of side effects that could influence children's testimony in unintended ways. Recently, one such program has been subjected to a systematic evaluation (Sas et al., 1991). In Canada, 120 alleged victims of abuse received either status quo services from the Victim Witness Assistance Program or individual preparation focused on demystifying the process with education and anxiety reduction techniques such as relaxation training. Children receiving the experimental preparation gained more knowledge of the legal system, showed less generalized fears, and less abuse-specific fears (e.g., fears of revictimization). Nevertheless, group differences in fears of testifying or fears specific to court were not found.

From this study, the effects of preparation on the accuracy of children's testimony could not be evaluated. This is because there was no record of the crime under investigation against which to compare the accuracy of the children's memory. When children from the preparation program testified in court, however, the case was more likely to be associated with a conviction than if children from the regular services group testified. Whether this can be linked to children's performance on the stand requires further investigation. Attorneys rated children from the preparation program as better witnesses; unfortunately, the attorneys were not blind raters and may have been invested in the success of the program to which they referred their clients. Despite the limitations in this study, it is the first of its kind and an important springboard for future research.

In addition to field studies of ongoing programs, there is a need for experimental analog studies that examine the effects of preparation on children's reports of previously staged or memorialized events. In this way, children's reports with and without preparation can be compared to a record of the event in question in order

to examine both positive and negative effects on accuracy. Recently, researchers have begun to examine the effects of legal education and anxiety reduction techniques on accuracy (Saywitz et al., 1993). Preliminary results suggest that although children learn a great deal about the system and appear less anxious when prepared, increased accuracy and reduced fear of testifying have been difficult to document. This is partially due to the lack of sensitive measurement instruments, young children's limited ability to report anxiety, and differences between "normal" research subjects and abused children (e.g., levels of motivation and anxiety). Hence, the efficacy of preparation for improved performance or reduced stress requires further investigation.

Researchers also are beginning to turn their attention to preparing children for the unique demands of answering questions in the forensic context according to legal rules of process and procedure. For example, techniques to increase children's resistance to suggestive questions have been studied (Saywitz & Moan-Hardie, 1994; Warren, Hulse-Trotter, & Tubbs, 1991). This kind of preparation is necessary because young children expect adults to be sincere in everyday conversation (Demorest, Meyer, Phelps, Gardner, & Winner, 1984). They may not anticipate the use of leading questions for adversarial purposes. In two studies, children participated in a school activity and then 2 weeks later were questioned (Saywitz & Moan-Hardie, 1994). Researchers prepared children, warning them that some of the questions might suggest an answer that reflects the questioner's guess. Children were informed that when questioners are not present at the event, they could not know what really happened. Then children practiced resisting by saying the answer when they knew it or saying "I don't know" when they did not. Children prepared in this manner resisted significantly more misleading questions than children in control groups.

In the first of the two studies, contrary to expectations, children who were prepared used the "I don't know" response more than control groups, even on non-leading questions. Perhaps they became more cautious about responding. This unintended side effect was eliminated with subsequent refinement of the method in the second study. Nonetheless, this result highlights the need for rigorous testing and refinement of preparation programs to ensure no harm is done to the reliability of children's testimony.

Preparation must be distinguished from coaching; effects on truth telling must be considered carefully at every turn. Many of the clinical approaches to anxiety reduction are thought to be helpful to child witnesses. Techniques such as deep breathing, guided imagery, self-monitoring, and self-statements ("I can do it") are found to have beneficial effects in other contexts. Examinations of their effects on recall is a fruitful area for further research. In designing the next generation of studies, researchers will need to consider the following: (a) the ecological validity of stimuli, retention tests, and retention intervals; (b) expanded theories of memory to account for effects of affect, motivation, and context; (c) the emotional and clinical realities of child-victim witnesses (e.g., effects of post-traumatic symptomatology); (d) the constraints of legal procedure and precedent; and (e) rights of the accused. This will allow a more comprehensive approach to the issue than previously has been the rule.

Reforming the investigative process. Studies have identified characteristics of the investigative process that can compromise memory for detail and interfere with a child's psychological recovery from trauma (Ceci & Bruck, 1993; Goodman, Pyle-Taub, et al., 1992; Tedesco & Schnell, 1987). These include protracted investigations, developmentally insensitive personnel, repeated interviews or court appearances, and multiple interviewers. Investigations conducted by multidisciplinary teams with a high level of coordination among law enforcement and social service agencies are thought to produce more accurate and complete information with less stress placed on children. When such teams are employed, a single interviewer (e.g., a police officer) may question the child, having consulted first with officials from relevant agencies (e.g., social services) on important questions to ask. In some settings, such officials watch behind a one-way mirror to reduce the need for subsequent interviews. One field study examined the effectiveness of such a team approach on the investigative process (California Attorney General's Office, 1994). Cases before and after the implementation of a Multidisciplinary Child

Interview Center (MDIC) were examined: 177 consecutive cases of suspected child sexual abuse reported to police in Sacramento County, California, were compared with 212 cases investigated after institution of a countywide MDIC. The center was associated with significantly fewer interviews, interviewers, and interview settings per case. Furthermore, children themselves rated the center-based interviews more positively than standard practices. Unfortunately, data were not collected on the number of additional interviews during the judicial phase of cases. Therefore, it is not possible to know how the MDIC affected interview patterns at later stages. There was no evidence that the MDIC affected the rates at which petitions on charges were filed in courts. Hence, factors thought to be associated with stress and contamination (repeated interviews) were reduced, but the costs associated with these benefits remain unknown.

The Need for and Use of Special Court Procedures

At present, most child witnesses are not given the benefits of special programs to prepare them to testify. Without such help, what are the effects on children of participation in the legal system? A number of studies suggest that, at least for a subset of children, involvement as witnesses in the criminal justice system is associated with the prolonging of emotional distress (e.g., DeFrancis, 1969; Goodman, Pyle-Taub, et al., 1992; Oates & Tong, 1987; Runyan, Everson, Edelsohn, Hunter, & Coulter, 1988). In contrast, involvement as a witness in the juvenile justice system has not been found to be associated with increased emotional problems (Runyan et al., 1988), although more research is needed before definitive statements can be made.

What measures can be taken to make the courtroom more "child friendly"? Goodman, Pyle-Taub, et al. (1992) found that when children testified in criminal court, they were better able to answer questions and looked less frightened when a parent or loved one was permitted to stay in the courtroom with them. The children also cried less when the courtroom was closed to spectators. In contrast, children who were more frightened of the defendant had more difficulty answering the prosecutor's questions and later expressed greater negativity about having been involved in the prosecution.

In an attempt to shelter children from the intimidation of facing the defendant and from testifying in open court, closed-circuit television can be used constitutionally in certain child sexual abuse cases (*Maryland v. Craig*, 1990). Such technology is being employed on an experimental basis in England with encouraging results. For example, children appear more fluent, confident, relaxed, and consistent witnesses when they testify via closed-circuit television (Davies & Noon, 1991; see also Cashmore, 1992). However, there is also an indication that jurors are more likely to mistrust a child's statements and that the child's testimony will have less impact on them when it is presented via closed-circuit television (Batterman-Faunce & Goodman, 1993; Davies & Noon, 1991; Goodman, Sachsenmaier, et al., 1992).

It is possible that other formats for obtaining children's testimony will be more beneficial to justice and to children; at least in the United States, there is evidence of public support for a variety of alternative means of gathering testimony from children (Batterman-Faunce & Goodman, 1993; Goodman et al., 1994), such as using children's courtrooms and having a neutral clinician rather than an attorney take the child's testimony. Strong empirical evidence that such procedures improve the fact-finding process are needed before the courts will be likely to consider them, because they represent drastic changes to traditional procedures.

Practice Implications

The results of child witness research have a number of implications for children's performance in pretrial interviews and legal proceedings. Below, we discuss implications for interviewing children in forensic settings and for presenting their testimony in court.

Questioning children. Studies suggest important age differences in children's responses to questioning. Different techniques will be required to elicit accurate information from children of different age groups. Interviewing protocols are needed that are sensitive to developmental differences in free recall, suggestibil-

ity, communicative competence, and socioemotional concerns (e.g., intimidation, embarrassment).

Interview protocols also must be sensitive to individual differences among children and to different cultural expectations across ethnic groups.

Interview protocols also must be sensitive to individual differences among children and to different cultural expectations across ethnic groups. Despite the need for further research in these areas, we present a number of general guidelines to consider, as a function of age, when interviewing children.

Preschool children. The reliability of reports from preschool children (3 to 5 years of age) particularly depends on the way in which children are questioned. Their responses appear to be especially vulnerable to the effects of the environment (e.g., familiarity, formality), the interviewer (e.g., supportive, intimidating, authoritative), the wording of questions (e.g., linguistic complexity, vocabulary, generality, specificity), type of information requested (e.g., central actions, peripheral details), and exposure to misleading postevent information. This is not to say that some 3- to 4-year-olds cannot provide accurate, detailed accounts of personally meaningful events, such as sexual molestation. Many can, even after direct and leading questions. However, intimidating interrogation in an unfamiliar environment with leading questions, especially regarding poorly remembered details, can contaminate children's reports. Such a questioning style is clearly dangerous and must be avoided. This style often is deemed necessary, for example, in cross-examination by defense lawyers to elicit inconsistencies in a child's statements. Unfortunately, it also can create inconsistencies that are a function of the questioning itself.

To bolster the reliability of preschoolers' reports, the following methods are indicated by the available research: (a) Misunderstandings can be minimized by keeping questions short, grammatical constructions simple, and vocabulary familiar. (b) Accuracy is promoted when questions concern events that are salient and meaningful to children and when question content is matched closely to children's knowledge and experience. (c) Accuracy can be facilitated when hesitant preschoolers are not pressured, coerced, or bullied into answering questions by authority figures. Inconsistencies can be probed by professing confusion, not by challenging children. (d) Suggestibility may be reduced when interviewers are neutral or supportive of children's efforts but do not praise them for providing specific content. (e) Interviewer bias can be reduced when interviewers take an objective, nonjudgmental stance on both nonverbal and verbal levels (e.g., tone of voice, facial expression, wording of questions). This does not preclude empathic comments to overcome children's anxiety. It does imply that an accusatory climate must be avoided—for example, one in which suspects are labeled as "bad" and assumed to have done "bad things" based on uncorroborated information provided by someone other than the child.

Preschoolers can be inconsistent in their retelling of past events across multiple interviews (Fivush, 1993; Fivush & Shukar, 1995). Different settings and different questioning styles can result in disclosure of different pieces of information at different points in time. For example, more complete and detailed renditions can be expected from children in familiar and informal settings than in unfamiliar, formal, and anxiety-provoking settings (Ceci, Bronfenbrenner, & Baker, 1988; Saywitz & Nathanson, 1993; Saywitz et al., 1993). Perhaps the clinical practice of equating inconsistency with false information should be reevaluated in light of these findings.

The use of leading questions with preschoolers remains a controversial issue. Strongly worded accusatory questions (e.g., "John hurt you, didn't he?") should be avoided. They can affect the child's memory as well as the child's credibility adversely. Although leading questions are to be avoided whenever possible, preschoolers are likely to benefit from specific questions to trigger memory of additional information not provided spontaneously. Children are often most resistant to leading questions about central actions, but at times even reports concerning central actions can be contaminated through use of leading questioning. Important individual differences exist in children's responses, with many

children retaining accuracy in the face of specific questioning, especially in regard to salient abuse-related actions such as nakedness. The majority of false reports that do occur in research studies are often limited to false affirmations of misleading yes-no questions (e.g., "He touched your private parts, didn't he?"), although some children will provide false detail as well, perhaps especially if repeated misleading questioning occurs. If interviewers use yes-no questions with children, follow-up questions to yes-no responses are critical (e.g., "What makes you think so?"), and interviewers must remain as open-minded as possible rather than pursue an "agenda," especially when corroborative evidence is lacking.

There are those who advocate the exclusive use of general questions to avoid any hint of suggestion; such questions, however, can elicit irrelevancies and inconsistencies from preschoolers. For example, when asked, "Did he put something in your mouth?" a young child is likely to answer "No." If asked more specifically, "Did he put a thermometer in your mouth?" the same child is likely to say "Yes," responding accurately about a physical examination (Saywitz et al., 1991). When asked if he or she saw a weapon after witnessing a shooting, a preschooler is likely to answer "No." If asked more specifically, "Did you see a gun?" the same child is likely to respond "Yes" when in fact the gun was present. Hierarchical, conceptual categories, such as *weapon*, may not be understood, but concrete, familiar objects, such as *gun*, may be understood well. Although the more general term is less leading, it can create inconsistencies and errors. Preschoolers reason on the basis of what they can see and visualize (specifics) rather than on abstract concepts and principles (generalities).

Obtaining the most complete and accurate reports from preschoolers remains a challenge. There is a pressing need for researchers and practitioners to determine how to elicit disclosures from children within this age group without contaminating their reports.

Elementary-age children. Elementary-age children (5 to 11 years of age) show both strengths and weaknesses. Under certain conditions, their performance may exceed that of adults (e.g., reporting details that go unnoticed by grown-ups). Under other conditions, elementary-age children show noteworthy limitations. Because children within this age range often can provide detailed narratives of events, pretrial inquiry can begin with open-ended questions to elicit free recall. Then, children can be prompted to elaborate on their narratives in a non-biased manner with comments such as "tell me a little more," "what happened next," or repeating the end of their last sentence with a rising intonation.

> *Although capable of providing accurate narratives, free recall is still likely to be incomplete, and specific follow-up questions may be necessary.*

Although capable of providing accurate narratives, free recall is still likely to be incomplete, and specific follow-up questions may be necessary. Research and clinical literature have suggested that interviewers proceed from narrative elaboration to open-ended, specific questions ("What was the weather like that night?" "What kinds of clothes was she wearing?") and then to specific, short-answer questions ("What color was her scarf?"), reserving closed questions (yes-no, multiple choice) for the end, if used at all (Lamb, 1994; Lamb et al., in press; *Memorandum of Good Practice*, 1992; Saywitz, 1994, 1995; Saywitz & Geiselman, in press). Research results suggest that yes-no questions must be dealt with cautiously but need not be avoided totally (Saywitz et al., 1991). Such questions can be followed by attempts to elicit elaboration ("Tell me more.") or justification ("What makes you think so?") to avoid misinterpretation. The ensuing explanation helps determine how much or how little weight to place on a child's response.

Some interviewers deem it necessary to ask specific questions about information that may not otherwise be reported (e.g., sexual or injurious contact) for a variety of reasons (e.g., the child's embarrassment or fear of retaliation). Research on elementary-age children's accuracy in the face of leading or misleading questions suggests that elementary-age children are more resistant than preschool children (e.g., Goodman & Reed, 1986). Interviewers also need to be aware of the possibility of lying or coaching.

Discussions regarding the use of specific or leading questions often are cast in extremes, pitting the notion that everything a child says is accurate against the notion that one misleading question invalidates a child's entire report. Individual practitioners will need to conduct a cost-benefit analysis on a case-by-case basis, combining clinical judgment with knowledge of the dangers of leading questions.

School-aged children may benefit from learning about the investigative and judicial process (Sas et al., 1991; Saywitz et al., 1993). They are likely to profit from a better understanding of the broader context in which the interview occurs, the purpose of questioning, the role of the interviewer, or the limits on confidentiality. This could facilitate increased familiarity and decreased anxiety, resulting in improved interview performance.

School-aged children benefit from a warning that they might not understand all the questions and from instructions to announce when they do not understand (Saywitz & Snyder, 1993). As discussed earlier, recent studies suggest that these children benefit most from preinterview practice with strategies for detecting and coping with noncomprehension (Saywitz & Snyder, 1993).

Inconsistencies or contradictions in children's statements can result from a variety of interview-induced sources, such as developmentally inappropriate wording of questions. These can be reduced or eliminated when questions are well-matched in vocabulary and linguistic complexity to the school-aged child's stage of language acquisition. For example, elementary-school children's knowledge of common legal terms cannot be assumed. Children may think they understand a term's meaning when, in fact, they and the adult interviewer have a different meaning in mind. When asked, "Do you know what testify means?" a child may answer "yes" but may be thinking about taking a test. In general, interviewers need to avoid or compensate for linguistic forms that are slow to develop.

If the child must testify, elementary-school children should be helped to reduce the gap between everyday rules of conversation and the language of the courtroom. For example, interview questions often jump from one topic to another without the necessary transition for children to switch frames of reference (Brennan & Brennan, 1988). Children become disoriented. They require transitional comments to signal a change of topic that may be rare in the courtroom context. For example, "Before, we were talking about school. Now I want to ask you about your vacation."

Adolescents. For many forensic purposes, the interview performance of children over 11 years of age can be expected to be comparable to that of a large number of adults, at least in terms of quantity and quality of memory, resistance to suggestion, legal knowledge, comprehension of questions, and formulation of verbal responses. Unfortunately, few studies directly concern teenagers' testimony about sexual matters. Therefore, developmental differences in interview performance due to the effects of emotions (e.g., embarrassment), self-image, and coping strategies have not been well-researched. Likewise, the interaction between interview performance and individual differences in expressions of stress and psychological disturbance (e.g., posttraumatic stress disorder) has yet to be investigated and understood fully. Even older children may differ substantially from adults in these respects. Because research on adolescents' testimony in regard to sexual abuse allegations is lacking, we hesitate to provide many guidelines concerning the interviewing of adolescents.

Limits of current knowledge. Despite the age-related trends described earlier, there is danger in generalizing to individual cases using research studies based on averages and probabilities. It is important to note that a given child may be delayed or advanced for her or his age in one or more domains of development. A child with excellent verbal skills for his or her age may nevertheless have poor retrieval strategies and inferior recall of details than agemates, especially if he or she is intimidated or frightened more easily. Moreover, the ecological validity of research studies is limited. For example, traumatic events may be recalled better than stimuli in laboratory studies, or they may be distorted for emotional reasons in ways that are not yet understood fully.

In addition, studies have not produced a single, proper method for interviewing child victim witnesses that can be held out as the standard by which all questioning should be conducted. Structured protocols have been proposed. None have been rigorously tested or shown to be reliable and valid for all children. Several appear promising (e.g., Boat & Everson,

1988; Jones & McQuiston, 1989; Saywitz et al., 1992; Sgroi, 1982), but more research is needed to determine their effects, both expected and unintended. Until researchers establish the type of interviewing that leads to accurate disclosure of actual abuse, we will not know how to balance the need for open-ended versus specific questioning. Even with the advent of more research, the judgment of experienced professionals will be needed to apply one or more of a variety of interviewing strategies differentially.

It seems fair to conclude that when children are questioned as if they were adults, their testimony can be contaminated and their credibility undermined; children misunderstand complex questions, adults misinterpret children's responses, and children fail to clarify their meaning. An accepting, unbiased environment that poses understandable questions in an objective yet empathic climate should be created to maximize reliability and minimize suggestibility. The interviewer builds a bridge between the world of the child and the world of the adult to create the best opportunity for the discovery of truth.

Court appearances. Recent research also permits implications to be drawn in regard to children's courtroom testimony. Special approaches for preparing children to testify and for reducing their anxiety hold promise in bolstering children's abilities to withstand the lengthy and stressful criminal justice system. However, such programs and approaches must be considered carefully in each jurisdiction to ensure that they meet with attorneys' approval so that challenges to children's credibility are minimized.

Legal professionals need to be aware that a certain subset of children who testify may be particularly vulnerable witnesses. Research indicates that such factors as lack of maternal support, the need to testify multiple times, harsh cross-examination, victim age, and fear of the defendant should be considered in predictions that children may suffer stress from the legal process itself (Goodman, Pyle-Taub, et al., 1992). For children who are at risk of stress from legal involvement, protective measures, such as testifying via closed-circuit television, may prove particularly important (Cashmore, 1992; Davies & Noon, 1991). Although such techniques may reduce children's credibility in jurors' eyes, they may be, at times, the only reasonable and fair way of entering into court the testimony of a frightened child witness.

Conclusion

Research on children's testimony has provided valuable insights regarding children's abilities and needs as witnesses. Although many pressing questions still need to be explored, the research base has grown substantially and provides a number of consistent findings. Perhaps the most important finding is that age alone is not a measure of a child's ability to provide accurate testimony or withstand court appearances. Instead, the context in which a child is questioned and in which the child testifies can help bolster or undermine a child's performance as well as a child's emotional resilience. The task for researchers is to find optimal interview techniques and contexts to help child witnesses be as accurate and resilient as possible.

References

Asher, S. (1976). Children's ability to appraise their own and other person's communication performance. *Developmental Psychology, 12,* 24-32.

Batterman-Faunce, J. M., & Goodman, G. S. (1993). Effects of context on the accuracy and suggestibility of child witnesses. In G. S. Goodman & B. L. Bottoms (Eds.), *Child victims, child witnesses* (pp. 301-330). New York: Guilford.

Boat, B., & Everson, M. (1988). Research issues in using anatomical dolls. *Annals of Sex Research, 1,* 191-204.

Bottoms, B. L., Shaver, P. R., & Goodman, G. S. (in press). An analysis of allegations of ritualistic and religion-related child abuse. *Law and Human Behavior.*

Brennan, M., & Brennan, R. (1988). *Strange language: Child victims under cross examination.* Riverina, Australia: Charles Stuart University.

Briere, J., & Conte, J. (1993). Self-reported amnesia for abuse in adults molested as children. *Journal of Traumatic Stress, 6,* 21-31.

Brigham, J., Vanverst, M., & Bothwell, R. (1986). Accuracy of children's eyewitness identifications in a field setting. *Basic and Applied Social Psychology, 7,* 295-306.

Bruck, M., Ceci, S. J., Francouer, E., & Renick, A. (1995). Anatomically detailed dolls do not facilitate preschoolers' reports of a pediatric examination involving genital touching. *Journal of Experimental Psychology: Applied, 1*(2), 95-109.

Bugental, D. B., Blue, J., Cortez, V., Fleck, K., & Rodriguez, A. (1992). Influences of witnessed affect on information processing in children. *Child Development, 63,* 774-786.

Bull, R. (1995). Innovative techniques for the questioning of child witnesses, especially those who are young and those with learning disabilities. In M. Zaragoza, J. R. Graham, G. C. N. Hall, R. Hirschman, & Y. S. Ben-Porath (Eds.), *Memory and testimony in the child witness* (pp. 179-194). Thousand Oaks, CA: Sage.

Bussey, K., Lee, K., & Grimbeek, E. (1993). Lies and secrets: Implications for children's reporting of sexual abuse. In G. S. Goodman & B. L. Bottoms (Eds.), *Child victims, child witnesses* (pp. 147-168). New York: Guilford.

California Attorney General's Office. (1994, July). *Child victim witness investigation pilot project: Research and evaluation, final report.* Sacramento: Author.

Carter, C. (1991). *Influences of language and emotional support on children's testimony.* Unpublished dissertation, SUNY-Buffalo.

Cashmore, J. (1992). *The use of closed circuit television for child witnesses in the act.* Sydney: Australian Law Reform Commission.

Cashmore, J., & Bussey, K. (1990). Children's conceptions of the witness role. In J. Spencer, G. Nicholson, R. Flin, & R. Bull (Eds.), *Children's evidence in legal proceedings: An international perspective* (pp. 177-188). Cambridge, UK: Cambridge University Faculty of Law.

Ceci, S. J., Bronfenbrenner, U., & Baker, J. C. (1988). *Memory in context: The case of prospective remembering.* In F. E. Weinert & M. Perlmutter (Eds.), *Universal changes and individual differences* (pp. 243-256). Hillsdale, NJ: Lawrence Erlbaum.

Ceci, S. J., & Bruck, M. (1993). The suggestibility of child witnesses. *Psychological Bulletin, 113,* 403-439.

Christiansson, S. A. (1992). Emotional stress and eyewitness memory: A critical review. *Psychological Bulletin, 12,* 284-309.

Clarke-Stewart, A., Thompson, L., & Lepore, S. (1989, April). Manipulating children's interpretations through interrogation. In G. S. Goodman (Chair), *Can children provide accurate testimony?* Symposium presented at the Society for Research in Child Development Meetings, Kansas City, MO.

Davies, G., & Noon, E. (1991). *An evaluation of the live link for child witnesses.* London: Home Office.

Davies, G., Stevenson, Y., & Flin, R. (1988). Telling tales out of school: Children's memory for an unexpected event. In M. Gruenberg, P. Morris, & R. Sykes (Eds.), *Practical aspects of memory* (pp. 122-127). New York: John Wiley.

DeFrancis, V. (1969). *Protecting the child victim of sex crimes committed by adults.* Denver, CO: American Humane Association.

Demorest, A., Meyer, C., Phelps, E., Gardner, H., & Winner, E. (1984). Words speak louder than actions: Understanding deliberately false remarks. *Child Development, 55,* 1527-1534.

Dent, H. (1977). Stress as a factor influencing person recognition in identification parades. *Bulletin of the British Psychological Society, 30,* 339-340.

Dent, H., & Flin, R. (1992). *Children as witnesses.* London: Wiley.

Dent, H., & Stephenson, G. (1979). An experimental study of the effectiveness of different techniques of questioning child witnesses. *British Journal of Social and Clinical Psychology, 18,* 41-51.

Donaldson, M. C. (1979). *Children's minds.* New York: Norton.

Feldman-Summers, S., & Pope, K. (1994). The experience of "forgetting" childhood abuse: A national survey of psychologists. *Journal of Consulting and Clinical Psychology, 62*(3), 636-639.

Fisher, R., & McCauley, M. (1995). Improving eyewitness testimony with the cognitive interview. In M. Zaragoza, J. R. Graham, G. C. N. Hall, R. Hirschman, & Y. S. Ben-Porath (Eds.), *Memory and testimony in the child witness* (pp. 141-159). Thousand Oaks, CA: Sage.

Fivush, R. (1993). Developmental perspectives on autobiographical recall. In G. S. Goodman & B. L. Bottoms (Eds.), *Child victims, child witnesses* (pp. 1-24). New York: Guilford.

Fivush, R., & Shukar, J. (1995). What young children recall: Issues of content, consistency, and coherence. In M. Zaragoza, J. R. Graham, G. C. N. Hall, R. Hirschman, & Y. S. Ben-Porath (Eds.), *Memory and testimony in the child witness* (pp. 5-23). Thousand Oaks, CA: Sage.

Flin, R. (1993). Hearing and testing children's evidence. In G. Goodman & B. Bottoms (Eds.), *Child victims, child witnesses* (pp. 279-299). New York: Guilford.

Flin, R., Stevenson, Y., & Davies, G. (1989). Children's knowledge of court proceedings. *British Journal of Psychology, 80,* 285-297.

Friedman, W. (1982). *The developmental psychology of time.* New York: Academic Press.

Gallagher, T. (1981). Contingent query sequences within adult-child discourse. *Journal of Child Language, 8,* 51-62.

Geiselman, E., & Fischer, R. (1989). The cognitive interview technique for victims and witnesses of crime. In D. Raskin (Ed.), *Psychological methods in criminal investigation and evidence.* New York: Springer.

Goodman, G. S. (1984). The child witness. *Journal of Social Issues, 40,* 1-175.

Goodman, G. S., & Aman, C. J. (1991). Children's use of anatomically detailed dolls to recount an event. *Child Development, 61,* 1859-1871.

Goodman, G. S., Batterman-Faunce, J. M., Quas, J. A., Riddlesberger, M. M., & Kuhn, J. (1994). Optimizing children's testimony: Research and social policy issues concerning allegations of child sexual abuse. In D. Cicchetti & S. Toth (Eds.), *Child abuse, child development, and social policy* (pp. 139-166). Norwood, NJ: Ablex.

Goodman, G. S., & Bottoms, B. L. (Eds.). (1993). *Child victims, child witnesses.* New York: Guilford.

Goodman, G. S., Bottoms, B. L., Schwartz-Kenney, B., & Rudy, L. (1991). Children's memory for a stressful event: Improving children's reports. *Journal of Narrative and Life History, 1,* 69-99.

Goodman, G. S., Hepps, D., & Reed, R. S. (1986). The child victim's testimony. In A. Haralambie (Ed.), *New issues for child advocates* (pp. 167-177). Phoenix: Arizona Council of Attorneys for Children.

Goodman, G. S., Hirschman, J., Hepps, D., & Rudy, L. (1991). Children's memory for stressful events. *Merrill-Palmer Quarterly, 37,* 109-158.

Goodman, G. S., Pyle-Taub, E. P., Jones, D. P. H., England, P., Port, L. K., Rudy, L., & Prado, L. (1992). The effects of criminal court testimony on child sexual assault victims. *Monographs of the Society for Research in Child Development, 57* (Serial No. 229), 1-163.

Goodman, G. S., & Reed, R. (1986). Age differences in eyewitness testimony. *Law and Human Behavior, 10,* 317-332.

Goodman, G. S., Sachsenmaier, T., Batterman-Faunce, J., Tobey, A., Thomas, S., Orcutt, H., & Schwartz-Kenney, B. (1992, August). *Impact of innovative court procedures on children's testimony*. In B. L. Bottoms & M. Levine (Chairs), *Children's eyewitness testimony*. Symposium presented at the annual meeting of the American Psychological Association, Washington, DC.

Gray, E. (1993). *Unequal justice.* New York: Free Press.

Hill, P., & Hill, S. (1987). Videotaping children's testimony: An empirical view. *Michigan Law Review, 85,* 809-833.

Jones, D. P. H., & McQuiston, M. (1989). *Interviewing the sexually abused child.* Denver, CO: Kempe Center.

Katz, S., & Mazur, M. A. (1979). *Understanding the rape victim.* New York: John Wiley.

Lamb, M. (1994). The investigation of child sexual abuse: An interdisciplinary consensus statement. *Journal of Child Sexual Abuse, 3*(4), 93-106.

Lamb, M., Hershkowitz, I., Sternberg, K., Esplin, P., Hovav, M., Manor, T., & Yudilevitch, L. (in press). Effects of investigative utterance types on Israeli children's responses. *International Journal of Behavioral Development.*

Lanning, K. (1991). Ritual abuse: A law enforcement view or perspective. *Child Abuse & Neglect, 15,* 171-173.

Leichtman, M., & Ceci, S. J. (1995). Effects of stereotypes and suggestions on preschoolers' reports. *Developmental Psychology, 31,* 568-578.

Leippe, M., Romanczyk, A., & Manion, A. (1992). Eyewitness memory for a touching experience: Accuracy differences between child and adult witnesses. *Journal of Applied Psychology, 76,* 367-379.

Loftus, E. F. (1979). *Eyewitness testimony.* Cambridge, MA: Harvard University Press.

Loftus, E. F. (1992, August). *The reality of repressed memories.* Paper presented at the annual meeting of the American Psychological Association, Washington, DC.

Malinoski, P., Lynn, S. J., Martin, D., Aronoff, A., Neufeld, J., & Gedeon, S. (1995, August). *Individual differences in early memory reports: An empirical investigation.* Paper presented at the annual meeting of the American Psychological Association, New York.

Marin, B. V., Holmes, D. L., Guth, M., & Kovac, P. (1979). The potential of children as eyewitness. *Law and Human Behavior, 3,* 295-305.

Markman, E. M. (1977). Realizing that you don't understand: A preliminary investigation. *Child Development, 48,* 986-992.

Maryland v. Craig (1990). 110 S. Ct. 3157, 3169.

Melton, G. (1981). Children's competence to testify. *Law and Human Behavior, 5,* 73-85.

Melton, G., Limber, S., Jacobs, J., & Oberlander, L. (1992). *Preparing sexually abused children for testimony: Children's perceptions of the legal process.* Final report to the National Center on Child Abuse & Neglect (Grant No 90-CA-1274). Lincoln: University of Nebraska-Lincoln.

Melton, G., & Thompson, R. (1987). Getting out of a rut: Detours to less traveled paths in child-witness research. In S. Ceci, M. Toglia, & D. Ross (Eds.), *Children's eyewitness memory* (pp. 209-229). New York: Springer-Verlag.

Memorandum of good practice on video-recorded interviews with child witnesses for criminal proceedings. (1992). London: Her Majesty's Stationery Office.

Oates, K., & Tong, L. (1987). Sexual abuse of children: An area with room for professional reform. *Medical Journal of Australia, 147,* 544-548.

Ornstein, P., Baker-Ward, L., Gordon, B., & Merritt, R. (1993, March). Children's memory for medical procedures. In N. Stein (Chair), *Children's memory for emotional events.* Symposium presented at the Society for Research in Child Development Meetings, New Orleans, LA.

Patterson, C., Massad, C., & Cosgrove, J. (1978). Children's referential communication: Components of plans for effective listening. *Developmental Psychology, 14,* 401-406.

Perry, N., & Wrightsman, L. (1991). *The child witness.* Newbury Park, CA: Sage.

Peters, D. (1991). The influence of stress and arousal on the child witness. In J. Doris (Ed.), *The suggestibility of children's recollections* (pp. 60-76). Washington, DC: American Psychological Association.

Pezdek, K. (1995, July). *Childhood memories: What types of false memories can be suggestively planted?* Paper presented at the Society for Applied Research in Memory and Cognition Meetings, Vancouver, Canada.

Pickell, J. (in press). The formation of false memories. *Psychiatric Annals.*

Pipe, M. E., Gee, S., & Wilson, C. (1993). Cues, props, and context: Do they facilitate children's reports. In G. S. Goodman & B. L. Bottoms (Eds.), *Child victims, child witnesses* (pp. 25-45). New York: Guilford.

Pynoos, R., & Eth, S. (1984). The child as witness to homicide. *Journal of Social Issues, 40,* 87-108.

Pynoos, R., hild && Nader, K. (1988). Children's memory and proximity to violence. *Journal of the American Academy of Child and Adolescent Psychiatry, 27,* 567-572.

Revelle, G., Wellman, H., & Karabenik, J. (1985). Comprehension monitoring in preschool children. *Child Development, 56,* 654-663.

Rogers, C. M. (1980, September). *Child sexual abuse and the courts: Empirical findings.* Paper presented at the annual meeting of the American Psychological Association, Montreal, Canada.

Runyan, D. K., Everson, M. D., Edelsohn, G. A., Hunter, W. M., & Coulter, M. L. (1988). Impact of legal intervention on sexually abused children. *Journal of Pediatrics, 113,* 647-653.

Sas, L., Hurley, P., Austin, G., & Wolfe, D. (1991). *Reducing the system-induced trauma for child sexual abuse victims through court preparation, assessment and follow-up.* Final Report for the National Welfare Grants Division, Health and Welfare (Project #4555-1-125), Canada.

Saywitz, K. (1989). Children's conceptions of the legal system: Court is place to play basketball. In S. Ceci, M. Toglia, & D. Ross (Eds.), *Perspectives on children's testimony* (pp. 131-157). New York: Springer-Verlag.

Saywitz, K. (1994). Questioning child witnesses. *Violence Update, 4*(7), 3-10.

Saywitz, K. (1995). Improving children's testimony: The question, the answer, and the environment. In M. S. Zaragoza, J. R. Graham, G. C. N. Hall, R. Hirschman, & Y. S. Ben-Porath (Eds.), *Memory and testimony in the child witness* (pp. 113-140). Thousand Oaks, CA: Sage.

Saywitz, K., & Geiselman, E. (in press). Interviewing the child witness: Maximizing completeness and minimizing error. In S. Lynn (Ed.), *Memory and truth.* New York: Guilford.

Saywitz, K., Geiselman, R., & Bornstein, G. (1992). Effects of cognitive interviewing and practice on children's recall performance. *Journal of Applied Psychology, 77*(5), 744-756.

Saywitz, K., Goodman, G. S., Nicholas, E., & Moan, S. (1991). Children's memories of physical examinations involving genital touch: Implications for reports of child sexual abuse. *Journal of Consulting and Clinical Psychology, 59,* 682-691.

Saywitz, K., Jaenicke, C., & Camparo, L. (1990). Children's knowledge of legal terminology. *Law and Human Behavior, 14*(6), 523-535.

Saywitz, K., & Moan-Hardie, S. (1994). Reducing the potential for distortion of childhood memories. *Consciousness and Cognition, 3,* 408-425.

Saywitz, K., & Nathanson, R. (1993). Children's testimony and their perceptions of stress in and out of the courtroom. *Child Abuse & Neglect, 17,* 613-622.

Saywitz, K., Nathanson, R., Snyder, L., & Lamphear, V. (1993). *Preparing children for the investigative and judicial process: Improving communication, memory, and emotional resiliency.* Final report to the National Center on Child Abuse & Neglect (Grant No. 90-CA-1179). Torrance: University of California, Los Angeles, Harbor-UCLA Medical Center, Department of Psychiatry.

Saywitz, K., & Snyder, L. (1993). Improving children's testimony with preparation. In G. Goodman & B. Bottoms (Eds.), *Child victims, child witnesses* (pp. 117-146). New York: Guilford.

Sgroi, S. (1982). *Handbook of clinical intervention in child sexual abuse.* New York: Heath.

Smith, B. (1993). *The prosecution of child sexual and physical abuse cases.* Final report to the National Center on Child Abuse & Neglect, Washington, DC.

Spencer, J., & Flin, R. (1990). *The evidence of children: The law and the psychology.* London: Blackstone.

Steward, M. (1992). Preliminary findings from the University of California, Davis, Child Memory Study. *APSAC Advisor, 5,* 11-13.

Tedesco, J., & Schnell, S. (1987). Children's reactions to sex abuse investigation and litigation. *Child Abuse & Neglect, 11,* 267-272.

Terr, L. (1988). What happens to early memories of trauma? A study of 20 children under age 5 at the time of the documented traumatic events. *Journal of the American Academy of Child and Adolescent Psychiatry, 27,* 96-104.

Terr, L. (1991). Childhood traumas: An outline and overview. *American Journal of Psychiatry, 148,* 10-20.

Tobey, A., & Goodman, G. S. (1992). Children's eyewitness memory: Effects of participation and forensic context. *Child Abuse & Neglect, 16,* 779-796.

Usher, J., & Neisser, U. (1993). Childhood amnesia and the beginnings of memory for four early life events. *Journal of Experimental Psychology General, 122,* 155-165.

U.S. Department of Health and Human Services. (1992). *National child abuse and neglect data system* (Working Paper No. 1, 1990 summary data component). Washington, DC: Author.

Walker, A. G. (1993). Questioning young children in court: A linguistic case study. *Law and Human Behavior, 17,* 59-81.

Warren, A., Hulse-Trotter, K., & Tubbs, E. (1991). Inducing resistance to suggestibility in children. *Law and Human Behavior, 15*(3), 273-285.

Warren-Leubecker, A. (1991). Commentary: The influence of stress and arousal on the child witness. In J. Doris (Ed.), *The suggestibility of children's recollections* (pp. 83-85). Washington, DC: American Psychological Association.

Warren-Leubecker, A., Tate, C., Hinton, I., & Ozbek, I. (1989). What do children know about the legal system and why do they know it? In S. Ceci, M. Toglia, D. Ross (Eds.), *Perspectives on children's testimony* (pp. 158-184). New York: Springer-Verlag.

Whitcomb, D., Runyan, D., De Vos, E., Hunter, W., Cross, T., Everson, M., Peeler, N., Porter, C., Toth, P., & Gropper, C. (1992). *Child victim as witness research and development program* (Grant No. 87-MC-CX-0026). Final report to the National Institute of Justice Educational Development Center. Boston, MA.

Williams, L. M. (1994). Recall of childhood trauma: A prospective study of women's memories of child sexual abuse. *Journal of Consulting and Clinical Psychology, 62*(6), 1167-1176.

17

Expert Testimony

JOHN E. B. MYERS

Child abuse is often difficult to prove in court. Abuse occurs in secret, and the child is usually the only eyewitness. Although many children are excellent witnesses, some are too young to testify, and others are ineffective on the witness stand. Because evidence of abuse is difficult to come by, expert testimony sometimes plays an important role in child abuse litigation, especially sexual abuse. This chapter describes the scope and limits of expert testimony.

Experts testify in criminal court, juvenile court, family court, and in other legal arenas. In many criminal cases there is a jury. Juries are not universal in criminal court, however, and when there is no jury, the judge fulfills the fact-finding responsibility normally entrusted to jurors. In juvenile and family court cases, there usually is no jury. In this chapter, the word *jury* is used for convenience to describe the fact-finder, whether that is a jury or a judge.

Lay and Expert Witnesses

Two types of witnesses testify in court: lay witnesses and experts. A lay witness is someone with personal knowledge of relevant facts. An example of a lay witness is an eyewitness to a bank robbery. The lay witness tells the jury what he or she saw or heard.

An expert witness is a person with special knowledge who helps the jury understand technical, clinical, or scientific issues. Depending on the type of case, an expert may or may not need personal knowledge of the facts of the case being litigated. An example of an expert witness is a mental health professional who helps the jury understand that many sexually abused children recant following disclosure.

In child abuse and neglect litigation, professionals provide both lay and expert testimony. For example, suppose a child discloses sexual abuse to a psychotherapist. The child's disclosure is relevant evidence, and the therapist is an eyewitness *to the disclosure*. In court, the therapist could testify as a lay witness to repeat the child's disclosure for the jury. In another case, the same therapist might testify as an expert. Indeed, in some cases the professional testifies as both a lay witness *and* an expert. Suppose, for example, that a child discloses sexual abuse to a nurse practitioner who is examining the child for possible sexual abuse. In court, the nurse practitioner testifies as a lay witness when repeating the child's disclosure. The nurse offers expert testimony when interpreting the results of the physical examination.

Two Categories of Evidence: Substantive and Rehabilitative

Cases are won and lost with evidence, which is defined as "any matter, verbal or physical, that can be used to support the existence of a factual proposition" (Lilly, 1987, p. 2). Thus, evidence includes testimony from lay and expert witnesses, written documents, photographs, and objects such as the gun used to hold up a bank. The admissibility of evidence is governed by complex rules administered by the judge.

Substantive evidence. Evidence offered in court to prove that a child was abused is called *substantive evidence*. For example, in a physical abuse case, the substantive evidence might consist of the child's hospital record and expert testimony on battered child syndrome. In a sexual abuse case, the substantive evidence might be the findings of a physical examination, the child's disclosure statement to a social worker, lay testimony from the child's mother, and expert testimony from a mental health professional that the child was abused. In both the physical and sexual abuse cases, the expert testimony is substantive evidence, that is, evidence that abuse occurred.

Rehabilitation. There is a second category of expert testimony. Testimony in the second category is *not* offered as substantive evidence of abuse but serves the more limited, although important, role of rehabilitating a child witness' credibility after the defense attorney attacks it.

The two categories of expert testimony—substantive evidence and rehabilitation—are discussed later in this chapter.

Expert Testimony in Criminal Versus Noncriminal Proceedings

On paper, similar rules govern expert testimony in criminal and noncriminal proceedings. In practice, however, judges often allow experts greater latitude in noncriminal cases, such as in juvenile court proceedings and family court litigation regarding child custody or visitation.

Thus, in a juvenile court proceeding, a judge might allow an expert to give an opinion the judge would not allow in a criminal case. Judges are most likely to limit or disallow expert testimony when there is a jury. Judges worry that some jurors defer too quickly to experts, thus abdicating the juror's responsibility to decide the case.

Principles of Expert Testimony

Expert testimony is allowed when members of the jury need help to understand technical, clinical, or scientific issues (Chadwick, 1990; Myers, 1992b). For example, in many physical abuse cases, the accused person claims that the child's injuries were accidental. The jury lacks the knowledge required to differentiate accidental from inflicted injuries. Thus, to help the jury, a physician is allowed to testify as an expert.

In the case of sexual abuse, children sometimes recant. Many jurors do not understand that recantation is common in abused children (Morison & Greene, 1992). The defense attorney may attack the child's credibility in an effort to convince the jury that the only explanation for recantation is that abuse did not occur. In such a case, an expert witness may rehabilitate the child's credibility by explaining that recantation may occur among sexually abused children.

Thus, expert witnesses are used to help jurors understand technical, clinical, and scientific issues. With help to the jury as the loadstar for expert testimony, the acronym HELP is useful to organize the metaprinciples that underlie expert testimony:

H—honesty
E—evenhandedness
L—limits of expertise
P—preparation

Honesty. Expert witnesses must be honest with the jury, the judge, the attorneys, and, in the final analysis, with themselves (Committee on Ethical Guidelines for Forensic Psychologists, 1991). The duty to provide honest testimony derives in part from the oath in which the expert swears to "tell the truth, the whole truth, and nothing but the truth." But honesty has deeper roots. Honesty lies at the core of professionalism and personal integrity. Experts who allow half-truths to go unchecked, or who shade the truth to favor one side in the litigation, undermine the very purpose of the law. Half-honest experts seldom help the jury.

Evenhandedness. In our legal system, an expert witness plays a very different role from an attorney. The attorney's job is to win the case for the client. To be sure, the ultimate goal of the legal system is truth, but the theory of our adversary system of justice is that the truth emerges through the courtroom confrontation of adversaries. Thus, attorneys are advocates for their clients and are not supposed to be objective.

Unlike attorneys, expert witnesses are not—or, at least, should not be—partisan advocates.

Unlike attorneys, expert witnesses are not—or, at least, should not be—partisan advocates. The expert's responsibility is not to win the case but to help the jury understand clinical, technical, or scientific issues. The expert's responsibility is to educate, not to claim victory. Experts who view litigation through advocate's eyes lose their bearings and sink to the level of "hired guns."

In the effort to avoid becoming an advocate, must experts aspire to complete objectivity? Is an expert irreparably sullied if the expert's sympathies lean toward one side or the other? Although it may be possible in theory to attain unqualified objectivity, such purity is rare in the "real world" of litigation (Saks, 1990). Moreover, in a system where each side retains its own expert, it is unrealistic to expect

professionals to be completely dispassionate about the outcome. What is important is not unconditional evenhandedness but the degree of objectivity that is compatible with honesty and professionalism.

Just as important as reasonable objectivity is a willingness to acknowledge one's biases and recognize the shaping influence such biases may exert on one's testimony. Finally, experts should not represent themselves as objective when, in fact, they are not. The latter requirement relates, of course, to the metaprinciple of honesty.

Limits of expertise. During the past 30 years, much has been learned about child abuse, yet many questions remain. With sexual abuse in particular, our knowledge is in the formative stage of development. For example, controversy continues about the meaning of various genital and anal findings (Adams & Wells, 1993). Even more uncertainty surrounds the diagnostic importance of behaviors such as nightmares, regression, and acting out.

Expert witnesses should be familiar with relevant literature and appreciate the limits of current knowledge. While on the witness stand, experts should acknowledge these limits and refuse to exceed them, even in the face of pressure from attorneys or the judge (Melton, Petrila, Poythress, & Slobogin, 1987).

In addition to understanding the limits of knowledge in the field, experts should have a clear fix on the limits of their own knowledge (Saks, 1990).

Preparation. Preparation is the key to effective expert testimony. The expert should evaluate all relevant information. Before testifying, the expert should meet with the attorney who solicited the testimony. Chadwick (1990) emphasizes that such meetings "are always desirable, and rarely impossible" (p. 963).

Before going to court, it is often necessary to review pertinent records. Reviewing records before trial, or using records while testifying, raises complex issues regarding the right of attorneys to inspect confidential records, and experts should be familiar with the rules on this topic in the locality where they testify (see Myers, 1993a).

Although expert witnesses are not expected to know the legal rules governing expert testimony, experts should know enough about the rules to avoid unnecessary and potentially costly mistakes. For example, professionals should understand that courts do not allow experts to testify that children told the truth when disclosing abuse.

Who Qualifies to Testify as an Expert Witness?

Before a person may testify as an expert witness, the judge must be convinced that the person possesses sufficient "knowledge, skill, experience, training, or education" to qualify as an expert (Fed. R. Evid. 702). Normally, proposed experts take the witness stand and answer questions about their educational accomplishments, specialized training, and relevant experience. A professional does not have to be a well-known authority to testify as an expert witness. For example, publication of books or articles is not required. The important question is whether the jury will be helped by the professional's testimony (Wigmore, 1974). The type and degree of expertise required depends on the testimony the expert offers.

The Form of Expert Testimony

Expert testimony usually takes one of the following forms: (a) an opinion, (b) an answer to a hypothetical question, (c) a lecture providing background information on a pertinent subject, or (d) some combination of the above.

Opinion Testimony

Lay witnesses generally confine their testimony to a description of what they saw or heard and refrain from offering opinions. Experts, by contrast, are permitted to offer opinions. For example, in a physical abuse case, a physician could testify that, in the doctor's opinion, a child has battered child syndrome, and the child's injuries are not accidental. Experts must be reasonably confident of their opinions. Lawyers and judges use the term *reasonable certainty* to describe the necessary degree of confidence. Thus, the question to an expert might be, "Do you have an opinion, based on a reasonable degree of certainty, about whether the child's injuries were accidental?"

Unfortunately, the reasonable certainty standard is not self-defining, and the law does little to elucidate the term. It is clear that expert witnesses may not speculate or guess (Wigmore, 1974). It is equally clear that experts do not have to be completely certain before offering opinions (Louisell & Mueller, 1988). Thus, the degree of certainty required for expert testimony lies between guesswork and absolute certainty. Unfortunately, locating reasonable certainty somewhere between guesswork and absolute certainty adds little to the concept, and, in the end, the reasonable certainty standard fails to provide a meaningful tool to evaluate the helpfulness of expert testimony.

A more productive approach to assessing the helpfulness of expert testimony looks beyond the rubric of reasonable certainty and asks questions such as the following:

1. In formulating an opinion, did the expert consider all relevant facts?
2. How much confidence can be placed in the facts underlying the expert's opinion?
3. Does the expert have an adequate understanding of pertinent clinical and scientific principles?
4. To the extent the expert's opinion rests on scientific principles, have the principles been subjected to rigorous testing?
5. Have the principles or theories relied on by the expert been published in peer-reviewed journals?
6. Are the principles or theories relied on by the expert generally accepted as reliable by experts in the field?
7. Did the expert employ appropriate methods of assessment?
8. Are the inferences and conclusions drawn by the expert defensible?
9. Is the expert reasonably objective?

In the final analysis, the important question is whether the expert's opinion is logical, consistent, explainable, objective, and defensible. The value of the expert's opinion depends on the answers to these questions (Black, 1988).

The Hypothetical Question

In bygone days, expert testimony often was elicited in response to a lengthy hypothetical question asked by an attorney. Such a question contains hypothetical facts that closely parallel the actual facts of the case. The hypothetical question has never been short of critics. Louisell and Mueller (1988) argued that hypothetical

> questions are generally at best an awkward means to get at the truth. They tend to be long, complicated, and difficult for all— judge, jury, counsel, witness—to understand. . . . Such questions often distort the truth, misrepresenting or stifling the actual opinion of the expert. (p. 711)

Although hypothetical questions are useful in some situations and are common in some states, this often cumbersome device is falling out of favor.

Expert Testimony in the Form of a Lecture

Rather than offer an opinion, an expert may testify in the form of "a dissertation or exposition of scientific or other principles relevant to the case, leaving to the [jury] to apply them to the facts" (Fed. R. Evid. 702, Advisory Committee Note). A common example of this form of expert testimony occurs in child sexual abuse cases in which an expert helps the jury understand that delayed reporting and recantation are common among sexually abused children.

Types of Information on Which Expert Witnesses May Rely to Form Opinions Offered in Court

Professionals draw from many sources of information to reach conclusions about child abuse. When it comes to expert testimony in court, the law generally allows professionals to base their testimony on the same sources of information they rely on in their normal, day-to-day practice. Thus, in a sexual abuse case, an expert may base expert testimony on the child's disclosure, the results of a child protective services (CPS) investigation, and consultation with colleagues. In a physical abuse case, the physician may form an opinion on the basis of an interview and physical examination of the child, statements of the parents, results of

laboratory tests and X-rays, and readings in the literature.

Expert Testimony Based on Scientific Principles or Techniques

A special rule governs the admissibility of expert testimony that is based on scientific principles or techniques that are novel or of dubious reliability. The purpose of the special rule is to exclude expert testimony based on unreliable scientific principles or techniques.

The rule takes two forms in the United States:

1. The general acceptance rule, commonly known as the *Frye* rule
2. Relevance analysis, commonly known as the *Daubert* rule

The two forms of the rule are described briefly below.

General Acceptance—Frye

The general acceptance rule takes its name from a 1923 case called *Frye v. United States*. In *Frye*, the court ruled that expert testimony based on a novel scientific principle is admissible only when the principle gains "general acceptance in the field in which it belongs" (p. 1014). An attorney offering expert testimony based on a novel scientific principle must convince the judge that the principle is generally accepted as reliable in the relevant professional community.

The general acceptance rule was once the dominant rule in the United States. In recent years, however, an increasing number of courts have rejected the general acceptance rule because the rule sometimes excludes scientific and clinical information that could help the jury.

Relevance Analysis—Daubert

The most promising alternative to the general acceptance rule is a rule commonly called relevance analysis. In 1993, the U.S. Supreme Court adopted relevance analysis for the federal courts, rejecting *Frye*'s general acceptance rule (*Daubert v. Merrell Dow Pharmaceuticals,*

Inc., 1993). Although the Supreme Court's *Daubert* ruling is not binding on state court judges, *Daubert* is likely to influence increasing numbers of state court judges to switch from general acceptance to relevance analysis.

With relevance analysis, the judge conducts a searching inquiry into the reliability[1] of scientific principles supporting expert testimony. To assess reliability, the judge considers the following:

- Whether the principle "can be (and has been) tested" to determine its reliability and validity (*Daubert,* p. 2796).
- How often the principle yields accurate results.
- Existence of standards governing use of the principle to ensure accurate results (e.g., clear diagnostic criteria).
- Degree to which expert testimony is based on subjective analysis, as opposed to objective analysis. Expert testimony based on subjective analysis may be of questionable reliability if it is difficult to evaluate the expert's subjective decision-making process.
- Publication in the peer-reviewed literature. The Supreme Court wrote,

Another pertinent consideration is whether the theory or technique has been subjected to peer review and publication. Publication (which is but one element of peer review) is not a *sine qua non* of admissibility; it does not necessarily correlate with reliability, . . . and in some instances well-grounded but innovative theories will not have been published. . . . Some propositions, moreover, are too particular, too new, or of too limited interest to be published. But submission to the scrutiny of the scientific community is a component of "good science," in part because it increases the likelihood that substantive flaws in methodology will be detected. . . . The fact of publication (or lack thereof) in a peer-reviewed journal thus will be a relevant, though not dispositive, consideration in assessing the scientific validity of a particular technique or methodology on which an opinion is premised." (*Daubert,* p. 2797)

- Whether the scientific or clinical principle is generally accepted by experts in the field (the *Frye* rule). The *Daubert* Court wrote that "widespread accep-

tance can be an important factor in ruling particular evidence admissible" (p. 2797).

- Whether the principle or technique is consistent with established and proven modes of analysis (Black, Francisco, & Saffran-Brinks, 1994).

When Does the Special Rule Governing Scientific Evidence Apply?

The special rule governing scientific evidence does not apply every time an expert's testimony is based in whole or in part on scientific principles. Many scientific principles are so well-established that the judge takes what is called judicial notice of the reliability of the principles. For example, battered child syndrome is an accepted medical diagnosis. Judges take judicial notice of the reliability of the syndrome, and expert testimony based on the syndrome is not subject to the rule governing scientific principles or techniques (Myers, 1992a).

Unfortunately, uncertainty abounds regarding application of the special rule to many aspects of expert testimony in child abuse litigation. For example, in most states it is unclear whether the rule applies to expert testimony based on clinical literature and judgment. It is equally unclear whether the rule applies to expert testimony based partly on clinical judgment and partly on scientific or empirical data. Should the rule apply to clinical judgment and admixtures of clinical and scientific information? Although reasonable minds can differ, I believe the search for truth would be aided by more frequent application of the rule (see Imwinkelried, 1992). It seems reasonable to apply the rule whenever expert testimony is based on scientific *or* clinical principles that are of doubtful or untested reliability.

When the rule applies, the attorney offering the expert testimony must convince the judge that the scientific or clinical principles underlying the testimony are sufficiently reliable.

Expert Testimony in Physical Abuse and Neglect Cases

Expert testimony regarding nonaccidental injury is a complex subject. Limitations of space preclude extended discussion of this interesting and important subject, and the reader is referred to other sources (see Helfer & Kempe, 1987; Ludwig & Kornberg, 1992; Reece, 1994).

Briefly, in physical child abuse litigation, accused individuals usually raise one of two defenses. The most common defense is that the child's injuries were accidental. Alternatively, the accused may acknowledge that the child was abused but claim someone else did it.

Expert testimony from medical professionals plays a key role in proving nonaccidental injury (Chadwick, 1990; Myers, 1992a). Physicians regularly provide testimony about bruises, bites, head injuries, abdominal injuries, burns, and fractures (Reece, 1994; Schmitt, 1987; see Chapter 12, this volume).

Expert Medical Testimony on Cause of Injury

A properly qualified medical professional may testify that a child's injuries were probably not accidental. In general, experts are allowed to describe the means used to inflict injury (Myers, 1992a, § 3.8). In *People v. Jackson* (1971), for example, the court wrote that "an expert medical witness may give his opinion as to the means used to inflict a particular injury, based on his deduction from the appearance of the injury itself" (p. 921). Thus, an expert could state that a skull fracture was probably caused by a blow from a blunt instrument or that injury probably was caused by a person of mature strength. An expert may offer an opinion on "whether the explanation given for the injuries is reasonable" (*Gideon v. State*, 1986, p. 1336). Finally, an expert may offer an opinion on the cause of death or the potential harm of injuries inflicted on certain portions of the body (Myers, 1992a, § 3.8).

Battered Child Syndrome

In their landmark article, Kempe and his colleagues coined the term *battered child syndrome* (Kempe, Silverman, Steele, Droegemueller, & Silver, 1962). Kempe et al. describe the battered child:

The battered child syndrome may occur at any age, but, in general the affected children are younger than 3 years. In some instances the clinical manifestations are limited to those resulting from a single episode of trauma, but more often the child's general health is below par, and he shows evidence of neglect, including poor skin hygiene, multiple soft tissue injuries, and malnutrition. One often obtains a history of previous episodes suggestive of parental neglect or trauma. A marked discrepancy between clinical findings and historical data as supplied by the parents is a major diagnostic feature of the battered-child syndrome. . . . Subdural hematoma, with or without fracture of the skull . . . is an extremely frequent finding even in the absence of fractures of the long bones. . . . The characteristic distribution of these multiple fractures and the observation that the lesions are in different stages of healing are of additional value in making the diagnosis. (p. 17)

Not all victims of physical abuse have injuries in various stages of healing. Kempe et al. noted that abusive injury sometimes results from "a single episode of trauma" (p. 17). Many child abuse fatalities lack a pattern of repeated injury. Zumwalt and Hirsch noted that "fatalities from an isolated or single beating are as common as fatalities from repeated physical assault" (1987, p. 258).

Expert testimony on battered child syndrome is admitted routinely. Physicians are permitted to state that a child has the syndrome and probably suffered nonaccidental injury.

Shaken Baby Syndrome

Frustrated caretakers sometimes grasp young children by the shoulders or under the arms and shake them. Neurological damage caused by violent shaking is called *shaken baby syndrome*. The syndrome is an accepted medical diagnosis and is not subject to the special rule governing scientific evidence. Expert testimony on shaken baby syndrome is admissible (Myers, 1992a, § 3.11).

Munchausen Syndrome by Proxy

Munchausen syndrome in adults is "a condition characterized by habitual presentation for hospital treatment of an apparent acute illness, the patient giving a plausible and dramatic history, all of which is false" (*Dorland's Illustrated Medical*

Dictionary, 1981, p. 1295). Munchausen syndrome by proxy occurs when adults use a child as the vehicle for fabricated illness. Zumwalt and Hirsch (1987) write that

> Munchausen syndrome by proxy occurs when a parent or guardian falsifies a child's medical history or alters a child's laboratory test or actually causes an illness or injury in a child in order to gain medical attention for the child which may result in innumerable harmful hospital procedures. (p. 276)

Courts allow expert testimony describing Munchausen syndrome by proxy (Myers, 1992a, § 3.15). In *People v. Phillips* (1981), for example, the court approved expert psychiatric testimony on the syndrome to establish the defendant's motive to poison her baby by putting large quantities of salt in the baby's food. The court ruled that the syndrome was not a scientific technique subject to the special rule governing such techniques.

Neglect Cases

Neglect is a broad concept, covering many types of maltreatment. Unfortunately, it is not possible in this short chapter to describe the various kinds of neglect and the role expert witnesses play in proving neglect. For in-depth treatment of neglect, see Helfer and Kempe (1987), Ludwig and Kornberg (1992), Reece (1994), and Chapter 10, this volume. For case law regarding neglect, see Myers (1992a, § 3.16 to § 3.27).

Expert Testimony in Sexual Abuse Litigation

Expert testimony plays an important role in some child sexual abuse litigation (Bulkley, 1992). At the outset, expert testimony regarding sexual abuse should be divided into three categories: (a) testimony describing medical evidence, (b) testimony based largely on the psychological effects of abuse, and (c) testimony based largely on developmental differences between children and adults.

Medical Evidence

The first category of expert testimony concerns medical evidence of sexual abuse, such as genital injury and sexually transmitted disease (Bays & Chadwick, 1993). Although medical evidence is found in a small percentage of cases, when such evidence exists, judges generally allow physicians and other qualified medical professionals to describe it.

Testimony Based Largely on the Psychological Effects of Sexual Abuse

Expert testimony regarding psychological effects falls into two subcategories: (a) substantive evidence and (b) rehabilitation (see p. 320 for definitions of substantive and rehabilitation evidence).

Substantive Evidence

Substantive expert testimony from mental health professionals takes several forms. The expert may offer an opinion that the child has a diagnosis of sexual abuse. The expert may avoid diagnostic terminology and offer an opinion that the child was abused. The expert may state that the child's symptoms are consistent with sexual abuse. Alternatively, the expert may state that the child demonstrates sexual knowledge that is unusual for children of that age. Finally, the expert may avoid mention of the child in the case at hand and confine testimony to a description of symptoms commonly seen in sexually abused children. Whatever form the testimony takes, it is offered as *substantive evidence* of abuse.

Controversy in the literature. Expert psychological testimony offered as substantive evidence is based on many factors, including the child's statements and the child's behavior and symptoms. There is controversy over whether mental health professionals should offer testimony in the form of substantive evidence of sexual abuse. Melton and Limber (1989) assert that "under no circumstances should a court admit the opinion of [a mental health professional] about whether a particular child has been abused" (p. 1230). By contrast, the writings of other professionals support the use of such testimony in some cases (Corwin, 1988; Faller, 1990;

Myers et al., 1989). Faller (1990) observes that "there appears to be a fair amount of consensus among mental health professionals about both the strategy and the criteria for deciding whether a child has been sexually victimized" (p. 115). Oberlander surveyed 31 Massachusetts mental health professionals who evaluate children for possible sexual abuse. Oberlander (1995) writes,

> Evaluators were asked whether it was possible to determine whether a child's behavior and symptoms were consistent with typical responses to sexual abuse. . . . In this sample, 67.7% said they believed it was possible to make such a determination, 9.7% said they were unsure or that it depends on the case, and 22.5% said they believed it was not possible to make such a determination.
>
> Evaluators were asked to indicate their opinions about whether evaluation results could establish that a child was sexually abused. . . . In this sample, 58.1% said they believed evaluation results could establish abuse, 12.9% said they were unsure or that it depends on the case, and 29.0% said they believed evaluation results could not establish abuse. (Most evaluators drew a distinction between "establish" and "prove," suggesting that their opinions are probabilistic.) (pp. 482-483)

In 1990, the American Professional Society on the Abuse of Children issued guidelines for the psychosocial evaluation of sexual abuse in young children. The guidelines state the following:

> Sexual abuse is known to produce both acute and long-term negative psychological effects requiring therapeutic intervention. Psychosocial assessments are a systematic process of gathering information and forming professional opinions about the source of statements, behavior, and other evidence that form the basis of concern about possible sexual abuse. Psychosocial evaluations are broadly concerned with understanding developmental, familial, and historical factors and events that may be associated with psychological adjustment. The results of such evaluations may be used to assist in legal decision making and in directing treatment planning. (APSAC, 1990, p. 1)

Controversy is likely to continue over the propriety of expert testimony offered

as substantive evidence of child sexual abuse.

The significance of symptoms commonly observed in sexually abused children. Among the many factors considered in evaluating possible sexual abuse, professionals consider psychological symptoms and cognitive reactions observed in many sexually abused children (Mosteller, 1989). Although there is no single set of symptoms observed in all sexually abused children, the presence of commonly observed symptoms often provides evidence of abuse.

Many psychological symptoms are observed in sexually abused children. Symptoms of anxiety are particularly common, including fear, sleep disturbances and nightmares, flashbacks, startle reactions, hypervigilance, regression, bed wetting, phobic behavior, withdrawal from usual activities, nervousness, and clinginess (Browne & Finkelhor, 1986; Kendall-Tackett, Williams, & Finkelhor, 1993; Mannarino & Cohen, 1986). Some sexually abused children are depressed (Lanktree, Briere, & Zaidi, 1991; Lipovsky, Saunders, & Murphy, 1989; Wozencraft, Wagner, & Pellegrin, 1991).

The fact that a child has nightmares and regression says little about sexual abuse, because other circumstances may cause such symptoms.

The fact that a child has nightmares and regression says little about sexual abuse, because other circumstances may cause such symptoms. In fact, if all we know about a child is that the child has nightmares and regression, it is more likely the child is *non*abused than abused. This conclusion flows from the base rate at which nightmares and regression occur in the total population of *non*abused children in the United States (Melton & Limber, 1989). The base rate of a symptom or behavior is essentially the prevalence of the symptom or behavior.

To illustrate the base rate effect, consider the following hypothetical case. (The population figures in this hypothetical are for illustration only and are not accurate.) Assume there are 30 million *non*abused children in the United States, and

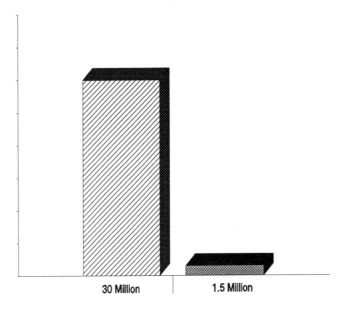

Figure 17.1. 30 Million Nonabused Children, 5% of Whom Have Nightmares and Regression

5% of these *non*abused children experience serious nightmares and regression. Thus, in the total population of *non*abused children, 1.5 million have nightmares and regression. Figure 17.1 illustrates the number of *non*abused children with nightmares and regression.

Now, shift your attention away from *non*abused children and concentrate on sexually abused children. Assume there are 300,000 sexually abused children in the United States, and 25% of them have serious nightmares and regression. Why the higher percentage for sexually abused children? Because sexual abuse does cause nightmares and regression in a substantial percentage of children. Thus, among sexually abused children, 75,000 experience nightmares and regression. Figure 17.2 illustrates the number of sexually abused children with nightmares and regression.

When the abused and the *non*abused children with nightmares and regression are combined, the total number of children with these symptoms is 1,575,000. Figure 17.3 illustrates the important point that in the *total* population of children with nightmares and regression, the great majority are *non*abused.

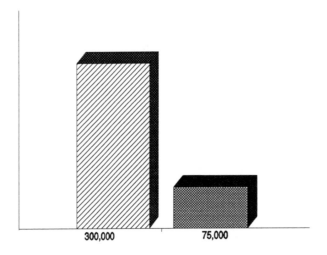

Figure 17.2. 300,000 Sexually Abused Children, 25% of Whom Have Nightmares and Regression

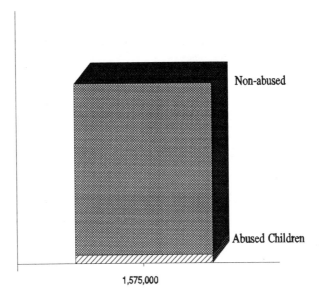

Figure 17.3. 1.5 Million Nonabused Children; 75,000 Abused Children

However, Figure 17.3 is misleading because the sexually abused children clearly remain distinguishable from the *non*abused children. To bring home the effect of the base rate, it is necessary to intermingle the 1.5 million symptomatic *non*abused children and the 75,000 abused children to form one large, undifferentiated group of children. Figure 17.4 illustrates the point.

If one reaches into this pool of 1,575,000 children with nightmares and regression and selects one child at random, the odds are great that the child is

*non*abused. Thus, the base rate explains why a child with nightmares and regression is more likely to be *non*abused than abused.

The base rate phenomenon is complex. Indeed, the foregoing example is an oversimplification. In some cases, nightmares and regression may say more about abuse than in other cases, although, in all cases, such behaviors—considered in isolation—say very little about abuse. Melton and Limber observe that "even psychologists who have had substantial statistical training often fail to appreciate

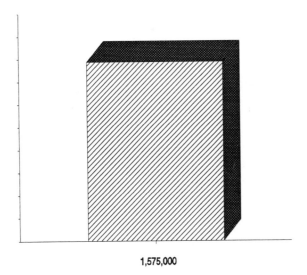

Figure 17.4. Abused *and* Nonabused Children With Nightmares and Regression

the significance of base rates" (1989, p. 1229). Once the base rate effect is understood, professionals should not base decisions about sexual abuse primarily on symptoms shared by abused and nonabused children. (For detailed discussion of base rates, see Wood, in press, and Wood & Wright, 1995.)

Although many symptoms observed in sexually abused children are found in nonabused children, some symptoms are more strongly associated with a personal or vicarious sexual experience. Examples of symptoms that have a closer connection to sexual abuse include developmentally unusual knowledge of sexual acts and sexualized play in young children (Beitchman, Zucker, Hood, daCosta, & Akman, 1991; Friedrich, 1993; Kolko & Moser, 1988; Mannarino & Cohen, 1986).

Friedrich and his colleagues gathered data on normative sexual behavior in children (Friedrich, Brambsch, Broughton, & Beilke, 1991) and noted,

> A relatively clear finding is that despite the fact that 2- through 12-year-old children exhibit a wide variety of sexual behaviors at relatively high frequencies, e.g., self-stimulatory behavior and exhibitionism, there are a number of behaviors that are quite unusual. . . . These tend to be those behaviors that are either more aggressive or more imitative of adult sexual behavior. (p. 462)

In Friedrich's study, the sexual behaviors observed *least* often in *non*abused children were placing the child's mouth on a sex part, asking to engage in sex acts, masturbating with an object, inserting objects in the vagina/anus, imitating intercourse, making sexual sounds, French kissing, undressing other people, asking to watch sexually explicit television, and imitating sexual behavior with dolls. However, the child's display of one or more of these uncommon sexual behaviors is by no means conclusive evidence of sexual abuse. According to Friedrich, "Sexual behavior in children is related to the child's family context, most specifically the sexual behavior in the family" (p. 462).

In a related study, Friedrich and his colleagues compared sexual behavior in *non*abused and abused children and discovered statistically significant differences for some behaviors (Friedrich, 1993; Friedrich et al., 1992).

Lindblad and colleagues (Lindblad, Gustafsson, Larsson, & Lundin, 1995) examined the frequency of sexual behaviors in a sample of 251 Swedish preschool children attending day care centers. The following behaviors are of interest: 99.6% of the children never attempted to make an adult at day care touch the child's genitals; 91.2% never attempted to touch a female staff member's breasts; 99.6% never attempted to touch an adult's genitals at day care; 91.6% of the children never exhibited their genitals at day care; 92.0% never played sexually explorative games such as "doctor"; 96.8% never initiated games simulating adult sexual activity.

Phipps-Yonas and her colleagues (Phipps-Yonas, Yonas, Turner, & Kauper, 1993) surveyed 564 licensed family day care providers in Minnesota regarding the providers' "observations of children's behavior and apparent sexual knowledge" (p. 2). Phipps-Yonas et al. write the following:

> We are all sexual creatures and sexual learning begins in early infancy. . . . Among preschoolers there is often considerable freedom regarding their bodies as well as touching of themselves, their peers, and family members. Children at this stage engage in games such as playing doctor or house which involve explorations through touch and sight of each other's so-called private parts.
>
> We asked people to answer how children aged one to three behave and how children aged four to six behave. . . . Older children were viewed as much more curious than the younger ones regarding the mechanics of sexual activities and reproduction. They were also much more likely to engage in exploratory "sexual" games such as "I'll show you mine, if you show me yours" or doctor or house.
>
> As other investigators have reported, touching of other children's genitals is relatively common. . . . Certain behaviors were reported as having a very low probability by the day care providers, especially for children under age four. These include: efforts to engage in pretend sexual intercourse; French-kissing; requests to have another suck, lick, or kiss their genitals; and attempts to insert objects into their own or another's buttocks or vaginas. (pp. 1, 3-4)

Conte and his colleagues surveyed 212 professionals who regularly evaluate children for possible sexual abuse (Conte, Sorenson, Fogarty, & Dalla Rosa, 1991).

The professionals were asked to rank the importance of 41 indicators of sexual abuse. The following indicators were thought to be important by more than 90% of the evaluators: medical evidence of abuse, age-inappropriate sexual knowledge, sexualized play during the interview, precocious or seductive behavior, excessive masturbation, consistency in the child's description over time, and the child's report of pressure or coercion.

Conte cautioned against placing undue confidence in his findings, however, noting that consensus among professionals "does not ensure that professional practice or professional beliefs are knowledge-based, and agreement among these respondents should not be assumed to validate various practices as reliable and effective" (Conte et al., 1991). Indeed, professional judgment based on clinical experience alone is often a poor foundation for decision making (Wood, in press; see Dawes, Faust, & Meehl, 1989; Garb, 1989).

Wells and colleagues studied symptoms in three groups of prepubescent females: nonabused, confirmed abuse, and suspected but unconfirmed abuse (Wells, McCann, Adams, Voris, & Ensign, 1995). The authors write,

Children with known or suspected sexual abuse were significantly more likely to have sudden emotional and behavioral change, to be fearful of being left with a particular person, to know more about sex and to be more interested and curious about sex matters or private parts. There were no differences between the groups on bed-wetting, headaches, constipation, or vaginal bleeding. Significant problems in concentration and changes in school performance were noted in those children with suspected sexual abuse, but there were no significant differences regarding bath habits, truancy or extracurricular involvement. No children in the nonabused sample were described as acting overly mature or adultlike for age, while 33% of children in the other groups had this reported by a parent. Similarly, there were no parents in the nonabused groups who reported that their child had become fearful of males or unusually self-conscious about her body. In contrast, 27% of children with suspected sexual abuse were reportedly fearful of males and 28% had become unusually self-conscious about their bodies. . . . Children with a perpetrator confession had significantly greater rates of reported

fearfulness of being left alone, fearfulness of males, and of being self-conscious about her body. . . . Nightmares, crying easily, and being fearful of being left alone were common symptoms in the nonabused sample, as were difficulties with bed-wetting, headaches and stomach aches. These symptoms do not appear to be necessarily reflective of abuse. In contrast, specific fears of a particular person, self-consciousness about her body and fearfulness of males appear to be questions that discriminate amongst abused and nonabused samples. . . . Sudden changes in children's behaviors and particularly increased and specific fears and heightened interest and curiosity regarding sexual matters appears to happen relatively infrequently in the nonabused sample, but are present in 30 to 66% of children who are suspected victims of abuse. (pp. 159-161)

Current research has limitations. Nevertheless, the findings of Friedrich, Lindblad, Phipps-Yonas, Conte, Wells, and others lay the beginnings of an empirical foundation for the conclusion that the presence of sexual behaviors that are seldom observed in nonabused children provides evidence of sexual abuse.

When evaluating children for sexual abuse, no single symptom or behavior—sexual or nonsexual—is pathognomonic of abuse.

When evaluating children for sexual abuse, no single symptom or behavior—sexual or nonsexual—is pathognomonic of abuse. Moreover, depending on the base rate of abuse in a population of children, individual symptoms or behaviors that normally provide relatively strong evidence of abuse may be of marginal probative value (Wood, in press).

When can one place the most confidence in an expert's opinion that a child was sexually abused? The greatest confidence often is warranted when the expert's opinion is based on a coalescence of five types of data:

1. Developmentally unusual sexual behavior, knowledge, or symptoms providing relatively strong evidence of sexual experience (e.g., 4-year-old with detailed

knowledge of fellatio, including ejaculation)

2. Nonsexual behavior or symptoms commonly observed in sexually abused children (e.g., symptoms such as nightmares and regression)
3. Medical evidence indicative of sexual abuse
4. Convincing disclosure by the child
5. Evidence that corroborates the abuse (e.g., incriminating statements by the alleged perpetrator)

Confidence in an expert's opinion typically (although not invariably) grows as the amount and quality of evidence increases. For example, confidence in an expert's opinion may grow as the number or persuasiveness of developmentally unusual sexual behaviors increases, the types of nonsexual symptoms expand, the strength of medical evidence increases, the corroborating evidence becomes more convincing, and when there is evidence that the professionals who interviewed the child used proper techniques.

Confidence in an expert's opinion about sexual abuse often (although, again, not invariably) declines as the amount and quality of evidence supporting the opinion decreases. The decline in confidence is particularly precipitous when evidence providing relatively strong evidence of abuse is lacking. For example, there may be no medical evidence, the child may demonstrate none of the developmentally unusual sexual behaviors that are related to sexual abuse, and there may be no corroborating evidence. In such a case, the expert's opinion about sexual abuse is based entirely on *non*sexual symptoms and the child's disclosure. Although one *may* place enough confidence in the expert's opinion to allow it in court, one may well have less confidence in an opinion that is not supported by medical evidence, sexualized behavior, or corroboration.

Some cases may be based on no medical evidence, no developmentally unusual sexual behavior, no corroboration, and no convincing disclosure. In such cases, the expert's opinion is based on one source of data: *non*sexual symptoms commonly observed in sexually abused children. One can have *no* confidence in such an opinion, however, because of the base rate effect.

One should not conclude from the foregoing that the *quantity* of evidence is a satisfactory basis for judging expert opinion. Rather, sound decision making rests on careful assessment of the quantity, quality, and context of the evidence.

Courts take three positions regarding expert testimony offered as substantive evidence of sexual abuse. Judges do not question the ability of mental health professionals to make *clinical* decisions about sexual abuse. However, the level of certainty that is sufficient for clinical purposes may not be sufficient for expert testimony that a child was abused. As outlined earlier, professionals have not achieved consensus on whether current knowledge is adequate to support mental health testimony offered as substantive evidence of abuse. Courts also are divided on the issue. With some oversimplification, it is possible to say that courts in the United States take three positions regarding expert testimony from mental health professionals offered as *substantive evidence* of sexual abuse.

One group of court decisions allows properly qualified professionals to offer *some forms* of substantive evidence of sexual abuse in *some cases*[2] (e.g., *Broderick v. King's Way Assembly of God Church*, 1991 [AK]; *Cohn v. State*, 1993 [TX]; *Commonwealth v. Trowbridge*, 1995 [MA]; *Glendening v. State*, 1988 [FL]; *Hall v. State*, 1992 [MS]; *In re Gina D.*, 1994 [NH]; *Rivera v. State*, 1992 [WY]; *Sciscoe v. State*, 1992 [AL]; *Shannon v. State*, 1989 [NV]; *State v. Butler*, 1995 [CT]; *State v. Charles*, 1990 [WV]; *State v. Florczak*, 1994 [WA]; *State v. Hammond*, 1993 [NC]; *State v. Hester*, 1988 [ID]; *State v. Hillman*, 1993 [LA]; *State v. Kallin*, 1994 [UT]; *State v. Schumpert*, 1993 [SC]; *State v. Silvey*, 1995 [MO]; *State v. Wilson*, 1993 [OR]).

A second group of decisions rejects some or all forms of substantive evidence from mental health professionals (e.g., *Commonwealth v. Dunkle*, 1992 [PA]; *Hall v. Commonwealth*, 1993 [KY]; *Johnson v. State*, 1987 [AR]; *People v. McAlpin*, 1991 [CA]; *People v. Singh*, 1992 [NY]; *State v. Anderson*, 1994 [TN]; *State v. Jones*, 1993 [WA]; *State v. Lamb*, 1988 [WI]; *State v. Schimpf*, 1989 [TN]).

A third group of decisions adopts a middle position. These courts treat substantive evidence from mental health professionals as a form of scientific evidence and subject it to the special rule applied to such evidence. This approach has much to commend it. By characterizing expert mental health testimony offered as substantive evidence as a form of scientific evidence, the courts leave the door open to such testimony *if and when* it is established as sufficiently reliable (see p. 323 for discussion of the special rule governing scientific evidence; e.g., *Gier v. Educational Service Unit No. 16*, 1994 [NE]; *In re Amber B.*, 1987 [CA]; *State v. Ballard*, 1993 [TN]; *State v. Cressey*, 1993 [NH]; *State v. Foret*, 1993 [LA]; *State v. Rimmasch*, 1989 [UT]).

Rehabilitation Expert Testimony

The second category of expert testimony from mental health professionals is testimony offered for the limited purpose of rehabilitating a child's credibility *after* it is attacked by the defense attorney. When expert testimony is limited to rehabilitation, the testimony is *not* offered as substantive evidence of sexual abuse.

Expert rehabilitation testimony serves a limited—although important—purpose: to help the jury accurately assess the child's credibility after it has been attacked.

How does the defense attorney attack the child's credibility? The defense attorney may assert that a child's behavior is inconsistent with abuse. For example, defense counsel may argue that a child should not be believed because the child did not report abuse for a substantial period of time or because the child recanted. When the defense concentrates on delay, recantation, and certain other behaviors, the judge may permit the prosecutor to respond with expert testimony to inform jurors that such behavior is common in sexually abused children.

Delay in reporting. Many victims of child sexual abuse never disclose their abuse (Russell, 1983). Of those who do disclose, delayed reporting is common (Finkelhor, 1979; Russell, 1986). The reasons for delay are apparent. In intrafamilial abuse, the child is relatively helpless and must accommodate to ongoing maltreatment (Summit, 1983). The abusing parent is often in a position to enforce secrecy. Many children are too embarrassed to disclose their victimization.

Recantation. When disclosure occurs, many children refrain from telling the whole story, revealing a little at a time to "test the water" and see how adults react (Sorensen & Snow, 1991). Jones and McQuiston (1985) write that

usually children disclose a small portion of their total experience initially in an apparent attempt to test the adult's response before letting them know more about the assault. If they receive a positive and supportive response, they may feel safe enough to disclose more about their experience. (pp. 3-4)

Following disclosure, many children recant. Sorensen and Snow (1991) studied 116 cases of confirmed child sexual abuse and found that "in approximately 22% of the cases, children recanted their allegations. . . . Of those who recanted, 92% reaffirmed their abuse allegations over time" (p. 11).

Ambivalence toward the abuser. In intrafamilial child sexual abuse, many victims are ambivalent toward the abuser, feeling love and anger at the same time. It is not uncommon for abused children to demonstrate affection toward the abusing parent and a desire to live with the perpetrator.

Nearly all states allow limited use of mental health expert testimony to rehabilitate children's credibility. When children's testimony is challenged, judges in most states selectively approve expert testimony that is designed to rehabilitate children's credibility. However, Pennsylvania, Kentucky, and Tennessee may disallow expert testimony offered to rehabilitate children's credibility (*Commonwealth v. Dunkle*, 1992).

Expert testimony generally is allowed to explain why sexually abused children delay reporting abuse, why children recant, why children's descriptions of abuse are sometimes inconsistent, why abused children are angry, why some children want to live with the person who abused them, why a child abuse victim might appear "emotionally flat" following the assault, and why a child might run away from home (Myers, 1992a, § 4.13).

Courts generally hold that expert rehabilitation testimony is not subject to the special rule governing scientific principles.

The following guidelines are offered regarding expert testimony to rehabilitate children's impeached credibility:

1. In some states, the prosecutor must tell the judge and the defense attorney which behavior(s) the expert will discuss (*People v. Bowker*, 1988). For example, if the defense attorney limits the attack on the child's credibility to delay in reporting, the prosecutor must let the

judge and defense counsel know that the expert's testimony will be limited to helping the jury understand delay. The expert should then limit testimony to the behavior emphasized by the defense attorney and should not offer a broad-ranging lecture on children's reactions to sexual abuse.

2. In most cases, expert rehabilitation testimony is limited to a description of behaviors seen in sexually abused children *as a group.* Unless asked to do so, it is wise to avoid describing any particular child and, in particular, to avoid describing the child in the present case.

3. If it is necessary to refer to the child in the present case, the expert should avoid using the word *victim.* Judges worry that referring to the child as a victim sends the jury a message that the expert believes the child was abused. (Remember, when expert testimony is limited to rehabilitation, the expert is *not* there to give the jury evidence on whether the child was abused.)

4. In most sexual abuse cases, the expert should avoid reference to syndromes, such as child sexual abuse accommodation syndrome. An expert does not need to use the loaded word *syndrome* to help the jury understand that delay in reporting, recantation, and inconsistency is common in sexually abused children.

Nonabusive *parents* sometimes delay reporting the abuse of their children. In *People v. McAlpin* (1991), the defendant was charged with molesting the daughter of the woman whom the defendant was dating. The child's mother did not break off her relationship with the defendant immediately after learning of the molestation. Moreover, the mother had sexual intercourse with the defendant a week following the molestation. At the defendant's trial, the defense counsel sought to impeach the mother's "credibility by strongly implying that her behavior after the alleged incident was inconsistent with that of a mother who believed her daughter had been molested" (*People v. McAlpin,* 1991, p. 570). The California Supreme Court approved expert "testimony that it is not unusual for a parent to refrain from reporting a known molestation of his or her child" (p. 569).

The degree of expertise required to testify as an expert depends on whether the testimony is offered as substantive evidence or for rehabilitation. Professionals with relatively little

experience and training can provide expert testimony to rehabilitate a child's credibility. In many cases, for example, rehabilitation testimony is limited to explaining that sexually abused children often recant or delay reporting. The expert does not venture an opinion that the child in the case at hand was abused. Indeed, with rehabilitation testimony, it is often unnecessary to refer to the child. Rehabilitation testimony is straightforward and simple. To provide such testimony, the only requirement is knowledge of relevant literature.

Although only limited expertise is required for rehabilitation testimony, a high level of expertise is required to offer substantive evidence of sexual abuse (APSAC, 1990). Only a small percentage of professionals working with sexually abused children are qualified to provide substantive evidence.

Expert Testimony Regarding Developmental Differences Between Children and Adults

Increasingly, defense attorneys seek to undermine children's credibility by arguing that developmental differences between adults and children render children *as a group* less credible than adults. The defense counsel may assert that children are highly suggestible and have poor memories (*Idaho v. Wright,* 1990; *State v. Michaels,* 1994). In some cases, the defense offers its own expert to discuss children's suggestibility or to challenge the way children were interviewed by professionals. In response to this strategy, the judge may allow the prosecutor to offer expert testimony to help jurors understand that children have good memories and are not as suggestible as many adults believe. In some cases, the prosecutor offers expert testimony about the complex task of interviewing young children.

Expert Testimony About Psychological Syndromes

The following section briefly discusses three psychological syndromes that play a role in child sexual abuse litigation (for a detailed discussion of this topic, see Myers, 1993b).

Child sexual abuse accommodation syndrome. In 1983, Summit described child sexual abuse accommodation syndrome (CSAAS). Summit noted five characteristics commonly observed in sexually abused children: (a) secrecy; (b) helplessness; (c) entrapment and accommodation; (d) delayed, conflicted, and unconvincing disclosure; and (e) retraction. Summit's purpose in describing the accommodation syndrome was to provide a "common language" for professionals working to protect sexually abused children. Summit did not intend the accommodation syndrome as a diagnostic device. Because of misunderstandings about application of the syndrome, Summit recently clarified that it cannot be used to determine whether a child has been sexually abused (Meinig, 1991). The accommodation syndrome does *not* detect sexual abuse. Rather, CSAAS assumes that abuse occurred and explains the child's reactions to it. Thus, the accommodation syndrome does not prove abuse and does not constitute substantive evidence.

The syndrome helps explain why many sexually abused children delay reporting their abuse and why many abused children recant allegations of abuse and deny that anything happened. When the syndrome is confined to these rehabilitative purposes, the accommodation syndrome serves a useful forensic function.

Rape trauma syndrome. Rape trauma syndrome (RTS) was described by Burgess and Holmstrom (1974) as "the acute phase and long-term reorganization process that occurs as a result of forcible rape or attempted forcible rape. This syndrome of behavioral, somatic, and psychological reactions is an acute stress reaction to a life-threatening situation" (p. 982). Although expert testimony on RTS is used most often in litigation involving adult victims, RTS is useful in child sexual abuse litigation involving older children and adolescents.

Expert testimony on RTS has been offered by prosecutors for two purposes: (a) as substantive evidence to prove lack of consent to sexual relations and (b) as rehabilitation to explain behavior such as delay in reporting rape, which jurors might misconstrue as evidence that rape did not occur.

RTS as substantive evidence of lack of consent. Courts are divided on the admissibility of RTS to prove lack of consent. Consent is not a defense to a charge of child sexual abuse. Nevertheless, consent sometimes plays a subsidiary role in child sexual abuse litigation. Several courts reject RTS to prove lack of consent (*Commonwealth v. Gallagher,* 1988; *People v. Bledsoe,* 1984; *People v. Taylor,* 1990; *State v. Black,* 1987).

Several courts allow expert testimony describing RTS when the defendant asserts that the victim consented (*State v. Alberico,* 1993; *State v. Allewalt,* 1986; *State v. Brodniak,* 1986; *State v. Huey,* 1985; *State v. Marks,* 1982; *State v. McCoy,* 1988; *United States v. Carter,* 1988). Courts that allow RTS to prove lack of consent place limits on the evidence. Thus, courts do not permit expert witnesses to testify that the alleged victim was, in fact, raped.

RTS to rehabilitate the victim's credibility. Most courts allow expert testimony on RTS to rehabilitate the victim's credibility (*People v. Hampton,* 1987; *State v. Graham,* 1990). In *People v. Bledsoe* (1984), the California Supreme Court wrote that "expert testimony on rape trauma syndrome may play a particularly useful role by disabusing the jury of some widely held misconceptions about rape and rape victims, so that it may evaluate the evidence free of the constraints of popular myths" (p. 457). In *People v. Taylor* (1990), the New York Court of Appeals approved expert testimony explaining why a rape victim might not appear upset following the assault.

Courts place limits on evidence of RTS offered to explain behaviors observed in rape victims. For example, several court decisions state that the expert should describe behaviors observed in rape victims *as a group* and should not refer to the victim in the case at hand (*People v. Coleman,* 1989).

Posttraumatic stress disorder. Evidence of posttraumatic stress disorder (PTSD) is sometimes admissible as substantive evidence of abuse. In addition, evidence of PTSD is sometimes admissible to rehabilitate the victim's credibility.

Expert Testimony That Judges Do Not Allow

All U.S. courts agree that expert witnesses are not to comment directly on the credibility of individual children or on the credibility of sexually abused children as a group. Thus, expert witnesses should not say that a child told the truth or was believable when describing abuse. The Oregon Supreme Court did not mince words in its condemnation of expert testimony on the truthfulness of children. The court wrote, "We have said before, and we will say it again, but this time with emphasis—we really mean it—*no psychotherapist may render an opinion on whether a witness is credible in any trial conducted in this state*. The assessment of credibility is for the trier of fact and not for psychotherapists" (*State v. Milbradt*, 1988, p. 624). Courts reject expert testimony on credibility because judges firmly believe that assessment of credibility must be the exclusive province of the jury. As one court put it, "The jury is the lie detector in the courtroom" (*United States v. Barnard*, 1973, p. 912).

Judges also do not permit expert witnesses to testify that a particular person perpetrated abuse.

Expert Testimony Regarding the Alleged Perpetrator

In the effort to prove that a person sexually abused a child, is the prosecutor allowed to offer expert testimony that the person fits the psychological profile of a sex offender or pedophile? For psychological as well as legal reasons, the answer should be "No."

From the *psychological perspective*, the clinical and scientific literature indicates that persons who sexually abuse children are a heterogeneous group with few shared characteristics apart from a predilection for deviant sexual behavior with children. Furthermore, no psychological test or device reliably detects persons who have or will sexually abuse children (Murphy, Rau, & Worley, 1994). Thus, under the current state of scientific knowledge, there is no profile of a "typical" child molester (Myers et al., 1989, p. 142).

From the *legal perspective*, the inappropriateness of profile testimony is supported by one of the basic rules of U.S. law. A prosecutor is generally not allowed to establish a person's guilt through evidence that the person has a particular character trait or propensity. Thus, evidence of a person's character is not allowed to prove that the person acted in conformity with character on a particular occasion.

The rule against character evidence is applicable in sexual abuse litigation.[3] The prosecutor cannot establish guilt through expert testimony that the accused person has a character trait or propensity for sexual abuse. Expert testimony that the accused person fits the profile of a "typical" sex offender is essentially character evidence and inadmissible for that reason.

In 1994, Congress changed federal law so that prosecutors in federal court trials can now offer evidence that the defendant abused other children in the past. Such evidence is used to prove that because the defendant has a track record of abuse, he or she probably abused the child in the case as at hand (Fed. R. Evid. 413-415). This new rule is a complete abrogation in sex offense cases of the well-established principle that prohibits the prosecutor from using character evidence to prove guilt. The rule will be challenged in federal court, and it remains to be seen whether state legislatures will adopt similar rules.

May the prosecutor offer expert testimony that there is *no* profile of a "typical" child molester? In *People v. McAlpin* (1991), the California Supreme Court said yes, at least in some cases. Such expert testimony helps the jury understand that child molesters come from all walks of life and backgrounds.

Unlike the prosecutor, the defendant in a criminal case *is* allowed to offer character evidence to prove innocence (Fed. R. Evid. 404[a][1]). With this rule in mind, should a person accused of child sexual abuse be allowed to offer expert testimony that the person does *not* fit the profile or share the character traits of child molesters? From the scientific perspective, the answer should be "No" (*Flanagan v. State*, 1993; *State v. Person*, 1989). However, despite the lack of a reliable profile, some mental health professionals are willing to describe profiles or testify that a person does not share the characteristics of individuals who typically abuse children, and a few courts allow such testimony (*People v. Stoll*, 1989).

Once the defendant offers expert testimony that the defendant does not share the characteristics of child molesters, the prosecutor is allowed to offer expert testimony to contradict the defendant's expert witness.

Conclusion

Expert testimony plays an important role in child abuse litigation. As long as experts realize the limits of their knowledge and keep their testimony within those limits, they will continue to help juries decide these difficult cases.

Notes

1. In *Daubert*, the Supreme Court used the word *reliable* to include both reliability and validity.

2. Before providing expert testimony offered as substantive evidence, the professional should confer with the attorney offering the professional's testimony on the scope and limits of such testimony under local law.

3. Quite a few states do allow a type of character evidence in child sexual abuse litigation. These states allow the prosecutor to prove that the accused person has committed sexual offenses for which the accused person is not now on trial. The use of the accused person's other sexual offenses is a type character evidence. Nevertheless, states allowing such evidence create an exception to the general rule that a person's guilt cannot be established with evidence of the person's character (see Myers, 1992a, § 6.10).

References

Adams, J. A., & Wells, R. (1993). Normal versus abnormal genital findings in children: How well do examiners agree? *Child Abuse & Neglect, 17,* 663-675.

American Professional Society on the Abuse of Children (APSAC). (1990). *Guidelines for psychosocial evaluation of suspected sexual abuse in young children.* Chicago: Author.

Bays, J., & Chadwick, D. L. (1993). Medical diagnosis of the sexually abused child. *Child Abuse & Neglect, 17,* 91-110.

Beitchman, J. H., Zucker, K. J., Hood, J. E., daCosta, G. A., & Akman, D. (1991). A review of the short-term effects of child sexual abuse. *Child Abuse & Neglect, 15,* 537-556.

Black, B. (1988). A unified theory of scientific evidence. *Fordham Law Review, 56,* 595-695.

Black, B., Francisco, J., & Saffran-Brinks, C. (1994). Science and the law in the wake of *Daubert:* A new search for scientific knowledge. *Texas Law Review, 72,* 715-802.

Broderick v. King's Way Assembly of God Church, 808 P.2d 1211 (Alaska 1991).

Browne, A., & Finkelhor, D. (1986). Impact of child sexual abuse: A review of the research. *Psychological Bulletin, 99,* 66-77.

Bulkley, J. A. (1992). The prosecution's use of social science expert testimony in child sexual abuse cases: National trends and recommendations. *Journal of Child Sexual Abuse, 1,* 73-93.

Burgess, A., & Holmstrom, L. (1974). Rape trauma syndrome. *American Journal of Psychiatry, 131,* 981-986.

Chadwick, D. L. (1990). Preparation for court testimony in child abuse cases. *Pediatric Clinics of North America, 37,* 955-970.

Cohn v. State, 849 S.W.2d 817 (Tex. Crim. App. 1993).

Committee on Ethical Guidelines for Forensic Psychologists. (1991). Specialty guidelines for forensic psychologists. *Law and Human Behavior, 15,* 655-665.

Commonwealth v. Dunkle, 602 A.2d 830 (Pa. 1992).

Commonwealth v. Gallagher, 547 A.2d 355 (Pa. 1988).

Commonwealth v. Trowbridge, 1995 WL 126087 (Mass. 1995).

Conte, J. R., Sorenson, E., Fogarty, L., & Dalla Rosa, J. (1991). Evaluating children's reports of sexual abuse: Results from a survey of professionals. *American Journal of Orthopsychiatry, 61,* 428.

Corwin, D. L. (1988). Early diagnosis of child sexual abuse: Diminishing the lasting effects. In G. E. Wyatt & G. J. Powell (Eds.), *Lasting effects of child sexual abuse* (pp. 251-269). Newbury Park, CA: Sage.

Daubert v. Merrell Dow Pharmaceuticals, Inc., 113 S. Ct. 2786 (1993).

Dawes, R. M., Faust, D., & Meehl, P. E. (1989). Clinical versus actuarial judgment. *Science, 243,* 1668-1674.

Dorland's illustrated medical dictionary (26th ed.). (1981). Philadelphia: Saunders.

Faller, K. C. (1990). *Understanding child sexual maltreatment*. Newbury Park, CA: Sage.

Federal rules of evidence. United States Code. Title 28.

Finkelhor, D. (1979). *Sexually victimized children*. New York: Free Press.

Flanagan v. State, 625 So.2d 827 (Fla. 1993).

Friedrich, W. N. (1993). Sexual victimization and sexual behavior in children: A review of recent literature. *Child Abuse & Neglect, 17,* 59-66.

Friedrich, W. N., Brambsch, P., Broughton, K., & Beilke, R. L. (1991). Normative sexual behavior in children. *Pediatrics, 88,* 456.

Friedrich, W. N., Grambsch, P., Damon, L., Hewitt, S., Koverola, C., Lang, R., Wolfe, V., & Broughton, D. (1992). The child sexual behavior inventory: Normative and clinical findings. *Psychological Assessment, 4,* 303-311.

Frye v. United States, 293 F. 1013 (D.C. Cir. 1923).

Garb, H. N. (1989). Clinical judgment, clinical training, and professional experience. *Psychological Bulletin, 105,* 387-396.

Gideon v. State, 721 P.2d 1336 (Okla. Crim. App. 1986).

Gier v. Educational Service Unit No. 16, 845 F. Supp. 1342 (D. Neb. 1994).

Glendening v. State, 536 So. 2d 212 (Fla. 1988).

Hall v. Commonwealth, 862 S.W.2d 321 (Ky. 1993).

Hall v. State, 611 So.2d 915 (Miss. 1992).

Helfer, R. E., & Kempe, R. S. (Eds.). (1987). *The battered child* (4th ed.). Chicago: University of Chicago Press.

Idaho v. Wright, 110 S. Ct. 3139 (1990).

Imwinkelried, E. (1992). Attempts to limit the scope of the *Frye* standard for the admission of scientific evidence: Confronting the real cost of the general acceptance test. *Behavioral Sciences and the Law, 10,* 441-454.

In re Amber B., 236 Cal. Rptr. 623 (1987).

In re Gina D., 645 A.2d 61 (N.H. 1994).

Johnson v. State, 732 S.W.2d 817 (Ark. 1987).

Jones, D. P. H., & McQuiston, M. (1985). *Interviewing the sexually abused child*. Denver, CO: C. Henry Kempe National Center for the Prevention and Treatment of Child Abuse and Neglect.

Kempe, C. H., Silverman, F. N., Steele, B. F., Droegemueller, W., & Silver, H. K. (1962). The battered-child syndrome. *Journal of the American Medical Association, 181,* 17-24.

Kendall-Tackett, K. A., Williams, L. M., & Finkelhor, D. (1993). Impact of sexual abuse on children: A review and synthesis of recent empirical studies. *Psychological Bulletin, 113,* 164-180.

Kolko, D. J., & Moser, J. T. (1988). Behavioral/emotional indicators of sexual abuse in child psychiatric inpatients: A controlled comparison with physical abuse. *Child Abuse & Neglect, 12,* 529-541.

Lanktree, C., Briere, J., & Zaidi, L. (1991). Incidence and impact of sexual abuse in a child outpatient sample: The role of direct inquiry. *Child Abuse & Neglect, 15,* 447-453.

Lilly, G. C. (1987). *An introduction to the law of evidence*. St. Paul, MN: West.

Lindblad, F., Gustafsson, P. A., Larsson, I., & Lundin, B. (1995). Preschoolers' sexual behavior at daycare centers: An epidemiological study. *Child Abuse & Neglect, 19,* 569-577.

Lipovsky, J. A., Saunders, B. E., & Murphy, S. M. (1989). Depression, anxiety, and behavior problems among victims of father-child sexual assault and nonabused siblings. *Journal of Interpersonal Violence, 4,* 452-468.

Louisell, D. W., & Mueller, C. B. (1988). *Federal evidence* (Vol. 3). San Francisco: Bancroft-Whitney.

Ludwig, S., & Kornberg, A. E. (Eds.). (1992). *Child abuse: A medical reference* (2nd ed.). New York: Churchill Livingstone.

Mannarino, A. P., & Cohen, J. A. (1986). A clinical-demographic study of sexually abused children. *Child Abuse & Neglect, 10,* 17-23.

Meinig, M. B. (1991). Profile of Roland Summit. *Violence Update, 1,* 6.

Melton, G. B., & Limber, S. (1989). Psychologists' involvement in cases of child maltreatment. *American Psychologist, 44*(9), 1225-1233.

Melton, G. B., Petrila, J., Poythress, N., & Slobogin, C. (1987). *Psychological evaluations for the courts.* New York: Guilford.

Morison, S., & Greene, E. (1992). Juror and expert knowledge of child sexual abuse. *Child Abuse & Neglect, 16,* 595-613.

Mosteller, R. P. (1989). Legal doctrines governing the admissibility of expert testimony concerning social framework evidence. *Law and Contemporary Problems, 52,* 85-132.

Murphy, W., Rau, T., & Worley, P. (1994). The perils and pitfalls of profiling child sex abusers. *APSAC Advisor, 7*, 3-4, 28-29.

Myers, J. E. B. (1992a). *Evidence in child abuse and neglect cases.* New York: John Wiley.

Myers, J. E. B. (1992b). *Legal issues in child abuse and neglect.* Newbury Park, CA: Sage.

Myers, J. E. B. (1993a). Confidentiality: Reviewing client records before testifying. *Violence Update, 3*, 3.

Myers, J. E. B. (1993b). Expert testimony regarding psychological syndromes. *Pacific Law Journal, 24*, 1449-1464.

Myers, J. E. B., Bays, J., Becker, J., Berliner, L., Corwin, D., & Saywitz, K. (1989). Expert testimony in child sexual abuse litigation. *Nebraska Law Review, 68*, 1-34.

Oberlander, L. B. (1995). Psycholegal issues in child sexual abuse evaluations: A survey of forensic mental health professionals. *Child Abuse & Neglect, 19*, 475-490.

People v. Bledsoe, 681 P.2d 291 (Cal. 1984).

People v. Bowker, 249 Cal. Rptr. 886 (1988).

People v. Coleman, 768 P.2d 32 (Cal. 1989).

People v. Hampton, 746 P.2d 947 (Colo. 1987).

People v. Jackson, 95 Cal. Rptr. 919 (Ct. App. 1971).

People v. McAlpin, 812 P.2d 563 (Cal. 1991).

People v. Phillips, 175 Cal. Rptr. 703 (Ct. App. 1981).

People v. Singh, 588 N.Y.S. 573 (A.D. 1992).

People v. Stoll, 783 P.2d 698 (Cal. 1989).

People v. Taylor, 552 N.E.2d 131, 552 N.Y.S.2d 883 (1990).

Phipps-Yonas, S., Yonas, A., Turner, M., & Kauper, M. (1993). Sexuality in early childhood: The observations and opinions of family day care providers. *University of Minnesota CURA Reporter, 23*, 1-5.

Reece, R. M. (Ed.). (1994). *Child abuse: Medical diagnosis and management.* Malvern, PA: Lea & Febiger.

Rivera v. State, 840 P.2d 933 (Wyo. 1992).

Russell, D. E. H. (1983). The incidence and prevalence of intrafamilial and extrafamilial sexual abuse of female children. *Child Abuse & Neglect, 7*, 133-146.

Russell, D. E. H. (1986). *The secret trauma: Incest in the lives of girls and women.* New York: Basic Books.

Saks, M. J. (1990). Expert witnesses, nonexpert witnesses, and nonwitness experts. *Law and Human Behavior, 14*, 291-313.

Schmitt, B. D. (1987). The child with nonaccidental trauma. In R. E. Helfer & R. S. Kempe (Eds.), *The battered child* (4th ed., pp. 178-196). Chicago: University of Chicago Press.

Sciscoe v. State, 606 So. 2d 202 (Ala. Crim. App. 1992).

Shannon v. State, 783 P.2d 942 (Nev. 1989).

Sorensen, T., & Snow, B. (1991). How children tell: The process of disclosure in child sexual abuse. *Child Welfare, 70*, 3-15.

State v. Alberico, 861 P.2d 192 (N.M. 1993).

State v. Allewalt, 517 A.2d 741 (Md. 1986).

State v. Anderson, 1994 WL 17069 (Tenn. Crim. App. 1994).

State v. Ballard, 855 S.W.2d 557 (Tenn. 1993).

State v. Black, 745 P.2d 12 (Wash. 1987).

State v. Brodniak, 718 P.2d 322 (Mont. 1986).

State v. Butler, 651 A.2d 1306 (Conn. App. 1995).

State v. Charles, 398 S.E.2d 123 (W. Va. 1990).

State v. Cressey, 628 A.2d 969 (N.H. 1993).

State v. Florczak, 882 P.2d 199 (Wash. Ct. App. 1994).

State v. Foret, 628 So.2d 1116 (La. 1993).

State v. Graham, 798 P.2d 314 (Wash. Ct. App. 1990).

State v. Hammond, 435 S.E.2d 798 (N.C. Ct. App. 1993).

State v. Hester, 760 P.2d 27 (Idaho 1988).

State v. Hillman, 613 So.2d 1053 (La. Ct. App. 1993).

State v. Huey, 699 P.2d 1290 (Ariz. 1985).

State v. Jones, 863 P.2d 85 (Wash. Ct. App. 1993).

State v. Kallin, 877 P.2d 138 (Utah 1994).

State v. Lamb, 427 N.W.2d 142 (Wis. 1988).

State v. McCoy, 366 S.E.2d 731 (W. Va. 1988).

State v. Marks, 647 P.2d 1292 (Kan. 1982).

State v. Michaels, 642 A.2d 1372 (N.J. 1994).

State v. Milbradt, 756 P.2d 620 (Or. 1988).

State v. Person, 564 A.2d 626 (Conn. Ct. App. 1989).

State v. Rimmasch, 775 P.2d 388 (Utah 1989).

State v. Schimpf, 782 S.W.2d 186 (Tenn. Crim. App. 1989).

State v. Schumpert, 435 S.E.2d 859 (S.C. 1993).

State v. Silvey, 1995 WL 124589 (Mo. 1995).

State v. Wilson, 855 P.2d 657 (Or. Ct. App. 1993).

Summit, R. C. (1983). The child sexual abuse accommodation syndrome. *Child Abuse & Neglect, 7,* 177-193.

United States v. Barnard, 490 F.2d 907 (9th Cir. 1973).

United States v. Carter, 26 M.J. 428 (C.M.A. 1988).

Wells, R. D., McCann, J., Adams, J., Voris, J., & Ensign, J. (1995). Emotional, behavioral, and physical symptoms reported by parents of sexually abused, nonabused, and allegedly abused prepubescent females. *Child Abuse & Neglect, 19,* 155-163.

Wigmore, J. (1974). *Evidence in trials at common law.* Boston: Little, Brown.

Wood, J. (in press). Weighing evidence in sexual abuse evaluations: An introduction to Bayes' Theorem. *Child Maltreatment.*

Wood, J. M., & Wright, L. (1995). Evaluation of children's sexual behaviors and incorporation of base rates in judgments of sexual abuse. *Child Abuse & Neglect, 19,* 1263-1273.

Wozencraft, T., Wagner, W., & Pellegrin, A. (1991). Depression and suicidal ideation in sexually abused children. *Child Abuse & Neglect, 15,* 505-511.

Zumwalt, R. E., & Hirsch, C. S. (1987). Pathology of fatal child abuse and neglect. In R. E. Helfer & R. S. Kempe (Eds.), *The battered child* (4th ed., pp. 247-285). Chicago: University of Chicago Press.

PART FIVE

Preventing and Reporting Abuse

Efforts to prevent and to report abuse stir as many ideological battles as practical challenges. Both raise the hotly debated issues of family privacy and parental rights. The chapters in Part Five review the research on each topic to provide information useful in addressing both the practical and ideological issues.

In Chapter 18, Deborah Daro points out that efforts to prevent physical abuse have a much longer history than parallel efforts in sexual abuse, the occurrence of which has only been recognized belatedly. Physical abuse prevention programs have focused on parent enhancement, including altering parents' view of themselves, providing basic child development information, and teaching parents how to use formal and informal social supports. Home visitation is undergoing intense reexamination as a very promising mode of physical abuse prevention.

Sexual abuse prevention efforts, typically called child assault prevention (CAP) programs, have mushroomed in response to the huge increase in sexual abuse reports—from 6,000 in 1976 to 490,000 in 1992, with the biggest increase occurring between 1976 and 1984. Daro discusses the challenges posed by the great heterogeneity of perpetrators and victims of child sexual abuse: It is hard to know when and whom to target. Just as efforts to prevent physical abuse have raised questions about the right of parents to be left alone, CAP programs have raised concerns about frightening children needlessly with talk of "bad touch" and introducing children prematurely to sexual concepts. Daro reviews the research about the efficacy of these programs and offers concrete suggestions for future program planning, policy development, and research.

In Chapter 19, Gail L. Zellman and Kathleen Coulborn Faller reveal that reporting may be even more politicized than preventing abuse. By 1973, when the federal government first required it, all 50 states already had on their books laws requiring certain professional groups to report suspected child abuse. No one, however, was prepared for the flood of abuse reports to public child protective services (CPS) agencies—from 670,000 in 1976 to 3,140,000 in 1994. Despite the huge number of reports, other sources of information reveal that much abuse is never known to authorities: Surveys of professionals have revealed that a high percentage fail to report abuse at some time; in population surveys, many more people report being subjected to child maltreatment than official reports indicate; and the 1986 National Incidence Study of Child Abuse and Neglect revealed that most children demonstrably endangered by abuse or neglect did not come to the attention of CPS. Overwhelmed by reports, many CPS agencies have narrowed definitions summarily to screen out less serious reports or reports better dealt with by other agencies. Zellman and Faller provide a reasoned, data-based discussion of the highly charged issues of high unsubstantiation rates, intentionally false reports, and the possibility that reporting laws should be modified. Despite the many problems occurring in the wake of mandated reporting laws, they argue, the laws have resulted in a great improvement in public awareness, professional knowledge, and our ability to identify people who need services.

—T.R.

18

Preventing Child Abuse and Neglect

DEBORAH DARO

Almost 3 million children were reported for suspected child abuse and neglect in 1992, more than 300% more than the number reported in 1976. More alarming is the increase in documented child abuse fatalities: An estimated 1,261 victims, essentially 3 children a day, were identified in 1992. This is 57% more than were documented in 1985 (McCurdy & Daro, 1994). Such increases reflect greater public awareness of the problem and a willingness to report suspected cases. However, many in the child welfare field also consider these numbers indicators of a growing problem and the limited success of treatment services (Cohn & Daro, 1988; U.S. Advisory Board, 1991). Regardless of whether one views these increases as real or merely a statistical artifact, calls for an expanded emphasis on prevention are widespread.

Prevention can occur at three levels: primary prevention—targeting services to the general population, with the objective of stopping any new reports of a given disease or condition; secondary prevention—targeting services to specific high-risk groups to avoid the continued spread of the disease or condition; and tertiary prevention—targeting services to victims of the disease or condition, with the intent of minimizing its negative consequences and avoiding reincidence

(Blum, 1974; Helfer, 1982). Child abuse prevention, therefore, has come to include such diverse efforts as public awareness campaigns, parent education and support services, safety education for children, and therapeutic interventions for perpetrators and victims. Others in this volume have focused on the strengths and weaknesses of various treatment or tertiary prevention strategies. Consequently, emphasis in this chapter will be limited to primary and secondary prevention efforts.

The bulk of the literature on prevention has focused on the development and assessment of strategies aimed at reducing the prevalence of physical abuse and neglect. To a large extent, this pattern reflects the field's major emphasis for the past 30 years. Until recently, professionals and public alike perceived maltreatment to involve problematic or damaging parenting practices. Excessive physical discipline, failure to provide children with basic necessities and care, and mismatches between a parent's expectations and a child's abilities have long been recognized as precursors to maltreatment. Whether these failures stemmed from limitations within the parent or within the surrounding social system, the most prevalent and best researched methods to prevent child abuse have been efforts to enhance parental capacity.

Beginning in the late 1970s, this singular focus was altered with the long overdue recognition of child sexual abuse. Reports of child sexual abuse increased from 6,000 in 1976 to an estimated 490,000 in 1992, with the bulk of this increase occurring between 1976 and 1984 (McCurdy & Daro, 1994). Prevalence studies on this problem estimate that as many as 20% of all females and 7% of all males will experience at least one episode of sexual abuse during their childhood (Peters, Wyatt, & Finkelhor, 1986). Furthermore, sexual abuse victims are a far more heterogeneous population than physical abuse or neglect victims. Risk factors with respect to perpetrator characteristics, victim characteristics, and sociodemographic variables are far from universal (Melton, 1992). Consequently, prevention advocates have had limited information to use in formulating effective prevention strategies targeted to potential perpetrators or communities.

Driven by a sense of urgency to respond to the sexual abuse problem, prevention advocates have focused their energies on strengthening potential victims, one of Finkelhor's (1984) four preconditions for sexual abuse. These efforts, generally identified under the rubric of child assault prevention education, provide classroom-based instruction for children of all ages on how to protect themselves from sexual assault and what to do if they experience actual or potential abuse. Although in most cases these strategies include informational sessions for parents and school personnel, their primary focus is strengthening a child's ability to resist assault.

Both the historic pool of prevention services (parent enhancement efforts) and the more recent efforts to strengthen potential victims (child assault prevention education) have undergone numerous evaluations. As noted elsewhere, the majority of these efforts are not controlled experiments, and many are fraught with serious methodological problems (Azar, 1988; Daro, 1994; Howing, Wodarski, Kurtz, & Gaudin, 1989). Such criticism is well-placed and underscores the need for more sophisticated and consistent evaluation efforts. However, limiting the pool of useful program evaluations to only those efforts that meet strict standards of scientific purity is impractical. Although the present pool of evaluative research has its limitations, it does offer preliminary guidelines for shaping programs and systems.

The purpose of this chapter, therefore, is to identify these guidelines as defined by repeated evaluations of various parent enhancement programs and child assault prevention efforts. In the following discussion, I review key questions of debate, evaluative data, and program implications. The chapter concludes with recommendations for future research and program development.

Interventions to Assist Parents: What Do We Know?

A number of factors determine an individual's parenting style. Efforts to model this process generally include some combination of developmental history, personality factors, social interactions or social networks, familial relationships, and child characteristics (Belsky & Vondra, 1990; Sameroff & Chandler, 1975; Sandler, 1979). Recognizing the complexity of how parenting patterns are formed, service goals in this area have included altering parents' view of themselves and their own parents, improving parents' understanding of basic child development and care, enhancing parents' child management and discipline skills, and teaching parents how to obtain formal and informal social supports. Determining how best to structure programs in light of these diverse objectives has hinged on issues of duration, structure, staffing, and cultural competence.

Questions of Duration

Prevention efforts to enhance parental capacity have long included both short-term and extended interventions. Very brief crisis intervention services, such as respite care centers and telephone hotlines, consistently have been viewed as cost-effective methods for conveying knowledge and providing support to parents under stress (Cherry & Kirby, 1971; Green, 1976; Kempe & Helfer, 1976). In an evaluation of a crisis respite center with a 90-day follow-up period, Vaughan and Loadman (1988) noted that 72% of participants reported a reduction in stress, 100% expressed less isolation, and no children served by the center were hospitalized for an abuse- or neglect-related incident for at least 90 days following program participation.

Positive findings also have been noted among prevention programs providing parenting services for less than 6 months (Rodriguez & Cortez, 1988; Wolfe, Edwards, Manion, & Koverola, 1988). Taylor and Beauchamp (1988) report notable differences in parenting knowledge, skills, and attitudes among participants receiving only four visits by a student nurse volunteer compared to a no-service control group. Those who received the visits scored significantly higher on tests of child development, expressed more democratic ideas regarding child rearing, and demonstrated more positive parent-infant interactions and greater problem-solving abilities.

Beyond these types of emergency and educational interventions, however, limited, short-term interventions generally produce limited, short-term gains (Barth, 1991; Daro, Jones, & McCurdy, 1993; Heinicke, Beckwith, & Thompson, 1988; Larson, 1980; Siegel, Bauman, Schaefer, & Saunders, 1980). Alteration of parental

practices, particularly with high-risk families, generally occurs only after more extensive efforts. For example, at least three longitudinal studies have found that comprehensive parenting services provided over 2 years produced initial gains that were strengthened over time (Polit & White, 1988; Seitz, Rosenbaum, & Apfel, 1985; Wieder, Poisson, Lourie, & Greenspan, 1988). Areas showing improvement included parenting skills, parent-child relationships, educational achievement, employment rates, and economic well-being. And, as presented below, a number of the most promising home-based and center-based child abuse prevention programs provide services for 1 to 2 years.

Questions of Structure

Looking across the full range of prevention services, the U.S. Advisory Board on Child Abuse and Neglect has identified home visiting services as the "best documented preventive effort" and the intervention holding the most promise (U.S. Advisory Board, 1991). Support for such a statement is strong. Indeed, a variety of home visitor programs using different types of providers (e.g., nurses, graduate students, paraprofessionals) and emphasizing different topics (e.g., health education, child development, social supports) have proven successful in reducing the likelihood for maltreatment and altering parental attitudes and behaviors (Olds & Kitzman, 1993).

One of strongest cases for this service model has been made by David Olds and his colleagues (Olds, Henderson, Chamberlain, & Tatelbaum, 1986) at the University of Rochester. The 400 participants in this study, all of whom were first-time mothers, were randomly assigned to one of four conditions in which the most intensive level of services involved regular pre- and postnatal home visits by a nurse practitioner. The nurse home visitor carried out three major activities: parent education regarding fetal and infant development, the involvement of family members and friends in child care and support of the mother, and the linkage of family members with other health and human services.

Those who received the most intensive intervention had a significantly lower incidence of reported child abuse over the 2-year postbirth study period. Although 19% of the group that received no home visitation services ($n = 32$) at the greatest risk for maltreatment (i.e., poor, unmarried teens) were reported for abuse or neglect, only 4% of their nurse-visited counterparts ($n = 22$) were reported. Of this 4%, half involved reports of neglect only and the other half involved reports of neglect and physical abuse.

In addition to having a lower reported rate of child abuse, infants whose mothers received ongoing nurse home visits had fewer accidents and were less likely to require emergency room care.

In addition to having a lower reported rate of child abuse, infants whose mothers received ongoing nurse home visits had fewer accidents and were less likely to require emergency room care. The mothers also reported a less frequent need to punish or restrict their children.

Reduction in child abuse rates also has been observed in repeated evaluations of Project 12-Ways, a multifaceted home-based service program in central Illinois. In this instance, services were provided in the client's home by advanced graduate students and covered such topics as parenting skills, stress management, self-control, assertiveness training, health maintenance, job placement, and marital counseling. In assessing the program, Lutzker and Rice (1984, 1987) have documented significantly fewer repeated abuse and neglect incidents among program recipients than among similar families not receiving this intervention. While enrolled in the program, only 2% of a randomly selected number of Project 12-Ways clients were reported for maltreatment compared to 11% of the control group. In the year following termination of services, 10% of the treatment families and 21% of the nontreatment families were reported for maltreatment.

Larson (1980) noted similar gains in an assessment of the Prenatal Intervention Project in Montreal, but only in cases in which such visits began prior to the child's birth. In this case, the home visitors were women with undergraduate degrees in child psychology who had received special training in preventive health care. The home visits were designed to provide information about general caretaking topics and the need for regular well-child care. Participants also were encouraged to talk to their infants and respond to their vocalizations. Children whose mothers began receiving services in the seventh month of pregnancy had a lower accident rate and exhibited fewer feeding problems. In addition, the mothers scored higher in assessments of maternal behavior and in providing appropriate and stimulating home environments.

Three other randomized trials found that home visits had little or no impact on the treatment group. For example, Gray, Cutler, Dean, and Kempe (1979) found no significant difference between the randomly assigned high-risk mothers who received home visits ($N = 50$) and those who did not ($N = 50$) with respect to reported cases of maltreatment. Siegel et al. (1980) found that nine home visits by paraprofessionals during the first 3 months of the child's life did not have a significant impact on subsequent rates of child maltreatment. Barth (1991) studied the Parent Child Enrichment Program (CREP), an early intervention program providing 6 months of home visits by paraprofessionals to at-risk mothers. Reports of child abuse and neglect did not vary by treatment condition, nor were there any significant differences in self-report measures of child abuse potential, use of community resources, child temperament, and child welfare.

In at least two of these cases (Barth, 1991; Siegel et al., 1980), the limited extent of the program may account for the absence of significant outcomes (Olds & Kitzman, 1993). In the third instance (Gray et al., 1979), weekly home visits were scheduled for 2 years postpartum, but it is not clear if the services actually were delivered with this frequency. Furthermore, although no significant differences in the number of child abuse reports were noted between the experimental and control groups in this study, those receiving services demonstrated enhanced mother-infant relationships and had fewer child hospitalizations for serious injury.

Like the Gray project, the Ford Foundation's Child Survival/Fair Start Initiative used well-trained community volunteers or paraprofessionals to provide services to families at risk. The six programs that participated in this effort were housed in community health clinics, child care and social service agencies, and small, independent organizations, all of which adopted a multidisciplinary approach in tackling problems of maternal and infant health and infant development. Parents participating in these programs demonstrated an increased ability to secure routine and preventive health care for their infants and a greater openness in discussing family problems and using community resources (Larner, 1990).

In addition to home visiting, parenting education and center-based services also have produced positive gains in overall parenting skills and in the use of community resources (Daro, 1988, 1993). Many of these programs are school based or use community-based organizations, thereby increasing their availability to high-risk populations (Furstenburg, 1970, 1980; Polit & White, 1988; Rodriguez & Cortez, 1988). The most notable outcomes of these efforts include an increase in positive parent-child interactions, more extensive use of social supports, less use of corporal punishment, and higher self-esteem and personal functioning. For teen mothers, positive outcomes also include fewer subsequent births, higher employment rates, and less welfare dependency (Dornbusch, Barr, & Seer, 1993; Ellwood, 1988).

In working with the most dysfunctional families, one successful approach has been to combine parenting instruction with a therapeutic approach (Gambrill, 1983). Testing this notion, Wolfe et al. (1988) achieved notable success by combining agency-based family support services with training in child management. Their sample included 30 women drawn from the caseload of a child protective services agency who were randomly assigned to receive either both individual and group services or group services alone.

Individual training sessions with the parent and child were scheduled weekly for 90 minutes, shifting to biweekly once gains were evident. The content was based on a social learning approach and aimed at emergent problems in child management and child development. Training was competency based, whereby the therapist progressed to more advanced skills once basic skills were achieved. In contrast to this intense individual service, informational sessions were held twice a week for 2 hours each in

groups of 8 to 10 participants. These sessions included social activities and informal discussion on a variety of parenting and personal topics, such as the mother's personal growth and maturity, improved self-esteem, and development of adequate social support. Children attended day care during the sessions.

At the 3-month follow-up for both groups, mothers who received individual parent training in addition to group services for an average of 20 weeks reported fewer and less intense child behavior problems and indicated fewer adjustment problems associated with the risk of maltreatment than did the controls who attended only the group services for an average of 18 weeks. The treatment group fell within the normal range on the Child Abuse Potential Inventory (Milner, 1980) at follow-up, whereas the controls, although improved, remained at risk. This pattern was supported by caseworker ratings at the 1-year follow-up, which showed greater improvement and a lowered risk of maltreatment among clients who received a combination of both interventions.

Questions of Staff Skills

A program's success often hinges on the qualifications and skills of its direct service providers. Successful providers tend to combine a variety of technical and interpersonal skills. A number of academic programs exists to teach the technical skills necessary to provide effective educational and support services. The most common disciplines found among prevention staff include social work, nursing, education, special education, psychology, and child development.

Although such professionals are assumed to be technically competent, it is less clear that formal training provides the interpersonal skills necessary to successfully engage and retain at-risk families. Professional interpersonal skills most successful in fostering positive and sustained client-provider relationships include an active interest in new ideas, an active interest in people and an ability to engage people socially, an ability to accept people's life situations without prejudging them, an ability to relate to a family's experiences without becoming enmeshed in the family's problem cycles, and relative stability in the professional's own personal life (Halpern & Larner, 1987).

Many programs create the structure of social support central to preventing child abuse by employing the services of individuals who come from within the same community.

Many programs create the structure of social support central to preventing child abuse by employing the services of individuals who come from within the same community and share many of the same values and experiences as program participants. The rationale for the use of paraprofessional service providers results, at least in part, from the belief that they are more likely than trained professionals to possess the interpersonal skills desired for effective service provision. Paraprofessionals also are used to enhance program efficiency and effectiveness (Austin, 1978). Underlying this rationale is that paraprofessionals are thought to provide more cost-effective services and relieve professionals from doing the work that can be done by those with less training and skills (Carkhuff, 1968).

The incorporation of paraprofessionals in the provision of child abuse and neglect treatment services has a long history. Both the initial work of the C. Henry Kempe Center for the Treatment and Prevention of Child Abuse and Neglect and the Ford Foundation Child Survival/ Fair Start Initiative found strong support for the use of lay counselors. In a final review of the Fair Start program, Larner (1990) noted that program supervisors felt that clients were "more open, relaxed and responsive with the lay workers than they would have been with professionals" (p. 9).

The use of paraprofessionals, however, has its problems. Despite the strong support for this staffing concept among those involved in the Ford Foundation's Child Survival/Fair Start Initiative, Halpern and Larner (1987) noted that paraprofessionals had difficulty providing all of the assistance clients needed in the areas of health care, child care, and mental health services. The high demand for therapeutic services among families

seeking assistance from prevention programs has led others to conclude that self-help methods offer families only limited support and should never be construed as an adequate substitute for professional intervention (Powell, 1979).

Over and above these skills and organizational issues are the personal problems paraprofessionals may experience. At times, the indigenous qualities of paraprofessionals may prove counterproductive. These include overidentification with the client, excessive dependence on the client, projections of one's own situation onto the client, or low expectations (Austin, 1978). Others have noted that the advantages of paraprofessionals may be overstated, adding that class and cultural barriers between provider and client can be overcome by carefully selecting providers who are compassionate and sensitive to differences in lifestyle and child-rearing methods. Olds and Henderson (1990) report that others have observed that parents are sometimes reluctant to reveal personal matters to indigenous workers from the neighborhood because they fear a loss of privacy, a problem that is reduced when parents communicate with professionals. Furthermore, professionals may be more successful in helping a family communicate with local health care, welfare, and educational systems.

Questions of Cultural Competence

The battle for culturally competent social services is long-standing. Debate has been particularly sharp in the area of family interventions and child welfare services.

Diverse cultures of families in the United States have led many professionals to speak against adopting too rigid a standard of family well-being and "correct" methods of parent-child interactions. Despite the longevity of this debate, many have noted that we lack adequate information about how cultural factors influence the occurrence of child maltreatment and the delivery of effective interventions (Cross, Bazron, Dennis, & Isaacs, 1989; Garbarino, Cohn, & Ebata, 1982; Mann, 1990).

Achieving a culturally competent service system requires service providers and agency administrators to acknowledge that cultural differences as well as similarities exist within the population. The process requires practitioners to be aware of the cultures represented among their caseload, understand the basic parameters of these cultures, and recognize that cultural diversity will affect a family's participation in service delivery (Anderson & Fenichel, 1989).

Of particular importance is the need for service providers to understand how the concept of family is defined in a given culture and recognize that individuals and families make different choices based on cultural forces. If service providers deny these choices or mislabel them, interventions can compound rather than resolve parenting dilemmas. Based on her assessment of the African American family, Slaughter (1988) noted three implications for service planners: to recognize and incorporate into the treatment plan the importance of the extended or augmented family, establish program goals in light of the cultural-ecological realities of racial and ethnic minority family life, and recognize the diversity within racial and ethnic minority communities. Looking across the range of responses different cultural groups might exhibit to certain risk factors for maltreatment, Derezotes and Snowden (1990) concurred with Slaughter that interventions must be selected in light of the family's cultural orientation and preferences. For example, when faced with an African American or Hispanic adult presenting problems of distress or personal dissatisfaction, they recommend drawing on the coping strategies most common in these cultures (e.g., religious institutions, extended families) rather than referring the client to psychotherapy.

The absence of significant empirical research on service impacts for families from different racial and cultural backgrounds limits the discussion of recommended practice standards. Although, theoretically, practitioners may need to be cognizant of the differences in family life and parenting responsibilities among people of different cultural groups, it remains unclear if such differences demand unique intervention systems. The requisite differences may be more a question of the manner, rather than the form, in which services are delivered. Furthermore, in certain cases, stronger predictors of success may lie in other key demographic characteristics. For example, a recent evaluation of child abuse prevention services targeting adolescent parents

found no significant differences in outcomes by the client's race. African American and white teens responded equally well (and equally poorly) to the various interventions tested. Age (i.e., under or over 16 years) and the initial point of service delivery (i.e., during pregnancy or postbirth) were far more accurate than race in predicting client outcomes (Center on Child Abuse Prevention Research, 1990). Such findings are far from conclusive. They merely suggest that the relationship between cultural competency and program outcomes requires a great deal of further study.

Key Conclusions

Several service features or components have been identified as increasing the probability of reducing physical abuse and neglect within diverse populations. The program evaluation literature reviewed earlier suggests the following promising design features:

- Supporting parents in their child-rearing responsibilities is best done by initiating services prior to or as close to the birth of the first child as possible.
- Parenting enhancement services need to be tied a child's specific developmental level and recognize the unique challenges involved in caring for and disciplining children of various ages.
- Regardless of service location, it is important to provide opportunities for parents to model the interactions or discipline methods being promoted through the intervention.
- Although child development knowledge can be transferred to parents in a relatively brief period of time (i.e., 6 to 12 weeks), changing attitudes and strengthening parenting and personal skills often require a longer time commitment (i.e., more than 6 months).
- An emphasis on social supports and the ability to obtain needed assistance is a critical element of programs seeking to ensure the safety of children beyond the immediate intervention period.
- A balance of home-based and group-based alternatives for parents are needed to address those isolated and uncomfortable in group settings as well as those who appreciate opportunities to share problems with other parents.

■ Programs need to recognize cultural differences in how families function and in the nature of parent-child interactions.

Child Assault Prevention Programs: What Do We Know?

As with parenting enhancement services, methods for providing child assault prevention instruction within a classroom setting vary along a number of key dimensions, including the characteristics and background of the instructor, the frequency of the presentations, and the specific content of the message. Most programs, however, provide direct instruction to the child on the distinction between good, bad, and questionable touching and the concept of body ownership or the rights of children to control who touches their bodies and where they are touched. Children are encouraged to tell if someone touches them, even if that person has told the child not to reveal the incident. Programs also offer children a range of resources they can use if they have been abused. In addition, most of the more popular curricula include some type of orientation or instruction for both parents and school personnel. These sessions cover a number of topics, including a review of the materials to be presented to the children, a summary of the local child abuse reporting systems, a discussion of what to do if you suspect a child has been mistreated, and a review of local services available to victims and their families (Berrick, 1988).

The major debates surrounding child assault prevention programs are substantially different from those surrounding parent enhancement services (Daro, 1994). Although a certain level of disagreement exists with respect to the appropriate length and staffing of child assault prevention efforts, fundamental questions of utility, client targeting, disclosure, and potential negative consequences have received the greatest attention.

Questions of Utility

At least six major review articles on child sexual assault and victimization programs have concluded that, on balance, most evaluations find significant gains in a child's knowledge of sexual abuse and how to respond (Carroll, Miltenberger, & O'Neill, 1992; Daro, 1991; Finkelhor & Strapko, 1992; Hazzard, 1990; Reppucci & Haugaard, 1989; Wurtele & Miller-Perrin, 1992). Furthermore, a meta-analysis that reviewed the findings from 30 such evaluations concluded that these programs produce a small but statistically significant gain in knowledge (Berrick & Barth, 1992). Although some of these gains have been noted following repeated presentation of the concepts over a 10- to 15-week period (Downer, 1984; Fryer, Kraizer, & Miyoski, 1987; Woods & Dean, 1986; Young, Liddell, Pecot, Siegenthaler, & Yamagishi, 1987), the majority of these gains have been realized after fewer than five brief presentations (Borkin & Frank, 1986; Conte, Rosen, Saperstein, & Shermack, 1985; Garbarino, 1987; Harvey, Forehand, Brown, & Holmes, 1988; Kolko, Moser, Litz, & Hughes, 1987; Nibert, Cooper, Fitch, & Ford, 1988; Plummer, 1984; Swan, Press, & Briggs, 1985).

As with all prevention efforts, these gains are distributed unevenly across concepts and participants. On balance, children have greater difficulty in accepting the idea that abuse can occur at the hands of someone they know than at the hands of strangers (Finkelhor & Strapko, 1992). Among younger participants, the more complex concepts such as secrets and dealing with ambiguous feelings often remain misunderstood (Gilbert, Duerr-Berrick, LeProhn, & Nyman, 1990). Although most children learn something from these efforts, a significant percentage of children fail to show progress in every area presented. For example, Conte noted that even the best performers in his study grasped only 50% of the concepts taught (Conte et al., 1985). Retention of the gains noted immediately following these instructions also varies. At least one evaluator discovered that although children have been found to retain increased awareness and knowledge of safety rules several months after receiving the instruction, they retain less information with respect to such key concepts as who can be a molester, the difference between physical abuse and sexual abuse, and the fact that sexual abuse, if it occurs, is not the victim's fault (Plummer, 1984).

Questions of Appropriate Target Populations

Significant debate has occurred over the potential of this intervention with a preschool population. A central feature of this debate has been the finding by several researchers that young children learn significantly less than their older counterparts. For example, Borkin and Frank (1986) found that virtually none of the 3-year-olds interviewed retained any of the information presented after only 1 week, and only 40% of the 4- and 5-year-olds retained any knowledge over this period. Similarly, Conte and his colleagues (1985) found significant differences in the level of information retained by the 4- and 5-year-olds in their sample versus the 6- to 10-year-olds. Gilbert and his colleagues (1990) found that between 25% and 65% of the 123 children participating in their evaluation of seven different preschool curricula remained at risk, depending on the outcome measures of concern.

Although apparently learning less than older children, sizable numbers of 4- and 5-year-olds do learn as a result of these interventions. A reanalysis of the Gilbert data cited above found that 90% of the participants provided more appropriate answers at posttest in at least one of the areas tested (Daro, 1989). Harvey et al. (1988) found that relative to a no-treatment control group, kindergarten children participating in a child assault prevention education program demonstrated more knowledge about preventing abuse and performed better on simulated scenes involving sexual abuse 3 weeks and 7 weeks after the intervention. Following a 5-day, behavioral-based prevention program for kindergarten, first-, and second-graders, Kraizer, Witte, and Fryer (1989) found significant improvements in all dimensions tested. Of particular note is that all 33 trained children indicated they would tell a responsible adult of the incident, both when coerced and when asked to keep the encounter a secret. Contrary to what one might expect, with increased training, kindergartners and first-graders enhanced their scores about equally, with the second-grade group having less notable gains.

Learning to tell an adult when confused may be among the most important concepts to convey to young children.

Similar to the Kraizer study, the most dramatic increase in an assessment of seven different programs targeting preschoolers was that a greater number of program recipients said they would encourage a fictional little bunny to tell an adult if something troubled it. Of the respondents, 75% showed improvement or repeated the correct response in this area at posttest (Daro, 1989). This pattern is particularly noteworthy, given research on perpetrator behavior. Sexual abuse offenders interviewed by Conte, Wolf, and Smith (1989) reported that children indicating they would tell a specific adult about the assault does have an impact on their behavior. Similarly, Gilgun and Connor (1989) and Budin and Johnson (1989) reported that perpetrators seek out passive, troubled, or lonely children who can be counted on to maintain the secret of an abusive relationship.

Questions of Disclosure

In addition to having a potential for primary prevention, child assault prevention instructions create environments in which children can disclose more easily prior to ongoing maltreatment. In other words, independent of the impact these programs may have on future behavior, they offer an opportunity for present victims to reach out for help, thereby preventing continued abuse (Leventhal, 1987). Even those who doubt that any useful prevention strategies can be developed with respect to sexual abuse admit that child assault prevention programs hold strong promise in obtaining earlier disclosures (Melton, 1992).

The few studies that have measured the extent to which these interventions result in increased disclosures have been promising. Kolko, Moser, and Hughes (1989) reported that in five of six schools in which prevention programs were offered, school guidance counselors received 20 confirmed reports of inappropriate sexual or physical touching in the 6 months following the intervention. In contrast, no reports were noted in the one control school in their study. Similarly, Hazzard, Webb, and Kleemeier (1988) found that 8 children reported ongoing sexual abuse, and 20 others reported past occurrences within 6 weeks of receiving a three-session prevention program.

Questions of Negative Consequences

Despite these and similar gains, some have questioned the advisability of raising the sensitive topic of sexual abuse with young children, the majority of whom will not experience sexual abuse by family members, friends, or strangers. Several studies that have looked explicitly for increased anxiety or fear on the part of program participants, however, have found very limited overt negative reactions (Hazzard et al., 1988; Kenning, Gallmeier, Jackson, & Plemons, 1987; Wurtele & Miller-Perrin, 1987). Others have found more disturbing trends. Garbarino (1987) found that more than one third of the second-, fourth-, and sixth-graders who participated in an evaluation of the National Committee to Prevent Child Abuse's Spiderman comic book reported being worried or anxious after completing the two stories on sexual abuse. Girls were more than twice as likely as boys to express these fears, perhaps reflecting the fact that very few girls reported prior experiences with Spiderman comics in general.

Although no study completed to date has documented any lasting increased anxiety as a result of child assault prevention instruction, several have found children exhibiting some behaviors that suggest caution is warranted in developing these programs. Swan and her colleagues (1985) noted that, following a presentation of the play *Bubbylonian Encounter,* 93% of the children recognized the potential within their own families for a coercive (i.e., nonviolent episode of child sexual abuse), and 88% saw the potential for violent sexual assault. One interpretation of this finding is that the children successfully grasped one of the program's key concepts: Sexual abuse is not something that only involves strangers. On the other hand, the finding also suggests that a large number of children are now questioning, perhaps unnecessarily, the safety of their own homes. Similarly, Gilbert and his colleagues (1990) noted that a greater number of preschool children participating in their study had more negative attitudes toward not only clearly negative touches (e.g., hitting) but also rather benign or natural touches (e.g., tickling and bathing).

A recent telephone survey of children who had received various types of safety education is particularly instructive on this issue. This survey found that children

and parents who reported elevated levels of fear or anxiety following the provision of the program also were most likely to rate the program as having an overall positive effect and to have used the concepts in their daily lives (Finkelhor & Dziuba-Leatherman, 1993). Based on this finding, the authors concluded that initial anxiety and fear may not be an indication that these programs have negative effects. Rather, children experience increased anxiety precisely because the programs have raised a real concern for them, one which they now feel better prepared to address.

Key Program Conclusions

The generally positive findings from the evaluations conducted to date suggest that some form of child-focused education is an important component in our efforts to reduce the likelihood a child will submit to ongoing sexual abuse or engage in violent behavior. Equally true, however, is the reality that preventing child abuse or violence requires much more than simply educating the next generation on appropriate conduct. Rather than offering definitive conclusions on the merits of these programs, the current pool of evaluative data suggests positive outcomes can be maximized if programs include the following features:

- Providing children with behavioral rehearsal of prevention strategies and offering feedback on their performance to facilitate children's depiction of their involvement in abusive as well as unpleasant interactions
- Developing curricula with a more balanced developmental perspective and tailoring training materials to a child's cognitive characteristics and learning ability
- For young children, presenting the material in a stimulating and varied manner to maintain their attention and reinforce the information learned
- Teaching generic concepts such as assertive behavior, decision-making skills, and communication skills that children can use in everyday situations, not just to fend off abuse
- Repeatedly stressing the need for children to tell every time someone continues to touch them in a way that makes them uneasy

- Developing longer programs that are better integrated into regular school curricula and practices
- Creating more formal and extensive parent and teacher training components, particularly when targeting young children
- Developing extended after-school programs and more in-depth discussion opportunities for certain high-risk groups (e.g., former victims, teen parents)

Implications for Future Prevention Planning

Despite prevention's intuitive appeal and promising outcomes, several conditions may hamper its further expansion. First, the growing discrepancy between the need to provide all identified victims with adequate therapeutic services and the resources available to fill this need present a double challenge to the prevention field. Not only are child welfare administrators failing in their treatment function, they are unable to devote any notable resources to intervening with a family before abuse or neglect occurs. Data collected by the National Committee to Prevent Child Abuse (NCPCA), as part of an annual survey of child welfare administrators in 1992, found that therapeutic services were provided, on average, to fewer than two thirds of those children identified as victims of maltreatment. This figure represents a 15% decline from the percentage of victims reported to be receiving services in 1990 (McCurdy & Daro, 1994). Furthermore, a recent assessment of the child welfare system conducted by Kamerman and Kahn (1990) found "no state providing enough family services to meet generally accepted standards of community responsibility. Most agencies focus almost exclusively on child and family crises."

Second, to the extent resources are allocated in a rational fashion, it becomes increasingly important for prevention services to document that they do indeed prevent child abuse. In the absence of large-scale longitudinal studies that include some direct observation of parent-child interactions, acceptance of the ultimate efficacy of prevention programs will remain more theoretical than empirical. Although programs can and should become more rigorous in how they assess changes in their clients, proving that such changes translate into fewer cases of maltreatment remains a challenging task. Limited resources, as well as the limited reliability and validity of existing assessment tools, suggest that a significant volume of research acceptable in the scientific community is unlikely to be developed in the immediate future.

Beyond these political and methodological concerns lie normative questions of family privacy and parental rights.

Beyond these political and methodological concerns lie normative questions of family privacy and parental rights. Intervening with a family or individual before abuse or neglect occurs runs the risk of violating the privacy of the family and the right of parents to determine the well-being of their children. A commonly recognized barrier to primary prevention is the right of people to be left alone (Gaylin, Glasser, Marcus, & Rothman, 1978). Without concrete evidence identifying a given condition as leading to maltreatment, prevention efforts are limited to serving families who have defined themselves as being at risk of abusing or neglecting their children or offering limited, nonintrusive universal services. Too often, however, such efforts represent "too little, too late" for many high-risk families.

Overcoming these barriers will require those committed to prevention to pursue new avenues. Several conditions need to be addressed for prevention to accomplish its mission. First, treatment services, particularly child protective services, need sufficient funding to ensure that all children identified as victims of maltreatment receive therapeutic intervention. The devastating impacts of maltreatment on one's ability to parent are clear. Looking across a number of retrospective studies, Kaufman and Zigler (1989) estimated that an abused child is six times more likely than his or her nonabused counterpart to be an abusive parent. In the most significant prospective study on the intergenerational cycle of maltreatment, the Minnesota Mother-Child Project reported dramatic maltreatment rates for mothers who had been abused as children. Of the 47 mothers in this category, 34% were identified as abusing their children, 6% exhibited other problematic behaviors, and 30% were classified as borderline caretakers. In contrast, of the 35 mothers in the sample judged to have been raised in an emotionally supportive family, only one mother currently was maltreating her child (Egeland, 1988). Unless treatment services are funded at a level commensurate with the task at hand, new victims will swamp whatever prevention systems are developed.

Second, prevention services need to reach broader populations. Although notable gains have been achieved in the areas of public awareness and prevention programming, measurable change in aggregate indicators of child and family well-being will not be realized until all parents, particularly those facing the greatest challenges, have access to key prevention services (Daro & Gelles, 1992). Although many efforts are needed, consensus has developed around the importance of establishing a national home visitation program for all new parents (Cohn, 1992; U.S. Advisory Board, 1991). As proposed by the U.S. Advisory Board on Child Abuse and Neglect, such a system would provide ongoing home visitation to all new parents who requested it and accept referrals from health and child welfare agencies of families who are at risk of developing—but have not yet developed—abusive behavior. This design would avoid stigmatization, a common problem of secondary prevention efforts, and provide an opportunity for more indepth screening of families to determine actual level of risk.

The National Committee to Prevent Child Abuse (NCPCA) launched a new initiative in 1992 to lay the foundation for such a system in partnership with Hawaii's Healthy Start Program, a model home visitation program developed by that state's Maternal and Child Health Division and Family Stress Center, a local community-based organization. At present, the Hawaii program serves more than 50% of the state's at-risk new parents and plans to be universal within the next 5 years. NCPCA's initiative, Healthy Families America (HFA), originally was designed to have at least 25 states initiate legislative activity in the next 3 years to support broad-based home visitation services for new parents. As of 1995, HFA programs had begun in 150 communities

in 25 states, and essentially all 50 states were engaged in planning activities.

In addition to reaching more families, existing prevention services need to expand their mission to address more of the causal factors associated with all forms of maltreatment. For example, rather than viewing parenting enhancement services as only addressing physical abuse and neglect, their potential to also address sexual abuse needs to be explored. To the extent sexual abuse is more common among families under stress or in transition, parent enhancement services targeting these populations should include sexual abuse indicators and methods of response within their service objectives. Assisting parents in addressing the broader issue of sexuality and appropriate sexual boundaries would provide families with a language and opportunity to discuss sexuality more openly, thereby making it more difficult to sustain the secrecy of sexual abuse.

Similarly, child assault prevention programs should cover all forms of maltreatment and offer skills training beyond saying no to maltreatment. These additional skills might include planning skills, assertiveness skills, negotiated conflict resolution, and peer resistance skills. To the extent that child assault prevention programs mature into curricula that offer explicit opportunities for this type of skill building, they become programs that prevent not only child abuse but also a host of other dilemmas children face.

All of these reforms—adequate funding for treatment, greatly expanded primarily prevention efforts, and more comprehensive service objectives—need to recognize explicitly the broader contextual issues that shape a child's ultimate environment. Children and their families do not live in isolation.

Enhancing parenting knowledge and skills or increasing a child's awareness of potential dangers are strategies that afford children some protection. However, sustained economic uncertainty, limited access to quality housing, education and medical care, and social acceptance of violence and prejudice may overcome even the most vigilant and protective parent. Although such systemic issues may lie beyond the scope of individual prevention services, advocating for change in the economic, cultural, and normative conditions that create environments harmful to children should not.

References

Anderson, P., & Fenichel, E. (1989). *Serving culturally diverse families of infants and toddlers with disabilities.* Washington, DC: National Center for Clinical Infant Programs.

Austin, M. J. (1978). *Professionals and paraprofessionals.* New York: Human Science Press.

Azar, S. (1988). Methodological considerations in treatment outcome research in child maltreatment. In G. Hotaling, D. Finkelhor, J. Kirkpatrick, & M. Straus (Eds.), *Coping with family violence: Research and policy perspectives* (pp. 288-289). Newbury Park, CA: Sage.

Barth, R. (1991). An experimental evaluation of in-home child abuse prevention services. *Child Abuse & Neglect, 15,* 363-376.

Belsky, J., & Vondra, J. (1990). Lessons for child abuse: The determinants of parenting. In D. Cicchetti & V. Carlson (Eds.), *Child maltreatment: Theory and research on the causes and consequences of child abuse and neglect* (pp. 153-202). New York: Cambridge University Press.

Berrick, J. (1988). Parental involvement in child abuse prevention training: What do they learn? *Child Abuse & Neglect, 12,* 543-553.

Berrick, J., & Barth, R. (1992). Child sexual abuse prevention: Research review and recommendations. *Social Work Research and Abstracts, 28*(4), 6-15.

Blum, H. (1974). *Planning for health: Development and application of social change theory.* New York: Human Sciences Press.

Borkin, J., & Frank, L. (1986). Sexual abuse prevention for preschoolers: A pilot program. *Child Welfare, 65,* 75-82.

Budin, L., & Johnson, C. (1989). Sex abuse prevention programs: Offenders' attitudes about their efficacy. *Child Abuse & Neglect, 13,* 77-87.

Carkhuff, R. (1968). Differential functioning of lay and professional helpers. *Journal of Counseling Psychology, 15*(2), 117-126.

Carroll, L., Miltenberger, R., & O'Neill, K. (1992). A review and critique of research evaluating child sexual abuse prevention programs. *Education and Treatment of Children, 15,* 335-354.

Center on Child Abuse Prevention Research. (1990). *Adolescent parent services evaluation: Final report* (Prepared for the William T. Grant Foundation under grant number 725.1162). Chicago: National Committee for Prevention of Child Abuse.

Cherry, B., & Kirby, A. (1971). Obstacles to the delivery of medical care to children of neglecting parents. *American Journal of Public Health, 61,* 568-573.

Cohn, A. (1992, April 2). Testimony presented before the U.S. House of Representative's Select Committee on Children, Youth and Families.

Cohn, A., & Daro, D. (1988). Is treatment too late: What ten years of evaluative research tell us. *Child Abuse & Neglect, 11,* 433-442.

Conte, J., Rosen, C., Saperstein, L., & Shermack, R. (1985). An evaluation of a program to prevent the sexual victimization of young children. *Child Abuse & Neglect, 9,* 329-334.

Conte, J., Wolf, S., & Smith, T. (1989). What sexual offenders tell us about prevention strategies. *Child Abuse & Neglect, 13,* 293-301.

Cross, T., Bazron, B., Dennis, K., & Isaacs, M. (1989). *Toward a culturally competent system of care.* Washington, DC: Georgetown University Child Development Center, Child and Adolescent Service System Program Technical Assistance Center.

Daro, D. (1988). *Confronting child abuse: Research for effective program design.* New York: Free Press.

Daro, D. (1989). When should prevention education begin? *Journal of Interpersonal Violence, 4*(2), 257-260.

Daro, D. (1991). Prevention programs. In C. Hollin & K. Howells (Eds.), *Clinical approaches to sex offenders and their victims* (pp. 285-306). New York: John Wiley.

Daro, D. (1993). Child maltreatment research: Implications for program design. In D. Cicchetti & S. Toth (Eds.), *Child abuse, child development and social policy* (pp. 331-367). Norwood, NJ: Ablex.

Daro, D. (1994). Prevention of childhood sexual abuse. *The Future of Children, 4*(2), 198-223.

Daro, D., & Gelles, R. (1992). Public attitudes and behaviors with respect to child abuse prevention. *Journal of Interpersonal Violence, 7*(4), 517-531.

Daro, D., Jones, E., & McCurdy, K. (1993). *Preventing child abuse: An evaluation of services to high-risk families* [Monograph]. Philadelphia: William Penn Foundation.

Derezotes, D., & Snowden, L. (1990). Cultural factors in the intervention of child maltreatment. *Child and Adolescent Social Work Journal, 7*(2), 161-175.

Dornbusch, S., Barr, J., & Seer, N. (1993). *The impact of education for parenting upon parents, children and family system.* Palo Alto, CA: Stanford Center for the Study of Families, Children and Youth.

Downer, A. (1984). *An evaluation of talking about touching.* Unpublished manuscript available from author, P.O. Box 15190, Seattle, WA 98115.

Egeland, B. (1988). Breaking the cycle of abuse: Implications for prediction and intervention. In K. Browne, C. Davies, & P. Stratton (Eds.), *Early prediction and prevention of child abuse* (pp. 87-102). New York: John Wiley.

Ellwood, A. (1988). Prove to me that MELD makes a difference. In H. Weiss & F. Jacobs (Eds.), *Evaluating family programs* (pp. 302-314). New York: Aldine.

Finkelhor, D. (1984). *Child sexual abuse: New theory and research.* New York: Free Press.

Finkelhor, D., & Dziuba-Leatherman, J. (1993). *Victimization prevention programs: A national survey on children's exposure and reactions.* Final report of the National Youth Victimization Prevention Study, funded by the Boy Scouts of America.

Finkelhor, D., & Strapko, N. (1992). Sexual abuse prevention education: A review of evaluation studies. In D. Willis, E. Holder, & M. Rosenberg (Eds.), *Child abuse prevention* (pp. 150-167). New York: John Wiley.

Fryer, G., Kraizer, S., & Miyoski, T. (1987). Measuring actual reduction of risk to child abuse: A new approach. *Child Abuse & Neglect, 11,* 173-179.

Furstenburg, F. (1970). *Unplanned parenthood.* New York: Free Press.

Furstenburg, F. (1980). Burdens and benefits: The impact of early childbearing on the family. *Journal of Social Issues, 36,* 64-87.

Gambrill, E. (1983). Behavioral interventions with child abuse and neglect. *Progress in Behavior Modification, 15,* 1-56.

Garbarino, J. (1987). Children's response to a sexual abuse prevention program: A study of the Spiderman comic. *Child Abuse & Neglect, 11,* 143-148.

Garbarino, J., Cohn, A., & Ebata, A. (1982). *The significance of cultural and ethnic factors in preventing child abuse: An exploration of research findings.* Chicago: National Committee for Prevention of Child Abuse.

Gaylin, W., Glasser, I., Marcus, S., & Rothman, D. (1978). *Doing good: The limits of benevolence.* New York: Pantheon.

Gilbert, N., Duerr-Berrick, J., LeProhn, N., & Nyman, N. (1990). *Protecting young children from sexual abuse: Does preschool training work?* Lexington, MA: Lexington Books.

Gilgun, J., & Connor, T. (1989). How perpetrators view child sexual abuse. *Social Work, 34*(3), 249-251.

Gray, J., Cutler, C. A., Dean, J. G., & Kempe, C. H. (1979). Prediction and prevention of child abuse and neglect. *Journal of Social Issues, 35*(2), 127-139.

Green, A. (1976). A psychodynamic approach to the study and treatment of child abusing parents. *Journal of the American Academy of Child Psychology, 15,* 414-442.

Halpern, R., & Larner, M. (1987). Lay family support during pregnancy and infancy: The Child Survival/Fair Start Initiative. *Infant Mental Health Journal, 8*(2), 130-143.

Harvey, P., Forehand, R., Brown, C., & Holmes, T. (1988). The prevention of sexual abuse: Examination of the effectiveness of a program with kindergarten-age children. *Behavior Therapy, 19,* 429-435.

Hazzard, A. (1990). Prevention of child sexual abuse. In R. Ammerman & M. Hersen (Eds.), *Treatment of family violence* (pp. 354-384). New York: John Wiley.

Hazzard, A., Webb, C., & Kleemeier, C. (1988). *Child sexual assault prevention programs: Helpful or harmful?* Unpublished manuscript, Emory University School of Medicine, Atlanta, GA.

Heinicke, C., Beckwith, L., & Thompson, A. (1988). Early intervention in the family system: A framework and review. *Infant Mental Health Journal, 9,* 111-141.

Helfer, R. (1982). A review of the literature on the prevention of child abuse and neglect. *Child Abuse & Neglect, 6,* 251-261.

Howing, P., Wodarski, J., Kurtz, P., & Gaudin, J. (1989). Methodological issues in child maltreatment research. *Social Work Research and Abstracts, 25*(3), 3-7.

Kamerman, S., & Kahn, A. (1990). Social services for children, youth and families in the United States. *Children and Youth Services Review* (Special issue), *12*(1/2).

Kaufman, J., & Zigler, E. (1989). The intergenerational transmission of child abuse. In D. Cicchetti & V. Carlson (Eds.), *Child maltreatment: Theory and research on the causes and consequences of child abuse and neglect* (pp. 129-150). Cambridge, NY: Cambridge University Press.

Kempe, H., & Helfer, R. (1976). *Child abuse and neglect: The family and community.* New York: Ballinger.

Kenning, M., Gallmeier, T., Jackson, T., & Plemons, S. (1987, July). *Evaluation of child sexual abuse prevention programs: A summary of two studies.* Paper presented at the Third National Conference on Family Violence, University of New Hampshire.

Kolko, D., Moser, J., & Hughes, J. (1989). Classroom training in sexual victimization awareness and prevention skills: An extension of the Red Flag/Green Flag people program. *Journal of Family Violence, 4,* 25-45.

Kolko, D., Moser, J., Litz, J., & Hughes, J. (1987). Promoting awareness and prevention of child sexual victimization using the Red Flag/Green Flag program: An evaluation with follow-up. *Journal of Family Violence, 2,* 11-35.

Kraizer, S., Witte, S., & Fryer, G. (1989). Child sexual abuse prevention programs: What makes them effective in protecting children? *Children Today, 18,* 23-27.

Larner, M. (1990). A "fair start" for parents and infants. *High Scope Review, 9*(1), 5-6, 8-10.

Larson, C. (1980). Efficacy of prenatal and postpartum home visits on child health and development. *Pediatrics, 66,* 191-197.

Leventhal, J. (1987). Programs to prevent sexual abuse: What outcomes should be measured? *Child Abuse & Neglect, 11,* 169-171.

Lutzker, J., & Rice, J. (1984). Project 12-Ways: Measuring outcome of a large in-home service for treatment and prevention of child abuse and neglect. *Child Abuse & Neglect, 8,* 519-524.

Lutzker, J., & Rice, J. (1987). Using recidivism data to evaluate Project 12-Ways: An ecobehavioral approach to the treatment and prevention of child abuse and neglect. *Journal of Family Violence, 2*(4), 283-290.

Mann, J. (1990). Drawing on cultural strengths to empower families. *Protecting Children, 7*(3), 3-5.

McCurdy, K., & Daro, D. (1994). Current trends in child abuse reporting and fatalities. *Journal of Interpersonal Violence, 9*(4), 75-94.

Melton, G. (1992). The improbability of prevention of sexual abuse. In D. Willis, E. Holden, & M. Rosenberg (Eds.), *Child abuse prevention* (pp. 168-192). New York: John Wiley.

Milner, J. (1980). *The child abuse potential inventory manual.* Webster, NC: Psytec.

Nibert, D., Cooper, S., Fitch, L., & Ford, J. (1988). *Prevention of abuse of young children: Exploratory evaluation of an abuse prevention program.* Columbus, OH: National Assault Prevention Center.

Olds, D. L., Henderson, C. R., Chamberlain, R., & Tatelbaum, R. (1986). Preventing child abuse and neglect: A randomized trial of nurse home visitation. *Pediatrics, 78,* 65-78.

Olds, D., & Henderson, C., Jr. (1990). The prevention of maltreatment. In D. Cicchetti & V. Carlson (Eds.), *Child maltreatment* (pp. 722-763). New York: Cambridge University Press.

Olds, D., & Kitzman, H. (1993). Review of research on home visiting for pregnant women and parents of young children. *The Future of Children, 3*(3), 53-92.

Peters, S. D., Wyatt, G. E., & Finkelhor, D. (1986). Prevalence. In D. Finkelhor (Ed.), *A sourcebook on child sexual abuse* (pp. 15-59). Newbury Park, CA: Sage.

Plummer, C. (1984, July). *Preventing sexual abuse: What in-school programs teach children.* Paper presented at the Second National Conference on Family Violence, University of New Hampshire.

Polit, D., & White, C. (1988). *The lives of young, disadvantaged mothers: The five year follow-up of the project redirection sample.* Saratoga Springs, NY: Human Analysis.

Powell, T. (1979). Comparison between self-help groups and professional services. *Social Casework, 60,* 561-565.

Reppucci, N., & Haugaard, J. (1989). Prevention of child sexual abuse: Myth or reality. *American Psychologist, 44*(10), 1266-1275.

Rodriguez, G., & Cortez, C. (1988). The evaluation experience of the Avancé Parent-Child Education Program. In H. Weiss & F. Jacobs (Eds.), *Evaluating family programs* (pp. 287-302). New York: Aldine.

Sameroff, A., & Chandler, M. (1975). Reproductive risk and the continuum of caretaking casualty. In F. Horowitz (Ed.), *Review of child development research* (Vol. 4). Chicago: University of Chicago Press.

Sandler, J. (1979). *Effects of adolescent pregnancy on mother-infant relations: A transactional model of reports to the Center for Population Research.* Bethesda, MD: National Institutes of Health.

Seitz, V., Rosenbaum, L., & Apfel, N. (1985). Effects of family support intervention: A ten-year follow-up. *Child Development, 56,* 376-391.

Siegel, E., Bauman, K., Schaefer, E., & Saunders, M. (1980). Hospital and home support during infancy: Impact on maternal attachment, child abuse and neglect, and health care utilization. *Pediatrics, 66,* 183-190.

Slaughter, D. (1988). Programs for racially and ethnically diverse American families: Some critical issues. In H. Weiss & F. Jacobs (Eds.), *Evaluating family programs* (pp. 461-476). New York: Aldine.

Swan, H., Press, A., & Briggs, S. (1985). Child sexual abuse prevention: Does it work? *Child Welfare, 64,* 395-405.

Taylor, D., & Beauchamp, C. (1988). Hospital-based primary prevention strategy in child abuse: A multi-level needs assessment. *Child Abuse & Neglect, 12,* 343-354.

U.S. Advisory Board on Child Abuse and Neglect. (1991). *Creating caring communities: Blueprint for an effective federal policy on child abuse and neglect.* Washington, DC: Department of Health and Human Services.

Vaughan, M., & Loadman, W. (1988, September 17). *Evaluating the effectiveness of a crisis nursery: Turning point's experiences to date.* Paper presented at the VII International Congress on Child Abuse and Neglect, Rio de Janeiro, Brazil.

Wieder, S., Poisson, S., Lourie, R., & Greenspan, S. (1988). Enduring gains: A five-year follow-up report on the Clinical Infant Development Program. *Zero to Three, 8*(4), 6-11.

Wolfe, D., Edwards, B., Manion, I., & Koverola, C. (1988). Early intervention for parents at risk of child abuse and neglect: A preliminary investigation. *Journal of Consulting and Clinical Psychology, 56*(1), 40-47.

Woods, S., & Dean, K. (1986). *Community-based options for maltreatment prevention: Augmenting self-sufficiency.* Prepared under contract to the U.S. Department of Health and Human Services, National Center on Child Abuse and Neglect.

Wurtele, S., & Miller-Perrin, C. (1987). An evaluation of side effects associated with participation in a child sexual abuse prevention program. *Journal of School Health, 57,* 228-231.

Wurtele, S., & Miller-Perrin, C. (1992). *Preventing child sexual abuse: Sharing the responsibility.* Lincoln: University of Nebraska Press.

Young, B., Liddell, T., Pecot, J., Siegenthaler, M., & Yamagishi, M. (1987). *Preschool sexual abuse prevention project: Executive summary.* Report prepared under a research grant funded by the U.S. Department of Heath and Human Services, Office of Human Development Services, Washington, DC.

19

Reporting of
Child Maltreatment

GAIL L. ZELLMAN

KATHLEEN COULBORN FALLER

The incidence and prevalence of child maltreatment are continuing concerns for those who advocate for children, those who provide services, and those who make funding and other relevant policies. And, as with other social problems that occur behind closed doors and often in families, determining the incidence and prevalence of child maltreatment is a difficult task.

A number of sources have been tapped to yield incidence and prevalence figures; as we shall see, each is flawed in its own way, and jointly the picture remains clouded. Official reports, which are mandated under state laws, provide an important national source of incidence and prevalence data. Their aggregation was facilitated by a provision of the Child Abuse Prevention Adoption and Family Service Act of 1988 (P.L. 100-294), which required the National Center on Child Abuse and Neglect (NCCAN) to establish a national data collection and analysis program on child maltreatment.[1]

Large, rigorous incidence studies funded by the federal government track cases and estimate the percentage that result in formal reports. Findings from these studies indicate that many cases do not eventuate in formal reports. Such findings emphasize the need for studies of would-be reporters who are required because of their professional position to report suspected maltreatment to appropriate authorities. Such studies validate the widespread failures to report found in the incidence studies and suggest the importance of a final type of prevalence indicator—surveys of adults about their experiences with maltreatment, either as perpetrators or as victims.

This chapter presents findings from each of these very different indicators and attempts to integrate their findings. Because officially reported cases have the clearest implications for the child protective system, we focus particularly on several important issues related to outcomes for officially reported cases.

History of Reporting Laws

Concerns about child maltreatment in the 1960s revivified an issue that had disappeared from the public policy agenda some 40 years before (Gordon, 1988). An article published in 1962 by Dr. C. Henry Kempe and his associates (Kempe, Silverman, Steele, Droegemueller, & Silver, 1962) at the Denver Medical Center marked the beginning of modern interest in child maltreatment.

Their paper argued that much of the accidental injury seen by pediatricians was in fact the result of intentional abuse. Kempe et al. relied on radiographic evidence of fractures in various stages of healing (e.g., Caffey, 1957, cited in Williams, 1983, p. 240) to shatter the widely held belief that abuse of children was a practice of the past (Williams, 1983, p. 240). By labeling the phenomenon the *battered child syndrome,* the paper convinced people that child maltreatment was a "disease" that could afflict anyone (Pleck, 1987, p. 172). The focus on physical abuse implied in the use of radiographic evidence served as well to reframe the meaning of child maltreatment: Long associated with neglect arising out of or in concert with poverty, physical abuse seemed far less tied to social class.

Kempe et al.'s arguments found an immediate and responsive audience. In an era marked by a growing concern for individual rights, increased sensitivity to injustice, and a belief that government had

the means and the obligation to improve the prospects of individuals and families, the paper stimulated a tremendous response in both professional and lay media.

This response was different from earlier ones. The older "cruelty" model of child maltreatment viewed perpetrating parents as miscreants; their crimes invoked criminal sanctions under cruelty laws. The reframing of child maltreatment as a medical condition implied more humane treatment. The battered child syndrome accorded parents greater compassion, care, and treatment by helping professionals and provided hope for a cure. A number of agencies organized to make this response.

In 1962, Dr. Kempe discussed the battered child syndrome at meetings held by the U.S. Children's Bureau, which had become interested in child abuse as a natural extension of its mission (Nelson, 1984). One product of these meetings was a model child abuse statute requiring that certain types of persons report known cases of child abuse and neglect to social services agencies (Nelson, 1984). Soon thereafter, the American Humane Association, the American Medical Association, and the Council of State Governments developed their own model statutes (Fraser, 1986).

The motivation for these laws was simple: Protection and services only could be provided when cases of child maltreatment became known. Reporting laws would provide the incentive to make such identification. The medicalizing of child maltreatment pointed to physicians as the obvious group to bring such cases to light. Physicians possessed expert skill and judgment, and they saw injured children regularly. The model laws would require physicians to report cases of suspected maltreatment. Statutory provisions would free them of any civil or criminal liability for doing so (Paulsen, Parker, & Adelman, 1966).

Implicit in the identification focus of the model laws was the assumption that child abuse only had to be identified to be "cured." Moreover, it was assumed that very few "cures" would be required: Child abuse, although serious, was believed to be rare. These two assumptions contributed to the unprecedented support garnered by the reporting legislation. Legislators in every state saw the reporting laws as an opportunity to demonstrate "no-cost rectitude" (Nelson, 1984, p. 75). No one thought at that time that the reporting laws would become a driving force for the expansion of child welfare services (Nelson, 1984).

No legislation in the history of this country had been so widely adopted in so little time. Within a 5-year span, every state had passed a child abuse reporting law, which required specified professionals likely to come in contact with children in the course of their work to report suspected maltreatment to child protective agencies. The framers of these laws, not unmindful of the ignorance, denial, and confidentiality concerns that had made such laws necessary, devised a number of provisions designed to remove legal impediments to reporting. These provisions included statutory immunity for good-faith reporting, abolition of doctor-patient privilege in situations of suspected maltreatment, language that required only reasonable suspicion or belief and that precluded investigation on the part of the reporting professional, anonymity provisions for reporters in some states, and assessment of criminal and/or civil penalties for failure to report as required by law (Davidson, 1988).

As knowledge and understanding of child maltreatment increased over time, it became evident that professionals other than physicians also might be in a position to identify maltreatment.

As knowledge and understanding of child maltreatment increased over time, it became evident that professionals other than physicians also might be in a position to identify maltreatment. Indeed, the framers of reporting legislation became aware that members of other professions might be able to detect maltreatment and bring it to the attention of authorities at an earlier juncture—before the occurrence of the severe injuries that often brought abuse to the attention of physicians (Fraser, 1986).

These new understandings led to a substantial increase in the number of professional groups designated in state laws as mandated reporters. In 1974, for example, all state reporting laws mandated

physicians to report suspected abuse and neglect, but only 25 states required social workers to report, and only 9 states required that police officers do so. By 1986, virtually every state included nurses, social workers, other mental health professionals, teachers, and school staff in the category of mandated reporters (Fraser, 1986).

The expansion of the ranks of mandated reporters was accompanied by a broadening of the concept of reportable maltreatment in the 1970s to include sexual abuse, emotional maltreatment, and neglect. Both of these changes were strongly influenced by the Child Abuse Prevention and Treatment Act (CAPTA) (P.L. 93-247) passed in 1974. In addition to the establishment of the National Center on Child Abuse and Neglect, CAPTA included a small state grant program. In order to obtain a grant, a state had to meet specified eligibility requirements. Key were the establishment of procedures for reporting and investigating child abuse reports and the assurance of treatment availability. These provisions speeded the creation of specialized child protective services (CPS) agencies and gave state child welfare agencies the power to remove a child if investigation suggested that the child was in danger (Pleck, 1987).

Impact of Laws on Identification of Maltreatment

The reporting laws clearly succeeded in encouraging the identification of abuse and neglect. The reporting rate—10.1 per 1,000 children in 1976—had climbed to 34.0 by 1987. More than 2 million reports were made in 1987, representing a 225% increase since 1976, when 669,000 reports were estimated to have been received.[2] In 1993, almost 3 million children were the subjects of reports of suspected maltreatment (Daro & McCurdy, 1994). Among victims of substantiated or indicated reports collected from state sources by NCCAN (1993), neglect was the most frequently reported kind of maltreatment. Forty-four percent of these children suffered deprivation of necessities. Physical injury accounted for 24% of all substantiated or indicated cases reported in that year; the figure for sexual abuse was 15%. Emotional maltreatment accounted for 6% of these cases; other maltreatment accounted for 11% of children (NCCAN, 1993). The relative rankings of types of abuse have not changed in recent years (American Humane Association, 1988).

As a direct result of reporting statutes, medical and mental health professionals, school staff, police, and other mandated reporters have reported suspected incidents of abuse to official agencies in growing numbers. Since 1984, professionals have accounted for the majority (mean = 53%) of reports (American Humane Association, 1988; NCCAN, 1993).

Recent data reveal that among professional reporters, school personnel were responsible for the largest number of reports (30% of all reports from professional sources). Law enforcement accounted for 22% of reports made by professionals. Medical personnel and social services workers accounted for 20% and 24% of reports, respectively. Child care providers accounted for the remaining 4% of reports made by professionals (American Humane Association, 1988; NCCAN, 1993). Again, these figures have changed little in recent years.

Impact of Laws on Protective Agencies

The success of the reporting laws created substantial and unanticipated problems for the protective agencies designated to receive those reports. Most simply lacked the capacity to respond adequately to a large share of the cases that flooded in. As Newberger (1983) notes, "No one could have foreseen that the prevalence of child abuse, however narrowly defined, was far greater than was believed at the time of the publication of the 'Battered Child Syndrome' paper or the signing of Public Law 93-247" (p. 308).

As idealists succeeded in expanding both the definition of child abuse and the numbers of professional groups required to make reports, the inability of protective agencies to respond occasioned a crisis. As the optimism of the 1960s and 1970s faded and government support for social programs declined, the ability of CPS agencies to materially assist children and families identified through child abuse reports was called into question.

Observers and actors from all points on the political spectrum began to worry publicly about the state of CPS. Agencies began to cut back on their caseloads by defining maltreatment more narrowly, by screening out less severe reports, and by setting priorities that precluded the provision of help to large numbers of children and families (Kamerman & Kahn, 1990; Zellman & Antler, 1990).

Professional Compliance With Reporting Laws

Although the number of reports increased dramatically, a sure sense that not all professionals were meeting the reporting mandate continued, and not all of even the most serious cases of child maltreatment were being reported. Such failures to report suspected maltreatment undermine the child abuse reporting system and its ability to help children in need of protection in many ways.

Most important, failure to report may deny children in need of protection any opportunity to receive it. This is particularly true when the abuse is severe and the harm imminent.

Widespread violation of the reporting mandate reduces wholehearted professional support for it. It is impossible for professionals to endorse fully to the public and to other professionals a law that many have knowingly violated (Finkelhor & Zellman, 1991). In addition, widespread failure to report actually may punish those professionals who do make reports by driving people who wish to avoid being reported to professionals known to violate the reporting law.

Failure to report also exposes professionals to anxiety and liability. Nevertheless, some knowledgeable professionals take this risk when they believe that a report threatens their relationship with a child and when they are fairly certain that the report will not result in any benefit to the child or the family, as discussed below.

Finally, cases handled covertly and outside the system do not come into the data collection process. Unreported cases distort the aggregate picture of child abuse and may reduce funding and policy support for children in need.

A number of studies using different methods consistently have confirmed widespread concerns that mandated reporter compliance with the reporting laws is far from complete (e.g., Finkelhor, Gomes-Schwartz, & Horowitz, 1984; James, Womack, & Stauss, 1978; Kalichman, Craig, & Follingstad, 1990; Morris, Johnson, & Clasen, 1985; Saulsbury & Campbell, 1985). Two studies in particular address this important issue and provide national data concerning the degree of compliance with the reporting mandate and the reasons that professionals may not report.

National Incidence Study

The first, the Study of the National Incidence and Prevalence of Child Abuse and Neglect (NIS) (DHHS, 1988), was commissioned by NCCAN in response to a specific congressional mandate in the Child Abuse Amendments of 1984 (P.L. 98-457).[3] This study, which followed an earlier one with the same goals (DHHS, 1981), was designed to assess the national incidence of child abuse and neglect and determine how the severity, frequency, and character of child maltreatment had changed since the earlier study was completed.

Community professionals in a national probability sample of 29 counties reported cases of child maltreatment to the study from their positions in CPS, schools, hospitals, police departments, juvenile probation, and other child-serving agencies. CPS provided information about all reported cases accepted for investigation during the study period. Participating professionals at other agencies served as "sentinels," looking for and reporting to the study cases of maltreatment that met the study's definitions (DHHS, 1988).

The NIS methodology is based on a model that depicts five levels of official recognition or public awareness of maltreatment:

1. Children reported to CPS.
2. Children not known to CPS but who are known to other "investigatory" agencies, such as police, courts, or public health departments. Although such children are known officially, they are not necessarily known as maltreated.
3. Maltreated children who are not known to CPS or to any investigatory agency but who have been recognized as maltreated by professionals in other major community institutions, such as schools,

hospitals, day care centers, and social services agencies.
4. Maltreated children known to people in the community, such as neighbors or other family members, but these people have not reported the maltreatment to any agency.
5. Children whose maltreatment has not been recognized by anyone.

The NIS-II collected data relevant to Levels 1 through 3 using both the definitions of maltreatment used in the first NIS and the expanded definitions consistent with the 1984 amendments. The earlier, narrower definition was based on demonstrable harm; the later, broader one was based on an endangerment standard.[4]

A unique contribution of the NIS studies is their ability to determine what proportion of cases known to professionals were also known to CPS. Thus, these data illuminate professional reporting practices, particularly compliance with the reporting laws.

NIS data reveal that under both the earlier, narrower definition of maltreatment and the later, more inclusive one, CPS learned of fewer than half of countable cases known to a professional in a non-CPS agency (44% under original definitions, 51% under expanded definitions).

Comparison of the 1986 findings with 1980 data reveals that although a larger percentage of countable cases was known to CPS in 1986 than in 1980, the percentage increase (from 33% to 44% under original definitions) was not statistically significant. The author cautions that the nonsignificance of this finding may be due in part to increased screening out of cases by CPS. Screened-out cases were not classified as "known to CPS," even though they had been reported to CPS. Thus, rates of acceptance for investigation have an effect to an unknown degree on the "known to CPS" figure.

Noninvestigatory agencies, including schools, hospitals, social services, and mental health agencies, recognized more than four and a half times the number of child victims than did investigatory agencies such as probation departments, courts, and law enforcement. Rates of reporting by agency type reveal widely varying proportions of cases reported to CPS of those recognized by someone in the agency. Hospitals and mental health agencies had the highest proportion of cases reported to cases recognized (100% and 82%, respectively). Rates for other agencies were far lower; for example, the proportions for social services, probation, courts, and schools were all less than 30%.

As discussed earlier, the meaning of the differences in these proportions across agency types is not entirely clear. As the NIS author notes, increased screenouts of reported cases by CPS may suppress them. Study data showing a significant increase in the number of unfounded cases that were countable under original definitions suggest that CPS agencies have tightened substantiation standards since 1980. Cases that might have been accepted for investigation in 1980 were less likely to be accepted in 1986, suppressing the number of cases considered known to CPS and the proportion of cases known to CPS of all cases known to professionals (see Ards & Harrell, 1993, for further discussion of this point).

If the increased numbers of screenouts are selective, this may magnify differences across agency types. If cases of mild abuse and neglect are less likely to be accepted for investigation (and increased use of risk assessment and screening approaches in CPS agencies suggest that this is likely the case; see below), agencies that tend to report milder abuse (e.g., schools) may appear to be reporting far lower percentages of known cases than they actually are reporting.[5] In contrast, agencies that tend to report more severe cases (e.g., hospitals and law enforcement) may produce higher proportions because the cases that they report are less likely to be screened out.

Despite ambiguities with regard to some of the data, NIS findings clearly show that a majority of children who are recognized as abused or neglected by mandated reporters do not enter the CPS report base. Most cases of suspected maltreatment known to professionals are not reported or investigated. With support from NCCAN, Zellman and her colleagues undertook a national survey of mandated reporters to understand why.

Mandated Reporter Study

Professionals in 15 states, sampled from directories of their various professional organizations, were mailed a questionnaire in the spring of 1987 that surveyed their reporting behavior and the nature of their professional work. At the very beginning of the survey form, each respondent read and responded to five vignettes, each of which briefly described a case of possible abuse or neglect. The vignettes provided common stimuli across respondents and permitted the exploration of the independent contributions of case characteristics to intended reporting and to other decisions that bear on reporting intentions.

A total of 1,196 general and family practitioners, pediatricians, child psychiatrists, clinical psychologists, social workers, public school principals, and heads of child care centers responded to the survey (59% response rate).

Reporting behavior. More than three fourths of respondents (77%) indicated that they had made a child abuse report at some time in their professional career. Rates of ever-reporting varied considerably by profession. Nearly all elementary school principals had reported at some time (92%). Rates of ever-reporting were nearly as high for child psychiatrists (90%) and pediatricians (89%). Rates for secondary school principals, social workers, and clinical psychologists were 84%, 70%, and 63%, respectively.

The majority of these reporters (56%) had made a report in the past year. Reporting rates in the past year by profession followed a pattern similar to that for ever-reporting.

Failure to report. Almost 40% of respondents admitted that at some time in their career they had suspected abuse or neglect but had decided not to make a report.

There were substantial differences across professional groups in failure-to-report (FTR) rates, with child psychiatrists most likely to have failed to report (58%) and child care providers and pediatricians least likely to have done so (24% and 30%, respectively). The majority of respondents (56%) who had ever failed to report had done so at least once in the past year, suggesting that failure to report was not simply an artifact of the lack of awareness about the reporting mandate that characterized the reporting environment as recently as 10 or 15 years ago.

Patterns of reporting behavior. To provide a clearer picture of reporting behavior, two variables that measured lifetime reporting behavior were combined into a single variable with four categories that described the respondents' reporting history: (a) never reported and never failed to report (outside system), (b) reported at least once and never failed to report (consistent reporting), (c) reported at least once and failed to report at least once (discretionary reporting), and (d) never reported but failed to report at least once (consistent failure to report). The most common lifetime reporting pattern in our sample was consistent reporting, which is what the law requires. Forty-four percent of respondents indicated that they had reported at some time and had never failed to do so when they suspected maltreatment. The second most common pattern was discretionary reporting. One third of the sample fell into this category. Seventeen percent had neither reported nor failed to report and thus remained outside the child abuse reporting system. Finally, 6% of respondents had a lifetime pattern that included no reporting but at least one instance of FTR (see Table 19.1).

Reasons for making reports. Those respondents who had ever reported rated the importance of a series of reasons for doing so. Ninety-two percent indicated that stopping maltreatment was a very important reason for past reporting; 89% indicated that getting help for the family was a very important motivator. The reporting law was cited as a strong reason for past reporting by 71%. Differences across professions revealed that family/general practitioners were less influenced by the reporting mandate and were less likely to cite workplace reporting policy as an important motivator for reports, in part because of their tendency to practice in private group or solo settings. Child psychiatrists and psychologists were less likely to believe that a report would help the child or family, help the family see the seriousness of the problem, or stop maltreatment. They were least likely of all professional groups to rate "bringing CPS expertise to bear" as an important reason for past reporting.

Analysis of the vignette data reveals additional factors that enter into professionals' reporting decisions (Zellman, 1992).[6] Respondents were significantly more likely to intend a report in cases of serious abuse (e.g., when there were physical injuries or intercourse had occurred), when the child was young rather than an adolescent, and when there was a history of previous maltreatment. When a teenager recanted an allegation of physical or sexual abuse after confrontation by an adult, respondents were significantly less likely to intend a report, despite growing awareness that recantation is a part of the child sexual abuse accommodation syndrome and should not be taken at face value (e.g., Summit, 1983).

Reasons for Failing to Report

Using factor analysis, we identified three clusters of reasons for failure to report. One cluster, which we labeled "bad for me," focuses on the perceived costs of reporting to the reporter. A second cluster, "I can do better than the system," includes a range of criticisms of CPS agencies *and* respondent beliefs that he or she could do more for the child than CPS could. The third cluster, "not reportable," includes a number of evidence-based reasons for not reporting.

Table 19.2 indicates levels of support by profession for several reasons from each of the three clusters. Reasons in the "not reportable" category were endorsed most commonly; reasons in the "bad for me" category received limited support. The most frequently endorsed reason for failing to report was a lack of sufficient evidence that maltreatment had occurred. This finding supports other work that shows that many reporters will not report solely on the basis of a "subjective state of suspicion" (Kalichman & Brosig, 1993). One third of respondents ascribed great importance to their judgment that the maltreatment that they suspected or had observed was not serious enough to report.

Nineteen percent considered the fact that a report would disrupt treatment to be an important reason for not having reported suspected maltreatment. A similar percentage ascribed considerable importance to the belief that they could help the child better themselves. Sixteen percent considered the poor quality of CPS services an important reason for not having reported.

The levels of endorsement of these reasons for FTR provide some important insights into how mandated professionals view the reporting laws. Reporting laws ask professionals to be reasonably vigilant and to report their suspicions or beliefs that maltreatment has occurred or is occurring. The laws are clear that no more

TABLE 19.1 Lifetime Prevalence and Annual Incidence of Child Abuse Reporting and Failure to Report by Profession (Percentages)

Behavior	Family/General Practitioners (N = 88)[a]	Pediatricians (N = 243)	Child Psychiatrists (N = 99)	Clinical Psychologists (N = 176)	Social Workers (N = 195)	Child Care Providers (N = 109)	Elementary Principals (N = 148)	Secondary Principals (N = 112)	Total Sample (N = 1,170)
				PROFESSIONAL GROUP					
Ever reported child abuse or neglect	75.0[b]	89.3	89.9	63.1	69.7	50.5	91.9	83.9	77.3
Reported in last year	43.2	70.5	67.0	38.6	38.7	33.6	83.8	67.9	56.0
Reported in last year/ever reported[c]	57.6	79.0	74.5	61.3	55.4	66.7	91.2	80.9	72.5
Ever failed to report child abuse or neglect	35.2	30.0	58.2	44.3	51.3	23.6	37.7	33.6	39.3
Failed to report in past year	19.5	17.2	32.0	22.7	27.0	13.2	23.0	23.4	22.1

a. These sample numbers apply to row 1 and may vary slightly for other rows depending on the amount of missing data.
b. Cell entries represent the percentage of respondents in the specified profession who indicated that they had performed the behavior in question.
c. Cell entries in this row are the percentage in each profession indicating they had reported in the past year divided by the percentage indicating they had ever reported. In the case of family/general practitioners, the cell entry 57.6 is the result of 43.2 divided by 75.0.

366

TABLE 19.2 Ratings of Reasons for Failing to Report by Those Who Had Ever Failed to Report by Profession (Percentages)

Reasons for Failure to Report	PROFESSIONAL GROUP								
	Family/General Practitioners (N = 34)[a]	Pediatricians (N = 90)	Child Psychiatrists (N = 54)	Clinical Psychologists (N = 75)	Social Workers (N = 100)	Child Care Providers (N = 28)	Elementary Principals (N = 61)	Secondary Principals (N = 40)	Total Sample (N = 492)
Bad for me									
Reports take too much time	2.9[b]	2.3	0.0	0.0	1.0	4.2	1.6	0.0	1.2
Fear of lawsuit for reporting	0.0	2.3	1.7	2.7	3.0	9.5	1.6	2.4	2.5
Discomfort with family	0.0	3.4	0.0	1.4	2.0	15.0	5.1	0.0	2.6
I can do better									
CPS overreacts to reports	5.9	11.5	7.1	12.2	12.0	4.8	0.0	8.0	8.0
CPS services are of poor quality	9.1	11.6	23.2	19.2	22.5	10.0	8.2	7.3	15.5
Could help the child better myself	2.9	18.4	21.1	24.0	29.1	14.8	13.3	10.0	19.3
Treatment was already accepted	12.1	16.3	33.3	32.9	40.2	5.3	6.7	20.0	24.2
Report would disrupt treatment	11.8	20.7	28.1	23.2	27.5	4.8	8.6	2.4	19.0
Not reportable									
Lacked sufficient evidence that abuse has occurred	67.6	63.6	57.9	55.1	49.5	76.0	59.7	73.8	59.9
Abuse or neglect not serious enough to report	25.7	35.6	38.6	28.4	36.3	28.0	37.3	27.5	33.4
Situation resolved itself	18.2	19.3	10.7	21.3	29.3	26.1	13.6	20.0	20.3
Case already reported	18.2	21.8	35.1	16.0	22.0	9.5	11.7	24.4	20.7

a. Sample numbers reflect the exclusion of respondents who indicated that they had never failed to report.
b. Cell entries represent the mean percentage of professionals in the specified group who rated the reason as "very important" in their decisions not to report suspected abuse or neglect.

is required: Indeed, professionals are precluded explicitly from conducting any further investigation, a prohibition reinforced by the short latency period before a report is required (Maney & Wells, 1988). Furthermore, they are not to exercise professional discretion in choosing which cases to report. The laws are mute regarding the efficacy of making reports, but it is clear in the prohibitions on professional discretion that the potential benefits of reports are not to be considered in the reporting decision.

These data reveal, however, that issues of efficacy are of considerable concern to would-be reporters. As noted earlier, a common reporting pattern among mandated reporters is discretionary reporting—reporting in some instances and deciding not to report in others. Indeed, discretionary reporters accounted for four fifths of all those who admitted having ever failed to report.

Discretionary reporters did not lack knowledge and experience. Unlike consistent nonreporters, who tended to have little child abuse training and limited child abuse knowledge, discretionary reporters were just as knowledgeable about and just as well trained in child abuse as the consistent reporters, a finding supported in subsequent work (e.g., Kalichman & Brosig, 1993). Discretionary reporters also expressed more confidence than other reporters in their own ability to treat child abuse. Moreover, the discretionary reporters were more likely than even consistent reporters to indicate that they served as their agency's child abuse resource person.

What most distinguished discretionary reporters from other groups was their beliefs that reports often had negative consequences for the children involved.

What most distinguished discretionary reporters from other groups was their negative opinion of the professionalism and capability of CPS staff and their beliefs that reports often had negative consequences for the children involved (Finkelhor & Zellman, 1991). Their experience and attitudes led them to conclude that it was better for the child not to make

a report in some cases. These cases often involved mild abuse or neglect that they knew would not receive adequate attention from overburdened CPS staff. At the same time, such reports would risk termination of treatment and loss of the opportunity to continue to monitor the family and perhaps provide the support or education that might reduce the likelihood of further maltreatment.

Perceived efficacy was a significant contributor to reporting intentions. When respondents believed that the child would be unlikely to benefit from a report, they were significantly less likely to intend to make one (Zellman, 1990). Despite the fact that the usefulness of an intended report is raised only rarely in law or training, would-be reporters clearly consider it when they decide whether to report suspected maltreatment.

Protective system incapacity increases concerns about the usefulness of reports. When the protective system becomes increasingly burdened as economic hard times both reduce agency budgets and increase the risk to children that arises from family stress occasioned by unemployment and economic worries, attention needs to be paid to this issue, as we do below.

Victim and Offender Disclosure of Maltreatment

Gathering information about maltreatment and its disclosure directly from the persons involved represents another way to learn about the extent of the problem. Population surveys have two particular advantages. First, they provide information about cases that may not come to professional attention. Second, they yield better data than incidence studies about the extent and effects of child abuse (Peters, Wyatt, & Finkelhor, 1986).

Most prevalence studies involve surveys of adults who are asked about victimization during their childhood. These may be studies of volunteers, community samples, or special populations (e.g., college students). Surveys of offenders are much smaller in number. Most of this research focuses on sexual abuse, although there are some important findings regarding physical abuse as well. The little work that investigates neglect and emotional maltreatment does so with clinical populations.

Prevalence of Physical Abuse

Research that addresses the prevalence of physical abuse examines both the use of violence by parents and victimization experiences of special populations, specifically college students and health care professionals.

Straus and colleagues (Gelles & Straus, 1988; Straus, Gelles, & Steinmetz, 1978) investigated rates of parental violence in national samples of adults in two-parent families in two surveys 10 years apart. Parents were asked about their use of tactics for resolving conflicts with their children, ranging from nonabusive to severely abusive. Conflict tactics characterized as "severe violence" and thus physically abusive included kicking, biting, punching, hitting or trying to hit the child with an object, beating up, threatening with a gun or knife, and using a gun or knife.

In 1975, 14% of 1,428 parents reported using severe violence, and in 1985, 11% of 1,146 parents did so. The difference in these two rates is small but statistically significant. The researchers have argued that this represents a decrease in parental abuse of children over the decade. An alternative explanation posits that differences in methodology and changes in reporting norms account for the decrease in rate. In the first study, data were collected using face-to-face interviews and in the second using telephone interviews. Moreover, adverse publicity about child abuse may have discouraged disclosure by parents by the time of the second survey.

Three studies that questioned college students about being abused as children (Graziano & Namaste, 1990; Henschel, Briere, & Morlau-Magallanes, 1990; Wiemers & Petretic-Jackson, 1991) focused on spankings, observable injury, and physical abuse. Findings suggest that the vast majority of the study populations experienced spankings, and 10% to 20% were victims of behaviors that we now would label physical abuse.

Nuttall and Jackson (1994) surveyed 646 health care professionals (169 social workers, 128 pediatricians, 176 psychologists, and 173 psychiatrists) about their own abuse victimization during childhood. Among their findings were that 7.1% reported physical abuse as children.

Psychiatrists reported significantly lower rates of physical abuse than did the other three disciplines.

Prevalence of Sexual Abuse

No researcher has directly questioned adults in nonclinical populations about their sexual abuse of children. However, Briere and Runtz (1989) surveyed college males about their sexual attraction to children and reported that 21% endorsed items indicating such arousal.

In contrast, the number of studies of victims of sexual abuse is considerable. The findings from these studies are quite varied. This variability derives from methodological differences in the various studies—specifically, definitions of sexual abuse, the number and structure of questions about sexual abuse, data collection strategies, populations studied, and sample selection. All of these influence prevalence rates. As might be expected, the broader the definition, the higher the rates of sexual abuse. Studies that focus largely on sexual abuse and ask more questions about it yield more disclosures. Face-to-face interviews, as opposed to telephone surveys or questionnaires, tend to result in increased rates, as do studies of "high-risk" populations, such as psychiatric patients, convicted felons, prostitutes, and abusive parents. Finally, higher proportions of females than males report sexual victimization.[7]

The rates for male sexual victimization range from as low as 3% when a single question about sexual abuse or forced sexual contact is asked (Burnam, 1985, personal communication, as cited in Finkelhor, 1986; Kercher & McShane, 1984; Murphy, 1987) to 30% in a survey of college students, using a nonspecific definition (Landis, 1956). Of particular interest is a study by Risin and Koss (1987) involving 2,972 male college students who were asked about their sexual experiences before age 14. The importance of this study is not so much its prevalence rate (7.3%) but its finding that close to half of the offenders were females and that almost 40% of the men reported that they did not feel victimized by the experience.

Prevalence rates across studies vary more dramatically for women. The study with the lowest rate involved 1,623 women, interviewed face-to-face by nonprofessional interviewers about issues of mental health. They were asked a single question about sexual assault prior to age 16; 6% indicated they had been assaulted (Burnam, 1985, personal communication, as cited in Finkelhor, 1986). The highest rate is reported by Wyatt in a study of 248 women focusing on their sexual experiences and using a broad definition of sexual abuse (Wyatt, 1985). Sixty-two percent of respondents reported sexual victimization; this figure was 45% when only contact behavior was considered. Wyatt's research involved face-to-face extended interviews, and the interviewers were matched with respondents on gender and race.

A larger study than Wyatt's, conducted about the same time with similar methodology and a slightly more restricted definition, yielded similar results (Russell, 1983, 1986). Fifty-four percent of 930 San Francisco-area women reported being sexually abused before 18; this figure was 35% when only contact behavior was considered.

The most recent data available on sexual abuse of women come from two surveys by Saunders and colleagues (Saunders et al., 1991; Saunders, Villeponteaux, Lipovsky, Kilpatrick, & Veronen, 1993). Both employed the same broad definition of sexual abuse but differed in data collection methods. One involved a representative national sample surveyed by trained female telephone interviewers. The second was a probability sample of women in Charleston County, South Carolina, interviewed face to face by trained female research assistants. The 4,008 (weighted) respondents in the national study reported a rate of child sexual abuse of 13.3%. In contrast, the 391 women in the Charleston study reported a rate of 33.5%.

The Relationship of Victim and Offender Reports to Official Reports

An important but not extensively studied issue is the relationship between estimates of the prevalence of maltreatment derived from victims and offenders in response to surveys and those derived from official reports. Limited data illuminate this issue.

Some prevalence researchers have asked respondents whether their cases were ever reported. Russell (1986), who, as noted earlier, surveyed 930 women in

the San Francisco area, obtained 648 disclosures of child sexual abuse. Of these, respondents indicated that only 30 cases (5%) were ever reported to the police. Saunders and colleagues (Saunders et al., 1991; Saunders et al., 1993) asked participants in both the Charleston, South Carolina, community survey and the national survey of adult women whether their sexual abuse was ever reported to the police or to other authorities. In the former study, only 5.7% of the 139 incidents described to researchers were ever reported. The proportion was a little higher for the national study: 12% of the 699 sexual assaults. But these data are less than illuminating in terms of reporting rates because many of the incidents described probably occurred before the advent of the mandatory reporting laws. In addition, victim studies usually ask about abuse during childhood, as opposed to, for example, abuse during a given year, which might more readily allow comparisons with official reporting data.

However, Straus and his colleagues (Gelles & Straus, 1988; Straus et al., 1978) asked in their surveys of parents not only if they had *ever* used severe violence tactics with their children but whether they had done so during the *previous year.* They found that when data from that same year were compared, the rates reported by parents were 50% higher than official estimates from NCCAN. Moreover, the authors contend that these parental reports are themselves underestimates, because parents may not remember or reveal abuse. They conclude that if parents reported *all* abuse, these rates would be two to three times higher than the 3.6% of parents surveyed in 1975 who reported using severe violence during the previous year and the 1.9% making such disclosures in 1985 (Gelles & Straus, 1988, p. 104).

Thus, both victim and offender surveys suggest that most abuse does not come to the attention of officials. Moreover, many researchers, including Straus and colleagues (e.g., Gelles & Straus, 1988; Peters et al., 1986), regard findings from general population prevalence surveys to be underestimates because respondents may be unwilling to disclose maltreatment, may not remember, or may not view these events as abuse. These findings indicate that failure to report by mandated professionals, as revealed by the National Incidence Studies and the Mandated Reporter Study, is not the only reason child maltreatment cases elude official identification and intervention.

Case Management and Disposition After Reporting

The purpose of child abuse reports is to bring potential abuse to the attention of CPS and to precipitate some CPS response when appropriate. The type and intensity of that response depend on the characteristics of the report and on the receiving agency's approach to organizing, classifying, and deploying its resources.

The nature of the reporting mandate and the state of child welfare services results in the receipt of some reports outside the CPS mandate. Because mandated reporters must act only on "reasonable suspicions" or "reasonable beliefs," some reports may be found not to constitute child maltreatment. Insufficient staffing of child welfare services in many communities has caused some reports that might have been accepted to be screened out (Wells, 1987). Such practices increase the number of uninvestigated or unsubstantiated reports. Given demand for investigation and services that far outstrips available resources, CPS must act to preserve and allocate these resources appropriately. Gatekeeping activities help CPS agencies do this. Gatekeeping in CPS agencies takes place at three points: the decision to investigate a report, the decision to substantiate a report after investigation, and the decision to provide agency service (Wells, 1987).

Screening is the first gatekeeping point. It occurs when a report is received; its final outcome is a decision about whether to conduct an official investigation. The decision to investigate hinges on whether a report of suspected maltreatment that the agency has received is determined to be a "valid report of abuse or neglect" (Wells, 1987, p. 2). This determination is a function of law, agency policies and procedures, local conditions, and practice (Wells, 1987, p. 2).

Screening serves several purposes for CPS agencies. First, screening is a tool to reduce investigative caseloads to a point that at least approaches, if not matches, available resources (Zellman & Antler,

1990). As the number of reports continues to increase and agency budgets remain steady at best, caseload management approaches take on increased urgency (Downing, Wells, & Fluke, 1990).

Second, screening may identify nonabusive families who are in need of support and preventive services; CPS can make referrals to agencies that can provide those services. As Wells, Stein, Fluke, and Downing (1989) note, many reports to CPS may be made in the belief that child welfare services are accessible only through an allegation of maltreatment. Often, reports motivated for this reason are unfounded on investigation. If screening occurs prior to investigation, nonabusive families in need of services may be referred without the potential stigma of an investigation to an agency that can provide needed services, although the availability of such services is far from certain.

Third, screening may help CPS agencies to manage caseloads and deploy limited investigational staff and resources to those cases in which the threat of harm is greatest. This third purpose is problematic for many: A triage approach to investigation institutionalizes the movement of CPS agencies away from the preventive goals that motivated the expansion of the reporting laws to include additional mandated reporter groups (Wells et al., 1989). Others applaud this more limited purview. Besharov (1988), for example, argues that because our ability to predict future danger to the child is so limited, agencies are best advised to focus resources on cases in which harm already has occurred or past parental behavior could have been harmful. This approach avoids the subjectivity implicit in responding to "threatened harm."

For the most part, the state reporting laws encourage or require the investigation of all bona fide reports. This stance complies with the federal statute that requires all reports of child abuse and neglect to be investigated (P.L. 93-247). Only a handful of state laws explicitly provide for the screening of complaints.

Nevertheless, the screening function is implicit in most of the reporting laws. Some laws circumscribe the investigatory responsibility of CPS through their definitions of maltreatment. For example, most states limit investigatory responsibility to reports of children 18 and younger by defining child maltreatment as something that occurs only to those in this age group. The identity and role of the alleged perpetrator vis á vis the child often figures into definitions of maltreatment as well. In most states, the alleged perpetrator must be a caretaker; in some states, alleged maltreatment in out-of-home care is explicitly a matter for the police rather than for CPS. In at least one state, the level of seriousness of the allegations figures into the definition of child abuse. Reports in which alleged physical or mental injury is not serious are not subject to investigation, because nonserious injuries are not defined as child maltreatment (Wells, 1987).

Other legislative criteria may permit CPS not to investigate. For example, in some states, complaints from reporters who refuse to give their name need not be investigated (Wells, 1987). Complaints may be rejected if the same person has made three previous unfounded reports concerning the same child and alleged perpetrator (Wells et al., 1989). Policies permit screen-out on the basis of incomplete information, outdated reports, absence of a specific incident or pattern of incidents, and "inappropriate referrals" (Wells, 1987, p. 6). Indeed, Wells's analysis of 45 state policies revealed that more than two thirds appear to allow some screening (Wells, 1987). Such widespread acknowledgment and acceptance of screening contrast with the lack of discussion or permission to screen in the state reporting laws.

Other empirical data confirm the prevalence of screening policies. In a survey of CPS administrators and intake supervisors in 100 local agencies in eight states, respondents revealed to Downing et al. (1990) that most agencies have written policies that delimit the nature of reports considered appropriate for investigation. At least half of each group reported that the policy permitted screen-outs when the alleged perpetrator was not a caregiver or when the complaint concerned the parents' behavior (e.g., parental drug use with no specific act of abuse or neglect alleged). Another common reason for screening out complaints is that the problem reported is not appropriate for CPS and is better handled by another agency. Alleged school truancy, failure to provide medical care, and a mother's psychiatric problems were examples frequently cited in this latter category.

Some state policies prohibit screening: All reports are to be investigated. Zellman and Antler (1990) found, however, that even when screening is not permitted, it may occur by default. Using formal or informal risk assessment tools, cases are assigned to be investigated urgently, immediately, or as soon as possible. Because of the press of new, more emergent cases, those cases in the last, least serious category may never be investigated at all. Although the agency's intent may be to respond to all reported cases, prioritization or risk assessment schemes may screen out the lowest-priority cases effectively (Wells, 1987). The danger in this, notes Giovannoni (1989), is that the ability to predict risk is "in its infancy"; therefore, screen-outs based on risk are ill-advised at this time.

Given the reality that screening does occur (e.g., Rosen, 1981), many argue that the process should be formalized and regulated (e.g., Barone, Adams, & Tooman, 1981). Besharov (1988) urges child protective agencies to develop policies that specify the kinds of reports that will be accepted for investigation. Daniel, Newberger, Reed, and Kotelchuk (1978) note that the use of screening tests focuses program efforts on high-risk populations and is thus a useful approach. As Wells (1987) notes, unless agencies have limitless funding, they cannot serve every child whose life is troubled or traumatic. Consequently, CPS can and should limit definitions of abuse and neglect.

Classification of Cases After Investigation

CPS ultimately must determine whether reports of suspected abuse and neglect describe valid maltreatment. The purpose of the investigation is to make this determination. Whether CPS will intervene in the family, refer to another agency for voluntary services, or withdraw completely depends on this decision.

The labels applied to this determination vary by child protection agency. The terms *substantiation, founding,* and *indicated* all describe similar but not identical decisions. Essentially, the decision following investigation is whether to process the case further into the system. "Substantiated" cases are opened for service after investigation; "unsubstantiated" cases are closed (Giovannoni, 1989).

The Substantiation Decision

States require a report to be substantiated with either "some credible evidence" or a sufficient reason to conclude that the child has been abused or neglected. Involuntary court-ordered services can be imposed, but state laws require either a "preponderance of the evidence" or "clear and convincing evidence" that maltreatment has occurred (Besharov, 1988, p. 9).

Unsubstantiated cases indicate only that CPS has decided to take no further action after investigation. "Unsubstantiated" is not synonymous with "false report" (Giovannoni, 1989). Cases may be unsubstantiated for a variety of reasons. Many of the reasons (e.g., inability to locate the address) are unrelated to the validity of the case. The many reasons for failure to substantiate are important to keep in mind, because substantiation rates have become a source of controversy, as discussed below.

Giovannoni (1989) argues that cases dismissed after investigation without further CPS involvement should be described using three categories:

■ No maltreatment or other evidence of family dysfunction found
■ No maltreatment found, but some evidence of family dysfunction or need for service found
■ Maltreatment found, but further CPS activity not indicated

The use of such categories would clarify what sorts of cases CPS is not pursuing and why. These data also would focus attention on an important group of cases—those in which service needs exist in the absence of maltreatment. Such cases should but rarely do receive social welfare services (e.g., Besharov, 1994).

A limited number of studies have attempted to understand the process of making substantiation decisions. The studies have relied on a range of methodologies, including case review, interviews with decision makers, and responses of CPS workers to case vignettes (Eckenrode, Powers, Doris, Munsch, & Bolger, 1988; Giovannoni, 1989).

Giovannoni reviewed 1,156 reports made to CPS. Several report variables significantly discriminated between cases that were and were not substantiated on investigation. A higher number of specific incidents of maltreatment alleged in the report was associated with substantiation. The availability of the address of the child and the alleged perpetrator increased the likelihood of a finding of maltreatment. Reports from absent spouses and reports of alleged drug or alcohol abuse by caretakers were less likely to be substantiated on investigation. Finally, reports from schools, law enforcement, and responsible caretakers were more likely to have had some maltreatment on investigation than reports from other sources.

Eckenrode and his colleagues (1988) reviewed a total of 1,974 cases in the New York State Registry, looking for factors that predicted substantiation. Multiple regression analyses revealed that the source of report, particularly whether the reporter was a professional or not, was a significant predictor of substantiation, with reports from professionals more likely to be substantiated. However, there were some important interactions between source of report and report type. For example, when sexual abuse was alleged by a caretaker mother, the likelihood of substantiation was the same as if the report had been made by a professional. Cases involving court action were more likely to be substantiated. The nature of the investigatory process also influenced substantiation probability, with the number of official contacts with the subjects of the report and the length of the investigation significantly contributing to substantiation probability. However, as Eckenrode et al. note, these process variables may reflect caseworker assessment of risk based on evidence available in the case, which complicates their meaning for the substantiation decision.

Substantiation Rates

As CPS resources shrink and numbers of reports continue to rise, the rate at which cases are substantiated has become an issue among those concerned with protecting children. Some argue that when large numbers of cases that are investigated are not substantiated, this represents a significant waste of limited CPS resources and poses a significant burden on the families that are investigated. Although there is consensus that some level of failure to substantiate is legitimate in a reporting system that accords mandated reporters no discretion and insists that reports be made on the basis of suspicions only, the amount that will or should be tolerated and the implications of higher rates are in considerable dispute.

Besharov (1986, 1988) has been among those most active in raising these concerns. Relying heavily on data reported by states (e.g., American Humane Association, 1988), he argues that there has been a steady increase in the percentage of "unfounded" reports since 1976 and finds these statistics troubling on several counts.

First, Besharov (1985) argues, investigations are "unavoidably traumatic" (p. 557). Second, conducting investigations of "minor" cases diverts inadequate resources from children in danger of serious maltreatment. These latter cases get more cursory investigation and less intensive supervision than they require because resources are being used to pursue "minor" cases. Third, would-be reporters may decide not to make reports to agencies that they know to be overtaxed.

Besharov argues that society's overambitious expectations about the ability of social agencies to identify and protect endangered children must be changed. He urges that state action should be limited to situations in which the parents have "already engaged in abusive or neglectful behavior" (p. 580) or done something that was capable of causing serious injury—in short, limited to situations in which seriously harmful behavior has occurred. These narrowed definitions should be accompanied by increased screening authority in CPS agencies.

Implementation of rigorous screening policies by experienced caseworkers would reduce the number of investigations initiated, raise the substantiation rate, and help more families receive services on a voluntary basis.

Implementation of rigorous screening policies by experienced caseworkers would reduce the number of investiga-

tions initiated, raise the substantiation rate, and help more families receive services on a voluntary basis.

The other side of this political coin is probably best represented by David Finkelhor (1990). He notes that the American Humane Association and state-level data that Besharov cites as evidence of declining substantiation rates are rife with methodological problems that make estimates difficult at best. Citing the methodologically far more rigorous NIS data, which indicate that substantiation rates significantly increased (from 43% in 1980 to 53% in 1986), Finkelhor suggests that substantiation rates may be largely unchanged over time or actually may be increasing. More important, he argues, the very different ways that substantiation rates are measured over jurisdictions and over time render these measures inappropriate bases for policy decisions. Revised definitions or screening policies can change reported substantiation rates in the absence of any other change.

Finkelhor makes a larger and more significant point about substantiation as well. He notes that the U.S. public repeatedly has demonstrated its willingness to tolerate some considerable inefficiency and intrusion in the pursuit of important policy goals. He points to the criminal justice system as an example of a system that demonstrates considerable inefficiency, with only about half of all arrests leading to convictions. Yet public opinion polls repeatedly indicate that Americans want more—not fewer—people arrested. And limited studies suggest that even those who are the subjects of maltreatment investigations understand the need for such activity. For example, Fryer, Bross, Krugman, Denson, and Baird (1990) conducted a consumer satisfaction survey of parents who had been investigated by CPS. The vast majority (more than 70%) rated the quality of services as excellent or good and felt that their family was better off as a result of CPS involvement.

Reasons for Failure to Substantiate

Politicization of substantiation statistics obscure a complex process that is not well-understood. There are many reasons why reports of child maltreatment are not substantiated; very little research has been conducted on this issue. Major studies that produce substantiation rates (e.g., American Humane Association,

1988; DHHS, 1988) provide no data concerning reasons for lack of substantiation. Clinical data and anecdotal information suggest a range of reasons why cases that are investigated are not substantiated.

Insufficient information. Many cases are not substantiated because there is insufficient information to make a determination about child maltreatment. In a substantial number of these cases, *no contact* is ever made with the family; most often this happens when families cannot be located. However, cases also may not be investigated because the allegations are too vague or no injury was reported (Finkelhor, 1990).

Cases also are denied after investigation because of insufficient information. Without clear-cut medical or other physical evidence, firsthand observations of home conditions or neglectful behavior, or a credible eyewitness, the CPS worker may not have enough information to conclude that the child has been maltreated, or it may not be possible to know whether the parent is responsible for the child's condition.

Data from one of the few studies that examined reasons for failing to substantiate (Jones & McGraw, 1987) revealed that 24% of the 576 sexual abuse cases examined were unfounded because of insufficient information.

Inappropriate referral. A case may be classified as unsubstantiated because the referral was not an appropriate one. A substantial number of these cases are in fact cases of child maltreatment.

The referral may be inappropriate for jurisdictional reasons. For example, the maltreatment occurred in one county, but the victim resides in another.

A case may be denied because the parties are not subject to the child protection act. Children may be too young or too old. Reports on unborn children or those over 16 may not be substantiated. Cases involving juvenile offenders or adults who are not the alleged victim's primary caretaker may be considered inappropriate referrals.

A case may be denied because services already are being received. These include cases subject to duplicate report (Finkelhor, 1990), new reports on already open cases, cases already receiving service from another agency, and cases already active in court (e.g., divorce court). In addition, some states only classify cases as substanti-

ated if protective action is taken in the juvenile court (Finkelhor, 1990).

The problem does not constitute child maltreatment. Two kinds of cases fall into this category: those in which the cause of the child's condition is not maltreatment and those in which the problem is a resource issue.

Designated professionals are mandated to report cases when they have "reasonable cause to suspect" child maltreatment. CPS investigation may determine that the suspicion was warranted but the child's problem was not caused by maltreatment. For example, an injury may be determined to have resulted from an accidental fall.

Pervasive cutbacks in social and welfare services in the past 10 years have resulted in both inappropriate referrals and inappropriate denials. In the first instance, there has been increased use of CPS reports to address problems that really do not constitute child maltreatment—for example, situations involving severely impaired children. Similarly, a family problem may be characterized as maltreatment in hopes of providing the family services only available through CPS.

In the second instance, scarce resources within CPS and increased referrals have led to a higher threshold for opening cases. CPS may decide that the standard of care in the family meets "minimum sufficient level," even though other community professionals and certainly the mandated reporter may not agree. Cases in which there is a risk of maltreatment, but no maltreatment has been found on investigation, may be denied.

Because of scarce resources, some CPS agencies tend to substantiate only when the maltreatment is severe enough to warrant removal of the child. A new trend to develop intensive, short-term, home-based services to prevent placement of children in foster care may reverse this pattern.

Child no longer at risk. Several types of cases are not substantiated because the child is deemed no longer at risk. These include cases in which maltreatment occurred too long ago (Finkelhor, 1990), family circumstances have changed, and the maltreatment is deemed minor and not likely to recur.

False allegations. Despite widespread concern about false allegations, little empirical data exist concerning them. Almost all of the available research on false allegations has been conducted on sexual abuse cases. These studies confront a range of difficult methodological problems, including defining and validating the falsity of reports and determining whether the reporter has made a knowingly false report.

False allegations appear to be rare (Faller, 1988; Goodwin, Sahd, & Rada, 1979; Horowitz, Salt, Gomes-Schwartz, & Sauzier, 1984; Jones & McGraw, 1987). Jones and McGraw (1987) concluded such reports represented only 6% of the sexual abuse cases that they examined. State data collected by NCCAN (1993) suggest that the number of intentionally false reports is very low. The percentage of intentionally filed false reports was less than 1% of all reports. However, with only four states reporting in this category, these data must be considered with caution.

False allegations are more likely to be made by adults than children. Jones and McGraw (1987) determined that only 1% of their reports represented false accounts by children. When children make intentionally false accusations, they are usually older children (Faller, 1988; Horowitz et al., 1984; Jones & McGraw, 1987).

False allegations appear to be more common surrounding divorce than in other contexts. However, even in divorce cases, between 50% and 75% of allegations of maltreatment appear to be valid (Faller, 1991; Faller, Corwin, & Olafson, 1993; Green, 1986; Thoennes & Tjaden, 1991). Those who report higher rates of false allegations either present no data (Blush & Ross, 1986; Gardner, 1989) or rely on small, biased samples (Benedek & Schetky, 1985; Green, 1986; Kaplan & Kaplan, 1981). Moreover, most of these authors do not differentiate between cases involving calculated lies and those in which parents' mental functioning led to a false accusation.

Even in divorce situations, calculated false allegations appear to be very rare. Thoennes and Tjaden (1991), in a sample of 9,000 divorces from 12 states with disputed custody or visitation, found that 169 (less than 2%) involved child sexual abuse allegations, and only 8 were judged to be knowing lies. Faller (1991), using a clinical sample of 136 sexual abuse allega-

tions in divorce, found only 3 cases that were judged to be calculated lies.

Proposals to Improve the Substantiation Process

A number of suggestions have been put forth for improving the substantiation process. Many argue that, along with informing professionals about their responsibility to report suspected maltreatment, training sessions also should include information about what levels of maltreatment constitute abuse that is likely to be acted on by CPS (e.g., Besharov, 1988; Winefield & Bradley, 1992). To do this, decision rules provided to professional reporters should be congruent with those used by child protective staffs. This way, training would not necessarily increase the number of reports but would likely increase the percentage of pursuable ones. Zellman (1990) argues that feedback from CPS to reporters on individual cases would serve a similar purpose. Such feedback also might increase professionals' sense that their reports would benefit the child or family, a key factor in reporting intentions (Zellman & Bell, 1990).

Kalichman and Brosig (1992) and Giovannoni (1989) warn that such efforts could be misdirected. Although clearer decision rules would likely increase substantiation rates, this might well occur at the cost of missing cases of maltreatment. Asking would-be reporters to use categories such as "serious" may inappropriately transfer some of the investigative function from CPS to them (Giovannoni, 1989).

Finkelhor and Zellman (1991) suggest that some level of professional discretion be built formally into the reporting system. They argue for the creation of a category of registered reporters, who by dint of their previous reporting history and child maltreatment expertise are accorded carefully bounded discretion in their reporting behavior. As Thompson-Cooper, Fugere, and Cormier (1993) note, Finkelhor and Zellman's proposal contains some of the essential elements of the "confidential doctor" system operating in the Netherlands since 1971. Under this system, there is no reporting mandate, and in most cases no child protection measures are imposed. Instead, once a notification is made, a trusted professional meets with those involved with the family to determine whether abuse has in fact taken place. According to Thompson-Cooper et al., the new system has resulted in more notifications, including a sharp rise in the number of parents and children applying for help. At the same time, the number of removals of children from their homes has dropped.

Hutchison (1993) and Besharov (1985, 1990) suggest that substantiation rates would increase and children would be better served if the grounds for CPS intervention were narrowed. But simply excluding cases would fail—and does fail—the many children living in troubled families. Children could be helped if the grounds for CPS intervention were narrowed and the net provided by social welfare services was widened. In this way, maltreatment need not be substantiated in order for a family to receive preventive and other family-focused services (Besharov, 1994; Giovannoni, 1989). Besharov argues that significant barriers exist to such an approach, including inertia, a lack of political will to advocate for expensive ongoing services that might prevent more harm, and lack of funds. Bergmann (1994) notes the contentions of those who claim that we "can't afford" such services because family support often obscures insufficient desire or will:

> The $150-500 billion savings and loan crisis has illuminated the lack of seriousness of the "can't afford" argument against child welfare programs. The public money to make the S&L depositors whole was forthcoming with no debate at all. . . . Until we change our notions of how desirable adequate child welfare programs are, the public purse, which opens so easily and lavishly for other purposes, will not be available for them. (p. 18)

Conclusion

Contemporary concerns about child maltreatment were expressed in the development of model reporting laws in the 1960s, which were adopted rapidly by every state. These laws succeeded in increasing both public awareness of child maltreatment and the number of maltreatment reports.

The success of the reporting laws has created substantial and unanticipated problems for the protective agencies that receive those reports. Most simply have lacked the capacity to respond adequately to a large share of the reports that have flooded in. This reality has resulted in calls to narrow the basis for reporting, increase the amount of screening in CPS agencies, and increase the availability of both protective and other child welfare services.

Although concerns about too many reports recently have dominated discussions of reporting, prevalence studies of victims and offenders indicate that official reports do not reflect the full extent of child maltreatment. In addition, there continues to be a sure sense supported by empirical data that not all professionals are meeting the reporting mandate and not all of even the most serious cases of child maltreatment are reported. The inability of protective agencies to respond to many reports has been implicated as a significant factor in professional decisions to withhold reports.

Few efforts have been made to do more than lament inadequacies in the current system. Proposals to limit reporting (e.g., Besharov, 1985; Hutchison, 1993; Thompson-Cooper et al., 1993) or to increase professional discretion in reporting (e.g., Crenshaw, Bartell, & Lichtenberg, 1994; Finkelhor & Zellman, 1991) are of concern to those who have worked hard to create a system in which individual, idiosyncratic decisions would be replaced by professional, universalistic ones. Proposals to increase the funding and reach of protective agencies have concerned those who worry about unwarranted intrusion into families and have disheartened those who realize that such expansion is very difficult in a time of fiscal retrenchment. A broader perspective on the delivery of all types of services to needy families that transfers many services from protective agencies back to social welfare agencies might help both families and the systems that attempt to serve them, as Besharov (1994) suggests. But the lack of political will to sell long-term programs with limited outcomes and, to a smaller extent, lack of funds (Bergmann, 1994) reduce the chances of substantial change any time soon.

From a longer historical perspective, however, there is reason for encouragement and self-congratulation. Although some reports do not receive the attention they deserve, and many maltreated children remain unidentified to protective agencies, the reporting laws have brought attention and services to many others. Research aimed at identifying rates of child maltreatment in national and community samples and in special populations has raised public and professional awareness about the pervasiveness of this problem. These studies and requirements for reporting and intervention also have established child maltreatment as an important policy concern that is not likely to be eclipsed in the near future.

Notes

1. The Child Abuse, Domestic Violence, Adoption, and Family Services Act of 1992 (P.L. 102-295) retained the provisions of the 1988 Act and also required NCCAN to develop a program that analyzes available state child abuse and neglect reporting information that is, to the extent possible, universal and case specific.

2. The numbers prior to 1976 are even lower but are available for only a limited number of states. American Humane statistics are obtained from state-level CPS programs that voluntarily provide data on officially reported child abuse and neglect. Differences across states in policy, definitions, and information collection procedures limit the comparability of data across states. Moreover, data on specific case measures are not available from many states. The recently reauthorized Child Abuse Prevention and Treatment Act, now called the Child Abuse, Domestic Violence, Adoption, and Family Services Act of 1992 (P.L. 102-295), mandated collection of state child abuse reports by NCCAN. This mandate, including its technical assistance provision, already has improved the quality of data about reported cases.

3. The original report of study findings contained inaccurate data due to weighting problems. The data below are drawn from the revised report (Sedlak, 1991).

4. We use the broader definition here, because that definition is closer to current usage than the earlier, narrower one. Although numbers obviously vary as a function of definition, with the new definition producing higher counts, the findings and conclusions change little as a result.

5. The particularly low rate for schools—one fourth—may reflect substantially higher rates of CPS nonacceptance of reports from school staff (see Zellman, 1990; Zellman & Antler, 1990, for more discussion of this point).

6. We were unable to measure reporting behavior in the vignettes but used reporting intentions as a reasonable proxy. Such intentions have been found to be significant predictors of actual behavior in a number of studies across a broad range of behaviors (e.g., Ajzen & Fishbein, 1980; Sheppard, Hartwick, & Warshaw, 1988).

7. For a thorough review of the studies of prevalence of sexual abuse and methodological issues, see Peters et al. (1986).

References

Ajzen, I., & Fishbein, M. (1980). *Understanding attitudes and predicting social behavior.* Englewood Cliffs, NJ: Prentice Hall.

American Humane Association. (1988). *Highlights of official child neglect and abuse reporting, 1986.* Denver, CO: Author.

Ards, S., & Harrell, A. (1993). Reporting of child maltreatment: A secondary analysis of the national incidence surveys. *Child Abuse & Neglect, 17*(3), 337-344.

Barone, N., Adams, W., & Tooman, P. (1981). The screening unit: An experimental approach to child protective services. *Child Welfare, 60*(3), 198-204.

Benedek, E., & Schetky, D. (1985). Allegations of sexual abuse in child custody and visitation disputes. In E. Benedek & D. Schetky (Eds.), *Emerging issues in child psychiatry and the law.* New York: Brunner/Mazel.

Bergmann, B. (1994, May). *Child care: The key to ending child poverty.* Paper presented at the Conference on Social Policies for Children, Princeton University, Woodrow Wilson School of Public and International Affairs, New Jersey.

Besharov, D. (1985). Doing something about child abuse: The need to narrow the grounds for state intervention. *Harvard Journal of Law & Public Policy, 8*(3), 539-589.

Besharov, D. (1986). Unfounded allegations—A new child abuse problem. *The Public Interest, 83,* 18-33.

Besharov, D. (1988). Child abuse and neglect reporting and investigation: Policy guidelines for decision making. *Family Law Quarterly, 22,* 1-15.

Besharov, D. (1990). Gaining control over child abuse reports. *Public Welfare, 48*(2), 34-40.

Besharov, D. (1994, May). *Don't call it child abuse if it's really poverty.* Paper presented at the Conference on Social Policies for Children, Princeton University, Woodrow Wilson School of Public and International Affairs, New Jersey.

Blush, G., & Ross, K. (1986). *SAID syndrome: Sexual allegations in divorce.* Unpublished manuscript.

Briere, J., & Runtz, M. (1989). University males' sexual interest in children: Predicting potential indices of "pedophilia" in a non-forensic sample. *Child Abuse & Neglect, 13,* 65-75.

Caffey, J. (1957). Some traumatic lesions in growing bones other than fractures and dislocations: Clinical and radiological features, the Mackenzie Davidson Memorial Lecture. *British Journal of Radiology, 30,* 225-238.

Child Abuse Prevention and Treatment Act (Public Law 93-247). (1974). *Congressional Record, 119.*

Crenshaw, W., Bartell, P., & Lichtenberg, J. (1994). Proposed revisions to mandatory reporting laws: An exploratory survey of child protective service agencies. *Child Welfare, 73*(1), 15-27.

Daniel, J., Newberger, E., Reed, R., & Kotelchuck, M. (1978). Child-abuse screening: Implications of the limited predictive power of abuse discriminants from a controlled family study of pediatric social illness. *Child Abuse & Neglect, 2*(4), 247-259.

Daro, D., & McCurdy, K. (1994). *Current trends in child abuse reporting and fatalities: The results of the 1993 annual fifty-state survey.* Chicago: National Committee for the Prevention of Child Abuse.

Davidson, H. (1988). Failure to report child abuse: Legal penalties and emerging issues. In A. Maney & S. Wells (Eds.), *Professional responsibility in protecting children.* New York: Praeger.

Downing, J., Wells, S., & Fluke, J. (1990). Gatekeeping in child protective services: A survey of screening policies. *Child Welfare, 69*(4), 357-369.

Eckenrode, J., Powers, J., Doris, J., Munsch, J., & Bolger, N. (1988). Substantiation of child abuse and neglect reports. *Journal of Consulting and Clinical Psychology, 56,* 9-16.

Faller, K. C. (1988). *Child sexual abuse: An interdisciplinary manual for diagnosis, case management, and treatment.* New York: Columbia University Press.

Faller, K. C. (1991). Possible explanations for sexual abuse allegations in divorce. *American Journal of Orthopsychiatry, 61*(1), 86-91.

Faller, K. C., Corwin, D., & Olafson, E. (1993). Research on false allegations of sexual abuse in divorce. *APSAC Advisor, 6*(3), 1-10.

Finkelhor, D. (1986). *A sourcebook on child sexual abuse.* Newbury Park, CA: Sage.

Finkelhor, D. (1990, Winter). Is child abuse overreported? *Public Welfare,* pp. 22-29.

Finkelhor, D., Gomes-Schwartz, B., & Horowitz, J. (1984). Professionals' responses. In D. Finkelhor (Ed.), *Child sexual abuse: New theory and research* (pp. 200-220). New York: Free Press.

Finkelhor, D., & Zellman, G. (1991). Flexible reporting options for skilled child abuse professionals. *Child Abuse & Neglect, 15,* 335-341.

Fraser, B. (1986). A glance at the past, a gaze at the present, a glimpse at the future: A critical analysis of the development of child abuse reporting statutes. *Journal of Juvenile Law, 10,* 641-686.

Fryer, G., Bross, D., Krugman, R., Denson, D., & Baird, D. (1990, Winter). Good news for EPS workers. *Public Welfare,* pp. 39-41.

Gardner, R. (1989). Differentiating between bona fide and fabricated allegations of sexual abuse of children. *Journal of the American Academy of Matrimonial Lawyers, 5,* 1-26.

Gelles, R., & Straus, M. (1988). *Intimate violence: The causes and consequences of abuse in the American family.* New York: Simon & Schuster.

Giovannoni, J. (1989). Substantiated and unsubstantiated reports of child maltreatment. *Children and Youth Services Review, 11*(4), 299-318.

Goodwin, J., Sahd, D., & Rada, R. (1979). Incest hoax. In W. Holder (Ed.), *Sexual abuse of children* (pp. 37-46). Denver, CO: American Humane Association.

Gordon, L. (1988). *Heroes of their own lives: The politics and history of family violence.* Boston: Viking.

Graziano, A., & Namaste, K. (1990). Parental use of physical force in child discipline. *Journal of Interpersonal Violence, 5*(4), 449-453.

Green, A. (1986). True and false allegations of sexual abuse in child custody disputes. *Journal of the American Academy of Child Psychiatry, 25*(4), 449-456.

Henschel, D., Briere, J., & Morlau-Magallanes, D. (1990, August). *Multivariate long-term correlates of childhood physical, sexual, and psychological abuse.* Paper presented at the annual meeting of the American Psychological Association, Boston.

Horowitz, J., Salt, P., Gomes-Schwartz, B., & Sauzier, M. (1984). Unconfirmed cases of sexual abuse. In Tufts New England Medical Center (Ed.), *Sexually exploited children* (Service and research project, final report). Washington, DC: Office of Juvenile Justice and Delinquency Prevention.

Hutchison, E. (1993). Mandatory reporting laws: Child protective case finding gone awry? *Social Work, 38*(1), 56-63.

James, J., Womack, W., & Stauss, F. (1978). Physician reporting of sexual abuse of children. *Journal of the American Medical Association, 181,* 17-24.

Jones, D., & McGraw, E. (1987). Reliable and fictitious accounts of sexual abuse to children. *Journal of Interpersonal Violence, 2*(1), 27-45.

Kalichman, S., & Brosig, C. (1992). Mandatory child abuse reporting laws: Issues and implications for policy. *Law and Policy, 14*(2-3), 153-168.

Kalichman, S., & Brosig, C. (1993). Practicing psychologists' interpretations of and compliance with child abuse reporting laws. *Law and Human Behavior, 17,* 83-93.

Kalichman, S., Craig, M., & Follingstad, D. (1990). Mental health professionals and suspected cases of child abuse: An investigation of factors influencing reporting. *Community Mental Health Journal, 24,* 43-51.

Kamerman, S., & Kahn, A. (1990). If CPS is driving child welfare, where do we go from here? *Public Welfare, 48*(1), 9-13.

Kaplan, S. L., & Kaplan, S. J. (1981). The child's accusation of sexual abuse during a divorce and custody struggle. *Hillside Journal of Clinical Psychiatry, 3,* 81-95.

Kempe, C., Silverman, F., Steele, B., Droegemueller, W., & Silver, H. (1962). The battered child syndrome. *Journal of the American Medical Association, 181,* 17-24.

Kercher, G., & McShane, M. (1984). *The prevalence of child sexual abuse victimization in an adult sample of Texas residents.* Huntsville, TX: Sam Houston State University.

Landis, J. (1956). Experiences of 500 children with adult sexual deviants. *Psychiatric Quarterly Supplement, 30,* 91-109.

Maney, A., & Wells, S. (1988). *Professional responsibilities in protecting children.* New York: Praeger.

Morris, J., Johnson, C., & Clasen, M. (1985). To report or not to report: Physicians' attitudes toward discipline and child abuse. *American Journal of Diseases of Children, 139,* 195-197.

Murphy, J. (1987, July). *Reports of sexual abuse in a community sample.* Paper presented at the National Family Violence Research Conference, Durham, NH.

National Center on Child Abuse and Neglect (NCCAN). (1993). *National child abuse and neglect data systems* (Working Paper No. 2, 1991 summary data component). Washington, DC: Government Printing Office.

Nelson, B. (1984). *Making an issue of child abuse.* Chicago: University of Chicago Press.

Newberger, E. (1983). The helping hand strikes again: Unintended consequences of child abuse reporting. *Journal of Clinical Child Psychology, 2,* 307-311.

Nuttall, R., & Jackson, H. (1994). Personal history of childhood abuse among clinicians. *Child Abuse & Neglect, 18,* 455-472.

Paulsen, M., Parker, G., & Adelman, L. (1966). Child abuse reporting laws: Some legislative history. *George Washington Law Review, 34,* 482-506.

Peters, S. D., Wyatt, G. E., & Finkelhor, D. (1986). Prevalence. In D. Finkelhor (Ed.), *A sourcebook on child sexual abuse* (pp. 15-59). Newbury Park, CA: Sage.

Pleck, E. (1987). *Domestic tyranny: The making of social policy against family violence from colonial times to the present.* New York: Oxford University Press.

Risin, L., & Koss, M. (1987). The sexual abuse of boys. *Journal of Interpersonal Violence, 2*(3), 309-323.

Rosen, H. (1981). How workers use cues to determine child abuse. *Social Work Research and Abstracts, 17*(4), 27-33.

Russell, D. E. H. (1983). The incidence and prevalence of intrafamilial and extrafamilial sexual abuse of female children. *Child Abuse & Neglect, 7*(2), 133-146.

Russell, D. E. H. (1986). *The secret trauma: Incest in the lives of girls and women.* New York: Basic Books.

Saulsbury, F., & Campbell, R. (1985). Evaluation of child abuse reporting by physicians. *American Journal of Diseases, 139,* 393-395.

Saunders, B., Kilpatrick, D., Lipovsky, J., Resnick, H., Best, C., & Sturgis, E. (1991, March). *Prevalence, case characteristics, and long-term psychological effects of sexual assault: A national survey.* Paper presented at the annual meeting of the American Orthopsychiatric Association, Toronto.

Saunders, B., Villeponteaux, L., Lipovsky, J., Kilpatrick, D., & Veronen, L. (1993). Child sexual abuse as a risk factor for mental disorders among women: A community survey. *Journal of Interpersonal Violence, 7*(2), 189-204.

Sedlak, A. (1991). *National incidence and prevalence of child abuse and neglect: 1988 revised report.* Rockville, MD: Westat.

Sheppard, B., Hartwick, J., & Warshaw, P. (1988). The theory of reasoned action: A meta-analysis of past research with recommendations of modifications and future research. *Journal of Consumer Research, 15,* 325-343.

Straus, M., Gelles, R., & Steinmetz, S. (1978). *Behind closed doors.* New York: Free Press.

Summit, R. (1983). The child abuse accommodation syndrome. *Child Abuse & Neglect, 7,* 177-193.

Thoennes, N., & Tjaden, P. (1991). The extent, nature, and validity of sexual abuse allegations in custody/visitation disputes. *Child Abuse & Neglect, 14,* 151-163.

Thompson-Cooper, I., Fugere, R., & Cormier, B. (1993). The child abuse reporting laws: An ethical dilemma for professionals. *Canadian Journal of Psychiatry, 38,* 557-562.

U.S. Department of Health and Human Services. (1981). *National study of the incidence and severity of child abuse and neglect.* Washington, DC: Author.

U.S. Department of Health and Human Services. (1988). *Study findings: Study of national incidence and prevalence of child abuse and neglect.* Washington, DC: Author.

Wells, S. (1987). *Screening practices in child protective services.* Washington, DC: National Legal Resource Center for Child Advocacy and Protection.

Wells, S., Stein, T., Fluke, J., & Downing, J. (1989). Screening in child protective services. *Social Work, 34*(1), 45-48.

Wiemers, K., & Petretic-Jackson, P. (1991, August). *Defining physical child abuse: Ratings of parental behaviors.* Paper presented at the annual meeting of the American Psychological Association, San Francisco.

Williams, G. (1983). Child protection: A journey into history. *Clinical Child Psychology, 12,* 236-243.

Winefield, H., & Bradley, P. (1992). Substantiation of reported child abuse or neglect: Predictors and implications. *Child Abuse & Neglect, 16,* 661-671.

Wyatt, G. (1985). The sexual abuse of Afro-American and white women in childhood. *Child Abuse & Neglect, 9,* 507-519.

Zellman, G. (1990). Linking schools and social services: The case of child abuse reporting. *Educational Evaluation and Policy Analysis, 12,* 41-56.

Zellman, G. (1992). The impact of case characteristics on child abuse reporting decisions. *Child Abuse & Neglect, 16,* 57-74.

Zellman, G., & Antler, S. (1990). Mandated reporters and child protective agencies: A study in frustration. *Public Welfare, 48*(1), 30-37.

Zellman, G., & Bell, R. (1990). *The role of professional background, case characteristics, and protective agency response in mandated child abuse reporting.* Santa Monica, CA: RAND.

Organization and Delivery of Services

The chapters in this final Part Six focus on practical public policy in response to child abuse and neglect. In Chapter 20, Patricia Schene reviews the history of child welfare activity in the United States, beginning with the earliest efforts of private, nonprofit organizations founded to "rescue" abused, neglected, and abandoned children. Schene continues by tracing the evolution of child welfare as a public concern through the federal legislation of the 1990s, noting the ongoing tension between those who have seen the work as primarily rescuing children from unfit parents and those who have seen it as giving troubled families the support they need to function well. Schene uses this framework to discuss current public policy. Acknowledging that some families cannot be rehabilitated, Schene argues that "child protection" and "family preservation" are generally compatible goals. She identifies as one of our biggest problems the transformation of CPS to primarily an investigative agency. Families seen by CPS have increasingly serious and complex problems and need access to comprehensive services. Schene sees a "paradigm shift" occurring, spurred partly by the 1993 Family Preservation and Support Services Act, in which communities are contemplating ways to reconfigure their resources to provide more comprehensive services to children and families. These holistic, community-based services will be offered before abuse is substantiated and will involve schools, courts, mental health, law enforcement, job training, substance abuse treatment, and so on.

In his chapter on the organization of services (Chapter 21), David L. Chadwick looks more closely at how such a comprehensive program might be implemented. Chadwick maintains that each unique community needs its own plan, and the process of protocol development is the first step in the process of interagency collaboration. This process forces managers to meet, clarify process and content issues, and begin building the habit of working together. Although each plan will be unique, Chadwick articulates several basic principles, including the need for continuing professional education, interdisciplinary cooperation, equitable service delivery, public-private cooperation, avoidance of duplication, and sharing of critical information about clients. Chadwick covers many other practical considerations, including the steps in the assessment of abuse reports, elements of fatal case assessment, characteristics of an adequate assessment site, and the involvement of sources for ongoing therapeutic and supportive services.

Both Schene and Chadwick stress the need for service delivery systems to be culturally competent. Certainly, if services are to be effective, they must be planned and delivered in a manner to which clients are receptive. With children and families of color overrepresented in the child welfare system and people of color underrepresented in the ranks of social service professionals, the awareness of cultural differences that can compromise service effectiveness becomes critical. In Chapter 22, Veronica D. Abney provides a conceptual framework for the development of culturally competent interventions. According to Abney, the search for an ethnic or racial "match" between service provider and recipient is less important than the service provider's ability to empathize with clients by inhabiting different worldviews. Abney maintains that culturally competent practice depends on practitioners' and policymakers' examination of their values, knowledge, and methods. Abney discusses multiple aspects of each of these critical areas, providing readers with a place to start their own self-assessment.

—T.R.

20

Child Abuse and Neglect Policy

History, Models, and Future Directions

PATRICIA SCHENE

The public system of intervention in cases of child abuse and neglect generally is known as child protective services (CPS) and resides in public departments of social services in almost all counties in the United States. This system of intervention did not originate with the state mandatory reporting laws of the 1960s but was made more commonly recognizable and universally dispersed through those laws as well as through the federal Child Abuse Prevention and Treatment Act (CAPTA) passed in 1974.

The CPS system has, in many ways, been surprisingly successful in a relatively short period of time. Every state has reporting laws mandating professionals who work with children to report their suspicions of child neglect and abuse to universally available CPS units that receive these reports and, if deemed necessary, "investigate" or "assess" the child's situation. This normally results in an "official report" that makes its way into a state- (or sometimes county-) run information system and also results in a decision on whether to "substantiate" the report and/or "open" the case for ongoing services or to close the case after investigation. As a result of the collection and automation of the reporting data, we have had more information over a longer period of time on CPS reports and cases than on any other part of our public social service system activity.

CPS is currently the subject of extensive examination and controversy. Some argue that no governmental agency should have the right to investigate parents, and others believe CPS is not doing enough to protect children from abuse and neglect. Definitional quandaries remain about what constitutes child abuse or child neglect and whether there ever can be agreement on definitions across communities. Many are concerned that our interventions are disrespectful of communities of color and lack the necessary cultural competence to understand and use the strengths of diverse communities. There is controversy surrounding the overall focus of our intervention—are the dual goals of child protection and family preservation compatible? Some believe that CPS should have primarily a quasi-law enforcement function—protecting "victims" and punishing "perpetrators." Others argue that child maltreatment emerges from the larger context of family problems; these individuals advocate supporting parents through services rather than punishing them and placing their children in foster care. Almost everyone recognizes that we have not placed sufficient resources in CPS in terms of well-trained staff, manageable workloads, treatment and services, and resources for adequate supervision and effective accountability. In 1990, the U.S. Advisory Board on Child Abuse and Neglect referred to child abuse as a "national emergency," requiring the "replacement of the existing child protection system" (1990, pp. vii-viii).

The CPS system is in transition and does not have the broad support necessary from the public, or even from many prominent child advocates, to respond effectively to the needs of neglected and abused children and their families. This chapter will examine the *history* and *development* of our public response to child abuse and neglect, outlining some of the continuity of policy concerns over time. We will then outline some generic models of CPS and lay out the current issues and challenges facing our protective services system. We will then explore where we are and where we need to be in child protective services and policy. We will conclude with a summary of what we need to consider and resolve in maintaining our public commitment to protect children from abuse and neglect.

Child Welfare:
The Historical Context

It may be difficult to imagine from a late 20th-century perspective, but the development of public concern and policy for dependent, abused, and neglected children began largely at the initiative of private, nonprofit agencies. One of the

remarkable aspects of this development of child welfare policy in the United States was the overlapping responsibilities of private and public agencies and the opportunity this presented for accountability as well as program development.

David Gil (in Laird & Hartman, 1985, p. 12) points out that the existence of "child welfare," as a field of service and practice, is an indicator of the absence of child welfare as a condition. There is a built-in "deficit" orientation to child welfare services. Child welfare services generally are understood to be a substitute for, and a supplement to, the functions of a natural family environment that has somehow become unable to carry out its responsibilities for the care of children. "A substitutive philosophy of child welfare implies that it is a substitute for failed family function" (Rice, 1985, p. 73).

Current progressive public policy purports to see child welfare services as a **support to** *the task of raising children, primarily in families.*

Current progressive public policy purports to see child welfare services as a *support to* the task of raising children, primarily in families. Yet our public service programs and funding levels currently do not accommodate a more general family support role. There is broad agreement that removing children and allowing them to grow up in substitute families not only is a prescription for instability but also may be unnecessarily alienating more children from the possibilities and potentials of their original family and social environment. Unfortunately, the roots of this family support orientation are not as deep as those of the "child rescue" orientation.

The complexity and significance of these issues can be seen as both a legacy and a consequence of the way child welfare policy has evolved. In addition, the large role played early in that evolution by private, nonprofit agencies may offer some path toward meeting the current challenge to forge the public-private partnerships essential to an effective system of child protection creatively.

Early Approaches to Child Welfare Services

> In colonial times when labor was in short supply and work sanctified, dependent children were indentured. It was understood that such children would earn their keep while learning a skill or trade. Later, when almshouses were developed, children, considered "little adults," were placed in congregate institutions with adults suffering a variety of physical and social ills. . . . And when Horace Greeley said, "Go west, young man," the agrarian myth was in full sway; children were rescued from the urban streets and sent to farm homes in the Midwest. Thus arrangements made for the welfare of children may serve as a metaphor for society's changing values. (Laird & Hartman, 1985, p. xxi)

In colonial days, poverty was considered a sin and work the way to salvation. Children of the "unworthy poor" had to be saved from developing slothful ways, often by separating them from their parents through indenture or placement in institutions and foster homes (Costin, 1985, p. 35).

The legal base for early "child-saving" was twofold: the power of the township overseer of the poor and the doctrine of *parens patrie* on which American guardianship law rests. Public responsibility for the poor was placed in local towns following the Elizabethan Poor Law of 1601. *Parens patrie*—the ruler's power to protect minors—came to be interpreted broadly in America as justification for governmental intervention into the parent-child relationship in an attempt to enforce parental duty or supply substitute care.

The English poor laws were the foundation for some of the earliest child welfare efforts in the colonies. These made the local parish or community responsible for supporting all individuals born within its precincts. Unwanted or abandoned children were the responsibility of the whole community.

From the mid-19th century, many private agencies—notably the Children's Aid Society—brought poor, vagrant children to good homes, often in other parts of the country. These agencies moved children from the industrial northeastern cities to the rural Midwest, where there was a demand for their labor. This was the forerunner of a general system of *foster care*—when children grow up in homes other than their birth homes.

There was no clear pattern of progression from institutionalizing needy children to serving them in their own homes. The philosophy behind both trends had common purposes. The belief was that the next generation deserved a clean slate, an opportunity to be housed, fed, educated, and exposed to "middle-class values" to compete in the world. If not an equal opportunity, then at least some kind of opportunity needed to be provided to the children of the desperately poor. The development of institutions for children had a broad base of popular support based on a position of equity—all children deserve a chance. It is hard to see many signs of compassion for the parents that would lead to broad programs of economic support, but there was a willingness to remove children when homes were not economically viable.

Another social response to the problems of poverty in the late 18th and 19th centuries was the almshouse—a facility to house the very poor. Homer Folks (1902) described almshouses as "half-retributive and wholly uncharitable" (p. 1). Almshouses were confined mostly to large cities and cared for *both children and adults*. In 1800, the Common Council in New York City formed a new set of rules related to children:

> The children of the house should be under the government of capable matrons. . . . They should be uniformed, housed and lodged in separate departments by sex; they should be kept as much as possible from the other paupers, habituated to decency, cleanliness and order, and carefully instructed in reading, writing and arithmetic. . . . When the children arrive at proper ages great care should be taken to furnish them with suitable places (indentured) that they may be instructed in some useful trade or occupation. (quoted in Folks, 1902, p. 5)

The community's responsibility for abandoned or unwanted babies led to the establishment of foundling hospitals in the early 19th century. The rise of the market society led to pregnant poor women being abandoned by their husbands in the search for opportunities to sell their labor; pregnancy was a very limiting factor in mobility, and often the wages were inadequate to support a family. Urbanization, industrialization, and immigration made child vagrancy highly visible. In the late 19th century in New York City, thousands of poor children wandered the streets without the care of their families. Private, charitable organizations emerged to assist these children in their own homes or, if homeless, in institutions until they could be indentured. Institutionalization of children became popular in the 19th century. The motivation of 19th-century policymakers has had public policy consequences that are definitely with us today. We seem to be more ready today to "protect" children from abuse and neglect than we are to support families. In addition, the children we "protect" are largely from the ranks of the very poor.

Child Abuse and Neglect: A Specialty Within Child Welfare

Child abuse and neglect were both a reason for intervention into family life and a rationale for separate child welfare services. Despite accelerated public interest in cruelty to children in the 19th century, there were no clear lines of responsibility among voluntary agencies or public officials for identifying abused or neglected children. There was a need for a separate agency to play the role of enforcing existing legislation. Private agencies focusing solely on the abuse and neglect of children developed in the late 19th century. Known broadly as the "anti-cruelty" societies, they engendered a large degree of public support with the proliferation of numerous local societies for the prevention of cruelty to children in almost every major city by the early 20th century. They became a part of the American Humane Association, a national agency focusing on both child and animal protection.

The primary tasks of these "societies for the prevention of cruelty to children" were investigating reports of neglect and cruelty, filing complaints against the perpetrators, and aiding the courts in their prosecution (Costin, 1985, pp. 44-45).

The origins of the "anti-cruelty movement" are still present in current public policy issues. Both law and social agency practice still reflect an ambivalence in relation to child rights versus parents rights. Traces of threat and punishment as a deterrent to cruelty to children can still be identified in

the work of child protective services. The [New York Society for the Prevention of Cruelty to Children's] adamant stand [in favor of] the exclusiveness of child protection versus collaboration with the broader functions of child welfare agencies left a troublesome legacy of resistance to the development of home-based services. (Costin, 1985, p. 46)

Prior to 1800, children rarely became the subjects of public care except in cases of severe parental poverty or their own wrongdoing. The responsibility of the public to intervene in cases of cruelty began to be recognized after 1825 but was rarely enforced. In 1882, Massachusetts laws allowed abused and neglected children to be taken into the "custody" of the State Board of Charities. In 1877, New York, at the urging of the Society for the Prevention of Cruelty to Children (SPCC), passed a law protecting children and preventing and punishing certain wrongs done to children (Folks, 1902, pp. 167-172).

Many viewed this "anti-cruelty movement" as largely a "middle-class movement directed against lower-class immigrant parents" (Costin, 1985, p. 43), but its impact was much broader. The New York SPCC "discovered" cases of child abuse and neglect by stationing agents in magistrate courts to investigate all cases involving children. They advised magistrates on the commitment of children; they were given police powers and could take custody of children pending the investigation. The funding for this effort was from both private and public sources.

In the 19th century, only one state, Indiana, created a governmental body to perform the duties elsewhere performed by SPCCs. In 1899, a law was passed authorizing the appointment of a "board of children's guardians" in townships and counties (six persons appointed by the circuit court) to investigate alleged abuse and neglect, bring perpetrators to trial, oversee the children, and place them in temporary homes (Folks, 1902, p. 177).

The early leaders in the child protection field came almost exclusively from private, secular agencies rather than religious or governmental groups. These organizations took an active role in protecting individual children and in advocating for better legislation and public sector commitments to safeguard children's interests.

The private child protective movement's initial adoption of a punitive, law enforcement emphasis gradually was replaced in some regions by a broader focus on family casework and the need to maintain and enrich family life through broad social supports. Child protection, initially isolated from the general child welfare movement, gradually became part of it. There were some significant holdouts, however; the New York Society for the Prevention of Cruelty to Children (NYSPCC) maintained it was not a "charity." "Child rescue is not child reformation. It is not technically charitable work" (Schultz, 1924, p. 202).

The Massachusetts Society for the Prevention of Cruelty to Children (MSPCC) was formed in 1878 and initially also operated "primarily as an arm of the law" (Antler & Antler, 1979, p. 184). Yet it did not deny its charitable functions but acknowledged that it was both a "prosecution and relief society." The MSPCC differed from the NYSPCC in that it stressed education and reformation of offenders, family rehabilitation, and the avoidance of institutionalization of children, and it also pursued close working relations with other child welfare agencies, state and local authorities, school officials, and the police (Antler & Antler, 1979, p. 184).

Under new leadership in the MSPCC (C. C. Carstens became executive director in 1907), "child rescue" was linked inseparably with the dual objectives of family rehabilitation and community reform. Carstens placed child protective work firmly in the camp of progressive social action (Antler & Antler, 1979, p. 187). By 1912, Carstens was clear that child protective societies had to organize not only against individual cases of abuse and neglect but prevent what he called "community neglect. . . . It therefore seems to be the duty of this Society, which would prevent cruelty and neglect, also to direct its attention to the improvement of better social conditions affecting child welfare" (MSPCC, 1911, quoted in Antler & Antler, 1979, p. 188).

The MSPCC was instrumental in the adoption of a state "mother's pension" law, as well as laws protecting illegitimate, abandoned, and neglected children (Antler & Antler, 1979, p. 188). The Children's Welfare League was organized in Roxbury in 1912 after the MSPCC had determined that Roxbury was the Boston district that had the greatest amount of dependency and delinquency. Financed by the MSPCC, and with 35 different agencies cooperating, the following was accomplished: A list of approved, affordable tenant housing and a placement bureau for youths were created; study houses were established at local libraries; land was donated for a playground; and a board of censorship to supervise movies was established. The MSPCC assumed that solutions to problems of cruelty and neglect required "community and family reconstruction" as well as judicial action.

Fabricating a synthesis of legal process and social work practice that served as a model for his contemporaries, Carstens developed a series of programs which enabled MSPCC to emphasize modern case work and community organization approaches to problems that had previously been solely within the domain of law enforcement. The dilemma Carstens never confronted, however, was how reformers could devise methods of family protection without imposing judgments based on their own narrow perceptions of acceptable family values and behaviors. (Antler & Antler, 1979, pp. 194-195)

In 1920, the Child Welfare League of America (CWLA) was founded and Carstens was elected its executive director. Through the CWLA and other agencies, a standardized national child welfare program was designed privately that stressed temporary rather than permanent institutional care for dependent children and attempted to preserve the natural family home wherever possible.

The Pennsylvania SPCC shared the "modern economic thought that the normal condition of the child is in the home," suggesting that the old idea of SPCC as a "hand offered to the arm of the law" be discarded (McCrea, 1910; Schultz, 1924). "The new type of Society must deal with the family as a unit of treatment. . . . It is a family rehabilitation society."

"Not to take the child from an unfit home, but to make the home fit for them and keep him in it is our aim" agreed the Children's Aid and SPCC of Essex County New Jersey (Schultz, 1924, p. 210).

At the 1909 White House Conference on Children, the U.S. Children's Bureau policy statement was that "no child should be removed from the home unless it is impossible so to construct family conditions or build and supplement family resources as to make the home safe for the child. . . . The ideal solution for the problem of the child in his home is the rehabilitation of the natural home" (Schultz, 1924, p. 209).

To rehabilitate and reconstruct family life, many anticruelty societies expanded their protecting efforts beyond the individual child.

To rehabilitate and reconstruct family life, many anticruelty societies expanded their protecting efforts beyond the individual child. The Pennsylvania society, for example, in association with other Philadelphia social agencies, was instrumental in forming a local Children's Bureau to consider the needs of any child in distress (McCrea, 1910).

The head of the Cleveland Humane Society in 1915, Cheney Jones, reiterated the role of child protective agencies to combat "the chronic indifference of people to social maladjustment and to efforts at reform."

> Ought not the private society, the juvenile Court and the state bureau of child protection join in sounding through the land an appeal for providing opportunity for parents to obtain employment at a living wage? . . . The injustice in our present industrial arrangements produces more neglected children than all our machinery can protect. (Jones, 1915, p. 163)

Four years later, Julia Lathrop, chief of the U.S. Children's Bureau, noted at the National Conference of Social Work that adequate child welfare standards had to be based on efforts at social amelioration such as "stabilizing employment, substituting good schools for work for all children, providing adequate care for the health and welfare of all mothers and children" (Lathrop, 1919, p. 8).

By 1919, even the NYSPCC had begun to broaden its program to include the rehabilitation and reconstruction of family life. By the 1930s, the "liberal" and "conservative" approaches truly converged, signified by the formulation of a set of standards for the American Humane Association that were based on the preventive principles pioneered by the Massachusetts Society (Antler & Antler, 1979, p. 199).

Governmental Efforts

The establishment of the U.S. Children's Bureau in 1909 within the federal government was a direct outcome of the first White House Conference on Children. The Children's Bureau took an early, active role in setting program standards, along with state and voluntary agencies, and generally acted as advocates for children and parents. The maternal and child health system was built by the Children's Bureau. They actively advocated for the inclusion of the Aid to Dependent Children (ADC) program in the Social Security Act in the 1930s.

By the 1930s, many of the older humane societies no longer performed protective services for children, their functions being taken over by a variety of public and voluntary organizations such as juvenile courts, juvenile protective associations, family welfare societies, children's aid, and local welfare boards. Some SPCCs and humane societies merged with public welfare agencies so that in many of the newly formed government boards, personnel long associated with the SPCC tradition continued to carry out policy (Carstens, 1923, pp. 92-96). The growing acceptance by states, counties, and municipalities of the responsibility for child protection symbolized a new era in the child welfare movement.

The Social Security Act of 1935 marked the first federal government venture into funding child welfare services. Title IVA (ADC, later Aid to Families With Dependent Children [AFDC]) specifically addressed the financial needs of children in families deprived of parental support. Title IVB (Child Welfare Services) encouraged states to develop, strengthen, or expand preventive and protective services for vulnerable children by providing limited federal funding to states through formula grants.

The major impact of Title IVB was on the substitute care system: Funds were available through IVB to pay for foster care of children but not to provide supportive services to families with children at home. Title IVB provided only financial assistance in the form of welfare payments to predominantly single parents, which many critics associated with the vastly increasing numbers of poor children born to single-parent households.

A corresponding development of social casework methods in the 1930s and

1940s provided a major impetus for moving child protection from a law enforcement, punitive issue to a social service, rehabilitative one. "Aggressive casework," the use of outreach and case finding, found increasing favor in the 1950s. As a result, social workers recognized that casework methods could be applied to families who had not of their own free will sought out service (Antler & Antler, 1979, pp. 201-206).

In the 1960s, largely due to the efforts of medical professionals, child abuse truly became an issue of national importance. Reporting laws were passed in all the states mandating professionals and others to identify children who needed protection and requiring public welfare departments to assume a social service investigation and a capacity to track families and perpetrators because they might "hospital-hop" or move from community to community.

The major issues surrounding the development of the reporting laws included (a) whether law enforcement or social services should be the primary respondent to the reports, (b) the value of including neglect or limiting reporting to physical abuse alone, (c) the definitions of child neglect and abuse, and (d) the approaches to accountability on the part of both county and state child welfare agencies, as well as mandated reporters.

The resolution of these issues gave social services the primary role, based on the expectation that abused and neglected children and their families needed services to change dysfunctional parenting practices. Definitions emphasizing the distinction between corporal punishment and physical abuse, as well as the severe side of neglect—the deprivation of a child's basic necessities—were included. To ensure accountability, mandated professionals were required to report suspicions of child maltreatment. In addition, the eligibility of federal funding for states was tied to the universality of a systematic response to reports of child abuse and neglect.

In 1974, the Child Abuse Prevention and Treatment Act (P.L. 93-247) was passed by Congress establishing the National Center on Child Abuse and Neglect (NCCAN) as an agency within the federal Department of Health, Education, and Welfare (currently the Department of Health and Human Services). This act provided funds to assist states, localities, and nonprofits to develop programs and services for abused and ne-

glected children and their families. The federal government was expected to play a leadership role in encouraging states to develop laws and policies based on national standards. States needed to meet specific federal reporting and procedural requirements to be eligible for federal grants. In general, it is agreed that NCCAN has been effective in producing changes in state policies relative to reports of abuse and neglect, as well as national awareness of the problem. However, this legislation did not provide services to those children and families reported. The size of the state grants was too small to fund service programs beyond demonstration efforts or training resources for social service workers.

The 1960s and early 1970s saw a rapid growth in overall federal financing of social services provided by the states. The 1962 amendments to the Social Security Act legislated federal-state cost sharing for social services aimed at reducing or preventing welfare dependency. Between 1967 and 1972, federal expenditures for social services grew from $281.6 million to $1.7 billion, a 504% increase (Burt & Pittman, 1985, p. 27). By the mid-1970s, federal dollars accounted for about half of the total public spending on child welfare services. A cap was placed on federal social service expenditures in 1972 due to the enormous increases—a doubling of expenditures in one year (1971-1972) from $741 million to $1.7 billion (Burt & Pittman, 1985, p. 30). This cap made it even more difficult for states to develop and use services to children as an alternative to foster care.

Congress made a major effort in 1975 to improve state services to families and reduce current and future dependency through the passage of another amendment to the Social Security Act (Title XX). States were given increased authority, responsibility, and flexibility in choosing the complex of social services to be provided with federal financial participation (75% federal share, 25% state share). The $2.5 billion cap on social service expenditures enacted in 1972 remained in effect, thus limiting opportunity for program developments. Title XX supplied approximately 30% of the budget for state child welfare services by 1982, compared to 52% from state, local, and private sources. Children received on average about one half of the Title XX dollars, yet by the end of the 1970s, nearly three fourths of all child welfare monies were devoted to foster care (Burt & Pittman, 1985, p. 31).

It was not until the enactment of P.L. 96-272, the Adoption Assistance and Child Welfare Act of 1980, however, that the federal government attempted to develop and implement a national child welfare policy. This act set forth a comprehensive set of standards for child welfare. By October 1983, states were to develop plans that demonstrated that reasonable preventive efforts were to be made for each child prior to out-of-home placement, and reasonable efforts would be made to reunite children with their families. A major goal was a reduction in the large numbers of children drifting permanently into the foster care system. Fiscal incentives were included to help move the service emphasis away from foster care. These included Medicaid coverage for adopted children with special needs. The new legislation made "permanency planning" a national goal for dependent children and facilitated action at the state level. P.L. 96-272 restrains professional authority by mandating external (generally citizen or judicial) case review procedures to ensure that there is a case plan for each child in foster care and that the plan is being followed.

In both fiscal 1982 and 1983, the Reagan Administration attempted to repeal P.L. 96-272 (Burt & Pittman, 1985, p. 36). As the Children's Defense Fund noted in its analysis of the 1984 federal budget, Congress was able to keep the legislation and most of the funding intact, but the Reagan Administration was able to undermine the Act by delaying both the issuance of final regulations and the review of states that had self-certified as being in compliance with the Act to receive additional funds (Children's Defense Fund, 1983).

Since the mid-1980s, the full implementation of P.L. 96-272 has been hindered by both the increasing numbers of children identified as abused and neglected and the serious limitations on service resources in most U.S. communities. Between 1976 and 1993, the number of reported children increased by 347%—to 2.9 million in 1993. Total resources to respond to these children and their families—federal, state, and local—increased by a far lower percentage.

In August 1993, President Clinton signed legislation that added to the Social Security Act a new entitlement—The Family Preservation and Family Support Act. This new legislation was meant to be a catalyst for building a system of publicly supported services for vulnerable children and families that can come into play prior to a report of child maltreatment and that also can respond energetically to families in crises that may lead to the removal of their children into foster care. The level of funding is modest, but the planning processes underway in states have involved a broad group of community agencies and resources.

Overview of Child Welfare Policy

Public child welfare policies in the United States have been aimed primarily at poor or dysfunctional families. It is significant, as Stephen Antler points out, that the major public and private institutions of the child welfare system evolved in response to the child-rearing difficulties encountered by a relatively well-defined group of poor, deprived families encountering unmanageable family crises (Antler, 1985, pp. 83-85). As of 1987, the last year case data were widely available, of the 2.2 million children officially reported in the United States in that one year, more than 40% were receiving public assistance (American Humane Association, 1988).

The development of a more expansive policy framework for providing supportive services to families is not yet well-rooted in our society in comparison with other developed countries, such as western European democracies. The impetus for our system of child welfare arose out of the philanthropic and "child-saving" motivations of the private, nonprofit sector. That sector has not manifested interest in developing widespread public support for families. Although there is an obvious connection between the needs of children and the conditions faced by their families, this connection has not been translated into broad support for services to maintain and enhance family functioning. The equally obvious connection between poverty and child welfare also does not serve to motivate private and public concern for services to families nor income supports beyond what is provided to largely single parents through the Aid to Dependent Children Program.

The development of societies for the prevention of cruelty to children in the early 20th century placed attention on the need for changes in the personal characteristics and behavior of parents, not on needed changes in the institutional arrangements of the larger society. There has been consistency in the main characteristics of the public's response to child maltreatment. It has been characterized by a focus on child rescue, not family support; by an emphasis on "judgment"—against parent perpetrators; by an unwillingness to directly address the impact of poverty on child maltreatment; and by an uneven focus on parental pathology as opposed to social and environmental deprivation.

The rhetoric accompanying policy development in these areas can support giving children a fresh start but *not* providing families with the minimum level of income, housing, and supportive services essential for rearing their own children.

Child welfare in the 1990s is once again experiencing a major transformation.

A cornerstone of today's child welfare system is the emphasis on the importance of the family and on the need to support and enhance rather than to hinder its capacities and competence.

A cornerstone of today's child welfare system is the emphasis on the importance of the family and on the need to support and enhance rather than to hinder its capacities and competence, to protect familial bonds, and to maintain children with their families of birth if at all possible. Changes can be seen most vividly in the growing emphasis on the prevention of placement; in the redefinition of foster care toward a focus on reunification; in the increased use of citizen, consumer, and self-help group participation in program development and service delivery; in a willingness to provide prevention and early intervention services; and in an emphasis on deepening the roots of child protection in the communities where children and families live.

Conceptual Models of Current Child Protective Services

It is difficult to describe the alternative ways child protective services currently are constituted in the absence of an empirical study and in the presence of a rapidly changing environment. However, it is possible to group CPS under two broad models:

1. CPS systems that begin with the intake of reports of child abuse and neglect, move on to their investigation, and end their role with the substantiation decision. If the child is in need of immediate out-of-home placement, this also would be handled normally by CPS, including the attendant court process, or
2. CPS systems that define the role as beginning with intake and ending when the case is closed for service. The process here normally includes intake, assessment/investigation, substantiation decision, service planning, service provision and/or referral, evaluation of client progress, and case closure. Placement decisions and court involvement also would be handled by CPS in this model at any point in the process.

Under the second broad type, variants include CPS systems in which some staff specialize in intake and investigation and others in ongoing services, once the decision is made to open a case for services. There also might be a separate (non-CPS) unit providing foster care.

Under the first broad type, there normally would be some capacity to "hand over" an opened case to a service provision unit, which would assign the case to foster care, a child welfare service worker, or a "family service" worker. The distinction would be whether this staff is separate (physically and functionally) from CPS. The tendency is that the more "separate," the longer the wait between the decision to open a case and the actual initiation of services.

Many variations or additional components characterize these broad categories of our public CPS systems. "In-home services" are specialized services focusing on the children who remain at home and their families. "Intensive family preservation services" are widely provided, usually but not always from private providers such as Homebuilders or Families First. These family preservation services are intensive short-term services to families in which children are at imminent risk of placement. Some public CPS agencies have the capacity to provide these services themselves.

Some CPS systems provide services directly; others focus on "case management" services whereby the CPS worker arranges direct services for the client from a variety of community agencies or treatment resources. Other key conceptual issues distinguishing CPS systems relate to their ability to serve "voluntary" as well as "involuntary" clients and the inclusion of "nonfamilial" (institutional abuse, school-based abuse, stranger/perpetrator cases, etc.) as well as "intrafamilial" cases under CPS responsibilities. Some CPS systems include voluntary and nonfamilial cases, but most do not.

There are many variants within each of the two broad models. The main distinction is that, in the first model, CPS limits itself primarily to investigation; in the second, CPS includes both investigation and service provision. Normally, neither model includes the foster care system. What is important, however, is that a response to a family in need of help generally cannot begin without a report of child maltreatment that makes it through the screening and case-opening criteria of a CPS agency. Many are concerned that CPS has become the gatekeeper for all children and family services. When Family Preservation and Family Support Act state plans are implemented in fiscal year 1996, there is some hope and expectation that this will change.

Current Issues

As a consequence of increased child neglect and abuse reporting, state and local CPS agencies are overwhelmed by their responsibilities for conducting investigations. As Kamerman and Kahn (1989) stated in their national study of children's services, "Child protective services today constitute the core public child and family service, the fulcrum and sometimes the totality of the system" (p. 10). Nationally, only about 42% of reported cases are substantiated, but enormous energy and resources go into the investigatory process, and a high proportion of "unsubstantiated" cases involve children and families in serious need of services. Moreover, many of the substantiated cases were reported previously and not substantiated, thus missing an opportunity for earlier intervention.

Equally disturbing is that many maltreated children never come to the attention of CPS. The 1986 National Incidence Study revealed that only an estimated 35% of children known to be harmed during that year actually were investigated by CPS (Sedlak, 1991, p. 13). Large numbers of children unknown to the child protection system have already suffered demonstrable harm due to abuse and neglect. The 1986 National Incidence Study estimated there were 1,424,400 children demonstrably endangered by abuse or neglect (Sedlak, 1991), *most* of whom did not come to the attention of public CPS.

Another major issue is that the public child welfare service system, including CPS, is not able to address the variety of treatment needs of abused and neglected children even when they are identified to CPS. The findings of a national evaluation of federally funded child abuse intervention projects of abused children under age 13 showed their extensive needs. The findings can be summarized (Daro, 1988, p. 154):

- Approximately 30% of the abused children had some type of cognitive or language disorder
- Approximately 14% of the abused children exhibited self-mutilative or other self-destructive behaviors
- More than half of the abused children had difficulty in school, including poor attendance and misconduct
- More than 22% had learning disorders requiring special education service
- Approximately 30% had chronic health problems

Daro also points out that the maltreated adolescents included in the study demonstrated an even wider range of problems and severe disorders than the younger group (Daro, 1988, p. 154).

With the passage of the Family Preservation and Family Support Act of 1993, we have turned a corner on public child welfare policy toward an emphasis on the importance of families. Yet even now, some would like to draw a distinction between "family preservation" and "child protection," as if they were opposing goals. The opposite of family preservation is permanent out-of-home care for children; the opposite of family preservation is not child protection. In fact, family preservation is an excellent tool for child protection. Family preservation programs normally do provide for the safety and protection of children in the home by being available 24 hours a day, by the training and preparation of the staff, and by the large number of hours every week in face-to-face contact with family members. The research on intensive family preservation services shows that children normally are kept safe at home during the time of services. However, home-based services were designed and promoted as an alternative to out-of-home placement for families at imminent risk of child placement. Experiments testing this proposition generally have not supported this hypothesis, leading to speculation that although the families were clearly in crisis and in need of services, placement was not actually necessary.

Today's child protective services system is dominated by its responsibility for investigating allegations of child maltreatment and for providing care for children who cannot safely remain in their own homes. CPS has become mainly an investigation rather than a service provision resource, and foster care has become the main intervention, even though only a small percentage of substantiated abuse and neglect reports result in out-of-home placement. CPS cannot draw on a larger array of community service resources even for its open cases. There are relatively few resources available for improving family functioning, treating the multiple service needs of abused and neglected children, and providing concrete assistance with housing, medical care, food, and other necessities, and there is almost no way for public social services to provide preventive or early intervention services to strengthen families before abuse or neglect takes hold. Neither the mandate nor the resources for these tasks are in place yet.

Our CPS systems increasingly deal with more serious, complex cases. Many children and families are living without the necessary familial and community supports in neighborhoods characterized by deprivation, substance abuse, and violence. The children who come into care are more likely to have been there before and their home conditions more likely to have deteriorated from those of the previous placement. It is becoming increasingly clear that we need to provide more consistent supports to children and families to prevent recurring crises.

There is a paradigm shift going on—away from individual agencies running *their* programs with *their* funding sources and toward *communities configuring their resources to achieve certain goals for children and families;* away from investigating, substantiating, and closing and toward assessing and providing services to strengthen families to prevent additional maltreatment.

Leaders all over the United States are beginning to speak with one voice in conceptualizing the child and family service system the United States needs. A consensus has emerged among many organizations, including the American Public Welfare Association, the American Humane Association, The Child Welfare League of America, the National Commission on Children, the U.S. Advisory Board on Child Abuse and Neglect, the National Governor's Association Policy Academy, the leading foundations concerned with child welfare, the National Association of Public Child Welfare Administrators, and the states' children's mental health association. The vision of the children and family service system of the future is quite different from what it is today.

This is what the consensus looks like:

1. We must have early intervention and prevention services to help children and families *before* problems intensify. Our response cannot *begin* with a report on child abuse.
2. A more comprehensive system of meeting basic needs of children and families for housing, health, food, clothing, and so on is essential.
3. The focus on intervention in child abuse and neglect has to move beyond investigation and placement to include assessment and services.
4. We need a more *comprehensive, holistic response,* moving away from *categorical programs* with separate eligible criteria to a *community system of care* in which schools, courts, mental health, law enforcement, social services, substance abuse treatment, and so on work together.
5. We must *destigmatize* or normalize parents' need for help. It does not make sense to have a *substantiated* report of child abuse and neglect be the normal access point to services. Who would de-

liberately design a system of service that required parents to abuse or neglect their children to obtain help? It is important to offer some *preventive* services to everyone, such as home visitation for new parents on a voluntary basis, as well as family resource centers and other community-based natural points of access to help.

6. We must become more *outcome oriented* instead of process oriented.

7. We must locate supports and services at the neighborhood and community levels.

8. We have to develop more ways to connect children and families to their neighborhoods and communities and connect people who want to help in more natural ways with people who need help.

9. Our service system must become more culturally competent. We have to use the natural identities of children and the richness of community cultural diversity more positively as resources for children and families.

The emerging consensus on the direction of child welfare reform does not mean controversy and alternative agendas do not exist. There is an ongoing and legitimate concern about the length of time that should be spent providing supports to families if they continue to abuse and neglect their children. Most child welfare professionals, as well as ordinary citizens, believe that children should be removed and placed permanently outside their homes if a pattern of maltreatment persists despite services. On the other hand, most children who grow up in foster care try to connect or reconnect to their families. The challenge is in developing ways for children to be safe and well-cared for while maintaining some continuity of family ties whenever possible.

The maltreatment of children is unacceptable to American values, and we consistently have supported policies that encourage the larger society—through public child protective services—to step in when children are in need of protection and their parents are unwilling or unable to offer that protection. Experience has taught us that, over the long run, it is far better to strengthen and preserve families whenever possible. This vital work requires a socially supported framework for decision making on cases, adequate resources in terms of community services and foster or group homes, and a CPS staff well-trained and well-supervised to make these important decisions. This is still a "work in progress." In most communities, all three of these necessary ingredients are not in place. Although it may be tempting to generate simple solutions, such as a return to orphanages, we have accumulated enough experience to know that such simple solutions will not work.

References

American Humane Association. (1988). *Highlights of official aggregate child neglect and abuse reporting, 1987.* Denver, CO: American Humane Association.

Antler, J., & Antler, S. (1979). From child rescue to family protection. *Children and Youth Services Review, 1,* 177-204.

Antler, S. (1985). The social policy context of child welfare. In J. Laird & A. Hartman (Eds.), *A handbook of child welfare* (pp. 77-99). New York: Free Press.

Burt, M., & Pittman, K. (1985). *Testing the social safety net.* Washington, DC: The Urban Institute Press.

Carstens, C. C. (1923). Who shall protect the children? *Survey, 51,* 92-96.

Children's Defense Fund. (1983). *A children's defense budget: An analysis of the president's FY 1984 budget and children.* Washington, DC: Author.

Costin, L. (1985). The historical context of child welfare. In J. Laird & A. Hartman (Eds.), *A handbook of child welfare* (pp. 34-60). New York: Free Press.

Daro, D. (1988). *Confronting child abuse: Research for effective program design.* New York: Free Press.

Folks, H. (1902). *The care of destitute, neglected and delinquent children.* New York: Macmillan.

Jones, C. (1915). The relation of private societies to juvenile courts and to state bureaus of protection. In *Proceedings of the National Conference of Charities and Correction.* Boston: National Conference of Charities and Correction.

Kamerman, S., & Kahn, A. (1989). *Social services for children, youth and families in the United States.* New York: Annie E. Casey Foundation.

Laird, J., & Hartman, A. (Eds.). (1985). *A handbook of child welfare.* New York: Free Press.

Lathrop, J. A. (1919). Child welfare standards: A test of democracy. In *Proceedings of the National Conference of Social Work, 1919*. Boston: National Conference of Charities and Correction.

McCrea, R. (1910). *The humane movement*. College Park, MD: McGrath.

Rice, R. (1985). The well-being of families and children—A context for child welfare. In J. Laird & A. Hartman (Eds.), *A handbook of child welfare* (pp. 61-76). New York: Free Press.

Schultz, W. J. (1924). *The humane movement in the United States, 1910-1922*. New York: Columbia University Press.

Sedlak, A. (1991). *National incidence and prevalence of child abuse and neglect, 1988: Revised report*. Rockville, MD: Westat.

U.S. Advisory Board on Child Abuse and Neglect. (1990). *Child abuse and neglect: Critical first steps in response to a national emergency*. Washington, DC: Department of Health and Human Services, Office of Human Development Services.

21

Community Organization of Services Needed to Deal With Child Abuse

DAVID L. CHADWICK

The recognition and the increasingly sophisticated definition of child abuse over the past 30 years have revealed a large number of needs and a growing list of services and interventions. However, resources have failed to grow along with the professionally perceived needs and the knowledge of presumed helpful remedies. Most communities now recognize abused children at a rate approximating 1% to 2% of all children each year (State of California, 1992; U.S. Department of Health and Human Services, 1988), and most provide a number of interventions and services that attempt to interrupt abuse, prevent it, or deal appropriately with its consequences. Although the services and interventions tend to be quite similar from one locale to another in the United States, the manner in which they are provided, the organization of services, and the ways in which they relate vary considerably.

The concept of interdisciplinary work in child abuse generally is well-accepted, and communication among different agencies and individuals who are attempting to manage individual cases is not a new idea (Bross, Krugman, Lenherr, Rosenberg, & Schmitt, 1988). However, the notion that communities might consciously attempt, at a political level, to organize all of the needed services in a coherent way is not standard practice. The development of services varies from one locality to another. Agencies and individuals have attempted to provide the services they believed to be needed and in ways that they found possible and to work out interagency agreements and protocols that suit the given community. Some centers that have specialized in providing various services and training have replicated their patterns in different sites, and this has resulted in what are called *models* for the provision of some services.

These models appear to work successfully in their own communities, but it would be premature to argue that any one of them should be adopted in all or most communities. There is, at present, no reliable way in which to assess how well each model or each community deals with the problem of child abuse.

Because many disciplines must contribute skills to the assessment and management of child abuse cases, most communities have informal or formal interdisciplinary networks of professionals who participate in these processes. An effect of these contacts is the development of a shared body of knowledge about child abuse that is regularly applied and allows the promulgation of guidelines and standards. Knowledge about child abuse was very limited a few decades ago but now is growing rapidly as a result of increased clinical experience and formal research. Sharing this new knowledge is vital. Any form of community organization must include a plan for the continuing education of participating professionals.

Principles for Organization

A few broad principles should be applied to ensure that programs are of good quality and reasonably free from wasteful duplication:

- Organization should result in the best possible long-term outcomes for many children and their families, recognizing that ideal outcomes often are not achievable for children who have been seriously abused or neglected. This requirement imposes a need to know what happens to children and families in the years that follow a report of child abuse. Few communities now have the capability to do this.
- Organization should provide services and interventions in an equitable manner to all children and families in the region being served.
- Organization should facilitate communication between agencies and individuals who work with abused children and their families. Confidentiality needs of affected persons must be respected, but confidentiality should never be used as an excuse for a failure to communicate essential information between professionals who are making decisions that may affect the lives of abused children and their families.
- Organization should result in efficiency and the avoidance of duplication and ensure the highest quality of service.
- Organization must adapt to local conditions and local capabilities and maximize local resources.
- Organization must provide services and interventions promptly. In particular, decisions about infants are always urgent.
- Given the existing realities of the availability of services in most U.S. communities, a number of different but independent governmental agencies and a number of services based in the private sector are needed in dealing with child abuse. Active cooperation between public and private sectors is essential and must be documented.
- Interventions that require the use of the authority to invade the privacy of citizens, detain persons against their will, or assume the responsibility for the care of children can be carried out only by agencies of the government.
- Services that require the development of close relationships and for which the person served normally can choose a provider are best provided in the private sector or in a publicly funded agency that can provide private, professional relationships.
- Planning can greatly increase the efficiency and effectiveness of services and

the development of community protocols that describe interagency agreements and define how services will be
provided.

Assessment Services

Recognition and Reporting of Maltreatment

This function requires a level of knowledge and awareness among persons who
encounter children as a result of their
work (mandated reporters) and a consciousness of abuse in the population at
large. The needed level of knowledge and
awareness usually has been sought by the
provision of continuing education programs for professionals who deal with
children and through publication of standards and guidelines for these professionals.

Mandated reporters of child abuse are
professional persons whose work makes it
likely that they will see abused children.
The professions involved are health care
(almost all types), education, child care,
welfare, law enforcement, and a few others. In most states, workers in these professions are required to report the "reasonable suspicion" of child abuse to a law
enforcement or child protective agency.

Mandated reporters often are experienced with children and families and capable of performing preliminary assessments of the cases they see so that their
reports may express more than "suspicion." They also are often connected to
the families of abused children in ways
that give them valuable insights into what
sort of interventions may be appropriate
in the cases they report. Often (although
not always) they want to be in a position
to recommend further steps in investigation or intervention. Whenever it is feasible, they should be offered opportunities
to participate in interdisciplinary discussions about the cases they have reported,
and, in almost all cases, they should be
provided with feedback about the case
they have reported as the case moves forward.

Although reporting of child abuse has
increased dramatically over the past two
or three decades, reporting rates for different jurisdictions still differ markedly
(State of California, 1992), suggesting
that reporting practices are not consistent from state to state or locality to locality. This situation confounds statisticians,
planners, and policymakers and indicates
a need for further research and education. Individual communities should
sponsor occasional multidisciplinary conferences on the reporting of child abuse
with the goal of promulgating uniform
guidelines.

Detailed Assessment of Children Suspected of Being Abused

The process that is sometimes called
substantiation requires a sufficient amount
of investigation to determine, at some
level of certainty, that the child in question has (or has not) been abused and to
acquire as much information as possible
about the abuse. A number of different
sorts of assessment techniques may be
needed, depending on the individual
case.

Often more than one type of professional and more than one agency is involved at this stage, and careful communication and coordination are vital. The
following list is a classification of the techniques and processes that may be needed
for substantiation:

- Interview of the initial reporter
- Interview of the parent(s) or other care-
  taker(s)
- Interview of the suspect(s)
- Interview of the child
- Interview of other witnesses
- Social assessment of the family
- Scene investigation (collection and ex-
  amination of physical evidence)
- Home visit to assess environment
- Medical history, examination, and test-
  ing (collection and examination of evi-
  dence)
- Autopsy and multidisciplinary review of
  fatal cases
- Conference with two or more profession-
  als or with a team
- Initiation of criminal legal process
- Initiation of protective legal process
- Arrest of a suspect
- Protective detention of a child in a shel-
  ter or a foster home
- Initiation of treatment for children who
  demonstrate treatable conditions result-
  ing from abuse or neglect

Many of these processes overlap, and,
without cooperation among professionals

and agencies, dealing with a child abuse case that calls for criminal investigation, child protective action, and care for a serious condition of the child will quickly become chaotic. Most communities should have protocols that describe the roles of different agencies and professionals in these processes.

New Case Assessment and Early Case Management

Liaison Between Law Enforcement and Children's Services

The mandated recipients of child abuse reports are law enforcement officers and child protective service workers. Because of the various forms of organization of public services, it is typical that the responsible law enforcement entity and the responsible child protective agency are in *different* governmental entities. Although these agencies almost always are allowed and often mandated to communicate freely about child abuse cases, it is not always easy for them to do so because of geographic or administrative considerations.

The roles and responsibilities of law enforcement and child protective services differ, but they both usually must work from the same base of information, and they easily can confound each other or work at cross-purposes. The best work may be done in those rare instances in which there is an on-site liaison between law enforcement and child protective services, and the quality of investigative work varies directly with the level of communication and confidence that connects investigators from the two disciplines.

The ability to share files and information quickly and efficiently can result in a substantial saving of stretched investigative resources, but this will not occur unless professionals trust one another.

The ability to share files and information quickly and efficiently can result in a substantial saving of stretched investigative resources, but this will not occur unless professionals trust one another.

Investigative Techniques and the Contribution of the Health Care System

Children whose verbal skills allow them to be interviewed should be interviewed whether the suspected problem is physical abuse, sexual abuse, emotional abuse, or neglect. Children should be interviewed under conditions that reduce their anxiety and make them feel safe to reveal abuse. For some children, there are no such conditions, but special child-oriented and "safe" settings should be available.

Skilled interviewers of children exist among physicians, social workers, law enforcement officers, attorneys, psychiatrists, psychologists, school teachers and counselors, nurses, and others. However, the needed skills are by no means universal in the persons who first encounter children suspected of being abused. The ability to interview children skillfully about maltreatment is not provided in the basic education of any of the involved disciplines, so it must be acquired in postgraduate settings. Interviewers must be comfortable with children and must know a good deal about child development. They must know a good deal about the sort of abuse that they are investigating, and they must be able to avoid the legal pitfalls that may invalidate the information gained from children. The knowledge and skills required to interview very young children are different from those needed for school-age and adolescent children.

There has been growing support for special facilities that allow audiotaping or videotaping of children's interviews. Some authorities prefer not to record interviews because taped interviews tend to be given greater weight than other statements children might make about their abuse experiences. In general, however, the videotaped record of the interview is extremely useful in providing a clear record that the interview was properly conducted and that the child was not led by the investigator to make untrue statements. It enables all parties to a litigated case to assess what the child is likely to say as a witness, and it may avoid the need for multiple interviews and sometimes for a trial.

Physical examination is needed in the substantiation process for most abused or neglected children. Physical abuse usually is defined by the physical damage seen in the victim, and a substantial fraction of sexual abuse victims also will have physical findings. In some cases, it will be provided by a physician who reports the case, but not all physicians are able and willing to provide this service, so communities must develop sites and recruit physicians who can provide the necessary service. Sometimes, the medical assessment can stand alone as an indicator of abuse, but in many cases it must be evaluated in the light of information gained from medical histories, specialized interviews, or statements by caretakers or other witnesses.

Seriously injured children with suspected internal injuries require specialized assessment by physicians familiar with the syndromes of inflicted injury. At present, most of the physicians who are qualified in this area are pediatricians. However, special contributions in the objective determination of injury mechanisms often can be provided by radiologists, neurosurgeons, neurologists, and critical care physicians.

Communities with organized trauma programs should include physical abuse diagnostic and substantiation services because physically abused children may surface in almost any primary care setting that is used by the public. For this reason, recognition skills must be widespread among primary care agencies.

Fatal Child Abuse Cases

Fatal child abuse cases require that communities establish "medical examiner" systems for the investigation of unexplained or suspicious deaths. Autopsies of such cases by forensic pathologists should be mandatory in all cases, including those infant deaths that appear to be related to sudden infant death syndrome (SIDS).

An infant death cannot be classified as SIDS unless an autopsy is performed (American Academy of Pediatrics, 1994). Forensic pathologists need to be very familiar with the syndromes of child physical abuse and with the knowledge that differentiates unintentional from inflicted injury after death.

Systematic review of all child fatalities is an excellent method for ensuring that deaths from inflicted injury are discovered. However, it will not work well in the absence of competent forensic pathology and training of pathologists about child abuse. Communities that still operate fa-

tality review systems under the direction of "lay coroners" should reexamine their systems carefully and attempt to secure knowledgeable forensic pathology through shared arrangements with neighboring communities or with statewide medical examiner systems.

The review of fatal cases that may be due to inflicted injuries also requires the participation of physicians and other health personnel who had contact with the case prior to death. Although this is most important in relationship to observations and care during the period immediately preceding death, medical data also may be needed going back to the time of birth. The observations of emergency medical providers who go into homes in response to calls from caretakers may be valuable, as may be the observations of nurses from the bedside care of hospitalized children. Scene data collected by law enforcement or protective service workers who visit the home also are valuable in many cases and almost indispensable in cases involving severe burns or suffocation.

Fatal case review has become standard in many states and communities (Granik, Durfee, & Wells, 1991). This process provides for the review of *all* unexplained or doubtful deaths by a multidisciplinary team with representation from health, law enforcement, children's services, and other agencies. Medical examiners should be in charge of this process in communities that have them. Communities lacking medical examiners should designate an official in the health department or in the hospital to oversee fatal case reviews.

The Assessment Site

Designated assessment sites for abused children and their families are now the standard in most communities. Large cities often have several sites, and the number that the city needs and can support varies. Rural areas and small communities often must share assessment sites. A single assessment site can serve a total population of 2 or 3 million comfortably. However, the ability to reach the site within 1 hour is a desirable feature. Small communities in lightly populated areas should have sites that serve smaller populations.

Sites are based in a variety of different facilities. Hospitals with emergency departments and with pediatric services often house assessment sites. They also may be offered in a "Safe House," which is typically a converted residence with a child-friendly ambience. Children's emergency shelters must be capable of providing basic health assessment to children at the site, and definitive evidential assessments also may be provided in emergency shelters.

> *Ideally, an assessment site provides a focal point in which many child abuse-related services can be offered.*

Ideally, an assessment site provides a focal point in which many child abuse-related services can be offered. The services should be oriented toward all forms of child maltreatment, physical abuse, sexual abuse, neglect, emotional abuse, and parent-initiated illness because of the high frequency with which the different forms overlap in given cases. The skills and services that can be provided include the following:

- Interviews of children
- Interviews of adults, parents, and caretakers of children
- Crisis management for families
- Medical examinations for physical abuse, sexual abuse, neglect, and malnutrition and assessment for medical neglect and parent-initiated illness
- Capability and qualification of all persons providing assessments to be expert witnesses in later court actions
- Investigative activities of law enforcement, children's services, prosecutors, and attorneys representing children
- Adjacent or nearby emergency care for injuries and illness (this requires a hospital)
- Adjacent or nearby mental health care for abused children and their families
- Spaces for law enforcement and children's services personnel to carry out desk work
- Facilities for interdisciplinary case conferences

If the facility is at a hospital, it should not be in the middle of the emergency department, where the sights and sounds may frighten children, but should be apart in a relatively quiet setting. However, abused children in need of emergency medical care have the early portions of the abuse-related assessment accomplished in the emergency department.

Definitive Decision Making About Intervention: Organization of the Courts

Many investigated cases are not substantiated and are closed without criminal or protective interventions. In many cases, no criminal interventions are sought and the protective interventions are accepted by responsible adults and instituted by the responsible agencies.

Criminal and protective interventions often are contested by affected parties, resulting in litigation or bargaining in the face of litigation. The courts provide the means for decision making in such cases. Depending on the nature of the child abuse case, any of a number of forms of litigation may occur. The most common and the most important are the protective action in the juvenile (or sometimes family) court and the criminal case brought against a suspected abuser. Domestic courts also are involved in many child abuse cases, and the determination of jurisdiction sometimes may cause problems.

For the courts also, planning and developing protocols are essential in avoiding unnecessary conflict and inefficiency. Courts also can set standards and guidelines for the participation of various professionals (especially attorneys) in child abuse work. The courts themselves must develop special knowledge and skills to provide competent judgments in child maltreatment cases.

Ongoing Interventions and Services to Families

After child abuse has been reported, investigated, and proven, any one or a large array of intervention, services, and treatments may be put in place. Some of these are voluntary for the persons affected, and some are court mandated.

Some of the interventions are incompatible with others—for example, a long period of confinement for an abusing parent may be incompatible with family preservation or with a reunification plan.

There also may be a tendency to consider a case as solved once the court actions are over and decisions made. However, regardless of the short-term dispositions, the underlying problems that led to the abuse are unlikely to be solved quickly. In the ongoing management of such cases, coordinated efforts are needed especially from social services, personal health services, preventive family support services, and mental health services. The same is true for families whose children have been removed and placed in foster care or kinship care and for whom reunification is planned, as well as for those children and families in which parental rights have been terminated and adoption or guardianship is being sought.

Community protocols describing the participation and responsibilities of the various agencies and professionals also should be developed for these later phases of care. Except for criminal sanctions, most of what is done after the proof of abuse is the promotion of healing, and these therapeutic and supportive services are best provided by the private sector.

Provision of Abuse-Focused Mental Health Services

Crisis counseling and sensitive support services should be available at the "assessment site." More definitive and prolonged services will be needed by many victims, perpetrators, and family members, and very few, if any, communities have the resources to provide these at the levels that are needed. Depending on community size, population distribution, and many other factors, these services may be organized or provided in a variety of ways. Because mental health services typically require frequent visits to the therapist over long periods of time, long travel times for access are likely to result in difficulties for families. Therefore, decentralization of these services is essential.

Mental health services for the persons affected by child abuse require that providers have specialized training or experience that provides familiarity with the problems that are likely to develop as a result of abuse and the therapies that are effective for them. A first principle in abuse-focused therapy is that the abusive acts should stop if a good outcome is to be achieved. The use of *insight therapy* in the face of ongoing abuse may do more harm than good.

Mental health services must be tailored to the mental health problems presented by clients who have a wide range of symptoms, behaviors, and degrees of severity. Services should meet these needs to the maximum extent that is compatible with available resources. The tendency for persons abused as children to repeat these behaviors as they grow up (Kaufman & Zigler, 1987) imposes a social mandate for treatment beyond the individual needs to relieve distressing symptoms. It also imposes a mandate for sufficient follow-up to determine the long-term outcome of as many cases as possible.

All of the conventional settings for mental health care are likely to be needed by certain abuse victims, including outpatient care, day care, residential and group home care, and in-patient and intensive care.

In addition, specialized services that focus on the needs of preschool children and infants also are needed badly, although rarely available. Many very young children are physically abused or neglected and some are sexually abused as well. The long-term disabling effects of early abuse are potentially profound but not inevitable. Therapeutic preschool settings appear to have great value in ameliorating these effects (Kempe, 1987), but mental health professionals with training and experience in treating abused infants and preschool children are in short supply. Most communities now settle for a system that attempts to interrupt the abuse and place the infant in a caring and supportive environment (typically foster or kinship care).

Mental health providers in the public and private sectors should work with the agencies involved in child abuse services to develop community protocols to ensure the provision of the best possible care to the largest number of children in a climate of scarcity.

Prevention Programs

Home-Based Programs

Recent research (Center for the Future of Children, 1993; Olds, Henderson, Chamberlain, & Tatelbaum, 1986) has demonstrated the feasibility and probable cost-effectiveness of some home-based services for the prevention of child abuse. Hawaii has developed a statewide program based on a combination of risk assessment and home-based services for high-risk families. The program is sponsored and funded by the state, but the provision of services is contracted to nonprofit entities, including a hospital. The close relationship of the home-based service program to the clients is an important feature of this program (Center for the Future of Children, 1993).

Nationally, a number of differing models for home-based programs are in use, and there is as yet no definitive research that compels the use of one in preference to another. It seems likely, however, that the same community organizational structures that address child abuse after the fact might work in developing programs for prevention. In the Elmira program (Olds et al., 1986), the home visitors were nurses, and their success suggests that health departments might play a major role in the provision of preventive services. However, the home visiting capability of health departments has declined in most jurisdictions over the past 20 years, and restoring this function to them is a major task of institutional rebuilding.

Most home-based prevention programs combine the education of parents about child rearing with support that allows parents to select nonabusive solutions to family problems. The most effective program that has been subjected to rigorous analysis employed a health-oriented approach and used nurses as home visitors (Olds et al., 1986). A focus on families with newborns and young children has been prominent in most primary prevention programs.

Home-based programs appear to focus on the prevention of physical abuse and neglect, and an important question relates to the extent to which they might (or might not) prevent child sexual abuse. To the extent that these programs reduce the isolation of families and increase the time that children spend with caring adults, they might be expected to reduce sexual abuse. However, this effect has not been studied yet.

Sexual abuse prevention programs have a long history (Wurtele, 1992) and usually have employed educational methods in which children and parents are informed about the definitions of sexual abuse and the methods of avoiding or deterring it. Finkelhor (Finkelhor, Asdigian, & Dziuba-Leatherman, 1995) has demonstrated the effectiveness of these prevention programs, although a number of

problems remain. One of these is that this form of prevention is not available to many children. Preventive education probably is best provided by schools. However, for many school districts, the development of this service is not financially feasible despite its relatively low cost. Under these conditions, any provider willing and capable of meeting standards for the provision of prevention education should be encouraged to do so.

Political and Economic Considerations

Problem Orientation

Communities and political jurisdictions are organized using historically defined departmental structures. The problems that present themselves to communities (such as child abuse) require the participation of many public and private components, and no political structure exists that can commit these components to common courses of action. This creates the need for interdisciplinary and interagency councils and other such bodies that provide for communication and the development of protocols, guidelines, and standards. Such councils are commonplace and essential in child abuse work, but they require constant nurturing by their communities if they are to be effective.

The political structures of state and local government must look to child abuse councils and to the private sector for much of the work that can ameliorate the problem of child abuse.

This does not mean that state and local governments can forget about the problem. It must, in fact, remain on their "problem list" for generations to come, along with such items as crime, family violence, homelessness, and unemployment. Elected leaders must expect regular reports from their law enforcement agencies, courts, children's services departments, and health departments about progress in dealing with child abuse. A component of these reports must be an analysis of long-term outcomes for children and families that have been reported. The reports from agencies to their executives and legislatures also should contain documentation of interdisciplinary activity and of public-private initiatives and ongoing work.

Better Information

State and local governmental entities also need to develop more accurate ways in which to assess the seriousness of the child abuse problem in their communities and determine trends. The gross confounding of statistics, based solely on counting child abuse reports, requires that this method be supplemented by hospital samples and by ongoing retrospective surveys using the memories of older children and adults about abusive events in their childhoods, as well as other methods. Governmental entities should use the epidemiological skills available in the health sector in the development of their statistical methodologies.

Along with more accurate and standardized methods of assessing the numbers of cases, governments must adopt methods for counting the costs of child abuse. Unless this is done the cost-benefit ratios for various interventions cannot be known, and the government will continue to make policies in a whimsical fashion based on the latest anecdote to emerge in the press.

Large jurisdictions need to improve the information systems that store and report data about child abuse cases. Although initiatives to accomplish this have begun in several states, most cities and counties remain unaffected and uninformed about what really is going on. Most managers in government would prefer to have very accurate information, although some of them recognize that these data may present an unflattering view of the governmental response to child abuse. The initial development of effective information systems is costly. However, a system developed in a single large jurisdiction probably can be exported to many others and to small jurisdictions at fairly low costs, so there is no longer any excuse for political leaders to remain in a state of ignorance about child abuse.

Specific Actions: Protocol Development

Throughout this chapter a recurrent recommendation has been for the development of protocols. These serve as both guidelines and commitments by and for the various involved agencies and professionals to carry out their work in ways that will meet high standards of practice and still provide an efficient and coordinated response to the occurrence of child abuse. Many communities already have done so, but most of these documents are not published formally nor are easily available for reference. Although the child abuse problem is similar in most parts of the United States, the resources available to deal with it differ considerably, so most communities are better advised to develop their own than to adopt one developed in another area.

In addition, the process of developing the protocol has great value, because it brings managers together from the involved agencies and organizations. In the course of communication during multiple meetings and over considerable time, the habit of working together and communicating freely about problems can become established.

It is possible to define a list of common elements that should be a part of most or all protocols for dealing with child abuse after the fact. This list should contain at least the following items:

- Definition of the agencies receiving child abuse reports
- Description of cross-reporting procedures between law enforcement and children's services agencies
- Definition of types of cases to be investigated by law enforcement, by children's services, and by both agencies
- Designation of private providers of services such as interviews of children, medical assessments and care, and mental health assessments
- Description of the communication links between agencies and providers that are to be used to move information quickly in the course of an investigation
- Commitments of the agencies and providers to follow certain procedures and to communicate about cases
- Reference to any contractual arrangements between agencies involving the provision of child abuse-related services
- Description of the precise roles of all participants in the process, including law enforcement, public children's services, private health care institutions and providers, mental health professionals, public health agencies, prosecutors, attor-

neys representing children and families, and the various courts that are involved in child abuse cases

■ Designation (by position) of the persons responsible for carrying out the provisions of the protocol

Commitment of Resources

At present, the costs of dealing with child abuse are difficult to track because they are merged with operating budgets of agencies that deal with many sorts of problems, and they may not be easily identifiable. Precise knowledge of the expenditures for the problem would be useful in policy development, and it is worthwhile to develop means for teasing out these costs. The knowledge, in a given community, that the expenditures for this purpose were dramatically higher or lower than a national average would be valuable.

If accurate cost information became available, political decision making might improve substantially as a result of guidance by accurate programmatic and financial data.

Although few child advocates believe that the resources for dealing with child abuse are sufficient, even fewer can calculate what is being spent and what needs to be spent or in what way. The process of consciously organizing community efforts and documenting organization with written protocols might lead to far greater knowledge and better decision making in the allocation of resources for this pervasive and debilitating societal problem.

Conclusion

Community organization for the effective provision of services that prevent, treat, or interrupt child abuse is necessarily idiosyncratic and related to individual community needs and resources; however, there are a number of useful principles and guidelines that communities can use to assure their citizens and the body politic that everything is being done that can and should be done.

In order to define a community's organization, a responsible group of providers from public and private sectors and from multiple disciplines must meet together and develop community protocols that describe how the different forms of abuse are to be handled in the given community. Minimally, the participants in this process must include public social service and law enforcement agencies, the hospitals, and health providers that frequently provide services to abused children, public health services, schools, preschools, and infant development programs, as well as services for developmentally disabled people, mental health service providers, foster parents, residential and group home care providers, and others.

The organization and the content of community protocols may vary considerably from one community to another, but all protocols should emphasize provision of services at the best level of quality that is possible, based on statements of standards from the American Professional Society on the Abuse of Children and from other professional associations such as the Child Welfare League of America, the American Medical Association, the American Academy of Pediatrics, the American Psychological Association, and the American Psychiatric Association, in addition to state and national associations that set standards for criminal justice practices, school practices, foster care practices, and the practices of other professions that serve abused children and their families.

Community protocols may require fairly frequent review and updating as scientific and professional knowledge affecting child maltreatment continues to advance.

References

American Academy of Pediatrics, Committee on Child Abuse and Neglect. (1994). Distinguishing sudden infant death syndrome from child abuse fatalities. *Pediatrics, 94,* 124-126.

Bross, D. C., Krugman, R. D., Lenherr, M. R., Rosenberg, D. A., & Schmitt, B. D. (1988). *The new child protection team handbook.* New York: Garland.

Center for the Future of Children. (1993). Home visiting. *The Future of Children, 3,* 3.

Finkelhor, D., Asdigian, N., & Dziuba-Leatherman, J. (1995). The effectiveness of victimization prevention instruction: An evaluation of children's responses to actual threats and assaults. *Child Abuse & Neglect, 19,* 141-153.

Granik, L. A., Durfee, M., & Wells, S. J. (1991). *Child death review teams: A manual for design and implementation.* Washington, DC: American Bar Association.

Kaufman, J., & Zigler, E. (1987). Do abused children become abusive parents? *American Journal of Orthopsychiatry, 57,* 186-192.

Kempe, R. S. (1987). A developmental approach to the treatment of the abused child. In R. E. Helfer & R. S. Kempe (Eds.), *The battered child* (4th ed., pp. 360-381). Chicago: University of Chicago Press.

Olds, D., Henderson, C. R., Chamberlain, R., & Tatelbaum, R. (1986). Preventing child abuse and neglect: A randomized trial of nurse home visitation. *Pediatrics, 78,* 65-78.

State of California, Department of Social Services. (1992). *Emergency response referrals received, calendar year ending December 1992* (Report SOC 291, Table 1). Sacramento: Author.

U.S. Department of Health and Human Services, National Center for Child Abuse and Neglect. (1988). *Study findings: Study of national incidence and prevalence of child abuse and neglect.* Washington, DC: Author.

Wurtele, S. (1992). *Preventing child abuse: Sharing the responsibility.* Lincoln: University of Nebraska Press.

22

Cultural Competency in the Field of Child Maltreatment

VERONICA D. ABNEY

Stolorow and Atwood's (1992) theory of intersubjectivity holds that the individual's subjective world evolves "organically from the person's encounter with the critical formative experiences that constitute his unique life history" (p. 2). These critical formative experiences include not only child maltreatment but also the effects of the culture in which the individual lives.

Culture is a set of beliefs, attitudes, values, and standards of behavior that are passed from one generation to the next. Culture includes language, worldview, dress, food, styles of communication, notions of wellness, healing techniques, child-rearing patterns, and self-identity. Human beings create culture, and each group develops its own over time. Culture is dynamic and changing, not static; it changes as the condition of the people change and as their interaction with the larger society changes. Every culture has a set of assumptions made up of beliefs that are so completely accepted by the group that they do not need to be stated, questioned, or defended.

Cultural identification has a crucial impact on an individual's response to traumatic stress because of its effect on

AUTHOR'S NOTE: This chapter is an elaboration of the article "Culture: A Rationale for Cultural Competency," written by Veronica D. Abney and Karen Gunn in the *APSAC Advisor, 6*(3), 1993.

the organization of experience (Parson, 1985). Therefore, cultural identification must be considered carefully when addressing practice issues in the field of child maltreatment. It determines the individual's view and disclosure of the trauma, expression of symptoms, and attitude toward treatment and recovery.

Discussions of cultural differences and issues regarding our competence as professionals in a cross-cultural context often evoke strong emotions that cause us considerable stress. This seems related in part to our nation's long history of racial and ethnic turmoil. These discussions also are stressful because there are certain risks inherent in such a pursuit. We risk disclosing that we have prejudices or may not have the knowledge or skill required to work cross-culturally. This leads to embarrassment and feelings of inadequacy. The greatest risk is that of change, moving from what we thought was a comfortable space to one filled with uncertainty and ambiguity.

This chapter explores how to improve therapeutic and professional interactions with those from other cultures. It will address *cultural competency* from a generic perspective, presenting a brief historical overview of human science's attempts to look at the role of culture, a rationale for cultural competency, and a tripartite approach to the culturally different client. Although the focus will be primarily at the practice level, what will be discussed can be generalized to the organizational level.

Throughout the chapter, there is frequent use of the term *ethnic group,* which is defined in sociology as "a group of people of the same race or nationality who share a common and distinctive culture" (*Random House Dictionary,* 1968). In common usage, ethnicity mistakenly is used to refer only to race, nationality, and land of origin, ignoring the important variable of culture. The term *people of color* is used to describe those viewed as *culturally different* in our society or those who are members of a "visible minority group" (Yamamoto, James, & Palley, 1968, p. 45). This term has largely political significance, focuses on color as a significant social factor in the United States, and is meant by me to include African Americans, Native Americans, Latinos, and Asian/Pacific Islanders in terms of their experience of oppression and discrimination. These experiences have an impact on virtually all of our intercultural interactions.

Historical Overview

Historically, there has been a tendency in the human sciences to explore cultural differences from either a perspective of *cultural deviance* or *cultural relativism.* This means that we are prone to view others from our own cultural perspective, either seeing our culture as superior or "normal" or seeing everything that is different in the other as related to culture and therefore acceptable. Both perspectives can be destructive when assessing child maltreatment and function as barriers to the delivery of culturally competent services.

The cultural deviance perspective is ethnocentric.

The cultural deviance perspective is ethnocentric. It blinds us to the strengths of a particular culture and alienates us in a way that limits our ability to help and empower. It also can cause us to view culturally based child-rearing practices as inappropriate or dangerous when they may well reflect parents' ways of protecting their children. A prime example of this is European culture's belief that infants should sleep separate from their parents and the pathologizing of parents who sleep with their children as lacking appropriate boundaries. New infant research is finding that, in addition to speculations about the emotional benefits of an infant sleeping with his or her parents, this practice may be physiologically safer and prevent sudden infant death syndrome (SIDS) (McKenna, 1990). Our Eurocentric belief that cultures in which children sleep with parents are "primitive" may have caused us to engage in and promote a child-rearing practice that, beyond its possible negative impact on attachment, may have even life-threatening consequences for high-risk infants.

The perspective of cultural relativism is based on the philosophical theory of relativism that holds that judgment criteria are relative and vary with each individual and his or her environment. This presents a difficulty, because it suggests that if a practice is sanctioned culturally, it is devoid of negative impact. Thus, practitioners may ignore the danger or destructiveness inherent in certain culturally approved child-rearing practices (e.g., infibulation, coining, foot binding, physical discipline, discouragement of displays of "weakness" in male children) and consequently leave children at risk for physical or psychological harm.

The *cultural variant* (Allen, 1978) or *culturally different* (Baratz & Baratz, 1970) model offers a potentially more valid and pluralistic perspective. It brings together the subjective worldview of a particular culture and that from a broader cross-cultural base (Korbin, 1981), avoiding both ethnocentrism and cultural relativism. It accepts that cultures vary and does not use one culture as the ideal norm. It also accepts that some cultural practices, despite having evolved to meet universal human needs, may be destructive. Such a model has particular significance in the field of child maltreatment. It offers us a theoretical basis to assess cultural practices with an understanding and appreciation of cultural variations. It is the core of cultural competency.

Rationale for Cultural Competency

In brief, cultural competency is the ability to understand, to the best of one's ability, the worldview of our culturally different clients (or peers) and adapt our practice accordingly. Cultural competency is good social work practice. In order to best meet clients' needs, the professional must understand the world from the clients' point of view and provide the help needed in a manner in which it can be used. Contemporary urgency regarding cultural competency by child treatment professionals is a response to three factors in the United States: (a) increasing cultural diversity, (b) the underrepresentation of professionals from diverse backgrounds, and (c) inadequate delivery of social and mental health services to maltreated children of color.

Increasing Cultural Diversity in the United States

The United States has seen a tremendous increase in ethnic diversity over the past decade as immigration from Asia, Europe, and Central and South America has increased and birthrates among cultural minorities have risen rapidly. The 1990 U.S. Census revealed that nearly one in four Americans are people of color. This is the largest change in racial and ethnic composition in any one decade during the 20th century. By the year 2050, the U.S. Bureau of the Census projects that the Anglo population will decrease from its current 76% to 52%, and people of color will constitute 48% of the U.S. population ("The Numbers Game," 1993). Given this rate of growth in U.S. racial and ethnic diversity, the likelihood of intercultural problems in service delivery increases. If our policies and clinical practices are not culturally proficient, the needs of maltreated children will be neglected.

Underrepresentation of Professionals From Diverse Backgrounds

Although people of color are overrepresented in child protective services (CPS) populations (see Table 22.1), professionals of color appear to be underrepresented in the fields of social work and psychology. In 1993, only 9.1% of the National Association of Social Work (NASW) members (Gilbelman & Schervish, 1993) and 5.1% of the American Psychological Association (APA) members (APA Education Directorate, 1993) were identified as people of color. These figures only indicate how many professionals of color are members of these organizations and therefore do not offer an exact percentage of professionals of color in the field. However, they do suggest a substantial shortage when looked at in conjunction with statistics such as those of the Council for Social Work Education, which reports that in 1991-1992, only 17.1% of those receiving a master's degree in social work were people of color (Lennon, 1993). These shortages may reflect a number of factors: Undergraduate and graduate programs in relevant areas may not recruit and retain students of color adequately, hiring and promotion practices may be discriminatory, and qualified candidates of color may be lured away by increased opportunities (Gilbelman & Schervish, 1993).

The relative scarcity of professionals of color in the fields is not a problem that can be solved easily or quickly, and recruiting more professionals of color is not the entire solution. Although there al-

TABLE 22.1 Comparative Rates of Substantiated Child Abuse Reports and U.S. Population by Ethnicity, 1990

Percentage	African American	Asian-Pacific Islander	Native American	Hispanic	White	Unknown/ Other
U.S. Census Report[a]	12.10	2.9	.80	9.00	80.3	4.00
Substantiated Reports AHA	24.44	.81	1.65	8.45	55.91	8.74

NOTE: a. Total exceeds 100% due to an individual's possible inclusion in multiple categories.

ways will be clients who desire ethnic match, it is not always feasible nor is it always a client's choice. The idea that being a member of a particular ethnic group makes one automatically cognizant of and sensitive to cultural issues is a myth. Within each cultural group, there is much heterogeneity resulting from varying levels of assimilation, acculturation, and socioeconomic status. The match or fit that we must aim for derives from expanding our worldview and increasing our empathy for those who are different from us. As increasing numbers of people of color enter the social service system, an increasing percentage of professionals of all colors must be able to respond to their needs in a culturally competent and sensitive manner.

Inadequate Delivery of Social and Mental Health Services

The failure of professionals to be culturally competent is reflected in a number of ways in the delivery of social and mental health services. One consequence of this failure, although not immediately seen as such, is the overrepresentation of children of color in the child protection system. The American Humane Association (AHA) national data for 1990 on substantiated reports of child maltreatment indicate that the ethnic diversity of children in the system is far greater than that found in the nation (NCCAN, 1990) (see Table 22.1). For instance, African Americans and Native Americans represent 12% and .8% of the U.S. population, respectively, yet represent 24% and 1.7% of substantiated child abuse reports—double their representation in the general population. In sharp contrast, whites and Asian/Pacific Islanders represent 80% and 3% of the population, respectively, but only 56% and .8% of substantiated

child maltreatment reports. Hispanic children are about equally represented in substantiated reports and in the general population.

Gathering data on the incidence and prevalence of child maltreatment in various ethnic groups is a methodological challenge, and, to date, our attempts have been flawed. This may be due, in part, to the difficulty of disentangling social class and cultural difference in a society in which people of color are more likely than whites to hold lower socioeconomic status and lack access to powerful institutions (Garbarino & Ebata, 1983). In addition, substantiation rates may be affected by factors such as sampling biases and professionals' perceptions of the behavior of those being reported. Racial and ethnic stereotypes, poverty, drug availability, and the culturally sanctioned use of physical discipline may leave African Americans and Native Americans more vulnerable to reporting and subsequent substantiation. In contrast, lower rates of substantiated reports for Asian American children may be due not only to the lower incidence of child abuse in these communities but also to professional stereotypes regarding Asian "passivity" and the view of Asians as the "model minority" (Sue & Sue, 1990, p. 192).

Although not definitive evidence, these disproportionate substantiation rates raise concerns about the cultural competence of professionals in the field of child protection. One could speculate that if professionals understood the worldview of their clients and had adequate awareness of their own stereotyped ideas and biases, these rates might be a closer approximation of the prevalence of child abuse in communities of color. Concern about the cultural competence of professionals is only heightened by the data on the delivery of social and mental health services.

As child abuse professionals, we are all concerned that social and mental health services be delivered in the most efficacious manner. Unfortunately, there is much evidence indicating that services for clients of color are inadequate. In a series of research studies done by Sue and associates in 1974 and 1975, it was revealed that 50% of people of color terminate treatment after just one contact with the mental health system as compared to a rate of 30% for whites. The primary reasons cited were the lack of nonwhite staff, the traditional way in which services were delivered, poor response to education and vocational needs of clients, and an antagonistic response to culture, class, and language-bound variables (Sue & Sue, 1990).

Reviewing the evidence on the fate of families of color in public social service systems, one researcher concluded, "Once children and families of color enter child welfare systems, there is evidence which indicates differential treatment with regard to what services are provided, both in terms of quantity and quality" (Harris, 1990). A 1980 study indicated that assessment and intervention is "harsher" for families of color. Another study cited higher rates of out-of-home placements for children of color than for Anglo children, different and more restrictive referral and diagnostic patterns for African American children, and a disproportionate number of these children in less desirable placements (Stehno, 1982). In Los Angeles County, the rate of African American children going into the CPS system is four times higher than that for whites (Swinger, 1993). Nationally, 50% of children in out-of-home care are children of color, even though they comprise only 20% of the population (Keys, 1991). These statistics suggest a link between inadequate service delivery and placement of children of color in more restricted levels of care.

These higher rates cannot be explained simply by a higher incidence or greater severity of child abuse in communities of color, but, more likely, they appear to be a consequence of greater poverty in communities of color.

Impoverished people depend more on publicly funded social and mental health systems that, when not culturally competent, result in overscrutiny and misunderstandings of people of color. In addition, poverty leaves people powerless to deal with these massive governmental systems, so that parents are less able to challenge removal of children from their homes.

Approaching Culturally Different Clients

Culture affects all levels of service delivery. Practitioners and administrators must take into account the culture of their service populations and the impact of their response to these populations to ensure effective service delivery. The challenges to service delivery encompass variables of culture, class, and language (Sue & Sue, 1990). For instance, white professionals in the field usually have Western world beliefs that are brought into the treatment room. As a result, their focus tends to be on the individual: They tend to stress cause and effect; value insight, openness, and verbal expressiveness; and believe that the best family is a nuclear family. As professionals, many of us, from all cultures, share middle-class values such as long-range planning and strict adherence to time schedules; we have a high tolerance for ambiguity and use only standard English.

What happens when the professional encounters the culturally different client?

What happens when the professional encounters the culturally different client? A poor working-class client often does not view self-disclosure as healthy or safe, due to numerous experiences with racism and oppression. These clients are more likely to believe in collectivism, have an intuitive approach to life, have a great reliance on extended family, think more about today than tomorrow, and believe there is little time for insight because they must figure out how to feed the children and pay the rent. Used to waiting endlessly at public institutions, clients arrive at the agency an hour late expecting to be seen and then do not speak a language or dialect the professional can understand easily. Because professional behavior is mediated by client behavior and vice versa

(Ridley, 1985), the fit needed to work effectively may not be possible.

Subtle or unconscious, stereotypical or value-laden attitudes of the professional and client may be communicated and responded to verbally or nonverbally, precipitating a potentially negative and destructive interactive dynamic. The subjective worldviews of client and professional, reflective of each individual's cultural experience, can collide and result in what Stolorow and Atwood (1992, p. 103) describe as "intersubjective dysjunction." Professional or client may assimilate the other's communications in such a way that the meaning of these communications can be altered grossly and lead to misunderstandings.

So how do we address the cultural needs of our clients in a culturally sensitive and competent fashion? There are three aspects to cultural competency, which when addressed at all levels of service will improve cross-cultural interactions and enable professionals to better provide services to the culturally different client: *value base, knowledge,* and *methods.*

Value Base

Value base describes the ideals, customs, attitudes, practices, and beliefs that one deems as worthy and useful and stimulate, within that individual, a strong emotional response. Each of us sees the world through culture-colored glasses. We compare others and process events based on our own value systems. A professional's value base should have an earnest appreciation of three factors: (a) the dynamics of difference, (b) the existence of individual and institutional biases and the sometimes subtle but immense power of myths of stereotypes in our interactions, and (c) the essential need to empower the disenfranchised. An appropriate value base is the most important aspect to culturally competent practice. Without it our knowledge and methods mean little.

Dynamics of Difference

More often than not, difference creates dynamics that in many cultures lead to negative learning experiences. Individuals become hostile when faced with someone different. Freud (1918) termed this *the narcissism of minor differences* and saw it as a result of narcissistic injury: "It is precisely the minor differences in people who are otherwise alike that form the basis of feelings of strangeness and hostility between them" (p. 199). Martin Luther King, Jr. (1964) linked this hostility to fear of the unknown. History is full of accounts depicting the inhumane treatment of those deemed by society as different (e.g., the Salem witch trials, the Holocaust, the lynching of African Americans, the treatment of Muslims in Bosnia).

In the field of mental health, difference often seems to become synonymous with pathology. When the behavior of a culturally different client is not understood, it may be labeled as a negative transference response or viewed as indicative of severe pathology. The following is a fictitious case example that is not atypical.

G. is an 8-year-old African American female who had been physically abused by her mother. She was referred by a white clinical social worker for educational and psychological testing after completion of the initial intake. The social worker reported that during the interview, G. was timid, shy, offered little verbal communication, and did not play and described G. as "immature and possibly, developmentally delayed." A week later, the newly assigned African American child welfare worker did a home visit and within this setting saw a very different child. He arrived to find G. crossing the street, laundry basket and siblings in tow. The worker accompanied G. to the laundromat, where he observed her counting money, washing the family's clothes, and disciplining her siblings. He was able to engage her in a lengthy conversation about home and school. Having read the social worker's evaluation, he left G. feeling very puzzled.

These contrasting pictures of G. can be explained by looking more closely at the different contexts within which these observations were made. The first view of G. was from a white social worker in a university clinic staffed primarily by whites and displaying artwork and media from the white culture. At best, this had to be alienating, frightening, and overwhelming for G., who was undoubtedly already anxious about having to disclose her mother's abusive behavior of her. The second view of G. was from an African American worker in an environment familiar to G., an environment she negotiated daily and within which she proved herself to be competent.

Research findings on the diagnosis of the culturally different client suggest increased pathologizing of these groups. Nonwhites are given more severe diagnoses than middle-class whites (Adebimpe, 1981; Carter, 1974; Marsella & Pedersen, 1981). Nonwhite children (ages 10-17) are hospitalized at a rate three times higher than that for whites (Shiloh & Selavan, 1974), and nonwhites (ages 11-43) are almost twice as likely as whites to be given a diagnosis of schizophrenia (DHEW, 1977). In addition, the culturally different patient is at high risk to receive inferior and biased treatment because many hold a lower socioeconomic status (Learner, 1972; Lorion, 1973, 1974; Pavkov, Lewis, & Lyons, 1989; Powell & Powell, 1983; Yamamoto et al., 1968).

Culturally different clients are faced with the fact of their difference from the moment they enter most treatment facilities or child welfare offices, which tend to display media from the white culture.

Culturally different clients are faced with the fact of their difference from the moment they enter most treatment facilities or child welfare offices, which tend to display media from the white culture and may require interactions with workers outside their particular culture. This makes a very powerful statement to clients, communicating a sense of their invisibility in this society and triggering feelings of alienation and hostility as described clearly in Ellison's *Invisible Man* (1947). It is the professional's role to explore such feelings empathically and attempt to understand the patient's subjective reality rather than to respond by pathologizing or defensively assuming no responsibility for the patient's response. Differences between client and professional can lead to positive learning experiences for professionals and a curative experience for the client, if responses of ignorance, fear, antagonism, and hostility are avoided. The culturally different client can enhance professional growth and

development, and if approached with *sustained empathic inquiry,* the mutually decided on goals of treatment can be attained (Stolorow, Brandchaft, & Atwood, 1987).

Accepting the Existence of Biases, Myths, and Stereotypes

The professional's value base must include room for the fact that individual and institutional biases do exist and that these biases slant toward the worldview, well-being, and desires of the majority culture. Accepting this fact will positively influence the care delivered at two levels. It allows the clinician to better meet particular needs of an individual client and offers the treating institution an opportunity to explore its own biases that directly affect a community's use of the facility.

The biases of the white culture affect the lives of people of color on a daily basis and at numerous levels (e.g., housing access, job availability, educational and social opportunities). Regardless of the presenting complaint, the culturally different client will bring this issue into treatment, at some point, on a manifest or latent level. As with other reality-based issues, the client will require support for this.

For instance, a Latina mother in a Parent's United program may complain it is taking her longer than Anglo mothers in similar situations to regain custody of her children. She believes this is the result of discrimination and consequently becomes depressed at what she views as the hopelessness of her predicament. The well-meaning clinician, who does not believe such biases exist in 1993 and knows that this patient tends to project, may, without malicious intent, invalidate the patient's complaint by ignoring it and encouraging her to look at her defensive behavior as the *real* cause of the problem. A more effective response is to first investigate the possibility of bias and, if needed, advocate for the woman. If after some investigation it appears bias is not the cause of delayed reunification, exploration and interpretation of the issue are appropriate.

The child maltreatment professional also must accept the power of myths and stereotypes in the field and in our society. All of us are affected in some way by these myths and stereotypes. Sue and Sue (1990) define *stereotypes* as "rigid preconceptions we hold about *all* people who are members of a particular group, whether it be defined along racial, religious, sexual, or other lines" (p. 47). Myths and stereotypes are perpetrated in a variety ways but most particularly by mass media and flawed research. For instance, studies have documented that white counselors often believe African Americans are paranoid and angry and more likely to suffer from the character disorders (Evans, 1985; Jones, 1985; Willie, Kramer, & Brown, 1973) and schizophrenia (Pavkov et al., 1989). The list of racial and ethnic myths and stereotypes is long and cannot be explored fully here, but no one can escape exposure to them. One of the most destructive beliefs is the assumption of homogeneity within minority ethnic groups. A mistake often is made in believing that all Asians, Native Americans, African Americans, or Latinos are alike, despite the fact that individuals within minority ethnic groups vary as much as those in majority ethnic groups.

Empowerment

The child maltreatment professional also must value the notion of empowerment as a treatment goal. It is a goal that has been recognized for more than a decade by the child welfare system as a crucial aspect of family preservation. Empowerment is a process that enables clients to exert their personal power to obtain needed emotional, physical, or social resources. Sue and Sue (1990) understand empowerment as a worldview that embraces the belief that the *locus of control* rests with the individual rather than an external force. Most clinicians would agree that this worldview is one that offers clients greater ability to master the environment and function in healthy ways.

Powerlessness is an ever-present and well-accepted effect of child abuse trauma. Powerlessness is also a feeling that people of color often are faced with because of their minority group status and overrepresentation in the poverty class. Research has documented that the poor and people of color tend to believe more in an external locus of control (Sue & Sue, 1990). Frequent discrimination, decreased employment and educational opportunities, racial and ethnic stereotypes, and poverty make it difficult for an individual to feel powerful, especially when combined with the effects of child-

hood trauma. Feelings of powerlessness are increased further when paternalistic public agencies must intervene in one's life.

Empowerment skills offer clients an opportunity to negotiate the various systems that affect their lives in ways that may provoke feelings of frustration and helplessness. In practice, a professional can model and teach clients how to use power by initially advocating openly for the client. However, later the professional needs to help clients move out of the passive role by sharing power with them. This means involving clients in the advocacy process that enables use of the client's power as an individual. Without clients' involvement, the professional risks becoming a patron and perpetuating clients' powerlessness (Pinderhughes, 1983). Solomon (1985) argues that an empowerment-based practice recognizes client strengths. It is a practice in which the client and clinician collaborate as peers in the solving of problems. Instead of telling a client how to change, the professional might better ask how the client would like to change and work toward that goal mutually.

Heger and Hunzeker (1988) point out the complexity of teaching empowerment skills to children whose "powerlessness is unavoidable because they lack experience, maturity, and the resources to meet their own needs" (p. 501). They suggest offering children experiences that encourage mastery and a sense of belonging:

> These include association with valued adults who demonstrate empowerment; strong ties with sources of identity, including biological kin, ethnic heritage, and religious tradition; age-appropriate participation in decisions; and involvement in building a network of relationships and institutional supports that will sustain children into adulthood. (p. 501)

Knowledge

The second key aspect of cultural competency requires that professionals be informed from a phenomenological point of view and have knowledge of several factors. First, it is important to understand the influence of culture on perceptions (including those formed in transference and countertransference responses), behaviors, sex roles, interactions, expectations, and modes of communication (verbal and nonverbal). Second, professionals should study the history of racism and oppression to gain an understanding of the individual's response and adaptation to it. Membership in an oppressed group has a profound effect on the individual's identity and life experience.

Third, the professional must gain knowledge of the individual client's culture by becoming familiar with its child-rearing practices, sex roles, family structure, religious beliefs, worldview, community characteristics, and levels of acculturation or assimilation. This knowledge must be used cautiously with an assumption that such information is only a generalization and should not be used to stereotype. Fourth, understanding social class and its impact is also crucial. Many factors that appear related to culture are better correlated with socioeconomic status, but separating the two is a difficult task. Fifth, professionals must work from an unbiased theoretical base. Contemporary relational theories, such as those of the interpersonal/cultural school, social constructivists, or intersubjectivity and cultural variance theory, lend themselves to working cross-culturally. Last, although there never may be agreement on a set of universal criteria of child abuse, as Korbin (1981) suggests, in determining what constitutes child maltreatment, professionals must take into account the physical and emotional harm done to a child, parental intent, and socialization goals of the culture.

Methods

The third aspect of cultural competency concerns the methods used in professional practice, research, and the development of human resources. Professionals must develop their ability to diagnose, determine, and adapt clinically to culturally based values, viewpoints, attitudes, and behavior patterns. Current research practices and databases must be improved and expanded. Resource development is needed within the workforce,

in the community, and at the funding level. For example, support systems and informal helping networks can be created through consultation with various members at different community levels. Finally, we must view cultural competency as an integral part of professional training programs and practice standards and develop tools, at all levels of practice, like that of the Northwest Indian Child Welfare Association (work in progress), which assesses an organization's level of cultural competency.

Conclusions

Although knowing all there is to know about a particular culture is not possible from an outsider's vantage point, it is possible to work effectively in a cross-cultural context if certain givens are accepted. The trauma of abuse and neglect is experienced and organized from the subjective viewpoint of the individual. It is a viewpoint derived from the individual's entire life experience, which includes cultural identification. The child maltreatment professional approaches clients from a viewpoint organized by similar factors. Both client and professional come to the interaction with values derived from cultural experience. The space in which the viewpoint of professional and client meets holds the potential for meaningful work and change. Through *sustained empathic inquiry* (Stolorow et al., 1987) and an appreciation of subjectivity and interactive dynamics, the professional can work competently with the culturally different client.

Social and mental health delivery for children and families of color have suffered from a lack of cultural awareness, acceptance, and professional competence. The increased diversity within the United States presents a challenge that only can be met if cultural competency is regarded as a standard professional skill supported by a valid theory, knowledge, and methods.

References

Adebimpe, V. (1981). Overview: White norms and psychiatric diagnosis of black patients. *American Journal of Psychiatry, 138,* 279-285.

Allen, W. R. (1978). The search for applicable theories of black family life. *Journal of Marriage and the Family, 40,* 117-129.

APA Education Directorate. (1993). *1993 APA directory survey.* Washington, DC: American Psychological Association.

Baratz, S., & Baratz, J. (1970). Early childhood intervention: The social sciences base of institutional racism. *Harvard Educational Review, 40,* 29-50.

Carter, J. (1974). Recognizing psychiatric symptoms in black Americans. *Geriatrics, 29,* 97-99.

DHEW. (1977). *Psychiatric services and the changing institutional scene, 1950-1975* (Publication No. [ADM] 717-433, NIMH Series B, No. 12). Washington, DC: Government Printing Office.

Ellison, R. (1947). *Invisible man.* New York: Random House.

Evans, D. A. (1985). Psychotherapy and black patients: Problems of training, trainees, and trainers. *Psychotherapy, 22,* 457-460.

Freud, S. (1918). The taboo of virginity. *Standard Edition, 11,* 191-208.

Garbarino, J., & Ebata, A. (1983). The significance of ethnic and cultural differences in child maltreatment. *Journal of Marriage and the Family, 45*(4), 773-783.

Gilbelman, M., & Schervish, P. H. (1993). *Who we are: The social work labor force as reflected in the NASW membership.* Washington, DC: NASW.

Harris, N. (1990). Dealing with diverse cultures in child welfare. *Protecting Children, 7*(3), 6-7.

Heger, R. L., & Hunzeker, J. M. (1988). Moving toward empowerment-based practice in public child welfare. *Social Work, 33,* 499-502.

Jones, A. C. (1985). Psychological functioning in black Americans: A conceptual guide for use in psychotherapy. *Psychotherapy, 22,* 363-369.

Keys, H. (1991). The CWLA cultural responsiveness initiative: A status report. *APSAC Advisor, 4*(3), 12-13.

King, M. L. (1964). *Why we can't wait.* New York: Penguin.

Korbin, J. (1981). *Child abuse and neglect: Cross-cultural perspectives.* Berkeley: University of California Press.

Learner, B. (1972). *Therapy in the ghetto.* Baltimore, MD: Johns Hopkins University Press.

Lennon, T. M. (1993). *Statistics of social work education in the United States: 1992.* Alexandria, VA: Council on Social Work Education.

Lorion, R. P. (1973). Socioeconomic status and treatment approaches reconsidered. *Psychological Bulletin, 79,* 263-280.

Lorion, R. P. (1974). Patient and therapist variables in the treatment of low-income patients. *Psychological Bulletin, 81,* 344-354.

Marsella, A., & Pedersen, P. (Eds.). (1981). *Cross-cultural counseling and psychotherapy.* Elmsford, NY: Pergamon.

McKenna, J. J. (1990). Evolution and sudden infant death syndrome (SIDS), part I: Infant responsivity to parental content. *Human Nature, 1*(2), 145-177.

NCCAN. (1990). *Summary data component* (Working paper no. 1). Washington, DC: Author.

Northwest Indian Child Welfare Association, Inc. (work in progress). *Organizational self-study on cultural competence for agencies addressing child abuse and neglect* (NCCAN Grant No. 90CA1443). Washington, DC: People of Color Leadership Institute.

The numbers game. (1993). *Time, 142*(21), 14-15.

Parson, E. R. (1985). Ethnicity and traumatic stress: The intersecting point in psychotherapy. In C. R. Figley (Ed.), *Trauma and its wake: The study and treatment of post-traumatic stress disorder* (Vol. 1, pp. 315-337). New York: Brunner/Mazel.

Pavkov, T. W., Lewis, D. A., & Lyons, J. S. (1989). Psychiatric diagnosis and racial bias: An empirical investigation. *Professional Psychology: Research & Practice, 20,* 364-368.

Pinderhughes, E. (1983). Empowerment for our clients and for ourselves. *Social Casework, 64,* 331-338.

Powell, G., & Powell, R. (1983). Poverty: The greatest and severest handicapping condition in childhood. In G. Powell (Ed.), *The psychosocial development of minority group children* (pp. 573-580). New York: Brunner/Mazel.

Random house dictionary of the English language: College edition. (1968). New York: Author.

Ridley, C. R. (1985). Pseudo-transference in interracial psychotherapy: an operant paradigm. *Journal of Contemporary Psychotherapy, 15*(1), 29-36.

Shiloh, A., & Selavan, I. C. (Eds.). (1974). *Ethnic groups in America: Their morbidity, mortality and behavior disorders: Vol. II. The blacks.* Springfield, IL: Charles C Thomas.

Solomon, B. B. (1985). How do we really empower families? New strategies for social work practitioners. *Family Resource Coalition—FRC Report, 3,* 2-3.

Stehno, S. M. (1982). Differential treatment of minority children in service systems. *Social Work,* *27*(1), 39-46.

Stolorow, R. D., & Atwood, G. E. (1992). *Contexts of being: The intersubjective foundations of psychological life.* Hillsdale, NJ: Analytic Press.

Stolorow, R. D., Brandchaft, B., & Atwood, G. E. (1987). *Psychoanalytic treatment: An intersubjective approach.* Hillsdale, NJ: Analytic Press.

Sue, D. W., & Sue, D. (1990). *Counselling the culturally different: Theory and practice.* New York: John Wiley.

Swinger, H. (1993, January). *Cross cultural considerations in working with African American families.* Paper presented at the San Diego Conference on Responding to Child Maltreatment, La Jolla, CA.

Willie, C. V., Kramer, B. M., & Brown, B. S. (1973). *Racism and mental health.* Pittsburgh: University of Pittsburgh Press.

Yamamoto, J., James, J. C., & Palley, N. (1968). Cultural problems in psychiatric therapy. *Archives of General Psychiatry, 19,* 45-59.

Epilogue

RICHARD D. KRUGMAN

Readers of this handbook will have found an enormous amount of useful information to enable them to recognize, assess, medically diagnose, treat, and even prevent the abuse of children effectively. The gap between what the ideal child protection system in the United States should be and what it is, however, is wide and getting wider every year. In June 1990, the U.S. Advisory Board on Child Abuse and Neglect, which had studied the problems faced by the child protection system in the United States, declared that the system was a national emergency. It still exists, unaddressed by nearly every executive and legislative branch on all levels of government in the United States.

First, to be clear, when the board used the words "child protection system," it described the multidisciplinary network of professionals, which includes social work, law enforcement, mental health, health, the judiciary, education, and any other professional or layperson who was part of a community's multidisciplinary network available to protect children. The board declared the emergency based on the following: (a) In spite of its avowed aim to protect children, the numbers of children abused and neglected annually had risen continuously for several decades to the point that well over a million children were *known* to have been abused and neglected in 1989. (b) Billions of dollars are being spent on the downstream effects of abuse and neglect of this and the last generation of children. (c) The system that was supposed to be protecting children was failing. It was overwhelmed with cases, underfunded, and staffed with individuals who were, for the most part, entry-level professionals with little training, huge caseloads, and inadequate support from either their own supervisory agencies or consultants from medicine, law, and mental health that should have been helping them.

How did this happen? And what might be done to reverse it?

In September 1991, the board's second report focused on the federal role in trying to address the emergency and, because the response of the federal government to the first report had been underwhelming, repeated several recommendations and called for, among other things, the stimulation of universal voluntary neonatal home visitation in an effort to prevent the physical abuse and neglect of children. The board, in a statement issued in September 1992, pointed out that the emergency still existed and that, in spite of Secretary Louis Sullivan's "initiative," the gap between what needed to be done for children and what was being done was growing wider every year.

The recognition of sexual abuse of children over the past decade and a half has in many ways exacerbated the inability of the child protection system to work effectively. Part of the difficulty is that unlike physical abuse and neglect, which has been for 20 years entirely dealt with through the civil court system and rarely treated as a criminal offense, sexual abuse of children is treated as a criminal offense universally (as it should be). This dichotomy has created significant difficulties for child protective services agencies, which were not used to criminal investigation, and it has created significant difficulties from a policy perspective because the criminal system requires higher standards of proof, and the nature of sexual abuse is such that those standards are difficult to meet.

In its September 1991 report, the board stated that one of the first priorities for the federal, state, and local governments would be to state their child protection policy clearly. It is my view that most communities (and many professionals) in the United States really have not decided how they want to protect children from sexual abuse, in part because sexual abuse is so emotionally distressing and also because it is so clearly a crime against children that society's inclination is to use the criminal justice system to try to punish those who sexually abuse children. As noted above, however, and throughout this handbook, the absence of physical findings (such as the fractures or burns found on physically abused children) and the usual absence of witnesses leave those wishing to prosecute this crime in a very difficult situation. The number of children who are sexually abused in the United States is substantially greater than the number of children whose sexual abuse cases come into the criminal justice system. That leaves the question for communities, professionals, and the country at large to answer how we are going to *protect* those children from ongoing sexual abuse. Although it is true that criminal prosecution of perpetrators will protect children from those perpetrators for the length of time that they are in jail, from a public health perspective, criminal prosecution is the least efficient method of protecting children from sexual abuse.

Twenty years ago, a coordinated child sexual abuse treatment program was described involving civil and criminal courts, the mental health system, child welfare, and law enforcement. This multidisciplinary approach also used self-help groups and combinations of individual and group treatment under civil and criminal court jurisdiction to treat incestuous families. Numerous communities throughout the country tried to replicate the Santa Clara County experience, and some were successful. The reality is, however, that the heterogeneity within the United States does not make it likely that programs that work in one area easily can be transplanted or replicated throughout the United States. For such a coordinated system to work, professionals in child welfare, law enforcement, mental health, and the civil and criminal judiciary must all agree to work together. Equally important, all need to have a common approach rooted in a community child protection policy that is supportable both politically and economically. In most parts of the country, it has been my experience that there is no agreement on what the child protection policy should be in that community. The net result is that children enter a system in which some of the professionals believe that, given enough money and enough time, the perpetrator and family can be treated. Other professionals believe that because they know of no effective treatment, the only approach that works is the incarceration of perpetrators. This polarization leads to an untenable situation in which the child usually falls through the cracks, gets no treatment, and, in the worst case, the abuse continues. What is missing in this country is a true child-centered, neighborhood-based child protection system. By *child-centered* (because some view this phrase suspiciously), I mean a system that recognizes that the best place for a child is in the family and that efforts need to be made to keep families together, but it does not use the child as an instrument for treating a family that is dysfunctional and disturbed. It also recognizes that some families are untreatable and grants quick no-fault divorces of children from these families. Such a system has yet to develop in the United States. In its 1993 report, the Advisory Board suggested a model system that might be adapted for use nationally in the coming decade.

To protect children from sexual abuse as well as the other forms of abuse and neglect will require at least a decade-long effort to rebuild a child protection system that has collapsed in this country. It will mean that every profession and every agency will have to join with APSAC in taking this rebuilding as a priority. In 1993, many had high hopes that with the change in administration, this process might have begun. Three years later, it hasn't. The sad history of child protection in the United States over the past 30 years, however, recognizes that no administration, political party, or political movement in the United States has *ever* made abused and neglected children a priority, nor have any significant problems of child abuse and neglect been addressed in a way that has offered any hope of success. Republicans and Democrats, conservatives and liberals have much to be ashamed of over the past 30 years. Lip service and "initiatives" have not been enough. It's time for action.

Author Index

Abel, G., 63, 175, 176, 177, 178, 179, 180, 182, 252
Aber, J., 9, 10, 13, 15, 16, 27, 28, 29, 32
Abramowitz, S., 28
Abueg, F., 152
Achenbach, T., 12
Ackman, D., 55
Acton, R., 34
Adam, T., 29
Adams, J., 321, 331
Adams, W., 372
Adams-Wescott, J., 121
Adebimpe, V., 415
Adelman, L., 360
Adler, R., 215
Adnopoz, J., 83
Ainsworth, M., 9, 10, 38, 77, 106, 159
Akman, D., 123, 330
Albanese, M., 209
Alessandri, S., 26, 28, 31
Alexander, P., 53, 61, 64, 105, 106-107, 129, 142, 149, 166, 180
Alexander, R., 213, 214, 221
Allen, D., 28, 29, 30, 36
Allen, J., 15, 28, 29
Allen, W., 411
Altemeier, W., 14
Alterman, A., 28
Alvarez, W., 62, 222
Aman, C., 299, 301
Ammerman, R., 21, 23, 24, 30, 231
Ammons, P., 162, 163, 232
Amundson, M., 35
Anderson, P., 349
Anderson, W., 177
Antler, J., 389, 390, 391
Antler, S., 362, 371, 372, 389, 390, 391, 392
Apfel, N., 84, 345
Apollo, J., 208, 214
Aragona, J., 133, 163, 231

Ards, S., 364
Aries, P., 121
Arkinson, M., 162
Arkowitz, H., 26
Armentrout, J., 177
Arnold, L., 177
Arrington, E., 41
Asdigian, N., 405
Asen, K., 35
Asher, S., 305
Atkenson, B., 14
Atkins, M., 56, 104
Atwood, G., 409, 414, 415, 417
Augoustinos, M., 28
Austin, G., 297
Austin, M., 348
Avery, L., 162
Ayoub, C., 35, 36, 41
Azar, S., 21, 23, 24, 26, 27, 28, 30, 31, 33, 34, 35, 37, 38, 160, 231, 232, 344

Baglow, L., 33, 36
Baily, F., 72, 168
Baily, W., 72, 168
Bain, J., 180
Baird, D., 374
Baird, P., 202
Baker, J., 311
Baker-Ward, L., 302
Baldwin, D., 26
Ball, W., 218
Ballantine, T., 215
Bandman, R., 212
Bandura, A., 179
Barahal, R., 30
Baratz, J., 411
Baratz, S., 411
Barbaree, H., 176, 177, 178, 179, 182, 185, 186
Barlow, B., 207
Barnes, K., 23
Barnett, D., 29, 36, 80, 109, 168
Barnett, M., 203

Barnum, R., 25
Baron, L., 53, 61
Barone, N., 372
Barr, J., 347
Barrett, K., 113
Barrett, M., 112, 126, 180
Barron, B., 212
Barsky, A., 203
Bartell, P., 377
Barth, R., 34, 35, 345, 346, 350
Basham, R., 14
Basta, S., 55
Bates, J., 32
Batterman-Faunce, J., 302, 310
Baum, C., 23
Bauman, K., 345
Bays, J., 326
Bays, L., 185
Bazron, B., 348
Beauchamp, C., 345
Beaver, B., 214
Becerra, R., 227
Beck, A., 134
Beck, S., 178
Becker, J., 63, 176, 178
Beckwith, L., 345
Beckworth, B., 84
Beezley, P., 8
Beilke, R., 56, 57, 104, 105, 111, 330
Beitchman, J., 55, 123, 128, 330
Bell, R., 14, 30, 376
Bell, T., 200
Belsky, J., 13, 14, 23, 24, 27, 28, 29, 31, 35, 38, 228, 231, 344
Benedek, E., 80, 376
Benedict, M., 231
Bentovim, A., 63, 180
Berdie, J., 132
Berdie, M., 132
Bergman, A., 31
Bergmann, B., 377
Berkowitz, C., 201, 236
Berkowitz, L., 38

Subject Index

About the Editors

John Briere, PhD, is Associate Professor in the Departments of Psychiatry and Psychology at the University of Southern California School of Medicine and a Clinical Psychologist in the Department of Emergency Psychiatric Services of the LAC-USC Medical Center. He is author of various articles and book chapters, primarily in the areas of child abuse, psychological trauma, and interpersonal violence. He is on the editorial boards of several scholarly journals and is a member of the board of directors of the American Professional Society on the Abuse of Children (APSAC) and the International Society for Traumatic Stress Studies (ISTSS). Dr. Briere is author of the books *Therapy for Adults Molested as Children: Beyond Survival* and *Child Abuse Trauma: Theory and Treatment of the Lasting Effects,* as well as an upcoming book for the American Psychological Association on assessing posttraumatic stress. He has edited two clinical sourcebooks titled *Treating Victims of Child Sexual Abuse* and *Assessing and Treating Victims of Violence.* He is author of the *Trauma Symptom Inventory* (TSI), a psychological test published by Psychological Assessment Resources, and the *Trauma Symptom Checklist for Children* (TSCC), due to be released by Psychological Assessment Resources in early 1996.

Lucy Berliner, MSW, is a Clinical Associate Professor at the University of Washington Graduate School of Social Work. Since 1973, she has worked at the Harborview Sexual Assault Center, a specialty clinic of a University of Washington teaching hospital. Her activities include clinical interventions with sexual assault victims/families, conducting research on various aspects of sexual victimization of children, lecturing, writing, and promoting public policy on behalf of sexual assault victims. She is Associate Editor of the *Journal of Interpersonal Violence,* on the editorial board of the *Journal of Child Abuse and Neglect,* on the board of directors at the National Center for Missing and Exploited Children, and on the advisory board at the National Resource Center on Child Sexual Abuse, the Association for the Treatment of Sexual Abusers, the American Professional Society on the Abuse of Children, and the National Center for the Prosecution of Child Abuse.

Josephine A. Bulkley, JD, is a consulting attorney with the American Bar Association's (ABA) Center on Children and the Law, where she has directed projects relating to the legal issues in child sexual abuse cases since 1979. She was responsible for some of the first legal writings and policy recommendations regarding sexual abuse of children, including *Child Sexual Abuse and the Law, Innovations in the Prosecution of Child Sexual Abuse Cases, Protecting Child Victim/Witnesses: Sample Laws and Materials,* and *Sexual Abuse Allegations in Custody and Visitation Cases.* She has published numerous articles, chapters, and ABA reports, and courts, legislatures, and prosecutors throughout the country have relied on her work. She has lectured throughout the United States and provided training and technical assistance to communities, attorneys, legislators, and judges, as well as other professionals involved in child abuse cases. She was on the founding Board of Directors of the American Professional Society on the Abuse of Children and has served as Legal Editor of the *APSAC Advisor* and on the editorial boards of various journals. In 1984, she was a staff person to the U.S. House of Representatives' Select Committee on Children, Youth and Families. Ms. Bulkley is a graduate of the National Cathedral School for Girls, holds a BA from the University of Michigan and her law degree from Antioch School of Law, and currently is seeking her master's degree in social work from the Catholic University of America.

Carole Jenny, MD, MBA, is the Director of the Child Advocacy and Protection Team at the Children's Hospital in Denver, Colorado, and is Associate Professor of Pediatrics at the University of Colorado School of Medicine. She also directs medical programs at the C. Henry Kempe National Center for the Prevention and Treatment of Child Abuse and Neglect. She recently served on the board of directors of the American Professional Society on the Abuse of Children and is Chair of the Executive Committee of the Section on Child Abuse and Neglect of the American Academy of Pediatrics. She attended the University of Missouri, Dartmouth Medical School, and the University of Washington. She was an intern in Pediatrics at the University of Colorado and a resident at the Children's Hospital of Philadelphia. After her residency, she was a Robert Wood Johnson Clinical Scholar at the University of Pennsylvania and received an MBA in Health Care from the Wharton School. Dr. Jenny's research interests include sexually transmitted diseases, head trauma in infants, and the use of colposcopy in the evaluation of sexual abuse and assault.

Theresa Reid, MA, is the Executive Director of the American Professional Society on the Abuse of Children (APSAC). She has directed the growth of the organization from start-up to the largest professional society in the field of child abuse and neglect. She edits and manages all APSAC publications, including the *APSAC Advisor, Child Maltreatment: Journal of the American Professional Society on the Abuse of Children,* and *APSAC Guidelines for Practice.* She oversees and facilitates the operation of 20 standing board committees, 40 APSAC state chapters, membership services, and planning for and implementation of APSAC's annual National Colloquium. Ms. Reid is a member of the American Association for Protecting Children, the American Society of Association Executives, and the International Society for the Prevention of Child Abuse and Neglect. She is on the research committee of the National Committee to Prevent Child Abuse and is a member of the State Advisory Group on National Child Abuse and Neglect Data Systems (NCANDS). Ms. Reid is finishing her doctorate in English at the University of Chicago.

About the Contributors

Veronica D. Abney, LCSW, BCD, is a licensed clinical social worker and board-certified diplomate on the staff and clinical faculty of UCLA's Neuropsychiatric Hospital and Institute in Los Angeles, where she is Coordinator of the Suspected Child Abuse and Neglect (SCAN) Team. She also has a private practice in Santa Monica specializing in the treatment of child, adolescent, and adult survivors of childhood sexual trauma. As a senior candidate member of the Institute of Contemporary Psychoanalysis, she is interested in the application of modern psychoanalytic theories in cross-cultural and adult survivor treatment. Ms. Abney is on the board of directors of the American Professional Society on the Abuse of Children and the California Professional Society on the Abuse of Children. She is an Associate Editor of *Child Maltreatment: Journal of the American Professional Society on the Abuse of Children* and the *APSAC Advisor.* Her publications include *Transference and Countertransference Issues Unique to Long-Term Group Psychotherapy of Adult Women Molested as Children: The Trials and Rewards, A Rationale for Cultural Competency,* and *African Americans and Sexual Child Abuse.*

Maureen Black, PhD, is an Associate Professor in the Department of Pediatrics at the University of Maryland School of Medicine and Director of the Growth and Nutrition Clinic. She is a developmental psychologist who specializes in intervention research involving the prevention of developmental and emotional problems among vulnerable children and their families. She is a Fellow of the American Psychological Association and a past president of the Division on Child, Youth, and Family Services.

Barbara L. Bonner, PhD, is a Clinical Child Psychologist, Associate Professor in the Department of Pediatrics at the University of Oklahoma Health Sciences Center, and Director of the Center on Child Abuse and Neglect. Her clinical and research interests include the assessment and treatment of abused children and adolescents, the prevention of child fatalities, and the treatment of children and adolescents with inappropriate or illegal sexual behavior. She established a treatment program for adolescent sex offenders in 1986 and has presented seminars on the program throughout the United States and in several foreign countries. Currently, she is directing a 5-year research project funded by the National Center on Child Abuse and Neglect to compare two approaches to treatment for children with sexual behavior problems.

Marla R. Brassard, PhD, is a faculty member in Developmental and Educational Psychology at Teachers College, Columbia University. She previously has been on the faculty at the Universities of Utah and Georgia and most recently has spent the past 9 years in the School and Counseling Psychology Program at the University of Massachusetts at Amherst. Clinically, she has consulted in the schools and a prison, directed the UMASS assessment clinic, and has a small forensic private practice. Her research has focused on issues of psychological assessment of children and their families and child maltreatment. She is particularly interested in the psychological maltreatment of children and the relational aspects of family life and school environments that promote and undermine children's interpersonal competence. She is the author of the book *The Psychological Maltreatment of Children and Youth,* more than 30 articles and chapters, and two scales related to psychological maltreatment and mental injury and is the coauthor of the APSAC *Practice Guidelines for the Psychosocial Evaluation of Suspected Psychological Maltreatment of Children and Adolescents.*

David L. Chadwick, MD, is Director of the Center for Child Protection at Children's Hospital in San Diego, one of the largest and most advanced health-based child abuse treatment centers in the United States. He has engaged in clinical work with abused children since 1960. Prior to his present position, he was Medical Director of Children's Hospital-San Diego for 17 years. Dr. Chadwick is the author or coauthor of many peer-reviewed articles dealing with a wide range of pediatric subjects as well as child abuse. He is the author of the chapter on child abuse in the textbook *Pediatrics* (18th ed.), edited by Abraham M. Rudolph. He lectures widely on child abuse to a variety of audiences and appears frequently in court as an expert witness in child abuse cases. He has been active in the American Academy of Pediatrics' efforts against child abuse and the American Medical Association's initiative to deal with violence as a health problem. He is a past president of the American Professional Society on the Abuse of Children and is a member of their advisory board.

Mark Chaffin, PhD, is a Psychologist at the University of Arkansas for Medical Sciences in Little Rock, where he serves on the faculty of the Department of Pediatrics. He is currently Director of the Arkansas Children's Hospital Family Treatment Program, which is a specialty clinic providing treatment for within-family child sexual abuse and sexual abusers. He is also director of the UAMS Adolescent Sexual Adjustment Program, which is a statewide network of residential and outpatient treatment programs for adolescent sexual abusers. He completed his

training at the University of Oklahoma and the University of Oklahoma Health Sciences Center. He has served on the board of directors of APSAC, as Executive Editor of the *APSAC Advisor,* and is currently Editor of *Child Maltreatment: Journal of the American Professional Society on the Abuse of Children.*

Patricia M. Crittenden, PhD, has a multidisciplinary background in developmental and clinical psychology as well as in special education. Her multidisciplinary experience includes teaching (normal and special education in high school, elementary school, and preschool); conducting social work, parent education, various types of intervention (individual, family, and group therapy; neighborhood support center); and administering the Miami Child Protection Team. Her empirical research is focused on maltreatment and attachment. Her research on maltreatment focuses on different subtypes of maltreatment (especially neglect and psychological maltreatment) and aspects of family functioning that vary by type of maltreatment. For this work, she received in 1994 the Gimbel Award for scholarship in the area of family and child violence. In her research on attachment, Dr. Crittenden is known for her work on atypical organizations of attachment associated with disturbed and maltreated infants and children. Her most recent work consists of a series of theoretical papers on the development of psychopathology across the life span. These papers address issues of multidimensional risk, the nonlinear process of development, and implications for prevention and treatment.

Deborah Daro, DSW, is the Director of the National Center on Child Abuse Prevention Research, a program of the National Committee to Prevent Child Abuse. Prior to this position, she served as the Director of the Family Welfare Research Group at the University of California, Berkeley, School of Social Welfare, and as a Vice-President of Berkeley Planning Associates, a private consulting firm in California. Throughout her career, Dr. Daro has sought to improve the quality of program evaluations through the development of innovative research designs and methods of data collection. These innovations include methods for comparing performance across different service models and obtaining reliable staff assessments on client functioning and progress. She has directed some of the largest multisite program evaluations completed in the field. The sizable samples generated through these efforts have allowed her to identify the most critical elements for effective service delivery with various maltreatment subpopulations. As both a lecturer and author, she has sought to translate research findings into products that are useful and relevant to the programmatic and policy issues facing direct service workers in the voluntary and public social service sectors.

Howard Dubowitz, MD, is Associate Professor of Pediatrics at the University of Maryland School of Medicine and Director of the Child Advocacy Program at the University of Maryland Hospital. He is Chair of the Maryland Academy of Pediatrics Committee on Child Maltreatment and on the Executive Committee of the American Professional Society for the Abuse of Children. He also serves on a number of other local and national boards. Dr. Dubowitz is involved in clinical work concerning physical and sexual abuse as well as neglect. He is very interested in physician education and has developed a model curriculum on child maltreatment for pediatric residents. His major research interests currently include a longitudinal study of child neglect, kinship care, and the mental health outcomes of sexual abuse. He is particularly interested in risk and protective factors in vulnerable children and families that are useful for clinical practice and public policy.

Byron Egeland, PhD, is the Irving B. Harris Professor of Child Development at the University of Minnesota. He is the Principal Investigator of the Mother-Child Project, a NIMH-funded, 19-year longitudinal study of high-risk children and their families. He and Martha Erickson were the coprincipal investigators of Project STEEP, a NIMH-funded prevention program for high-risk parents and their infants. He is one of the coinvestigators involved in the national evaluation and study of the JOBS and New Chance Programs for families on welfare. He is a fellow in the American Psychological Association, the American Psychological Society, and the American Association of Applied and Preventive Psychology. He is

on the board of directors of the National Committee for Prevention of Child Abuse, Children's Division of the American Humane Association, and the Youth Advisory Board, Boy Scouts of America. He has published articles and book chapters in the areas of child maltreatment, the development of high-risk children, factors influencing developmental and educational outcomes, child psychopathology, and intervention with high-risk families.

Diana M. Elliott, PhD, is Director of Training and Research at the Harbor-UCLA Child Abuse Crisis Center and Assistant Clinical Professor of Psychiatry at UCLA School of Medicine. At Harbor-UCLA, she conducts forensic evaluations of child victims of interpersonal violence. She also supervises psychotherapy trainees in crisis interventions with child rape and abuse victims, conducts long-term therapy with adult survivors of abuse, and provides training to residents and fellows on the evaluation and impact of interpersonal violence. In addition, she regularly provides training to law enforcement agencies, district attorneys, and defense counsel in the evaluation of children in forensic contexts. Dr. Elliott earned her PhD in clinical psychology from Biola University and completed a postdoctoral fellowship in family violence at Harvard Medical School. She has published a number of research articles and chapters on the short- and long-term impacts of interpersonal trauma.

Martha Farrell Erickson, PhD, is Director of the Children, Youth, and Family Consortium at the University of Minnesota, a national resource for bringing diverse professionals and concerned citizens together to work for the well-being of children and families. In partnership with coauthor Byron Egeland, she also is a developer of the award-winning STEEP program, a preventive intervention program for high-risk parents and infants that is based on attachment theory and research. Dr. Erickson's professional writing and speaking focus on parent-child attachment, child abuse and violence prevention, program evaluation, and community-based approaches for strengthening families and promoting resiliency. She also writes the weekly newspaper column and radio feature *Growing Concerns* and appears weekly on television as the child and family expert for the *KARE 11 Today Show.* Dr. Erickson serves on the boards of Father to Father, the American Professional Society on the Abuse of Children, the Minnesota Committee for Prevention of Child Abuse, the PBS television show *Parenting Works,* and is president of the Board of Trustees of Washburn Child Guidance Center in Minneapolis.

Kathleen Coulborn Faller, PhD, ACSW, is Professor of Social Work, Director of the Family Assessment Clinic, Codirector of the Interdisciplinary Project on Child Abuse and Neglect, and Faculty Coordinator of the CIVITAS Partnership at the University of Michigan. She is the author of *Social Work With Abused and Neglected Children* (1981), *Child Sexual Abuse: An Interdisciplinary Manual for Diagnosis, Case Management, and Treatment* (1988), *Understanding Child Sexual Maltreatment* (1990), and *Child Sexual Abuse: Intervention and Treatment Issues* (1993), as well as numerous articles. Presently, she is on the board of directors and on the executive committee of the American Professional Society on the Abuse of Children.

Jane Nusbaum Feller is a staff attorney at the American Bar Association Center on Children and the Law. She is Editor of the *ABA Juvenile & Child Welfare Law Reporter,* a monthly publication that summarizes appellate decisions, analyzes legal issues, and tracks legislative and policy developments related to children. In addition, she provides legal expertise on Center projects involving child abuse and foster care. She wrote *Working With the Courts in Child Protection,* a manual for the National Center on Child Abuse and Neglect's User Manual series. She also has contributed to numerous manuals and monographs, including New York's manual on the interdisciplinary handling of child sexual abuse cases and *Child Sexual Abuse Judicial Training Manual: A Curriculum for Judges* (1993). Prior to joining the ABA, she worked as a family lawyer in Buffalo, New York.

David Finkelhor, PhD, is the Codirector of the Family Research Laboratory and the Family Violence Research Program at the University of New Hampshire. His publications include *A Sourcebook on Child Sexual Abuse* (1986), a widely used compilation of research on the subject of sexual abuse, and *Nursery Crimes* (1988), a study of sexual abuse in day care. He has been studying the problem of family violence since 1977 and has published three other books—*Stopping Family Violence* (1988), *License to Rape* (1985), and *Child Sexual Abuse: New Theory and Research* (1984)—and more than two dozen articles on the subject. He is coeditor of *Dark Side of Families* (1983), *Coping With Family Violence: New Research* (1988), and *New Directions in Family Violence and Abuse Research* (1988) and is the recipient of grants from the National Institute of Mental Health and the National Center on Child Abuse and Neglect.

William N. Friedrich, PhD, ABPP, is Professor and Consultant in the Department of Psychiatry and Psychology at the Mayo Clinic and the Mayo Medical School in Rochester, Minnesota. His position at Mayo includes clinical practice as well as teaching, consultation, and training. Prior to moving to the Mayo Clinic, he was a faculty member at the University of Washington in the Department of Psychology. He is a Diplomate with the American Board of Professional Psychology in both clinical psychology and family psychology. He has authored more than 100 publications, including four books. He also has written more than a dozen published short stories. Three of his books are directly related to sexual abuse—*Psychotherapy of Sexually Abused Children and Their Families, Casebook of Sexual Abuse Treatment,* and *Psychotherapy With Sexually Abused Boys.*

Gail S. Goodman, PhD, is Professor of Psychology at the University of California, Davis. She has published numerous scientific articles, books, and chapters on child abuse, child witnesses, and children's testimony. In addition, she has served as President of the Division of Child, Youth, and Family Services of the American Psychological Association (APA) and is a founding member of the American Professional Society on the Abuse of Children (APSAC). She also has received a variety of awards for her writings, including the 1994 Robert Chin Award from the Society for the Psychological Study of Social Issues of APA and APSAC's 1992 Research Career Achievement Award. Dr. Goodman obtained her doctoral degree in Developmental Psychology from UCLA in

1977 and conducted postdoctoral research at the University of Denver and the Universite Rene Descartes in Paris, France. She formerly served on the faculties of the University of Denver and the State University of New York at Buffalo.

Stuart N. Hart, PhD, is Director of the Office for the Study of the Psychological Rights of the Child and Professor in the Indiana University School of Education at Indiana University—Purdue University at Indianapolis. He directed the International Conference on Psychological Abuse of Children and Youth (1983) and an NCCAN, U.S. Department of Health and Human Services supported research project to develop operationally defined measures of emotional maltreatment (1986-1989). He is chair of the Task Force on Psychological Maltreatment of the American Professional Society on Abuse of Children (APSAC) and a member of the Working Group on Child Abuse and Neglect of the American Psychological Association. He coedited and contributed to the book *Psychological Maltreatment of Children and Youth,* has written many book chapters and journal articles on the topic of psychological maltreatment, and codirected the development of the *Practice Guidelines: Psychosocial Evaluation of Suspected Psychological Maltreatment in Children and Adolescents* of APSAC.

Charles F. Johnson, MD, is Professor of Pediatrics at The Ohio State University School of Medicine and became Director of the Child Abuse Program at Columbus Children's Hospital in 1980. The program at Children's Hospital, which was recognized as a Center of Excellence by the Ohio Department of Human Services in 1993, is dedicated to service, research, teaching, and prevention. His research interests include primary prevention of child abuse through preparation for parenting, unusual manifestations of physical and sexual abuse, sexual abuse perpetrator modus operandi, females as abuse perpetrators, male and female sexual abuse victims, and improving professional knowledge, skills, and attitudes in child abuse identification and reporting. Dr. Johnson has served as an expert witness in abuse cases, has presented abuse topics at national child abuse conferences, is Editor of the Newsletter of the American Academy of Pediatrics (AAP) Section on

Child Abuse, and has served as cochair for scientific programs. He is a medical consultant to abuse programs in three foreign countries. In 1994, he was appointed to the AAP Committee on Child Abuse.

Henry C. Karlson, JD, is Professor of Law at the Indiana University School of Law. He is a member of the Coalition on Law Enforcement, legal adviser for the Johnson County prosecutor's office, and on the board of examiners of the National Board of Trial Advocacy. From 1983 to 1988, he was Chair of the Indiana Supreme Court Rules Subcommittee on Changes in Rules of Criminal Procedure, and from 1992 to 1993 he was a member of the Indiana Supreme Court Committee on Rules of Evidence. He is the author or coauthor of numerous book chapters and articles, including "Recent Developments in the Law of Evidence" (1995), "Attorney Attitudes Regarding Behaviors Associated With Child Sexual Abuse" (1994), and "Recent Case Law Developments in Indiana Evidence" (1994).

Susan J. Kelley, RN, PhD, is Director of Research and Professor, College of Health Sciences, at Georgia State University. She has been involved in the field of child abuse since 1979 and has published more than 30 journal articles and book chapters on child abuse. She is the author of *Pediatric Emergency Nursing* (2nd ed.). Her research has focused on stress responses of children to sexual victimization, the relationship between child abuse and substance abuse, and grandparents raising grandchildren as a result of child maltreatment. Dr. Kelley is on the board of directors of the American Professional Society on the Abuse of Children and is Editor-in-Chief of the *APSAC Advisor.*

David J. Kolko, PhD, is Associate Professor of Child Psychiatry and Psychology in the Department of Psychiatry at the University of Pittsburgh Medical Center. He is also Director of the Child and Parent Behavior Clinic at Western Psychiatric Institute and Clinic, a specialty program serving children and families involved in antisocial and violent behavior. He is a member of APSAC's Board of Directors and is Co-Chair of its research committee. He is a member of the editorial boards of journals dealing with child abuse and family violence, including *Child Maltreatment,: Journal of the American Professional Society on the Abuse of Children,* and has conducted research on treatment and service delivery funded by the National Institute of Mental Health and the National Center on Child Abuse and Neglect. His clinical research interests are in the areas of conduct disorder/antisocial behavior in children/adolescents, youth and family violence, child physical abuse, and child firesetting.

Richard D. Krugman, MD, is Dean of the University of Colorado School of Medicine and has held a variety of administrative positions, including director of admissions and codirector of the Child Health Associate Program, director of the University's SEARCH/AHEC program, and vice-chairman for clinical affairs in the Department of Pediatrics. As a Professor of Pediatrics, he served as director of the C. Henry Kempe National Center for the Prevention and Treatment of Child Abuse and Neglect from 1981-1992 and has gained international prominence in the field of child abuse. Dr. Krugman is a graduate of Princeton University and earned his medical degree at New York University School of Medicine. A board-certified pediatrician, he did his internship and residency in pediatrics at the University of Colorado School of Medicine. He has earned many honors in the field of child abuse and neglect and headed the U.S. Advisory Board of Child Abuse and Neglect from 1988-1991, which issued a landmark national report in 1991. More recently, he is working with the Association of American Colleges (AAMC) task forces on generalist physician education, violence, and the financing of medical education.

Kenneth V. Lanning, MS, is a Supervisory Special Agent assigned to the Behavioral Science Unit at the FBI Academy in Quantico, Virginia, and has been involved in studying the criminal aspects of deviant sexual behavior since 1973. He has specialized in the study of the sexual victimization of children since 1981. He is a founding member of the board of directors of the American Professional Society on the Abuse of Children (APSAC) and is currently a member of the APSAC Advisory Board. He is also a member of the U.S. Interagency Task Force on Child

Abuse and Neglect, the advisory board of the National Resource Center on Child Sexual Abuse, and the Boy Scouts of America Youth Protection Expert Advisory Panel. He has published articles in the *FBI Law Enforcement Bulletin* and other professional journals. He is a chapter author in Burgess's *Child Pornography and Sex Rings,* Zillman and Bryant's *Pornography: Research Advances and Policy Considerations,* Hazelwood and Burgess's *Practical Aspects of Rape Investigation,* and Sakheim and Devine's *Out of Darkness.*

Louanne Lawson, RN, is on the faculty at the University of Arkansas for Medical Sciences, College of Nursing, where she is Course Coordinator for the Psychiatric/ Mental Health Nursing courses. She trains staff in psychiatric hospitals, residential treatment facilities, and therapeutic foster homes in the milieu management of trauma-related maladaptive behaviors. She has provided nursing care to families where abuse is a problem since 1985. She was the first nurse practitioner on the child abuse team at Arkansas Children's Hospital. She participated in developing a program for teaching family practice and emergency medicine to pediatric residents who evaluate children who may have been abused. She developed a protocol for preparing sexually abused children for physical evaluation. She provided follow-up physical and emotional care for children and their families. She contributed to the development of the Family Treatment Program and provided services to men who had molested children, nonoffending mothers, and adolescent survivors and perpetrators. Currently, she is participating in a research project to develop a psychometric assessment tool for use with male intrafamilial sexual child abusers.

William D. Murphy, PhD, is Professor in the Department of Psychiatry, Division of Clinical Psychology, at the University of Tennessee, Memphis. He serves as Director of the Special Problems Unit—an evaluation, treatment, and research program for sexual offenders—and is the Director of the APA-approved University of Tennessee Professional Psychology Internship Consortium. He is a board member and President-Elect of the Association for the Treatment of Sexual Abusers and serves on the advisory board of the Memphis and Shelby County Child Sexual Abuse Council. He is a member of the editorial boards of *Sexual Abuse: A Journal of Research and Treatment, Child Maltreatment: Journal of the American Professional Society on the Abuse of Children,* and *Acta Sexologica.*

John E. B. Myers, JD, is Professor of Law at the University of the Pacific, McGeorge School of Law in Sacramento, California. He is the editor of *The Backlash: Child Protection Under Fire* (1994) and the author of *Evidence in Child Abuse and Neglect Cases* (1992, 1995), *Legal Issues in Child Abuse and Neglect* (1992), and *Legal and Educational Issues Affecting Autistic Children* (with W. Jenson & W. McMahon, 1986). He has written many articles on child maltreatment, and his writing has been cited by more than 125 courts, including the U.S. Supreme Court. Professor Myers is on the faculty of the National Judicial College, the National Council of Juvenile and Family Court Judges, and the National Center for Prosecution of Child Abuse. He has received awards recognizing his work in child protection. In 1992, he was named Child Abuse Professional of the Year by the California Consortium for the Prevention of Child Abuse. In 1993, he received the Distinguished Faculty Award from the University of the Pacific. In 1994, he received the Outstanding Service Award from the American Professional Society on the Abuse of Children.

Rebecca Roe, JD, received her degree from the University of Puget Sound School of Law in 1977. Currently, she litigates civil cases dealing with discrimination, sexual harassment and abuse, employment law, and professional negligence at Schroeter, Goldmark & Bender. Prior to joining Schroeter, Goldmark & Bender, she concluded a 15-year career as the chief of the nationally recognized special-assault unit of the King County prosecutor's office. In this capacity, she prosecuted cases of sexual assault and violence against women and children. She is the only public lawyer to have been named top trial attorney of the year by the Seattle-King County Bar Association. She also was named by *Parade* magazine as one of the toughest prosecutors in the nation and was featured in the cover story of *Pacific* magazine. She is a member of the Washington State Bar Association, the Washington Association of Prosecuting Attorneys, the Washington State Trial Lawyers Association, and the American Trial Lawyers Association and a board member of the Washington Council on Crime & Delinquency and the King County Sexual Assault Resource Center.

Karen J. Saywitz, PhD, is Associate Professor of Psychiatry at the University of California, Los Angeles, School of Medicine. She is Director of Child and Adolescent Psychology at the Harbor-UCLA Medical Center. She is a clinical and developmental psychologist. Dr. Saywitz is the author of numerous articles regarding the capabilities, limitations, and needs of child victim-witnesses. In her research on interviewing children and preparing them for court, she develops and tests innovative interventions to enhance children's memory performance, communicative competence, emotional resilience, and their resistance to suggestive questions. She is also on the faculty of the National Judicial College, where she teaches principles of child development for judicial application. She has coauthored a brief of amici curiae to the U.S. Supreme Court and a benchguide for California judges. Her articles have been cited by more than 40 appellate courts. In 1993, she was named Child Abuse Professional of the Year by the California Consortium for the Prevention of Child Abuse and Outstanding Teacher of the Year by the California State Psychological Association. She is currently coauthoring a book with Diana Elliott titled *Interviewing Children in the Forensic Context.*

Patricia Schene, PhD, has been working in the field of children and family services for 25 years as a state administrator, private agency director, researcher, and teacher. For 17 years she had been the Director of the Children's Division of the American Humane Association. She has had the opportunity to be involved and to lead many national forums on the response to child abuse and neglect in our society and has had a leadership role in national system development, policy changes at the state level, definition and measurement of outcomes in child welfare, risk assessment, and curriculum development to prepare staff and supervisors in public child protective services. She serves as Vice-President of the board of directors of the National Committee to Prevent Child Abuse (NCPCA), has been a member of the executive committee of the National Association of Public Child Welfare Administrators, and is a consultant to the Edna McConnell Clark Foundation in their new initiative in child protective services. Dr. Schene received her doctorate in Public Administration with a specialization in nonprofit agencies from the University of Colorado and a Master's in Political Science from the University of California, Berkeley.

Timothy A. Smith, MEd, has been a Counselor since 1972 and has worked in crisis clinics, drug treatment programs, psychiatric hospitals, and in private practice. Since 1977, he has specialized in the assessment and treatment of forensic clients, their spouses, and families. He is licensed as a Certified Sex Offender Treatment Provider in the State of Washington. He has worked in both private and public programs dealing with sex abusers. His current practice includes consultations and training for treatment programs and providers as well as providing evaluations and individual and group treatment for sexual offenders, sexual addicts, and adult male survivors of sexual assault.

Paul Stern, JD, is Senior Deputy Prosecuting Attorney for Snohomish County, Washington. He has been a prosecutor since 1981. He has tried numerous cases involving interpersonal violence and has prosecuted dozens of cases of child sexual abuse, physical abuse, assault, rape, and murder. He serves on the executive committee of the board of directors for the American Professional Society on the Abuse of Children. He is past-president of the Washington Professional Society on the Abuse of Children. He is a frequent lecturer at conferences dealing with child abuse and neglect issues. He has testified several times before legislative committees, has published several articles about expert witnesses and child abuse issues, and has served as legal editor for the *APSAC Advisor* and *Violence Update*. He is also on the editorial board of *Child Maltreatment: Journal of the American Professional Society on the Abuse of Children*. A graduate of Ithaca College and Rutgers-Camden Law School, Mr. Stern is admitted to practice law in Washington, New Jersey, and before the U.S. Supreme Court.

Bill Walsh is a 17-year veteran of the Dallas Police Department and Commander of the Investigation Section, which includes the Child Abuse Unit, the Family Violence Unit, and the Child Exploitation Unit. In 1989, he cofounded the Dallas Children's Advocacy Center and currently serves on its board of trustees. He also serves on the national boards of the American Professional Society on the Abuse of Children (APSAC) and the National Network of Children's Advocacy Centers. In addition, his current memberships include the Committee on the Assessment of Family Violence Interventions of the National Research Council, the National Institute of Justice (NIJ) Family Violence Program Review Team, and the Texas Child Fatality Review Team Project Committee. He also serves as a trainer and consultant to the Office of Juvenile Justice and Delinquency Prevention (OJJDP) and the National Resource Center on Child Sexual Abuse. Lt. Walsh recently was appointed to serve on the U.S. Advisory Board on Child Abuse and Neglect.

Karen Boyd Worley, PhD, is an instructor at the University of Arkansas for Medical Sciences, where she is Clinical Director for the Adolescent Sexual Adjustment Program at Arkansas Children's Hospital. She coordinates a multiagency network providing a continuum of services to adolescents with sexual behavior disorders. She also serves as psychotherapist and diagnostician for the Family Treatment Program at UAMS/ACH, working with families in which a parent has molested a child. For 12 years, Dr. Worley has been an active participant in a series of state-level commissions addressing the problem of child abuse in Arkansas. She has published articles on child abuse and working with families. She has trained extensively at the state level on these topics and has served as a board member for several agencies that deal with maltreated children. She received her doctorate in Clinical Psychology from Texas Tech University in 1983. She has completed an internship at the Kansas City V.A. Medical Center and has worked with abused children and their families for more than 15 years.

Gail L. Zellman, PhD, is a social and clinical psychologist at RAND, a public policy research institution. There, her work includes study of a range of youth and family policies, including teenage pregnancy and contraceptive use, substance use and prevention, delinquency prevention, and rape. She also has studied the implementation of policy innovations in such diverse organizations as public schools, the military, and HMOs. With support from NCCAN, she conducted a national study of mandated reporters that produced a number of articles and a RAND report. Her current work focuses on prenatal substance exposure, family contributions to children's cognitive and emotional outcomes, and child care. She also maintains a small therapy practice in which she specializes in work with couples and families.